Learning Python

Other resources from O'Reilly

Related titles

Programming Python
Python in a Nutshell
Python Cookbook
Python Pocket Reference

Jython Essentials
Python & XML
Python Programming on Win32

oreilly.com

oreilly.com is more than a complete catalog of O'Reilly books. You'll also find links to news, events, articles, weblogs, sample chapters, and code examples.

oreillynet.com is the essential portal for developers interested in open and emerging technologies, including new platforms, programming languages, and operating systems.

Conferences

O'Reilly & Associates brings diverse innovators together to nurture the ideas that spark revolutionary industries. We specialize in documenting the latest tools and systems, translating the innovator's knowledge into useful skills for those in the trenches. Visit *conferences.oreilly.com* for our upcoming events.

Safari Bookshelf (*safari.oreilly.com*) is the premier online reference library for programmers and IT professionals. Conduct searches across more than 1,000 books. Subscribers can zero in on answers to time-critical questions in a matter of seconds. Read the books on your Bookshelf from cover to cover or simply flip to the page you need. Try it today with a free trial.

SECOND EDITION

Learning Python

Mark Lutz and David Ascher

O'REILLY®

Beijing · Cambridge · Farnham · Köln · Paris · Sebastopol · Taipei · Tokyo

Learning Python, Second Edition
by Mark Lutz and David Ascher

Copyright © 2004, 1999 O'Reilly Media, Inc. All rights reserved.
Printed in the United States of America.

Published by O'Reilly Media, Inc., 1005 Gravenstein Highway North, Sebastopol, CA 95472.

O'Reilly Media, Inc. books may be purchased for educational, business, or sales promotional use. On-line editions are also available for most titles (*safari.oreilly.com*). For more information, contact our corporate/institutional sales department: (800) 998-9938 or *corporate@oreilly.com*.

Editors:	Linda Mui and Paula Ferguson
Production Editor:	Matt Hutchinson
Production Services:	Argosy Publishing
Cover Designer:	Edie Freedman
Interior Designer:	David Futato

Printing History:

March 1999:	First Edition.
December 2003:	Second Edition.

 This book uses RepKover™, a durable and flexible lay-flat binding.

ISBN: 0-596-00281-5
[M]   [12/05]

To the late Frank Willison, our mentor, friend,
and first editor.

Table of Contents

Part VI.   Classes and OOP

Preface

This book provides an introduction to the Python programming language. Python is a popular object-oriented language used for both standalone programs and scripting applications in a variety of domains. It is free, portable, powerful, and remarkably easy to use.

Whether you are new to programming or a professional developer, this book's goal is to bring you up to speed on the core Python language in a hurry.

About This Second Edition

In the four years after the first edition of this book was published in late 1998, there have been substantial changes in both the Python language and in the topics presented by the authors in Python training sessions. Although we have attempted to retain as much of the original version as possible, this new edition reflects recent changes in both Python and Python training.

On the language front, this edition has been thoroughly updated to reflect Python 2.2, and all changes to the language since publication of the first edition. In addition, discussion of anticipated changes in the upcoming 2.3 release have been incorporated throughout. Some of the major language topics for which you'll find new or expanded coverage in this edition are:

- List comprehension (Chapter 14)
- Class exceptions (Chapter 25)
- String methods (Chapter 5)
- Augmented assignment (Chapter 8)
- Classic, true, and floor division (Chapter 4)
- Package imports (Chapter 17)
- Nested function scopes (Chapter 13)
- Generators and iterators (Chapter 14)
- Unicode strings (Chapter 5)

- Subclass types (Chapters 7 and 23)
- Static and class methods (Chapter 23)
- Pseudo-private class attributes (Chapter 23)
- Extended print and import statements (Chapters 8 and 18)
- New built-ins such as `zip` and `isinstance` (Chapters 7 and 10)
- New-style classes (Chapter 23)
- New configuration and launch options, and *.pth* files (Chapter 3 and Appendix A)
- New development tools such as IDLE, Psyco, Py2exe, and Installer (Chapters 2, 3, and 29)
- New testing and documentation tools such as PyDoc, PyUnit, and doctest (Chapter 26)

Smaller language changes (e.g., long integer promotion, module export lists) appear throughout the book. Besides such language changes, we augmented the core language parts of this edition (Parts I–VII) with new topics and examples presented in the Python training sessions Mark has held in recent years. For example, you'll find:

- A new OOP introduction (Chapter 19)
- A new dynamic typing overview (Chapter 4)
- A new development tools summary (Chapter 26)
- New material on program architecture and execution (Chapters 2, 3, and 15)
- New coverage of documentation sources (Chapter 11)

Many core language part additions and changes were made with beginners in mind. You'll also find that the coverage of many original core language topics has been substantially expanded in this edition, with new discussion and examples. Because this text has largely become the primary resource for learning the core Python language, we've taken liberties with making that coverage more complete than before, and added new use cases throughout. Likewise, we updated Part VIII to reflect recent Python application domains, and modern usage patterns.

In addition, this entire edition integrates a new set of Python tips and tricks, gleaned from both teaching classes over the last seven years, and using Python for real work over the last decade. The exercises have been updated and expanded to reflect current Python practice, new language features, and common beginner mistakes we've witnessed first-hand in recent years. Overall, this edition is bigger, both because Python is bigger, and because we've added context that has proved to be important in practice.

To accommodate the fact that this edition is more complete, we've split most of the original chapters into bite-sized chunks. That is, we've reorganized the core language section into many multichapter parts, to make the material easier to tackle. Types and statements, for instance, are now two top-level parts, with one chapter for each major type and statement topic. This new structure is designed to allow us to say more, without intimidating readers. In the process, exercises and gotchas were moved from chapter ends to part ends; they now appear at the end of the last chapter in each part.

Despite all the new topics, this book is still oriented toward Python newcomers, and is designed to be a first Python text for programmers.* It retains much of the first edition's material, structure, and focus. Where appropriate, we have expanded introductions for newcomers, and isolated the more advanced new topics from the main thread of discussion to avoid obscuring the fundamentals. Moreover, because it is largely based on time-tested training experience and materials, this edition, like the first, can still serve as a self-paced introductory Python class.

Prerequisites

There are none to speak of, really. This book has been used successfully by both absolute beginners, and crusty programming veterans. In general, though, we have found that any exposure to programming or scripting before this text can be helpful, even if not required for every reader.

This book is designed to be an introductory level Python text for programmers. It may not be an ideal text for someone who has never touched a computer before (for instance, we're not going to spend any time explaining what a computer is), but we haven't made many assumptions about your programming background or education.

On the other hand, we won't insult readers by assuming they are "dummies" either, whatever that means; it's easy to do useful things in Python, and we hope to show you how. The text occasionally contrasts Python with languages such as C, C++, Java, and Pascal, but you can safely ignore these comparisons if you haven't used such languages in the past.

One thing we should probably mention up front: Python's creator, Guido van Rossum, named it after the BBC comedy series *Monty Python's Flying Circus*. This legacy has inevitably added a humorous flavor to many Python examples. For instance, the traditional "foo" and "bar" become "spam" and "eggs" in the Python world, and in some of the code you'll see in this book. The occasional "Brian," "Ni," and "shrubbery" likewise owe their appearances to this namesake. You don't need to be familiar with the series to make sense of such examples (symbols are symbols), but it can't hurt.

---

* And by "programmer," we mean anyone who has written a single line of code in any programming or scripting language in the past. If you don't meet this test, you will probably find this book useful anyhow. But we'll spend more time teaching Python than programming fundamentals.

This Book's Scope

Although this book covers all the essentials of the Python language, we've kept its scope narrow in the interest of speed and size. To keep things simple, this book focuses on core concepts, uses small and self-contained examples to illustrate points, and sometimes omits the small details that are readily available in reference manuals. Because of that, this book is probably best described as both an introduction and a stepping stone to more advanced and complete texts.

For example, we won't say much about Python/C integration—a complex topic, which is nevertheless central to many Python-based systems. We also won't talk much about Python's history or development processes. And popular Python applications such as GUIs, system tools, and network scripting get only a short survey, if they are mentioned at all. Naturally, this scope misses some of the big picture.

By and large, Python is about raising the quality bar a few notches in the scripting world. Some of its ideas require more context than can be provided here, and we'd be remiss if we didn't recommend further study after you finish this book. We hope that most readers of this book will eventually go on to gain a more complete understanding of application-level programming from other texts.

Because of its beginners' focus, *Learning Python* is designed to be naturally complemented by O'Reilly's other Python books. For instance, *Programming Python*, Second Edition provides larger and more advanced application-level examples, and was explicitly designed to be a follow-up text to the one you are reading now. Roughly, the second editions of *Learning Python* and *Programming Python* reflect the two halves of Mark's training materials—the core language and applications programming. In addition, O'Reilly's *Python Pocket Reference*, Second Edition, serves as a quick reference supplement for looking up the fine details we will largely skip here.

Other followup Python books can also help provide additional examples, explore specific Python domains, and serve as references. We recommend O'Reilly's *Python in a Nutshell* and New Riders' *Python Essential Reference* as references, and O'Reilly's *Python Cookbook* as an example library. Regardless of which books you choose, you should keep in mind that the rest of the Python story requires studying examples that are more realistic than there is space for here. There are roughly 40 English language Python books available today, along with a few dozen foreign language texts. Because books are a subjective experience, we invite you to browse all available texts to find one that suits your needs.

But despite its limited scope (and perhaps because of it), we think you'll find this book to be a good first text on Python. You'll learn everything you need to get started writing useful standalone Python programs and scripts. By the time you've finished this book, you will have learned not only the language itself, but also how to apply it to day-to-day tasks. And you'll be equipped to tackle more advanced topics and examples as they come your way.

This Book's Style and Structure

Much of this book is based on training materials developed for a three-day hands-on Python course. You'll find exercises at the end of the last chapter of the core language parts, with solutions to all exercises in Appendix B. The exercises are designed to get you coding right away, and are usually one of the highlights of the course.

We strongly recommend working through the exercises along the way, not only to gain Python programming experience, but also because some exercises raise issues not covered elsewhere in the book. The solutions in Appendix B should help if you get stuck (and we encourage you to "cheat" as much and as often as you like). Naturally, you'll need to install Python to run the exercises.

Because this text is designed to introduce language basics quickly, we've organized the presentation by major language features, not examples. We'll take a bottom-up approach here: from built-in object types, to statements, to program units, and so on. Each chapter is fairly self-contained, but later chapters use ideas introduced in earlier ones (e.g., by the time we get to classes, we'll assume you know how to write functions), so a linear reading makes the most sense. From a broader perspective, this book is divided into the following functional areas, and their corresponding parts.

Core Language

This portion of the book presents the Python language, in a bottom-up fashion. It is organized with one part per major language feature—types, functions, and so forth—and most of the examples are small and self-contained (some might also call the examples in this section artificial, but they illustrate the points we're out to make). This section represents the bulk of the text, which tells you something about the focus of the book. It is composed of the following parts:

Part I, *Getting Started*
> We begin with a general overview of Python, that answers commonly asked initial questions—why people use the language, what it's useful for, and so on. The first chapter introduces the major ideas underlying the technology, to give you some background context.
>
> This part then begins the technical material of the book, by exploring the ways that both you and Python run programs. Its goal is to give you just enough information to be able to work along with later examples and exercises. If you need more help getting started, additional configuration details are available in Appendix A.

Part II, *Types and Operations*
> Next, we begin our tour of the Python language, by studying Python's major built-in object types in depth: numbers, lists, dictionaries, and so on. You can get a lot done in Python with these tools alone.

Part III, *Statements and Syntax*

The next part moves on to introduce Python's statements—the code you type to create and process objects in Python. It also presents Python's general syntax model.

Part IV, *Functions*

This part begins our look at Python's higher-level program structure tools. Functions turn out to be a simple way to package code for reuse.

Part V, *Modules*

Python modules let you organize statements and functions into larger components, and this part illustrates how to create, use, and reload modules.

Part VI, *Classes and OOP*

Here we explore Python's object-oriented programming (OOP) tool, the class. As you'll see, OOP in Python is mostly about looking up names in linked objects.

Part VII, *Exceptions and Tools*

We wrap up the core language coverage of this book section with a look at Python's exception handling model and statements, and a brief overview of development tools. This comes last, because exceptions can be classes if you want them to be.

Outer Layers

Part VIII samples Python's built-in tools, and puts them to use in a collection of small example programs. Common tasks are demonstrated in Python to give you some real-world context, using both the language itself, and its standard libraries and tools.

Chapter 27, *Common Tasks in Python*

This chapter presents a selection of the modules and functions that are included in the default Python installation. By definition, they comprise the minimum set of modules you can reasonably expect any Python user to have access to. Knowing the contents of this standard toolset will likely save you weeks of work.

Chapter 28, *Frameworks*

This chapter presents a few real applications. By building on the language core explained in earlier parts and the built-in tools described in Chapter 27, we present many small but useful programs that show how to put it all together. We cover three areas that are of interest to most Python users: basic tasks, text processing, and system interfaces. We close with a brief discussion of Jython, the Java port of Python, and a substantial Jython program.

Chapter 29, *Python Resources*

This chapter discusses the layers of the Python community and specialized libraries that are either part of the standard Python distribution or freely available from third parties.

Appendixes

The book ends with appendixes that give platform-specific tips for using Python on various platforms (Appendix A), and provide solutions to exercises that appear at the end of the last chapter in each part (Appendix B). Note that the index and table of contents can be used to hunt for details, but there are no reference appendixes in this book. As mentioned earlier, the *Python Pocket Reference*, Second Edition (O'Reilly), as well as other books and the free Python reference manuals maintained at *http://www.python.org*, fill in syntax and built-in tool details.

Book Updates

Improvements happen (and so do mis^H^H^H typos). Updates, supplements, and corrections for this book will be maintained (or referenced) on the Web at one of the following sites:

- *http://www.oreilly.com* (O'Reilly's site)
- *http://www.rmi.net/~lutz* (Mark's site)
- *http://starship.python.net/~da* (David's site)
- *http://www.python.org* (Python's main site)
- *http://www.rmi.net/~lutz/about-lp.html* (book's web page)

If we could be more clairvoyant, we would, but the Web changes faster than printed books.

Font Conventions

This book uses the following typographical conventions:

Italic
> For email addresses, filenames, URLs, for emphasizing new terms when first introduced, and for some comments within code sections

`Constant width`
> Shows the contents of files or the output from commands and to designate modules, methods, statements, and commands

`Constant width bold`
> In code sections to show commands or text that would be typed

`Constant width italic`
> Shows replaceables in code sections

`<Constant width>`
> Represents syntactic units that you replace with real code

Indicates a tip, suggestion, or general note relating to the nearby text.

 Indicates a warning or caution relating to the nearby text.

In our examples, the % character at the start of a system command line stands for the system's prompt, whatever that may be on your machine (e.g., C:\Python22> in a DOS window). Don't type the % character yourself! Similarly, in interpreter interaction listings, do not type the >>> and ... characters shown at the start of lines—these are prompts that Python displays. Type just the text after these prompts. To help you remember this, user inputs are shown in bold font in this book. Also, you normally don't need to type text that starts with a # in listings; as we'll explain later, these are comments, not executable code.

About the Programs in This Book

This book, and all the program examples in it, are based on Python Version 2.2, and reflect the upcoming 2.3 release. But since we'll stick to the core language, you can be fairly sure that most of what we have to say won't change very much in later releases of Python. Most of this book applies to earlier Python versions too, except when it does not; naturally, if you try using extensions added after the release you've got, all bets are off. As a rule of thumb, the latest Python is the best Python. Because this book focuses on the core language, most of it also applies to Jython, the Java-based Python language implementation, as well other Python implementations, described in Chapter 2.

Source code for the book's examples, as well as exercise solutions, can be fetched from the book's web site at *http://www.oreilly.com/catalog/lpython2/*. So how do you run the examples? We'll get into startup details in Chapter 3, so please stay tuned for the details on this front.

Using Code Examples

This book is here to help you get your job done. In general, you may use the code in this book in your programs and documentation. You do not need to contact us for permission unless you're reproducing a significant portion of the code. For example, writing a program that uses several chunks of code from this book does not require permission. Selling or distributing a CD-ROM of examples from O'Reilly books *does* require permission. Answering a question by citing this book and quoting example code does not require permission. Incorporating a significant amount of example code from this book into your product's documentation *does* require permission.

We appreciate, but do not require, attribution. An attribution usually includes the title, author, publisher, and ISBN. For example: "*ActionScript: The Definitive Guide*, Second Edition, by Colin Moock. Copyright 2001 O'Reilly & Associates, Inc., 0-596-00369-X."

If you feel your use of code examples falls outside fair use or the permission given above, feel free to contact us at *permissions@oreilly.com*.

How to Contact Us

Please address comments and questions concerning this book to the publisher:

O'Reilly & Associates, Inc.
1005 Gravenstein Highway North
Sebastopol, CA 95472
(800) 998-9938 (in the United States or Canada)
(707) 829-0515 (international or local)
(707) 829-0104 (fax)

We have a web page for this book, where we list errata, examples, and any additional information. You can access this page at:

http://www.oreilly.com/catalog/lpython2

To comment or ask technical questions about this book, send email to:

bookquestions@oreilly.com

For more information about our books, conferences, Resource Centers, and the O'Reilly Network, see our web site at:

http://www.oreilly.com

Mark and David are also both happy to answer book questions from readers, though you're more likely to get a response by sending "Core Language" questions to Mark, and "Outer Layer" queries to David, the two area's respective primary authors. You can find both of the authors' email addresses at the book's web site.

(Throughout this book, we normally use "we" to refer to both authors, but occasionally slip into a specific author's name for personal anecdotes—usually Mark in the Core Language parts, and David in the Outer Layers parts, reflecting the primary author of each part. Although this book was a joint effort of many, each author sometimes steps out of the collective.)

Acknowledgments

We'd like to express our gratitude to all the people who played a part in developing this book. First of all, we'd like to thank the editors that worked on this project: Laura Lewin, Paula Ferguson, and finally Linda Mui. We'd also like to thank O'Reilly in general, for supporting another Python book project. We're glad to be a part of what is now a full and growing Python product line at O'Reilly.

Thanks also to everyone who took part in the early review of this book—Guido van Rossum, Alex Martelli, Anna Ravenscroft, Sue Giller, and Paul Prescod.

And for creating such an enjoyable and useful language, we owe an especially large debt to Guido, and the rest of the Python community; like most open source systems, Python is the product of many heroic efforts.

We'd also like to give a special thanks to our original editor on this book, the late Frank Willison. Frank had a profound impact on both the Python world, and our own personal careers. It is not an overstatement to say that Frank was responsible for much of the fun and success of Python's early days. In fact, this very book was his idea. In recognition of his vision and friendship, we dedicate this update to him. Hack on, Frank.

Mark Also Says:

When I first met Python in 1992, I had no idea what an impact it would have on the next decade of my life. After writing the first edition of Programming Python in 1995, I began traveling around the country and world teaching Python to both beginners and experts. Since finishing the first edition of this book in 1999, I've been a full-time, independent Python trainer and writer, thanks largely to Python's exponentially growing popularity.

As I write these words in early 2003, I've taught roughly 90 Python training sessions, in the U.S., Europe, Canada, and Mexico, and met over one thousand students along the way. Besides racking up frequent flyer miles, these classes helped me refine my contributions to this book, especially the core language material. These parts of the book mostly come straight from my current course materials.

I'd like to thank all the students who have participated in my courses over the last seven years. Together with recent Python changes, your feedback played a huge role in shaping my contributions to this text. There's nothing quite as instructive as watching one thousand students repeat the same beginners' mistakes! The core language section of this second edition owes its changes primarily to classes held after 1999; I'd like to single out Hewlett-Packard, Intel, and Seagate for multiple sessions held in this timeframe. And I'd especially like to thank the clients who hosted classes in Dublin, Mexico City, Barcelona, and Puerto Rico; better perks would be hard to imagine.

I'd like to thank O'Reilly for giving me a chance to work on now six book projects; it's been net fun (and only feels a little like the movie *Groundhog Day*). I also want to thank coauthor David Ascher, for his work and patience on this project. Besides this book and his day job developing Python tools at ActiveState, David also donates his time to organizing conferences, editing other books, and much more.

Finally, a few personal notes of thanks. To all the people I worked with at various companies earlier in my career. To the Boulder public library, in which I hid while writing parts of this edition. To the late Carl Sagan, for inspiration in youth. To Jimmy Buffet, for perspective at the dawn of middle age. To a woman from New Mexico on a flight from Oklahoma, for reminding me of the importance of having a dream. To the Denver Broncos, for winning the big one (twice). To Sharp and Sony, for making such sweet machines. And most of all, to my children, Michael, Samantha, and Roxanne, for making me a truly rich man.

Longmont and Boulder, Colorado
July 2003

David Also Says:

In addition to the previous thanks, I'd like to extend special thanks to the following.

First, thanks to Mark Lutz for inviting me to work with him on this book and for supporting my efforts as a Python trainer. Additional thanks to the impressive array of Python folks who encouraged me in my early days understanding the language, especially Guido, Tim Peters, Don Beaudry, and Andrew Mullhaupt. It's amazing how a little encouragement at the right time can have long-lasting impact.

I used to teach Python and Jython, much like Mark still does. The students in these courses have helped me identify the parts of Python that are the trickiest to learn, as well as remind me of the aspects of the language that make it so pleasant to use, and I thank them for their feedback and encouragement. I would also like to thank those who gave me the chance to develop these courses: Jim Anderson (Brown University), Cliff Dutton (then at Distributed Data Systems), Geoffrey Philbrick (then at Hibbitt, Karlsson & Sorensen, Inc.), Paul Dubois (Lawrence Livermore National Labs), and Ken Swisz (KLA-Tencor). While I'm no longer regularly teaching Python, that experience is one I rely on still when coaching novices.

Thanks to my scientific advisors, Jim Anderson, Leslie Welch, and Norberto Grzywacz, who have all kindly supported my efforts with Python in general and this book in particular, not necessarily understanding why I was doing it but trusting me nonetheless. Any of the lessons they taught me are still relevant daily.

The first victims of my Python evangelization efforts deserve gold stars for tolerating my most enthusiastic (some might say fanatical) early days: Thanassi Protopapas, Gary Strangman, and Steven Finney. Thanassi also gave his typically useful feedback on an early draft of the book. Several Activators (known to civilians as "ActiveState employees") have been tremendous colleagues and friends these last three years—I'll single out Mark Hammond, Trent Mick, Shane Caraveo, and Paul Prescod. Each of them have taught me much, about Python and otherwise. ActiveState as a whole has provided me with an amazing environment in which to build a career, learn new things from fascinating people every day, and still program in Python.

Thanks to my family: my parents JacSue and Philippe for always encouraging me to do what I want to do; my brother Ivan for reminding me of some of my early encounters with programming texts (after hours of effort, realizing that a program listing in Byte magazine was buggy had a 13-year-old boy crying out of frustration); my wife Emily for her constant support and utter faith that writing a book was something I could do; our children, Hugo and Sylvia, for sharing the computers with me—they approach computers with such ease that I can't wait to see what their generation comes up with.

Finally, thinking about this edition in particular, I want to thank everyone who has contributed to the Python community. It is striking to compare Python now with Python five years ago—the language has changed a little, while the world in which it lives is so much broader and richer. It bubbles with enthusiasm, code, and ideas (from amazingly bright people and crackpots alike), while remaining respectful and cheerful. Let's keep on doing that.

Vancouver, British Columbia, Canada
November 2003

Getting Started

Part I begins by exploring some of the ideas behind Python, the Python execution model, and ways to launch program code. We won't actually start writing code until the next part, but make sure you have at least a basic understanding of Python's design goals and program launch techniques covered here before moving ahead to language details.

## CHAPTER 1

A Python Q&A Session

If you've bought this book, you may already know what Python is, and why it's an important tool to learn. If not, you probably won't be sold on Python until you've learned the language by reading the rest of this book and have done a project or two. But before jumping into details, the first few pages briefly introduce some of the main reasons behind Python's popularity. To begin sculpting a definition of Python, this chapter takes the form of a question and answer session, which poses some of the most common non-technical questions asked by beginners.

Why Do People Use Python?

Because there are many programming languages available today, this is the usual first question of newcomers. Given the hundreds of thousands of Python users out there today, there really is no way to answer this question with complete accuracy. The choice of development tools is sometimes based on unique constraints or personal preference.

But after teaching Python to roughly one thousand students and almost 100 companies in recent years, some common themes have emerged. The primary factors cited by Python users seem to be these:

Software quality

> For many, Python's focus on readability, coherence, and software quality in general, sets it apart from "kitchen sink" style languages like Perl. Python code is designed to be readable, and hence maintainable—much more so than traditional scripting languages. In addition, Python has deep support for software reuse mechanisms such as object oriented programming (OOP).

Developer productivity

> Python boosts developer productivity many times beyond compiled or statically typed languages such as C, C++, and Java. Python code is typically 1/3 to 1/5 the size of equivalent C++ or Java code. That means there is less to type, less to

debug, and less to maintain after the fact. Python programs also run immediately, without the lengthy compile and link steps of some other tools.

Program portability

Most Python programs run unchanged on all major computer platforms. Porting Python code between Unix and Windows, for example, is usually just a matter of copying a script's code between machines. Moreover, Python offers multiple options for coding portable graphical user interfaces.

Support libraries

Python comes with a large collection of prebuilt and portable functionality, known as the standard library. This library supports an array of application-level programming tasks, from text pattern matching, to network scripting. In addition, Python can be extended with both home-grown libraries, as well as a vast collection of third-party application support software.

Component integration

Python scripts can easily communicate with other parts of an application, using a variety of integration mechanisms. Such integrations allow Python to be used as a product customization and extension tool. Today, Python code can invoke C and C++ libraries, can be called from C and C++ programs, can integrate with Java components, can communicate over COM, Corba, and .NET, and can interact over networks with interfaces like SOAP and XML-RPC.

Enjoyment

Because of Python's ease of use and built-in toolset, it can make the act of programming more pleasure than chore. Although this may be an intangible benefit, its effect on productivity at large is an important asset.

Of these factors, the first two, quality and productivity, are probably the most compelling benefits to most Python users.

Software Quality

By design, Python implements both a deliberately simple and readable syntax, and a highly coherent programming model. As a slogan at a recent Python conference attests, the net result is that Python seems to just "fit your brain"—that is, features of the language interact in consistent and limited ways, and follow naturally from a small set of core concepts. This makes the language easier to learn, understand, and remember. In practice, Python programmers do not need to constantly refer to manuals when reading or writing code; it's an orthogonal design.

By philosophy, Python adopts a somewhat *minimalist* approach. This means that although there are usually multiple ways to accomplish a coding task, there is usually just one obvious way, a few less obvious alternatives, and a small set of coherent interactions everywhere in the language. Moreover, Python doesn't make arbitrary decisions for you; when interactions are ambiguous, explicit intervention is preferred over "magic." In the Python way of thinking, explicit is better than implicit, and simple is better than complex.*

Beyond such design themes, Python includes tools such as modules and OOP that naturally promote code reusability. And because Python is focused on quality, so too, naturally, are Python programmers.

Developer Productivity

During the great Internet boom of the mid-to-late 1990s, it was difficult to find enough programmers to implement software projects; developers were asked to implement systems as fast as the Internet evolved. Now, in the post-boom era of layoffs and economic recession, the picture has shifted. Today, programming staffs are forced to accomplish the same tasks with fewer people.

In both of these scenarios, Python has shined as a tool that allows programmers to get more done with less effort. It is deliberately optimized for *speed of development*—its simple syntax, dynamic typing, lack of compile steps, and built-in toolset allow programmers to develop programs in a fraction of the development time needed for some other tools. The net effect is that Python typically boosts developer productivity many times beyond that of traditional languages. That's good news both in boom times and bust.

Is Python a Scripting Language?

Python is a general purpose programming language that is often applied in scripting roles. It is commonly defined as an *object-oriented scripting language*—a definition that blends support for OOP with an overall orientation toward scripting roles. In fact, people often use the word "script" instead of "program" to describe a Python code file. In this book, the terms "script" and "program" are used interchangeably, with a slight preference for "script" to describe a simpler top-level file and "program" to refer to a more sophisticated multifile application.

Because the term "scripting" has so many different meanings to different observers, some would prefer that it not be applied to Python at all. In fact, people tend to think of three very different definitions when they hear Python labeled a "scripting" language, some of which are more useful than others:

Shell tools
Tools for coding operating system–oriented scripts. Such programs are often launched from console command-lines, and perform tasks such as processing

---

* For a more complete look at the Python philosophy, type the command **import this** at any Python interactive prompt (you'll see how in Chapter 2). This invokes an easter egg hidden in Python, a collection of Python design principles. The acronym EIBTI has lately become fashionable for the "explicit is better than implicit" rule.

text files and launching other programs. Python programs can serve such roles, but this is just one of dozens of common Python application domains. It is not just a better shell script language.

Control language

A "glue" layer used to control and direct (i.e., script) other application components. Python programs are indeed often deployed in the context of a larger application. For instance, to test hardware devices, Python programs may call out to components that give low-level access to a device. Similarly, programs may run bits of Python code at strategic points, to support end-user product customization, without having to ship and recompile the entire system's source code. Python's simplicity makes it a naturally flexible control tool. Technically, though, this is also just a common Python role; many Python programmers code standalone scripts, without ever using or knowing about any integrated components.

Ease of use

A simple language used for coding tasks quickly. This is probably the best way to think of Python as a scripting language. Python allows programs to be developed much quicker than compiled languages like C++. Its rapid development cycle fosters an exploratory, incremental mode of programming that has to be experienced to be appreciated. Don't be fooled, though—Python is not just for simple tasks. Rather, it makes tasks simple, by its ease of use and flexibility. Python has a simple feature set, but allows programs to scale up in sophistication as needed.

So, is Python a scripting language or not? It depends on whom you ask. In general, the term scripting is probably best used to describe the rapid and flexible mode of development that Python supports, rather than a particular application domain.

Okay, But What's the Downside?

Perhaps the only downside to Python is that, as currently implemented, its execution speed may not always be as fast as compiled languages such as C and C++.

We'll talk about implementation concepts later in this book. But in short, the standard implementations of Python today compile (i.e., translate) source code statements to an intermediate format known as *byte code*, and then interpret the byte code. Byte code provides portability, as it is a platform-independent format. However, because Python is not compiled all the way down to binary machine code (e.g., instructions for an Intel chip), some programs will run more slowly in Python than in a fully compiled language like C.

Whether you will ever *care* about the execution speed difference depends on what kinds of programs you write. Python has been optimized numerous times, and Python code runs fast enough by itself in most application domains. Furthermore, whenever you do something "real" in a Python script, like process a file or construct a GUI, your program is actually running at C speed since such tasks are immediately dispatched to compiled C code inside the Python interpreter. More fundamentally, Python's speed-of-development gain is often far more important than any speed-of-execution loss, especially given modern computer speeds.

Even at today's CPU speeds there still are some domains that do require optimal execution speed. Numeric programming and animation, for example, often need at least their core number-crunching components to run at C speed (or better). If you work in such a domain, you can still use Python—simply split off the parts of the application that require optimal speed into *compiled extensions*, and link those into your system for use in Python scripts.

We won't talk about extensions much in this text, but this is really just an instance of the Python-as-control-language role that we discussed earlier. A prime example of this dual language strategy is the *NumPy* numeric programming extension for Python; by *combining* compiled and optimized numeric extension libraries with the Python language, NumPy turns Python into a numeric programming tool that is both efficient and easy to use. You may never need to code such extensions in your own Python work, but they provide a powerful optimization mechanism if you ever do.

Who Uses Python Today?

At this writing, in 2003, the best estimate anyone can seem to make of the size of the Python user base is that there are between 500,000 and 1 million Python users around the world today (plus or minus a few). This estimate is based on various statistics like downloads and comparative newsgroup traffic. Because Python is open source, a more exact count is difficult—there are no license registrations to tally. Moreover, Python is automatically included with Linux distributions and some products and computer hardware, further clouding the user base picture. In general, though, Python enjoys a large user base, and a very active developer community. Because Python has been around for over a decade and has been widely used, it is also very stable and robust.

Besides individual users, Python is also being applied in real revenue-generating products, by real companies. For instance, Google and Yahoo! currently use Python in Internet services; Hewlett-Packard, Seagate, and IBM use Python for hardware testing; Industrial Light and Magic and other companies use Python in the production of movie animation; and so on. Probably the only common thread behind companies using Python today is that Python is used all over the map, in terms of application domains. Its general purpose nature makes it applicable to almost all fields, not just one. For more details on companies using Python today, see Python's web site at *http://www.python.org*.

What Can I Do with Python?

Besides being a well-designed programming language, Python is also useful for accomplishing real world tasks—the sorts of things developers do day in and day out. It's commonly used in a variety of domains, as a tool for both scripting other components and implementing standalone programs. In fact, as a general purpose language, Python's roles are virtually unlimited.

However, the most common Python roles today seem to fall into a few broad categories. The next few sections describe some of Python's most common applications today, as well as tools used in each domain. We won't be able to describe all the tools mentioned here; if you are interested in any of these topics, see Python online or other resources for more details.

Systems Programming

Python's built-in interfaces to operating-system services make it ideal for writing portable, maintainable system-administration tools and utilities (sometimes called shell tools). Python programs can search files and directory trees, launch other programs, do parallel processing with processes and threads, and so on.

Python's standard library comes with POSIX bindings, and support for all the usual OS tools: environment variables, files, sockets, pipes, processes, multiple threads, regular expression pattern matching, command-line arguments, standard stream interfaces, shell-command launchers, filename expansion, and more. In addition, the bulk of Python's system interfaces are designed to be portable; for example, a script that copies directory trees typically runs unchanged on all major Python platforms.

GUIs

Python's simplicity and rapid turnaround also make it a good match for GUI (graphical user interface) programming. Python comes with a standard object-oriented interface to the Tk GUI API called Tkinter, which allows Python programs to implement portable GUIs with native look and feel. Python/Tkinter GUIs run unchanged on MS Windows, X Windows (on Unix and Linux), and Macs. A free extension package, PMW, adds advanced widgets to the base Tkinter toolkit. In addition, the wxPython GUI API, based on a C++ library, offers an alternative toolkit for constructing portable GUIs in Python.

Higher-level toolkits such as *PythonCard* and *PMW* are built on top of base APIs such as wxPython and Tkinter. With the proper library, you can also use other GUI toolkits in Python such as Qt, GTK, MFC, and Swing. For applications that run in web browsers or have simple interface requirements, both Jython and Python server-side CGI scripts provide additional user interface options.

Internet Scripting

Python comes with standard Internet modules that allow Python programs to perform a wide variety of networking tasks, in both client and server modes. Scripts can communicate over sockets; extract form information sent to a server-side CGI script; transfer files by FTP; process XML files; send, receive, and parse email; fetch web pages by URLs; parse the HTML and XML of fetched web pages; communicate over XML-RPC, SOAP, and telnet; and more. Python's libraries make these tasks remarkably simple.

In addition, there is a large collection of third party tools on the web for doing Internet programming in Python. For instance, the *HTMLGen* system generates HTML files from Python class-based descriptions; the *win32all* Windows extensions package allows Python code to be embedded in HTML files in the spirit of JavaScript; the mod_python package runs Python efficiently within the Apache web server; and the Jython system provides for seamless Python/Java integration, and supports coding of server-side applets that run on clients. In addition, full-blown web development packages for Python such as Zope, WebWare, and Quixote, support quick construction of web sites.

Component Integration

We discussed the component integration role earlier, when describing Python as a control language. Python's ability to be extended by and embedded in C and C++ systems makes it useful as a flexile glue language, for scripting the behavior of other systems and components. For instance, by integrating a C library into Python, Python can test and launch its components. And by embedding Python in a product, on-site customizations can be coded without having to recompile the entire product, or ship its source code at all.

Tools such as the SWIG code generator can automate much of the work needed to link compiled components into Python for use in scripts. And larger frameworks such as Python's COM support on MS Windows, the Jython Java-based implementation, the Python.NET system, and various CORBA toolkits for Python provide alternative ways to script components. On Windows, for example, Python scripts can use frameworks to script MS Word and Excel, and serve the same sorts of roles as Visual Basic.

Database Programming

Python's standard `pickle` module provides a simple *object persistence* system—it allows programs to easily save and restore entire Python objects to files and file-like objects. For more traditional database demands, there are Python interfaces to Sybase, Oracle, Informix, ODBC, MySQL, and more.

The Python world has also defined a *portable database API* for accessing SQL database systems from Python scripts, which looks the same on a variety of underlying database systems. For instance, because vendor interfaces implement the portable API, a script written to work with the free MySQL system will work largely unchanged on other systems such as Oracle by simply replacing the underlying vendor interface. On the web, you'll also find a third-party system named *gadfly* that implements a SQL database for Python programs, and a complete object-oriented database system called *ZODB*.

Rapid Prototyping

To Python programs, components written in Python and C look the same. Because of this, it's possible to prototype systems in Python initially and then move components to a compiled language such as C or C++ for delivery. Unlike some prototyping tools, Python doesn't require a complete rewrite once the prototype has solidified. Parts of the system that don't require the efficiency of a language such as C++ can remain coded in Python for ease of maintenance and use.

Numeric Programming

The *NumPy* numeric programming extension for Python mentioned earlier includes such advanced tools as an array object, interfaces to standard mathematical libraries, and much more. By integrating Python with numeric routines coded in a compiled language for speed, NumPy turns Python into a sophisticated yet easy-to-use numeric programming tool, which can often replace existing code written in traditional compiled languages such as FORTRAN or C++. Additional numeric tools for Python support animation, 3D visualization, and so on.

Gaming, Images, AI, XML, and More

Python is commonly applied in more domains than can be mentioned here. For example, you can do graphics and game programming in Python with the *pygame* system; image processing with the *PIL* package and others; AI programming with neural network simulators and expert system shells; XML parsing with the xml library package, the xmlrpclib module, and third-party extensions; and even play solitaire with the *PySol* program. You'll find support for many such fields at the Vaults of Parnassus web site (linked from *http://www.python.org*). (The Vaults of Parnassus is a large collection of links to third-party software for Python programming. If you need to do something special with Python, the Vaults is usually the best first place to look for resources.)

In general, many of these specific domains are largely just instances of Python's component integration role in action again. By adding Python as a frontend to libraries of components written in a compiled language such as C, Python becomes useful for scripting in a wide variety of domains. As a general purpose language that supports integration, Python is widely applicable.

What Are Python's Technical Strengths?

Naturally, this is a developer's question. If you don't already have a programming background, the words in the next few sections may be a bit baffling—don't worry, we'll explain all of these in more detail as we proceed through this book. For developers, though, here is a quick introduction to some of Python's top technical features.

It's Object-Oriented

Python is an object-oriented language, from the ground up. Its class model supports advanced notions such as polymorphism, operator overloading, and multiple inheritance; yet in the context of Python's simple syntax and typing, OOP is remarkably easy to apply. In fact, if you don't understand these terms, you'll find they are much easier to learn with Python than with just about any other OOP language available.

Besides serving as a powerful code structuring and reuse device, Python's OOP nature makes it ideal as a scripting tool for object-oriented systems languages such as C++ and Java. For example, with the appropriate glue code, Python programs can subclass (specialize) classes implemented in C++ or Java. Of equal significance, OOP is an *option* in Python; you can go far without having to become an object guru all at once.

It's Free

Python is free. Just like other open source software, such as Tcl, Perl, Linux, and Apache, you can get the entire Python system for free on the Internet. There are no restrictions on copying it, embedding it in your systems, or shipping it with your products. In fact, you can even sell Python's source code, if you are so inclined.

But don't get the wrong idea: "free" doesn't mean "unsupported." On the contrary, the Python online community responds to user queries with a speed that most commercial software vendors would do well to notice. Moreover, because Python comes with complete source code, it empowers developers, and creates a large team of implementation experts. Although studying or changing a programming language's implementation isn't everyone's idea of fun, it's comforting to know that it's available as a final resort and ultimate documentation source. You're not dependent on a commercial vendor.

Python development is performed by a community, which largely coordinates its efforts over the Internet. It consists of Python's creator—Guido van Rossum, the officially anointed Benevolent Dictator For Life (BDFL) of Python—plus a cast of thousands.

Language changes must both follow a formal enhancement procedure (known as the PEP process), and be scrutinized by the BDFL. Happily, this tends to make Python more conservative with changes than some other languages.

It's Portable

The standard implementation of Python is written in portable ANSI C, and compiles and runs on virtually every major platform in use today. For example, Python programs run today on everything from PDAs to supercomputers. As a partial list, Python is available on Unix systems, Linux, MS-DOS, MS Windows (95, 98, NT, 2000, XP, etc.), Macintosh (classic and OS X), Amiga, AtariST, BeOS, OS/2, VMS, QNX, Vxworks, PalmOS, PocketPC and Windows CE, Cray supercomputers, IBM mainframes, PDAs running Linux, and more.

Besides the language interpreter itself, the set of standard library modules that ship with Python are also implemented to be as portable across platform boundaries as possible. Further, Python programs are automatically compiled to portable byte code, which runs the same on any platform with a compatible version of Python installed (more on this in the next chapter).

What that means is that Python programs using the core language and standard libraries run the same on Unix, MS Windows, and most other systems with a Python interpreter. Most Python ports also contain platform-specific extensions (e.g., COM support on MS Windows), but the core Python language and libraries work the same everywhere. As mentioned earlier, Python also includes an interface to the Tk GUI toolkit called Tkinter, which allows Python programs to implement full-featured graphical user interfaces that run on all major GUI platforms without program changes.

It's Powerful

From a features perspective, Python is something of a hybrid. Its tool set places it between traditional scripting languages (such as Tcl, Scheme, and Perl), and systems development languages (such as C, C++, and Java). Python provides all the simplicity and ease of use of a scripting language, along with more advanced software engineering tools typically found in compiled languages. Unlike some scripting languages, this combination makes Python useful for large-scale development projects. As a preview, here are some of the main things we'll find in Python's toolbox:

Dynamic typing
> Python keeps track of the kinds of objects your program uses when it runs; it doesn't require complicated type and size declarations in your code. In fact, as we'll see in Chapter 4, there is no such thing as a type or variable declaration anywhere to be found in Python.

Automatic memory management

Python automatically allocates and reclaims ("garbage collects") objects when no longer used, and most grow and shrink on demand. Python keeps track of low-level memory details so you don't have to.

Programming-in-the-large support

For building larger systems, Python includes tools such as modules, classes, and exceptions. These tools allow you to organize systems into components, use OOP to reuse and customize code, and handle events and errors gracefully.

Built-in object types

Python provides commonly used data structures such as lists, dictionaries, and strings, as an intrinsic part of the language; as we'll see, they're both flexible and easy to use. For instance, built-in objects can grow and shrink on demand, can be arbitrarily nested to represent complex information, and more.

Built-in tools

To process all those object types, Python comes with powerful and standard operations, including concatenation (joining collections), slicing (extracting sections), sorting, mapping, and more.

Library utilities

For more specific tasks, Python also comes with a large collection of pre-coded library tools that support everything from regular-expression matching to networking. Python's library tools are where much of the application-level action occurs.

Third-party utilities

Because Python is freeware, it encourages developers to contribute precoded tools that support tasks beyond Python's built-ins; you'll find free support for COM, imaging, CORBA ORBs, XML, database vendors, and much more.

Despite the array of tools in Python, it retains a remarkably simple syntax and design. The result is a powerful programming tool, which retains the usability of a scripting language.

It's Mixable

Python programs can be easily "glued" to components written in other languages, in a variety of ways. For example, Python's C API lets C programs call and be called by Python programs flexibly. That means you can add functionality to the Python system as needed, and use Python programs within other environments or systems.

For example, by mixing Python with libraries coded in languages such as C or C++, it becomes an easy-to-use frontend language and customization tool. As mentioned earlier, this also makes Python good at rapid prototyping; systems may be implemented in Python first to leverage its speed of development, and later moved to C for delivery, one piece at a time, according to performance demands.

It's Easy to Use

To run a Python program, you simply type it and run it. There are no intermediate compile and link steps like there are for languages such as C or C++. Python executes programs immediately, which makes for both an interactive programming experience and rapid turnaround after program changes.

Of course, development cycle turnaround is only one aspect of Python's ease of use. It also provides a deliberately simple syntax and powerful high-level built-in tools. In fact, some have gone so far as to call Python "executable pseudocode." Because it eliminates much of the complexity in other tools, Python programs are simpler, smaller, and more flexible than equivalent programs in language like C, C++, and Java.

It's Easy to Learn

This brings us to the topic of this book: compared to other programming languages, the core Python language is remarkably easy to learn. In fact, you can expect to be coding significant Python programs in a matter of days (and perhaps in just hours, if you're already an experienced programmer). That's good news both for professional developers seeking to learn the language to use on the job, as well as for end users of systems that expose a Python layer for customization or control. Today, many systems rely on the fact that end users can quickly learn enough Python to tailor their Python customization's code onsite, with little or no support.

How Does Python Stack Up to Language X?

Finally, in terms of what you may already know, people sometimes compare Python to languages such as Perl, Tcl, and Java. We talked about performance earlier, so here the focus is on functionality. While other languages are also useful tools to know and use, we think that Python:

- Is more powerful than Tcl. Python's support for "programming in the large" makes it applicable to larger systems development.
- Has a cleaner syntax and simpler design than Perl, which makes it more readable and maintainable, and helps reduce program bugs.
- Is simpler and easier to use than Java. Python is a scripting language, but Java inherits much of the complexity of systems languages such as C++.
- Is simpler and easier to use than C++, but often doesn't compete with C++ either; as a scripting language, Python often serves different roles.
- Is both more powerful and more cross-platform than Visual Basic. Its open source nature also means it is not controlled by a single company.
- Has the dynamic flavor of languages like SmallTalk and Lisp, but also has a simple, traditional syntax accessible to developers and end users.

Especially for programs that do more than scan text files, and that might have to be read in the future by others (or by you!), we think Python fits the bill better than any other scripting language available today. Furthermore, unless your application requires peak performance, Python is often a viable alternative to systems development languages such as C, C++, and Java; Python code will be much less difficult to write, debug, and maintain.

Of course, both of the authors are card-carrying Python evangelists, so take these comments as you may. They do, however, reflect the common experience of many developers who have taken time to explore what Python has to offer.

And that concludes the hype portion of this book. The best way to judge a language is to see it in action, so the next two chapters turn to a strictly technical introduction to the language. There, we explore ways to run Python programs, peek at Python's byte code execution model, and introduce the basics of module files for saving your code. Our goal will be to give you just enough information to run the examples and exercises in the rest of the book. As mentioned earlier, you won't really start programming until Chapter 4, but make sure you have a handle on the startup details before moving on.

CHAPTER 2

How Python Runs Programs

This chapter and the next give a quick look at program execution—how you launch code, and how Python runs it. In this chapter, we explain the Python interpreter. Chapter 3 will show you how to get your own programs up and running.

Startup details are inherently platform-specific, and some of the material in this chapter may not apply to the platform you work on, so you should feel free to skip parts not relevant to your intended use. In fact, more advanced readers who have used similar tools in the past, and prefer to get to the meat of the language quickly, may want to file some of this chapter away for future reference. For the rest of you, let's learn how to run some code.

Introducing the Python Interpreter

So far, we've mostly been talking about Python as a programming language. But as currently implemented, it's also a software package called an *interpreter*. An interpreter is a kind of program that executes other programs. When you write Python programs, the Python interpreter reads your program, and carries out the instructions it contains. In effect, the interpreter is a layer of software logic between your code and the computer hardware on your machine.

When the Python package is installed on your machine, it generates a number of components—minimally, an interpreter and a support library. Depending on how you use it, the Python interpreter may take the form of an executable program, or a set of libraries linked into another program. Depending on which flavor of Python you run, the interpreter itself may be implemented as a C program, a set of Java classes, or other. Whatever form it takes, the Python code you write must always be run by this interpreter. And to do that, you must first install a Python interpreter on your computer.

Python installation details vary per platform, and are covered in depth in Appendix A. In short:

- Windows users fetch and run a self-installing executable file, which puts Python on their machine. Simply double-click and say Yes or Next at all prompts.

- Linux and Unix users typically either install Python from RPM files, or compile it from its full source-code distribution package.

- Other platforms have installation techniques relevant to that platform. For instance, files are synched on Palm Pilots.

Python itself may be fetched from the downloads page at Python's web site, *www.python.org*. It may also be found through various other distribution channels. You may have Python already available on your machine, especially on Linux and Unix. If you're working on Windows, you'll usually find Python in the Start menu, as captured in Figure 2-1 (we'll learn what these menu items mean in a moment). On Unix and Linux, Python probably lives in your */usr* directory tree.

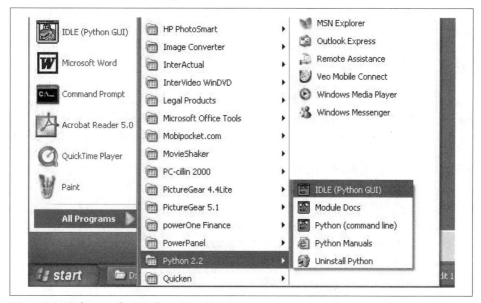

Figure 2-1. Python on the Windows Start menu

Because installation details are so platform-specific, we'll finesse the rest of this story here. (For more details on the installation process, consult Appendix A.) For the purposes of this chapter and the next, we'll assume that you've got Python ready to go.

Program Execution

What it means to write and run a Python script depends on whether you look at these tasks as a programmer or as a Python interpreter. Both views offer important perspective on Python programming.

The Programmer's View

In its simplest form, a Python program is just a text file containing Python statements. For example, the following file, named *script1.py*, is one of the simplest Python scripts we could dream up, but it passes for an official Python program:

```
print 'hello world'
print 2 ** 100
```

This file contains two Python print statements, which simply print a string (the text in quotes) and a numeric expression result (2 to the power 100) to the output stream. Don't worry about the syntax of this code yet—for this chapter, we're interested only in getting it to run. We'll explain the print statement, and why you can raise 2 to the power 100 in Python without overflowing, in later parts of this book.

You can create such a file of statements with any text editor you like. By convention, Python program files are given names that end in ".py"; technically, this naming scheme is required only for files that are "imported," as shown later in this book, but most Python files have *.py* names for consistency.

After you've typed these statements into a text file in one way or another, you must tell Python to *execute* the file—which simply means to run all the statements from top to bottom in the file, one after another. Python program files may be launched by command lines, by clicking their icons, and with other standard techniques. We'll demonstrate how to invoke this execution in the next chapter. If all goes well, you'll see the results of the two print statements show up somewhere on your computer—by default, usually in the same window you were in when you ran the program:

```
hello world
1267650600228229401496703205376
```

For example, here's how this script ran from a DOS command line on a Windows laptop, to make sure it didn't have any silly typos:

```
D:\temp>python script1.py
hello world
1267650600228229401496703205376
```

We've just run a Python script that prints a string and a number. We probably won't win any programming awards with this code, but it's enough to capture the basics of program execution.

Python's View

The brief description of the prior section is fairly standard for scripting languages, and is usually all that most Python programmers need to know. You type code into text files, and run those files through the interpreter. Under the hood, though, a bit more happens when you tell Python to "go." Although knowledge of Python internals is not strictly required for Python programming, a basic understanding of the runtime structure of Python can help you grasp the bigger picture of program execution.

When you instruct Python to run your script, there are a few steps that Python carries out before your code actually starts crunching away. Specifically, it's first compiled to something called byte code, and then routed to something called a virtual machine.

Byte code compilation

Internally, and almost completely hidden from you, Python first compiles your *source code* (the statements in your file) into a format known as *byte code*. Compilation is simply a translation step, and byte code is a lower-level, and platform-independent, representation of your source code. Roughly, each of your source statements is translated into a group of byte code instructions. This byte code translation is performed to speed execution—byte code can be run much quicker than the original source code statements.

You'll notice the prior paragraph said that this is *almost* completely hidden from you. If the Python process has write-access on your machine, it will store the byte code of your program in files that end with a *.pyc* extension (".pyc" means compiled ".py" source). You will see these files show up on your computer after you've run a few programs. Python saves byte code like this as a startup speed optimization. The next time you run your program, Python will load the *.pyc* and skip the compilation step, as long as you haven't changed your source code since the byte code was saved. Python automatically checks the time stamps of source and byte code files to know when it must recompile.

If Python cannot write the byte code files to your machine, your program still works—the byte code is generated in memory and simply discarded on program exit.* However, because *.pyc* files speed startup time, you'll want to make sure they are written for larger programs. Byte code files are also one way to ship Python programs—Python is happy to run a program if all it can find are *.pyc* files, even if the original *.py* source files are absent. (See the section "Frozen Binaries" later in this chapter for another shipping option.)

Python Virtual Machine (PVM)

Once your program has been compiled to byte code (or the byte code has been loaded from *.pyc* files), it is shipped off for execution to something generally known as the Python Virtual Machine (PVM, for the more acronym-inclined among you). The PVM sounds more impressive than it is; really, it's just a big loop that iterates through your byte code instructions, one by one, to carry out their operations. The PVM is the runtime engine of Python; it's always present as part of the Python system, and is the

---

* And strictly speaking, byte code is saved only for files that are imported, not for the top-level file of a program. We'll explore imports in Chapter 3, and again in Part V. Byte code is also never saved for code typed at the interactive prompt, which is described in Chapter 3.

component that truly runs your scripts. Technically, it's just the last step of what is called the Python interpreter.

Figure 2-2 illustrates the runtime structure described. Keep in mind that all of this complexity is deliberately hidden to Python programmers. Byte code compilation is automatic, and the PVM is just part of the Python system that you have installed on your machine. Again, programmers simply code and run files of statements.

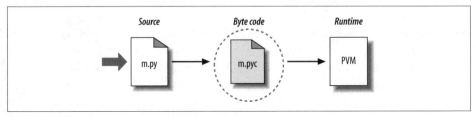

Figure 2-2. Runtime execution model

Performance implications

Readers with a background in fully compiled languages such as C and C++ might notice a few differences in the Python model. For one thing, there is usually no build or "make" step in Python work: code runs immediately after it is written. For another, Python byte code is not binary machine code (e.g., instructions for an Intel chip). Byte code is a Python-specific representation.

This is why some Python code may not run as fast as C or C++, as described in Chapter 1—the PVM loop, not the CPU chip, still must interpret the byte code, and byte code instructions require more work than CPU instructions. On the other hand, unlike classic interpreters, there is still a compile step internally—Python does not need to reanalyze and reparse each source statement repeatedly. The net effect is that pure Python code runs somewhere between a traditional compiled language, and a traditional interpreted language. See Chapter 1 for more on Python performance.

Development implications

Another ramification of Python's execution model is that there is really no distinction between the development and execution environments. That is, the systems that compile and execute your source code are really one in the same. This similarity may have a bit more significance to readers with a background in traditional compiled languages; but in Python, the compiler is always present at runtime, and is part of the system that runs programs.

This makes for a much more rapid development cycle—there is no need to precompile and link before execution may begin. Simply type and run the code. This also adds a much more dynamic flavor to the language—it is possible, and often very convenient, for Python programs to construct and execute other Python programs at runtime. The eval and exec built-ins, for instance, accept and run strings containing

Python program code. This structure is also why Python lends itself to product customization—because Python code can be changed on the fly, users can modify the Python parts of a system onsite, without needing to have or compile the entire system's code.

Execution Model Variations

Before moving on, we should point out that the internal execution flow described in the prior section reflects the standard implementation of Python today, and is not really a requirement of the Python language itself. Because of that, the execution model is prone to change with time. In fact, there are already a few systems that modify the picture in Figure 2-2 somewhat. Let's take a few moments to explore the most prominent of these variations.

Python Implementation Alternatives

Really, as this book is being written, there are two primary implementations of the Python language—*CPython* and *Jython*—along with a handful of secondary implementations such as *Python.NET*. CPython is the standard implementation; all the others have very specific purposes and roles. All implement the same Python language, but execute programs in different ways.

CPython

The original, and standard, implementation of Python is usually called CPython, when you want to contrast it with the other two. Its name comes from the fact that it is coded in portable ANSI C language code. This is the Python that you fetch from *www.python.org*, get with the ActivePython distribution, and have automatically in most Linux machines. If you've found a preinstalled version of Python on your machine, it's probably CPython as well, unless your company is using Python in very specialized ways.

Unless you want to script Java or .NET applications with Python, you probably want to use the standard CPython system. Because it is the reference implementation of the language, it tends to run fastest, be the most complete, and be more robust than the alternative systems. Figure 2-2 reflects CPython's runtime architecture.

Jython

The Jython system (originally known as JPython) is an alternative implementation of the Python language, targeted for integration with the Java programming language. Jython consists of Java classes that compile Python source code to Java byte code, and then route the resulting byte code to the Java Virtual Machine (JVM). Programmers still code Python statements in *.py* text files as usual; the Jython system essentially just replaces the rightmost two bubbles in Figure 2-2 with Java-based equivalents.

Jython's goal is to allow Python code to script Java applications, much as CPython allows Python to script C and C++ components. Its integration with Java is remarkably seamless. Because Python code is translated to Java byte code, it looks and feels like a true Java program at runtime. Jython scripts can serve as web applets and servlets, build Java-based GUIs, and so on. Moreover, Jython includes integration support that allows Python code to import and use Java classes, as though they were coded in Python. Because Jython is slower and less robust than CPython, it is usually seen as a tool of interest primarily to Java developers.

Python.NET

A third, and still somewhat experimental implementation of Python, is designed to allow Python programs to integrate with applications coded to Microsoft's .NET framework. .NET and its C# programming language runtime system are designed to be a language-neutral object communication layer, in the spirit of Microsoft's earlier COM model. Python.NET allows Python programs to act as both client and server components, accessible from other .NET languages.

By implementation, Python.NET is very much like Jython—it replaces the last two bubbles in Figure 2-2 for execution in the .NET environment. Also like Jython, Python.NET has a special focus—it is primarily of interest to developers integrating Python with .NET components. (Python.NET's evolution is unclear as we write this; for more details, consult Python online resources.)

The Psyco Just-in-Time Compiler

CPython, Jython, and Python.NET all implement the Python language in similar ways: by compiling source code to byte code, and executing the byte code on an appropriate virtual machine. The *Psyco* system is not another Python implementation, but a component that extends the byte code execution model to make programs run faster. In terms of Figure 2-2, Psyco is an enhancement to the PVM, which collects and uses type information while the program runs, to translate portions of the program's byte code all the way down to real binary machine code for faster execution. Psyco accomplishes this translation without requiring either changes to the code, or a separate compilation step during development.

Roughly, while your program runs, Psyco collects information about the kinds of objects being passed around; that information can be used to generate highly-efficient machine code tailored for those object types. Once generated, the machine code then replaces the corresponding part of the original byte code, to speed your program's overall execution. The net effect is that, with Psyco, your program becomes much quicker over time, and as it is running. In ideal cases, some Python code may become as fast as compiled C code under Psyco.

Because this translation from byte code happens at program runtime, Psyco is generally known as a *just-in-time* (JIT) compiler. Psyco is actually a bit more than JIT compilers you may have seen for the Java language. Really, Psyco is a *specializing JIT compiler*—it generates machine code tailored to the data types that your program actually uses. For example, if a part of your program uses different data types at different times, Psyco may generate a different version of machine code to support each different type combination.

Psyco has been shown to speed Python code dramatically. According to its web page, Psyco provides "2× to 100× speed-ups, typically 4×, with an unmodified Python interpreter and unmodified source code, just a dynamically loadable C extension module." Of equal significance, the largest speedups are realized for algorithmic code written in pure Python—exactly the sorts of code you might normally migrate to C to optimize. With Psyco, such migrations become even less important.

Psyco is also not yet a standard part of Python; you will have to fetch and install it separately. It is also still something of a research project, so you'll have to track its evolution online. For more details on the Psyco extension, and other JIT efforts that may arise, consult *http://www.python.org*; Psyco's home page currently resides at *http://psyco.sourceforge.net*.

Frozen Binaries

Sometimes when people ask for a "real" Python compiler, what they really seek is simply a way to generate a standalone binary executable from their Python programs. This is more a packaging and shipping idea than an execution-flow concept, but is somewhat related. With the help of third-party tools that you can fetch off the Web, it is possible to turn your Python programs into true executables—known as *frozen binaries* in the Python world.

Frozen binaries bundle together the byte code of your program files, along with the PVM (interpreter) and any Python support files your program needs, into a single package. There are some variations on this theme, but the end result can be a single binary executable program (e.g., an *.exe* file on Windows), which may be shipped easily to customers. In Figure 2-2, it is as though the byte code and PVM are merged into a single component—a frozen binary file.

Today, three primary systems are capable of generating frozen binaries: *Py2exe* (for Windows), *Installer* (similar, but works on Linux and Unix too, and is also capable of generating self-installing binaries), and *freeze* (the original). You may have to fetch these tools separately from Python itself, but they are available free of charge. They are also constantly evolving, so see *http://www.python.org* and the Vaults of Parnassus web site for more on these tools. To give you an idea of the scope of these systems,

Py2exe can freeze standalone programs that use the Tkinter, Pmw, wxPython, and PyGTK GUI libraries; programs that use the *pygame* game programming toolkit; win32com client programs; and more.

Frozen binaries are not the same as the output of a true compiler—they run byte code through a virtual machine. Hence, apart from a possible startup improvement, frozen binaries run at the same speed as the original source files. Frozen binaries are also not small (they contain a PVM), but are not unusually large by current standards of large. Because Python is embedded in the frozen binary, Python does not have to be installed on the receiving end in order to run your program. Moreover, because your code is embedded in the frozen binary, it is effectively hidden from recipients.

This single file-packaging scheme is especially appealing to developers of commercial software. For instance, a Python-coded user interface program based on the Tkinter toolkit can be frozen into an executable file, and shipped as a self-contained program on CD or on the Web. End users do not need to install, or even have to know about, Python.

Future Possibilities?

Finally, note that the runtime execution model sketched here is really an artifact of the current implementation, and not the language itself. For instance, it's not impossible that a full, traditional compiler for Python source to machine code may appear during the shelf life of this book (although one has not in over a decade). New byte code formats and implementation variants may also be adopted in the future. For instance:

- The emerging *Parrot* project aims to provide a common byte code format, virtual machine, and optimization techniques, for a variety of programming languages (see *http://www.python.org*).

- The *Stackless Python* system is a standard CPython implementation variant, which does not save state on the C language call stack. This makes Python more easily ported to small stack architectures, and opens up novel programming possibilities such as co-routines.

- The new *PyPy* project is an attempt to reimplement the PVM in Python itself, in order to enable new implementation techniques.

Although such future implementation schemes may alter the runtime structure of Python somewhat, it seems likely that the byte code compiler will still be the standard for some time to come. The portability and runtime flexibility of byte code are important features to many Python systems. Moreover, adding type constraint declarations to support static compilation would break the flexibility, conciseness, simplicity, and overall spirit of Python coding. Due to Python's highly dynamic nature, any future implementation will likely retain many artifacts of the current PVM.

## CHAPTER 3

How You Run Programs

Okay, it's time to start running some code. Now that you have a handle on program execution, you're finally ready to start some real Python programming. At this point, we'll assume that you have Python installed on your computer; if not, see Appendix A for installation and configuration hints.

There are a variety of ways to tell Python to execute the code you type. This chapter discusses all the program launching techniques in common use today. Along the way, you'll learn both how to type code *interactively*, and save it in *files* to be run with command lines, Unix tricks, icon clicks, IDEs, imports, and more.

If you just want to find out how to run a Python program quickly, you may be tempted to just read the parts that pertain to your platform and move on to Chapter 4. But don't skip the material on module imports, since that's essential to understanding Python's architecture. And we encourage you to at least skim the sections on IDLE and other IDEs, so you know what tools are available once you start developing more sophisticated Python programs.

Interactive Coding

Perhaps the simplest way to run Python programs is to type them at Python's interactive command line. There are a variety of ways to start this command line—in an IDE, from a system console, and so on. Assuming the interpreter is installed as an executable program on your system, the most platform-neutral way to start an interactive interpreter session is usually to type just "python" at your operating system's prompt, without any arguments. For example:

```
% python
Python 2.2 (#28, Dec 21 2001, 12:21:22) [MSC 32 bit (Intel)] on win32
Type "help", "copyright", "credits" or "license" for more information.
>>>
```

Here the word "python" is typed at your system shell prompt, to begin an interactive Python session (the "%" character stands for your system's prompt, not your input). The notion of a *system shell prompt* is generic, but varies per platform:

- On Windows, you can type **python** in a DOS console window (a.k.a. Command Prompt), or the Start/Run... dialog box.
- On Unix and Linux, you might type this in a shell window (e.g., in an *xterm* or console, running a shell such as *ksh* or *csh*).
- Other systems may use similar or platform-specific devices. On PalmPilots, for example, click the Python home icon to launch an interactive session; on a Zaurus PDA, open a Terminal window.

If you have not set your shell's PATH environment variable to include Python, you may need to replace the word "python" with the full path to the Python executable on your machine. For instance, on Windows, try typing **C:\Python22\python** (or **C:\ Python23\python** for Version 2.3); on Unix and Linux, **/usr/local/bin/python** (or **/usr/ bin/python**) will often suffice.

Once the Python interactive session starts, it begins by printing two lines of informational text (which we normally omit in our examples to save space), and prompts for input with >>> when it's waiting for you to type a new Python statement or expression. When working interactively, the results of your code are displayed after the >>> lines—here are the results of two Python print statements:

```
% python
>>> print 'Hello world!'
Hello world!
>>> print 2 ** 8
256
```

Again, don't worry about the details of the print statements shown here yet (we'll start digging into syntax in the next chapter). In short, they print a Python string and an integer, as shown by the output lines that appear after each >>> input line.

When working interactively like this, we can type as many Python commands as we like; each is run immediately after entered. Moreover, because the interactive session automatically prints the results of expressions typed, we don't usually need to say "print" explicitly at this prompt:

```
>>> lumberjack = 'okay'
>>> lumberjack
'okay'
>>> 2 ** 8
256
>>>                    use Ctrl-D or Ctrl-Z to exit
%
```

Here, the last two lines typed are expressions (lumberjack and 2 ** 8), and their results are displayed automatically. To exit an interactive session like this one and return to your system shell prompt, type Ctrl-D on Unix-like machines; on MS-DOS and Windows systems, type Ctrl-Z to exit. In the IDLE GUI discussed later, either type Ctrl-D, or simply close the window.

Now, we're not doing much in this session's code: we type Python print and assignment statements, and a few expressions, which we'll study in detail later. The main thing to notice is that the code entered is executed immediately by the interpreter, when the Enter key is pressed at the end of the line.

For instance, after typing the first print statement at the >>> prompt, the output (a Python string) is echoed back right away. There's no need to run the code through a compiler and linker first, as you'd normally do when using a language such as C or C++. As you'll see in later chapters, you can also run multiline statements at the interactive prompt; the statement runs immediately after you've entered all its lines.

Besides typing **python** in a shell window, you can also begin similar interactive sessions by starting IDLE's main window, or on Windows via the Start button menus for Python and select the Python (command-line) menu option as shown in Figure 2-1. Both spawn a >>> prompt with equivalent functionality—code is run as it is typed.

Testing Code at the Interactive Prompt

Because code is executed immediately, the interactive prompt turns out to be a great place to experiment with the language. It will be used often in this book to demonstrate smaller examples. In fact, this is the first rule of thumb to remember: if you're ever in doubt about how a piece of Python code works, fire up the interactive command line and try it out to see what happens. Chances are good that you won't break anything. (You need to know more about system interfaces before you will become dangerous.)

Although you won't do the bulk of your coding in interactive sessions (because the code you type there is not saved), the interactive interpreter is a great place to test code you've put in files. You can import your module files interactively, and run tests on the tools they define by typing calls at the interactive prompt. More generally, the interactive prompt is a place to test program components, regardless of their source—you can type calls to linked-in C functions, exercise Java classes under Jython, and more. Partly because of this interactive nature, Python supports an experimental and exploratory programming style you'll find convenient when starting out.

Using the Interactive Prompt

Although simple to use, there are a few ways that the interactive prompt seems to trip up beginners:

Type Python commands only. First of all, remember that you can only type Python code at the Python prompt, not system commands. There are ways to run system commands from within Python code (e.g., os.system), but they are not as direct as simply typing the command itself.

Print statements are required only in files. Because the interactive interpreter automatically prints the results of expressions, you do not need to type complete print statements interactively. This is a nice feature, but tends to confuse users when they move on to writing code in files: within a code file, you really must use print statements to see your output, because expression results are not automatically echoed. You must say print in files, but not interactively.

Don't indent at the interactive prompt (yet). When typing Python programs, either interactively or into a text file, be sure to start all your unnested statements in column 1 (that is, all the way to the left). If you don't, Python may print a "SyntaxError" message. Until Chapter 9, all statements will be unnested, so this includes everything for now. This seems to be a recurring confusion in introductory Python classes. A leading space generates an error message.

Prompts and compound statements. We won't meet compound (multiline) statements until Chapter 9, but as a preview, you should know that when typing lines two and beyond of a compound statement interactively, the prompt may change. In the simple shell window interface, the interactive prompt changes to ... instead of >>> for lines 2 and beyond; in the IDLE interface, lines after the first are automatically indented. In either case, a blank line (hitting the Enter key at the start of a line) is needed to tell interactive Python that you're done typing the multiline statement; by contrast, blank lines are ignored in files.

You'll see why this matters in Chapter 9. For now, if you happen to come across a ... prompt or blank line when entering your code, it probably means that you've somehow confused interactive Python into thinking you're typing a multiline statement. Try hitting the Enter key, or a Ctrl-C combination to get back to the main prompt. The >>> and ... prompts can also be changed (they are available in built-in module sys), but we'll assume they have not been in our examples.

System Command Lines and Files

Although the interactive prompt is great for experimenting and testing, it has one big disadvantage: programs you type there go away as soon as the Python interpreter executes them. The code you type interactively is never stored in a file, so you can't run it again without retyping it from scratch. Cut-and-paste and command recall can help some here, but not much, especially when you start writing larger programs. To cut and paste code from an interactive session, you have to edit out Python prompts, program outputs, and so on.

To save programs permanently, you need to write your code in files, usually known as *modules*. Modules are simply text files containing Python statements. Once coded, you can ask the Python interpreter to execute the statements in such a file any number of times, and in a variety of ways—by system command lines, by file icon clicks, by options in the IDLE user interface, and more. However they are run, Python executes all the code in a module file from top to bottom, each time you run the file. Such files are often referred to as *programs* in Python—a series of precoded statements.

The next few sections explore ways to run code typed into module files. In this section we run files in the most basic way: by listing their names in a python command line entered at a system prompt. As a first example, suppose we start our favorite text editor (e.g., vi, notepad, or the IDLE editor) and type two Python statements into a text file named *spam.py*:

```
print 2 ** 8                          # Raise to a power.
print 'the bright side ' + 'of life'   # + means concatenation.
```

This file contains two Python print statements and Python *comments* to the right. Text after a # is simply ignored as a human-readable comment, and is not part of the statement's syntax. Again, ignore the syntax of code in this file for now. The point to notice is that we've typed code into a file, rather than at the interactive prompt. In the process, we've coded a fully-functional Python script.

Once we've saved this text file, we can ask Python to run it by listing its full filename as a first argument on a python command, typed at the system shell's prompt:

```
% python spam.py
256
the bright side of life
```

Here again, you will type such a system shell command in whatever your system provides for command-line entry—a DOS console window, an xterm, or similar. Remember to replace "python" with a full directory path if your PATH setting is not configured. The output of this little script shows up after the command is typed—it's the result of the two print statements in the text file.

Notice that the module file is called *spam.py*. As for all top-level files, it could also be called simply *spam*, but files of code we want to import into a client have to end with a *.py* suffix. We'll study imports later in this chapter. Because you may want to import a file in the future, it's a good idea to use *.py* suffixes for most Python files that you code. Some text editors also detect Python files by their *.py* suffix; if the suffix is not present, you may not get things like syntax colorization and automatic indentation.

Because this scheme uses shell command lines to start Python programs, all the usual shell syntax applies. For instance, we can route the output of a Python script to a file in order to save it, by using special shell syntax:

```
% python spam.py > saveit.txt
```

In this case, the two output lines shown in the prior run show up in file *saveit.txt*, instead of being printed. This is generally known as *stream redirection*; it works for both input and output text, and works on both Windows and Unix-like systems. It also has little to do with Python (Python simply supports it), so we will skip further details on redirection here.

If you are working on a Windows or MS-DOS platform, this example works the same, but the system prompt is normally different:

```
C:\Python22>python spam.py
256
the bright side of life
```

As usual, be sure to type the full path to Python if you haven't set your PATH environment variable:

```
D:\temp>C:\python22\python spam.py
256
the bright side of life
```

(On some versions of Windows, you can also type just the name of your script, regardless of the directory you work in. Because newer Windows systems use the Windows registry to find a program with which to run a file, you don't need to list it on the command line explicitly.)

Finally, remember to give the full path to your script file if it lives in a different directory than the one you are working in. For example, the following system command line, run from *D:\other*, assumes Python is on your system path, but runs a file located elsewhere:

```
D:\other>python c:\code\myscript.py
```

Using Command Lines and Files

Running program files from system command lines is also a fairly straightforward launch option, especially if you are familiar with command lines in general from prior Unix or DOS work. Here are a few pointers about common beginner traps before moving on:

Beware of automatic extensions on Windows. If you use the Notepad program to code program files on Windows, be careful to pick type All Files when it comes time to save your file, and give your file a *.py* suffix explicitly. Otherwise, Notepad saves your file with a ".txt" extension (e.g., as spam.py.txt), making it difficult to run in some launching schemes.

Worse, Windows hides file extensions by default unless you have changed your view options, so you may not even notice that you've coded a text file, not a Python file. The file's icon may give this away—if it's not a snake, you may have trouble. Un-colored code in IDLE and files that open to edit instead of run when clicked are other symptoms of this problem.

MS Word similarly adds a *.doc* extension by default; much worse, it adds formatting characters that are not legal Python syntax. As a rule of thumb, always pick All Files when saving under Windows, or use more programmer-friendly text editors such as IDLE. IDLE does not even add a *.py* suffix automatically—a feature programmers like, and users do not.

Use file extensions at system prompts, but not imports. Don't forget to type the full name of your file in system command lines, that is, use `python spam.py`. This differs from Python import statements we'll meet later in this chapter, which omit both the *.py* file suffix, and directory path: `import spam`. This may seem simple, but it's a common mistake.

At the system prompt, you are in a system shell, not Python, so Python's module file search rules do not apply. Because of that, you must give the *.py* extension, and can optionally include a full directory path leading to the file you wish to run. For instance, to run a file that resides in a different directory than the one you are working in, you will typically list its full path name (`C:\python22>python d:\tests\spam.py`). Within Python code, you say just `import spam`, and rely on the Python module search path to locate your file.

Use print statements in files. Yes, this was already mentioned in the prior section, but it is so important that it should be said again here. Unlike interactive coding, you generally must use `print` statements to see output from program files.

Unix Executable Scripts (#!)

If you are going to use Python on a Unix, Linux, or Unix-like system, you can also turn files of Python code into executable programs, much as you would for programs coded in a shell language such as *csh* or *ksh*. Such files are usually called executable scripts; in simple terms, Unix-style executable scripts are just normal text files containing Python statements, but with two special properties:

Their first line is special. Scripts usually start with a first line that begins with the characters #! (often called "hash bang") followed by the path to the Python interpreter on your machine.

They usually have executable privileges. Script files are usually marked as executable, to tell the operating system that they may be run as top-level programs. On Unix systems, a command such as `chmod +x file.py` usually does the trick.

Let's look at an example. Suppose we use a text editor again, to create a file of Python code called `brian`:

```
#!/usr/local/bin/python
print 'The Bright Side of Life...'        # Another comment here
```

The special line at the top of the file tells the system where the Python interpreter lives. Technically, the first line is a Python comment. As mentioned earlier, all comments in Python programs start with a # and span to the end of the line; they are a place to insert extra information for human readers of your code. But when a comment such as the first line in this file appears, it's special, since the operating system uses it to find an interpreter for running the program code in the rest of the file.

Also, this file is called simply `brian`, without the *.py* suffix used for the module file earlier. Adding a *.py* to the name wouldn't hurt (and might help us remember that this is a Python program file); but since we don't plan on letting other modules import the code in this file, the name of the file is irrelevant. If we give the file executable privileges with a `chmod +x brian` shell command, we can run it from the operating system shell as though it were a binary program:

```
% brian
The Bright Side of Life...
```

A note for Windows users: the method described here is a Unix trick, and may not work on your platform. Not to worry; just use the basic command-line technique explored earlier. List the file's name on an explicit python command line:*

```
C:\book\tests> python brian
The Bright Side of Life...
```

In this case, you don't need the special #! comment at the top (although Python just ignores it if it's present), and the file doesn't need to be given executable privileges. In fact, if you want to run files portably between Unix and MS Windows, your life will probably be simpler if you always use the basic command-line approach, not Unix-style scripts, to launch programs.

Clicking Windows File Icons

On Windows, Python automatically registers itself to be the program that opens Python program files when they are clicked. Because of that, it is possible to launch the Python programs you write by simply clicking (or double-clicking) on their file icons with your mouse.

On Windows, icon clicks are made easy by the Windows registry. On non-Windows systems, you will probably be able to perform a similar trick, but the icons, file explorer, navigation schemes, and more may differ slightly. On some Unix systems, for instance, you may need to register the *.py* extension with your file explorer GUI, make your script executable using the #! trick of the prior section, or associate the file MIME type with an application or command by editing files, installing programs, or

---

* As seen when exploring command lines, modern Windows versions also let you type just the name of a *.py* file at the system command line—they use the registry to know to open the file with Python (e.g., typing brian.py is equivalent to typing python brian.py). This command-line mode is similar in spirit to the Unix #!. Note that some *programs* may actually interpret and use a first #! line on Windows much like Unix, but the DOS system shell and Windows itself ignores it completely.

using other tools. See your file explorer's documentation for more details, if clicks do not work correctly right off the bat.

Clicking Icons on Windows

To illustrate, suppose we create the following program file with our text editor, and save it as filename *script4.py*:

```
# A comment
import sys
print sys.platform
print 2 ** 100
```

There's not much new here—just an import and two prints again (sys.platform is just a string that identifies the kind of computer you're working on; it lives in a module called sys, which we must import to load). In fact, we can run this file from a system command line:

```
D:\OldVaio\LP-2ndEd\Examples>c:\python22\python script4.py
win32
1267650600228229401496703205376
```

Icon clicks allow us to run this file without any typing at all. If we find this file's icon—for instance, by selecting My Computer, and working our way down on the D drive—we will get the file explorer picture captured in Figure 3-1 and shown on Windows XP. Python source files show up as snakes on Windows, and byte code files as snakes with eyes closed (or with a reddish color in Version 2.3). You will normally want to click (or otherwise run) the source code file, in order to pick up your most recent changes. To launch the file here, simply click on the icon for *script4.py*.

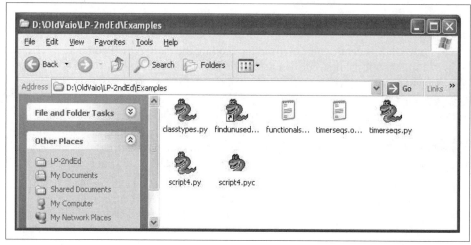

Figure 3-1. Python file icons on Windows

The raw_input Trick

Unfortunately, on Windows, the result of clicking on file icons may not be incredibly satisfying. In fact, as is, this example script generates a perplexing "flash" when clicked—not the sort of feedback that budding Python programmers usually hope for! This is not a bug, but has to do with the way the Windows port handles printed output.

By default, Python generates a pop-up black DOS console window to serve as a clicked file's input and output. If a script prints and exits, then, well, it just prints and exits—the console window appears, and text is printed there, but the console window closes and disappears on program exit. Unless you are very fast or your machine is very slow, you won't get to see your output at all. Although this is normal behavior, it's probably not what you had in mind.

Luckily, it's easy to work around this. If you need your script's output to stick around when launched with clicks, simply put a call to the built-in raw_input function at the very bottom of your script. For example:

```
# A comment
import sys
print sys.platform
print 2 ** 100
raw_input()              # ADDED
```

In general, raw_input reads the next line of standard input, and waits if there is none yet available. The net effect in this context will be to pause the script, thereby keeping the output window shown in Figure 3-2 open, until we press the Enter key.

Now that we've shown you this trick, keep in mind that it is usually only required for Windows, and then only if your script prints text and exits, and only if you will

Figure 3-2. Clicked program output with raw_input

launch this script by clicking its file icon. You should only add this call to the bottom of your top-level files, if and only if all of these three conditions apply. There is no reason to add this call in any other contexts.*

Before moving ahead, note that the raw_input call applied here is the input counterpart of using the print statement for outputs. It is the simplest way to read user input, and is more general than this example implies. For instance, raw_input:

- Optionally accepts a string that will be printed as a prompt (e.g., raw_input('Press Enter to exit'))
- Returns to your script the line of text read as a string (e.g., nextinput = raw_input( ))
- Supports input stream redirections at the system shell level (e.g., python spam.py < input.txt), just as the print statement does for output.

We'll use raw_input in more advanced ways later in this text; see Chapter 10 for an example of using it in an interactive loop.

Other Icon Click Limitations

Even with the raw_input trick, clicking file icons is not without its perils. You also may not get to see Python *error messages*. If your script generates an error, the error message text is written to the pop-up console window—which then immediately disappears as before. Worse, adding a raw_input call to your file will not help this time, because your script will likely abort long before it reaches this call. In other words, you won't be able to tell what went wrong.

Because of these limitations, it is probably best to view icon clicks as a way to launch programs after they have been debugged. Especially when starting out, use other techniques, such as system command lines and IDLE (later in this chapter), so that you can see generated error messages, and view your normal output without resorting to

---

* It is also possible to completely suppress the pop-up DOS console window for clicked files on Windows. Files whose names end in a *.pyw* extension will display only windows constructed by your script, not the default DOS console window. *.pyw* files are simply *.py* source files that have this special operational behavior on Windows. They are mostly used for Python-coded user interfaces that build windows of their own, and often in conjunction with various techniques for saving printed output and errors to files.

coding tricks. When we meet exceptions later in this book, we'll also learn that it is possible to intercept and recover from errors, so that they do not terminate our programs. Watch for the discussion of the try statement later in this book for an alternative way to keep the console window from closing on errors.

Module Imports and Reloads

So far, we've been calling files of code "modules," and using the word "import," without explaining what these terms mean. We'll study modules and larger program architecture in depth in Part V. Because imports are also a way to launch programs, this section introduces enough module basics to get you started.

In simple terms, every file of Python code whose name ends in a *.py* extension is a *module*. Other files can access the items defined by a module by *importing* that module; import operations essentially load another file, and grant access to the file's contents. Furthermore, the contents of a module are made available to the outside world through its *attributes*, a term we'll define next.

This module-based services model turns out to be the core idea behind program architecture in Python. Larger programs usually take the form of multiple module files, which import tools from other module files. One of the modules is designated as the main or top-level file, and is the one launched to start the entire program.

We'll delve into such architecture issues in more detail later in this book. This chapter is mostly interested in the fact that import operations *run* the code in a file that is being loaded, as a final step. Because of this, importing a file is yet another way to launch it.

For instance, if we start an interactive session (in IDLE, from a command line, or otherwise), we can run the original *script4.py* file that appeared earlier with a simple import:

```
D:\LP-2ndEd\Examples>c:\python22\python
>>> import script4
win32
126765060022822940149670320537б
```

This works, but only once per session (really, process), by default. After the first import, later imports do nothing, even if we change and save the module's source file again in another window:

```
>>> import script4
>>> import script4
```

This is by design; imports are too expensive an operation to repeat more than once per program run. As we'll learn in Chapter 15, imports must find files, compile to byte code, and run the code. If we really want to force Python to rerun the file again in the same session (without stopping and restarting the session), we need to instead call the built-in reload function:

```
>>> reload(script4)
win32
65536
<module 'script4' from 'script4.py'>
>>>
```

The reload function loads and runs the current version of your file's code, if you've changed it in another window. This allows you to edit and pick up new code on the fly, within the current Python interactive session. In this session, for example, the second print statement in script4.py was changed in another window to print 2 ** 16, between the time of the first import and the reload call.

The reload function expects the name of an already-loaded module object, so you have to have successfully imported once, before you reload. Notice that reload also expects parenthesis around the module object name, whereas import does not—reload is a function that is *called*, and import is a statement. That's why we must pass the module name as an argument in parenthesis, and is why we get back an extra output line when reloading. The last output line is just the print representation of the reload call's return value, a Python module object. More on functions in Chapter 12.

The Grander Module Story: Attributes

Imports and reloads provide a natural program launch option, because files are executed by import operations as a last step. In the broader scheme of things, though, modules serve the role of *libraries* of tools, as we'll learn in Part V. More generally, a module is mostly just a package of names, known as a *namespace*. And the names within that package are called *attributes*—variable names that are attached to a specific object.

In typical use, importers gain access to all the names assigned at the top level of a module's file. These names are usually assigned to services exported by the module—functions, classes, variables, and so on—which are intended to be used in other files and other programs. Outside a file, its names can be fetched with two Python statements: import and from, as well as the reload call.

To illustrate, suppose we use a text editor to create the one-line Python module file *myfile.py*, shown in the following example. This may be one of the world's simplest Python modules (it contains a single assignment statement), but it's enough to illustrate the basics. When this file is imported, its code is run to generate the module's attribute—this file's assignment statement creates a module attribute named title:

```
title = "The Meaning of Life"
```

Now, we can access this module's attribute `title` in other components in two different ways. With the `import` statement, we get back the module as a whole, and *qualify* the module name by the attribute name to access:

```
% python                    Start Python.
>>> import myfile           Run file; load module as a whole.
>>> print myfile.title      Use its attribute names: '.' to qualify.
The Meaning of Life
```

In general, the dot expression syntax `object.attribute` lets us fetch any attribute attached to any object, and is a common operation in Python code. Here, we use it to access the string variable `title` inside module `myfile`—that is, `myfile.title`. Alternatively, we can fetch (really, copy) names out of a module with `from` statements:

```
% python                        Start Python.
>>> from myfile import title    Run file; copy its names.
>>> print title                 Use name directly: no need to qualify.
The Meaning of Life
```

As we'll see in more detail later, `from` is just like an `import`, with an extra assignment to names in the importing component. Because it also copies names from the imported file, though, we use imports directly without going through the original module name. Technically, `from` copies a module's *attributes*, such that they become simple *variables* in the recipient—we simply refer to the imported string this time as `title` (a variable) instead of `myfile.title` (an attribute reference).[*]

Whether we use `import` or `from` to invoke an import operation, the statements in the module file *myfile.py* are executed, and the importing component (here, the interactive prompt) gains access to names assigned at the top level of the file. There's only one such name in this simple example—the variable `title`, assigned to a string—but the concept will be more useful when we start defining more useful objects such as functions and classes in our modules. Such objects become reusable software components accessed by name from one or more client modules.

In practice, module files usually define more than one name to be used in and outside the file. Here's an example that defines three:

```
a = 'dead'         # Define three attributes.
b = 'parrot'       # Exported to other files
c = 'sketch'
print a, b, c      # Also used in this file
```

This file, *threenames.py*, assigns three variables, and so generates three attributes for the outside world. It also uses its own three variables in a `print` statement, as we see when we run this as a top-level file:

```
% python threenames.py
dead parrot sketch
```

---

[*] Notice that `import` and `from` both list the name of the module file as simply *myfile*, *without* its *.py* suffix. As we'll learn in Part V, when Python looks for the actual file, it knows to include the suffix in its search procedure. Again, remember to include the suffix in system shell command lines, but not in import statements.

When this file is imported elsewhere, all its code runs as usual the first time it is imported (by either an import or from). Clients of this file that use import get a module with attributes; clients that use from get copies of the file's names:

```
% python
>>> import threenames                    Grab the whole module.
dead parrot sketch
>>>
>>> threenames.b, threenames.c
('parrot', 'sketch')
>>>
>>> from threenames import a, b, c       Copy multiple names.
>>> b, c
('parrot', 'sketch')
```

The results here are printed in parenthesis, because they are really *tuples*—a kind of object covered in the next part of this book.

Once you start coding modules with multiple names like this, the built-in dir function starts to come in handy to fetch a list of the names available inside a module:

```
>>> dir(threenames)
['__builtins__', '__doc__', '__file__', '__name__', 'a', 'b', 'c']
```

When the dir function is called with the name of an imported module passed in parentheses like this, it returns all the attributes inside that module. Some of the names it returns are names you get "for free": names with leading and trailing double underscores are built-in names that are always predefined by Python, and have special meaning to the interpreter. The variables our code defined by assignment—a, b, and c, show up last in the dir result.

Import and Reload Usage Notes

For some reason, once people find out about running by imports and reloads, many tend to focus on this alone, and forget about other launch options that always run the current version of the code (e.g., icon clicks, IDLE menu options, and command lines). This can lead to confusion quickly—you need to remember when you've imported to know if you can reload, need to remember to use parenthesis in reload (only), and need to remember to use reload in the first place to get the current version of your code to run.

Because of these complications (and others we'll meet later), avoid the temptation to launch by imports and reloads for now. The IDLE Edit/RunScript menu option, for example, provides a simpler and less error-prone way to run your files. On the other hand, imports and reloads have proven to be a popular testing technique in Python classes, so you be the judge. If you find yourself running into a wall, though, stop.

There is more to the module story than exposed here, and you may run into trouble if you use modules in unusual ways at this point in the book; for instance, if you try to import a module file that is stored in a directory other than the one you're working in, you'll have to skip ahead to Chapter 15, and learn about the *module search path*. For now, if you must import, try to keep all your files in the directory you are working in, to avoid complications.

The IDLE User Interface

IDLE is a graphical user interface for doing Python development, and is a standard and free part of the Python system. It is usually referred to as an *Integrated Development Environment* (IDE), because it binds together various development tasks into a single view.*

In short, IDLE is a GUI that lets you edit, run, browse, and debug Python programs, all from a single interface. Moreover, because IDLE is a Python program that uses the Tkinter GUI toolkit, it runs portably on most Python platforms: MS Windows, X Windows (Unix, Linux), and Macs. For many, IDLE is an easy-to-use alternative to typing command lines, and a less problem-prone alternative to clicking on icons.

IDLE Basics

Let's jump right into an example. IDLE is easy to start under Windows—it has an entry in the Start button menu for Python (see Figure 2-1); it can also be selected by right-clicking on a Python program icon. On some Unix-like systems, you may need to launch IDLE's top-level script from a command line or icon click—start file *idle.pyw* in the *idle* subdirectory of Python's *Tools* directory.†

Figure 3-3 shows the scene after starting IDLE on Windows. The Python Shell window at the bottom is the main window, which runs an interactive session (notice the >>> prompt). This works like all interactive sessions—code you type here is run immediately after you type it—and serves as a testing tool.

IDLE uses familiar menus with keyboard shortcuts for most of its operations. To make (or edit) a script under IDLE, open text edit windows—in the main window, select the File menu pulldown, and pick New window to open a text edit window (or Open... to edit an existing file). The window at the top of Figure 3-3 is an IDLE text edit window, where the code for file *script3.py* was entered.

Although this may not show up fully in this book, IDLE uses syntax-directed *colorization* for the code typed in both the main window, and all text edit windows—keywords

---

* IDLE is a corruption of IDE, named in honor of Monty Python member Eric Idle.

† IDLE is a Python program that uses the standard library's Tkinter GUI toolkit to build the IDLE GUI. This makes IDLE portable, but also means that you'll need to have Tkinter support in your Python to use IDLE. The Windows version of Python does by default, but Linux and Unix users occasionally need to install the appropriate Tkinter support (see the installation hints in Appendix A for details).

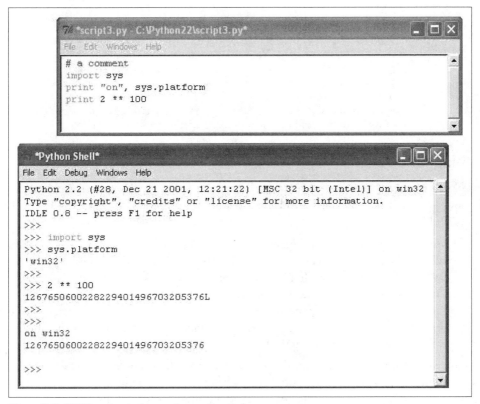

Figure 3-3. IDLE main window and text edit window

are one color, literals are another, and so on. This helps give you a better picture of the components in your code.

To run a file of code that you are editing in IDLE, select the file's text edit window, pick that window's Edit menu pulldown, and choose the Run Script option there (or use the equivalent keyboard shortcut, listed in the menu). Python will let you know that you need to save your file first, if you've changed it since it was opened or last saved. (In Python 2.3, the menu structure changes slightly: the Run Module option in the new Run menu has the same effect as the prior version's Edit/Runscript menu selection. See the sidebar "IDLE Changes in 2.3" later in this chapter.)

When run this way, the output of your script, and any error messages it may generate, shows up back in the main interactive window. In Figure 3-3, for example, the last two lines in the bottom interactive window reflect an execution of the script in the top text edit window.

Hint of the day: To repeat prior commands in IDLE's main interactive window, use Alt-P to scroll backwards through command history and Alt-N to scroll forwards. Your prior commands are recalled and displayed, and may be edited and rerun. You can also recall commands by positioning the cursor on them, or use cut-and-paste operations, but these tend to be more work. Outside IDLE, you may be able to recall commands in an interactive session with the arrow keys on Windows, if you're running doskey or using a recent version of Windows.

Using IDLE

IDLE is free, easy to use, and portable. But it is also somewhat limited compared to more advanced commercial IDEs. Here are a list of common issues that seem to trip up IDLE beginners:

You must add ".py" explicitly when saving your files. We mentioned this when talking about files in general, but it's a common IDLE stumbling block, especially for Windows users. IDLE does not automatically add a *.py* extension to file names when files are saved. Be careful to type the *.py* extension at the end of filenames yourself, when saving them for the first time. If you don't, you will be able to run your file from IDLE (and command lines), but will not be able to import your file either interactively or from other modules.

Make sure you're not looking at old error messages. IDLE currently does not do a good job of separating the output of each script execution in the interactive window—there is no blank line between the outputs. Because of that, many a beginner has been fooled by a prior run's error message into thinking that their script is still failing, when in fact it is silently succeeding. Make sure the error messages you see are not old—typing an empty line in the interactive window helps.

Run scripts from text edit windows, not the interactive window. To run a file of code under IDLE, always select the Edit/RunScript menu option from within the *text edit window* where you are editing the code to be run—not from within the main interactive window where the >>> prompt appears. The RunScript option should arguably not be available in the interactive window at all (and in fact seems to have disappeared in the recent release); if you select it there, you'll wind up trying to run a log of your interactive session, with less than desirable results!

Tkinter GUI programs may not work well with IDLE. Because IDLE is a Python/Tkinter program, it can be hung if you use it to run certain types of Python/Tkinter programs, especially if your code runs a Tkinter mainloop call. Your code may not exhibit such problems, but as a rule of thumb, it's always safe if you use IDLE to edit GUI programs, but launch them using other options such as clicks or command lines.

Other programs may not work well with IDLE either. More generally, because IDLE currently (in 2.2) runs your code in the same process that IDLE itself runs in, it's not impossible to hang IDLE with non-GUI programs as well. In fact, because IDLE uses neither processes nor threads to launch scripts, an infinite loop may render IDLE completely unresponsive. As a rule of thumb, if you can't find a reason for a program failure under IDLE, try running the program outside IDLE to make sure your problem is not really an IDLE problem.

This may improve over time (see the sidebar "IDLE Changes in 2.3"). The upside to this structure today is that, because your script is run in IDLE's environment, variables in your code show up automatically in the IDLE interactive session—you don't always need to run import commands to access names at the top level of files you've already run.

Run scripts by Edit/Run Script, not imports and reloads. In the prior section, we saw that it's also possible to run a file by importing it interactively. However, this scheme can grow complex because you are required to manually reload files after changes. By contrast, the Edit/RunScript option in IDLE always runs the most current version of your file. It also prompts you to save it first, if needed—another common mistake outside IDLE.

Technically speaking, IDLE's Edit/Runscript option always runs the current version of the top-level file only; imported files may still need to be interactively reloaded when changed. In general, though, Edit/Runscript eliminates common confusions surrounding imports. If you choose to use the import and reload technique instead, remember to use Alt-P/Alt-N key combinations to recall prior commands.

Customizing IDLE. To change the text fonts and colors in IDLE, edit the configuration files in IDLE's source directory. For example, for Python 2.2 on Windows, the file *C:\Python22\Tools\idle\config-win.txt* specifies text font and size. See file *config.txt* in that directory or IDLE's help pulldown menu for more hints. Also see the sidebar "IDLE Changes in 2.3".

There is currently no clear-screen in IDLE. This seems to be a frequent request (perhaps because of similar IDEs), and might be added eventually. Today, though, there is no way to clear the interactive window's text. If you want the window's text to go away, you can press and hold the Enter key, or type a Python loop to print blank lines.

Besides the basic edit and run functions, IDLE provides more advanced features, including a point-and-click program debugger and an object browser. Figure 3-4, for example, shows the IDLE debugger and object browser windows in action. The browser allows you to navigate through the module search path to files and objects in files; clicking on a file or object opens the corresponding source in a text edit window.

IDLE debugging is initiated by selecting the Debug/Debugger menu option in the main window, and then starting your script by selecting the Edit/Run Script option in the text edit window; once started, you can set breakpoints in your code that stop its execution by right-clicking on lines in the text edit windows, show variable values, and so on. You can also watch program execution when debugging—selecting the debugger's source toggle will cause the active line to be highlighted in the text edit window, as you step through your code.

In addition, IDLE's text editor offers a large collection of programmer-friendly tools, including automatic indentation, advanced text and file search operations, and more. Because IDLE uses intuitive GUI interactions, experiment with the system live to get a feel for its other tools.

Other IDEs

Because IDLE is free, portable, and a standard part of Python, it's a nice first development tool to become familiar with if you want to use an IDE at all. Use IDLE for this book's exercises if you're just starting out. There are, however, a handful of alternative IDEs for Python developers, some of which are substantially more powerful and robust than IDLE. Among the most commonly used today are these four:

Komodo

A full-featured development environment GUI for Python (and other languages). Komodo includes standard syntax-coloring text editing, debugging, and so on. In addition, Komodo offers many advanced features that IDLE does not, including

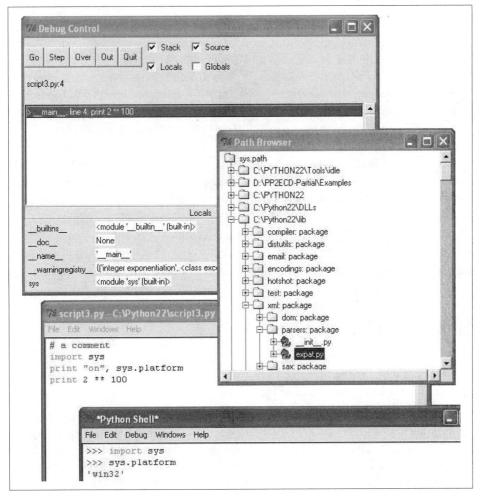

Figure 3-4. IDLE debugger and path/object browser

project files, source-control integration, regular expression debugging, and a drag-and-drop GUI builder which generates Python/Tkinter code to implement the GUIs you design interactively. Komodo is not free as we write this; it is available at *http://www.activestate.com*.

PythonWorks

Another full-featured development environment GUI. PythonWorks also has standard IDE tools, and provides a Python/Tkinter GUI builder that generates Python code. In addition, it supports unique features such as automatic code refactoring, for optimal maintenance and reuse. This is also a commercial product; see *http://www.pythonware.com* for details.

PythonWin

A free IDE that ships as part of ActiveState's ActivePython distribution (and may also be fetchable separately from *http://www.python.org* resources). PythonWin is a Windows-only IDE for Python; it is roughly like IDLE, with a handful of useful Windows-specific extensions added in. For instance, PythonWin has support for COM objects. It also adds basic user interface features beyond IDLE, such as object attribute list popups. Further, PythonWin serves as an example of using the Windows extension package's GUI library. See *http://www.activestate.com*.

Visual Python

ActiveState also sells a system called Visual Python, which is a plug-in that adds Python support to Microsoft's Visual Studio development environment. This is also a Windows-only solution, but is appealing to developers with a prior intellectual investment in Visual Studio. See ActiveState's web site for details.

There are roughly half a dozen other well-known IDEs that we are aware of (e.g., WingIDE, PythonCard), and more will probably appear over time. Rather than trying to document them all here, see the resources available at *http://www.python.org*, as well as the Vaults of Parnassus web site.

Embedding Calls

So far, we've seen how to run code typed interactively, and how to launch code saved in files with command lines, icon clicks, IDEs, module imports, and Unix executable scripts. That covers most of the cases we'll see in this book.

But in some specialized domains, Python code may also be run by an enclosing system. In such cases, we say that Python programs are *embedded* in (i.e., run by) another program. The Python code itself may be entered into a text file, stored in a database, fetched from an HTML page, parsed from an XML document, and so on. But from an operational perspective, another system—not you—may tell Python to run the code you've created.

For example, it's possible to create and run strings of Python code from a C program by calling functions in the Python runtime API (a set of services exported by the libraries created when Python is compiled on your machine):

```
#include <Python.h>
...
Py_Initialize();
PyRun_SimpleString("x = brave + sir + robin");
```

In this C code snippet, a program coded in the C language embeds the Python interpreter by linking in its libraries, and passes it a Python assignment statement string to run. C programs may also gain access to Python objects, and process or execute them using other Python API tools.

This book isn't about Python/C integration, but you should be aware that, depending on how your organization plans to use Python, you may or may not be the one who actually starts the Python programs you create.* Regardless, you can still likely use the interactive and file-based launching techniques described here, to test code in isolation from those enclosing systems that may eventually use it.

Frozen Binary Executables

Frozen binary executables are packages that combine your program's byte code and the Python interpreter into a single executable program. With these, programs can be launched in the same ways that you would launch any other executable program (icon clicks, command lines, etc.). While this option works well for delivery of products, it is not really intended for use during program development. You normally freeze just before shipping, and after development is finished.

Text Editor Launch Options

Many programmer-friendly text editors have support for editing, and possibly running, Python programs. Such support may be either built-in, or fetchable on the web. For instance, if you are familiar with the emacs text editor, you can do all your Python editing and launching from inside the text editor itself. See the text editor resources page at *http://www.python.org/editors* for more details.

Other Launch Options

Depending on your platform, there may be additional ways that you can start Python programs. For instance, on some Macintosh systems, you may be able to drag Python program file icons onto the Python interpreter icon, to make them execute. And on Windows, you can always start Python scripts with the Run... option in the Start menu. Finally, the Python standard library has utilities that allow Python programs to be started by other Python programs (e.g., execfile, os.popen, os.system); however, these tools are beyond the scope of the present chapter.

Future Possibilities?

Although this chapter reflects current practice, much of it has been both platform- and time-specific. Indeed, many of the execution and launch details presented arose

---

* See *Programming Python* (O'Reilly) for more details on embedding Python in C/C++. The embedding API can call Python functions directly, load modules, and more. Also note that the Jython system allows Java programs to invoke Python code, using a Java-based API (a Python interpreter class).

between this book's first and second editions. As for program execution, it's not impossible that new program launch options may arise over time.

New operating systems, and new versions of them, may also provide execution techniques beyond those outlined here. In general, because Python keeps pace with such changes, you should be able to launch it in whatever way makes sense for the machines you use, both now and in the future—be that drawing on tablet PCs or PDAs, grabbing icons in a virtual reality, or shouting a script's name over your coworkers' conversations.

Implementation changes may also impact launch schemes somewhat (e.g., a full compiler could produce normal executables, launched much like frozen binaries today). If we knew what the future truly held, though, we would probably be talking to a stock broker instead of writing these words.

Which Option Should I Use?

With all these options, the question naturally arises: Which one is best for me? In general, use the IDLE interface for development, if you are just getting started with Python. It provides a user-friendly GUI environment, and can hide some of the underlying configuration details. It also comes with a platform-neutral text editor for coding your scripts, and is a standard and free part of the Python system.

If instead, you are an experienced programmer, you might be more comfortable with simply the text editor of your choice in one window, and another window for launching the programs you edit, by system command lines or icon clicks. Because development environments are a very subjective choice, we can't offer much more in the way of universal guidelines; in general, the environment you like to use is usually the best to use.

Part I Exercises

It's time to start doing a little coding on your own. This first exercise session is fairly simple, but a few of these questions hint at topics to come in later chapters. Remember, check Appendix B for the answers; the exercises and their solutions sometimes contain supplemental information not discussed in the main part of the chapter. In other words, you should peek, even if you can manage to get all the answers on your own.

1. *Interaction.* Using a system command line, IDLE, or other, start the Python interactive command line (>>> prompt), and type the expression: "Hello World!" (including the quotes). The string should be echoed back to you. The purpose of this exercise is to get your environment configured to run Python. In some scenarios, you may need to first run a cd shell command, type the full path to the python executable, or add its path to your PATH environment variable. If desired, you can set it in your *.cshrc* or *.kshrc* file to make Python permanently available

on Unix systems; on Windows use a *setup.bat*, *autoexec.bat*, or the environment variable GUI. See Appendix A for help with environment variable settings.

2. *Programs*. With the text editor of your choice, write a simple module file—a file containing the single statement: `print 'Hello module world!'`. Store this statement in a file named *module1.py*. Now, run this file by using any launch option you like: running it in IDLE, clicking on its file icon, passing it to the Python interpreter program on the system shell's command line, and so on. In fact, experiment by running your file with as many of the launch techniques seen in this chapter as you can. Which technique seems easiest? (There is no right answer to this one.)

3. *Modules*. Next, start the Python interactive command line (>>> prompt) and import the module you wrote in Exercise 2. Try moving the file to a different directory and importing it again from its original directory (i.e., run Python in the original directory when you import); what happens? (Hint: is there still a file named *module1.pyc* in the original directory?)

4. *Scripts*. If your platform supports it, add the #! line to the top of your `module1.py` module, give the file executable privileges, and run it directly as an executable. What does the first line need to contain? Skip that if you are working on a Windows machine (#! usually only has meaning on Unix and Linux); instead try running your file by listing just its name in a DOS console window (this works on recent versions of Windows), or the Start/Run... dialog box.

5. *Errors*. Experiment with typing mathematical expressions and assignments at the Python interactive command line. First type the expression: `1 / 0`; what happens? Next, type a variable name you haven't assigned a value to yet; what happens this time?

   You may not know it yet, but you're doing exception processing, a topic we'll explore in depth in Part VII. As you'll learn there, you are technically triggering what's known as the *default exception handler*—logic that prints a standard error message.

   For full-blown source code *debugging* chores, IDLE includes a GUI debugging interface introduced in this chapter (see the advanced IDLE usage section), and a Python standard library module named `pdb` provides a command-line debugging interface (more on `pdb` in the standard library manual). When first starting out, Python's default error messages will probably be as much error handling as you need—they give the cause of the error, as well as showing the lines in your code that were active when the error occurred.

6. *Breaks*. At the Python command line, type:
   ```
   L = [1, 2]
   L.append(L)
   L
   ```

What happens? If you're using a Python newer than Release 1.5, you'll probably see a strange output that we'll describe in the next part of the book. If you're using a Python version older than 1.5.1, a Ctrl-C key combination will probably help on most platforms. Why do you think this occurs? What does Python report when you type the Ctrl-C key combination? Warning: if you do have a Python older than Release 1.5.1, make sure your machine can stop a program with a break-key combination of some sort before running this test, or you may be waiting a long time.

7. *Documentation*. Spend at least 17 minutes browsing the Python library and language manuals before moving on, to get a feel for the available tools in the standard library, and the structure of the documentation set. It takes at least this long to become familiar with the location of major topics in the manual set; once you do, it's easy to find what you need. You can find this manual in the Python Start button entry on Windows, in the Help pulldown menu in IDLE, or online at *http://www.python.org/doc*. We'll also have a few more words to say about the manuals and other documentation sources available (including PyDoc and the help function), in Chapter 11. If you still have time, go explore the Python web site (*http://www.python.org*), and the Vaults of Parnassus site link you'll find there. Especially check out the python.org documentation and search pages; they can be crucial resources in practice.

Types and Operations

In Part II, we study Python's built-in core data types, sometimes called object types. Although there are more kinds of objects in Python than we will meet in this part, the types discussed here are generally considered the core data types—the main subjects of almost every Python script you're likely to read or write.

This part of the book is organized around major core types, but watch for related topics, such as dynamic typing and general object categories, to also appear along the way. Because chapters in this part lay the groundwork assumed by later chapters, this part will work best if read in a linear fashion.

## CHAPTER 4

Numbers

This chapter begins our tour of the Python language. In Python, data takes the form of objects—either built-in objects that Python provides, or objects we create using Python and C tools. Since objects are the most fundamental notion in Python programming, we'll start this chapter with a survey of Python's built-in object types before concentrating on numbers.

Python Program Structure

By way of introduction, let's first get a clear picture of how this chapter fits into the overall Python picture. From a more concrete perspective, Python programs can be decomposed into modules, statements, expressions, and objects, as follows:

1. Programs are composed of modules.
2. Modules contain statements.
3. Statements contain expressions.
4. Expressions create and process objects.

We introduced the highest level of this hierarchy when we learned about modules in Chapter 3. This part's chapters begin at the bottom, exploring both built-in *objects*, and the *expressions* you can code to use them.

Why Use Built-in Types?

If you've used lower-level languages such as C or C++, you know that much of your work centers on implementing *objects*—also known as *data structures*—to represent the components in your application's domain. You need to lay out memory structures, manage memory allocation, implement search and access routines, and so on. These chores are about as tedious (and error prone) as they sound, and usually distract from your programs' real goals.

In typical Python programs, most of this grunt work goes away. Because Python provides powerful object types as an intrinsic part of the language, there's no need to code object implementations before you start solving problems. In fact, unless you have a need for special processing that built-in types don't provide, you're almost always better off using a built-in object instead of implementing your own. Here are some reasons why:

Built-in objects make simple programs easy to write. For simple tasks, built-in types are often all you need to represent the structure of problem domains. Because you get things such as collections (lists) and search tables (dictionaries) for free, you can use them immediately. You can get a lot of work done with Python's built-in object types alone.

Python provides objects and supports extensions. In some ways, Python borrows both from languages that rely on built-in tools (e.g., LISP), and languages that rely on the programmer to provide tool implementations or frameworks of their own (e.g., C++). Although you can implement unique object types in Python, you don't need to do so just to get started. Moreover, because Python's built-ins are standard, they're always the same; frameworks tend to differ from site to site.

Built-in objects are components of extensions. For more complex tasks you still may need to provide your own objects, using Python statements or C language interfaces. But as we'll see in later parts, objects implemented manually are often built on top of built-in types such as lists and dictionaries. For instance, a stack data structure may be implemented as a class that manages a built-in list.

Built-in objects are often more efficient than custom data structures. Python's built-in types employ already optimized data structure algorithms that are implemented in C for speed. Although you can write similar object types on your own, you'll usually be hard-pressed to get the level of performance built-in object types provide.

In other words, not only do built-in object types make programming easier, they're also more powerful and efficient than most of what can be created from scratch. Regardless of whether you implement new object types or not, built-in objects form the core of every Python program.

Table 4-1 previews the built-in object types and some of the syntax used to code their *literals*—expressions that generate objects.[*] Some of these types will probably seem familiar if you've used other languages. For instance, numbers and strings represent numeric and textual values, respectively, and files provide an interface for processing files stored on your computer.

---

[*] In this book, the term *literal* simply means an expression whose syntax generates an object—sometimes also called a *constant*. If you hear these called constants, it does not imply objects or variables that can never be changed (i.e., this is unrelated to C++'s const, or Python's "immutable"—a topic explored later in this part of the book).

Table 4-1. Built-in objects preview

Object type	Example literals/creation
Numbers	3.1415, 1234, 999L, 3+4j
Strings	'spam', "guido's"
Lists	[1, [2, 'three'], 4]
Dictionaries	{'food': 'spam', 'taste': 'yum'}
Tuples	(1,'spam', 4, 'U')
Files	text = open('eggs', 'r').read( )

The object types in Table 4-1 are more general and powerful than what you may be accustomed to. For instance, you'll find that lists and dictionaries obviate most of the work you do to support collections and searching in lower-level languages. Lists are ordered collections of other objects, and indexed by positions that start at 0. Dictionaries are collections of other objects that are indexed by key instead of position. Both dictionaries and lists may be nested, can grow and shrink on demand, and may contain objects of any type. For the full story, though, you'll have to read on.

Numbers

The first object type on the tour is Python numbers. In general, Python's number types are fairly typical and will seem familiar if you've used almost any other programming language in the past. They can be used to keep track of your bank balance, the distance to Mars, the number of visitors to your web site, and just about any other numeric quantity.

Python supports the usual numeric types (known as *integer* and *floating point*), as well as literals for creating numbers, and expressions for processing them. In addition, Python provides more advanced numeric programming support, including a complex number type, an unlimited precision integer, and a variety of numeric tool libraries. The next few sections give an overview of the numeric support in Python.

Number Literals

Among its basic types, Python supports the usual numeric types: both integer and floating-point numbers, and all their associated syntax and operations. Like the C language, Python also allows you to write integers using hexadecimal and octal literals. Unlike C, Python also has a complex number type, as well as a long integer type with unlimited precision (it can grow to have as many digits as your memory space allows). Table 4-2 shows what Python's numeric types look like when written out in a program (that is, as literals).

Table 4-2. Numeric literals

Literal	Interpretation
`1234, -24, 0`	Normal integers (C longs)
`9999999999999999999L`	Long integers (unlimited size)
`1.23, 3.14e-10, 4E210, 4.0e+210`	Floating-point (C doubles)
`0177, 0x9ff, 0XFF`	Octal and hex literals
`3+4j, 3.0+4.0j, 3J`	Complex number literals

In general, Python's numeric types are straightforward, but a few coding concepts are worth highlighting here:

Integer and floating-point literals

Integers are written as a string of decimal digits. Floating-point numbers have an embedded decimal point, and/or an optional signed exponent introduced by an e or E. If you write a number with a decimal point or exponent, Python makes it a floating-point object and uses floating-point (not integer) math when it's used in an expression. The rules for writing floating-point numbers are the same as in the C language.

Numeric precision and long integers

Plain Python integers (row 1 of Table 4-2) are implemented as C "longs" internally (i.e., at least 32 bits), and Python floating-point numbers are implemented as C "doubles"; Python numbers get as much precision as the C compiler used to build the Python interpreter gives to longs and doubles.[*]

Long integer literals

On the other hand, if an integer literal ends with an l or L, it becomes a Python long integer (not to be confused with a C long) and can grow as large as needed. In Python 2.2, because integers are converted to long integers on overflow, the letter L is no longer strictly required.

Hexadecimal and octal literals

The rules for writing hexadecimal (base 16) and octal (base 8) integers are the same as in C. Octal literals start with a leading zero (0), followed by a string of digits 0–7; hexadecimals start with a leading 0x or 0X, followed by hexadecimal digits 0–9, and A–F. In hexadecimal literals, hex digits may be coded in lower- or uppercase.

Complex numbers

Python complex literals are written as realpart+imaginarypart, where the imaginarypart is terminated with a j or J. The realpart is technically optional, and the imaginarypart can come first. Internally, they are implemented as a pair

---

[*] That is, the standard CPython implementation. In the Jython Java-based implementation, Python types are really Java classes.

of floating-point numbers, but all numeric operations perform complex math when applied to complex numbers.

Built-in Tools and Extensions

Besides the built-in number literals shown in Table 4-2, Python provides a set of tools for processing number objects:

Expression operators
    +, *, >>, **, etc.

Built-in mathematical functions
    pow, abs, etc.

Utility modules
    random, math, etc.

We'll meet all of these as we go along. Finally, if you need to do serious number-crunching, an optional extension for Python called *NumPy* (Numeric Python) provides advanced numeric programming tools, such as a matrix data type and sophisticated computation libraries. Hardcore scientific programming groups at places like Lawrence Livermore and NASA use Python with NumPy to implement the sorts of tasks they previously coded in C++ or FORTRAN.

Because it's so advanced, we won't say more about NumPy in this chapter. (See the examples in Chapter 29.) You will find additional support for advanced numeric programming in Python at the Vaults of Parnassus site. Also note that NumPy is currently an optional extension; it doesn't come with Python and must be installed separately.

Python Expression Operators

Perhaps the most fundamental tool that processes numbers is the *expression*: a combination of numbers (or other objects) and operators that computes a value when executed by Python. In Python, expressions are written using the usual mathematical notation and operator symbols. For instance, to add two numbers X and Y, say X+Y, which tells Python to apply the + operator to the values named by X and Y. The result of the expression is the sum of X and Y, another number object.

Table 4-3 lists all the operator expressions available in Python. Many are self-explanatory; for instance, the usual mathematical operators are supported: +, −, *, /, and so on. A few will be familiar if you've used C in the past: % computes a division remainder, << performs a bitwise left-shift, & computes a bitwise and result, etc. Others are more Python-specific, and not all are numeric in nature: the is operator tests object identity (i.e., address) equality, lambda creates unnamed functions, and so on. More on some of these later.

Table 4-3. Python expression operators and precedence

Operators	Description
`lambda args: expression`	Anonymous function generation
`x or y`	Logical or (y is evaluated only if x is false)
`x and y`	Logical and (y is evaluated only if x is true)
`not x`	Logical negation

`x < y, x <= y, x > y, x >= y,`
`x == y, x <> y, x != y,`
`x is y, x is not y,`
`x in y, x not in y`
	Comparison operators, value equality operators, object identity tests, and sequence membership

`x	y`	Bitwise or
`x ^ y`	Bitwise exclusive or
`x & y`	Bitwise and
`x << y, x >> y`	Shift x left or right by y bits
`-x + y, x - y`	Addition/concatenation, subtraction
`x * y, x % y, x / y, x // y`	Multiplication/repetition, remainder/format, division[a]
`-x, +x, ~x, x ** y`	Unary negation, identity, bitwise complement; binary power
`x[i], x[i:j], x.attr, x(...)`	Indexing, slicing, qualification, function calls
`(...), [...], {...}, `...``	Tuple, list,[b] dictionary, conversion to string[c]

[a] Floor division (X // Y), new in 2.2, always truncates fractional remainders. This is further described in the section "Division: Classic, Floor, and True."

[b] Beginning with Python 2.0, the list syntax ([...]) can represent either a list literal, or a *list comprehension* expression. The latter of these is a newer addition to Python, which performs an implied loop and collects expression results in a new list. Because they are often best understood in conjunction with functions, list comprehensions are postponed until Chapter 14.

[c] Conversion of objects to their print strings can also be accomplished with the more readable str and repr built-in functions, which are described in the section "Numeric Representation."

Mixed Operators: Operator Precedence

As in most languages, more complex expressions are coded by stringing together the operator expressions in Table 4-3. For instance, the sum of two multiplications might be written as a mix of variables and operators:

```
A * B + C * D
```

So how does Python know which operator to perform first? The solution to this lies in *operator precedence*. When you write an expression with more than one operator, Python groups its parts according to what are called precedence rules, and this grouping determines the order in which expression parts are computed. In Table 4-3, operators lower in the table have higher precedence and so bind more tightly in mixed expressions.

For example, if you write X + Y * Z, Python evaluates the multiplication first (Y * Z), then adds that result to X, because * has higher precedence (is lower in the table) than

+. Similarly, in this section's original example, both multiplications (A * B and C * D) will happen before their results are added.

Parentheses Group Subexpressions

You can forget about precedence completely if you're careful to group parts of expressions with parentheses. When you enclose subexpressions in parentheses, you override Python precedence rules; Python always evaluates expressions in parentheses first, before using their results in the enclosing expressions.

For instance, instead of coding X + Y * Z, write one of the following to force Python to evaluate the expression in the desired order:

```
(X + Y) * Z
X + (Y * Z)
```

In the first case, + is applied to X and Y first, because it is wrapped in parentheses. In the second case, the * is performed first (just as if there were no parentheses at all). Generally speaking, adding parentheses in big expressions is a great idea; it not only forces the evaluation order you want, but it also aids readability.

Mixed Types: Converted Up

Besides mixing operators in expressions, you can also mix numeric types. For instance, you can add an integer to a floating-point number:

```
40 + 3.14
```

But this leads to another question: what type is the result—integer or floating-point? The answer is simple, especially if you've used almost any other language before: in mixed type expressions, Python first converts operands *up* to the type of the most complicated operand, and then performs the math on same-type operands. If you've used C, you'll find this similar to type conversions in that language.

Python ranks the complexity of numeric types like so: integers are simpler than long integers, which are simpler than floating-point numbers, which are simpler than complex numbers. So, when an integer is mixed with a floating-point, as in the example, the integer is converted up to a floating-point value first, and floating-point math yields the floating-point result. Similarly, any mixed-type expression where one operand is a complex number results in the other operand being converted up to a complex number that yields a complex result.

As you'll see later in this section, as of Python 2.2, Python also automatically converts normal integers to long integers, whenever their values are too large to fit in a normal integer. Also keep in mind that all these mixed type conversions only apply when mixing *numeric* types around an operator or comparison (e.g., an integer and a floating-point number). In general, Python does not convert across other type boundaries. Adding a string to an integer, for example, results in an error, unless you manually convert one or the other; watch for an example when we meet strings in Chapter 5.

Preview: Operator Overloading

Although we're focusing on built-in numbers right now, keep in mind that all Python operators may be overloaded (i.e., implemented) by Python classes and C extension types, to work on objects you create. For instance, you'll see later that objects coded with classes may be added with + expressions, indexed with [i] expressions, and so on.

Furthermore, some operators are already overloaded by Python itself; they perform different actions depending on the type of built-in objects being processed. For example, the + operator performs addition when applied to numbers, but performs concatenation when applied to sequence objects such as strings and lists.[*]

Numbers in Action

Probably the best way to understand numeric objects and expressions is to see them in action. So, start up the interactive command line and type some basic, but illustrative operations.

Basic Operations and Variables

First of all, let's exercise some basic math. In the following interaction, we first assign two *variables* (a and b) to integers, so we can use them later in a larger expression. Variables are simply names—created by you or Python—that are used to keep track of information in your program. We'll say more about this later, but in Python:

- Variables are created when first assigned a value.
- Variables are replaced with their values when used in expressions.
- Variables must be assigned before they can be used in expressions.
- Variables refer to objects, and are never declared ahead of time.

In other words, the assignments cause these variables to spring into existence automatically.

```
% python
>>> a = 3          # Name created
>>> b = 4
```

---

[*] This is usually called *polymorphism*—the meaning of an operation depends on the type of objects being operated on. We'll revisit this word when we explore functions in Chapter 12, because it becomes a much more obvious feature there.

We've also used a *comment* here. In Python code, text after a # mark and continuing to the end of the line is considered to be a comment, and is ignored by Python. Comments are a place to write human-readable documentation for your code. Since code you type interactively is temporary, you won't normally write comments there, but they are added to examples to help explain the code.* In the next part of this book, we'll meet a related feature—documentation strings—that attaches the text of your comments to objects.

Now, let's use the integer objects in expressions. At this point, a and b are still 3 and 4, respectively; variables like these are replaced with their values whenever used inside an expression, and expression results are echoed back when working interactively:

```
>>> a + 1, a - 1          # Addition (3+1), subtraction (3-1)
(4, 2)

>>> b * 3, b / 2          # Multiplication (4*3), division (4/2)
(12, 2)

>>> a % 2, b ** 2         # Modulus (remainder), power
(1, 16)

>>> 2 + 4.0, 2.0 ** b     # Mixed-type conversions
(6.0, 16.0)
```

Technically, the results being echoed back here are *tuples* of two values, because lines typed at the prompt contain two expressions separated by commas; that's why the result is displayed in parenthesis (more on tuples later). Notice that the expressions work because the variables a and b within them have been assigned values; if you use a different variable that has never been assigned, Python reports an error rather than filling in some default value:

```
>>> c * 2
Traceback (most recent call last):
  File "<stdin>", line 1, in ?
NameError: name 'c' is not defined
```

You don't need to predeclare variables in Python, but they must be assigned at least once before you can use them at all. Here are two slightly larger expressions to illustrate operator grouping and more about conversions:

```
>>> b / 2 + a            # Same as ((4 / 2) + 3)
5
>>> print b / (2.0 + a)  # Same as (4 / (2.0 + 3))
0.8
```

In the first expression, there are no parentheses, so Python automatically groups the components according to its precedence rules—since / is lower in Table 4-3 than +,

---

* If you're working along, you don't need to type any of the comment text from # through the end of the line; comments are simply ignored by Python, and not a required part of the statements we run.

it binds more tightly, and so is evaluated first. The result is as if the expression had parenthesis as shown in the comment to the right of the code. Also notice that all the numbers are integers in the first expression; because of that, Python performs integer division and addition.

In the second expression, parentheses are added around the + part to force Python to evaluate it first (i.e., before the /). We also made one of the operands floating-point by adding a decimal point: 2.0. Because of the mixed types, Python converts the integer referenced by a to a floating-point value (3.0) before performing the +. It also converts b to a floating-point value (4.0) and performs a floating-point division; (4.0/5.0) yields a floating-point result of 0.8. If all the numbers in this expression were integers, it would invoke integer division (4/5), and the result would be the truncated integer 0 (in Python 2.2, at least—see the discussion of true division ahead).

Numeric Representation

By the way, notice that we used a print statement in the second example; without the print, you'll see something that may look a bit odd at first glance:

```
>>> b / (2.0 + a)          # Auto echo output: more digits
0.80000000000000004

>>> print b / (2.0 + a)    # print rounds off digits.
0.8
```

The whole story behind this has to do with the limitations of floating-point hardware, and its inability to exactly represent some values. Since computer architecture is well beyond this book's scope, though, we'll finesse this by saying that all of the digits in the first output are really there, in your computer's floating-point hardware; it's just that you're not normally accustomed to seeing them. We're using this example to demonstrate the difference in output formatting—the interactive prompt's automatic result echo shows more digits than the print statement. If you don't want all the digits, say print.

Note that not all values have so many digits to display:

```
>>> 1 / 2.0
0.5
```

And there are more ways to display the bits of a number inside your computer than prints and automatic echoes:

```
>>> num = 1 / 3.0
>>> num                     # Echoes
0.33333333333333331
>>> print num               # Print rounds
0.333333333333

>>> "%e" % num              # String formatting
'3.333333e-001'
```

```
>>> "%2.2f" % num          # String formatting
'0.33'
```

The last two of these employ *string formatting*—an expression that allows for format flexibility, explored in the upcoming chapter on strings.

Str and Repr Display Formats

Technically, the difference between default interactive echoes and prints corresponds to the difference between the built-in repr and str functions:

```
>>> repr(num)              # Used by echoes: as code form
'0.333333333333331'
>>> str(num)               # Used by print: user-friendly form
'0.333333333333'
```

Both of these convert arbitrary objects to their string representation: repr (and the interactive prompt) produces results that look as though they were code; str (and the print statement) converts to a typically more user-friendly format. This notion will resurface when we study strings; more on these built-ins in general later in the book.

Division: Classic, Floor, and True

Now that you've seen how division works, you should know that it is scheduled for a slight change in a future Python release (currently, in 3.0, scheduled to appear years after this edition is released). In Python 2.3, things work as just described, but there are actually two different division operators, one of which will change:

X / Y

> *Classic* division. In Python 2.3 and earlier, this operator truncates results down for integers, and keeps remainders for floating-point numbers, as described here. This operator will be changed to *true* division—always keeping remainders regardless of types—in a future Python release (3.0).

X // Y

> *Floor* division. Added in Python 2.2, this operator always truncates fractional remainders down to their floor, regardless of types.

Floor division was added to address the fact that the result of the current classic division model is dependent on operand types, and so can sometimes be difficult to anticipate in a dynamically-typed language like Python.

Due to possible backward compatibility issues, this is in a state of flux today. In version 2.3, / division works as described by default, and // floor division has been added to truncate result remainders to their floor regardless of types:

```
>>> (5 / 2), (5 / 2.0), (5 / -2.0), (5 / -2)
(2, 2.5, -2.5, -3)
```

```
>>> (5 // 2), (5 // 2.0), (5 // -2.0), (5 // -2)
(2, 2.0, -3.0, -3)

>>> (9 / 3), (9.0 / 3), (9 // 3), (9 // 3.0)
(3, 3.0, 3, 3.0)
```

In a future Python release, / division will likely be changed to return a true division result which always retains remainders, even for integers—for example, 1/2 will be 0.5, not 0, and 1//2 will still be 0.

Until this change is incorporated completely, you can see the way that the / will likely work in the future, by using a special import of the form: from __future__ import division. This turns the / operator into a true division (keeping remainders), but leaves // as is. Here's how / will eventually behave:

```
>>> from __future__ import division

>>> (5 / 2), (5 / 2.0), (5 / -2.0), (5 / -2)
(2.5, 2.5, -2.5, -2.5)

>>> (5 // 2), (5 // 2.0), (5 // -2.0), (5 // -2)
(2, 2.0, -3.0, -3)

>>> (9 / 3), (9.0 / 3), (9 // 3), (9 // 3.0)
(3.0, 3.0, 3, 3.0)
```

Watch for a simple prime number while loop example in Chapter 10, and a corresponding exercise at the end of Part IV, which illustrate the sort of code that may be impacted by this / change. In general, any code that depends on / truncating an integer result may be affected (use the new // instead). As we write this, this change is scheduled to occur in Python 3.0, but be sure to try these expressions in your version to see which behavior applies. Also stay tuned for more on the special from command used here in Chapter 18.

Bitwise Operations

Besides the normal numeric operations (addition, subtraction, and so on), Python supports most of the numeric expressions available in the C language. For instance, here it's at work performing bitwise shift and Boolean operations:

```
>>> x = 1          # 0001
>>> x << 2         # Shift left 2 bits: 0100
4
>>> x | 2          # bitwise OR: 0011
3
>>> x & 1          # bitwise AND: 0001
1
```

In the first expression, a binary 1 (in base 2, 0001) is shifted left two slots to create a binary 4 (0100). The last two operations perform a binary or (0001|0010 = 0011), and a binary and (0001&0001 = 0001). Such bit masking operations allow us to encode multiple flags and other values within a single integer.

We won't go into much more detail on "bit-twiddling" here. It's supported if you need it, but be aware that it's often not as important in a high-level language such as Python as it is in a low-level language such as C. As a rule of thumb, if you find yourself wanting to flip bits in Python, you should think about which language you're really coding. In general, there are often better ways to encode information in Python than bit strings.[*]

Long Integers

Now for something more exotic: here's a look at long integers in action. When an integer literal ends with a letter L (or lowercase l), Python creates a *long integer*. In Python, a long integer can be arbitrarily big—it can have as many digits as you have room for in memory:

```
>>> 99999999999999999999999999999999999999L + 1
100000000000000000000000000000000000000L
```

The L at the end of the digit string tells Python to create a long integer object with unlimited precision. As of Python 2.2, even the letter L is largely optional—Python automatically converts normal integers up to long integers, whenever they overflow normal integer precision (usually 32 bits):

```
>>> 99999999999999999999999999999999999999 + 1
100000000000000000000000000000000000000L
```

Long integers are a convenient built-in tool. For instance, you can use them to count the national debt in pennies in Python directly (if you are so inclined and have enough memory on your computer). They are also why we were able to raise 2 to such large powers in the examples of Chapter 3:

```
>>> 2L ** 200
1606938044258990275541962092341162602522202993782792835301376L
>>>
>>> 2 ** 200
1606938044258990275541962092341162602522202993782792835301376L
```

Because Python must do extra work to support their extended precision, long integer math is usually substantially slower than normal integer math (which usually maps directly to the hardware). If you need the precision, it's built in for you to use; but there is a performance penalty.

[*] As for most rules, there are exceptions. For instance, if you interface with C libraries that expect bit strings to be passed in, this doesn't apply.

A note on version skew: prior to Python 2.2, integers were not automatically converted up to long integers on overflow, so you really had to use the letter L to get the extended precision:

```
>>> 999999999999999999999999999999999999999 + 1        # Before 2.2
OverflowError: integer literal too large

>>> 999999999999999999999999999999999999999L + 1       # Before 2.2
1000000000000000000000000000000000000000L
```

In Version 2.2 the L is mostly optional. In the future, it is possible that using the letter L may generate a warning. Because of that, you are probably best off letting Python convert up for you automatically when needed, and omitting the L.

Complex Numbers

Complex numbers are a distinct core object type in Python. If you know what they are, you know why they are useful; if not, consider this section optional reading. Complex numbers are represented as two floating-point numbers—the real and imaginary parts—and are coded by adding a j or J suffix to the imaginary part. We can also write complex numbers with a nonzero real part by adding the two parts with a +. For example, the complex number with a real part of 2 and an imaginary part of -3 is written: 2 + -3j. Here are some examples of complex math at work:

```
>>> 1j * 1J
(-1+0j)
>>> 2 + 1j * 3
(2+3j)
>>> (2+1j)*3
(6+3j)
```

Complex numbers also allow us to extract their parts as attributes, support all the usual mathematical expressions, and may be processed with tools in the standard cmath module (the complex version of the standard math module). Complex numbers typically find roles in engineering-oriented programs. Since they are an advanced tool, check Python's language reference manual for additional details.

Hexadecimal and Octal Notation

As mentioned at the start of this section, Python integers can be coded in hexadecimal (base 16) and octal (base 8) notation, in addition to the normal base 10 decimal coding:

- Octal literals have a leading 0, followed by a string of octal digits 0–7, each of which represents 3 bits.

- Hexadecimal literals have a leading 0x or 0X, followed by a string of hex digits 0–9 and upper- or lowercase A–F, each of which stands for 4 bits.

Keep in mind that this is simply an alternative syntax for specifying the value of an integer object. For example, the following octal and hexadecimal literals produce normal integers, with the specified values:

```
>>> 01, 010, 0100          # Octal literals
(1, 8, 64)
>>> 0x01, 0x10, 0xFF       # Hex literals
(1, 16, 255)
```

Here, the octal value 0100 is decimal 64, and hex 0xFF is decimal 255. Python prints in decimal by default, but provides built-in functions that allow you to convert integers to their octal and hexadecimal digit strings:

```
>>> oct(64), hex(64), hex(255)
('0100', '0x40', '0xff')
```

The oct function converts decimal to octal, and hex to hexadecimal. To go the other way, the built-in int function converts a string of digits to an integer; an optional second argument lets you specify the numeric base:

```
>>> int('0100'), int('0100', 8), int('0x40', 16)
(100, 64, 64)
```

The eval function, which you'll meet later in this book, treats strings as though they were Python code. It therefore has a similar effect (but usually runs more slowly—it actually compiles and runs the string as a piece of a program):

```
>>> eval('100'), eval('0100'), eval('0x40')
(100, 64, 64)
```

Finally, you can also convert integers to octal and hexadecimal strings with a string formatting expression:

```
>>> "%o %x %X" % (64, 64, 255)
'100 40 FF'
```

This is covered in Chapter 5.

One warning before moving on, be careful to not begin a string of digits with a leading zero in Python, unless you really mean to code an octal value. Python will treat it as base 8, which may not work as you'd expect—010 is always decimal 8, not decimal 10 (despite what you might think!).

Other Numeric Tools

Python also provides both built-in functions and built-in modules for numeric processing. Here are examples of the built-in math module and a few built-in functions at work.

```
>>> import math
>>> math.pi, math.e
(3.1415926535897931, 2.7182818284590451)
```

```
>>> math.sin(2 * math.pi / 180)
0.034899496702500969

>>> abs(-42), 2**4, pow(2, 4)
(42, 16, 16)

>>> int(2.567), round(2.567), round(2.567, 2)
(2, 3.0, 2.5699999999999998)
```

The `math` module contains most of the tools in the C language's math library. As described earlier, the last output here will be just 2.57 if we say `print`.

Notice that built-in modules such as `math` must be imported, but built-in functions such as abs are always available without imports. In other words, modules are external components, but built-in functions live in an implied namespace, which Python automatically searches to find names used in your program. This namespace corresponds to the module called `__builtin__`. There is much more about name resolution in Part IV, Functions; for now, when you hear "module," think "import."

The Dynamic Typing Interlude

If you have a background in compiled or statically-typed languages like C, C++, or Java, you might find yourself in a perplexed place at this point. So far, we've been using variables without declaring their types—and it somehow works. When we type a = 3 in an interactive session or program file, how does Python know that a should stand for an integer? For that matter, how does Python know what a even is at all?

Once you start asking such questions, you've crossed over into the domain of Python's *dynamic typing* model. In Python, types are determined automatically at runtime, not in response to declarations in your code. To you, it means that you never declare variables ahead of time, and that is perhaps a simpler concept if you have not programmed in other languages before. Since this is probably the most central concept of the language, though, let's explore it in detail here.

How Assignments Work

You'll notice that when we say a = 3, it works, even though we never told Python to use name a as a variable. In addition, the assignment of 3 to a seems to work too, even though we didn't tell Python that a should stand for an integer type object. In the Python language, this all pans out in a very natural way, as follows:

Creation
> A variable, like a, is created when it is first assigned a value by your code. Future assignments change the already-created name to have a new value. Technically, Python detects some names before your code runs; but conceptually, you can think of it as though assignments make variables.

Types

A variable, like a, never has any type information or constraint associated with it. Rather, the notion of type lives with objects, not names. Variables always simply refer to a particular object, at a particular point in time.

Use

When a variable appears in an expression, it is immediately replaced with the object that it currently refers to, whatever that may be. Further, all variables must be explicitly assigned before they can be used; use of unassigned variables results in an error.

This model is strikingly different from traditional languages, and is responsible for much of Python's conciseness and flexibility. When you are first starting out, dynamic typing is usually easier to understand if you keep clear the distinction between names and objects. For example, when we say this:

```
>>> a = 3
```

At least conceptually, Python will perform three distinct steps to carry out the request, which reflect the operation of all assignments in the Python language:

1. Create an object to represent the value 3.

2. Create the variable a, if it does not yet exist.

3. Link the variable a to the new object 3.

The net result will be a structure inside Python that resembles Figure 4-1. As sketched, variables and objects are stored in different parts of memory, and associated by links—shown as a pointer in the figure. Variables always link to objects (never to other variables), but larger objects may link to other objects.

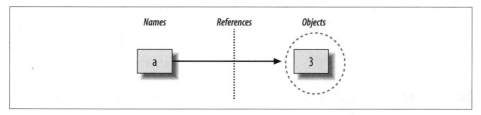

Figure 4-1. Names and objects, after a = 3

These links from variables to objects are called *references* in Python—a kind of association.* Whenever variables are later used (i.e., referenced), the variable-to-object

---

* Readers with a background in C may find Python references similar to C pointers (memory addresses). In fact, references are implemented as pointers, and often serve the same roles, especially with objects that can be changed in place (more on this later). However, because references are always automatically dereferenced when used, you can never actually do anything useful with a reference itself; this is a feature, which eliminates a vast category of C bugs. But, you can think of Python references as C "void*" pointers, which are automatically followed whenever used.

links are automatically followed by Python. This is all simpler than its terminology may imply. In concrete terms:

- *Variables* are simply entries in a search table, with space for a link to an object.
- *Objects* are just pieces of allocated memory, with enough space to represent the value they stand for, and type tag information.

At least conceptually, each time you generate a new value in your script, Python creates a new object (i.e., a chunk of memory) to represent that value. Python caches and reuses certain kinds of unchangeable objects like small integers and strings as an optimization (each zero is not really a new piece of memory); but it works as though each value is a distinct object. We'll revisit this concept when we meet the == and is comparisons in the section "Comparisons, Equality, and Truth" in Chapter 7.

Let's extend the session and watch what happens to its names and objects:

```
>>> a = 3
>>> b = a
```

After typing these two statements, we generate the scene captured in Figure 4-2. As before, the second line causes Python to create variable b; variable a is being used and not assigned here, so it is replaced with the object it references (3); and b is made to reference that object. The net effect is that variables a and b wind up referencing the same object (that is, pointing to the same chunk of memory). This is called a *shared reference* in Python—multiple names referencing the same object.

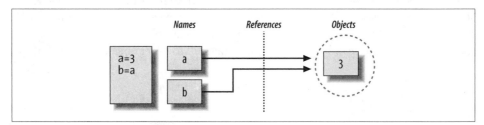

Figure 4-2. Names and objects, after b = a

Next, suppose we extend the session with one more statement:

```
>>> a = 3
>>> b = a
>>> a = 'spam'
```

As for all Python assignments, this simply makes a new object to represent the string value "spam", and sets a to reference this new object. It does not, however, change the value of b; b still refers to the original object, the integer 3. The resulting reference structure is as in Figure 4-3.

The same sort of thing would happen if we changed b to "spam" instead—the assignment would only change b, and not a. This example tends to look especially

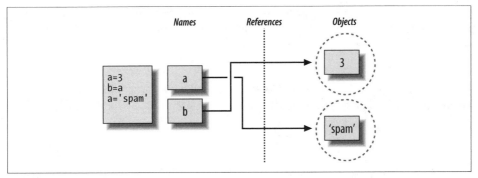

Figure 4-3. Names and objects, after a = 'spam'

odd to ex-C programmers—it seems as though the *type* of a changed from integer to string, by saying a = 'spam'. But not really. In Python, things work more simply: types live with objects, not names. We simply change a to reference a different object.

This behavior also occurs if there are no type differences at all. For example, consider these three statements:

```
>>> a = 3
>>> b = a
>>> a = 5
```

In this sequence, the same events transpire: Python makes variable a reference the object 3, and makes b reference the same object as a, as in Figure 4-2. As before, the last assignment only sets a to a completely different object, integer 5. It does not change b as a side effect. In fact, there is no way to ever overwrite the value of object 3 (integers can never be changed in place—a property called *immutability*). Unlike some languages, Python variables are always pointers to objects, not labels of changeable memory areas.

References and Changeable Objects

As you'll see later in this part's chapters, though, there are objects and operations that perform in-place object changes. For instance, assignment to offsets in lists actually changes the list object itself (in-place), rather than generating a brand new object. For objects that support such in-place changes, you need to be more aware of shared references, since a change from one name may impact others. For instance, list objects support in-place assignment to positions:

```
>>> L1 = [2,3,4]
>>> L2 = L1
```

As noted at the start of this chapter, lists are simply collections of other objects, coded in square brackets; L1 here is a list containing objects 2, 3, and 4. Items inside a list are accessed by their positions; L1[0] refers to object 2, the first item in the list L1.

Lists are also objects in their own right, just like integers and strings. After running the two prior assignments, L1 and L2 reference the same object, just like the prior example (see Figure 4-2). Also as before, if we now say this:

```
>>> L1 = 24
```

then L1 is simply set to a different object; L2 is still the original list. If instead we change this statement's syntax slightly, however, it has radically different effect:

```
>>> L1[0] = 24
>>> L2
[24, 3, 4]
```

Here, we've changed a component of the *object* that L1 references, rather than changing L1 itself. This sort of change overwrites part of the list object in-place. The upshot is that the effect shows up in L2 as well, because it shares the same object as L1.

This is usually what you want, but you should be aware of how this works so that it's expected. It's also just the default: if you don't want such behavior, you can request that Python copy objects, instead of making references. We'll explore lists in more depth, and revisit the concept of shared references and copies, in Chapters 6 and 7.*

References and Garbage Collection

When names are made to reference new objects, Python also reclaims the old object, if it is not referenced by any other name (or object). This automatic reclamation of objects' space is known as *garbage collection*. This means that you can use objects liberally, without ever needing to free up space in your script. In practice, it eliminates a substantial amount of bookkeeping code compared to lower-level languages such as C and C++.

To illustrate, consider the following example, which sets name x to a different object on each assignment. First of all, notice how the name x is set to a different *type* of object each time. It's as though the type of x is changing over time; but not really, in Python, types live with objects, not names. Because names are just generic references to objects, this sort of code works naturally:

```
>>> x = 42
>>> x = 'shrubbery'      # Reclaim 42 now (?)
>>> x = 3.1415           # Reclaim 'shrubbery' now (?)
>>> x = [1,2,3]          # Reclaim 3.1415 now (?)
```

Second of all, notice that references to *objects* are discarded along the way. Each time x is assigned to a new object, Python reclaims the prior object. For instance, when x is assigned the string 'shrubbery', the object 42 will be immediately reclaimed, as

---

* Objects that can be changed in-place are known as *mutables*—lists and dictionaries are mutable built-ins, and hence susceptible to in-place change side-effects.

long as it is not referenced anywhere else—the object's space is automatically thrown back into the free space pool, to be reused for a future object.

Technically, this collection behavior may be more conceptual than literal, for certain types. Because Python caches and reuses integers and small strings as mentioned earlier, the object 42 is probably not literally reclaimed; it remains to be reused the next time you generate a 42 in your code. Most kinds of objects, though, are reclaimed immediately when no longer referenced; for those that are not, the caching mechanism is irrelevant to your code.

Of course, you don't really need to draw name/object diagrams with circles and arrows in order to use Python. When you are starting out, though, it sometimes helps you understand some unusual cases, if you can trace their reference structure. Moreover, because *everything* seems to be assignment and references in Python, a basic understanding of this model helps in many contexts—as we'll see, it works the same in assignment statements, for loop variables, function arguments, module imports, and more.

CHAPTER 5

Strings

The next major built-in type is the Python *string*—an ordered collection of characters, used to store and represent text-based information. From a functional perspective, strings can be used to represent just about anything that can be encoded as text: symbols and words (e.g., your name), contents of text files loaded into memory, Internet addresses, Python programs, and so on.

You may have used strings in other languages too; Python's strings serve the same role as character arrays in languages such as C, but Python's strings are a somewhat higher level tool than arrays. Unlike C, Python strings come with a powerful set of processing tools. Also unlike languages like C, Python has no special type for single characters (like C's char), only one-character strings.

Strictly speaking, Python strings are categorized as *immutable sequences*—meaning that they have a left-to-right positional order (*sequence*), and cannot be changed in place (*immutable*). In fact, strings are the first representative of the larger class of objects called sequences. Pay special attention to the operations introduced here, because they will work the same on other sequence types we'll see later, such as lists and tuples.

Table 5-1 introduces common string literals and operations. Empty strings are written as two quotes with nothing in between, and there are a variety of ways to code strings. For processing, strings support *expression* operations such as concatenation (combining strings), slicing (extracting sections), indexing (fetching by offset), and so on. Besides expressions, Python also provides a set of string *methods* that implement common string-specific tasks, as well as a string *module* that mirrors most string methods.

Table 5-1. Common string literals and operations

Operation	Interpretation
s1 = ''	Empty string
s2 = "spam's"	Double quotes
block = """...""""	Triple-quoted blocks

Table 5-1. Common string literals and operations (continued)

Operation	Interpretation
s3 = r'\temp\spam'	Raw strings
s4 = u'spam'	Unicode Strings
s1 + s2 s2 * 3	Concatenate, repeat
s2[i] s2[i:j] len(s2)	Index, slice, length
"a %s parrot" % 'dead'	String formatting
s2.find('pa') s2.replace('pa', 'xx') s1.split( )	String method calls
for x in s2 'm' in s2	Iteration, membership

Methods and modules are discussed later in this section. Beyond the core set of string tools, Python also supports more advanced pattern-based string processing with the standard library's re (regular expression) module, introduced in Chapter 27. This section starts with an overview of string literal forms and basic string expressions, and then looks at more advanced tools such as string methods and formatting.

String Literals

By and large, strings are fairly easy to use in Python. Perhaps the most complicated thing about them is that there are so many ways to write them in your code:

- Single quotes: 'spa"m'
- Double quotes: "spa'm"
- Triple quotes: '''... spam ...''', """... spam ..."""
- Escape sequences: "s\tp\na\0m"
- Raw strings: r"C:\new\test.spm"
- Unicode strings: u'eggs\u0020spam'

The single- and double-quoted forms are by far the most common; the others serve specialized roles. Let's take a quick look at each of these options.

Single- and Double-Quoted Strings Are the Same

Around Python strings, single and double quote characters are interchangeable. That is, string literals can be written enclosed in either two single or two double quotes—

the two forms work the same, and return the same type of object. For example, the following two strings are identical, once coded:

```
>>> 'shrubbery', "shrubbery"
('shrubbery', 'shrubbery')
```

The reason for including both is that it allows you to embed a quote character of the other variety inside a string, without escaping it with a backslash: you may embed a single quote character in a string enclosed in double quote characters, and vice-versa:

```
>>> 'knight"s', "knight's"
('knight"s', "knight's")
```

Incidentally, Python automatically concatenates adjacent string literals, although it is almost as simple to add a + operator between them, to invoke concatenation explicitly.

```
>>> title = "Meaning " 'of' " Life"
>>> title
'Meaning of Life'
```

Notice in all of these outputs that Python prefers to print strings in single quotes, unless they embed one. You can also embed quotes by escaping them with backslashes:

```
>>> 'knight\'s', "knight\"s"
("knight's", 'knight"s')
```

But to understand why, we need to explain how escapes work in general.

Escape Sequences Code Special Bytes

The last example embedded a quote inside a string by preceding it with a backslash. This is representative of a general pattern in strings: backslashes are used to introduce special byte codings, known as *escape sequences*.

Escape sequences let us embed byte codes in strings that cannot be easily typed on a keyboard. The character \, and one or more characters following it in the string literal, are replaced with a single character in the resulting string object, which has the binary value specified by the escape sequence. For example, here is a five-character string that embeds a newline and a tab:

```
>>> s = 'a\nb\tc'
```

The two characters \n stand for a single character—the byte containing the binary value of the newline character in your character set (usually, ASCII code 10). Similarly, the sequence \t is replaced with the tab character. The way this string looks when printed depends on how you print it. The interactive echo shows the special characters as escapes, but print interprets them instead:

```
>>> s
'a\nb\tc'
>>> print s
a
b        c
```

To be completely sure how many bytes are in this string, you can use the built-in len function—it returns the actual number of bytes in a string, regardless of how it is displayed.

```
>>> len(s)
5
```

This string is five bytes long: an ASCII "a" byte, a newline byte, an ASCII "b" byte, and so on; the original backslash characters are not really stored with the string in memory.

For coding such special bytes, Python recognizes a full set of escape code sequences, listed in Table 5-2. Some sequences allow you to embed absolute binary values into the bytes of a string. For instance, here's another five-character string that embeds two binary zero bytes:

```
>>> s = 'a\0b\0c'
>>> s
'a\x00b\x00c'
>>> len(s)
5
```

Table 5-2. String backslash characters

Escape	Meaning
\newline	Ignored (continuation)
\\	Backslash (keeps a \)
\'	Single quote (keeps ')
\"	Double quote (keeps ")
\a	Bell
\b	Backspace
\f	Formfeed
\n	Newline (linefeed)
\r	Carriage return
\t	Horizontal tab
\v	Vertical tab
\N{id}	Unicode dbase id
\uhhhh	Unicode 16-bit hex
\Uhhhh...	Unicode 32-bit hex[a]
\xhh	Hex digits value hh
\ooo	Octal digits value
\0	Null (doesn't end string)
\other	Not an escape (kept)

[a] The \Uhhhh... escape sequence takes exactly eight hexadecimal digits (h); both \u and \U can be used only in Unicode string literals.

In Python, the zero (null) byte does not terminate a string the way it typically does in C. Instead Python keeps both the string's length and text in memory. In fact, no character terminates a string in Python; here's one that is all absolute binary escape codes—a binary 1 and 2 (coded in octal), followed by a binary 3 (coded in hexadecimal):

```
>>> s = '\001\002\x03'
>>> s
'\x01\x02\x03'
>>> len(s)
3
```

This becomes more important to know when you process binary data files in Python. Because their contents are represented as string in your scripts, it's okay to process binary files that contain any sort of binary byte values. More on files in Chapter 7.*

Finally, as the last entry in Table 5-2 implies, if Python does not recognize the character after a "\" as being a valid escape code, it simply keeps the backslash in the resulting string:

```
>>> x = "C:\py\code"      # keeps \ literally
>>> x
'C:\\py\\code'
>>> len(x)
10
```

Unless you're able to commit all of Table 5-2 to memory, you probably shouldn't rely on this behavior; to code literal backslashes, double up ("\\" is an escape for "\"), or use raw strings, described in the next section.

Raw Strings Suppress Escapes

As we've seen, escape sequences are handy for embedding special byte codes within strings. Sometimes, though, the special treatment of backslashes for introducing escapes can lead to trouble. It's suprisingly common, for instance, to see Python newcomers in classes trying to open a file with a filename argument that looks something like this:

```
myfile = open('C:\new\text.dat', 'w')
```

thinking that they will open a file called *text.dat* in directory *C:\new*. The problem here is that \n is taken to stand for a newline character, and \t is replaced with a tab. In effect, the call tries to open a file named *C:(newline)ew(tab)ext.dat*, with usually less than stellar results.

This is just the sort of thing that *raw strings* are useful for. If the letter "r" (uppercase or lowercase) appears just before the opening quote of a string, it turns off the escape

---

* But if you're especially interested in binary data files: the chief distinction is that you open them in binary mode (use open mode flags with a "b", such as "rb", "wb", and so on). See also the standard struct module, which can parse binary data loaded from a file.

mechanism—Python retains your backslashes literally, exactly as you typed them. To fix the filename problem, just remember to add the letter "r" on Windows:

```
myfile = open(r'C:\new\text.dat', 'w')
```

Because two backslashes are really an escape sequence for one backslash, you can also keep your backslashes by simply doubling-up, without using raw strings:

```
myfile = open('C:\\new\\text.dat', 'w')
```

In fact, Python itself sometimes uses this doubled scheme when it prints strings with embedded backslashes:

```
>>> path = r'C:\new\text.dat'
>>> path                       # Show as Python code.
'C:\\new\\text.dat'
>>> print path                 # User-friendly format
C:\new\text.dat
>>> len(path)                  # String length
15
```

There really is just one backslash in the string where Python printed two in the first output of this code. As with numeric representation, the default format at the interactive prompt prints results as if they were code, but the print statement provides a more user-friendly format. To verify, check the result of the built-in len function again, to see the number of bytes in the string, independent of display formats. If you count, you'll see that there really is just one character per backslash for a total of 15.

Besides directory paths on Windows, raw strings are also commonly used for regular expressions (text pattern matching, supported with module re); you'll meet this feature later in this book. Also note that Python scripts can usually use *forward* slashes in directory paths on both Windows and Unix, because Python tries to interpret paths portably. Raw strings are useful if you code paths using native Windows backslashes.

Triple Quotes Code Multiline Block Strings

So far, you've seen single quotes, double quotes, escapes, and raw strings. Python also has a triple-quoted string literal format, sometimes called a *block string*, which is a syntactic convenience for coding multiline text data. This form begins with three quotes (of either the single or double variety), is followed by any number of lines of text, and is closed with the same triple quote sequence that opened it. Single and double quotes in the text may be, but do not have to be, escaped. For example:

```
>>> mantra = """Always look
...  on the bright
... side of life."""
>>>
>>> mantra
'Always look\n on the bright\nside of life.'
```

This string spans three lines (in some interfaces, the interactive prompt changes to "..." on continuation lines; IDLE simply drops down one line). Python collects all the triple-quoted text into a single multiline string, with embedded newline characters (\n) at the places that your code has line breaks. Notice that the second line in the result has a leading space as it did in the literal—what you type is truly what you get.

Triple-quoted strings are handy any time you need multiline text in your program, for example, to code error messages or HTML and XML code. You can embed such blocks directly in your script, without resorting to external text files or explicit concatenation and newline characters.

Unicode Strings Encode Larger Character Sets

The last way to write strings in your scripts is perhaps the most specialized, and the least commonly used. Unicode strings are sometimes called "wide" character strings. Because each character may be represented with more than one byte in memory, Unicode strings allow programs to encode richer character sets than standard strings.

Unicode strings are typically used to support *internationalization* of applications (sometimes referred to as "i18n", to compress the 18 characters between the first and last characters of the term). For instance, they allow programmers to directly support European or Asian character sets in Python scripts. Because such character sets have more characters than a single byte can represent, Unicode is normally used to process these forms of text.

In Python, Unicode strings may be coded in your script by adding the letter "U" (lower or uppercase), just before the opening quote of a string:

```
>>> u'spam'
u'spam'
```

Technically, this syntax generates a Unicode string object, which is a different data type than normal strings. However, Python allows you to freely mix Unicode and normal strings in expressions, and converts up to Unicode for mixed-type results (more on + concatenation in the next section):

```
>>> 'ni' + u'spam'        # Mixed string types
u'nispam'
```

In fact, Unicode strings are defined to support all the usual string processing operations you'll meet in the next section, so the difference in types is often trivial to your code. Like normal strings, Unicode may be concatenated, indexed, sliced, matched with the re module, and so on, and cannot be changed in place. If you ever do need to convert between the two types explicitly, you can use the built-in str and unicode functions:

```
>>> str(u'spam')          # Unicode to normal
'spam'
>>> unicode('spam')       # Normal to unicode
u'spam'
```

Because Unicode is designed to handle multibyte characters, you can also use the special \u and \U escapes to encode binary character values that are larger than 8 bits:

```
>>> u'ab\x20cd'          # 8-bit/1-byte characters
u'ab cd'
>>> u'ab\u0020cd'        # 2-byte characters
u'ab cd'
>>> u'ab\U00000020cd'    # 4-byte characters
u'ab cd'
```

The first of these embeds the binary code for a space character; its binary value in hexadecimal notation is x20. The second and third do the same, but give the value in 2-byte and 4-byte Unicode escape notation.

Even if you don't think you will need Unicode, you might use them without knowing it. Because some programming interfaces (e.g., the COM API on Windows) represent text as Unicode, it may find its way into your script as API inputs or results, and you may sometimes need to convert back and forth between normal and Unicode types. Since Python treats the two string types interchangeably in most contexts, the presence of Unicode strings is often transparent to your code—you can largely ignore the fact that text is being passed around as Unicode objects, and use normal strings operations.

Unicode is a useful addition to Python; because it is built-in, it's easy to handle such data in your scripts when needed. Unfortunately, from this point forward, the Unicode story becomes fairly complex. For example:

- Unicode objects provide an encode method that converts a Unicode string into a normal 8-bit string using a specific encoding.
- The built-in function unicode and module codecs support registered Unicode "codecs" (for "COders and DECoders").
- The module unicodedata provides access to the Unicode character database.
- The sys module includes calls for fetching and setting the default Unicode encoding scheme (the default is usually ASCII)
- You may combine the raw and unicode string formats (e.g., ur'a\b\c').

Because Unicode is a relatively advanced and rarely used tool, we will omit further details in this introductory text. See the Python standard manual for the rest of the Unicode story.

Strings in Action

Once you've written a string, you will almost certainly want to do things with it. This section and the next two demonstrate string basics, formatting, and methods.

Basic Operations

Let's begin by interacting with the Python interpreter to illustrate the basic string operations listed in Table 5-1. Strings can be concatenated using the + operator, and repeated using the * operator:

```
% python
>>> len('abc')         # Length: number items
3
>>> 'abc' + 'def'      # Concatenation: a new string
'abcdef'
>>> 'Ni!' * 4          # Repetition: like "Ni!" + "Ni!" + ...
'Ni!Ni!Ni!Ni!'
```

Formally, adding two string objects creates a new string object, with the contents of its operands joined; repetition is like adding a string to itself a number of times. In both cases, Python lets you create arbitrarily sized strings; there's no need to predeclare anything in Python, including the sizes of data structures.* The len built-in function returns the length of strings (and other objects with a length).

Repetition may seem a bit obscure at first, but it comes in handy in a surprising number of contexts. For example, to print a line of 80 dashes, you can either count up to 80 or let Python count for you:

```
>>> print '------- ...more... ---'    # 80 dashes, the hard way
>>> print '-'*80                       # 80 dashes, the easy way
```

Notice that operator overloading is at work here already: we're using the same + and * operators that are called addition and multiplication when using numbers. Python does the correct operation, because it knows the types of objects being added and multiplied. But be careful: this isn't quite as liberal as you might expect. For instance, Python doesn't allow you to mix numbers and strings in + expressions: 'abc'+9 raises an error, instead of automatically converting 9 to a string.

As shown in the last line in Table 5-1, you can also iterate over strings in loops using for statements and test membership with the in expression operator, which is essentially a search:

```
>>> myjob = "hacker"
>>> for c in myjob: print c,    # Step through items.
...
h a c k e r
>>> "k" in myjob                # 1 means true (found).
1
>>> "z" in myjob                # 0 means false (not found).
0
```

---

* Unlike C character arrays, you don't need to allocate or manage storage arrays when using Python strings. Simply create string objects as needed, and let Python manage the underlying memory space. Python reclaims unused objects' memory space automatically, using a reference-count garbage collection strategy. Each object keeps track of the number of names, data-structures, etc. that reference it; when the count reaches zero, Python frees the object's space. This scheme means Python doesn't have to stop and scan all of memory to find unused space to free (an additional garbage component also collects cyclic objects).

The for loop assigns a variable to successive items in a sequence (here, a string), and executes one or more statements for each item. In effect, the variable c becomes a cursor stepping across the string here. But further details on these examples will be discussed later.

Indexing and Slicing

Because strings are defined as an ordered collection of characters, we can access their components by position. In Python, characters in a string are fetched by *indexing*— providing the numeric offset of the desired component in square brackets after the string. You get back the one-character string.

As in the C language, Python offsets start at zero and end at one less than the length of the string. Unlike C, Python also lets you fetch items from sequences such as strings using *negative* offsets. Technically, negative offsets are added to the length of a string to derive a positive offset. You can also think of negative offsets as counting backwards from the end.

```
>>> S = 'spam'
>>> S[0], S[-2]                # Indexing from front or end
('s', 'a')
>>> S[1:3], S[1:], S[:-1]      # Slicing: extract section
('pa', 'pam', 'spa')
```

The first line defines a four-character string and assigns it the name S. The next line indexes it two ways: S[0] fetches the item at offset 0 from the left (the one-character string 's'), and S[-2] gets the item at offset 2 from the end (or equivalently, at offset (4 + −2) from the front). Offsets and slices map to cells as shown in Figure 5-1.[*]

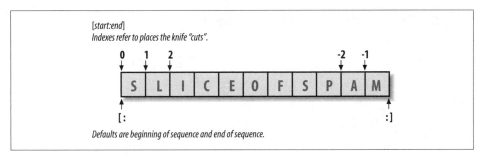

Figure 5-1. Using offsets and slices

The last line in the example above is our first look at *slicing*. Probably the best way to think of slicing is that it is a form of *parsing* (analyzing structure), especially when applied to strings—it allows us to extract an entire section (substring) in a single step. Slices can extract columns of data, chop off leading and trailing text, and more.

---

[*] More mathematically minded readers (and students in my classes) sometimes detect a small asymmetry here: the leftmost item is at offset 0, but the rightmost is at offset −1. Alas, there is no such thing as a distinct −0 value in Python.

Here's how slicing works. When you index a sequence object such as a string on a pair of offsets separated by a colon, Python returns a new object containing the contiguous section identified by the offsets pair. The left offset is taken to be the lower bound (inclusive), and the right is the upper bound (noninclusive). Python fetches all items from the lower bound, up to but not including the upper bound, and returns a new object containing the fetched items. If omitted, the left and right bound default to zero, and the length of the object you are slicing, respectively.

For instance, in the example above, S[1:3] extracts items at offsets 1 and 2. It grabs the second and third items, and stops before the fourth item at offset 3. Next S[1:] gets *all items past the first*—the upper bound defaults to the length of the string. Finally, S[:-1] fetches *all but the last item*—the lower bound defaults to zero, and −1 refers to the last item, non-inclusive.

This may seem confusing on first glance, but indexing and slicing are simple and powerful to use, once you get the knack. Remember, if you're unsure about what a slice means, try it out interactively. In the next chapter, you'll see that it's also possible to change an entire section of a certain object in one step, by assigning to a slice. Here's a summary of the details for reference:

Indexing (S[i]) fetches components at offsets

- The first item is at offset 0.
- Negative indexes mean to count backwards from the end or right.
- S[0] fetches the first item.
- S[-2] fetches the second from the end (like S[len(S)-2]).

Slicing (S[i:j]) extracts contiguous sections of a sequence

- The upper bound is noninclusive.
- Slice boundaries default to 0 and the sequence length, if omitted.
- S[1:3] fetches from offsets 1 up to, but not including, 3.
- S[1:] fetches from offset 1 through the end (length).
- S[:3] fetches from offset 0 up to, but not including, 3.
- S[:-1] fetches from offset 0 up to, but not including, the last item.
- S[:] fetches from offsets 0 through the end—a top-level copy of S.

We'll see another slicing-as-parsing example later in this section. The last item listed here turns out to be a very common trick: it makes a full top-level *copy* of a sequence object—an object with the same value, but a distinct piece of memory. This isn't very useful for immutable objects like strings, but comes in handy for objects that may be changed, such as lists (more on copies in Chapter 7). Later, we'll also see that the syntax used to index by offset (the square brackets) is used to index dictionaries by key as well; the operations look the same, but have different interpretations.

In Python 2.3, slice expressions support an optional third index, used as a step (sometimes called a stride). The step is added to the index of each item extracted. For instance, X[1:10:2] will fetch every *other* item in X from offsets 1–9; it will collect items from offsets 1, 3, 5, and so on. Similarly, the slicing expression "hello"[::-1] returns the new string "olleh". For more details, see Python's standard documentation, or run a few experiments interactively.

Why You Will Care: Slices

Throughout the core language parts of this book, we include sidebars such as this to give you a peek at how some of the language features being introduced are typically used in real programs. Since we can't show much of real use until you've seen most of the Python picture, these sidebars necessarily contain many references to topics not introduced yet; at most, you should consider them previews of ways you may find these abstract language concepts useful for common programming tasks.

For instance, you'll see later that the argument words listed on a command line used to launch a Python program are made available in the argv attribute of the built-in sys module:

```
# File echo.py
import sys
print sys.argv

% python echo.py -a -b -c
['echo.py', '-a', '-b', '-c']
```

Usually, you're only interested in inspecting the arguments past the program name. This leads to a very typical application of slices: a single slice expression can strip off all but the first item of the list. Here, sys.argv[1:] returns the desired list, ['-a', '-b', '-c']. You can then process without having to accommodate the program name at the front.

Slices are also often used to clean up lines read from input files; if you know that a line will have an end-of-line character at the end (a '\n' newline marker), you can get rid of it with a single expression such as line[:-1], which extracts all but the last character in the line (the lower limit defaults to 0). In both cases, slices do the job of logic that must be explicit in a lower-level language.

String Conversion Tools

You cannot add a number and a string together in Python, even if the string looks like a number (i.e., is all digits):

```
>>> "42" + 1
TypeError: cannot concatenate 'str' and 'int' objects
```

This is by design: because + can mean both addition and concatenation, the choice of conversion would be ambiguous. So, Python treats this as an error. In Python, magic is generally omitted, if it would make your life more complex.

What to do, then, if your script obtains a number as a text string from a file or user interface? The trick is that you need to employ conversion tools before you can treat a string like a number, or vice versa. For instance:

```
>>> int("42"), str(42)         # Convert from/to string.
(42, '42')
>>> string.atoi("42"), `42`    # Same, but older techniques
(42, '42')
```

The int and string.atoi functions both convert a string to a number, and the str function and *backquotes* around any object convert that object to its string representation (e.g., `42` converts a number to a string). Of these, int and str are the newer, and generally prescribed conversion techniques, and do not require importing the string module.

Although you can't mix strings and number types around operators such as +, you can manually convert before that operation if needed:

```
>>> int("42") + 1              # Force addition.
43
>>> "spam" + str(42)           # Force concatenation.
'spam42'
```

Similar built-in functions handle floating-point number conversions:

```
>>> str(3.1415), float("1.5")
('3.1415', 1.5)

>>> text = "1.234E-10"
>>> float(text)
1.2340000000000001e-010
```

Later, we'll further study the built-in eval function; it runs a string containing Python expression code, and so can convert a string to any kind of object. The functions int, string.atoi, and their relatives convert only to numbers, but this restriction means they are usually faster. As seen in Chapter 4, the string formatting expression provides another way to convert numbers to strings.

Changing Strings

Remember the term—immutable sequence? The immutable part means that you can't change a string in-place (e.g., by assigning to an index):

```
>>> S = 'spam'
>>> S[0] = "x"
Raises an error!
```

So how do you modify text information in Python? To change a string, you just need to build and assign a new string using tools such as concatenation and slicing, and possibly assigning the result back to the string's original name.

```
>>> S = S + 'SPAM!'        # To change a string, make a new one.
>>> S
'spamSPAM!'
>>> S = S[:4] + 'Burger' + S[-1]
>>> S
'spamBurger!'
```

The first example adds a substring at the end of S, by concatenation; really, it makes a new string, and assigns it back to S, but you can usually think of this as changing a string. The second example replaces four characters with six by slicing, indexing, and concatenating. Later in this section, you'll see how to achieve a similar effect with string method calls. Finally, it's also possible to build up new text values with string formatting expressions:

```
>>> 'That is %d %s bird!' % (1, 'dead')    # like C sprintf
That is 1 dead bird!
```

The next section shows how.

String Formatting

Python overloads the % binary operator to work on strings (the % operator also means remainder-of-division modulus for numbers). When applied to strings, it serves the same role as C's sprintf function; the % provides a simple way to format values as strings, according to a format definition string. In short, this operator provides a compact way to code multiple string substitutions.

To format strings:

1. Provide a format string on the left of the % operator with embedded conversion targets that start with a % (e.g., "%d").

2. Provide an object (or objects in parenthesis) on the right of the % operator that you want Python to insert into the format string on the left at its conversion targets.

For instance, in the last example of the prior section, the integer 1 replaces the %d in the format string on the left, and the string 'dead' replaces the %s. The result is a new string that reflects these two substitutions.

Technically speaking, the string formatting expression is usually optional—you can generally do similar work with multiple concatenations and conversions. However, formatting allows us to combine many steps into a single operation. It's powerful enough to warrant a few more examples:

```
>>> exclamation = "Ni"
>>> "The knights who say %s!" % exclamation
'The knights who say Ni!'
```

```
>>> "%d %s %d you" % (1, 'spam', 4)
'1 spam 4 you'

>>> "%s -- %s -- %s" % (42, 3.14159, [1, 2, 3])
'42 -- 3.14159 -- [1, 2, 3]'
```

The first example here plugs the string "Ni" into the target on the left, replacing the %s marker. In the second, three values are inserted into the target string. When there is more than one value being inserted, you need to group the values on the right in parentheses (which really means they are put in a tuple). Keep in mind that formatting always makes a new string, rather than changing the string on the left; since strings are immutable, it must.

Notice that the third example inserts three values again—an integer, floating-point, and list object—but all of the targets on the left are %s, which stands for conversion to string. Since every type of object can be converted to a string (the one used when printing), every object works with the %s conversion code. Because of this, unless you will be doing some special formatting, %s is often the only code you need to remember.

Advanced String Formatting

For more advanced type-specific formatting, you can use any of the conversion codes listed in Table 5-3 in formatting expressions. C programmers will recognize most of these, because Python string formatting supports all the usual C printf format codes (but returns the result, instead of displaying it like printf). Some of the format codes in the table provide alternative ways to format the same type; for instance, %e, %f, and %g, provide alternative ways to format floating-point numbers.

Table 5-3. String formatting codes

Code	Meaning
%s	String (or any object)
%r	s, but uses repr( ), not str( )
%c	Character
%d	Decimal (integer)
%i	Integer
%u	Unsigned (integer)
%o	Octal integer
%x	Hex integer
%X	x, but prints uppercase
%e	Floating-point exponent
%E	e, but prints uppercase
%f	Floating-point decimal
%g	Floating-point e or f

Table 5-3. String formatting codes (continued)

Code	Meaning
%G	Floating-point E or f
%%	Literal '%'

In fact, conversion targets in the format string on the expression's left side support a variety of conversion operations, with a fairly sophisticated syntax all their own. The general structure of conversion targets looks like this:

```
%[(name)][flags][width][.precision]code
```

The character codes in Table 5-3 show up at the end of the target string. Between the % and the character code, we can give a dictionary key; list flags that specify things like left justification (–), numeric sign (+), and zero fills (0); give total field width and the number of digits after a decimal point; and more.

Formatting target syntax is documented in full elsewhere, but to demonstrate commonly-used format syntax, here are a few examples. The first formats integers by default, and then in a six-character field with left justification and zero padding:

```
>>> x = 1234
>>> res = "integers: ...%d...%-6d...%06d" % (x, x, x)
>>> res
'integers: ...1234...1234  ...001234'
```

The %e, %f, and %g formats display floating-point numbers in different ways, such as:

```
>>> x = 1.23456789
>>> x
1.2345678899999999

>>> '%e | %f | %g' % (x, x, x)
'1.234568e+000 | 1.234568 | 1.23457'
```

For floating-point numbers, we can achieve a variety of additional formatting effects by specifying left justification, zero padding, numeric signs, field width, and digits after the decimal point. For simpler tasks, you might get by with simply converting to strings with a format expression or the str built-in function shown earlier:

```
>>> '%-6.2f | %05.2f | %+06.1f' % (x, x, x)
'1.23   | 01.23 | +001.2'

>>> "%s" % x, str(x)
('1.23456789', '1.23456789')
```

String formatting also allows conversion targets on the left to refer to the keys in a *dictionary* on the right, to fetch the corresponding value. We haven't told you much about dictionaries yet, but here's the basics for future reference:

```
>>> "%(n)d %(x)s" % {"n":1, "x":"spam"}
'1 spam'
```

Here, the (n) and (x) in the format string refer to keys in the dictionary literal on the right, and fetch their associated values. This trick is often used in conjunction with the vars built-in function, which returns a dictionary containing all the variables that exist in the place it is called:

```
>>> food = 'spam'
>>> age = 40
>>> vars()
{'food': 'spam', 'age': 40, ...many more... }
```

When used on the right of a format operation, this allows the format string to refer to variables by name (i.e., by dictionary key):

```
>>> "%(age)d %(food)s" % vars()
'40 spam'
```

We'll say much more about dictionaries in Chapter 6. See also the section "Numbers" in Chapter 4 for examples that convert to hexadecimal and octal strings with the %x and %o formatting target codes.

String Methods

In addition to expression operators, strings provide a set of *methods* that implement more sophisticated text processing tasks. Methods are simply functions that are associated with a particular object. Technically, they are attributes attached to objects, which happen to reference a callable function. In Python, methods are specific to object types; string methods, for example, only work on string objects.

Functions are packages of code, and method calls combine two operations at once—an attribute fetch, and a call:

Attribute fetches
> An expression of the form object.attribute means "fetch the value of attribute in object."

Call expressions
> An expression of the form function(arguments) means "invoke the code of function, passing zero or more comma-separated argument objects to it, and returning the function's result value."

Putting these two together allows us to call a method of an object. The method call expression object.method(arguments) is evaluated from left to right—Python will first fetch the method of the object, and then call it, passing in the arguments. If the method computes a result, it will come back as the result of the entire method call expression.

As you'll see throughout Part II, most objects have callable methods, and all are accessed using this same method call syntax. To call an object method, you have to go through an existing object; let's move on to some examples to see how.

String Method Examples: Changing Strings

Table 5-4 summarizes the call patterns for built-in string methods. They implement higher-level operations, like splitting and joining, case conversions and tests, and substring searches. Let's work through some code that demonstrates some of the most commonly used methods in action, and presents Python text-processing basics along the way.

Table 5-4. String method calls

S.capitalize( )	S.ljust(width)
S.center(width)	S.lower( )
S.count(sub [, start [, end]])	S.lstrip( )
S.encode([encoding [,errors]])	S.replace(old, new [, maxsplit])
S.endswith(suffix [, start [, end]])	S.rfind(sub [,start [,end]])
S.expandtabs([tabsize])	S.rindex(sub [, start [, end]])
S.find(sub [, start [, end]])	S.rjust(width)
S.index(sub [, start [, end]])	S.rstrip( )
S.isalnum( )	S.split([sep [,maxsplit]])
S.isalpha( )	S.splitlines([keepends])
S.isdigit( )	S.startswith(prefix [, start [, end]])
S.islower( )	S.strip( )
S.isspace( )	S.swapcase( )
S.istitle( )	S.title( )
S.isupper( )	S.translate(table [, delchars])
S.join(seq)	S.upper( )

Because strings are immutable, they cannot be changed in-place directly. To make a new text value, you can always construct a new string with operations such as slicing and concatenating. For example, to replace two characters in the middle of a string:

```
>>> S = 'spammy'
>>> S = S[:3] + 'xx' + S[5:]
>>> S
'spaxxy'
```

But if you're really just out to replace a substring, you can use the string replace method instead:

```
>>> S = 'spammy'
>>> S = S.replace('mm', 'xx')
>>> S
'spaxxy'
```

The replace method is more general than this code implies. It takes as arguments the original substring (of any length), and the string (of any length) to replace it with, and performs a global search-and-replace:

```
>>> 'aa$bb$cc$dd'.replace('$', 'SPAM')
'aaSPAMbbSPAMccSPAMdd'
```

In such roles, replace can be used to implement template replacement sorts of tools (e.g., form letters). Notice how the result simply prints this time, instead of assigning it to a name; you need to assign results to names only if you want to retain them for later use. If you need to replace one fixed-size string that can occur at any offset, you either can do replacement again, or search for the substring with the string find method and slice:

```
>>> S = 'xxxxSPAMxxxxSPAMxxxx'
>>> where = S.find('SPAM')          # Search for position
>>> where                           # Occurs at offset 4
4
>>> S = S[:where] + 'EGGS' + S[(where+4):]
>>> S
'xxxxEGGSxxxxSPAMxxxx'
```

The find method returns the offset where the substring appears (by default, searching from the front), or −1 if it is not found. Another way is to use replace with a third argument to limit it to a single substitution:

```
>>> S = 'xxxxSPAMxxxxSPAMxxxx'
>>> S.replace('SPAM', 'EGGS')       # Replace all
'xxxxEGGSxxxxEGGSxxxx'

>>> S.replace('SPAM', 'EGGS', 1)    # Replace one
'xxxxEGGSxxxxSPAMxxxx'
```

Notice that replace is returning a new string each time here. Because strings are immutable, methods never really change the subject string in-place, even if they are called "replace."

In fact, one potential downside of using either concatenation or the replace method to change strings, is that they both generate new string objects, each time they are run. If you have to apply many changes to a very large string, you might be able to improve your script's performance by converting the string to an object that does support in-place changes:

```
>>> S = 'spammy'
>>> L = list(S)
>>> L
['s', 'p', 'a', 'm', 'm', 'y']
```

The built-in list function (or an object construction call), builds a new list out of the items in any sequence—in this case, "exploding" the characters of a string into a list.

Once in this form, you can make multiple changes, without generating copies of the string for each change:

```
>>> L[3] = 'x'              # Works for lists, not strings
>>> L[4] = 'x'
>>> L
['s', 'p', 'a', 'x', 'x', 'y']
```

If, after your changes, you need to convert back to a string (e.g., to write to a file), use the string join method to "implode" the list back into a string:

```
>>> S = ''.join(L)
>>> S
'spaxxy'
```

The join method may look a bit backward at first sight. Because it is a method of strings (not the list of strings), it is called through the desired delimiter. join puts the list's strings together, with the delimiter between list items; in this case, using an empty string delimiter to convert from list back to string. More generally, any string delimiter and strings list will do:

```
>>> 'SPAM'.join(['eggs', 'sausage', 'ham', 'toast'])
'eggsSPAMsausageSPAMhamSPAMtoast'
```

String Method Examples: Parsing Text

Another common role for string methods is as a simple form of text *parsing*—analyzing structure and extracting substrings. To extract substrings at fixed offsets, we can employ slicing techniques:

```
>>> line = 'aaa bbb ccc'
>>> col1 = line[0:3]
>>> col3 = line[8:]
>>> col1
'aaa'
>>> col3
'ccc'
```

Here, the columns of data appear at fixed offsets, and so may be sliced out of the original string. This technique passes for parsing, as long as your data has fixed positions for its components. If the data is separated by some sort of delimiter instead, we can pull out its components by splitting, even if the data may show up at arbitrary positions within the string:

```
>>> line = 'aaa bbb   ccc'
>>> cols = line.split()
>>> cols
['aaa', 'bbb', 'ccc']
```

The string split method chops up a string into a list of substrings, around a delimiter string. We didn't pass a delimiter in the prior example, so it defaults to whitespace—the string is split at groups of one or more spaces, tabs, and newlines, and we get back a list of the resulting substrings. In other applications, the data may be separated by more tangible delimiters, such as keywords or commas:

```
>>> line = 'bob,hacker,40'
>>> line.split(',')
['bob', 'hacker', '40']
```

This example splits (and hence parses) the string at commas, a separator common in data returned by some database tools. Delimiters can be longer than a single character too:

```
>>> line = "i'mSPAMaSPAMlumberjack"
>>> line.split("SPAM")
["i'm", 'a', 'lumberjack']
```

Although there are limits to the parsing potential of slicing and splitting, both run very fast, and can handle basic text extraction chores.

You'll meet additional string examples later in this book. For more details, also see the Python library manual and other documentation sources, or simply experiment with these interactively on your own. Note that none of the string methods accept *patterns*—for pattern-based text processing, you must use the Python re standard library module. Because of this limitation, though, string methods sometimes run more quickly than the re module's tools.

The Original Module

Python's string method story is somewhat convoluted by history. For roughly the first decade of Python's existence, it provided a standard library module called string, which contained functions that largely mirror the current set of string object methods. Later, in Python 2.0 (and the short-lived 1.6), these functions were made available as methods of string objects, in response to user requests. Because so many people wrote so much code that relied on the original string module, it is retained for backward compatibility.

The upshot of this legacy is that today, there are usually two ways to invoke advanced string operations—by calling object methods, or calling string module functions and passing in the object as an argument. For instance, given a variable X assigned to a string object, calling an object method:

```
X.method(arguments)
```

is usually equivalent to calling the same operation through the module:

```
string.method(X, arguments)
```

provided that you have already imported the module string. Here's an example of both call patterns in action—first, the method scheme:

```
>>> S = 'a+b+c+'
>>> x = S.replace('+', 'spam')
```

```
>>> x
'aspambspamcspam'
```

To access the same operation through the module, you need to import the module (at least once in your process), and pass in the object:

```
>>> import string
>>> y = string.replace(S, '+', 'spam')
>>> y
'aspambspamcspam'
```

Because the module approach was the standard for so long, and because strings are such a central component of most programs, you will probably see both call patterns in Python code you come across.

Today, though, the general recommendation is to use methods instead of the module. The module call scheme requires you to import the `string` module (methods do not). The string module makes calls a few characters longer to type (at least when you load the module with `import`, but not for `from`). In addition, the module may run more slowly than methods (the current module maps most calls back to the methods, and so incurs an extra call along the way).

On the other hand, because the overlap between module and method tools is not exact, you may still sometimes need to use either scheme—some methods are only available as methods, and some as module functions. In addition, some programmers prefer to use the module call pattern, because the module's name makes it more obvious that code is calling string tools: `string.method(x)` seems more self-documenting than `x.method( )` to some. As always, the choice should ultimately be yours to make.

General Type Categories

Now that we've seen the first collection object, the string, let's pause to define a few general type concepts that will apply to most of the types from here on. In regard to built-in types, it turns out that operations work the same for all types in a category, so we only need to define most ideas once. We've only seen numbers and strings so far; but because they are representative of two of the three major type categories in Python, you already know more about other types than you think.

Types Share Operation Sets by Categories

Strings are immutable sequences: they cannot be changed in place (the *immutable* part), and are positionally-ordered collections that are accessed by offsets (the *sequence* part). Now, it so happens that all the sequences seen in this part of the book respond to the same sequence operations shown at work on strings—concatenation, indexing, iteration, and so on. More formally, there are three type (and operation) categories in Python:

Numbers
Support addition, multiplication, etc.

Sequences
Support indexing, slicing, concatenation, etc.

Mappings
Support indexing by key, etc.

We haven't seen mappings yet (dictionaries are discussed in the next chapter), but other types are going to be mostly more of the same. For example, for any sequence objects X and Y:

- X + Y makes a new sequence object with the contents of both operands.
- X * N makes a new sequence object with N copies of the sequence operand X.

In other words, these operations work the same on any kind of sequence—strings, lists, tuples, and some user-defined object types. The only difference is that you get back a new result object that is the same type as the operands X and Y—if you concatenate lists, you get back a new list, not a string. Indexing, slicing, and other sequence operations work the same on all sequences too; the type of the objects being processed tells Python which task to perform.

Mutable Types Can Be Changed in-Place

The immutable classification is an important constraint to know yet it tends to trip up new users. If an object type is immutable, you cannot change its value in-place; Python raises an error if you try. Instead, run code to make a new object for a new value. Generally, immutable types give some degree of integrity, by guaranteeing that an object won't be changed by another part of a program. You'll see why this matters when shared object references are discussed in Chapter 7.

## CHAPTER 6

Lists and Dictionaries

This chapter presents the list and dictionary object types—collections of other objects, which are the main workhorses in almost all Python scripts. As we'll see, both of these types are remarkably flexible: they can be changed, can grow and shrink on demand, and may contain and be nested in any other kind of object. By leveraging these types, we can build up and process arbitrarily rich information structures in our scripts.

Lists

The next stop on the built-in object tour is the Python *list*. Lists are Python's most flexible ordered collection object type. Unlike strings, lists can contain any sort of object: numbers, strings, even other lists. Python lists do the work of most of the collection data structures you might have to implement manually in lower-level languages such as C. In terms of some of their main properties, Python lists are:

Ordered collections of arbitrary objects
> From a functional view, lists are just a place to collect other objects, so you can treat them as a group. Lists also define a left-to-right positional ordering of the items in the list.

Accessed by offset
> Just as with strings, you can fetch a component object out of a list by indexing the list on the object's offset. Since items in lists are ordered by their positions, you can also do such tasks as slicing and concatenation.

Variable length, heterogeneous, arbitrarily nestable
> Unlike strings, lists can grow and shrink in place (they can have variable length), and may contain any sort of object, not just one-character strings (they're heterogeneous). Because lists can contain other complex objects, lists also support arbitrary nesting; you can create lists of lists of lists.

Of the category mutable sequence

In terms of our type category qualifiers, lists can be both changed in place (they're mutable) and respond to all the sequence operations used with strings like indexing, slicing, and concatenation. In fact, sequence operations work the same on lists. Because lists are mutable, they also support other operations strings don't, such as deletion and index assignment.

Arrays of object references

Technically, Python lists contain zero or more references to other objects. Lists might remind you of arrays of pointers (addresses). Fetching an item from a Python list is about as fast as indexing a C array; in fact, lists really are C arrays inside the Python interpreter. Python always follows a reference to an object whenever the reference is used, so your program only deals with objects. Whenever you insert an object into a data structure or variable name, Python always stores a reference to the object, not a copy of it (unless you request a copy explicitly).

Table 6-1 summarizes common list object operations.

Table 6-1. Common list literals and operations

Operation	Interpretation
L1 = [ ]	An empty list
L2 = [0, 1, 2, 3]	Four items: indexes 0..3
L3 = ['abc', ['def', 'ghi']]	Nested sublists
L2[i] L3[i][j] L2[i:j] len(L2)	Index, index of index slice, length
L1 + L2 L2 * 3	Concatenate, repeat
for x in L2 3 in L2	Iteration, membership
L2.append(4) L2.extend([5,6,7]) L2.sort( ) L2.index(1) L2.reverse( )	Methods: grow, sort, search, reverse, etc.
del L2[k] del L2[i:j] L2.pop( ) L2[i:j] = [ ]	Shrinking
L2[i] = 1 L2[i:j] = [4,5,6]	Index assignment, slice assignment
range(4) xrange(0, 4)	Make lists/tuples of integers
L4 = [x**2 for x in range(5)]	List comprehensions (Chapter 14)

When written down, lists are coded as a series of objects (or expressions that return objects) in square brackets, separated by commas. For instance, the second row in Table 6-1 assigns variable L2 to a four-item list. Nested lists are coded as a nested square-bracketed series (row 3), and the empty list is just a square-bracket pair with nothing inside (row 1).[*]

Many of the operations in Table 6-1 should look familiar, since they are the same sequence operations put to work on strings—indexing, concatenation, iteration, and so on. Lists also respond to list-specific method calls (which provide utilities such as sorting, reversing, adding items on the end, etc.), as well as in-place change operations (deleting items, assignment to indexes and slices, and so forth). Lists get the tools for change operations because they are a mutable object type.

Lists in Action

Perhaps the best way to understand lists is to see them at work. Let's once again turn to some simple interpreter interactions to illustrate the operations in Table 6-1.

Basic List Operations

Lists respond to the + and * operators much like strings; they mean concatenation and repetition here too, except that the result is a new list, not a string. In fact, lists respond to all of the general sequence operations used for strings.

```
% python
>>> len([1, 2, 3])                  # Length
3
>>> [1, 2, 3] + [4, 5, 6]           # Concatenation
[1, 2, 3, 4, 5, 6]
>>> ['Ni!'] * 4                     # Repetition
['Ni!', 'Ni!', 'Ni!', 'Ni!']
>>> 3 in [1, 2, 3]                  # Membership (1 means true)
1
>>> for x in [1, 2, 3]: print x,    # Iteration
...
1 2 3
```

We talk more about for iteration and the range built-ins in Chapter 10, because they are related to statement syntax; in short, for loops step through items in a sequence. The last entry in Table 6-1, *list comprehensions*, are covered in Chapter 14; they are a way to build lists by applying expressions to sequences, in a single step.

---

[*] In practice, you won't see many lists written out like this in list-processing programs. It's more common to see code that processes lists constructed dynamically (at runtime). In fact, although literal syntax is important to master, most data structures in Python are built by running program code at runtime.

Although + works the same for lists and strings, it's important to know that it expects the same sort of sequence on both sides—otherwise you get a type error when the code runs. For instance, you cannot concatenate a list and a string, unless you first convert the list to a string using backquotes, str, or % formatting. You could also convert the string to a list; the list built-in function does the trick:

```
>>> `[1, 2]` + "34"        # Same as "[1, 2]" + "34"
'[1, 2]34'
>>> [1, 2] + list("34")    # Same as [1, 2] + ["3", "4"]
[1, 2, '3', '4']
```

Indexing, Slicing, and Matrixes

Because lists are sequences, indexing and slicing work the same way, but the result of indexing a list is whatever type of object lives at the offset you specify, and slicing a list always returns a new list:

```
>>> L = ['spam', 'Spam', 'SPAM!']
>>> L[2]                          # Offsets start at zero.
'SPAM!'
>>> L[-2]                         # Negative: count from the right.
'Spam'
>>> L[1:]                         # Slicing fetches sections.
['Spam', 'SPAM!']
```

One note here: because you can nest lists (and other types) with lists, you will sometimes need to string together index operations to go deeper into a data structure. For example, one of the simplest ways to represent matrixes (multidimensional arrays) in Python, is as lists with nested sublists. Here's a basic, list-based, 3-by-3, two-dimensional array:

```
>>> matrix = [[1, 2, 3], [4, 5, 6], [7, 8, 9]]
```

With one index, you get an entire row (really, a nested sublist); with two, you get a item within the row:

```
>>> matrix[1]
[4, 5, 6]
>>> matrix[1][1]
5
>>> matrix[2][0]
7
>>> matrix = [[1, 2, 3],
...           [4, 5, 6],
...           [7, 8, 9]]
>>> matrix[1][1]
5
```

Notice the last portion of this example; lists can naturally span multiple lines if you want them to. Later in this chapter, you'll also see a dictionary-based matrix representation. The *NumPy* extension mentioned earlier provides other ways to handle matrixes.

Changing Lists in-Place

Because lists are mutable, they support operations that change a list object in-place; that is, the operations in this section all modify the list object directly, without forcing you to make a new copy as you had to for strings. But since Python only deals in object references, the distinction between in-place changes and new objects does matter; if you change an object in place, you might impact more than one reference to it at the same time.

Index and slice assignment

When using a list, you can change its contents by assigning to a particular item (offset), or an entire section (slice):

```
>>> L = ['spam', 'Spam', 'SPAM!']
>>> L[1] = 'eggs'                 # Index assignment
>>> L
['spam', 'eggs', 'SPAM!']
>>> L[0:2] = ['eat', 'more']      # Slice assignment: delete+insert
>>> L                             # Replaces items 0,1
['eat', 'more', 'SPAM!']
```

Both index and slice assignments are in-place changes—they modify the subject list directly, rather than generating a new list object for the result. Index assignment works much as it does in C, and most other languages: Python replaces the object reference at the designated offset with a new one.

Slice assignment, the last operation in the preceding example, replaces an entire section of a list in a single step. Because it can be a bit complex, it is perhaps best thought of as the combination of two steps:

1. *Deletion.* The slice you specify on the left of the = is deleted.
2. *Insertion.* The new items on the right are inserted into the list on the left, at the place where the old slice was deleted.

This isn't what really happens,* but it tends to help clarify why the number of items inserted doesn't have to match the number of items deleted. For instance, given a list L that has the value [1,2,3], the assignment L[1:2]=[4,5] sets L to the list [1,4,5,3]. Python first deletes the 2 (a one-item slice), then inserts items 4 and 5 where the deleted 2 used to be. It also explains why L[1:2]=[ ] is really a deletion operation.

List method calls

Like strings, Python list objects also support type-specific method calls:

```
>>> L.append('please')           # Append method call.
>>> L
```

---

* This description needs elaboration when the value and slice being assigned overlap: L[2:5]=L[3:6], for instance, works fine, because the value to be inserted is fetched before the deletion happens on the left.

```
['eat', 'more', 'SPAM!', 'please']
>>> L.sort()                        # Sort list items ('S' < 'e').
>>> L
['SPAM!', 'eat', 'more', 'please']
```

Methods were introduced in Chapter 5. In brief, they are functions (or attributes that reference functions) that are associated with a particular object. Methods provide type-specific tools; the list methods presented here, for instance, are only available for lists.

The list append method simply tacks a single item (object reference) onto the end of the list. Unlike concatenation, append expects you to pass in a single object, not a list. The effect of L.append(X) is similar to L+[X], but the former changes L in place, and the latter makes a new list.* The sort method orders a list in-place; by default, it uses Python standard comparison tests (here, string comparisons), and sorts in ascending fashion. You can also pass in a comparison function of your own to sort.

(Beware that append and sort change the associated list object in-place, but don't return the list as a result (technically, they both return a value called None). If you say something like L=L.append(X), you won't get the modified value of L (in fact, you'll lose the reference to the list altogether); when you use attributes such as append and sort, objects are changed as a side effect, so there's no reason to reassign.)

As for strings, other list methods perform other specialized operations. For instance, reverse reverses the list in-place, and the extend and pop methods insert multiple items at the end, and delete an item from the end, respectively:

```
>>> L = [1, 2]
>>> L.extend([3,4,5])      # Append multiple items.
>>> L
[1, 2, 3, 4, 5]
>>> L.pop()                # Delete, return last item.
5
>>> L
[1, 2, 3, 4]
>>> L.reverse()           # In-place reversal.
>>> L
[4, 3, 2, 1]
```

In some types of programs, the list pop method used here is often used in conjuction with append to implement a quick last-in-first-out *stack* structure. The end of the list serves as the top of the stack:

```
>>> L = []
>>> L.append(1)                    # Push onto stack.
>>> L.append(2)
>>> L
```

---

* Unlike + concatenation, append doesn't have to generate new objects, and so is usually faster. You can also mimic append with clever slice assignments: L[len(L):]=[X] is like L.append(X), and L[:0]=[X] is like appending at the front of a list. Both delete an empty slice and insert X, changing L in place quickly like append.

```
[1, 2]
>>> L.pop()                          # Pop off stack.
2
>>> L
[1]
```

Finally, because lists are mutable, you can also use the del statement to delete an item or section:

```
>>> L
['SPAM!', 'eat', 'more', 'please']
>>> del L[0]                         # Delete one item.
>>> L
['eat', 'more', 'please']
>>> del L[1:]                        # Delete an entire section.
>>> L                                # Same as L[1:] = [ ]
['eat']
```

Since slice assignment is a deletion plus an insert, you can also delete sections of lists by assigning an empty list to a slice (L[i:j]=[ ]); Python deletes the slice named on the left and then inserts nothing. Assigning an empty list to an index, on the other hand, just stores a reference to the empty list in the specified slot, rather than deleting it:

```
>>> L = ['Already', 'got', 'one']
>>> L[1:] = [ ]
>>> L
['Already']
>>> L[0] = [ ]
>>> L
[[ ]]
```

Here are a few pointers before moving on. Although all the operations above are typical, there are additional list methods and operations not illustrated here (including methods for inserting and searching). For a comprehensive and up-to-date list of type tools, you should always consult Python's manuals, or the *Python Pocket Reference* (O'Reilly) and other reference texts described in the Preface.

We'd also like to remind you one more time that all the in-place change operations above work only for mutable objects: they won't work on strings (or tuples, discussed ahead), no matter how hard you try.

Dictionaries

Besides lists, *dictionaries* are perhaps the most flexible built-in data type in Python. If you think of lists as ordered collections of objects, dictionaries are unordered collections; their chief distinction is that items are stored and fetched in dictionaries by *key*, instead of positional offset.

Being a built-in type, dictionaries can replace many of the searching algorithms and data structures you might have to implement manually in lower-level languages—

indexing a dictionary is a very fast search operation. Dictionaries also sometimes do the work of records and symbol tables used in other languages, can represent sparse (mostly empty) data structures, and much more. In terms of their main properties, dictionaries are:

Accessed by key, not offset

Dictionaries are sometimes called associative arrays or hashes. They associate a set of values with keys, so that you can fetch an item out of a dictionary using the key that stores it. You use the same indexing operation to get components in a dictionary, but the index takes the form of a key, not a relative offset.

Unordered collections of arbitrary objects

Unlike lists, items stored in a dictionary aren't kept in any particular order; in fact, Python randomizes their order in order to provide quick lookup. Keys provide the symbolic (not physical) location of items in a dictionary.

Variable length, heterogeneous, arbitrarily nestable

Like lists, dictionaries can grow and shrink in place (without making a copy), they can contain objects of any type, and support nesting to any depth (they can contain lists, other dictionaries, and so on).

Of the category mutable mapping

Dictionaries can be changed in place by assigning to indexes, but don't support the sequence operations that work on strings and lists. Because dictionaries are unordered collections, operations that depend on a fixed order (e.g., concatenation, slicing) don't make sense. Instead, dictionaries are the only built-in representative of the mapping type category—objects that map keys to values.

Tables of object references (hash tables)

If lists are arrays of object references, dictionaries are unordered tables of object references. Internally, dictionaries are implemented as hash tables (data structures that support very fast retrieval), which start small and grow on demand. Moreover, Python employs optimized hashing algorithms to find keys, so retrieval is very fast. Dictionaries store object references (not copies), just like lists.

Table 6-2 summarizes some of the most common dictionary operations (see the library manual for a complete list). Dictionaries are written as a series of key:value pairs, separated by commas, and enclosed in curly braces.* An empty dictionary is an empty set of braces, and dictionaries can be nested by writing one as a value inside another dictionary, or within a list or tuple.

---

* The same note about the relative rarity of literals applies here: dictionaries are often built up by assigning to new keys at runtime, rather than writing literals. But see the following section on changing dictionaries; lists and dictionaries are grown in different ways. Assignment to new keys works for dictionaries, but fails for lists (lists are grown with append instead).

Table 6-2. Common dictionary literals and operations

Operation	Interpretation
D1 = { }	Empty dictionary
D2 = {'spam': 2, 'eggs': 3}	Two-item dictionary
D3 = {'food': {'ham': 1, 'egg': 2}}	Nesting
D2['eggs'] D3['food']['ham']	Indexing by key
D2.has_key('eggs'), 'eggs' in D2 D2.keys( ) D2.values( ) D2.copy( ) D2.get(key, default) D2.update(D1)	Methods: membership test, keys list, values list, copies, defaults, merge, etc.
len(D1)	Length (number stored entries)
D2[key] = 42 del D2[key]	Adding/changing, deleting
D4 = dict(zip(keyslist, valslist))	Construction (Chapter 10)

Dictionaries in Action

As Table 6-2 suggests, dictionaries are indexed by key, and nested dictionary entries are referenced by a series of indexes (keys in square brackets). When Python creates a dictionary, it stores its items in any order it chooses; to fetch a value back, supply the key that it is associated with. Let's go back to the interpreter to get a feel for some of the dictionary operations in Table 6-2.

Basic Dictionary Operations

In normal operation, you create dictionaries and store and access items by key:

```
% python
>>> d2 = {'spam': 2, 'ham': 1, 'eggs': 3}   # Make a dictionary.
>>> d2['spam']                              # Fetch value by key.
2
>>> d2                                       # Order is scrambled.
{'eggs': 3, 'ham': 1, 'spam': 2}
```

Here, the dictionary is assigned to variable d2; the value of the key 'spam' is the integer 2. We use the same square bracket syntax to index dictionaries by key as we did to index lists by offsets, but here it means access by key, not position.

Notice the end of this example: the order of keys in a dictionary will almost always be different than what you originally typed. This is on purpose—to implement fast key lookup (a.k.a. hashing), keys need to be randomized in memory. That's why operations that assume a left-to-right order do not apply to dictionaries (e.g., slicing, concatenation); you can only fetch values by key, not position.

The built-in len function works on dictionaries too; it returns the number of items stored away in the dictionary, or equivalently, the length of its keys list. The dictionary has_key method allows you to test for key existence, and the keys method returns all the keys in the dictionary, collected in a list. The latter of these can be useful for processing dictionaries sequentially, but you shouldn't depend on the order of the keys list. Because the keys result is a normal list, however, it can always be sorted if order matters:

```
>>> len(d2)                    # Number of entries in dictionary
3
>>> d2.has_key('ham')          # Key membership test (1 means true)
1
>>> 'ham' in d2                # Key membership test alternative
1
>>> d2.keys()                  # Create a new list of my keys.
['eggs', 'ham', 'spam']
```

Notice the third expression in this listing: the in membership test used for strings and lists also works on dictionaries—it checks if a key is stored in the dictionary, like the has_key method call of the prior line. Technically, this works because dictionaries define *iterators* that step through their keys lists. Other types provide iterators that reflect their common uses; files, for example, have iterators that read line by line; more on iterators in Chapters 14 and 21.

In Chapter 10, you'll see that the last entry in Table 6-2 is another way to build dictionaries by passing lists of tuples to the new dict call (really, a type constructor), when we explore the zip function. It's a way to construct a dictionary from key and value lists in a single call.

Changing Dictionaries in-Place

Dictionaries are mutable, so you can change, expand, and shrink them in-place without making new dictionaries, just like lists. Simply assign a value to a key to change or create the entry. The del statement works here too; it deletes the entry associated with the key specified as an index. Notice the nesting of a list inside a dictionary in this example (the value of key "ham"); all collection data types in Python can nest inside each other arbitrarily:

```
>>> d2['ham'] = ['grill', 'bake', 'fry']      # Change entry.
>>> d2
{'eggs': 3, 'spam': 2, 'ham': ['grill', 'bake', 'fry']}

>>> del d2['eggs']                            # Delete entry.
>>> d2
{'spam': 2, 'ham': ['grill', 'bake', 'fry']}

>>> d2['brunch'] = 'Bacon'                    # Add new entry.
>>> d2
{'brunch': 'Bacon', 'spam': 2, 'ham': ['grill', 'bake', 'fry']}
```

As with lists, assigning to an existing index in a dictionary changes its associated value. Unlike lists, whenever you assign a *new* dictionary key (one that hasn't been assigned before), you create a new entry in the dictionary, as was done in the previous example for key 'brunch'. This doesn't work for lists, because Python considers an offset out of bounds if it's beyond the end of a list, and throws an error. To expand a list, you need to use such tools as the append method or slice assignment instead.

More Dictionary Methods

Besides has_key, dictionary methods provide a variety of tools. For instance, the dictionary values and items methods return lists of the dictionary's values and (key,value) pair tuples, respectively.

```
>>> d2.values(), d2.items()
([3, 1, 2], [('eggs', 3), ('ham', 1), ('spam', 2)])
```

Such lists are useful in loops that need to step through dictionary entries one by one. Fetching a nonexistent key is normally an error, but the get method returns a default value (None, or a passed-in default) if the key doesn't exist.

```
>>> d2.get('spam'), d2.get('toast'), d2.get('toast', 88)
(2, None, 88)
```

The update method provides something similar to concatenation for dictionaries; it merges the keys and values of one dictionary into another, blindly overwriting values of the same key:

```
>>> d2
{'eggs': 3, 'ham': 1, 'spam': 2}
>>> d3 = {'toast':4, 'muffin':5}
>>> d2.update(d3)
>>> d2
{'toast': 4, 'muffin': 5, 'eggs': 3, 'ham': 1, 'spam': 2}
```

Dictionaries also provide a copy method; more on this method in the next chapter. In fact, dictionaries come with more methods than those listed in Table 6-2; see the Python library manual or other documentation sources for a comprehensive list.

A Languages Table

Here is a more realistic dictionary example. The following example creates a table that maps programming language names (the keys) to their creators (the values). You fetch a creator name by indexing on language name:

```
>>> table = {'Python':  'Guido van Rossum',
...          'Perl':    'Larry Wall',
...          'Tcl':     'John Ousterhout' }
...
>>> language = 'Python'
>>> creator  = table[language]
```

```
>>> creator
'Guido van Rossum'

>>> for lang in table.keys():
...     print lang, '\t', table[lang]
...
Tcl     John Ousterhout
Python  Guido van Rossum
Perl    Larry Wall
```

The last command uses a for loop, which we haven't covered yet. If you aren't familiar with for loops, this command simply iterates through each key in the table and prints a tab-separated list of keys and their values. See Chapter 10 for more on for loops.

Because dictionaries aren't sequences, you can't iterate over them directly with a for statement, in the way you can with strings and lists. But if you need to step through the items in a dictionary it's easy: calling the dictionary keys method returns a list of all stored keys you can iterate through with a for. If needed, you can index from key to value inside the for loop as done in this code.

Python also lets us step through a dictionary's keys list without actually calling the keys method in most for loops. For any dictionary D, saying for key in D: works the same as saying the complete for key in D.keys():. This is really just another instance of the iterators mentioned earlier, which allow the in membership to work on dictionaries as well.

Dictionary Usage Notes

Here are a few additional details you should be aware of when using dictionaries:

Sequence operations don't work. Dictionaries are mappings, not sequences; because there's no notion of ordering among their items, things like concatenation (an ordered joining) and slicing (extracting contiguous section) simply don't apply. In fact, Python raises an error when your code runs, if you try to do such things.

Assigning to new indexes adds entries. Keys can be created either when you write a dictionary literal (in which case they are embedded in the literal itself), or when you assign values to new keys of an existing dictionary object. The end result is the same.

Keys need not always be strings. Our examples used strings as keys, but any other *immutable* objects (not lists) work just as well. In fact, you could use integers as keys, which makes a dictionary look much like a list (when indexing, at least). Tuples are sometimes used as dictionary keys too, allowing for compound key values. And class instance objects (discussed in Part VI) can be used as keys too, as long as they have the proper protocol methods; roughly, they need to tell Python that their values won't change, or else they would be useless as fixed keys.

Using dictionaries to simulate flexible lists

When you use lists, it is illegal to assign to an offset that is off the end of the list:

```
>>> L = [ ]
>>> L[99] = 'spam'
Traceback (most recent call last):
  File "<stdin>", line 1, in ?
IndexError: list assignment index out of range
```

Although you could use repetition to pre-allocate as big a list as you'll need (e.g., [0]*100), you can also do something that looks similar with dictionaries, which does not require such space allocations. By using integer keys, dictionaries can emulate lists that seem to grow on offset assignment:

```
>>> D = { }
>>> D[99] = 'spam'
>>> D[99]
'spam'
>>> D
{99: 'spam'}
```

Here, it almost looks as if D is a 100-item list, but it's really a dictionary with a single entry; the value of key 99 is the string 'spam'. You're able to access this structure with offsets much like a list, but you don't have to allocate space for all the positions you might ever need to assign values to in the future.

Using dictionaries for sparse data structures

In a similar way, dictionary keys are also commonly leveraged to implement *sparse* data structures—for example, multidimensional arrays, where only a few positions have values stored in them:

```
>>> Matrix = { }
>>> Matrix[(2,3,4)] = 88
>>> Matrix[(7,8,9)] = 99
>>>
>>> X = 2; Y = 3; Z = 4          # ; separates statements.
>>> Matrix[(X,Y,Z)]
88
>>> Matrix
{(2, 3, 4): 88, (7, 8, 9): 99}
```

Here, we use a dictionary to represent a three-dimensional array, all of which are empty except for the two positions, (2,3,4) and (7,8,8). The keys are *tuples* that record the coordinates of nonempty slots. Rather than allocating a large and mostly empty three-dimensional matrix, we can use a simple two-item dictionary. In this scheme, accessing empty slots triggers a nonexistent key exception—these slots are not physically stored:

```
>>> Matrix[(2,3,6)]
Traceback (most recent call last):
  File "<stdin>", line 1, in ?
KeyError: (2, 3, 6)
```

If we want to fill in a default value instead of getting an error message here, there are at least three ways we can handle such cases. We can either test for keys ahead of time in if statements, use the try statement to catch and recover from the exception explicitly, or simply use the dictionary get method shown earlier to provide a default for keys that do not exist:

```
>>> if Matrix.has_key((2,3,6)):      # Check for key before fetch.
...     print Matrix[(2,3,6)]
... else:
...     print 0
...
0
>>> try:
...     print Matrix[(2,3,6)]        # Try to index.
... except KeyError:                 # Catch and recover.
...     print 0
...
0
>>> Matrix.get((2,3,4), 0)           # Exists; fetch and return.
88
>>> Matrix.get((2,3,6), 0)           # Doesn't exist; use default arg.
0
```

We'll study the if and try statements later.

Using dictionaries as "records"

As you can see, dictionaries can play many roles in Python. In general, they can replace search data structures (since indexing by key is a search operation), and represent many types of structured information. For example, dictionaries are one of many ways to describe the properties of an item in your program's domain; they can serve the same role as "records" or "structs" in other languages:

```
>>> rec = {}
>>> rec['name'] = 'mel'
>>> rec['age']  = 41
>>> rec['job']  = 'trainer/writer'
>>>
>>> print rec['name']
mel
```

This example fills out the dictionary by assigning to new keys over time. Especially when nested, Python's built-in data types allow us to easily represent structured information:

```
>>> mel = {'name': 'Mark',
...        'jobs': ['trainer', 'writer'],
...        'web':  'www.rmi.net/~lutz',
...        'home': {'state': 'CO', 'zip':80501}}
```

This example uses a dictionary to capture object properties again, but has coded it all at once (rather than assigning to each key separately), and has nested a list and a dictionary to represent structure property values. To fetch components of nested objects, simply string together indexing operations:

```
>>> mel['name']
'Mark'
>>> mel['jobs']
['trainer', 'writer']
>>> mel['jobs'][1]
'writer'
>>> mel['home']['zip']
80501
```

Finally, note that more ways to build dictionaries may emerge over time. In Python 2.3, for example, the calls dict(name='mel', age=41) and dict([('name','bob'), ('age',30)]) also build two-key dictionaries. See Chapters 10, 13, and 27 for more details.

Why You Will Care: Dictionary Interfaces

Besides being a convenient way to store information by key in your programs, some Python extensions also present interfaces that look and work the same as dictionaries. For instance, Python's interface to dbm access-by-key files looks much like a dictionary that must be opened; strings are stored and fetched using key indexes:

```
import anydbm
file = anydbm.open("filename")   # Link to file.
file['key'] = 'data'             # Store data by key.
data = file['key']               # Fetch data by key.
```

Later, you'll see that we can store entire Python objects this way too, if we replace anydbm in the above with shelve (shelves are access-by-key databases of persistent Python objects). For Internet work, Python's CGI script support also presents a dictionary-like interface; a call to cgi.FieldStorage yields a dictionary-like object, with one entry per input field on the client's web page:

```
import cgi
form = cgi.FieldStorage()        # Parse form data.
if form.has_key('name'):
    showReply('Hello, ' + form['name'].value)
```

All of these (and dictionaries) are instances of mappings. More on CGI scripts later in this book.

CHAPTER 7

Tuples, Files, and Everything Else

This chapter rounds out our look at the core object types in Python, by introducing the *tuple* (a collection of other objects that cannot be changed), and the *file* (an interface to external files on your computer). As you'll see, the tuple is a relatively simple object that largely performs operations you've already learned about for strings and lists. The file object is a commonly-used and full-featured tool for processing files; further file examples appear in later chapters of this book.

This chapter also concludes this part of the book by looking at properties common to all the core datatypes we've met—the notions of equality, comparisons, object copies, and so on. We'll also briefly explore other object types in the Python toolbox; as we'll see, although we've met all the primary built-in types, the object story in Python is broader than we've implied thus far. Finally, we'll close this part with a set of common datatype pitfalls, and exercises that will allow you to experiment with the ideas you've learned.

Tuples

The last collection type in our survey is the Python tuple. Tuples construct simple groups of objects. They work exactly like lists, except that tuples can't be changed in-place (they're immutable) and are usually written as a series of items in parentheses, not square brackets. Although they don't support any method calls, tuples share most of their properties with lists. Tuples are:

Ordered collections of arbitrary objects
Like strings and lists, tuples are a positionally-ordered collection of objects; like lists, they can embed any kind of object.

Accessed by offset
Like strings and lists, items in a tuple are accessed by offset (not key); they support all the offset-based access operations, such as indexing and slicing.

Of the category immutable sequence

Like strings, tuples are immutable; they don't support any of the in-place change operations applied to lists. Like strings and lists, tuples are sequences; they support many of the same operations.

Fixed length, heterogeneous, arbitrarily nestable

Because tuples are immutable, they cannot grow or shrink without making a new tuple; on the other hand, tuples can hold other compound objects (e.g., lists, dictionaries, other tuples) and so support arbitrary nesting.

Arrays of object references

Like lists, tuples are best thought of as object reference arrays; tuples store access points to other objects (references), and indexing a tuple is relatively quick.

Table 7-1 highlights common tuple operations. Tuples are written as a series of objects (really, expressions that generate objects), separated by commas, and enclosed in parentheses. An empty tuple is just a parentheses pair with nothing inside.

Table 7-1. Common tuple literals and operations

Operation	Interpretation
( )	An empty tuple
t1 = (0,)	A one-item tuple (not an expression)
t2 = (0, 'Ni', 1.2, 3)	A four-item tuple
t2 = 0, 'Ni', 1.2, 3	Another four-item tuple (same as prior line)
t3 = ('abc', ('def', 'ghi'))	Nested tuples
t1[i] t3[i][j] t1[i:j] len(t1)	Index, index of index slice, length
t1 + t2 t2 * 3	Concatenate, repeat
for x in t2 3 in t2	Iteration, membership

Notice that tuples have no methods (e.g., an append call won't work here), but do support the usual sequence operations that we saw for strings and lists:

```
>>> (1, 2) + (3, 4)          # Concatenation
(1, 2, 3, 4)

>>> (1, 2) * 4               # Repitition
(1, 2, 1, 2, 1, 2, 1, 2)

>>> T = (1, 2, 3, 4)         # Indexing, slicing
>>> T[0], T[1:3]
(1, (2, 3))
```

The second and fourth entries in Table 7-1 merit a bit more explanation. Because parentheses can also enclose expressions (see the section "Numbers" in Chapter 4), you need to do something special to tell Python when a single object in parentheses is a tuple object and not a simple expression. If you really want a single-item tuple, simply add a trailing comma after the single item and before the closing parenthesis:

```
>>> x = (40)          # An integer
>>> x
40
>>> y = (40,)         # A tuple containing an integer
>>> y
(40,)
```

As a special case, Python also allows you to omit the opening and closing parentheses for a tuple in contexts where it isn't syntactically ambiguous to do so. For instance, the fourth line of the table simply listed four items, separated by commas. In the context of an assignment statement, Python recognizes this as a tuple, even though it didn't have parentheses. For beginners, the best advice is that it's probably easier to use parentheses than it is to figure out when they're optional. Many programmers also find that parentheses tend to aid script readability.

Apart from literal syntax differences, tuple operations (the last three rows in Table 7-1) are identical to strings and lists. The only differences worth noting are that the +, *, and slicing operations return new *tuples* when applied to tuples, and tuples don't provide the methods you saw for strings, lists, and dictionaries. If you want to sort a tuple, for example, you'll usually have to first convert it to a list to gain access to a sorting method call, and make it a mutable object:

```
>>> T = ('cc', 'aa', 'dd', 'bb')
>>> tmp = list(T)
>>> tmp.sort( )
>>> tmp
['aa', 'bb', 'cc', 'dd']
>>> T = tuple(tmp)
>>> T
('aa', 'bb', 'cc', 'dd')
```

Here, the list and tuple built-in functions were used to convert to a list, and then back to a tuple; really, both calls make new objects, but the net effect is like a conversion. Also note that the rule about tuple immutability only applies to the top-level of the tuple itself, not to its contents; a list inside a tuple, for instance, can be changed as usual:

```
>>> T = (1, [2, 3], 4)
>>> T[1][0] = 'spam'              # Works
>>> T
(1, ['spam', 3], 4)
>>> T[1] = 'spam'                 # Fails
TypeError: object doesn't support item assignment
```

Why Lists and Tuples?

This seems to be the first question that always comes up when teaching beginners about tuples: why do we need tuples if we have lists? Some of it may be historic. But the best answer seems to be that the immutability of tuples provides some *integrity*—you can be sure a tuple won't be changed through another reference elsewhere in a program. There's no such guarantee for lists.

Tuples can also be used in places that lists cannot—for example, as dictionary *keys* (see the sparse matrix example in Chapter 6). Some built-in operations may also require or imply tuples, not lists. As a rule of thumb, lists are the tool of choice for ordered collections that might need to change; tuples handle the other cases.

Files

Most readers are probably familiar with the notion of *files*—named storage compartments on your computer that are managed by your operating system. This last built-in object type provides a way to access those files inside Python programs. The built-in open function creates a Python file object, which serves as a link to a file residing on your machine. After calling open, you can read and write the associated external file, by calling file object methods. The built-in name `file` is a synonym for open, and files may be opened by calling either name.

Compared to the types you've seen so far, file objects are somewhat unusual. They're not numbers, sequences, or mappings; instead, they export methods only for common file processing tasks.

Table 7-2 summarizes common file operations. To open a file, a program calls the open function, with the external name first, followed by a processing mode (`'r'` to open for input—the default; `'w'` to create and open for output; `'a'` to open for appending to the end; and others we'll omit here). Both arguments must be Python strings. The external file name argument may include a platform-specific and absolute or relative directory path prefix; without a path, the file is assumed to exist in the current working directory (i.e., where the script runs).

Table 7-2. Common file operations

Operation	Interpretation
`output = open('/tmp/spam', 'w')`	Create output file (`'w'` means write).
`input  = open('data', 'r')`	Create input file (`'r'` means read).
`S = input.read()`	Read entire file into a single string.
`S = input.read(N)`	Read N bytes (1 or more).
`S = input.readline()`	Read next line (through end-line marker).
`L = input.readlines()`	Read entire file into list of line strings.
`output.write(S)`	Write string S into file.

Table 7-2. Common file operations (continued)

Operation	Interpretation
output.writelines(L)	Write all line strings in list L into file.
output.close( )	Manual close (done for you when file collected).

Once you have a file object, call its methods to read from or write to the external file. In all cases, file text takes the form of strings in Python programs; reading a file returns its text in strings, and text is passed to the write methods as strings. Reading and writing both come in multiple flavors; Table 7-2 gives the most common.

Calling the file close method terminates your connection to the external file. In Python, an object's memory space is automatically reclaimed as soon as the object is no longer referenced anywhere in the program. When file objects are reclaimed, Python also automatically closes the file if needed. Because of that, you don't need to always manually close your files, especially in simple scripts that don't run long. On the other hand, manual close calls can't hurt and are usually a good idea in larger systems. Strictly speaking, this auto-close-on-collection feature of files is not part of the language definition, and may change over time. Because of that, manual file close method calls are a good habit to form.

Files in Action

Here is a simple example that demonstrates file-processing basics. It first opens a new file for output, writes a string (terminated with an newline marker, '\n'), and closes the file. Later, the example opens the same file again in input mode, and reads the line back. Notice that the second readline call returns an empty string; this is how Python file methods tell you that you've reached the end of the file (empty lines in the file come back as strings with just a newline character, not empty strings).

```
>>> myfile = open('myfile', 'w')          # Open for output (creates).
>>> myfile.write('hello text file\n')     # Write a line of text.
>>> myfile.close( )

>>> myfile = open('myfile', 'r')          # Open for input.
>>> myfile.readline( )                     # Read the line back.
'hello text file\n'
>>> myfile.readline( )                     # Empty string: end of file
''
```

There are additional, more advanced file methods not shown in Table 7-2; for instance, seek resets your current position in a file (the next read or write happens at the position), flush forces buffered output to be written out to disk (by default, files are always buffered), and so on.

The sidebar "Why You Will Care: File Scanners" in Chapter 10 sketches common file-scanning loop code patterns, and the examples in later parts of this book discuss larger file-based code. In addition, the Python standard library manual and the reference books described in the Preface provide a complete list of file methods.

Type Categories Revisited

Now that we've seen all of Python's core built-in types, let's take a look at some of the properties they share.

Table 7-3 classifies all the types we've seen, according to the type categories we introduced earlier. Objects share operations according to their category—for instance, strings, lists, and tuples all share sequence operations. Only mutable objects may be changed in-place. You can change lists and dictionaries in-place, but not numbers, strings, or tuples. Files only export methods, so mutability doesn't really apply (they may be changed when written, but this isn't the same as Python type constraints).

Table 7-3. Object classifications

Object type	Category	Mutable?
Numbers	Numeric	No
Strings	Sequence	No
Lists	Sequence	Yes
Dictionaries	Mapping	Yes
Tuples	Sequence	No
Files	Extension	n/a

Why You Will Care: Operator Overloading

Later, we'll see that objects we implement with classes can pick and choose from these categories arbitrarily. For instance, if you want to provide a new kind of specialized sequence object that is consistent with built-in sequences, code a class that overloads things like indexing and concatenation:

```
class MySequence:
    def __getitem__(self, index):
        # Called on self[index], others
    def __add__(self, other):
        # Called on self + other
```

and so on. You can also make the new object mutable or not, by selectively implementing methods called for in-place change operations (e.g., __setitem__ is called on self[index]=value assignments). It's also possible to implement new objects in C, as C extension types. For these, you fill in C function pointer slots to choose between number, sequence, and mapping operation sets.

Object Generality

We've seen a number of compound object types (collections with components). In general:

- Lists, dictionaries, and tuples can hold any kind of object.
- Lists, dictionaries, and tuples can be arbitrarily nested.
- Lists and dictionaries can dynamically grow and shrink.

Because they support arbitrary structures, Python's compound object types are good at representing complex information in a program. For example, values in dictionaries may be lists, which may contain tuples, which may contain dictionaries, and so on—as deeply nested as needed to model the data to be processed.

Here's an example of nesting. The following interaction defines a tree of nested compound sequence objects, shown in Figure 7-1. To access its components, you may include as many index operations as required. Python evaluates the indexes from left to right, and fetches a reference to a more deeply nested object at each step. Figure 7-1 may be a pathologically complicated data structure, but it illustrates the syntax used to access nested objects in general:

```
>>> L = ['abc', [(1, 2), ([3], 4)], 5]
>>> L[1]
[(1, 2), ([3], 4)]
>>> L[1][1]
([3], 4)
>>> L[1][1][0]
[3]
>>> L[1][1][0][0]
3
```

References Versus Copies

"The Dynamic Typing Interlude" section in Chapter 4 mentioned that assignments always store references to objects, not copies. In practice, this is usually what you want. But because assignments can generate multiple references to the same object, you sometimes need to be aware that changing a mutable object in-place may affect other references to the same object elsewhere in your program. If you don't want such behavior, you'll need to tell Python to copy the object explicitly.

For instance, the following example creates a list assigned to X, and another assigned to L that embeds a reference back to list X. It also creates a dictionary D that contains another reference back to list X:

```
>>> X = [1, 2, 3]
>>> L = ['a', X, 'b']            # Embed references to X's object.
>>> D = {'x':X, 'y':2}
```

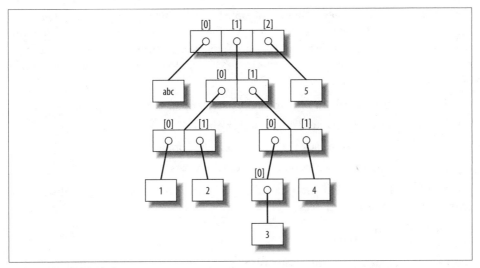

Figure 7-1. A nested object tree

At this point, there are three references to the first list created: from name X, from inside the list assigned to L, and from inside the dictionary assigned to D. The situation is illustrated in Figure 7-2.

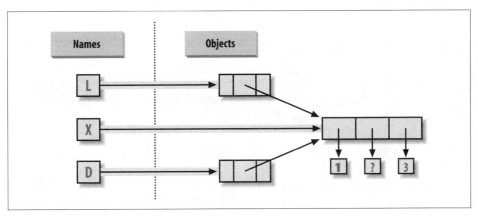

Figure 7-2. Shared object references

Since lists are mutable, changing the shared list object from any of the three references changes what the other two reference:

```
>>> X[1] = 'surprise'        # Changes all three references!
>>> L
['a', [1, 'surprise', 3], 'b']
>>> D
{'x': [1, 'surprise', 3], 'y': 2}
```

References are a higher-level analog of pointers in other languages. Although you can't grab hold of the reference itself, it's possible to store the same reference in more than one place: variables, lists, and so on. This is a feature—you can pass a large object around a program without generating copies of it along the way. If you really do want copies, you can request them:

- Slice expressions with empty limits copy sequences.
- The dictionary copy method copies a dictionary.
- Some built-in functions such as list also make copies.
- The copy standard library module makes full copies.

For example, if you have a list and a dictionary, and don't want their values to be changed through other variables:

```
>>> L = [1,2,3]
>>> D = {'a':1, 'b':2}
```

simply assign copies to the other variables, not references to the same objects:

```
>>> A = L[:]            # Instead of: A = L (or list(L))
>>> B = D.copy()        # Instead of: B = D
```

This way, changes made from other variables change the copies, not the originals:

```
>>> A[1] = 'Ni'
>>> B['c'] = 'spam'
>>>
>>> L, D
([1, 2, 3], {'a': 1, 'b': 2})
>>> A, B
([1, 'Ni', 3], {'a': 1, 'c': 'spam', 'b': 2})
```

In terms of the original example, you can avoid the reference side effects by slicing the original list, instead of simply naming it:

```
>>> X = [1, 2, 3]
>>> L = ['a', X[:], 'b']        # Emded copies of X's object.
>>> D = {'x':X[:], 'y':2}
```

This changes the picture in Figure 7-2—L and D will point to different lists than X. The net effect is that changes made through X will impact only X, not L and D; similarly, changes to L or D will not impact X.

One note on copies: empty-limit slices and the copy method of dictionaries still only make a *top-level* copy—they do not copy nested data structures, if any are present. If you need a complete, fully independent copy of a deeply nested data structure, use the standard copy module: import copy, and say X=copy.deepcopy(Y) to fully copy an arbitrarily nested object Y. This call recursively traverses objects to copy all their parts. This is the much more rare case, though (which is why you have to say more to make it go). References are usually the behaviour you will want; when they are not, slices and copy methods are usually as much copying as you'll need to do.

Comparisons, Equality, and Truth

All Python objects also respond to the comparisons: test for equality, relative magnitude, and so on. Python comparisons always inspect all parts of compound objects, until a result can be determined. In fact, when nested objects are present, Python automatically traverses data structures to apply comparisons *recursively*—left to right, and as deep as needed.

For instance, a comparison of list objects compares all their components automatically:

```
>>> L1 = [1, ('a', 3)]        # Same value, unique objects
>>> L2 = [1, ('a', 3)]
>>> L1 == L2, L1 is L2        # Equivalent? Same object?
(1, 0)
```

Here, L1 and L2 are assigned lists that are equivalent, but distinct objects. Because of the nature of Python references (studied in Chapter 4), there are two ways to test for equality:

The == operator tests value equivalence.   Python performs an equivalence test, comparing all nested objects recursively

The is operator tests object identity.   Python tests whether the two are really the same object (i.e., live at the same address in memory).

In the example, L1 and L2 pass the == test (they have equivalent values because all their components are equivalent), but fail the is check (they are two different objects, and hence two different pieces of memory). Notice what happens for short strings:

```
>>> S1 = 'spam'
>>> S2 = 'spam'
>>> S1 == S2, S1 is S2
(1, 1)
```

Here, we should have two distinct objects that happen to have the same value: == should be true, and is should be false. Because Python internally caches and reuses short strings as an optimization, there really is just a single string, 'spam', in memory, shared by S1 and S2; hence, the is identity test reports a true result. To trigger the normal behavior, we need to use longer strings that fall outside the cache mechanism:

```
>>> S1 = 'a longer string'
>>> S2 = 'a longer string'
>>> S1 == S2, S1 is S2
(1, 0)
```

Because strings are immutable, the object caching mechanism is irrelevent to your code—string can't be changed in-place, regardless of how many variables refer to them. If identity tests seem confusing, see the section "The Dynamic Typing Interlude" in Chapter 4 for a refresher on object reference concepts.

As a rule of thumb, the == operator is what you will want to use for almost all equality checks; is is reserved for highly specialized roles. We'll see cases of both operators put to use later in the book.

Notice that relative magnitude comparisons are also applied recursively to nested data structures:

```
>>> L1 = [1, ('a', 3)]
>>> L2 = [1, ('a', 2)]
>>> L1 < L2, L1 == L2, L1 > L2      # less,equal,greater: tuple of results
(0, 0, 1)
```

Here, L1 is greater than L2 because the nested 3 is greater than 2. The result of the last line above is really a tuple of three objects—the results of the three expressions typed (an example of a tuple without its enclosing parentheses).

The three values in this tuple represent true and false values; in Python, an integer 0 represents false and an integer 1 represents true. Python also recognizes any empty data structure as false, and any nonempty data structure as true. More generally, the notions of true and false are intrinsic properties of every object in Python—each object is true or false, as follows:

- Numbers are true if nonzero.
- Other objects are true if nonempty.

Table 7-4 gives examples of true and false objects in Python.

Table 7-4. Example object truth values

Object	Value
"spam"	True
""	False
[ ]	False
{ }	False
1	True
0.0	False
None	False

Python also provides a special object called None (the last item in Table 7-4), which is always considered to be false. None is the only value of a special data type in Python; it typically serves as an empty placeholder, much like a NULL pointer in C.

For example, recall that for lists, you cannot assign to an offset unless that offset already exists (the list does not magically grow if you assign out of bounds). To pre-allocate a 100-item list such that you can add to any of the 100 offsets, you can fill one with None objects:

```
>>> L = [None] * 100
>>>
```

```
>>> L
[None, None, None, None, None, None, None, . . . ]
```

The New Boolean Type in 2.3

Python 2.3 introduces a new explicit Boolean data type called `bool`, with values `True` and `False` available as new preassigned built-in names. Because of the way this new type is implemented, this is really just a minor extension to the notions of true and false outlined in this chapter, designed to make truth values more explicit. Most programmers were preassigning `True` and `False` to 1 and 0 anyway, so the new type makes this a standard. For instance, an infinite loop can now be coded as `while True:` instead of the less intuitive `while 1:`. Similarly, flags can be initialized with `flag = False`.

Internally, the new names `True` and `False` are instances of `bool`, which is in turn just a subclass of the built-in integer data type `int`. `True` and `False` behave exactly like integers 1 and 0, except that they have customized printing logic—they print themselves as the words `True` and `False`, instead of the digits 1 and 0 (technically, `bool` redefines its `str` and `repr` string formats.) Because of this customization, the output of Boolean expressions typed at the interactive prompt print as the words `True` and `False` as of Python 2.3, instead of the 1 and 0 you see in this book.

For all other practical purposes, you can treat `True` and `False` as though they are predefined variables set to integer 1 and 0 (e.g., `True + 3` yields 4). In truth tests, True and False evaluate to true and false, because they truly are just specialized versions of integers 1 and 0. Moreover, you are not required to use only Boolean types in if statements; all objects are still inherently true or false, and all the Boolean concepts mentioned in this chapter still work as before. More on Booleans in Chapter 9.

In general, Python compares types as follows:

- Numbers are compared by relative magnitude.
- Strings are compared lexicographically, character-by-character ("abc" < "ac").
- Lists and tuples are compared by comparing each component, from left to right.
- Dictionaries are compared as though comparing sorted (key, value) lists.

In later chapters, we'll see other object types that can change the way they get compared.

Python's Type Hierarchies

Figure 7-3 summarizes all the built-in object types available in Python and their relationships. We've looked at the most prominent of these; most other kinds of objects in Figure 7-3 either correspond to program units (e.g., functions and modules), or exposed interpreter internals (e.g., stack frames and compiled code).

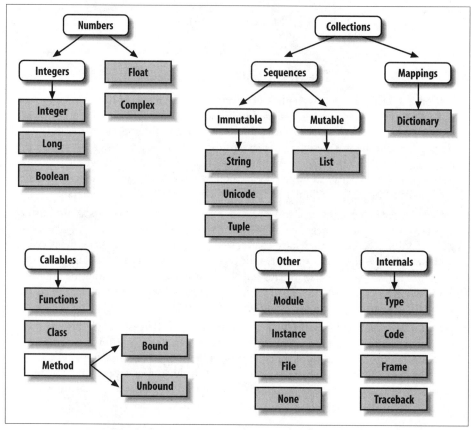

Figure 7-3. Built-in type hierarchies

The main point to notice here is that everything is an object type in a Python system and may be processed by your Python programs. For instance, you can pass a class to a function, assign it to a variable, stuff it in a list or dictionary, and so on.

Even types are an object type in Python: a call to the built-in function type(X) returns the type object of object X. Type objects can be used for manual type comparisons in Python if statements. However, for reasons to be explained in Part IV, manual type testing is usually not the right thing to do in Python.

A note on type names: as of Python 2.2, each core type has a new built-in name added to support type subclassing: dict, list, str, tuple, int, long, float, complex, unicode, type, and file (file is a synonym for open). Calls to these names are really object constructor calls, not simply conversion functions.

The types module provides additional type names (now largely synonyms for the built-in type names), and it is possible to do type tests with the isinstance function. For example, in Version 2.2, all of the following type tests are true:

```
isinstance([1],list)
type([1])==list
type([1])==type([ ])
type([1])==types.ListType
```

Because types can be subclassed in 2.2, the isinstance technique is generally recommended. See Chapter 23 for more on subclassing built-in types in 2.2 and later.

Other Types in Python

Besides the core objects studied in this chapter, a typical Python installation has dozens of other object types available as linked-in C extensions or Python classes. You'll see examples of a few later in the book—regular expression objects, DBM files, GUI widgets, and so on. The main difference between these extra tools and the built-in types just seen is that the built-ins provide special language creation syntax for their objects (e.g., 4 for an integer, [1,2] for a list, the open function for files). Other tools are generally exported in a built-in module that you must first import to use. See Python's library reference for a comprehensive guide to all the tools available to Python programs.

Built-in Type Gotchas

Part II concludes with a discussion of common problems that seem to bite new users (and the occasional expert), along with their solutions.

Assignment Creates References, Not Copies

Because this is such a central concept, it is mentioned again: you need to understand what's going on with shared references in your program. For instance, in the following example, the list object assigned to name L is referenced both from L and from inside the list assigned to name M. Changing L in-place changes what M references too:

```
>>> L = [1, 2, 3]
>>> M = ['X', L, 'Y']          # Embed a reference to L.
>>> M
['X', [1, 2, 3], 'Y']

>>> L[1] = 0                    # Changes M too
>>> M
['X', [1, 0, 3], 'Y']
```

This effect usually becomes important only in larger programs, and shared references are often exactly what you want. If they're not, you can avoid sharing objects by copying them explicitly; for lists, you can always make a top-level copy by using an empty-limits slice:

```
>>> L = [1, 2, 3]
>>> M = ['X', L[:], 'Y']      # Embed a copy of L.
>>> L[1] = 0                  # Changes only L, not M
>>> L
[1, 0, 3]
>>> M
['X', [1, 2, 3], 'Y']
```

Remember, slice limits default to 0 and the length of the sequence being sliced; if both are omitted, the slice extracts every item in the sequence, and so makes a top-level copy (a new, unshared object).

Repetition Adds One-Level Deep

Sequence repetition is like adding a sequence to itself a number of times. That's true, but when mutable sequences are nested, the effect might not always be what you expect. For instance, in the following, X is assigned to L repeated four times, whereas Y is assigned to a list *containing* L repeated four times:

```
>>> L = [4, 5, 6]
>>> X = L * 4          # Like [4, 5, 6] + [4, 5, 6] + ...
>>> Y = [L] * 4        # [L] + [L] + ... = [L, L,...]

>>> X
[4, 5, 6, 4, 5, 6, 4, 5, 6, 4, 5, 6]
>>> Y
[[4, 5, 6], [4, 5, 6], [4, 5, 6], [4, 5, 6]]
```

Because L was nested in the second repetition, Y winds up embedding references back to the original list assigned to L, and is open to the same sorts of side effects noted in the last section:

```
>>> L[1] = 0           # Impacts Y but not X
>>> X
[4, 5, 6, 4, 5, 6, 4, 5, 6, 4, 5, 6]
>>> Y
[[4, 0, 6], [4, 0, 6], [4, 0, 6], [4, 0, 6]]
```

Solutions

This is really another way to create the shared mutable object reference case, so the same solutions as above apply here. And if you remember that repetition, concatenation, and slicing copy only the top level of their operand objects, these sorts of cases make much more sense.

Cyclic Data Structures

We actually encountered this gotcha in a prior exercise: if a collection object contains a reference to itself, it's called a cyclic object. Python prints a "[...]" whenever it detects a cycle in the object, rather than getting stuck in an infinite loop:

```
>>> L = ['grail']              # Append reference to same object.
>>> L.append(L)                # Generates cycle in object: [...]
>>> L
['grail', [...]]
```

Besides understanding that the three dots represent a cycle in the object, this case is worth knowing about in general because it can lead to gotchas—cyclic structures may cause code of your own to fall into unexpected loops if you don't anticipate them. For instance, some programs keep a list or dictionary of items already visited, and check it to know if they have reached a cycle. See the solutions to Part I exercises in Appendix B for more on the problem, and the reloadall.py program at the end of Chapter 18 for a solution.

Don't use a cyclic reference, unless you need to. There are good reasons to create cycles, but unless you have code that knows how to handle them, you probably won't want to make your objects reference themselves very often in practice.

Immutable Types Can't Be Changed in-Place

Finally, you can't change an immutable object in-place:

```
T = (1, 2, 3)
T[2] = 4              # Error!
T = T[:2] + (4,)      # Okay: (1, 2, 4)
```

Construct a new object with slicing, concatenation, and so on, and assign it back to the original reference if needed. That might seem like extra coding work, but the upside is that the previous gotchas can't happen when using immutable objects such as tuples and strings; because they can't be changed in-place, they are not open to the sorts of side effects that lists are.

Part II Exercises

This session asks you to get your feet wet with built-in object fundamentals. As before, a few new ideas may pop up along the way, so be sure to flip to Appendix B when you're done (and even when you're not). If you have limited time, we suggest starting with exercise 11 (the most practical of the bunch), and then working from first to last as time allows. This is all fundamental material, though, so try to do as many of these as you can.

1. *The basics*. Experiment interactively with the common type operations found in the tables in Part II. To get started, bring up the Python interactive interpreter,

type each of the expressions below, and try to explain what's happening in each case:

```
2 ** 16
2 / 5, 2 / 5.0

"spam" + "eggs"
S = "ham"
"eggs " + S
S * 5
S[:0]
"green %s and %s" % ("eggs", S)

('x',)[0]
('x', 'y')[1]

L = [1,2,3] + [4,5,6]
L, L[:], L[:0], L[-2], L[-2:]
([1,2,3] + [4,5,6])[2:4]
[L[2], L[3]]
L.reverse(); L
L.sort(); L
L.index(4)

{'a':1, 'b':2}['b']
D = {'x':1, 'y':2, 'z':3}
D['w'] = 0
D['x'] + D['w']
D[(1,2,3)] = 4
D.keys(), D.values(), D.has_key((1,2,3))

[[]], ["",[],(),{},None]
```

2. *Indexing and slicing.* At the interactive prompt, define a list named L that contains four strings or numbers (e.g., L=[0,1,2,3]). Then, experiment with some boundary cases.

    a. What happens when you try to index out of bounds (e.g., L[4])?

    b. What about slicing out of bounds (e.g., L[-1000:100])?

    c. Finally, how does Python handle it if you try to extract a sequence in reverse—with the lower bound greater than the higher bound (e.g., L[3:1])? Hint: try assigning to this slice (L[3:1]=['?']) and see where the value is put. Do you think this may be the same phenomenon you saw when slicing out of bounds?

3. *Indexing, slicing, and del.* Define another list L with four items again, and assign an empty list to one of its offsets (e.g., L[2]=[ ]). What happens? Then assign an empty list to a slice (L[2:3]=[ ]). What happens now? Recall that slice assignment deletes the slice and inserts the new value where it used to be. The del statement deletes offsets, keys, attributes, and names. Use it on your list to

delete an item (e.g., del L[0]). What happens if you del an entire slice (del L[1:])? What happens when you assign a nonsequence to a slice (L[1:2]=1)?

4. *Tuple assignment.* Type this sequence:

```
>>> X = 'spam'
>>> Y = 'eggs'
>>> X, Y = Y, X
```

What do you think is happening to X and Y when you type this sequence?

5. *Dictionary keys.* Consider the following code fragments:

```
>>> D = {}
>>> D[1] = 'a'
>>> D[2] = 'b'
```

We learned that dictionaries aren't accessed by offsets, so what's going on here? Does the following shed any light on the subject? (Hint: strings, integers, and tuples share which type category?)

```
>>> D[(1, 2, 3)] = 'c'
>>> D
{1: 'a', 2: 'b', (1, 2, 3): 'c'}
```

6. *Dictionary indexing.* Create a dictionary named D with three entries, for keys 'a', 'b', and 'c'. What happens if you try to index a nonexistent key (D['d'])? What does Python do if you try to assign to a nonexistent key d (e.g., D['d']='spam')? How does this compare to out-of-bounds assignments and references for lists? Does this sound like the rule for variable names?

7. *Generic operations.* Run interactive tests to answer the following questions:

    a. What happens when you try to use the + operator on different/mixed types (e.g., string + list, list + tuple)?

    b. Does + work when one of the operands is a dictionary?

    c. Does the append method work for both lists and strings? How about using the keys method on lists? (Hint: What does append assume about its subject object?)

    d. Finally, what type of object do you get back when you slice or concatenate two lists or two strings?

8. *String indexing.* Define a string S of four characters: S = "spam". Then type the following expression: S[0][0][0][0][0]. Any clues as to what's happening this time? (Hint: recall that a string is a collection of characters, but Python characters are one-character strings.) Does this indexing expression still work if you apply it to a list such as: ['s', 'p', 'a', 'm']? Why?

9. *Immutable types.* Define a string S of 4 characters again: S = "spam". Write an assignment that changes the string to "slam", using only slicing and concatenation. Could you perform the same operation using just indexing and concatenation? How about index assignment?

10. *Nesting.* Write a data-structure that represents your personal information: name (first, middle, last), age, job, address, email address, and phone number. You may build the data structure with any combination of built-in object types you like: lists, tuples, dictionaries, strings, numbers. Then access the individual components of your data structures by indexing. Do some structures make more sense than others for this object?

11. *Files.* Write a script that creates a new output file called *myfile.txt* and writes the string "Hello file world!" into it. Then write another script that opens *myfile.txt*, and reads and prints its contents. Run your two scripts from the system command line. Does the new file show up in the directory where you ran your scripts? What if you add a different directory path to the filename passed to open? Note: file `write` methods do not add newline characters to your strings; add an explicit '\n' at the end of the string if you want to fully terminate the line in the file.

12. *The dir function revisited.* Try typing the following expressions at the interactive prompt. Starting with Version 1.5, the `dir` function has been generalized to list all attributes of any Python object you're likely to be interested in. If you're using an earlier version than 1.5, the `__methods__` scheme has the same effect. If you're using Python 2.2, `dir` is probably the only of these that will work.

```
[].__methods__      # 1.4 or 1.5
dir([])             # 1.5 and later

{}.__methods__      # Dictionary
dir({})
```

Statements and Syntax

In Part III, we study Python's procedural statement set: statements that select from alternative actions, repeat operations, print objects, and so on. Since this is our first formal look at statements, we will also explore Python's general syntax model. As we'll see, Python has a familiar and simple syntax model, though we often type much less in Python statements than in some other languages.

We'll also meet the boolean expressions in conjunction with conditional statements and loops, and learn about Python documentation schemes while studying the syntax of documentation strings and comments. At an abstract level, the statements we'll meet here are used to create and process the objects in Part II. By the end of this part, you will be able to code and run substantial Python program logic.

## CHAPTER 8

Assignment, Expressions, and Print

Now that we've seen Python's core built-in object types, this chapter explores its fundamental statement forms. In simple terms, statements are the things you write to tell Python what your programs should do. If programs do *things* with *stuff*, statements are the way you specify what sort of *things* a program does. Python is a procedural, statement-based language; by combining statements, you specify a procedure that Python performs to satisfy a program's goals.

Another way to understand the role of statements is to revisit the concept hierarchy introduced in Chapter 4, which talked about built-in objects and the expressions used to manipulate them. This chapter climbs the hierarchy to the next level:

1. Programs are composed of modules.
2. Modules contain statements.
3. Statements contain expressions.
4. Expressions create and process objects.

At its core, Python syntax is composed of statements and expressions. Expressions process objects, and are embedded in statements. Statements code the larger *logic* of a program's operation—they use and direct expressions to process the objects we've already seen. Moreover, statements are where objects spring into existence (e.g., in expressions within assignment statements), and some statements create entirely new kinds of objects (functions, classes, and so on). Statements always exist in modules, which themselves are managed with statements.

Table 8-1 summarizes Python's statement set. Part III deals with entries in the table through break and continue. You've informally been introduced to a few of the statements in Table 8-1. Part III will fill in details that were skipped earlier, introduce the rest of Python's procedural statement set, and cover the overall syntax model.

Table 8-1. Python statements

Statement	Role	Example
Assignment	Creating references	curly, moe, larry = 'good', 'bad', 'ugly'
Calls	Running functions	stdout.write("spam, ham, toast\n")
print	Printing objects	print 'The Killer', joke
if/elif/else	Selecting actions	if "python" in text: print text
for/else	Sequence iteration	for x in mylist: print x
while/else	General loops	while 1: print 'hello'
pass	Empty placeholder	while 1: pass
break, continue	Loop jumps	while 1: if not line: break
try/except/ finally	Catching exceptions	try: action( ) except: print 'action error'
raise	Triggering exception	raise endSearch, location
import, from	Module access	import sys; from sys import stdin
def, return, yield	Building functions	def f(a, b, c=1, *d): return a+b+c+d[0] def gen(n): for i in n, yield i*2
class	Building objects	class subclass: staticData = [ ]
global	Namespaces	def function( ): global x, y; x = 'new'
del	Deleting references	del data[k]; del data[i:j]; del obj.attr
exec	Running code strings	exec "import " + modName in gdict, ldict
assert	Debugging checks	assert X > Y

Statements that have to do with larger program units—functions, classes, modules, and exceptions—lead to larger programming ideas, so they will each have a section of their own. More exotic statements like exec (which compiles and executes code constructed as strings) are covered later in the book, or in Python standard documentation.

Assignment Statements

We've been using the Python assignment statement already, to assign objects to names. In its basic form, you write a *target* of an assignment on the left of an equals sign and an *object* to be assigned on the right. The target on the left may be a name or object component, and the object on the right can be an arbitrary expression that computes an object. For the most part, assignment is straightforward to use, but here are a few properties to keep in mind:

Assignments create object references. Python assignment stores references to objects in names or data structure slots. It always creates references to objects, instead of copying objects. Because of that, Python variables are much more like pointers than data storage areas.

Names are created when first assigned. Python creates variable names the first time you assign them a value (an object reference). There's no need to predeclare names ahead of time. Some (but not all) data structure slots are created when assigned too (e.g., dictionary entries, some object attributes). Once assigned, a name is replaced by the value it references whenever it appears in an expression.

Names must be assigned before being referenced. Conversely, it's an error to use a name you haven't assigned a value to yet. Python raises an exception if you try, rather than returning some sort of ambiguous (and hard to notice) default value.

Implicit assignments: `import`, `from`, `def`, `class`, `for`, *function arguments.* In this section, we're concerned with the = statement, but assignment occurs in many contexts in Python. For instance, we'll see later that module imports, function and class definitions, `for` loop variables, and function arguments, are all implicit assignments. Since assignment works the same everywhere it pops up, all these contexts simply bind names to object references at runtime.

Table 8-2 illustrates the different assignment statements in Python. In addition to this table, Python includes a set of assignment statement forms known as *augmented assignment.*

Table 8-2. Assignment statement forms

Operation	Interpretation
`spam = 'Spam'`	Basic form
`spam, ham = 'yum', 'YUM'`	Tuple assignment (positional)
`[spam, ham] = ['yum', 'YUM']`	List assignment (positional)
`spam = ham = 'lunch'`	Multiple-target

The first line in Table 8-2 is by far the most common: binding a single object to a name (or data-structure slot). The other table entries represent special forms:

Tuple and list unpacking assignments
> The second and third lines are related. When you code tuples or lists on the left side of the =, Python pairs objects on the right side with targets on the left and assigns them from left to right. For example, in the second line of the table, name `spam` is assigned the string `'yum'`, and name `ham` is bound to string `'YUM'`. Internally, Python makes a tuple of the items on the right first, so this is often called tuple (and list) unpacking assignment.

Multiple-target assignments
> The last line in Table 8-2 shows the multiple-target form of assignment. In this form, Python assigns a reference to the same object (the object farthest to the right) to all the targets on the left. In the table, names `spam` and `ham` would both be assigned a reference to the same string object `'lunch'`, and so share the same reference to the object. The effect is the same as if you had coded `ham='lunch'`, followed by `spam=ham`, since `ham` evaluates to the original string object.

We've already used basic assignment. Here are a few simple examples of unpacking assignment in action:

```
% python
>>> nudge = 1
>>> wink  = 2
>>> A, B = nudge, wink          # Tuple assignment
>>> A, B                        # Like A = nudge; B = wink
(1, 2)
>>> [C, D] = [nudge, wink]      # List assignment
>>> C, D
(1, 2)
```

Tuple assignment leads to a common coding trick in Python that was introduced in a solution to the exercises from Part II. Since Python creates a temporary tuple that saves the values on the right, unpacking assignments are also a way to *swap* two variables' values without creating a temporary of your own:

```
>>> nudge = 1
>>> wink  = 2
>>> nudge, wink = wink, nudge   # Tuples: swaps values
>>> nudge, wink                 # Like T = nudge; nudge = wink; wink = T
(2, 1)
```

The tuple and list assignment forms are generalized to accept any type of sequence on the right, as long as it is of the same length. You can assign a tuple of values to a list of variables, a string of characters to a tuple of variables, and so on. In all cases, Python assigns items in the sequence on the right to variables in the sequence on the left by position, from left to right:

```
>>> [a, b, c] = (1, 2, 3)
>>> a, c
(1, 3)
>>> (a, b, c) = "ABC"
>>> a, c
('A', 'C')
```

Unpacking assignment also gives rise to another common coding idiom in Python: assigning an integer series to a set of variables:

```
>>> red, green, blue = range(3)
>>> red, blue
(0, 2)
```

This initializes the three names to integer codes 0, 1, and 2, respectively (it's Python's equivalent of *enumerated* data types you may have seen in other languages). To make sense of this, you also need to know that the range built-in function generates a list of successive integers:

```
>>> range(3)
[0, 1, 2]
```

Since range is commonly used in for loops, we'll say more about it in Chapter 10.

Variable Name Rules

Now that we've seen assignment statements, it is also time to get more formal in the use of variable names. In Python, names come into existence when you assign values to them, but there are a few rules to follow when picking names for things in our program:

Syntax: (underscore or letter) + (any number of letters, digits, or underscores)
> Variable names must start with an underscore or letter, and be followed by any number of letters, digits, or underscores. _spam, spam, and Spam_1 are legal names, but 1_Spam, spam$, and @#! are not.

Case matters: SPAM is not the same as spam
> Python always pays attention to case in programs, both in names you create and in reserved words. For instance, names X and x refer to two different variables.

Reserved words are off limits
> Names we define cannot be the same as words that mean special things in the Python language. For instance, if we try to use a variable name like class, Python will raise a syntax error, but klass and Class work fine. Table 8-3 lists the words that are reserved (and hence off limits) in Python.

Table 8-3. Python reserved words

and	del	for	is	raise
assert	elif	from	lambda	return
break	else	global	not	try
class	except	if	or	while
continue	exec	import	pass	yield[a]
def	finally	in	print	

[a] yield is an optional extension in Version 2.2, but is a standard keyword in 2.3. It is used in conjunction with generator functions, a newer feature discussed in Chapter 14.

Python's reserved words are always all lowercase. And they are truly reserved; unlike names in the built-in scope that you will meet in the next part, you cannot redefine reserved words by assignment (e.g., and=1 is a syntax error).[*] Furthermore, because module names in import statements become variables in your script, this constraint extends to your module filenames—you can code a file called *and.py*, but cannot import it; we'll revisit this idea in Part V.

Naming conventions

Besides these rules, there is also a set of naming *conventions*—rules which are not required, but are used in normal practice. For instance, because names with two

---

[*] In the Jython Java-based implementation of Python, though, user-defined variables can sometimes be the same as Python reserved words.

leading and trailing underscores (e.g., __name__) generally have special meaning to the Python interpreter, you should avoid this pattern for your own names. Here is a list of all the conventions Python follows:

- Names that begin with a single underscore (_X) are not imported by a from module import * statement (described in Chapter 16).

- Names that have two leading and trailing underscores (__X__) are system-defined names, which have special meaning to the interpreter.

- Names that begin with two underscores and do not end with two more (__X) are localized ("mangled") to enclosing classes (described in Chapter 23).

- The name that is just a single underscore (_) retains the result of the last expression, when working interactively.

In addition to these Python interpreter conventions, we'll meet other conventions that Python programmers usually follow as well. In Part VI, for instance, we'll see class names commonly start with an uppercase letter, and that the name self, though not reserved, usually has a special role. And in Part IV, we'll study another class of names known as the *built-ins*, which are predefined but not reserved (and so can be reassigned: open=42 works, though you might wish it didn't).

Names have no type, but objects do

It's crucial to keep Python's distinction between names and objects clear. As described in the section "The Dynamic Typing Interlude" in Chapter 4, objects have a type (e.g., integer, list), and may be mutable or not. Names (a.k.a. variables), on the other hand, are always just references to objects; they have no notion of mutability and have no associated type information, apart from the type of the object they happen to reference at a given point in time.

In fact, it's perfectly okay to assign the same name to different kinds of objects at different times:

```
>>> x = 0          # x bound to an integer object
>>> x = "Hello"    # Now it's a string.
>>> x = [1, 2, 3]  # And now it's a list.
```

In later examples, you'll see that this generic nature of names can be a decided advantage in Python programming.* In Part IV, you'll learn that names also live in something called a *scope*, which defines where they can be used; the place you assign a name determines where it is visible.

---

* If you've used C++, you may be interested to know that there is no notion of C++'s const declaration in Python; certain objects may be immutable, but names can always be assigned. Python also has ways to hide names in classes and modules, but they're not the same as C++'s declarations.

Augmented Assignment Statements

Beginning with Python 2.0, a set of additional assignment statement formats, listed in Table 8-4, are now available. Known as *augmented assignment*, and borrowed from the C language, these formats are mostly just shorthand. They imply the combination of a binary expression and an assignment. For instance, the following two formats are now roughly equivalent:

```
X = X + Y        # Traditional form
X += Y           # Newer augmented form
```

Table 8-4. Augmented assignment statements

X += Y	X &= Y	X -= Y	X |= Y
X *= Y	X ^= Y	X /= Y	X »= Y
X %= Y	X «= Y	X **= Y	X //= Y

Augmented assignment works on any type that supports the implied binary expression. For example, here are two ways to add 1 to a name:

```
>>> x = 1
>>> x = x + 1        # Traditional
>>> x
2
>>> x += 1           # Augmented
>>> x
3
```

When applied to a string, the augmented form performs concatenation instead—exactly as if you had typed the longer: S = S + "SPAM":

```
>>> S = "spam"
>>> S += "SPAM"        # Implied concatenation
>>> S
'spamSPAM'
```

As shown in Table 8-4, there are analogous augmented assignment forms for every Python binary expression operator (an operator with values on the left and right side). For instance, X*=Y multiplies and assigns, X>>=Y shifts right and assigns, and so on. X //= Y (for floor division) is new in Version 2.2. Augmented assignments have three advantages:[*]

There's less for you to type.   Need we say more?

They only need to evaluate the left side once.   In X+=Y, X could be a complicated object expression. In the augmented form, it need only be evaluated once. In the long form, X=X+Y, X appears twice, and must be run twice.

---

[*] C/C++ programmers take note: although Python now has things like X+=Y, it still does not have C's auto-increment/decrement operators (e.g., X++, --X). These don't quite map to the Python object model, because there is no notion of an in-place change to immutable objects like numbers.

They automatically choose the optimal technique. For objects that support in-place changes, the augmented forms automatically perform in-place change operations, instead of slower copies.

The last point here requires a bit more explanation. For augment assignments, in-place operations may be applied for mutable objects as an optimization. Recall that lists can be extended in a variety of ways. To add a single item to the end of a list, we can concatenate or append:

```
>>> L = [1, 2]
>>> L = L + [3]          # Concatenate: slower
>>> L
[1, 2, 3]
>>> L.append(4)          # Faster, but in-place
>>> L
[1, 2, 3, 4]
```

And to add a set of items at the end, we may either concatenate again, or call the list extend method:*

```
>>> L = L + [5, 6]       # Concatenate: slower
>>> L
[1, 2, 3, 4, 5, 6]
>>> L.extend([7, 8])     # Faster, but in-place
>>> L
[1, 2, 3, 4, 5, 6, 7, 8]
```

In all of these, concatenation is less prone to the side effects of shared object references, but will generally run slower than the in-place equivalent. Concatenation must create a new object, copy in the list on the left, and then copy in the list on the right. By contrast, in-place method calls simply add items at the end of a memory block.

When augmented assignment is used to extend a list, we can forget these details—Python automatically calls the quicker extend method, instead of the slower concatenation operation implied by +:

```
>>> L += [9, 10]         # Mapped to L.extend([9, 10])
>>> L
[1, 2, 3, 4, 5, 6, 7, 8, 9, 10]
```

Expression Statements

In Python, you can use expressions as statements too. But since the result of the expression won't be saved, it makes sense to do so only if the expression does

---

* As suggested in Chapter 6, we can also use slice assignment: L[len(L):] = [11,12,13], but this works roughly the same as the simpler list extend method.

something useful as a side effect. Expressions are commonly used as statements in two situations:

For calls to functions and methods
> Some functions and methods do lots of work without returning a value. Since you're not interested in retaining the value they return, you can call such functions with an expression statement. Such functions are sometimes called procedures in other languages; in Python, they take the form of functions that don't return a value.

For printing values at the interactive prompt
> Python echoes back the results of expressions typed at the interactive command line. Technically, these are expression statements too; they serve as a shorthand for typing print statements.

Table 8-5 lists some common expression statement forms in Python. Calls to functions and methods are coded with zero or more argument objects (really, expressions that evaluate to objects) in parentheses, after the function or method.

Table 8-5. Common Python expression statements

Operation	Interpretation
spam(eggs, ham)	Function calls
spam.ham(eggs)	Method calls
Spam	Interactive print
spam < ham and ham != eggs	Compound expressions
spam < ham < eggs	Range tests

The last line in the table is a special form: Python lets us string together magnitude comparison tests, in order to code chained comparisons such as range tests. For instance, the expression (A < B < C) tests whether B is between A and C; it's equivalent to the Boolean test (A < B and B < C) but is easier on the eyes (and keyboard). Compound expressions aren't normally written as statements, but it's syntactically legal to do so and can even be useful at the interactive prompt if you're not sure of an expression's result.

Beware that although expressions can appear as statements in Python, statements can't be used as expressions. For instance, Python doesn't allow us to embed assignment statements (=) in other expressions. The rationale for this is that it avoids common coding mistakes; you can't accidentally change a variable by typing = when you really mean to use the == equality test. You'll see how to code around this when you meet the Python while loop in Chapter 10.

Print Statements

The print statement simply prints objects. Technically, it writes the textual representation of objects to the standard output stream. The standard output stream is the same as the C language's stdout; it is usually mapped to the window where you started your Python program (unless redirected to a file in your system's shell).

In Chapter 7, we also saw file methods that write text. The print statement is similar, but more focused: print writes objects to the stdout stream (with some default formatting), but file write methods write strings to files. Since the standard output stream is available in Python as the stdout object in the built-in sys module (i.e., sys.stdout), it's possible to emulate print with file writes, but print is easier to use.

Table 8-6 lists the print statement's forms. We've seen the basic print statement in action already. By default, it adds a space between the items separated by commas, and adds a linefeed at the end of the current output line:

```
>>> x = 'a'
>>> y = 'b'
>>> print x, y
a b
```

Table 8-6. Print statement forms

Operation	Interpretation
print spam, ham	Print objects to sys.stdout; add a space between.
print spam, ham,	Same, but don't add newline at end of text.
print >> myfile, spam, ham	Send text to myfile.write, not to sys.stdout.write.

This formatting is just a default; you can choose to use it or not. To suppress the linefeed (so you can add more text to the current line later), end your print statement with a comma, as shown in the second line of Table 8-6. To suppress the space between items, you can instead build up an output string yourself using the string concatenation and formatting tools covered in Chapter 5, and print the string all at once:

```
>>> print x + y
ab
>>> print '%s...%s' % (x, y)
a...b
```

The Python "Hello World" Program

To print a hello world message, you simply print it:

```
>>> print 'hello world'          # Print a string object.
hello world
```

Since expression results are echoed in the interactive command line, you often don't even need to use a print statement there; simply type expressions you'd like to have printed and their results are echoed back:

```
>>> 'hello world'                    # Interactive echoes
'hello world'
```

Really, the print statement is just an ergonomic feature of Python—it provides a user-friendly interface to the sys.stdout object, with a bit of default formatting. You can also code print operations this way:

```
>>> import sys                       # Printing the hard way
>>> sys.stdout.write('hello world\n')
hello world
```

This code explicitly calls the write method of sys.stdout—an attribute preset when Python starts up to an open file object connected to the output stream. The print statement hides most of those details. It provides a simple tool for simple printing tasks.

Redirecting the Output Stream

The sys.stdout print equivalent turns out to be basis of a common technique in Python. In general, print and sys.stdout are related as follows:

```
print X
```

is equivalent to the longer:

```
import sys
sys.stdout.write(str(X) + '\n')
```

that manually performs a string conversion with str, adds a newline with +, and calls the output stream's write method. The long form isn't all that useful for printing by itself. However, it is useful to know that this is exactly what print statements do, because it is possible to reassign sys.stdout to something different than the standard output stream. In other words, this equivalence provides a way for making your print statements send their text to other places. For example:

```
import sys
sys.stdout = open('log.txt', 'a')      # Redirects prints to file
...
print x, y, x                          # Shows up in log.txt
```

Here, we reset sys.stdout to a manually-opened output file object opened in append mode. After the reset, every print statement anywhere in the program will write its text to the end of file log.txt, instead of the original output stream. The print statements are happy to keep calling sys.stdout's write method, no matter what sys.stdout happens to refer to.

In fact, as this chapter's sidebar on print and stdout will explain, we can even reset sys.stdout to nonfile objects, as long as they have the expected protocol (a write method); when those objects are classes, printed text can be routed and processed arbitrarily.

Why You Will Care: print and stdout

The equivalence between the print statement and writing to sys.stdout is important to notice. It makes it possible to reassign sys.stdout to a user-defined object that provides the same methods as files (e.g., write). Since the print statement just sends text to the sys.stdout.write method, you can capture printed text in your programs by assigning sys.stdout to an object whose write method processes the text in arbitrary ways.

For instance, you can send printed text to a GUI window by defining an object with a write method that does the routing. You'll see an example of this trick later in the book, but abstractly, it looks like this:

```
class FileFaker:
    def write(self, string):
        # Do something with the string.

import sys
sys.stdout = FileFaker()
print someObjects          # Sends to the class write method
```

This works because print is what we will call a *polymorphic* operation in the next part of this book—it doesn't care what sys.sytdout is, only that it has a method (i.e., interface) called write. This redirection to objects is even simpler:

```
myobj = FileFaker()
print >> myobj, someObjects   # Does not reset sys.stdout
```

Python's built-in raw_input( ) function reads from the sys.stdin file, so you can intercept read requests in a similar way—using classes that implement file-like read methods. See the raw_input and while loop example in Chapter 10 for more background on this.

Notice that since print text goes to the stdout stream, it's the way to print HTML in CGI scripts. It also means you can redirect Python script input and output at the operating system's command line, as usual:

```
python script.py < inputfile > outputfile
python script.py | filterProgram
```

The print>>file extension

This trick of redirecting printed text by assigning sys.stdout was so commonly used that Python's print statement has an extension to make it easier. One potential problem with the last section's code is that there is no direct way to restore the original output stream, should you need to switch back after printing to a file. We can always save and restore as needed:[*]

```
import sys
temp = sys.stdout                    # Save for restoring.
sys.stdout = open('log.txt', 'a')    # Redirects prints to file
...
print x, y, x                        # Print to file.
...
sys.stdout = temp
print a, b, c                        # Print to original stdout.
```

But this is just complicated enough that a print extension was added to make the save and restore unnecessary. When a print statement begins with a >> followed by an output file (or other) object, that single print statement sends its text to the object's write method, but does not reset sys.stdout. Because the redirection is temporary, normal print statements keep printing to the original output stream:

```
log = open('log.txt', 'a')
print >> log, x, y, z                # Print to a file-like object.
print a, b, c                        # Print to original stdout.
```

The >> form of the print is handy if you need to print to both files and the standard output stream. If you use this form, be sure to give it a file object (or an object that has the same write method as a file object), not a file's name string.

---

[*] We can also use the relatively new __stdout__ attribute in module sys, which refers to the original value sys.stdout had at program start-up time. We still need to restore sys.stdout to sys.__stdout__ to go back to this original stream value, though. See the sys module in the library manual for more details.

CHAPTER 9

if Tests

This chapter presents the Python if statement—the main statement used for select-ing from alternative actions based on test results. Because this is our first exposure to *compound statements*—statements which embed other statements—we will also explore the general concepts behind the Python statement syntax model here. And because the if statement introduces the notion of tests, we'll also use this chapter to study the concepts of truth tests and Boolean expressions in general.

if Statements

In simple terms, the Python if statement selects actions to perform. It's the primary selection tool in Python and represents much of the *logic* a Python program pos-sesses. It's also our first compound statement; like all compound Python statements, the if may contain other statements, including other ifs. In fact, Python lets you combine statements in a program both sequentially (so that they execute one after another), and arbitrarily nested (so that they execute only under certain conditions).

General Format

The Python if statement is typical of most procedural languages. It takes the form of an if test, followed by one or more optional elif tests (meaning "else if"), and ends with an optional else block. Each test and the else have an associated block of nested statements indented under a header line. When the statement runs, Python executes the block of code associated with the first test that evaluates to true, or the else block if all tests prove false. The general form of an if looks like this:

```
if <test1>:            # if test
    <statements1>      # Associated block
elif <test2>:          # Optional elifs
    <statements2>
else:                  # Optional else
    <statements3>
```

Examples

Let's look at a few simple examples of the `if` statement at work. All parts are optional except the initial `if` test and its associated statements; in the simplest case, the other parts are omitted:

```
>>> if 1:
...     print 'true'
...
true
```

Notice how the prompt changes to "..." for continuation lines in the basic interface used here (in IDLE, you'll simply drop down to an indented line instead—hit Backspace to back up); a blank line terminates and runs the entire statement. Remember that 1 is Boolean true, so this statement's test always succeeds; to handle a false result, code the `else`:

```
>>> if not 1:
...     print 'true'
... else:
...     print 'false'
...
false
```

Now, here's an example of the most complex kind of `if` statement—with all its optional parts present:

```
>>> x = 'killer rabbit'
>>> if x == 'roger':
...     print "how's jessica?"
... elif x == 'bugs':
...     print "what's up doc?"
... else:
...     print 'Run away! Run away!'
...
Run away! Run away!
```

This multiline statement extends from the `if` line, through the `else` block. When run, Python executes the statements nested under the first test that is true, or the `else` part if all tests are false (in this example, they are). In practice, both the `elif` and `else` parts may be omitted, and there may be more than one statement nested in each section. Moreover, the words `if`, `elif`, and `else` are associated by the fact that they line up vertically, with the same indentation.

Multiway branching

If you've used languages like C or Pascal, you might be interested to know that there is no "switch" or "case" statement in Python that selects an action based on a variable's value. Instead, *multiway branching* is coded as either a series of if/elif tests as done in the prior example, or by indexing dictionaries or searching lists.

Since dictionaries and lists can be built at runtime, they're sometimes more flexible than hardcoded if logic:

```
>>> choice = 'ham'
>>> print {'spam': 1.25,          # A dictionary-based 'switch'
...        'ham':  1.99,          # Use has_key() or get() for default.
...        'eggs': 0.99,
...        'bacon': 1.10}[choice]
1.99
```

Although it usually takes a few moments for this to sink in the first time you see it, this dictionary is a multiway branch—indexing on key choice branches to one of a set of values much like a "switch" in C. An almost equivalent and more verbose Python if statement might look like this:

```
>>> if choice == 'spam':
...     print 1.25
... elif choice == 'ham':
...     print 1.99
... elif choice == 'eggs':
...     print 0.99
... elif choice == 'bacon':
...     print 1.10
... else:
...     print 'Bad choice'
...
1.99
```

Notice the else clause on the if here to handle the *default* case when no key matches. As we saw in Chapter 6, dictionary defaults can be coded with has_key tests, get method calls, or exception catching. All of the same techniques can be used here to code a default action in a dictionary-based multiway branch. Here's the get scheme at work with defaults:

```
>>> branch = {'spam': 1.25,
...           'ham':  1.99,
...           'eggs': 0.99}

>>> print branch.get('spam', 'Bad choice')
1.25
>>> print branch.get('bacon', 'Bad choice')
Bad choice
```

Dictionaries are good at associating values with keys, but what about more complicated actions you can code in if statements? In Part IV, you'll learn that dictionaries can also contain *functions* to represent more complex branch actions, and implement general jump tables. Such functions appear as dictionary values, are often coded as lambdas, and are called by adding parenthesis to trigger their action.

Python Syntax Rules

In general, Python has a simple, statement-based syntax. But there are a few properties you need to know:

Statements execute one after another, until you say otherwise. Python normally runs statements in a file or nested block from first to last, but statements like the if (and, as you'll see, loops) cause the interpreter to jump around in your code. Because Python's path through a program is called the control flow, things like the if that affect it are called control-flow statements.

Block and statement boundaries are detected automatically. There are no braces or "begin/end" delimiters around blocks of code; instead, Python uses the indentation of statements under a header to group the statements in a nested block. Similarly, Python statements are not normally terminated with a semicolon; rather, the end of a line usually marks the end of the statements coded on that line.

Compound statements = header, ":", indented statements. All compound statements in Python follow the same pattern: a header line terminated with a colon, followed by one or more nested statements usually indented under the header. The indented statements are called a *block* (or sometimes, a suite). In the if statement, the elif and else clauses are part of the if, but are header lines with nested blocks of their own.

Blank lines, spaces, and comments are usually ignored. Blank lines are ignored in files (but not at the interactive prompt). Spaces inside statements and expressions are almost always ignored (except in string literals and indentation). Comments are always ignored: they start with a # character (not inside a string literal) and extend to the end of the current line.

Docstrings are ignored but saved, and displayed by tools. Python supports an additional comment form called documentation strings (*docstrings* for short), which, unlike # comments, are retained. Docstrings are simply strings that show up at the top of program files and some statements, and are automatically associated with objects. Their contents are ignored by Python, but they are automatically attached to objects at runtime, and may be displayed with documentation tools. Docstrings are part of Python's larger documentation and are covered at the end of Part III.

As you've seen, there are no variable type declarations in Python; this fact alone makes for a much simpler language syntax than what you may be used to. But for most new users, the lack of braces and semicolons to mark blocks and statements seems to be the most novel syntactic feature of Python, so let's explore what this means in more detail here.

Block Delimiters

Python detects block boundaries automatically, by line *indentation*—the empty space to the left of your code. All statements indented the same distance to the right belong to the same block of code. In other words, the statements within a block line up vertically. The block ends at a line less indented or the end of the file, and more deeply nested blocks are simply indented further to the right than the statements in the enclosing block.

For instance, Figure 9-1 demonstrates the block structure of the following code:

```
x = 1
if x:
    y = 2
    if y:
        print 'block2'
    print 'block1'
print 'block0'
```

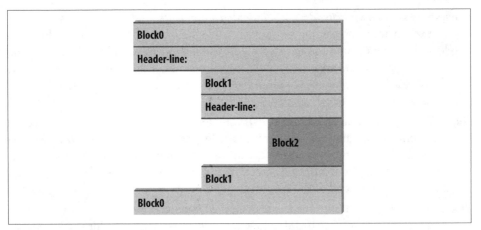

Figure 9-1. Nested code blocks

This code contains three blocks: the first (the top-level of the file) is not indented at all; the second (within the outer if statement) is indented four spaces; and the third (the print statement under the nested if) is indented eight spaces.

In general, top-level (unnested) code must start in column 1. Nested blocks can start in any column; indentation may consist of any number of spaces and tabs, as long as it's the same for all the statements in a given block. That is, Python doesn't care how you indent your code; it only cares that it's done consistently. Technically, tabs count for enough spaces to move the current column number up to a multiple of 8, but it's usually not a good idea to mix tabs and spaces within a block—use one or the other.

Indentation to the left of your code is the only major place in Python where whitespace matters; in most other contexts, space can be coded or not. However, indentation is really part of Python syntax, not just a stylistic suggestion: all the statements within any given single block must be indented the same, or Python reports a syntax error. This is on purpose—because you don't need to explicitly mark the start and end of a nested block of code, it removes some of the syntactic clutter found in other languages.

This syntax model also enforces indentation consistency, a crucial component of readability in structured programming languages like Python. Python's syntax is sometimes called the "what you see is what you get" of languages—the indentation of code unambiguously tells readers what it is associated with. Python's consistent appearance makes code easier to maintain.

Consistently-indented code always satisfies Python's rules. Moreover, most text editors (including IDLE) make it easy to follow Python's indentation model, by automatically indenting code as you type it.

Statement Delimiters

Statements normally end at the end of the line they appear on. This covers the vast majority of the Python statements you'll code. When statements are too long to fit on a single line, though, a few special rules may be used to make them span multiple continuation lines:

Statements may span lines if you're continuing an open syntactic pair. For statements that are too long to fit on one line, Python lets you continue typing the statement on the next line, if you're coding something enclosed in ( ), { }, or [ ] pairs. For instance, expressions in parenthesis and dictionary and list literals can span any number of lines; your statement doesn't end until the line on which you type the closing part of the pair ( ), }, or]). Continuation lines can start at any indentation level.

Statements may span lines if they end in a backslash. This is a somewhat outdated feature, but if a statement needs to span multiple lines, you can also add a backslash (\) at the end of the prior line to indicate you're continuing on the next line. But since you can also continue by adding parentheses around long constructs, backslashes are almost never needed.

Other rules. Very long string literals can span lines arbitrarily. In fact, the triple-quoted string blocks we met in Chapter 5 are designed to do so. Although uncommon, you can also terminate statements with a semicolon—this is sometimes used to squeeze more than one simple statement on a single line. Finally, comments and blank lines can appear anywhere.

A Few Special Cases

Here's what a continuation line looks like, using the open pairs rule; we can span delimited constructs across any number of lines:

```
L = ["Good",
     "Bad",
     "Ugly"]                       # Open pairs may span lines.
```

This works for anything in parentheses too: expressions, function arguments, functions headers (see Chapter 12), and so on. If you like using backslashes to continue you can, but it's not usually necessary:

```
if a == b and c == d and    \
   d == e and f == g:
    print 'olde'                   # Backslashes allow continuations.
```

Because any expression can be enclosed in parenthesis, you can usually simply wrap something in parenthesis anytime you need to span multiple lines:

```
if (a == b and c == d and
    d == e and e == f):
    print 'new'                    # But parentheses usually do too.
```

As a special case, Python allows you to write more than one non-compound statement (i.e., statements without nested statements) on the same line, separated by semicolons. Some coders use this form to save program file real estate, but it usually makes for more readable code if you stick to one statement per line for most of your work:

```
x = 1; y = 2; print x        # More than one simple statement
```

And finally, Python lets you move a compound statement's body up to the header line, provided the body is just a simple (non-compound) statement. You'll see this most often used for simple if statements with a single test and action:

```
if 1: print 'hello'          # Simple statement on header line
```

You can combine some of these special cases to write code that is difficult to read, but we don't recommend it; as a rule of thumb, try to keep each statement on a line of its own, and indent all except the simplest of blocks. Six months down the road, you'll be happy you did.

Truth Tests

We introduced the notions of comparison, equality, and truth values in Chapter 7. Since if statements are the first statement that actually uses test results, we'll expand on some of these ideas here. In particular, Python's Boolean operators are a bit different from their counterparts in languages like C. In Python:

- True means any nonzero number or nonempty object.
- False means not true: a zero number, empty object, or None.

- Comparisons and equality tests are applied recursively to data structures.
- Comparisons and equality tests return 1 or 0 (true or false).
- Boolean and and or operators return a true or false operand object.

In short, Boolean operators are used to combine the results of other tests. There are three Boolean expression operators in Python:

X and Y

> Is true if both X and Y are true

X or Y

> Is true if either X or Y are true

not X

> Is true if X is false (the expression returns 1 or 0)

Here, X and Y may be any truth value or an expression that returns a truth value (e.g., an equality test, range comparison, and so on). Boolean operators are typed out as words in Python (instead of C's &&, ||, and !). Boolean and and or operators return a true or false *object* in Python, not an integer 1 or 0. Let's look at a few examples to see how this works:

```
>>> 2 < 3, 3 < 2        # Less-than: return 1 or 0
(1, 0)
```

Magnitude comparisons like these return an integer 1 or 0 as their truth value result. But and and or operators always return an object instead. For or tests, Python evaluates the operand objects from left to right, and returns the first one that is true. Moreover, Python stops at the first true operand it finds; this is usually called *short-circuit evaluation*, since determining a result short-circuits (terminates) the rest of the expression:

```
>>> 2 or 3, 3 or 2      # Return left operand if true.
(2, 3)                  # Else return right operand (true or false).
>>> [] or 3
3
>>> [] or {}
{}
```

In the first line above, both operands are true (2, 3), so Python always stops and returns the one on the left. In the other two tests, the left operand is false, so Python simply evaluates and returns the object on the right (which will happen to have a true or false value if tested). Also, and operations stop as soon as the result is known; in this case, Python evaluates operands from left to right and stops at the first false object:

```
>>> 2 and 3, 3 and 2    # Return left operand if false.
(3, 2)                  # Else return right operand (true or false).
>>> [] and {}
[]
>>> 3 and []
[]
```

Here, both operands are true in the first line, so Python evaluates both sides and returns the object on the right. In the second test, the left operand is false ([ ]), so Python stops and returns it as the test result. In the last test, the left side is true (3), so Python evaluates and returns the object on the right (which happens to be a false [ ]).

The end result of all this is the same as in C and most other languages—you get a value that is logically true or false, if tested in an if or while. However, in Python, Booleans return either the left or right object, not an integer flag.

One final note: as described in Chapter 7, Python 2.3 includes a new Boolean type, named bool, which is internally a subclass of the int integer type, with values True and False. These two instances are really just customized versions of integers 1 and 0, which yield the words True and False when printed or otherwise converted to strings. The only time you'll generally notice this change is when you see Boolean outputs printed as True and False. More on type subclassing in Chapter 23.

Why You Will Care: Booleans

One common way to use the unique behaviour of Python Boolean operators is to select from a set of objects with an or. A statement:

```
X = A or B or C or None
```

sets X to the first nonempty (that is, true) object among A, B, and C, or None if all are empty. This turns out to be a fairly common coding paradigm in Python: to select a nonempty among a fixed size set, simply string them together in an or expression.

Short-circuit evaluation is also important to understand, because expressions on the right of a Boolean operator might call functions that do much work or have side effects that won't happen if the short-circuit rule takes effect:

```
if f1() or f2(): ...
```

Here, if f1 returns a true (or nonempty) value, Python will never run f2. To guarantee that both functions will be run, call them before the or:

```
tmp1, tmp2 = f1(), f2()
if tmp1 or tmp2: ...
```

You'll see another application of this behavior in Chapter 14: because of the way Booleans work, the expression ((A and B) or C) can be used to emulate an if/else statement—almost. Also notice that because all objects are inherently true or false, it's common and easier in Python to test an object directly (if X:) rather than comparing it to an empty value (if X != '':). For a string, the two tests are equivalent.

---

while and for Loops

In this chapter, we meet Python's two main *looping* constructs—statements that repeat an action over and over. The first of these, the while loop, provides a way to code general loops; the second, the for statement, is designed for stepping through the items in a sequence object and running a block of code for each item.

There are other kinds of looping operations in Python, but the two statements covered here are the primary syntax provided for coding repeated actions. We'll also study a few unusual statements such as break and continue here, because they are used within loops.

while Loops

Python's while statement is its most general iteration construct. In simple terms, it repeatedly executes a block of indented statements, as long as a test at the top keeps evaluating to a true value. When the test becomes false, control continues after all the statements in the while block; the body never runs if the test is false to begin with.

The while statement is one of two looping statements (along with the for). It is called a loop because control keeps looping back to the start of the statement, until the test becomes false. The net effect is that the loop's body is executed repeatedly while the test at the top is true. Besides statements, Python also provides a handful of tools that implicitly loop (iterate): the map, reduce, and filter functions; the in membership test; list comprehensions; and more. We'll explore most of these in Chapter 14.

General Format

In its most complex form, the while statement consists of a header line with a test expression, a body of one or more indented statements, and an optional else part that is executed if control exits the loop without running into a break statement.

Python keeps evaluating the test at the top, and executing the statements nested in the while part, until the test returns a false value:

```
while <test>:            # Loop test
    <statements1>        # Loop body
else:                    # Optional else
    <statements2>        # Run if didn't exit loop with break
```

Examples

To illustrate, here are a few simple while loops in action. The first just prints a message forever, by nesting a print statement in a while loop. Recall that an integer 1 means true; since the test is always true, Python keeps executing the body forever or until you stop its execution. This sort of behavior is usually called an *infinite loop*:

```
>>> while 1:
...     print 'Type Ctrl-C to stop me!'
```

The next example keeps slicing off the first character of a string, until the string is empty and hence false. It's typical to test an object directly like this, instead of using the more verbose equivalent: while x != '':. Later in this chapter, we'll see other ways to step more directly through the items in a string with a for.

```
>>> x = 'spam'
>>> while x:
...     print x,
...     x = x[1:]        # Strip first character off x.
...
spam pam am m
```

The code below counts from the value of a, up to but not including b. We'll see an easier way to do this with a Python for and range later.

```
>>> a=0; b=10
>>> while a < b:         # One way to code counter loops
...     print a,
...     a += 1           # Or, a = a+1
...
0 1 2 3 4 5 6 7 8 9
```

break, continue, pass, and the Loop else

Now that we've seen our first Python loop, we should introduce two simple statements that have a purpose only when nested inside loops—the break and continue statements. We will also study the loop else clause here because it is intertwined with break, and Python's empty placeholder statement, the pass. In Python:

break
> Jumps out of the closest enclosing loop (past the entire loop statement)

continue
> Jumps to the top of the closest enclosing loop (to the loop's header line)

pass

　　Does nothing at all: it's an empty statement placeholder

Loop else *block*

　　Runs if and only if the loop is exited normally—without hitting a break

General Loop Format

Factoring in break and continue statements, the general format of the while loop looks like this:

```
while <test1>:
    <statements1>
    if <test2>: break        # Exit loop now, skip else.
    if <test3>: continue     # Go to top of loop now.
else:
    <statements2>            # If we didn't hit a 'break'
```

break and continue statements can appear anywhere inside the while (and for) loop's body, but they are usually coded further nested in an if test, to take action in response to some sort of condition.

Examples

Let's turn to a few simple examples to see how these statements come together in practice. The pass statement is used when the syntax requires a statement, but you have nothing useful to say. It is often used to code an empty body for a compound statement. For instance, if you want to code an infinite loop that does nothing each time through, do it with a pass:

```
while 1: pass    # Type Ctrl-C to stop me!
```

Since the body is just an empty statement, Python gets stuck in this loop.[*] pass is roughly to statements as None is to objects—an explicit nothing. Notice that the while loop's body is on the same line as the header, after the colon; as in the if, this only works if the body isn't a compound statement.

The continue statement is an immediate jump to the top of a loop. It sometimes lets you avoid statement nesting; the next example uses continue to skip odd numbers. This code prints all even numbers less than 10 and greater than or equal to 0. Remember, 0

---

[*] This code does nothing, forever. It probably isn't the most useful Python program ever written, unless you want to test a CPU meter, or warm up your laptop computer on a cold winter's day. Frankly, though, we couldn't think of a better pass example. We'll see other places where it makes sense later in the book (for instance, in Chapter 22, to define empty classes that implement objects that behave like "structs" and "records" in other languages).

means false, and % is the remainder-of-division operator, so this loop counts down to zero, skipping numbers that aren't multiples of two (it prints 8 6 4 2 0):

```
x = 10
while x:
    x = x-1                     # Or, x -= 1
    if x % 2 != 0: continue     # Odd?--skip print
    print x,
```

Because continue jumps to the top of the loop, you don't need to nest the print statement inside an if test; the print is only reached if the continue is not run. If this sounds similar to a "goto" in other languages it should; Python has no goto statement, but because continue lets you jump about in a program, many of the warnings about readability and maintainability you may have heard about goto apply. continue should probably be used sparingly, especially when you're first getting started with Python; the example above, for instance, might be clearer if the print were nested under the if:

```
x = 10
while x:
    x = x-1
    if x % 2 == 0:              # Even?-- print
        print x,
```

The break statement is an immediate loop exit. Because code below it is never reached, the break can also sometimes avoid nesting. For example, here is a simple interactive loop, which inputs data with raw_input, and exits when the user enters "stop" for the name request:

```
>>> while 1:
...     name = raw_input('Enter name:')
...     if name == 'stop': break
...     age  = raw_input('Enter age: ')
...     print 'Hello', name, '=>', int(age) ** 2
...
Enter name:mel
Enter age: 40
Hello mel => 1600
Enter name:bob
Enter age: 30
Hello bob => 900
Enter name:stop
```

Notice how this code converts the age input to an integer before raising it to the second power, with int; raw_input returns user input as a string. In Chapter 22, you'll see that it also raises an exception on end-of-file (e.g., if users type Ctrl-Z or Ctrl-D); if it matters, wrap raw_input in try statements.

When combined with the loop else, the break statement can often eliminate the search status flags used in other languages. For instance, the following piece of code determines if a positive integer number y is prime by searching for factors greater than 1:

```
x = y / 2                          # For some y > 1
while x > 1:
    if y % x == 0:                 # Remainder
        print y, 'has factor', x
        break                      # Skip else
    x = x-1
else:                              # Normal exit
    print y, 'is prime'
```

Rather than setting a flag to be tested when the loop is exited, insert a break where a factor is found. This way, the loop else can assume that it will be executed only if no factor was found; if you don't hit the break, the number is prime.*

The loop else is also run if the body of the loop is never executed, since you don't run a break in that event either; in a while loop, this happens if the test in the header is false to begin with. In the example above, you still get the "is prime message" if x is initially less than or equal to 1 (e.g., if y is 2).

More on the Loop else

Because the loop else clause is unique to Python, it tends to perplex some newcomers on first glance. In more general terms, the loop else provides explicit syntax for a common coding scenario—it is a coding structure that lets you catch the "other" way out of a loop, without setting and checking flags or conditions.

Suppose, for instance, that you are writing a loop to search a list for a value, and need to know whether the value was found after you exit the loop. You might code such a task this way:

```
found = 0
while x and not found:
    if match(x[0]):                # Value at front?
        print 'Ni'
        found = 1
    else:
        x = x[1:]                  # Slice off front and repeat.
if not found:
    print 'not found'
```

---

* More or less. Numbers less than 2 are not considered prime by the strict mathematical definition. To be really picky, this code also fails for negatives, fails for floating-point numbers, and will be broken by the future / "true" division change mentioned in Chapter 4. If you want to experiment with this code, be sure to see the exercise at the end of Part IV, which wraps it in a function.

Here, we initialize, set, and later test a flag, to know if the search succeeded or not. This is valid Python code, and does work; but it's exactly the sort of structure that the loop else is there to handle. Here's an else equivalent:

```
while x:                        # Exit when x empty.
    if match(x[0]):
        print 'Ni'
        break                   # Exit, go around else.
    x = x[1:]
else:
    print 'Not found'           # Only here if exhausted x.
```

Here, the flag is gone, and we replaced the if test at loop end with an else (lined up vertically with the word while, by indentation). Because the break inside the main part of the while exits the loop and goes around the else, this serves as a more structured way to catch the search failure case.

Some readers might notice that the prior example's else could be replaced with a test for an empty x after the loop (e.g., if not x:). Although that's true in this example, the else provides explicit syntax for this coding pattern (it's more obviously a search failure clause here), and such an explicit empty test may not apply in some cases. Moreover, the loop else becomes even more useful when used in conjunction with the for loop, because sequence iteration is not under your control.

for Loops

The for loop is a generic sequence iterator in Python: it can step through the items in any ordered sequence object. The for works on strings, lists, tuples, and new objects we'll create later with classes.

General Format

The Python for loop begins with a header line that specifies an assignment target (or targets), along with an object you want to step through. The header is followed by a block of indented statements, which you want to repeat:

```
for <target> in <object>:   # Assign object items to target.
    <statements>            # Repeated loop body: use target
else:
    <statements>            # If we didn't hit a 'break'
```

When Python runs a for loop, it assigns items in the sequence object to the *target*, one by one, and executes the loop body for each. The loop body typically uses the assignment target to refer to the current item in the sequence, as though it were a cursor stepping through the sequence.

The name used as the assignment target in a for header line is usually a (possibly new) variable in the scope where the for statement is coded. There's not much special about it; it can even be changed inside the loop's body, but will be automatically set to the next item in the sequence when control returns to the top of the loop again. After the loop, this variable normally still refers to the last item visited, which is the last item in the sequence unless the loop exits with a break statement.

The for also supports an optional else block, which works exactly as it does in while loops; it's executed if the loop exits without running into a break statement (i.e., if all items in the sequence were visited). In fact, the break and continue statements introduced above work the same in the for loop as they do in the while. The for loop's complete format can be described this way:

```
for <target> in <object>:     # Assign object items to target.
    <statements>
    if <test>: break          # Exit loop now, skip else.
    if <test>: continue       # Go to top of loop now.
else:
    <statements>              # If we didn't hit a 'break'
```

Examples

Let's type a few for loops interactively. In the first example, the name x is assigned to each of the three items in the list in turn, from left to right, and the print statement is executed for each. Inside the print statement (the loop body), the name x refers to the current item in the list:

```
>>> for x in ["spam", "eggs", "ham"]:
...     print x,
...
spam eggs ham
```

The next two examples compute the sum and product of all the items in a list. In the next chapter, we'll see built-ins that apply operations like + and * to items in a list automatically, but it's usually just as easy to use a for:

```
>>> sum = 0
>>> for x in [1, 2, 3, 4]:
...     sum = sum + x
...
>>> sum
10
>>> prod = 1
>>> for item in [1, 2, 3, 4]: prod *= item
...
>>> prod
24
```

For loops work on strings and tuples too—any sequence works in a for:

```
>>> S, T = "lumberjack", ("and", "I'm", "okay")

>>> for x in S: print x,
...
l u m b e r j a c k

>>> for x in T: print x,
...
and I'm okay
```

If you're iterating through a sequence of tuples, the loop target can actually be a *tuple* of targets. This is just another case of tuple unpacking assignment at work; remember, the for assigns items in the sequence to the target, and assignment works the same everywhere:

```
>>> T = [(1, 2), (3, 4), (5, 6)]
>>> for (a, b) in T:                    # Tuple assignment at work
...     print a, b
...
1 2
3 4
5 6
```

Here, the first time through the loop, it's like writing: (a,b) = (1,2); the second time (a,b) is assigned (3,4), and so on. This isn't a special case; any assignment target works syntactically after the word for.

Now, let's look at something a bit more sophisticated. The next example illustrates both the loop else in a for and statement nesting. Given a list of objects (items) and a list of keys (tests), this code searches for each key in the objects list, and reports on the search's outcome:

```
>>> items = ["aaa", 111, (4, 5), 2.01]      # A set of objects
>>> tests = [(4, 5), 3.14]                   # Keys to search for
>>>
>>> for key in tests:                        # For all keys
...     for item in items:                   # For all items
...         if item == key:                  # Check for match.
...             print key, "was found"
...             break
...     else:
...         print key, "not found!"
...
(4, 5) was found
3.14 not found!
```

Since the nested if runs a break when a match is found, the loop else can assume that the search has failed. Notice the nesting here: when this code runs, there are two loops going at the same time. The outer loop scans the keys list, and the inner loop scans the items list for each key. The nesting of the loop else is critical; it's indented at the same level as the header line of the inner for loop, so it's associated with the inner loop (not the if or outer for).

By the way, this example is easier to code if we employ the in operator to test membership. Since in implicitly scans a list looking for a match, it replaces the inner loop:

```
>>> for key in tests:                        # For all keys
...     if key in items:                     # Let Python check for a match.
...         print key, "was found"
...     else:
...         print key, "not found!"
...
(4, 5) was found
3.14 not found!
```

In general, it's a good idea to let Python do as much of the work as possible, for the sake of both brevity and performance. The next example performs a typical data-structure task with a for—collecting common items in two sequences (strings). It's roughly a simple set intersection routine; after the loop runs, res refers to a list that contains all the items found in both seq1 and seq2:

```
>>> seq1 = "spam"
>>> seq2 = "scam"
>>>
>>> res = []                                 # Start empty.
```

```
>>> for x in seq1:                # Scan first sequence.
...     if x in seq2:             # Common item?
...         res.append(x)         # Add to result end.
...
>>> res
['s', 'a', 'm']
```

Unfortunately, this code is equipped to work only on two specific variables: seq1 and seq2. It would be nice if this loop could be somehow generalized into a tool you could use more than once. As you'll see, that simple idea leads us to functions, the topic of Part IV.

Loop Variations

The for loop subsumes most counter-style loops. It's generally simpler to code and quicker to run than a while, so it's the first tool you should reach for whenever you need to step through a sequence. But there are also situations where you will need to iterate in a more specialized way. For example, what if you need to visit every second or third item in a list, or change the list along the way? How about traversing more than one sequence in parallel, in the same for loop?

You can always code such unique iterations with a while loop and manual indexing, but Python provides two built-ins that allow you to specialize the iteration in a for:

- The built-in range function returns a list of successively higher integers, which can be used as indexes in a for.[*]

- The built-in zip function returns a list of parallel-item tuples, which can be used to traverse multiple sequences in a for.

Let's look at each of these built-ins in turn.

Counter Loops: range

The range function is really independent of for loops; although it's used most often to generate indexes in a for, you can use it anywhere you need a list of integers:

```
>>> range(5), range(2, 5), range(0, 10, 2)
([0, 1, 2, 3, 4], [2, 3, 4], [0, 2, 4, 6, 8])
```

With one argument, range generates a list with integers from zero up to but not including the argument's value. If you pass in two arguments, the first is taken as the lower bound. An optional third argument can give a *step*; if used, Python adds the

---

[*] Python also provides a built-in called xrange that generates indexes one at a time instead of storing all of them in a list at once like range does. There's no speed advantage to xrange, but it's useful as a space optimization if you have to generate a huge number of values.

Why You Will Care: File Scanners

In general, loops come in handy any place you need to repeat or process something more than once. Since files contain multiple characters and lines, they are one of the more typical uses for loops. To load a file's contents into a string all at once, you simply call read:

```
file = open('test.txt', 'r')
print file.read()
```

But in order to load a file in pieces, it's common to code either a while loop with breaks on end-of-file, or a for. To read by characters:

```
file = open('test.txt')
while 1:
    char = file.read(1)         # Read by character.
    if not char: break
    print char,


for char in open('test.txt').read():
    print char
```

The for here also processes each character, but loads the file into memory all at once. To read by lines or blocks with a while loop:

```
file = open('test.txt')
while 1:
    line = file.readline()      # Read line by line.
    if not line: break
    print line,

file = open('test.txt', 'rb')
while 1:
    chunk = file.read(10)       # Read byte chucks.
    if not chunk: break
    print chunk,
```

To read text files line by line, though, the for loop tends to be easiest to code, and quickest to run:

```
for line in open('test.txt').readlines(): print line
for line in open('test.txt').xreadlines():print line
for line in open('test.txt'):            print line
```

readlines loads a file all at once into a line-string list; xreadlines instead loads lines on demand, to avoid filling memory for large files; and the last example here relies on new file *iterators*, to achieve the equivalent of xreadlines (iterators will be covered in Chapter 14). The name open in all of the above can also be replaced with name file as of Python 2.2. See the library manual for more on the calls used here. As a general rule of thumb, the larger the size of data you read on each step, the quicker your program will run.

step to each successive integer in the result (steps default to one). Ranges can also be nonpositive, and nonascending, if you want them to be:

```
>>> range(-5, 5)
[-5, -4, -3, -2, -1, 0, 1, 2, 3, 4]

>>> range(5, -5, -1)
[5, 4, 3, 2, 1, 0, -1, -2, -3, -4]
```

Although such range results may be useful all by themselves, they tend to come in most handy within for loops. For one thing, they provide a simple way to repeat an action a specific number of times. To print three lines, for example, use a range to generate the appropriate number of integers:

```
>>> for i in range(3):
...     print i, 'Pythons'
...
0 Pythons
1 Pythons
2 Pythons
```

range is also commonly used to iterate over a sequence indirectly. The easiest and fastest way to step through a sequence exhaustively is always with a simple for; Python handles most of the details for you:

```
>>> X = 'spam'
>>> for item in X: print item,        # Simple iteration
...
s p a m
```

Notice the trailing comma on the print statement here, to suppress the default line feed (each print keeps adding to the current output line). Internally, the for handles the details of the iteration automatically. If you really need to take over the indexing logic explicitly, you can do it with a while loop:

```
>>> i = 0
>>> while i < len(X):                  # while loop iteration
...     print X[i],; i += 1
...
s p a m
```

You can also do manual indexing with a for, if you use range to generate a list of indexes to iterate through:

```
>>> X
'spam'
>>> len(X)                             # Length of string
4
>>> range(len(X))                      # All legal offsets into X
[0, 1, 2, 3]
>>>
```

```
>>> for i in range(len(X)): print X[i],    # Manual for indexing
...
s p a m
```

The example here is stepping over a list of *offsets* into X, not the actual *items* of X; we need to index back into X within the loop to fetch each item.

Nonexhaustive Traversals: range

The last example of the prior section works, but it probably runs more slowly than it has to. Unless you have a special indexing requirement, you're always better off using the simple for loop form in Python—use for instead of while whenever possible, and don't resort to range calls in for loops except as a last resort.

However, the same coding pattern used in that prior example also allows us to do more specialized sorts of traversals:

```
>>> S = 'abcdefghijk'
>>> range(0, len(S), 2)
[0, 2, 4, 6, 8, 10]

>>> for i in range(0, len(S), 2): print S[i],
...
a c e g i k
```

Here, we visit every *second* item in string S, by stepping over the generated range list. To visit every third item, change the third range argument to be 3, and so on. In effect, range used this way lets you skip items in loops, while still retaining the simplicity of the for. See also Python 2.3's new optional third slice limit, in the section "Indexing and Slicing" in Chapter 5. In 2.3, a similar effect may be achieved with:

```
for x in S[::2]: print x
```

Changing Lists: range

Another common place you may use range and for combined is in loops that change a list as it is being traversed. The following example needs an index to be able to assign an updated value to each position as we go:

```
>>> L = [1, 2, 3, 4, 5]
>>>
>>> for i in range(len(L)):         # Add one to each item in L
...     L[i] += 1                    # Or L[i] = L[i] + 1
...
>>> L
[2, 3, 4, 5, 6]
```

There is no way to do the same with a simple for x in L: style loop here, because such a loop iterates through actual items, not list positions. The equivalent while requires a bit more work on our part:[*]

```
>>> i = 0
>>> while i < len(L):
...     L[i] += 1
...     i += 1
...
>>> L
[3, 4, 5, 6, 7]
```

Parallel Traversals: zip and map

The range trick traverses sequences with for in nonexhaustive fashion. The built-in zip function allows us to use for loops to visit multiple sequences in *parallel*. In basic operation, zip takes one or more sequences, and returns a list of tuples that pair up parallel items taken from its arguments. For example, suppose we're working with two lists:

```
>>> L1 = [1,2,3,4]
>>> L2 = [5,6,7,8]
```

To combine the items in these lists, we can use zip:

```
>>> zip(L1,L2)
[(1, 5), (2, 6), (3, 7), (4, 8)]
```

Such a result may be useful in other contexts. When wedded with the for loop, though, it supports parallel iterations:

```
>>> for (x,y) in zip(L1, L2):
...     print x, y, '--', x+y
...
1 5 -- 6
2 6 -- 8
3 7 -- 10
4 8 -- 12
```

Here, we step over the result of the zip call—the pairs of items pulled from the two lists. This for loop uses tuple assignment again to unpack each tuple in the zip result (the first time through, it's as though we run (x,y)=(1,5)). The net effect is that we scan *both* L1 and L2 in our loop. We could achieve a similar effect with a while loop that handles indexing manually, but it would be more to type, and may be slower than the for/zip approach.

---

[*] A *list comprehension* expression of the form [x+1 for x in L] would do similar work here as well, albeit without changing the original list in-place (we could assign the expression's new list object result back to L, but this would not update any other references to the original list). See Chapter 14 for more on list comprehensions.

The zip function is more general than this example suggests. For instance, it accepts any type of sequence, and more than two arguments:

```
>>> T1, T2, T3 = (1,2,3), (4,5,6), (7,8,9)
>>> T3
(7, 8, 9)
>>> zip(T1,T2,T3)
[(1, 4, 7), (2, 5, 8), (3, 6, 9)]
```

zip truncates result tuples at the length of the shortest sequence, when argument lengths differ:

```
>>> S1 = 'abc'
>>> S2 = 'xyz123'
>>>
>>> zip(S1, S2)
[('a', 'x'), ('b', 'y'), ('c', 'z')]
```

The related, and older, built-in map function pairs items from sequences in a similar fashion, but pads shorter sequences with None if argument lengths differ:

```
>>> map(None, S1, S2)
[('a', 'x'), ('b', 'y'), ('c', 'z'), (None, '1'), (None, '2'), (None,'3')]
```

The example is actually using a degenerate form of the map built-in. Normally, map takes a function, and one or more sequence arguments, and collects the results of calling the function with parallel items taken from the sequences. When the function argument is None (as here), it simply pairs items like zip. map and similar function-based tools are covered in Chapter 14.

Dictionary Construction with zip

Dictionaries can always be created by coding a dictionary literal, or assigning to keys over time:

```
>>> D1 = {'spam':1, 'eggs':3, 'toast':5}
>>> D1
{'toast': 5, 'eggs': 3, 'spam': 1}

>>> D1 = {}
>>> D1['spam']  = 1
>>> D1['eggs']  = 3
>>> D1['toast'] = 5
```

What to do, though, if your program obtains dictionary keys and values in *lists* at runtime, after you've coded your script?

```
>>> keys = ['spam', 'eggs', 'toast']
>>> vals = [1, 3, 5]
```

One solution to go from the lists to a dictionary is to zip the lists and step through them in parallel with a for loop:

```
>>> zip(keys, vals)
[('spam', 1), ('eggs', 3), ('toast', 5)]

>>> D2 = {}
>>> for (k, v) in zip(keys, vals): D2[k] = v
...
>>> D2
{'toast': 5, 'eggs': 3, 'spam': 1}
```

It turns out, though, that you can skip the for loop altogether, and simply pass the zipped keys/values lists to the built-in dict constructor call in Python 2.2:

```
>>> keys = ['spam', 'eggs', 'toast']
>>> vals = [1, 3, 5]

>>> D3 = dict(zip(keys, vals))
>>> D3
{'toast': 5, 'eggs': 3, 'spam': 1}
```

The built-in name dict is really a type name in Python; calling it is something like a list-to-dictionary conversion, but really is an object construction request (more about type names in Chapter 23). Also, in Chapter 14, we'll meet a related but richer concept, the *list comprehension*, which builds lists in a single expression.

## CHAPTER 11

Documenting Python Code

This chapter concludes Part III with a look at techniques and tools used for documenting Python code. Although Python code is designed to be readable in general, a few well-placed human-readable comments can do much to help others understand the workings of your programs. To support comments, Python includes both syntax and tools to make documentation easier. Although this is something of a tools-related concept, the topic is presented here, partly because it involves Python's syntax model, and partly as a resource for readers struggling to understand Python's toolset. As usual, this chapter ends with pitfalls and exercises.

The Python Documentation Interlude

By this point in the book you're probably starting to realize that Python comes with an awful lot of prebuilt functionality—built-in functions, exceptions, predefined object attributes, standard library modules, and more. Moreover we've really only scratched the surface of each of these categories.

One of the first questions that bewildered beginners often ask is: how do I find information on all the built-in tools? This section provides hints on the various documentation sources available in Python. It also presents documentation strings and the *PyDoc* system that makes use of them. These topics are somewhat peripheral to the core language itself, but become essential knowledge as soon as your code reaches the level of the examples and exercises in this chapter.

Documentation Sources

As summarized in Table 11-1, there are a variety of places to look for information in Python, with generally increasing verbosity. Since documentation is such a crucial tool in practical programming, let's look at each of these categories.

Table 11-1. Python documentation sources

Form	Role
# comments	In-file documentation
The dir function	Lists of attributes available on objects
Docstrings: __doc__	In-file documentation attached to objects
PyDoc: The help function	Interactive help for objects
PyDoc: HTML reports	Module documentation in a browser
Standard manual set	Official language and library descriptions
Web resources	Online tutorial, examples, and so on
Published books	Commercially-available reference texts

Comments

Hash-mark comments are the most basic way to document your code. All the text following a # (that is not inside a string literal) is simply ignored by Python. Because of that, this provides a place for you to write and read words meaningful to programmers. Such comments are only accessible in your source files; to code comments that are more widely available, use docstrings.

The dir Function

The built-in dir function is an easy way to grab a list that shows all the attributes available inside an object (i.e., its methods, and simple data items). It can be called with any object that has atributes. For example, to find out what's available in the standard library's sys module, import it and pass to dir:

```
>>> import sys
>>> dir(sys)
['__displayhook__', '__doc__', '__excepthook__', '__name__',
'__stderr__', '__stdin__', '__stdout__', '_getframe', 'argv',
'builtin_module_names', 'byteorder', 'copyright', 'displayhook', 'dllhandle',
'exc_info', 'exc_type', 'excepthook',
...more names omitted...]
```

Only some of the many names are displayed; run these statements on your machine to see the full list. To find out what attributes are provided in built-in object types, run dir on a literal of that type. For example, to see list and string attributes, you can pass empty objects:

```
>>> dir([ ])
['__add__', '__class__', ...more...
'append', 'count', 'extend', 'index', 'insert', 'pop', 'remove',
'reverse', 'sort']

>>> dir('')
['__add__', '__class__', ...more...
```

```
'capitalize', 'center', 'count', 'decode', 'encode', 'endswith', 'expandtabs',
'find', 'index', 'isalnum', 'isalpha', 'isdigit',
'islower', 'isspace', 'istitle', 'isupper', 'join', 'ljust',
...more names omitted...]
```

dir results for built-in types include a set of attributes that are related to the implementation of the type (technically, operator overloading methods); they all begin and
end with double underscores to make them distinct, and can be safely ignored at this
point in the book, so they are not shown here.

Incidentally, you can achieve the same effect by passing a type name to dir instead of
a literal:

```
>>> dir(str) == dir('')      # Same result as prior example
1
>>> dir(list) == dir([ ])
1
```

This works, because functions like str and list that were once type converters are
actually names of types; calling them invokes their constructor to generate an
instance of that type. More on constructors and operator overloading methods when
we meet classes in Part VI.

The dir function serves as a sort of memory-jogger—it provides a list of attribute
names, but does not tell you anything about what those names mean. For such extra
information, we need to move on to the next topic.

Docstrings: _ _doc_ _

Besides # comments, Python supports documentation that is retained at runtime for
inspection, and automatically attached to objects. Syntactically, such comments are
coded as strings at the top of module files, and the top of both function and class
statements, before any other executable code. Python automatically stuffs the string,
known as a *docstring*, into the _ _doc_ _ attribute of the corresponding object.

User-defined docstrings

For example, consider the following file, *docstrings.py*. Its docstrings appear at the
beginning of the file, and at the start of a function and class within it. Here, we use
triple-quoted block strings for multiline comments in the file and function, but any
sort of string will work. We haven't studied the def or class statements yet, so ignore
everything about them, except the strings at their tops:

```
"""
Module documentation
Words Go Here
"""

spam = 40
```

```
def square(x):
    """
    function documentation
    can we have your liver then?
    """
    return x **2

class employee:
    "class documentation"
    pass

print square(4)
print square.__doc__
```

The whole point of this documentation protocol is that your comments are retained for inspection in _ _doc_ _ attributes, after the file is imported:

```
>>> import docstrings
16

    function documentation
    can we have your liver then?

>>> print docstrings.__doc__

Module documentation
Words Go Here

>>> print docstrings.square.__doc__

    function documentation
    can we have your liver then?

>>> print docstrings.employee.__doc__
class documentation
```

Here, after importing, we display the docstrings associated with the module and its objects, by printing their _ _doc_ _ attributes, where Python has saved the text. Note that you will generally want to explicitly say print to docstrings; otherwise, you'll get a single string with embedded newline characters.

You can also attach docstrings to methods of classes (covered later), but because these are just def statements nested in a class, they're not a special case. To fetch the docstring of a method function inside a class within a module, follow the path and go through the class: module.class.method._ _doc_ _ (see the example of method docstrings in Chapter 22).

Docstring standards

There is no broad standard about what should go into the text of a docstring (although some companies have internal standards). There have been various mark-up language and template proposals (e.g., HTML), but they seem to have not caught on in the Python world.

This is probably related to the priority of documentation among programmers in general. Usually, if you get any comments in a file at all, you count yourself lucky; asking programmers to hand-code HTML or other formats in their comments seems unlikely to fly. Of course, we encourage you to document your code liberally.

Built-in docstrings

It turns out that built-in modules and objects in Python use similar techniques to attach documentation above and beyond the attribute lists returned by dir. For example, to see actual words that give a human readable description of a built-in module, import and print its _ _doc_ _ string:

```
>>> import sys
>>> print sys.__doc__
This module provides access to some objects
used or maintained by the interpreter and to
...more text omitted...

Dynamic objects:

argv -- command line arguments; argv[0] is the script pathname if known
path -- module search path; path[0] is the script directory, else ''
modules -- dictionary of loaded modules
...more text omitted...
```

Similarly, functions, classes, and methods within built-in modules have attached words in their _ _doc_ _ attributes as well:

```
>>> print sys.getrefcount.__doc__
getrefcount(object) -> integer

Return the current reference count for the object.
...more text omitted...
```

In addition, you can read about built-in functions via their docstrings:

```
>>> print int.__doc__
int(x[, base]) -> integer

Convert a string or number to an integer, if possible.
...more text omitted...

>>> print open.__doc__
file(name[, mode[, buffering]]) -> file object

Open a file.  The mode can be 'r', 'w' or 'a' for reading
...more text omitted...
```

PyDoc: The help Function

The docstring technique proved to be so useful that Python ships with a tool that makes them even easier to display. The standard PyDoc tool is Python code that knows how to extract and format your docstrings, together with automatically extracted structural information, into nicely arranged reports of various types.

There are a variety of ways to launch PyDoc, including command-line script options. Perhaps the two most prominent Pydoc interfaces are the built-in help function, and the PyDoc GUI/HTML interface. The newly introduced help function invokes PyDoc to generate a simple textual report (which looks much like a manpage on Unix-like systems):

```
>>> import sys
>>> help(sys.getrefcount)
Help on built-in function getrefcount:

getrefcount(...)
    getrefcount(object) -> integer

    Return the current reference count for the object.
...more omitted...
```

Note that you do not have to import sys in order to call help, but you do have to import sys to get help on sys. For larger objects such as modules and classes, the help display is broken down into multiple sections, a few of which are shown here. Run this interactively to see the full report.

```
>>> help(sys)
Help on built-in module sys:

NAME
    sys

FILE
    (built-in)

DESCRIPTION
    This module provides access to some objects used
    or maintained by the interpreter and to functions
    ...more omitted...

FUNCTIONS
    __displayhook__ = displayhook(...)
        displayhook(object) -> None

        Print an object to sys.stdout and also save it
    ...more omitted...
DATA
    __name__ = 'sys'
    __stderr__ = <open file '<stderr>', mode 'w' at 0x0082BEC0>
    ...more omitted...
```

Some of the information in this report is docstrings, and some of it (e.g., function call patterns) is structural information that Pydoc gleans automatically by inspecting objects' internals. You can also use `help` on built-in functions, methods, and types. To get help for a built-in type, use the type name (e.g., `dict` for dictionary, `str` for string, `list` for list); you'll get a large display that describes all the methods available for that type:

```
>>> help(dict)
Help on class dict in module __builtin__:

class dict(object)
 |  dict() -> new empty dictionary.
 ...more omitted...

>>> help(str.replace)
Help on method_descriptor:

replace(...)
    S.replace (old, new[, maxsplit]) -> string

    Return a copy of string S with all occurrences
    ...more omitted...

>>> help(ord)
Help on built-in function ord:

ord(...)
    ord(c) -> integer

    Return the integer ordinal of a one-character string.
```

Finally, the `help` function works just as well on your modules as built-ins. Here it is reporting on the `docstrings.py` file coded in the prior section; again, some of this is docstrings, and some is automatic by structure:

```
>>> help(docstrings.square)
Help on function square in module docstrings:

square(x)
    function documentation
    can we have your liver then?

>>> help(docstrings.employee)
...more omitted...

>>> help(docstrings)
Help on module docstrings:

NAME
    docstrings

FILE
    c:\python22\docstrings.py
```

```
DESCRIPTION
    Module documentation
    Words Go Here

CLASSES
    employee
    ...more ommitted...

FUNCTIONS
    square(x)
        function documentation
        can we have your liver then?

DATA
    __file__ = 'C:\\PYTHON22\\docstrings.pyc'
    __name__ = 'docstrings'
    spam = 40
```

PyDoc: HTML Reports

The help function is nice for grabbing documentation when working interactively. For a more grandiose display, PyDoc also provides a GUI interface (a simple, but portable Python/Tkinter script), and can render its report in HTML page format, viewable in any web browser. In this mode, PyDoc can run locally or as a remote server, and reports contain automatically-created hyperlinks that allow you to click your way through the documentation of related components in your application.

To start PyDoc in this mode, you generally first launch the search engine GUI captured in Figure 11-1. You can start this by either selecting the Module Docs item in Python's Start button menu on Windows, or launching the pydocgui script in Python's tools directory. Enter the name of a module you're interested in knowing about, and press the Enter key; PyDoc will march down your module import search path looking for references to the module.

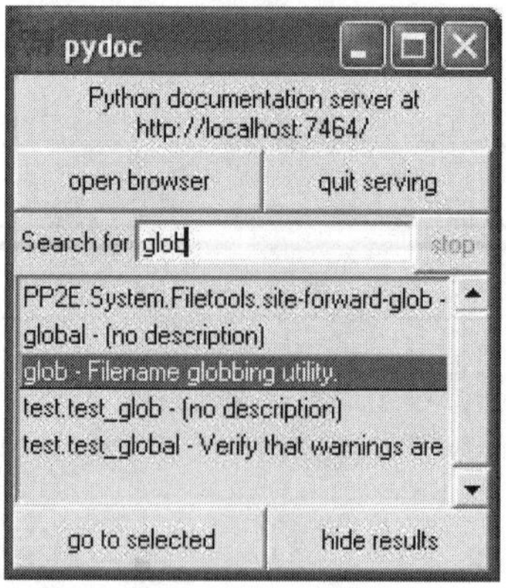

Figure 11-1. Pydoc GUI top-level search interface

Once you've found a promising entry, select and click "go to selected"; PyDoc spawns a web browser on your machine to display the report rendered in HTML format. Figure 11-2 shows information PyDoc displays for the built-in glob module.

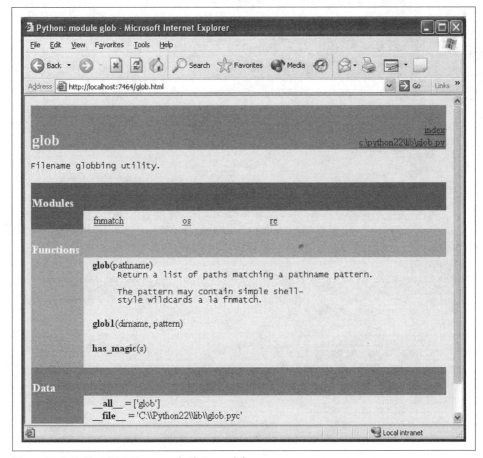

Figure 11-2. PyDoc HTML report, built-in module

Notice the hyperlinks in the Modules section of this page—click these to jump to the PyDoc pages for related (imported) modules. For larger pages, PyDoc also generates hyperlinks to sections within the page. As for the help function interface, the GUI interface works on user-defined modules as well; Figure 11-3 shows the page generated for the *docstrings.py* module file.

PyDoc can be customized and launched in various ways. The main thing to take away from this section is that PyDoc essentially gives you implementation reports "for free"—if you are good about using docstrings in your files, PyDoc does all the work of collecting and formatting them for display. PyDoc also provides an easy way to access a middle level of documentation for built-in tools—its reports are more useful than raw attribute lists, and less exhaustive than the standard manuals.

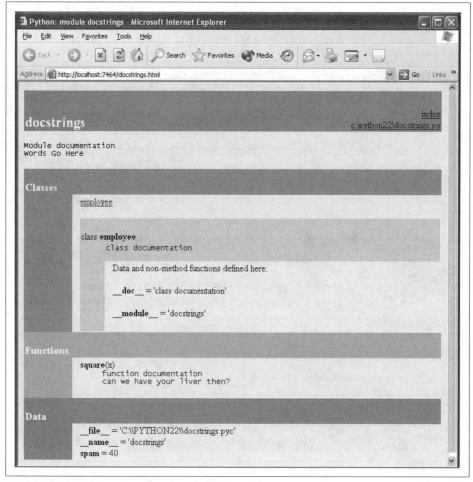

Figure 11-3. PyDoc HTML report, user-defined module

Standard Manual Set

For the complete and most up-to-date description of the Python language and its tool set, Python's standard manuals stand ready to serve. Python's manuals ship in HTML format and are installed with the Python system on Windows—they are available in your Start button's menu for Python, and can also be opened from the Help menu within IDLE. You can also fetch the manual set separately at *http://www. python.org* in a variety of formats, or read them online at that site (follow the Documentation link).

When opened, the HTML format of the manuals displays a root page like that in Figure 11-4. The two most important entries here are most likely the Library Reference (which documents built-in types, functions, exceptions, and standard library modules) and the Language Reference (which provides a formal description of language-level details). The tutorial listed on this page also provides a brief introduction for newcomers.

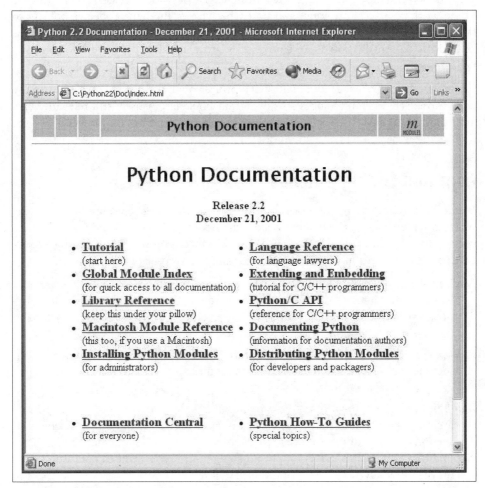

Figure 11-4. Python's standard manual set

Web Resources

At *http://www.python.org* you'll find links to various tutorials, some of which cover special topics or domains. Look for the Documentation and Newbies (i.e., newcomers) links. This site also lists non-English Python resources.

Published Books

Finally, you can today choose from a collection of reference books for Python. In general, books tend to lag behind the cutting edge of Python changes, partly because of the work involved in writing, and partly because of the natural delays built in to the publishing cycle. Usually, by the time a book comes out, it's six or more months behind the current Python state. Unlike standard manuals, books are also generally not free.

For many, the convenience and quality of a professionally published text is worth the cost. Moreover, Python changes so slowly that books are usually still relevant years after they are published, especially if their authors post updates on the Web. See the Preface for more pointers on Python books.

Common Coding Gotchas

Before the programming exercises for this part of the book, here are some of the most common mistakes beginners make when coding Python statements and programs. You'll learn to avoid these once you've gained a bit of Python coding experience; but a few words might help you avoid falling into some of these traps initially.

Don't forget the colons.   Don't forget to type a : at the end of compound statement headers (the first line of an if, while, for, etc.). You probably will at first anyhow (we did too), but you can take some comfort in the fact that it will soon become an unconscious habit.

Start in column 1.   Be sure to start top-level (unnested) code in column 1. That includes unnested code typed into module files, as well as unnested code typed at the interactive prompt.

Blank lines matter at the interactive prompt.   Blank lines in compound statements are always ignored in module files, but, when typing code, end the statement at the interactive prompt. In other words, blank lines tell the interactive command line that you've finished a compound statement; if you want to continue, don't hit the Enter key at the ... prompt until you're really done.

Indent consistently.   Avoid mixing tabs and spaces in the indentation of a block, unless you know what your text editor system does with tabs. Otherwise, what you see in your editor may not be what Python sees when it counts tabs as a number of spaces. It's safer to use all tabs or all spaces for each block.

Don't code C in Python.   A note to C/C++ programmers: you don't need to type parentheses around tests in if and while headers (e.g., if (X==1):); you can if you like (any expression can be enclosed in parentheses), but they are fully superfluous in this context. Also, do not terminate all your statements with a semicolon; it's technically legal to do this in Python as well, but is totally useless, unless you're placing more than one statement on a single line (the end of a line normally terminates a statement). And remember, don't embed assignment statements in while loop tests, and don't use { } around blocks (indent your nested code blocks consistently instead).

Use simple for loops instead of while or range. A simple for loop (e.g., for x in seq:) is almost always simpler to code, and quicker to run than a while or range-based counter loop. Because Python handles indexing internally for a simple for, it can sometimes be twice as fast as the equivalent while.

Don't expect results from functions that change objects in-place. In-place change operations like the list.append() and list.sort() methods of Chapter 6 do not return a value (other than None); call them without assigning the result. It's not uncommon for beginners to say something like mylist=mylist.append(X) to try to get the result of an append; instead, this assigns mylist to None, rather than the modified list (in fact, you'll lose a reference to the list altogether).

A more devious example of this pops up when trying to step through dictionary items in sorted fashion. It's fairly common to see this sort of code: for k in D.keys().sort():. This almost works: the keys method builds a keys list, and the sort method orders it—but since the sort method returns None, the loop fails because it is ultimately a loop over None (a nonsequence). To code this correctly, split the method calls out to statements: Ks = D.keys(), then Ks.sort(), and finally for k in Ks:. This, by the way is one case where you'll still want to call the keys method explicitly for looping, instead of relying on the dictionary iterators.

Always use parenthesis to call a function. You must add parentheses after a function name to call it, whether it takes arguments or not (e.g., use function( ), not function). In Part IV, we'll see that functions are simply objects that have a special operation—a call, that you trigger with the parentheses.

In classes, this seems to occur most often with files. It's common to see beginners type file.close to close a file, rather than file.close( ); because it's legal to reference a function without calling it, the first version with no parenthesis succeeds silently, but does not close the file!

Don't use extensions or paths in imports and reloads. Omit directory paths and file suffixes in import statements (e.g., say import mod, not import mod.py). (We met module basics in Chapter 6, and will continue studying them in Part V.) Because modules may have other suffixes besides *.py* (a *.pyc*, for instance), hardcoding a particular suffix is not only illegal syntax, it doesn't make sense. And platform-specific directory path syntax comes from module search path settings, not the import statement.

Part III Exercises

Now that you know how to code basic program logic, the exercises ask you to implement some simple tasks with statements. Most of the work is in exercise 4, which lets you explore coding alternatives. There are always many ways to arrange statements, and part of learning Python is learning which arrangements work better than others.

1. *Coding basic loops.*

    a. Write a for loop that prints the ASCII code of each character in a string named S. Use the built-in function ord(character) to convert each character to an ASCII integer. (Test it interactively to see how it works.)

    b. Next, change your loop to compute the sum of the ASCII codes of all characters in a string.

    c. Finally, modify your code again to return a new list that contains the ASCII codes of each character in the string. Does this expression have a similar effect—map(ord,S)? (Hint: see Part IV.)

2. *Backslash characters.* What happens on your machine when you type the following code interactively?

```
for i in range(50):
    print 'hello %d\n\a' % i
```

Beware that if run outside of the IDLE interface, this example may beep at you, so you may not want to run it in a crowded lab. IDLE prints odd characters instead (see the backslash escape characters in Table 5-2).

3. *Sorting dictionaries.* In Chapter 6, we saw that dictionaries are unordered collections. Write a for loop that prints a dictionary's items in sorted (ascending) order. Hint: use the dictionary keys and list sort methods.

4. *Program logic alternatives.* Consider the following code, which uses a while loop and found flag to search a list of powers of 2, for the value of 2 raised to the 5th power (32). It's stored in a module file called *power.py.*

```
L = [1, 2, 4, 8, 16, 32, 64]
X = 5

found = i = 0
while not found and i < len(L):
    if 2 ** X == L[i]:
        found = 1
    else:
        i = i+1

if found:
    print 'at index', i
else:
    print X, 'not found'
```

```
C:\book\tests> python power.py
at index 5
```

As is, the example doesn't follow normal Python coding techniques. Follow the steps below to improve it. For all the transformations, you may type your code interactively or store it in a script file run from the system command line (using a file makes this exercise much easier).

a. First, rewrite this code with a while loop else, to eliminate the found flag and final if statement.

b. Next, rewrite the example to use a for loop with an else, to eliminate the explicit list indexing logic. Hint: to get the index of an item, use the list index method (L.index(X) returns the offset of the first X in list L).

c. Next, remove the loop completely by rewriting the examples with a simple in operator membership expression. (See Chapter 6 for more details, or type this to test: 2 in [1,2,3].)

d. Finally, use a for loop and the list append method to generate the powers-of-2 list (L), instead of hard-coding a list literal.

e. Deeper thoughts: (1) Do you think it would improve performance to move the 2**X expression outside the loops? How would you code that? (2) As we saw in Exercise 1, Python also includes a map(function, list) tool that can generate the powers-of-2 list too: map(lambda x: 2**x, range(7)). Try typing this code interactively; we'll meet lambda more formally in Chapter 14.

Functions

In Part IV, we study the Python function—a package of code that can be called repeatedly, with different inputs and outputs each time. We've already been calling functions earlier in the book: open, to make a file object, for instance. Here, the emphasis will be on coding user-defined functions, which compute values, perform part of a program's overall logic, or otherwise wrap code for easy reuse.

CHAPTER 12

Function Basics

In Part III, we looked at basic procedural statements in Python. Here, we'll move on to explore a set of additional statements that create functions of our own. In simple terms, a function is a device that groups a set of statements, so they can be run more than once in a program. Functions also let us specify parameters that serve as function inputs, and may differ each time a function's code is run. Table 12-1 summarizes the primary function-related tools we'll study in this part of the book.

Table 12-1. Function-related statements and expressions

Statement	Examples
Calls	myfunc("spam", ham, "toast")
def, return, yield	def adder(a, b=1, *c): return a+b+c[0]
global	def function(): global x; x = 'new'
lambda	funcs = [lambda x: x**2, lambda x: x*3]

Why Use Functions?

Before going into the details, let's get a clear picture of what functions are about. Functions are a nearly universal program-structuring device. Most of you have probably come across them before in other languages, where they may have been called subroutines or procedures. But as a brief introduction, functions serve two primary development roles:

Code reuse

As in most programming languages, Python functions are the simplest way to package logic you may wish to use in more than one place and more than one time. Up until now, all the code we've been writing runs immediately; functions allow us to group and generalize code to be used arbitrarily many times later.

Procedural decomposition

Functions also provide a tool for splitting systems into pieces that have a well-defined role. For instance, to make a pizza from scratch, you would start by mixing the dough, rolling it out, adding toppings, baking, and so on. If you were programming a pizza-making robot, functions would help you divide the overall "make pizza" task into chunks—one function for each subtask in the process. It's easier to implement the smaller tasks in isolation than it is to implement the entire process at once. In general, functions are about procedure—how to do something, rather than what you're doing it to. We'll see why this distinction matters in Part VI.

In this part of the book, we explore the tools used to code functions in Python: function basics, scope rules, and argument passing, along with a few related concepts. As we'll see, functions don't imply much new syntax, but they do lead us to some bigger programming ideas.

Coding Functions

Although it wasn't made very formal, we've already been using functions in earlier chapters. For instance, to make a file object, we call the built-in open function. Similarly, we use the len built-in function to ask for the number of items in a collection object.

In this chapter, we will learn how to write *new* functions in Python. Functions we write behave the same way as the built-ins already seen: they are called in expressions, are passed values, and return results. But writing new functions requires a few additional ideas that haven't yet been applied. Moreover, functions behave very differently in Python than they do in compiled languages like C. Here is a brief introduction to the main concepts behind Python functions, which we will study in this chapter:

def *is executable code.*   Python functions are written with a new statement, the def. Unlike functions in compiled languages such as C, def is an executable statement—your function does not exist until Python reaches and runs the def. In fact, it's legal (and even occasionally useful) to nest def statements inside if, loops, and even other defs. In typical operation, def statements are coded in module files, and are naturally run to generate functions when the module file is first imported.

def *creates an object and assigns it to a name.*   When Python reaches and runs a def statement, it generates a new function object and assigns it to the function's name. As with all assignments, the function name becomes a reference to the function object. There's nothing magic about the name of a function—as we'll see, the function object can be assigned to other names, stored in a list, and so on. Functions may also be created with the lambda expression—a more advanced concept deferred until later in this chapter.

return *sends a result object back to the caller.* When a function is called, the caller stops until the function finishes its work and returns control to the caller. Functions that compute a value send it back to the caller with a return statement; the returned value becomes the result of the function call. Functions known as generators may also use the yield statement to send a value back and suspend their state, such that they may be resumed later; this is also an advanced topic covered later in this chapter.

Arguments are passed by assignment (object reference). In Python, arguments are passed to functions by assignment (which, as we've learned, means object reference). As we'll see, this isn't quite like C's passing rules or C++'s reference parameters—the caller and function share objects by references, but there is no name aliasing. Changing an argument name does not also change a name in the caller, but changing passed-in mutable objects can change objects shared by the caller.

global *declares module-level variables that are to be assigned.* By default, all names assigned in a function are local to that function and exist only while the function runs. To assign a name in the enclosing module, functions need to list it in a global statement. More generally, names are always looked up in *scopes*—places where variables are stored—and assignments bind names to scopes.

Arguments, return values, and variables are not declared. As with everything in Python, there are no type constraints on functions. In fact, nothing about a function needs to be declared ahead of time: we can pass in arguments of any type, return any kind of object, and so on. As one consequence, a single function can often be applied to a variety of object types.

If some of the preceding words didn't sink in, don't worry—we'll explore all these concepts with real code in this chapter. Let's get started by expanding on these ideas, and looking at a few first examples along the way.

def Statements

The def statement creates a function object and assigns it to a name. Its general format is as follows:

```
def <name>(arg1, arg2,... argN):
    <statements>
```

As with all compound Python statements, def consists of a header line, followed by a block of statements, usually indented (or a simple statement after the colon). The statement block becomes the function's *body*—the code Python executes each time the function is called. The header line specifies a function *name* that is assigned the function object, along with a list of zero or more *arguments* (sometimes called parameters) in parenthesis. The argument names in the header will be assigned to the objects passed in parentheses at the point of call.

Function bodies often contain a return statement:

```
def <name>(arg1, arg2,... argN):
    ...
    return <value>
```

The Python return statement can show up anywhere in a function body; it ends the function call and sends a result back to the caller. It consists of an object expression that gives the function's result. The return is optional; if it's not present, a function exits when control flow falls off the end of the function body. Technically, a function without a return returns the None object automatically, but it is usually ignored.

def Executes at Runtime

The Python def is a true executable statement: when it runs, it creates and assigns a new function object to a name. Because it's a statement, it can appear anywhere a statement can—even nested in other statements. For instance, it's completely legal to nest a function def inside an if statement, to select between alternative definitions:

```
if test:
    def func():          # Define func this way.
        ...
else:
    def func():          # Or else this way instead.
        ...
...
func()                   # Call the version selected and built.
```

One way to understand this code is to realize that the def is much like an = statement: it simply assigns a name at runtime. Unlike compiled languages like C, Python functions do not need to be fully defined before the program runs. More generally, defs are not evaluated until reached and run, and code *inside* defs is not evaluated until the function is later called.

Because function definition happens at runtime, there's nothing special about the function name, only the object it refers to:

```
othername = func         # Assign function object.
othername()              # Call func again.
```

Here, the function was assigned to a different name, and called through the new name. Like everything else in Python, functions are just objects; they are recorded explicitly in memory at program execution time.

A First Example: Definitions and Calls

Apart from such runtime concepts (which tend to seem most unique to programmers with backgrounds in traditional compiled languages), Python functions are straightforward to use. Let's code a first real example to demonstrate the basics. Really, there are two sides to the function picture: a *definition*—the def that creates a function, and a *call*—an expression that tells Python to run the function's body.

Definition

Here's a definition typed interactively that defines a function called times, which returns the product of its two arguments:

```
>>> def times(x, y):        # Create and assign function.
...     return x * y        # Body executed when called.
...
```

When Python reaches and runs this def, it creates a new function object that packages the function's code, and assign the object to the name times. Typically, this statement is coded in a module file, and it would run when the enclosing file is imported; for something this small, though, the interactive prompt suffices.

Calls

After the def has run, the program can call (run) the function by adding parentheses after the function's name; the parentheses may optionally contain one or more object arguments, to be passed (assigned) to the names in the function's header:

```
>>> times(2, 4)             # Arguments in parentheses
8
```

This expression passes two arguments to times: the name x in the function header is assigned the value 2, y is assigned 4, and the function's body is run. In this case, the body is just a return statement, which sends back the result as the value of the call expression. The returned object is printed here interactively (as in most languages, 2*4 is 8 in Python); it could also be assigned to a variable if we need to use it later:

```
>>> x = times(3.14, 4)      # Save the result object.
>>> x
12.56
```

Now, watch what happens when the function is called a third time, with very different kinds of objects passed in:

```
>>> times('Ni', 4)          # Functions are "typeless."
'NiNiNiNi'
```

In this third call, a string and an integer are passed to x and y, instead of two numbers. Recall that * works on both numbers and sequences; because you never declare the types of variables, arguments, or return values, you can use `times` to *multiply* numbers or *repeat* sequences.

Polymorphism in Python

In fact, the very meaning of the expression x * y in the simple `times` function depends completely upon the kinds of objects that x and y are—it means multiplication first and repetition second. Python leaves it up to the *objects* to do something reasonable for this syntax.

This sort of type-dependent behavior is known as *polymorphism*—which means that the meaning of operations depends on the objects being operated upon. Because Python is a dynamically typed language, polymorphism runs rampant: every operation is a polymorphic operation in Python.

This is a deliberate thing, and accounts for much of the language's flexibility. A single function, for instance, can generally be applied to a whole category of object types. As long as those objects support the expected *interface* (a.k.a. protocol), they can be processed by the function. That is, if the objects passed in to a function have the expected methods and operators, they are plug-and-play compatible with the function's logic.

Even in our simple `times` function, this means that *any* two objects that support a * will work, no matter what they may be, and no matter when they may be coded. Moreover, if the objects passed in do *not* support this expected interface, Python will detect the error when the * expression is run, and raise an exception automatically. It's pointless to code error checking ourselves here.

This turns out to be a crucial philosophical difference between Python and statically typed languages like C++ and Java: in Python, your code is *not supposed to care* about specific data types. If it does, it will be limited to work on just the types you anticipated when you wrote your code. It will not support other compatible object types coded in the future. Although it is possible to test for types with tools like the type built-in function, doing so breaks your code's flexibility. By and large, we code to object *interfaces* in Python, not data types.

A Second Example: Intersecting Sequences

Let's look at a second function example that does something a bit more useful than multiplying arguments, and further illustrates function basics.

In Chapter 10, we saw a for loop that collected items in common in two strings. We noted there that the code wasn't as useful as it could be because it was set up to work only on specific variables and could not be rerun later. Of course, you could cut and paste the code to each place it needs to be run, but this solution is neither good nor general—you'd still have to edit each copy to support different sequence names, and changing the algorithm then requires changing multiple copies.

Definition

By now, you can probably guess that the solution to this dilemma is to package the for loop inside a function. Functions offer a number of advantages over simple top-level code:

- By putting the code in a function, it becomes a tool that can be run as many times as you like.
- By allowing callers to pass in arbitrary arguments, you make it general enough to work on any two sequences you wish to intersect.
- By packaging the logic in a function, you only have to change code in one place if you ever need to change the way intersection works.
- By coding the function in a module file, it can be imported and reused by any program run on your machine.

In effect, wrapping the code in a function makes it a general intersection utility:

```
def intersect(seq1, seq2):
    res = [ ]                    # Start empty.
    for x in seq1:              # Scan seq1.
        if x in seq2:          # Common item?
            res.append(x)      # Add to end.
    return res
```

The transformation from the simple code of Chapter 10 to this function is straight-forward; we've just nested the original logic under a def header and made the objects on which it operates passed-in parameter names. Since this function computes a result, we've also added a return statement to send a result object back to the caller.

Calls

Before you can call the function, you have to make the function. Run its def statement by typing it interactively, or by coding it in a module file and importing the file. Once you've run the def one way or another, you call the function by passing any two sequence objects in parenthesis:

```
>>> s1 = "SPAM"
>>> s2 = "SCAM"

>>> intersect(s1, s2)              # Strings
['S', 'A', 'M']
```

Here, the code passes in two strings, and gets back a list containing the characters in common. The algorithm the function uses is simple: "for every item in the first argument, if that item is also in the second argument, append the item to the result." It's a little shorter to say that in Python than in English, but it works out the same.

Polymorphism Revisited

Like all functions in Python, intersect is polymorphic—it works on arbitrary types, as long as they support the expected object interface:

```
>>> x = intersect([1, 2, 3], (1, 4))    # Mixed types
>>> x                                    # Saved result object
[1]
```

This time, we pass in different types of objects to our function—a list and a tuple (mixed types)—and it still picks out the common items. Since you don't have to specify the types of arguments ahead of time, the intersect function happily iterates through any kind of sequence objects you send it, as long as they support the expected interfaces.

For intersect, this means that the first argument has to support the for loop, and the second has to support the in membership test—any two such objects will work. If you pass in objects that do not support these interfaces (e.g., passing in numbers), Python will automatically detect the mismatch and raise an exception for you— exactly what you want, and the best you could do on your own if you coded explicit type tests. The intersect function will even work on class-based objects you code, which you will learn how to build in Part VI.*

Local Variables

The variable res inside intersect is what in Python is called a *local variable*—a name that is only visible to code inside the function def, and only exists while the function runs. In fact, because all names *assigned* in any way inside a function are classified as local variables by default, nearly all the names in intersect are local variables:

- Because res is obviously assigned, it is a local variable.
- Because arguments are passed by assignment, so too are seq1 and seq2.
- Because the for loop assigns items to a variable, so is name x.

All these local variables appear when the function is called, and disappear when the function exits—the return statement at the end of intersect sends back the result *object*, but *name* res goes away. To fully understand the notion of locals, though, we need to move on to Chapter 13.

---

* Technically, intersect works on any object that responds to either the iteration protocol (discussed later in this chapter), or indexing. The for loop and in test work by either requesting an iterator object, or repeatedly indexing an object; when we study classes in Part VI, you'll see how to implement these protocols for user-defined objects, and hence support for and in. When so equipped, you can pass instances of your classes into the intersect function as well, even classes you code in the future, long after the function has been debugged.

## CHAPTER 13

Scopes and Arguments

Chapter 12 looked at basic function definition and calls. As we've seen, the basic function model is simple to use in Python. This chapter presents the details behind Python's *scopes*—the places where variables are defined, as well as *argument passing*—the way that objects are sent to functions as inputs.

Scope Rules

Now that you will begin to write your own functions, we need to get more formal about what names mean in Python. When you use a name in a program, Python creates, changes, or looks up the name in what is known as a *namespace*—a place where names live. When we talk about the search for a name's value in relation to code, the term *scope* refers to a namespace—the location of a name's assignment in your code determines the scope of the name's visibility to your code.

Just about everything related to names happens at assignment in Python—even scope classification. As we've seen, names in Python spring into existence when they are first assigned a value, and must be assigned before they are used. Because names are not declared ahead of time, Python uses the location of the assignment of a name to associate it with (i.e., *bind* it to) a particular namespace. That is, the place where you assign a name determines the namespace it will live in, and hence its scope of visibility.

Besides packaging code, functions add an extra namespace layer to your programs—by default, all names assigned inside a function are associated with that function's namespace, and no other. This means that:

- Names defined inside a `def` can only be seen by the code within that `def`. You cannot even refer to such names from outside the function.

- Names defined inside a `def` do not clash with variables outside the `def`, even if the same name is used elsewhere. A name `X` assigned outside a `def` is a completely different variable than a name `X` assigned inside the `def`.

The net effect is that function scopes help avoid name clashes in your programs, and help to make functions more self-contained program units.

Python Scope Basics

Before you started writing functions, all code was written at the top-level of a module (i.e., not nested in a def), so the names either lived in the module itself, or were built-ins that Python predefines (e.g., open).* Functions provide a nested namespace (i.e., a scope), which localizes the names they use, such that names inside the function won't clash with those outside (in a module or other function). Functions define a local scope, and modules define a global scope. The two scopes are related as follows:

The enclosing module is a global scope. Each module is a global scope—a namespace where variables created (assigned) at the top level of a module file live. Global variables become attributes of a module object to the outside world, but can be used as simple variables within a file.

The global scope spans a single file only. Don't be fooled by the word "global" here—names at the top level of a file are only global to code within that single file. There is really no notion of a single, all-encompassing global file-based scope in Python. Instead, names are partitioned into modules, and you always must import a file explicitly if you want to be able to use the names its file defines. When you hear "global" in Python, think "my module."

Each call to a function is a new local scope. Every time you call a function, you create a new local scope—a namespace where names created inside the function usually live. You can roughly think of this as though each def statement (and lambda expression) defines a new local scope. However, because Python allows functions to call themselves to loop—an advanced technique known as recursion—the local scope technically corresponds to a function call. Each call creates a new local namespace. Recursion is useful when processing structures whose shape can't be predicted ahead of time

Assigned names are local, unless declared global. By default, all the names assigned inside a function definition are put in the local scope (the namespace associated with the function call). If you need to assign a name that lives at the top-level of the module enclosing the function, you can do so by declaring it in a global statement inside the function.

All other names are enclosing locals, globals, or built-ins. Names not assigned a value in the function definition are assumed to be enclosing scope locals (in an

---

* Code typed at the interactive command line is really entered into a built-in module called __main__, so interactively created names live in a module too, and thus follow the normal scope rules. There's more about modules in Part V.

---

enclosing def), globals (in the enclosing module's namespace) or built-in (in the predefined _ _builtin_ _ names module Python provides).

Note that any type of assignment within a function classifies a name as local: = statements, imports, defs, argument passing, and so on. Also notice that in-place changes to objects do not classify names as locals; only actual name assignments do. For instance, if name L is assigned to a list at the top level of a module, a statement like L.append(X) within a function will not classify L as a local, whereas L = X will. In the former case, L will be found in the global scope as usual, and change the global list.

Name Resolution: The LEGB Rule

If the prior section sounds confusing, it really boils down to three simple rules:

- Name references search at most four scopes: local, then enclosing functions (if any), then global, then built-in.
- Name assignments create or change local names by default.
- Global declarations map assigned names to an enclosing module's scope.

In other words, all names assigned inside a function def statement (or lambda—an expression we'll meet later) are locals by default; functions can use both names in *lexically* (i.e., physically) enclosing functions and the global scope, but they must declare globals to change them. Python's name resolution is sometimes called the LEGB rule, after the scope names:

- When you use an unqualified name inside a function, Python searches up to four scopes—the local (*L*), then the local scope of any enclosing (*E*) defs and lambdas, then the global (*G*), and then the built-in (*B*)—and stops at the first place the name is found. If it is not found during this search, Python reports an error. As we learned in Chapter 4, names must be assigned before they can be used.
- When you assign a name in a function (instead of just referring to it in an expression), Python always creates or changes the name in the local scope, unless it's declared to be global in that function.
- When outside a function (i.e., at the top-level of a module or at the interactive prompt), the local scope is the same as the global—a module's namespace.

Figure 13-1 illustrates Python's four scopes. Note that the second "E" scope lookup layer—enclosing defs or lambdas—technically can correspond to more than one lookup layer. It only comes into play when you nest functions within functions.[*]

---

[*] The scope lookup rule was known as the "LGB" rule in the first edition of this book. The enclosing def layer was added later in Python, to obviate the task of passing in enclosing scope names explicitly—something usually of marginal interest to Python beginners.

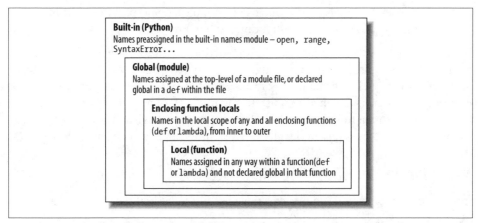

Figure 13-1. The LEGB scope lookup rule

Also, keep in mind that these rules only apply to simple *variable* names (such as spam). In Parts V and VI, we'll see that the rules for qualified *attribute* names (such as object.spam) live in a particular object and follow a completely different set of lookup rules than the scope ideas covered here. Attribute references (names following periods) search one or more objects, not scopes, and may invoke something called inheritance discussed in Part VI.

Scope Example

Let's look at an example that demonstrates scope ideas. Suppose we write the following code in a module file:

```
# Global scope
X = 99                 # X and func assigned in module: global

def func(Y):           # Y and Z assigned in function: locals
    # local scope
    Z = X + Y          # X is a global.
    return Z

func(1)                # func in module: result=100
```

This module, and the function it contains, use a number of names to do their business. Using Python's scope rules, we can classify the names as follows:

Global names: X, func

X is a global because it's assigned at the top level of the module file; it can be referenced inside the function without being declared global. func is global for the same reason; the def statement assigns a function object to the name func at the top level of the module.

Local names: Y, Z

Y and Z are local to the function (and exist only while the function runs), because they are both assigned a value in the function definition; Z by virtue of the = statement, and Y because arguments are always passed by assignment.

The whole point behind this name segregation scheme is that local variables serve as temporary names you need only while a function is running. For instance, the argument Y and the addition result Z exist only inside the function; these names don't interfere with the enclosing module's namespace (or any other function, for that matter).

The local/global distinction also makes a function easier to understand; most of the names it uses appear in the function itself, not at some arbitrary place in a module. Because you can be sure that local names are not changed by some remote function in your program, they also tend to make programs easier to debug.

The Built-in Scope

We've been talking about the built-in scope in the abstract, but it's a bit simpler than you may think. Really, the built-in scope is just a prebuilt standard library module called __builtin__, which you can import and inspect if you want to see which names are predefined:

```
>>> import __builtin__
>>> dir(__builtin__)
['ArithmeticError', 'AssertionError', 'AttributeError', 'DeprecationWarning',
'EOFError', 'Ellipsis',
    ...many more names ommitted...
'str', 'super', 'tuple', 'type', 'unichr', 'unicode',
'vars', 'xrange', 'zip']
```

The names in this list are the built-in scope in Python; roughly the first half are built-in exceptions, and the second are built-in functions. Because Python automatically searches this module last in its LEGB lookup rule, you get all the names in this list for free—they can be used without importing any module. In fact, there are two ways to refer to a built-in function: by the LEGB rule, or by manually importing:

```
>>> zip                    # The normal way
<built-in function zip>

>>> import __builtin__     # The hard way
>>> __builtin__.zip
<built-in function zip>
```

The second of these is sometimes useful in advanced work. The careful reader might also notice that, because the LEGB lookup procedure takes the first occurrence of a name that it finds, names in the local scope may override variables of the same name in both the global and built-in scopes, and global names may override built-ins. A function can, for instance, create a local variable called open by assigning to it:

```
def hider():
    open = 'spam'      # Local variable, hides built-in
    ...
```

However, this will hide the built-in function called open that lives in the built-in (outer) scope. It's also usually a bug, and a nasty one at that, because Python will not issue a message about it—there are times in advanced programming where you may really want to replace a built-in name by redefining it in your code.

Functions can similary hide global variables of the same name with locals:

```
X = 88          # Global X

def func():
    X = 99      # Local X: hides global

func()
print X         # Prints 88: unchanged
```

Here, the assignment within the function creates a local X that is a competely different variable than the global X in the module outside the function. Because of this, there is no way to change a name outside the function, without adding a global declaration to the def—as described in the next section.

The global Statement

The global statement is the only thing that's remotely like a declaration statement in Python. It's not a type or size declaration, though, it's a namespace declaration. It tells Python that a function plans to change global names—names that live in the enclosing module's scope (namespace). We've talked about global in passing already; as a summary:

- global means "a name at the top-level of the enclosing module file."
- Global names must be declared only if they are assigned in a function.
- Global names may be referenced in a function without being declared.

The global statement is just the keyword global, followed by one or more names separated by commas. All the listed names will be mapped to the enclosing module's scope when assigned or referenced within the function body. For instance:

```
X = 88          # Global X

def func():
    global X
    X = 99      # Global X: outside def

func()
print X         # Prints 99
```

We've added a global declaration to the example here, such that the X inside the def now refers to the X outside the def; they are the same variable this time. Here is a slightly more involved example of global at work:

```
y, z = 1, 2          # Global variables in module

def all_global():
    global x          # Declare globals assigned.
    x = y + z         # No need to declare y,z: LEGB rule
```

Here, x, y, and z are all globals inside the function all_global. y and z are global because they aren't assigned in the function; x is global because it was listed in a global statement to map it to the module's scope explicitly. Without the global here, x would be considered local by virtue of the assignment.

Notice that y and z are not declared global; Python's LEGB lookup rule finds them in the module automatically. Also notice that x might not exist in the enclosing module before the function runs; if not, the assignment in the function creates x in the module.

If you want to change names outside functions, you have to write extra code (global statements); by default, names assigned in functions are locals. This is by design—as is common in Python, you have to say more to do the "wrong" thing. Although there are exceptions, changing globals can lead to well-known software engineering problems: because the values of variables are dependent on the order of calls to arbitrarily distant functions, programs can be difficult to debug. Try to minimize use of globals in your code.

Scopes and Nested Functions

It's time to take a deeper look at the letter "E" in the LEGB lookup rule. The "E" layer takes the form of the local scopes of any and all enclosing function defs. This layer is a relatively new addition to Python (added in Python 2.2), and is sometimes called *statically nested scopes*. Really, the nesting is a lexical one—nested scopes correspond to physically nested code structures in your program's source code.

Nested Scope Details

With the addition of nested function scopes, variable lookup rules become slightly more complex. Within a function:

Assignment: X=value

Creates or changes name X in the current local scope by default. If X is declared global within the function, it creates or changes name X in the enclosing module's scope instead.

Reference: X

Looks for name X in the current local scope (function), then in the local scopes of all lexically enclosing functions from inner to outer (if any), then in the current global scope (the module file), and finally in the built-in scope (module __builtin__). global declarations make the search begin in the global scope instead.

Notice that the global declaration still maps variables to the enclosing module. When nested functions are present, variables in enclosing functions may only be referenced, not changed. Let's illustrate all this with some real code.

Nested Scope Examples

Here is an example of a nested scope:

```
def f1():
    x = 88
    def f2():
        print x
    f2()

f1()                    # Prints 88
```

First off, this is legal Python code: the def is simply an executable statement that can appear anywhere any other statement can—including nested in another def. Here, the nested def runs while a call to function f1 is running; it generates a function and assigns it to name f2, a local variable within f1's local scope. In a sense, f2 is a temporary function, that only lives during the execution of (and is only visible to code in) the enclosing f1.

But notice what happens inside f2: when it prints variable x, it refers to the x that lives in the enclosing f1 function's local scope. Because functions can access names in all physically enclosing def statements, the x in f2 is automatically mapped to the x in f1, by the LEGB lookup rule.

This enclosing scope lookup works even if the enclosing function has already returned. For example, the following code defines a function that makes and returns another:

```
def f1():
    x = 88
    def f2():
        print x
    return f2

action = f1()           # Make, return function.
action()                # Call it now: prints 88
```

In this code, the call to action is really running the function we named f2 when f1 ran. f2 remembers the enclosing scope's x in f1, even though f1 is no longer active. This sort of behavior is also sometimes called a closure—an object that remembers values in enclosing scopes, even though those scopes may not be around any more. Although classes (described in Part VI) are usually best at remembering state, such functions provide another alternative.

In earlier versions of Python, all this sort of code failed, because nested defs did not do anything about scopes—a reference to a variable within f2 would search local (f2), then global (the code outside f1), and then built-in. Because it skipped the scopes of enclosing functions, an error would result. To work around this, programmers typically used *default argument values* to pass-in (remember) the objects in an enclosing scope:

```
def f1():
    x = 88
    def f2(x=x):
        print x
    f2()

f1()                    # Prints 88
```

This code works in all Python releases, and you'll still see this pattern in much existing Python code. We'll meet defaults in more detail later in this chapter; in short, the syntax arg=val in a def header means that argument arg will default to value val, if no real value is passed to arg in a call.

In the modified f2, the x=x means that argument x will default to the value of x in the enclosing scope—because the second x is evaluated before Python steps into the nested def, it still refers to the x in f1. In effect, the default remembers what x was in f1, the object 88.

That's fairly complex, and depends entirely on the timing of default value evaluations. That's also why the nested scope lookup rule was added to Python, to make defaults unnecessary for this role. Today, Python automatically remembers any values required in the enclosing scope, for use in nested defs.

Of course, the best prescription here is probably just don't do that. Programs are much simpler if you do not nest defs within defs. Here's an equivalent of the prior example, which banishes the notion of nesting; notice that it's okay to call a function (see following) defined after the one that contains the call like this, as long as the second def runs before the call of the first function—code inside a def is never evaluated until the function is actually called:

```
>>> def f1():
...     x = 88
...     f2(x)
...
>>> def f2(x):
...     print x
...
>>> f1()
88
```

If you avoid nesting this way, you can almost forget about the nested scopes concept in Python, at least for defs. However, you are even more likely to care about such things when you start coding lambda expressions. We also won't meet lambda in depth until Chapter 14; in short, lambda is an expression that generates a new function to be called later, much like a def statement (because it's an expression, it can be used in places that def cannot, such as within list and dictionary literals).

Also like a def, lambda expressions introduce a new local scope. With the enclosing scopes lookup layer, they can see all the variables that live in the function in which they are coded. The following works today, only because the nested scope rules are now applied:

```
def func():
    x = 4
    action = (lambda n: x ** n)          # x in enclosing def
    return action

x = func()
print x(2) # Prints 16
```

Prior to the introduction of nested function scopes, programmers used defaults to pass values from an enclosing scope into lambdas, as for defs. For instance, the following works on all Python releases:

```
def func():
    x = 4
    action = (lambda n, x=x: x ** n)      # Pass x in manually.
```

Because lambdas are expressions, they naturally (and even normally) nest inside enclosing defs. Hence, they are perhaps the biggest beneficiary of the addition of enclosing function scopes in the lookup rules; in most cases, it is no longer necessary to pass values into lambdas with defaults. We'll have more to say about both defaults and lambdas later, so you may want to return and review this section later.

Before ending this discussion, note that scopes nest arbitrarily, but only enclosing functions (not classes, described in Part VI) are searched:

```
>>> def f1():
...     x = 99
...     def f2():
...         def f3():
...             print x        # Found in f1's local scope!
...         f3()
...     f2()
...
>>> f1()
99
```

Python will search the local scopes of *all* enclosing defs, after the referencing function's local scope, and before the module's global scope. However, this sort of code seems less likely in practice.

Passing Arguments

Let's expand on the notion of argument passing in Python. Earlier, we noted that arguments are passed by assignment; this has a few ramifications that aren't always obvious to beginners:

Arguments are passed by automatically assigning objects to local names. Function arguments are just another instance of Python assignment at work. Function arguments are references to (possibly) shared objects referenced by the caller.

Assigning to argument names inside a function doesn't affect the caller. Argument names in the function header become new, local names when the function runs, in the scope of the function. There is no aliasing between function argument names and names in the caller.

Changing a mutable object argument in a function may impact the caller. On the other hand, since arguments are simply assigned to passed-in objects, functions can change passed-in mutable objects, and the result may affect the caller.

Python's pass-by-assignment scheme isn't the same as C++'s reference parameters, but it turns out to be very similar to C's arguments in practice:

Immutable arguments act like C's "by value" mode. Objects such as integers and strings are passed by object reference (assignment), but since you can't change immutable objects in place anyhow, the effect is much like making a copy.

Mutable arguments act like C's "by pointer" mode. Objects such as lists and dictionaries are passed by object reference, which is similar to the way C passes arrays as pointers—mutable objects can be changed in place in the function, much like C arrays.

Of course, if you've never used C, Python's argument-passing mode will be simpler still—it's just an assignment of objects to names, which works the same whether the objects are mutable or not.

Arguments and Shared References

Here's an example that illustrates some of these properties at work:

```
>>> def changer(x, y):        # Function
...     x = 2                 # Changes local name's value only
...     y[0] = 'spam'         # Changes shared object in place
...
>>> X = 1
>>> L = [1, 2]                # Caller
>>> changer(X, L)            # Pass immutable and mutable
>>> X, L                      # X unchanged, L is different
(1, ['spam', 2])
```

In this code, the changer function assigns to argument name x and a component in the object referenced by argument y. The two assignments within the function are only slightly different in syntax, but have radically different results:

- Since x is a local name in the function's scope, the first assignment has no effect on the caller—it simply changes local variable x, and does not change the binding of name X in the caller.

- Argument y is a local name too, but it is passed a mutable object (the list called L in the caller). Since the second assignment is an in-place object change, the result of the assignment to y[0] in the function impacts the value of L after the function returns.

Figure 13-2 illustrates the name/object bindings that exist immediately after the function has been called, and before its code has run.

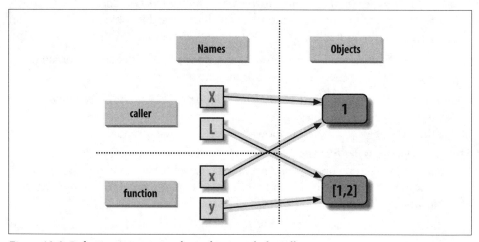

Figure 13-2. References: arguments share objects with the caller

If you recall some of the discussion about shared mutable objects in Chapters 4 and 7, you'll recognize that this is the exact same phenomenon at work: changing a mutable object in-place can impact other references to the object. Here, its effect is to make one of the arguments work like an *output* of the function.

Avoiding Mutable Argument Changes

If you don't want in-place changes within functions to impact objects you pass to them, simply make explicit copies of mutable objects, as we learned in Chapter 7. For function arguments, we can copy the list at the point of call:

```
L = [1, 2]
changer(X, L[:])        # Pass a copy, so my L does not change.
```

We can also copy within the function itself, if we never want to change passed-in objects, regardless of how the function is called:

```
def changer(x, y):
    y = y[:]              # Copy input list so I don't impact caller.
    x = 2
    y[0] = 'spam'         # Changes my list copy only
```

Both of these copying schemes don't stop the function from changing the object—they just prevent those changes from impacting the caller. To really prevent changes, we can always convert to immutable objects to force the issue. Tuples, for example, throw an exception when changes are attempted:

```
L = [1, 2]
changer(X, tuple(L))    # Pass a tuple, so changes are errors.
```

This scheme uses the built-in tuple function, which builds a new tuple out of all the items in a sequence. It's also something of an extreme—because it forces the function to be written to never change passed in arguments, it might impose more limitation on the function than it should, and should often be avoided. You never know when changing arguments might come in handy for other calls in the future. The function will also lose the ability to call any list-specific methods on the argument, even methods that do not change the object in-place.

Simulating Output Parameters

We've already discussed the return statement, and used it in a few examples. But here's a trick: because return sends back any sort of object, it can return multiple values, by packaging them in a tuple. In fact, although Python doesn't have what some languages label call-by-reference argument passing, we can usually simulate it by returning tuples, and assigning results back to the original argument names in the caller:

```
>>> def multiple(x, y):
...     x = 2                    # Changes local names only
...     y = [3, 4]
...     return x, y              # Return new values in a tuple.
...
>>> X = 1
>>> L = [1, 2]
>>> X, L = multiple(X, L)        # Assign results to caller's names.
>>> X, L
(2, [3, 4])
```

It looks like the code is returning two values here, but it's just one—a two-item tuple, with the optional surrounding parentheses omitted. After the call returns, use tuple assignment to unpack the parts of the returned tuple. (If you've forgotten why, flip back to the sections "Tuples" in Chapter 7 and "Assignment Statements" in Chapter 8.)The net effect of this coding pattern is to simulate the output parameters of other languages, by explicit assignments. X and L change after the call, but only because the code said so.

Special Argument Matching Modes

Arguments are always passed by *assignment* in Python; names in the def header are assigned to passed-in objects. On top of this model, though, Python provides additional tools that alter the way the argument objects in the call are *matched* with argument names in the header prior to assignment. These tools are all optional, but allow you to write functions that support more flexible calling patterns.

By default, arguments are matched by position, from left to right, and you must pass exactly as many arguments as there are argument names in the function header. But you can also specify a match by name, default values, and collectors for extra arguments.

Some of this section gets complicated, and before going into syntactic details, we'd like to stress that these special modes are optional and only have to do with matching objects to names; the underlying passing mechanism is still assignment, after the matching takes place. But here's a synopsis of the available matching modes:

Positionals: matched left to right
> The normal case used so far is to match arguments by position.

Keywords: matched by argument name
> Callers can specify which argument in the function is to receive a value by using the argument's name in the call, with a name=value syntax.

Varargs: catch unmatched positional or keyword arguments
> Functions can use special arguments preceded with * characters to collect arbitrarily extra arguments (much like, and often named for, the *varargs* feature in the C language, which supports variable-length argument lists).

Defaults: specify values for arguments that aren't passed
> Functions may also specify default values for arguments to receive if the call passes too few values, using a name=value syntax.

Table 13-1 summarizes the syntax that invokes the special matching modes.

Table 13-1. Function argument-matching forms

Syntax	Location	Interpretation
func(value)	Caller	Normal argument: matched by position
func(name=value)	Caller	Keyword argument: matched by name
def func(name)	Function	Normal argument: matches any by position or name
def func(name=value)	Function	Default argument value, if not passed in the call
def func(*name)	Function	Matches remaining positional args (in a tuple)
def func(**name)	Function	Matches remaining keyword args (in a dictionary)

In a call (the first two rows of the table), simple names are matched by position, but using the name=value form tells Python to match by name instead; these are called *keyword arguments*.

In a function header, a simple name is matched by position or name (depending on how the caller passes it), but the name=value form specifies a default value, the *name collects any extra positional arguments in a tuple, and the **name form collects extra keyword arguments in a dictionary.

As a result, special matching modes let you be fairly liberal about how many arguments must be passed to a function. If a function specifies defaults, they are used if you pass too few arguments. If a function uses the *varargs* (variable argument list) form, you can pass too many arguments; the varargs names collect the extra arguments in a data structure.

Keyword and Default Examples

Python matches names by position by default, like most other languages. For instance, if you define a function that requires three arguments, you must call it with three arguments:

```
>>> def f(a, b, c): print a, b, c
...
```

Here, we pass them by position: a is matched to 1, b is matched to 2, and so on:

```
>>> f(1, 2, 3)
1 2 3
```

In Python, though, you can be more specific about what goes where when you call a function. Keyword arguments allow us to match by *name*, instead of position:

```
>>> f(c=3, b=2, a=1)
1 2 3
```

Here, the c=3 in the call means match this against the argument named c in the header. The net effect of this call is the same as the prior, but notice that the left to right order no longer matters when keywords are used, because arguments are matched by name, not position. It's even possible to combine positional and keyword arguments in a single call—all positionals are matched first from left to right in the header, before keywords are matched by name:

```
>>> f(1, c=3, b=2)
1 2 3
```

When most people see this the first time, they wonder why one would use such a tool. Keywords typically have two roles in Python. First of all, they make your calls a bit more self-documenting (assuming that you use better argument names than a, b, and c). For example, a call of this form:

```
func(name='Bob', age=40, job='dev')
```

is much more meaningful than a call with three naked values separated by commas—the keywords serve as labels for the data in the call. The second major use of keywords occurs in conjunction with defaults.

We introduced defaults earlier when discussing nested function scopes. In short, defaults allow us to make selected function arguments optional; if not passed a value, the argument is assigned its default before the function runs. For example, here is a function that requires one argument, and defaults two:

```
>>> def f(a, b=2, c=3): print a, b, c
...
```

When called, we must provide a value for a, either by position or keyword; if we don't pass values to b and c, they default to 2 and 3, respectively:

```
>>> f(1)
1 2 3
>>> f(a=1)
1 2 3
```

If we pass two values, only c gets its default; with three values, no defaults are used:

```
>>> f(1, 4)
1 4 3
>>> f(1, 4, 5)
1 4 5
```

Finally, here is how the keyword and default features interact: because they subvert the normal left-to-right positional mapping, keywords allow us to essentially skip over arguments with defaults:

```
>>> f(1, c=6)
1 2 6
```

Here a gets 1 by position, c gets 6 by keyword, and b, in between, defaults to 2.

Arbitrary Arguments Examples

The last two matching extensions, * and **, are designed to support functions that take any number of arguments. The first collects unmatched positional arguments into a tuple:

```
>>> def f(*args): print args
```

When this function is called, Python collects all the positional arguments into a new tuple, and assigns the variable args to that tuple. Because it is a normal tuple object, it might be indexed, stepped through with a for loop, and so on:

```
>>> f()
()
>>> f(1)
(1,)
>>> f(1,2,3,4)
(1, 2, 3, 4)
```

The ** feature is similar, but only works for keyword arguments—it collects them into a new dictionary, which can then be processed with normal dictionary tools. In a sense, the ** form allows you to convert from keywords to dictionaries:

```
>>> def f(**args): print args
...
>>> f()
{}
>>> f(a=1, b=2)
{'a': 1, 'b': 2}
```

Finally, function headers can combine normal arguments, the *, and the **, to implement wildly flexible call signatures:

```
>>> def f(a, *pargs, **kargs): print a, pargs, kargs
...
>>> f(1, 2, 3, x=1, y=2)
1 (2, 3) {'y': 2, 'x': 1}
```

In fact, these features can be combined in more complex ways that almost seem ambiguous at first glance—an idea we will revisit later in this chapter.

Combining Keywords and Defaults

Here is a slightly larger example that demonstrates both keywords and defaults in action. In the following, the caller must always pass at least two arguments (to match spam and eggs), but the other two are optional; if omitted, Python assigns toast and ham to the defaults specified in the header:

```
def func(spam, eggs, toast=0, ham=0):    # First 2 required
    print (spam, eggs, toast, ham)

func(1, 2)                               # Output: (1, 2, 0, 0)
func(1, ham=1, eggs=0)                   # Output: (1, 0, 0, 1)
func(spam=1, eggs=0)                     # Output: (1, 0, 0, 0)
func(toast=1, eggs=2, spam=3)            # Output: (3, 2, 1, 0)
func(1, 2, 3, 4)                         # Output: (1, 2, 3, 4)
```

Notice that when keyword arguments are used in the call, the order in which arguments are listed doesn't matter; Python matches by name, not position. The caller must supply values for spam and eggs, but they can be matched by position or name. Also notice that the form name=value means different things in the call and def: a keyword in the call, and a default in the header.

The min Wakeup Call

To make this more concrete, let's work through an exercise that demonstrates a practical application for argument matching tools: suppose you want to code a function that is able to compute the minimum value from an arbitrary set of arguments, and an arbitrary set of object datatypes. That is, the function should accept zero or more arguments—as many as you wish to pass. Moreover, the function should work for all kinds of Python object types—numbers, strings, lists, lists of dictionaries, files, even None.

The first part of this provides a natural example of how the * feature can be put to good use—we can collect arguments into a tuple, and step over each in turn with a simple for loop. The second part of this problem definition is easy: because every object type supports comparisons, we don't have to specialize the function per type (an application of *polymorphism*); simply compare objects blindly, and let Python perform the correct sort of comparison.

Full credit

The following file shows three ways to code this operation, at least one of which was suggested by a student at some point along the way:

- In the first function, take the first argument (args is a tuple), and traverse the rest by slicing off the first (there's no point in comparing an object to itself, especially if it might be a large structure).

- The second version lets Python pick off the first and rest of the arguments automatically, and so avoids an index and a slice.

- The third converts from tuple to list with the built-in list call, and employing the list sort method.

Because the sort method is so quick, this third scheme is usually fastest, when this has been timed. File *mins.py* contains the solution code:

```
def min1(*args):
    res = args[0]
    for arg in args[1:]:
        if arg < res:
            res = arg
    return res

def min2(first, *rest):
    for arg in rest:
        if arg < first:
            first = arg
    return first

def min3(*args):
    tmp = list(args)
    tmp.sort( )
    return tmp[0]

print min1(3,4,1,2)
print min2("bb", "aa")
print min3([2,2], [1,1], [3,3])
```

All three produce the same result, when we run this file. Try typing a few calls interactively to experiment with these on your own.

```
C:\Python22>python mins.py
1
aa
[1, 1]
```

Notice that none of these three variants test for the case where no arguments are passed in. They could, but there's no point in doing so here—in all three, Python will automatically raise an exception if no arguments are passed in. The first raises an exception when we try to fetch item 0; the second, when Python detects an argument list mismatch; and the third, when we try to return item 0 at the end.

This is exactly what we want to happen, though—because these functions support any data type, there is no valid sentinel value that we could pass back to designate an error. There are exceptions to this rule (e.g., if you have to run expensive actions before you reach the error); but in general, it's better to assume that arguments will work in your functions' code, and let Python raise errors for you when they do not.

Bonus points

Students and readers can get bonus points here for changing these functions to compute the *maximum*, rather than minimum values. Alas, this one is too easy: the first two versions only require changing < to >, and the third only requires that we return tmp[-1] instead of tmp[0]. For extra points, be sure to set the function name to "max" as well (though this part is strictly optional).

It is possible to generalize a single function like this to compute either a minimum or maximum, by either evaluating comparison expression strings with tools like the eval built-in function to evaluate a dynamically constructed string of code (see the library manual), or by passing in an arbitrary comparison function. File *minmax.py* shows how to implement the latter scheme:

```
def minmax(test, *args):
    res = args[0]
    for arg in args[1:]:
        if test(arg, res):
            res = arg
    return res

def lessthan(x, y): return x < y      # see also: lambda
def grtrthan(x, y): return x > y

print minmax(lessthan, 4, 2, 1, 5, 6, 3)
print minmax(grtrthan, 4, 2, 1, 5, 6, 3)

% python minmax.py
1
6
```

Functions are another kind of object that can be passed into another function like this. To make this a max (or other), we simply pass in the right sort of test function.

The punch line

Of course, this is just a coding exercise. There's really no reason to code either min or max functions, because both are built-ins in Python! The built-in versions work almost exactly like ours, but are coded in C for optimal speed.

A More Useful Example: General Set Functions

Here's a more useful example of special argument-matching modes at work. Earlier in the chapter, we wrote a function that returned the intersection of two sequences (it picked out items that appeared in both). Here is a version that intersects an arbitrary number of sequences (1 or more), by using the varargs matching form *args to collect all arguments passed. Because the arguments come in as a tuple, we can process them in a simple for loop. Just for fun, we've also coded an arbitrary-number-arguments union function too; it collects items that appear in any of the operands:

```
def intersect(*args):
    res = []
    for x in args[0]:              # Scan first sequence
        for other in args[1:]:     # for all other args.
            if x not in other: break  # Item in each one?
        else:                      # No:  break out of loop
            res.append(x)          # Yes: add items to end
    return res

def union(*args):
    res = []
    for seq in args:               # For all args
        for x in seq:              # For all nodes
            if not x in res:
                res.append(x)      # Add new items to result.
    return res
```

Since these are tools worth reusing (and are too big to retype interactively), we've stored the functions in a module file called *inter2.py* (more on modules in Part V). In both functions, the arguments passed in at the call come in as the args tuple. As in the original intersect, both work on any kind of sequence. Here they are processing strings, mixed types, and more than two sequences:

```
% python
>>> from inter2 import intersect, union
>>> s1, s2, s3 = "SPAM", "SCAM", "SLAM"

>>> intersect(s1, s2), union(s1, s2)          # Two operands
(['S', 'A', 'M'], ['S', 'P', 'A', 'M', 'C'])

>>> intersect([1,2,3], (1,4))                 # Mixed types
[1]
```

```
>>> intersect(s1, s2, s3)                       # Three operands
['S', 'A', 'M']

>>> union(s1, s2, s3)
['S', 'P', 'A', 'M', 'C', 'L']
```

Argument Matching: The Gritty Details

If you choose to use and combine the special argument matching modes, Python will ask you to follow two ordering rules:

- In a call, all keyword arguments must appear after all non-keyword arguments.
- In a function header, the *name must appear after normal arguments and defaults, and **name must appear last.

Moreover, Python internally carries out the following steps to match arguments before assignment:

1. Assign non-keyword arguments by position.
2. Assign keyword arguments by matching names.
3. Assign extra non-keyword arguments to *name tuple.
4. Assign extra keyword arguments to **name dictionary.
5. Assign default values to unassigned arguments in header.

This is as complicated as it looks, but tracing Python's matching algorithm helps to understand some cases, especially when modes are mixed. We'll postpone additional examples of these special matching modes until we do the exercises at the end of Part IV.

Why You Will Care: Keyword Arguments

Keyword arguments play an important role in Tkinter, the de facto standard GUI API for Python. We meet Tkinter later in this book, but as a preview, keyword arguments set configuration options when GUI components are built. For instance, a call of the form:

```
from Tkinter import *
widget = Button(text="Press me", command=someFunction)
```

creates a new button and specifies its text and callback function, using the text and command keyword arguments. Since the number of configuration options for a widget can be large, keyword arguments let you pick and choose. Without them, you might have to either list all possible options by position or hope for a judicious positional argument defaults protocol that handles every possible option arrangement.

As you can see, advanced argument matching modes can be complex. They are also entirely optional; you can get by with just simple positional matching, and it's probably a good idea to do so if you're just starting out. However, because some Python tools make use of them, they're important to know in general.

## CHAPTER 14

Advanced Function Topics

This chapter introduces a collection of more advanced function-related topics: the lambda expression, functional programming tools such as map and list comprehensions, generators, and more. Part of the art of using functions lies in the interfaces between them, so we will also explore some general function design principles here. Because this is the last chapter in Part IV, we'll close with the usual sets of gotchas and exercises to help you start coding the ideas you've read about.

Anonymous Functions: lambda

So far, we've seen what it takes to write our own functions in Python. The next sections turn to a few more advanced function-related ideas. Most of these are optional features, but can simplify your coding tasks when used well.

Besides the def statement, Python also provides an *expression* form that generates function objects. Because of its similarity to a tool in the LISP language, it's called lambda.* Like def, this expression creates a function to be called later, but returns it instead of assigning it to a name. This is why lambdas are sometimes known as anonymous (i.e., unnamed) functions. In practice, they are often used as a way to inline a function definition, or defer execution of a piece of code.

lambda Expressions

The lambda's general form is the keyword lambda, followed by one or more arguments (exactly like the arguments list you enclose in parenthesis in a def header), followed by an expression after a colon:

```
lambda argument1, argument2,... argumentN : expression using arguments
```

---

* The name "lambda" seems to scare people more than it should. It comes from Lisp, which got it from the lambda calculus, which is a form of symbolic logic. In Python, though, it's really just a keyword that introduces the expression syntactically.

Function objects returned by running lambda expressions work exactly the same as those created and assigned by def. But the lambda has a few differences that make it useful in specialized roles:

lambda *is an expression, not a statement*. Because of this, a lambda can appear in places a def is not allowed by Python's syntax—inside a list literal or function call, for example. As an expression, the lambda returns a value (a new function), which can be assigned a name optionally; the def statement always assigns the new function to the name in the header, instead of returning it as a result.

lambda *bodies are a single expression, not a block of statements*. The lambda's body is similar to what you'd put in a def body's return statement; simply type the result as a naked expression, instead of explicitly returning it. Because it is limited to an expression, lambda is less general than a def; you can only squeeze so much logic into a lambda body without using statements such as if (read on for more on this). This is by design, to limit program nesting: lambda is designed for coding simple functions, and def handles larger tasks.

Apart from those distinctions, the def and lambda do the same sort of work. For instance, we've seen how to make functions with def statements:

```
>>> def func(x, y, z): return x + y + z
...
>>> func(2, 3, 4)
9
```

But you can achieve the same effect with a lambda expression, by explicitly assigning its result to a name through which you can later call:

```
>>> f = lambda x, y, z: x + y + z
>>> f(2, 3, 4)
9
```

Here, f is assigned the function object the lambda expression creates; this is how def works too, but its assignment is automatic. Defaults work on lambda arguments, just like the def:

```
>>> x = (lambda a="fee", b="fie", c="foe": a + b + c)
>>> x("wee")
'weefiefoe'
```

The code in a lambda body also follows the same scope lookup rules as code inside a def—lambda expressions introduce a local scope much like a nested def, which automatically sees names in enclosing functions, the module, and the built-in scope (via the LEGB rule):

```
>>> def knights():
...     title = 'Sir'
...     action = (lambda x: title + ' ' + x)    # Title in enclosing def
...     return action                            # Return a function.
...
>>> act = knights()
```

```
>>> act('robin')
'Sir robin'
```

Prior to Release 2.2, the value for name title would typically be passed in as a default argument value instead; flip back to the scopes coverage of Chapter 13 if you've forgotten why.

Why lambda?

Generally speaking, lambdas come in handy as a sort of function shorthand that allows you to embed a function's definition within the code that uses it. They are entirely optional (you can always use def instead), but tend to be a simpler coding construct in scenarios when you just need to embed small bits of executable code.

For instance, we'll see later that callback handlers are frequently coded as in-line lambda expressions embedded directly in a registration call's arguments list, instead of being defined with a def elsewhere in a file and referenced by name (see the callbacks sidebar for an example).

lambdas are also commonly used to code *jump tables*—lists or dictionaries of actions to be performed on demand. For example:

```
L = [(lambda x: x**2), (lambda x: x**3), (lambda x: x**4)]

for f in L:
    print f(2)      # Prints 4, 8, 16

print L[0](3)       # Prints 9
```

The lambda expression is most useful as a shorthand for def, when you need to stuff small pieces of executable code in places where statements are illegal syntactically. This code snippet, for example, builds up a list of three functions by embedding lambda expressions inside a list literal; def won't work inside a list literal like this, because it is a statement, not an expression.

You can do the same sort of thing with dictionaries and other data structures in Python, to build up action tables:

```
>>> key = 'got'
>>> {'already': (lambda: 2 + 2),
...  'got':     (lambda: 2 * 4),
...  'one':     (lambda: 2 ** 6)
... }[key]()
8
```

Here, when Python makes the dictionary, each of the nested lambdas generates and leaves behind a function to be called later; indexing by key fetches one of those functions, and parenthesis force the fetched function to be called. When coded this way, a dictionary becomes a more general *multiway branching* tool than what we could show you in Chapter 9's coverage of if statements.

To make this work without `lambda`, you'd need to instead code three `def` statements somewhere else in your file, and outside the dictionary in which the functions are to be used:

```
def f1( ): ...
def f2( ): ...
def f3( ): ...
...
key = ...
{'already': f1, 'got': f2, 'one': f3}[key]( )
```

This works too, and avoids `lambda`s; but your `def`s may be arbitrarily far away in your file, even if they are just little bits of code. The *code proximity* that `lambda`s provide is especially useful for functions that will only be used in a single context—if the three functions here are not useful anywhere else, it makes sense to embed their definition within the dictionary as `lambda`s.

`lambda`s also come in handy in function argument lists, as a way to inline temporary function definitions not used anywhere else in your program; we'll meet examples of such other uses later in this chapter when we study `map`.

How (Not) to Obfuscate Your Python Code

The fact that the body of a `lambda` has to be a single expression (not statements) would seem to place severe limits on how much logic you can pack into a `lambda`. If you know what you're doing, though, you can code almost every statement in Python as an expression-based equivalent.

For example, if you want to print from the body of a `lambda` function, simply say `sys.stdout.write(str(x)+'\n')`, instead of `print x`. (See Chapter 8 if you've forgotten why.) Similarly, it's possible to emulate an `if` statement by combining Boolean operators in expressions. The expression:

```
((a and b) or c)
```

is roughly equivalent to:

```
if a:
    b
else:
    c
```

and is almost Python's equivalent to the C language's `a?b:c` ternary operator. (To understand why, you need to have read the discussion of Boolean operators in Chapter 9.) In short, Python's `and` and `or` short-circuit (they don't evaluate the right side, if the left determines the result), and always return either the value on the left, or the value on the right. In code:

```
>>> t, f = 1, 0
>>> x, y = 88, 99
```

```
>>> a = (t and x) or y          # If true, x
>>> a
88
>>> a = (f and x) or y          # If false, y
>>> a
99
```

This works, but only as long as you can be sure that x will not be false too (otherwise, you will always get y). To truly emulate an if statement in an expression, you must wrap the two possible results so as to make them non-false, and then index to pull out the result at the end:[*]

```
>>> ((t and [x]) or [y])[0]     # If true, x
88
>>> ((f and [x]) or [y])[0]     # If false, y
99
>>> (t and f) or y              # Fails: f is false, skipped
99
>>> ((t and [f]) or [y])[0]     # Works: f returned anyhow
0
```

Once you've muddled through typing this a few times, you'll probably want to wrap it for reuse:

```
>>> def ifelse(a, b, c): return ((a and [b]) or [c])[0]
...
>>> ifelse(1, 'spam', 'ni')
'spam'
>>> ifelse(0, 'spam', 'ni')
'ni'
```

Of course, you can get the same results by using an if statement here instead:

```
def ifelse(a, b, c):
    if a: return b
    else: return c
```

But expressions like these can be placed inside a lambda, to implement selection logic:

```
>>> lower = (lambda x, y: (((x < y) and [x]) or [y])[0])
>>> lower('bb', 'aa')
'aa'
>>> lower('aa', 'bb')
'aa'
```

Finally, if you need to perform loops within a lambda, you can also embed things like map calls and *list comprehension* expressions—tools we'll meet later in this section:

```
>>> import sys
>>> showall = (lambda x: map(sys.stdout.write, x))
```

---

[*] As we write this, a debate rages on *comp.lang.python* about adding a more direct ternary conditional expression to Python; see future release notes for new developments on this front. Note that you can almost achieve the same effect as the and/or with an expression ((falsevalue,truevalue)[condition]), except that this does not short-circuit (both possible results are evaluated every time), and the condition must be 0 or 1.

```
>>> t = showall(['spam\n', 'toast\n', 'eggs\n'])
spam
toast
eggs
```

But now that we've shown you these tricks, we need ask you to please only use them as a last resort. Without due care, they can lead to unreadable (a.k.a. *obfuscated*) Python code. In general, simple is better than complex, explicit is better than implicit, and full statements are better than arcane expressions. On the other hand, you may find these useful, when taken in moderation.

Nested lambdas and Scopes

lambdas are the main beneficiaries of nested function scope lookup (the E in the LEGB rule). In the following, for example, the lambda appears inside a def—the typical case—and so can access the value that name x had in the enclosing function's scope, at the time that the enclosing function was called:

```
>>> def action(x):
...     return (lambda y: x + y)          # Make, return function.

>>> act = action(99)
>>> act
<function <lambda> at 0x00A16A88>
>>> act(2)
101
```

What we didn't illustrate in the prior discussion is that a lambda also has access to the names in any enclosing lambda. This case is somewhat obscure, but imagine if we recoded the prior def with a lambda:

```
>>> action = (lambda x: (lambda y: x + y))
>>> act = action(99)
>>> act(3)
102
>>> ((lambda x: (lambda y: x + y))(99))(4)
103
```

Here, the nested lambda structure makes a function that makes a function when called. In both cases, the nested lambda's code has access to variable x in the enclosing lambda. This works, but it's fairly convoluted code; in the interest of readability, nested lambdas are generally best avoided.

Applying Functions to Arguments

Some programs need to call arbitrary functions in a generic fashion, without knowing their names or arguments ahead of time. We'll see examples of where this can be useful later, but by way of introduction, both the apply built-in function, and the special call syntax, do the job.

The apply Built-in

You can call generated functions by passing them as arguments to apply, along with a tuple of arguments:

```
>>> def func(x, y, z): return x + y + z
...
>>> apply(func, (2, 3, 4))
9
>>> f = lambda x, y, z: x + y + z
>>> apply(f, (2, 3, 4))
9
```

The function apply simply calls the passed-in function in the first argument, matching the passed-in arguments tuple to the function's expected arguments. Since the arguments list is passed in as a tuple (i.e., a data structure), it can be built at runtime by a program.[*]

---

[*] Be careful not to confuse apply with map, the topic of the next section. apply runs a single function call, passing arguments to the function object just once. map calls a function many times instead, for each item in a sequence.

The real power of apply is that it doesn't need to know how many arguments a function is being called with; for example, you can use if logic to select from a set of functions and argument lists, and use apply to call any:

```
if <test>:
    action, args = func1, (1,)
else:
    action, args = func2, (1, 2, 3)
. . .
apply(action, args)
```

More generally, apply is useful any time you cannot predict the arguments list ahead of time. If your user selects an arbitrary function via a user interface, for instance, you may be unable to hardcode a function call when writing your script. Simply build up the arguments list with tuple operations and call indirectly through apply:

```
>>> args = (2,3) + (4,)
>>> args
(2, 3, 4)
>>> apply(func, args)
9
```

Passing keyword arguments

The apply call also supports an optional third argument, where you can pass in a dictionary that represents keyword arguments to be passed to the function:

```
>>> def echo(*args, **kwargs): print args, kwargs

>>> echo(1, 2, a=3, b=4)
(1, 2) {'a': 3, 'b': 4}
```

This allows us to construct both positional and keyword arguments, at runtime:

```
>>> pargs = (1, 2)
>>> kargs = {'a':3, 'b':4}
>>> apply(echo, pargs, kargs)
(1, 2) {'a': 3, 'b': 4}
```

Apply-Like Call Syntax

Python also allows you to accomplish the same effect as an apply call with special syntax at the call, which mirrors the arbitrary arguments syntax in def headers that we met in Chapter 13. For example, assuming the names of this example are still as assigned earlier:

```
>>> apply(func, args)          # Traditional: tuple
9
>>> func(*args)                # New apply-like syntax
9
>>> echo(*pargs, **kargs)      # Keyword dictionaries too
(1, 2) {'a': 3, 'b': 4}
```

```
>>> echo(0, *pargs, **kargs)         # Normal, *tuple, **dictionary
(0, 1, 2) {'a': 3, 'b': 4}
```

This special call syntax is newer than the apply function. There is no obvious advantage of the syntax over an explicit apply call, apart from its symmetry with def headers, and a few less keystrokes.

Mapping Functions Over Sequences

One of the more common things programs do with lists and other sequences is to apply an operation to each item, and collect the results. For instance, updating all the counters in a list can be done easily with a for loop:

```
>>> counters = [1, 2, 3, 4]
>>>
>>> updated = [ ]
>>> for x in counters:
...     updated.append(x + 10)          # Add 10 to each item.
...
>>> updated
[11, 12, 13, 14]
```

Because this is such a common operation, Python provides a built-in that does most of the work for you. The map function applies a passed-in function to each item in a sequence object, and returns a list containing all the function call results. For example:

```
>>> def inc(x): return x + 10          # function to be run
...
>>> map(inc, counters)                 # Collect results.
[11, 12, 13, 14]
```

We introduced map as a parallel loop traversal tool in Chapter 10, where we passed in None for the function argument to pair items up. Here, we make better use of it by passing in a real function to be applied to each item in the list—map calls inc on each list item, and collects all the return values into a list.

Since map expects a function to be passed in, it also happens to be one of the places where lambdas commonly appear:

```
>>> map((lambda x: x + 3), counters)          # Function expression
[4, 5, 6, 7]
```

Here, the function adds 3 to each item in the counters list; since this function isn't needed elsewhere, it was written inline as a lambda. Because such uses of map are equivalent to for loops, with a little extra code, you could always code a general mapping utility yourself:

```
>>> def mymap(func, seq):
...     res = [ ]
...     for x in seq: res.append(func(x))
...     return res
...
```

```
>>> map(inc, [1, 2, 3])
[11, 12, 13]
>>> mymap(inc, [1, 2, 3])
[11, 12, 13]
```

However, since map is a built-in, it's always available, always works the same way, and has some performance benefits (in short, it's faster than a for). Moreover, map can be used in more advanced ways than shown; for instance, given multiple sequence arguments, it sends items taken from sequences in parallel as distinct arguments to the function:

```
>>> pow(3, 4)
81
>>> map(pow, [1, 2, 3], [2, 3, 4])        # 1**2, 2**3, 3**4
[1, 8, 81]
```

Here, the pow function takes two arguments on each call—one from each sequence passed to map. Although we could simulate this generality too, there is no obvious point in doing so, when map is built-in and quick.

Functional Programming Tools

The map function is the simplest representative of a class of Python built-ins used for *functional programming*—which mostly just means tools that apply functions to sequences. Its relatives filter out items based on a test function (filter), and apply functions to pairs of items and running results (reduce). For example, the following filter call picks out items in a sequence greater than zero:

```
>>> range(-5, 5)
[-5, -4, -3, -2, -1, 0, 1, 2, 3, 4]

>>> filter((lambda x: x > 0), range(-5, 5))
[1, 2, 3, 4]
```

Items in the sequence for which the function returns true are added to the result list. Like map, it's roughly equivalent to a for loop, but is built-in and fast:

```
>>> res = [ ]
>>> for x in range(-5, 5):
...     if x > 0:
...         res.append(x)
...
>>> res
[1, 2, 3, 4]
```

Here are two reduce calls computing the sum and product of items in a list:

```
>>> reduce((lambda x, y: x + y), [1, 2, 3, 4])
10
>>> reduce((lambda x, y: x * y), [1, 2, 3, 4])
24
```

At each step, reduce passes the current sum or product, along with the next item from the list, to the passed in lambda function. By default, the first item in the sequence initializes the starting value. Here's the for loop equivalent to the first of these, with the addition hardcoded inside the loop:

```
>>> L = [1,2,3,4]
>>> res = L[0]
>>> for x in L[1:]:
...     res = res + x
...
>>> res
10
```

If this has sparked your interest, also see the built-in operator module, which provides functions that correspond to built-in expressions, and so comes in handy for some uses of functional tools:

```
>>> import operator
>>> reduce(operator.add, [2, 4, 6])      # function-based +
12
>>> reduce((lambda x, y: x + y), [2, 4, 6])
12
```

Some observers might also extend the functional programming toolset in Python to include lambda and apply, and list comprehensions (discussed in the next section).

List Comprehensions

Because mapping operations over sequences and collecting results is such a common task in Python coding, Python 2.0 sprouted a new feature—the *list comprehension* expression—that can make this even simpler than using map and filter. Technically, this feature is not tied to functions, but we've saved it for this point in the book, because it is usually best understood by analogy to function-based alternatives.

List Comprehension Basics

Let's work through an example that demonstrates the basics. Python's built-in ord function returns the integer ASCII code of a single character:

```
>>> ord('s')
115
```

The chr built-in is the converse—it returns the character for an ASCII code integer. Now, suppose we wish to collect the ASCII codes of *all* characters in an entire string. Perhaps the most straightforward approach is to use a simple for loop, and append results to a list:

```
>>> res = []
>>> for x in 'spam':
...     res.append(ord(x))
...
```

```
>>> res
[115, 112, 97, 109]
```

Now that we know about map, we can achieve similar results with a single function call without having to manage list construction in the code:

```
>>> res = map(ord, 'spam')        # Apply func to seq.
>>> res
[115, 112, 97, 109]
```

But as of Python 2.0, we get the same results from a list comprehension expression:

```
>>> res = [ord(x) for x in 'spam']    # Apply expr to seq.
>>> res
[115, 112, 97, 109]
```

List comprehensions collect the results of applying an arbitrary expression to a sequence of values, and return them in a new list. Syntactically, list comprehensions are enclosed in square brackets (to remind you that they construct a list). In their simple form, within the brackets, you code an expression that names a variable, followed by what looks like a for loop header that names the same variable. Python collects the expression's results, for each iteration of the implied loop.

The effect of the example so far is similar to both the manual for loop, and the map call. List comprehensions become more handy, though, when we wish to apply an arbitrary expression to a sequence:

```
>>> [x ** 2 for x in range(10)]
[0, 1, 4, 9, 16, 25, 36, 49, 64, 81]
```

Here, we've collected the squares of the numbers 0 to 9. To do similar work with a map call, we would probably invent a little function to implement the square operation. Because we won't need this function elsewhere, it would typically be coded inline, with a lambda:

```
>>> map((lambda x: x**2), range(10))
[0, 1, 4, 9, 16, 25, 36, 49, 64, 81]
```

This does the same job, and is only a few keystrokes longer than the equivalent list comprehension. For more advanced kinds of expressions, though, list comprehensions will often be less for you to type. The next section shows why.

Adding Tests and Nested Loops

List comprehensions are more general than shown so far. For instance, you can code an if clause after the for, to add selection logic. List comprehensions with if clauses can be thought of as analogous to the filter built-in of the prior section—they skip sequence items for which the if clause is not true. Here are both schemes picking up even numbers from 0 to 4; like map, filter invents a little lambda function for the test expression. For comparison, the equivalent for loop is shown here as well:

```
>>> [x for x in range(5) if x % 2 == 0]
[0, 2, 4]
```

```
>>> filter((lambda x: x % 2 == 0), range(5))
[0, 2, 4]

>>> res = []
>>> for x in range(5):
...     if x % 2 == 0: res.append(x)
...
>>> res
[0, 2, 4]
```

All of these are using modulus (remainder of division) to detect evens: if there is no remainder after dividing a number by two, it must be even. The filter call is not much longer than the list comprehension here either. However, the *combination* of an if clause and an arbitrary expression gives list comprehensions the effect of a filter and a map, in a single expression:

```
>>> [x**2 for x in range(10) if x % 2 == 0]
[0, 4, 16, 36, 64]
```

This time, we collect the squares of the even numbers from 0 to 9—the for loop skips numbers for which the attached if clause on the right is false, and the expression on the left computes squares. The equivalent map call would be more work on our part: we would have to combine filter selections with map iteration, making for a noticeably more complex expression:

```
>>> map((lambda x: x**2), filter((lambda x: x % 2 == 0), range(10)))
[0, 4, 16, 36, 64]
```

In fact, list comprehensions are even more general still. You may code nested for loops, and each may have an associated if test. The general structure of list comprehensions looks like this:

```
[ expression for target1 in sequence1 [if condition]
             for target2 in sequence2 [if condition] ...
             for targetN in sequenceN [if condition] ]
```

When for clauses are nested within a list comprehension, they work like equivalent nested for loop statements. For example, the following:

```
>>> res = [x+y for x in [0,1,2] for y in [100,200,300]]
>>> res
[100, 200, 300, 101, 201, 301, 102, 202, 302]
```

has the same effect as the substantially more verbose equivalent statements:

```
>>> res = []
>>> for x in [0,1,2]:
...     for y in [100,200,300]:
...         res.append(x+y)
...
>>> res
[100, 200, 300, 101, 201, 301, 102, 202, 302]
```

Although list comprehensions construct a list, remember that they can iterate over any sequence type. Here's a similar bit of code that traverses strings instead of lists of numbers, and so collects concatenation results:

```
>>> [x+y for x in 'spam' for y in 'SPAM']
['sS', 'sP', 'sA', 'sM', 'pS', 'pP', 'pA', 'pM',
 'aS', 'aP', 'aA', 'aM', 'mS', 'mP', 'mA', 'mM']
```

Finally, here is a much more complex list comprehension. It illustrates the effect of attached if selections on nested for clauses:

```
>>> [(x,y) for x in range(5) if x%2 == 0 for y in range(5) if y%2 == 1]
[(0, 1), (0, 3), (2, 1), (2, 3), (4, 1), (4, 3)]
```

This expression permutes even numbers from 0 to 4, with odd numbers from 0 to 4. The if clauses filter out items in each sequence iteration. Here's the equivalent statement-based code—nest the list comprehension's for and if clauses inside each other to derive the equivalent statements. The result is longer, but perhaps clearer:

```
>>> res = []
>>> for x in range(5):
...     if x % 2 == 0:
...         for y in range(5):
...             if y % 2 == 1:
...                 res.append((x, y))
...
>>> res
[(0, 1), (0, 3), (2, 1), (2, 3), (4, 1), (4, 3)]
```

The map and filter equivalent would be wildly complex and nested, so we won't even try showing it here. We'll leave its coding as an exercise for Zen masters, ex-LISP programmers, and the criminally insane.

Comprehending List Comprehensions

With such generality, list comprehensions can quickly become, well, incomprehensible, especially when nested. Because of that, our advice would normally be to use simple for loops when getting started with Python, and map calls in most other cases (unless they get too complex). The "Keep It Simple" rule applies here, as always; code conciseness is much less important a goal than code readability.

However, there is currently a substantial performance advantage to the extra complexity in this case: based on tests run under Python 2.2, map calls are roughly twice as fast as equivalent for loops, and list comprehensions are usually very slightly faster than map. This speed difference owes to the fact that map and list comprehensions run at C language speed inside the interpreter, rather than stepping through Python for loop code within the PVM.

Because for loops make logic more explicit, we recommend them in general on grounds of simplicity. map, and especially list comprehensions, are worth knowing if your application's speed is an important consideration. In addition, because map and list comprehensions are both expressions, they can show up syntactically in places that for loop statements cannot, such as in the bodies of lambda functions, within list and dictionary literals, and more. Still, you should try to keep your map calls and list comprehensions simple; for more complex tasks, use full statements instead.

Why You Will Care: List Comprehensions and map

Here's a more realistic example of list comprehensions and map in action. Recall that the file readlines method returns lines with their \n end-line character at the end:

```
>>> open('myfile').readlines()
['aaa\n', 'bbb\n', 'ccc\n']
```

If you don't want the end-line, you can slice off all lines in a single step, with either a list comprehension or a map call:

```
>>> [line[:-1] for line in open('myfile').readlines()]
['aaa', 'bbb', 'ccc']

>>> [line[:-1] for line in open('myfile')]
['aaa', 'bbb', 'ccc']

>>> map((lambda line: line[:-1]), open('myfile'))
['aaa', 'bbb', 'ccc']
```

The last two of these make use of *file iterators* (it essentially means you don't need a method call to grab all the lines, in iteration contexts such as these). The map call is just slightly longer than list comprehensions, but neither has to manage result list construction explicitly.

List comprehensions can also be used as a sort of column projection operation. Python's standard SQL database API returns query results as a list of tuples—the list is the table, tuples are rows, and items in tuples are column values, much like the following list:

```
listoftuple = [('bob', 35, 'mgr'), ('mel', 40, 'dev')]
```

A for loop could pick up all values from a selected column manually, but map and list comprehensions can do it in a single step, and faster:

```
>>> [age for (name, age, job) in listoftuple]
[35, 40]
>>> map((lambda (name, age, job): age), listoftuple)
[35, 40]
```

Both of these make use of tuple assignment to unpack row tuples in the list. See other books and resources for more on Python's database API.

Generators and Iterators

It is possible to write functions that may be resumed after they send a value back. Such functions are known as *generators* because they generate a sequence of values over time. Unlike normal functions that return a value and exit, generator functions automatically suspend and resume their execution and state around the point of value generation. Because of that, they are often a useful alternative to both computing an entire series of values up front, and manually saving and restoring state in classes.

The chief code difference between generator and normal functions is that generators yield a value, rather than returning one—the `yield` statement suspends the function and sends a value back to the caller, but retains enough state to allow the function to resume from where it left off. This allows functions to produce a series of values over time, rather than computing them all at once, and sending them back in something like a list.

Generator functions are bound up with the notion of iterator protocols in Python. In short, functions containing a `yield` statement are compiled specially as generators; when called, they return a generator object that supports the iterator object interface.

Iterator objects, in turn, define a `next` method, which returns the next item in the iteration, or raises a special exception (`StopIteration`) to end the iteration. Iterators are fetched with the `iter` built-in function. Python `for` loops use this iteration interface protocol to step through a sequence (or sequence generator), if the protocol is supported; if not, `for` falls back on repeatedly indexing sequences instead.

Generator Example

Generators and iterators are an advanced language feature, so please see the Python library manuals for the full story on generators.

To illustrate the basics, though, the following code defines a generator function that can be used to generate the squares of a series of numbers over time:[*]

```
>>> def gensquares(N):
...     for i in range(N):
...         yield i ** 2              # Resume here later.
```

This function yields a value, and so returns to its caller, each time through the loop; when it is resumed, its prior state is restored, and control picks up again immediately after the `yield` statement. For example, when used as the sequence in a `for` loop, control will resume the function after its `yield` statement, each time through the loop:

```
>>> for i in gensquares(5):        # Resume the function.
...     print i, ':',              # Print last yielded value.
...
0 : 1 : 4 : 9 : 16 :
>>>
```

---

[*] Generators are available in Python releases after version 2.2; in 2.2, they must be enabled with a special import statement of the form: `from __future__ import generators`. (See Chapter 18 for more on this statement form.) Iterators were already available in 2.2, largely because the underlying protocol did not require the new, non-backward-compatible keyword, `yield`.

To end the generation of values, functions use either a return statement with no value, or simply fall off the end of the function body. If you want to see what is going on inside the for, call the generator function directly:

```
>>> x = gensquares(10)
>>> x
<generator object at 0x0086C378>
```

You get back a generator object that supports the *iterator protocol*—it has a next method, which starts the function, or resumes it from where it last yielded a value:

```
>>> x.next()
0
>>> x.next()
1
>>> x.next()
4
```

for loops work with generators in the same way—by calling the next method repeatedly, until an exception is caught. If the object to be iterated over does not support this protocol, for loops instead use the indexing protocol to iterate.

Note that in this example, we could also simply build the list of yielded values all at once:

```
>>> def buildsquares(n):
...     res = []
...     for i in range(n): res.append(i**2)
...     return res
...
>>> for x in buildsquares(5): print x, ':',
...
0 : 1 : 4 : 9 : 16 :
```

For that matter, we could simply use any of the for loop, map, or list comprehension techniques:

```
>>> for x in [n**2 for n in range(5)]:
...     print x, ':',
...
0 : 1 : 4 : 9 : 16 :

>>> for x in map((lambda x:x**2), range(5)):
...     print x, ':',
...
0 : 1 : 4 : 9 : 16 :
```

However, especially when result lists are large, or when it takes much computation to produce each value, generators allow functions to avoid doing all the work up front. They distribute the time required to produce the series of values among loop iterations. Moreover, for more advanced generator uses, they provide a simpler alternative to manually saving the state between iterations in class objects (more on classes later in Part VI); with generators, function variables are saved and restored automatically.

Iterators and Built-in Types

Built-in datatypes are designed to produce iterator objects in response to the iter built-in function. Dictionary iterators, for instance, produce key list items on each iteration:

```
>>> D = {'a':1, 'b':2, 'c':3}
>>> x = iter(D)
>>> x.next()
'a'
>>> x.next()
'c'
```

In addition, all iteration contexts, including for loops, map calls, and list comprehensions, are in turn designed to automatically call the iter function to see if the protocol is supported. That's why you can loop through a dictionary's keys without calling its keys method, step through lines in a file without calling readlines or xreadlines, and so on:

```
>>> for key in D:
...     print key, D[key]
...
a 1
c 3
b 2
```

For file iterators, Python 2.2 simply uses the result of the file xreadlines method; this method returns an object that loads lines from the file on demand, and reads by chunks of lines instead of loading the entire file all at once:

```
>>> for line in open('temp.txt'):
...     print line,
...
Tis but
a flesh wound.
```

It is also possible to implement arbitrary objects with classes, which conform to the iterator protocol, and so may be used in for loops and other iteration contexts. Such classes define a special __iter__ method that return an iterator object (preferred over the __getitem__ indexing method). However, this is well beyond the scope of this chapter; see Part VI for more on classes in general, and Chapter 21 for an example of a class that implements the iterator protocol.

Function Design Concepts

When you start using functions, you're faced with choices about how to glue components together—for instance, how to decompose a task into functions (*cohesion*), how functions should communicate (*coupling*), and so on. Some of this falls into the category of structured analysis and design. Here are a few general hints for Python beginners:

Coupling: use arguments for inputs and return for outputs.   Generally, you should strive to make a function independent of things outside of it. Arguments and return statements are often the best ways to isolate external dependencies.

Coupling: use global variables only when truly necessary.   Global variables (i.e., names in the enclosing module) are usually a poor way for functions to communicate. They can create dependencies and timing issues that make programs difficult to debug and change.

Coupling: don't change mutable arguments unless the caller expects it.   Functions can also change parts of mutable objects passed in. But as with global variables, this implies lots of coupling between the caller and callee, which can make a function too specific and brittle.

Cohesion: each function should have a single, unified purpose.   When designed well, each of your functions should do one thing—something you can summarize in a simple declarative sentence. If that sentence is very broad (e.g., "this function implements my whole program"), or contains lots of conjunctions (e.g., "this function gives employee raises *and* submits a pizza order"), you might want to think about splitting it into separate and simpler functions. Otherwise, there is no way to reuse the code behind the steps mixed together in such a function.

Size: each function should be relatively small.   This naturally follows from the cohesion goal, but if your functions start spanning multiple pages on your display, it's probably time to split. Especially given that Python code is so concise to begin with, a function that grows long or deeply nested is often a symptom of design problems. Keep it simple, and keep it short.

Figure 14-1 summarizes the ways functions can talk to the outside world; inputs may come from items on the left side, and results may be sent out in any of the forms on the right. Some function designers usually only use arguments for inputs and return statements for outputs.

There are plenty of exceptions, including Python's OOP support—as you'll see in Part VI, Python classes *depend* on changing a passed-in mutable object. Class functions set attributes of an automatically passed-in argument called `self`, to change per-object state information (e.g., `self.name='bob'`). Moreover, if classes are not used, global variables are often the best way for functions in modules to retain state between calls. Such side effects aren't dangerous if they're expected.

Functions Are Objects: Indirect Calls

Because Python functions are objects at runtime, you can write programs that process them generically. Function objects can be assigned, passed to other functions,

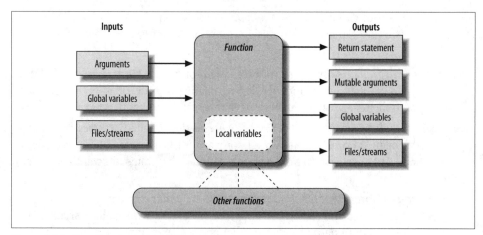

Figure 14-1. Function execution environment

stored in data structures, and so on, as if they were simple numbers or strings. We've seen some of these uses in earlier examples. Function objects happen to export a special operation—they can be called by listing arguments in parentheses after a function expression. But functions belong to the same general category as other objects.

For instance, there's really nothing special about the name used in a def statement: it's just a variable assigned in the current scope, as if it had appeared on the left of an = sign. After a def runs, the function name is a reference to an object; you can reassign that object to other names and call it through any reference—not just the original name:

```
>>> def echo(message):        # Echo assigned to a function object.
...     print message
...
>>> x = echo                  # Now x references it too.
>>> x('Hello world!')         # Call the object by adding ().
Hello world!
```

Since arguments are passed by assigning objects, it's just as easy to pass functions to other functions, as arguments; the callee may then call the passed-in function just by adding arguments in parentheses:

```
>>> def indirect(func, arg):
...     func(arg)                     # Call the object by adding ().
...
>>> indirect(echo, 'Hello jello!')    # Pass function to a function.
Hello jello!
```

You can even stuff function objects into data structures, as though they were integers or strings. Since Python compound types can contain any sort of object, there's no special case here either:

```
>>> schedule = [ (echo, 'Spam!'), (echo, 'Ham!') ]
>>> for (func, arg) in schedule:
```

```
...        func(arg)
...
Spam!
Ham!
```

This code simply steps through the schedule list, calling the echo function with one argument each time through. Python's lack of type declarations makes for an incredibly flexible programming language. Notice the tuple unpacking assignment in the for loop header, introduced in Chapter 8.

Function Gotchas

Here are some of the more jagged edges of functions you might not expect. They're all obscure, and a few have started to fall away from the language completely in recent releases, but most have been known to trip up a new user.

Local Names Are Detected Statically

Python classifies names assigned in a function as locals by default; they live in the function's scope and exist only while the function is running. What we didn't tell you is that Python detects locals statically, when it compiles the def's code, rather than by noticing assignments as they happen at runtime. This leads to one of the most common oddities posted on the Python newsgroup by beginners.

Normally, a name that isn't assigned in a function is looked up in the enclosing module:

```
>>> X = 99
>>> def selector():        # X used but not assigned
...     print X            # X found in global scope
...
>>> selector()
99
```

Here, the X in the function resolves to the X in the module outside. But watch what happens if you add an assignment to X after the reference:

```
>>> def selector():
...     print X            # Does not yet exist!
...     X = 88             # X classified as a local name (everywhere)
...                        # Can also happen if "import X", "def X",...
>>> selector()
Traceback (most recent call last):
  File "<stdin>", line 1, in ?
  File "<stdin>", line 2, in selector
UnboundLocalError: local variable 'X' referenced before assignment
```

You get an undefined name error, but the reason is subtle. Python reads and compiles this code when it's typed interactively or imported from a module. While compiling, Python sees the assignment to X and decides that X will be a local name everywhere in the function. But later, when the function is actually run, the assignment hasn't yet happened when the print executes, so Python says you're using an undefined name. According to its name rules, it should; local X is used before being assigned. In fact, any assignment in a function body makes a name local. Imports, =, nested defs, nested classes, and so on, are all susceptible to this behavior.

The problem occurs because assigned names are treated as locals everywhere in a function, not just after statements where they are assigned. Really, the previous example is ambiguous at best: did you mean to print the global X and then create a local X, or is this a genuine programming error? Since Python treats X as a local everywhere, it is an error; but if you really mean to print global X, you need to declare it in a global statement:

```
>>> def selector():
...     global X          # Force X to be global (everywhere).
...     print X
...     X = 88
...
>>> selector()
99
```

Remember, though, that this means the assignment also changes the global X, not a local X. Within a function, you can't use both local and global versions of the same simple name. If you really meant to print the global and then set a local of the same name, import the enclosing module and qualify to get to the global version:

```
>>> X = 99
>>> def selector():
...     import __main__       # Import enclosing module.
...     print __main__.X      # Qualify to get to global version of name.
...     X = 88                # Unqualified X classified as local.
...     print X               # Prints local version of name.
...
>>> selector()
99
88
```

Qualification (the .X part) fetches a value from a namespace object. The interactive namespace is a module called __main__, so __main__.X reaches the global version of X. If that isn't clear, check out Part V.[*]

Defaults and Mutable Objects

Default argument values are evaluated and saved when the def statement is run, not when the resulting function is called. Internally, Python saves one object per default argument, attached to the function itself.

---

[*] Python has improved on this story somewhat, by issuing the more specific "unbound local" error message for this case shown in the example listing (it used to simply raise a generic name error); this gotcha is still present in general, though.

That's usually what you want; because defaults are evaluated at def time, it lets you save values from the enclosing scope if needed. But since defaults retain an object between calls, you have to be careful about changing mutable defaults. For instance, the following function uses an empty list as a default value and then changes it in place each time the function is called:

```
>>> def saver(x=[ ]):          # Saves away a list object
...     x.append(1)            # Changes same object each time!
...     print x
...
>>> saver([2])                 # Default not used
[2, 1]
>>> saver( )                   # Default used
[1]
>>> saver( )                   # Grows on each call!
[1, 1]
>>> saver( )
[1, 1, 1]
```

Some see this behavior as a feature—because mutable default arguments retain their state between function calls, they can serve some of the same roles as *static* local function variables in the C language. In a sense, they work something like global variables, but their names are local to the function, and so will not clash with names elsewhere in a program.

To most observers, though, this seems like a gotcha, especially the first time they run into this. There are better ways to retain state between calls in Python (e.g., using classes, which will be discussed in Part VI).

Moreover, mutable defaults are tricky to remember (and understand at all). They depend upon the timing of default object construction. In the example, there is just one list object for the default value—the one created when the def was executed. You don't get a new list every time the function is called, so the list grows with each new append; it is not reset to empty on each call.

If that's not the behavior you wish, simply make copies of the default at the start of the function body, or move the default value expression into the function body; as long as the value resides in code that's actually executed each time the function runs, you'll get a new object each time through:

```
>>> def saver(x=None):
...     if x is None:          # No argument passed?
...         x = [ ]            # Run code to make a new list.
...     x.append(1)            # Changes new list object
...     print x
...
>>> saver([2])
[2, 1]
>>> saver( )                   # Doesn't grow here
[1]
>>> saver( )
[1]
```

By the way, the `if` statement in the example could *almost* be replaced by the assignment x = x or [ ], which takes advantage of the fact that Python's or returns one of its operand objects: if no argument was passed, x defaults to None, so the or returns the new empty list on the right.

However, this isn't exactly the same. When an empty list is passed in, the or expression would cause the function to extend and return a newly created list, rather than extending and returning the passed-in list like the previous version. (The expression becomes [ ] or [ ], which evaluates to the new empty list on the right; see the section "Truth Tests" in Chapter 9 if you don't recall why). Real program requirements may call for either behavior.

Functions Without Returns

In Python functions, return (and `yield`) statements are optional. When a function doesn't return a value explicitly, the function exits when control falls off the end of the function body. Technically, all functions return a value; if you don't provide a return, your function returns the None object automatically:

```
>>> def proc(x):
...     print x        # No return is a None return.
...
>>> x = proc('testing 123...')
testing 123...
>>> print x
None
```

Functions such as this without a return are Python's equivalent of what are called "procedures" in some languages. They're usually invoked as a statement, and the None result is ignored, since they do their business without computing a useful result.

This is worth knowing, because Python won't tell you if you try to use the result of a function that doesn't return one. For instance, assigning the result of a list append method won't raise an error, but you'll really get back None, not the modified list:

```
>>> list = [1, 2, 3]
>>> list = list.append(4)      # append is a "procedure."
>>> print list                 # append changes list in-place.
None
```

As mentioned in the "Common Coding Gotchas" section of Chapter 11, such functions do their business as a side effect, and are usually designed to be run as a statement, not an expression.

Part IV Exercises

We're going to start coding more sophisticated programs in these exercises. Be sure to check solutions in Appendix B, and be sure to start writing your code in module files. You won't want to retype these exercises from scratch if you make a mistake.

---

1. *The basics.* At the Python interactive prompt, write a function that prints its single argument to the screen and call it interactively, passing a variety of object types: string, integer, list, dictionary. Then try calling it without passing any argument. What happens? What happens when you pass two arguments?

2. *Arguments.* Write a function called adder in a Python module file. The function adder should accept two arguments and return the sum (or concatenation) of its two arguments. Then add code at the bottom of the file to call the function with a variety of object types (two strings, two lists, two floating points), and run this file as a script from the system command line. Do you have to print the call statement results to see results on your screen?

3. *varargs.* Generalize the adder function you wrote in the last exercise to compute the sum of an arbitrary number of arguments, and change the calls to pass more or less than two. What type is the return value sum? (Hints: a slice such as S[:0] returns an empty sequence of the same type as S, and the type built-in function can test types; but see the min examples in Chapter 13 for a simpler approach.) What happens if you pass in arguments of different types? What about passing in dictionaries?

4. *Keywords.* Change the adder function from Exercise 2 to accept and add three arguments: def adder(good, bad, ugly). Now, provide default values for each argument and experiment with calling the function interactively. Try passing one, two, three, and four arguments. Then, try passing keyword arguments. Does the call adder(ugly=1, good=2) work? Why? Finally, generalize the new adder to accept and add an arbitrary number of keyword arguments, much like Exercise 3, but you'll need to iterate over a dictionary, not a tuple. (Hint: the dict.keys() method returns a list you can step through with a for or while.)

5. Write a function called copyDict(dict) that copies its dictionary argument. It should return a new dictionary with all the items in its argument. Use the dictionary keys method to iterate (or, in Python 2.2, step over a dictionary's keys without calling keys). Copying sequences is easy (X[:] makes a top-level copy); does this work for dictionaries too?

6. Write a function called addDict(dict1, dict2) that computes the union of two dictionaries. It should return a new dictionary, with all the items in both its arguments (assumed to be dictionaries). If the same key appears in both arguments, feel free to pick a value from either. Test your function by writing it in a file and running the file as a script. What happens if you pass lists instead of dictionaries? How could you generalize your function to handle this case too? (Hint: see the type built-in function used earlier.) Does the order of arguments passed matter?

7. *More argument matching examples.* First, define the following six functions (either interactively, or in a module file that can be imported):

```
def f1(a, b): print a, b          # Normal args

def f2(a, *b): print a, b         # Positional varargs
```

```
def f3(a, **b): print a, b          # Keyword varargs

def f4(a, *b, **c): print a, b, c   # Mixed modes

def f5(a, b=2, c=3): print a, b, c  # Defaults

def f6(a, b=2, *c): print a, b, c   # Defaults and positional varargs
```

Now, test the following calls interactively and try to explain each result; in some cases, you'll probably need to fall back on the matching algorithm shown in Chapter 13. Do you think mixing matching modes is a good idea in general? Can you think of cases where it would be useful?

```
>>> f1(1, 2)
>>> f1(b=2, a=1)

>>> f2(1, 2, 3)
>>> f3(1, x=2, y=3)
>>> f4(1, 2, 3, x=2, y=3)

>>> f5(1)
>>> f5(1, 4)

>>> f6(1)
>>> f6(1, 3, 4)
```

8. *Primes revisited*. Recall the code snippet we saw in Chapter 10, which simplistically determines if a positive integer is prime:

```
x = y / 2                         # For some y > 1
while x > 1:
    if y % x == 0:                # Remainder
        print y, 'has factor', x
        break                     # Skip else
    x = x-1
else:                             # Normal exit
    print y, 'is prime'
```

Package this code as a reusable function in a module file, and add some calls to your function at the bottom of your file. While you're at it, replace the first line's / operator with //, to make it handle floating point numbers too, and be immune to the "true" division change planned for the / operator in Python 3.0 as described in Chapter 4. What can you do about negatives and 0 and 1? How about speeding this up? Your outputs should look something like this:

```
13 is prime
13.0 is prime
15 has factor 5
15.0 has factor 5.0
```

9. *List comprehensions*. Write code to build a new list containing the square roots of all the numbers in this list: [2, 4, 9, 16, 25]. Code this as a for loop first, then as a map call, and finally as a list comprehension. Use the sqrt function in the built-in math module to do the calculation (i.e., import math, and say math.sqrt(x)). Of the three, which approach do you like best?

Modules

Part V explores Python modules. Modules are packages of names that usually correspond to source files and serve as libraries of tools for use in other files and programs. We introduced modules very early (in Part I) as a way to retain and run code. Here, we fill in the remaining details on this subject, and study some advanced module-related topics, such as package (directory) imports.

CHAPTER 15

Modules: The Big Picture

This chapter begins our look at the Python *module*, the highest-level program organization unit, which packages program code and data for reuse. In concrete terms,
modules usually correspond to Python program files (or C extensions). Each file is a
module, and modules import other modules to use the names they define. Modules
are processed with two new statements and one important built-in function:

import
    Lets a client (importer) fetch a module as a whole

from
    Allows clients to fetch particular names from a module

reload
    Provides a way to reload a module's code without stopping Python

We introduced module fundamentals in Chapter 3, and have been using them ever
since. Part V begins by expanding on core module concepts, and then moves on to
explore more advanced module usage. This first chapter begins with a general look at
the role of modules in overall program structure. In the next and following chapters,
we'll dig into the coding details behind the theory.

Along the way, we'll flesh out module details we've omitted so far: reloads, the
__name__ and __all__ attributes, package imports, and so on. Because modules and
classes are really just glorified namespaces, we formalize namespace concepts here as
well.

Why Use Modules?

Modules provide an easy way to organize components into a system, by serving as
packages of names. From an abstract perspective, modules have at least three roles:

Code reuse
    As we saw in Chapter 3, modules let us save code in files permanently. Unlike
    code you type at the Python interactive prompt, which goes away when you exit

Python, code in module files is persistent—it can be reloaded and rerun as many times as needed. More to the point, modules are a place to define names, or attributes, that may be referenced by external clients.

System namespace partitioning

Modules are also the highest-level program organization unit in Python. Fundamentally, they are just packages of names. Modules seal up names into self-contained packages that avoid name clashes—you can never see a name in another file, unless you explicitly import it. In fact, everything "lives" in a module: code you execute and objects you create are always implicitly enclosed by a module. Because of that, modules are a natural tool for grouping system components.

Implementing shared services or data

From a functional perspective, modules also come in handy for implementing components that are shared across a system, and hence only require a single copy. For instance, if you need to provide a global object that's used by more than one function or file, you can code it in a module that's imported by many clients.

To truly understand the role of modules in a Python system, though, we need to digress for a moment and explore the general structure of a Python program.

Python Program Architecture

So far in this book, we've sugar-coated some of the complexity in our descriptions of Python programs. In practice, programs usually are more than just one file; for all but the simplest scripts, your programs will take the form of multifile systems. And even if you can get by with coding a single file yourself, you will almost certainly wind up using external files that someone else has already written.

This section introduces the general architecture of Python programs—the way you divide a program into a collection of source files (a.k.a. modules), and link the parts into a whole. Along the way, we also define the central concepts of Python modules, imports, and object attributes.

How to Structure a Program

Generally, a Python program consists of multiple text files containing Python statements. The program is structured as one main, *top-level* file, along with zero or more supplemental files known as *modules* in Python.

In a Python program, the top-level file contains the main flow of control of your program—the file you run to launch your application. The module files are libraries of tools, used to collect components used by the top-level file, and possibly elsewhere. Top-level files use tools defined in module files, and modules use tools defined in other modules. In Python, a file *imports* a module to gain access to the tools it defines. And the tools defined by a module are known as its *attributes*—variable names attached to objects such as functions. Ultimately, we import modules, and access their attributes to use their tools.

Imports and Attributes

Let's make this a bit more concrete. Figure 15-1 sketches the structure of a Python program composed of three files: *a.py*, *b.py*, and *c.py*. The file *a.py* is chosen to be the top-level file; it will be a simple text file of statements, which is executed from top to bottom when launched. Files *b.py* and *c.py* are modules; they are simple text files of statements as well, but are usually not launched directly. Rather, modules are normally imported by other files that wish to use the tools they define.

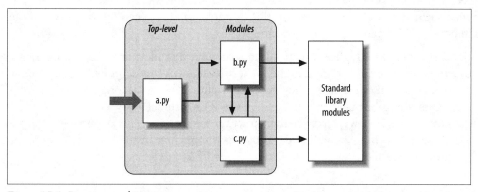

Figure 15-1. Program architecture

For instance, suppose file *b.py* in Figure 15-1 defines a *function* called spam, for external use. As we learned in Part IV, *b.py* would contain a Python def statement to generate the function, which is later run by passing zero or more values in parenthesis after the function's name:

```
def spam(text):
    print text, 'spam'
```

Now, if *a.py* wants to use spam, it might contain Python statements such as the following:

```
import b
b.spam('gumby')
```

The first of these two, a Python import statement, gives file *a.py* access to everything defined in file *b.py*. It roughly means: "load file *b.py* (unless it's already loaded), and give me access to all its attributes through name b." import (and as you'll see later, from) statements execute and load another file at runtime. In Python, cross-file module linking is not resolved until such import statements are executed.

The second of these statements calls the function spam defined in module b using object attribute notation. The code b.spam means: "fetch the value of name spam that lives within object b." This happens to be a callable function in our example, so we pass a string in parenthesis ('gumby'). If you actually type these files and run *a.py*, the words "gumby spam" are printed.

More generally, you'll see the notation object.attribute throughout Python scripts—most objects have useful attributes that are fetched with the "." operator. Some are callable things like functions, and others are simple data values that give object properties (e.g., a person's name).

The notion of importing is also general throughout Python. Any file can import tools from any other file. For instance, file *a.py* may import *b.py* to call its function, but *b.py* might also import *c.py* in order to leverage different tools defined there. Import chains can go as deep as you like: in this example, module a can import b, which can import c, which can import b again, and so on.

Besides serving as a highest organization structure, modules (and module packages, described in Chapter 17) are also the highest level of *code reuse* in Python. By coding components in module files, they become useful in both the original program, as well as in any other program you may write. For instance, if after coding the program in Figure 15-1 we discover that function b.spam is a general purpose tool, we can reuse it in a completely different program; simply import file *b.py* again, from the other program's files.

Standard Library Modules

Notice the rightmost portion of Figure 15-1. Some of the modules that your programs will import are provided by Python itself, not files you will code. Python automatically comes with a large collection of utility modules known as the *Standard Library*.

This collection, roughly 200 modules large at last count, contains platform independent support for common programming tasks: operating system interfaces, object persistence, text pattern matching, network and Internet scripting, GUI construction, and much more. None of these are part of the Python language itself, but can be used by importing the appropriate modules on any standard Python installation.

In this book, you will meet a few of the standard library modules in action in the examples, but for a complete look, you should browse the standard Python Library Reference Manual, available either with your Python installation (they are in IDLE and your Python Start button entry on Windows), or online at *http://www.python.org*.

Because there are so many modules, this is really the only way to get a feel for what tools are available. You can also find Python library materials in commercial books, but the manuals are free, viewable in any web browser (they ship in HTML format), and updated each time Python is re-released.

How Imports Work

The prior section talked about importing modules, without really explaining what happens when you do so. Since imports are at the heart of program structure in Python, this section goes into more detail on the import operation to make this process less abstract.

Some C programmers like to compare the Python module import operation to a C #include, but they really shouldn't—in Python, imports are not just textual insertions of one file into another. They are really runtime operations that perform three distinct steps the first time a file is imported by a program:

1. *Find* the module's file.
2. *Compile* it to byte-code (if needed).
3. *Run* the module's code to build the objects it defines.

All three of these steps are only run the first time a module is imported during a program's execution; later imports of the same module bypass all of these and simply fetch the already-loaded module object in memory. To better understand module imports, let's explore each of these steps in turn.

1. Find It

First off, Python must locate the module file referenced by your import statement. Notice the import statement in the prior section's example names the file without a *.py* suffix and without its directory path. It says just import b, instead of something like import c:\dir1\b.py. Import statements omit path and suffix details like this on purpose; you can only list a simple name.* Instead, Python uses a standard *module search path* to locate the module file corresponding to an import statement.

The module search path

In many cases, you can rely on the automatic nature of the module import search path and need not configure this path at all. If you want to be able to import files across user-defined directory boundaries, though, you will need to know how the

---

* In fact, it's syntactically illegal to include path and suffix detail in an import. In Chapter 17, we'll meet *package imports*, which allow import statements to include part of the directory path leading to a file, as a set of period-separated names. However, package imports still rely on the normal module search path, to locate the leftmost directory in a package path. They also cannot make use of any platform-specific directory syntax in the import statement; such syntax only works on the search path. Also note that module file search path issues are not as relevant when you run *frozen executables* (discussed in Chapter 2); they typically embed byte code in the binary image.

search path works, in order to customize it. Roughly, Python's module search path is automatically composed as the concatenation of these major components:

1. The home directory of the top-level file.
2. PYTHONPATH directories (if set).
3. Standard library directories.
4. The contents of any *.pth* files (if present).

The first and third of these are defined automatically. Because Python searches the concatenation of these from first to last, the second and fourth can be used to extend the module search path to include your own directories. Here is how Python uses each of these path components:

Home directory

Python first looks for the imported file in the home directory. Depending on how you are launching code, this is either the directory containing your program's top-level file, or the directory in which you are working interactively. Because this is always searched first, if a program is located entirely in a single directory, all its imports will work automatically, with no path configuration required.

PYTHONPATH *directories*

Next, Python searches all directories listed in your PYTHONPATH envronment variable setting, from left to right (assuming you have set this at all). In brief, PYTHONPATH is simply set to a list of user-defined and platform-specific names of directories that contain Python code files. Add all the directories that you wish to be able to import from; Python uses your setting to extend the module search path.

Because Python searches the home directory first, you only need to make this setting to import files across directory boundaries—that is, to import a file that is stored in a different directory than the file that imports it. In practice, you probably will make this setting once you start writing substantial programs. When you are first starting out, though, if you save all your module files in the directory that you are working in (i.e., the home directory), your imports will work without making this setting at all.

Standard library directories

Next, Python will automatically search the directories where the standard library modules are installed on your machine. Because these are always searched, they normally do not need to be added to your PYTHONPATH.

.pth file directories

Finally, a relatively new feature of Python allows users to add valid directories to the module search path by simply listing them, one per line, in a text file whose name ends in a *.pth* suffix (for "path"). These path configuration files are a somewhat advanced installation-related feature, which we will not discuss fully here.

In short, a text file of directory names, dropped in an appropriate directory, can serve roughly the same role as the PYTHONPATH environment variable setting. For instance, a file named *myconfig.pth*, may be placed at the top level of the Python install directory on Windows (e.g., in C:\Python22), to extend the module search path. Python will add the directories listed on each line of the file, from first to last, near the end of the module search path list. Because they are based on files instead of shell settings, path files can also apply to all users of an installation, instead of just one user or shell.

This feature is more sophisticated than we will describe here. We recommend that beginners use either PYTHONPATH or a single *.pth* file, and then only if you must import across directories. See the Python library manual for more details on this feature, especially its documentation for standard library module site.

See also Appendix A for examples of common ways to extend your module search path with PYTHONPATH or *.pth* files on various platforms. Depending on your platform, additonal directories may be automatically added to the module search path as well. In fact, this description of the module search path is accurate, but generic; the exact configuration of the search path is prone to change over both platforms and Python releases.

For instance, Python may add an entry for the *current working directory*—the directory from which you launched your program—in the search path, after the PYTHONPATH directories, and before standard library entries. When launching from a command line, the current working directory may not be the same as the *home directory* of your top-level file—the directory where your program file resides. (See Chapter 3 for more on command lines.) Since the current working directory can vary each time your program runs, you normally shouldn't depend on its value for import purposes.

The sys.path list

If you want to see how the path is truly configured on your machine, you can always inspect the module search path as it is known to Python, by printing the built-in sys.path list (that is, attribute path, of built-in module sys). This Python list of directory name strings is the actual search path; on imports, Python searches each directory on this list, from left to right.

Really, sys.path *is* the module search path. It is configured by Python at program startup, using the four path components just described. Python automatically merges any PYTHONPATH and *.pth* file path settings you've made into this list, and always sets the first entry to identify the home directory of the top-level file, possibly as an empty string.

Python exposes this list for two good reasons. First of all, it provides a way to verify the search path settings you've made—if you don't see your settings somewhere on this list, you need to recheck your work. Secondly, if you know what you're doing, this list also provides a way for scripts to tailor their search paths manually. As you'll see later in this part, by modifying the sys.path list, you can modify the search path for all future imports. Such changes only last for the duration of the script, however; PYTHONPATH and *.pth* files are more permanent ways to modify the path.*

Module file selection

Keep in mind that filename *suffixes* (e.g., *.py*) are omitted in import statements, intentionally. Python chooses the first file it can find on the search path that matches the imported name. For example, an import statement of the form import b, might load:

- Source file *b.py*
- Byte-code file *b.pyc*
- A directory named *b*, for package imports
- A C extension module (e.g., b.so on Linux)
- An in-memory image, for frozen executables
- A Java class, in the Jython system
- A zip file component, using the zipimport module

Some standard library modules are actually coded in C. C extensions, Jython, and package imports all extend imports beyond simple files. To importers, though, the difference in loaded file type is completely transparent, both when importing and fetching module attributes. Saying import b gets whatever module b is, according to your module search path, and b.attr fetches an item in the module, be that a Python variable or a linked-in C function. Some standard modules we will use in this book, for example, are coded in C, not Python; their clients don't have to care.

If you have both a *b.py* and a *b.so* in different directories, Python will always load the one on the first (leftmost) directory on your module search path, during the left to right search of sys.path. But what happens if there is both a *b.py* and *b.so* in the *same* directory? Python follows a standard picking order, but it is not guaranteed to stay the same over time. In general, you should not depend on which type of file Python will choose within a given directory—make your module names distinct, or use module search path configuration to make module selection more obvious. It is also possible

---

* Some programs really need to change sys.path, though. Scripts that run on web servers, for example, usually run as user "nobody" to limit machine access. Because such scripts cannot usually depend on "nobody" to have set PYTHONPATH in any particular way, they often set sys.path manually to include required source directories, prior to running any import statements.

to redefine much of what an import operation does in Python, with what are known as *import hooks*. These hooks can be used to make imports do useful things such as load files from zip archives, perform decryption, and so on (in fact, Python 2.3 includes a `zipimport` standard module, which allows files to be directly imported from zip archives). Normally, though, imports work as described in this section. Python also supports the notion of *.pyo* optimized byte-code files, created and run with the -0 Python command-line flag; because these run only slightly faster than normal *.pyc* files (typically 5% faster), they are infrequently used. The Psyco system (see Chapter 2) provides more substantial speedups.

2. Compile It (Maybe)

After finding a source code file that matches an import statement according to the module search path, Python next compiles it to byte code, if necessary. (We discussed byte code in Chapter 2.)

Python checks file timestamps and skips the source to byte code compile step, if it finds a *.pyc* byte code file that is not older than the corresponding *.py* source file. In addition, if Python finds only a byte code file on the search path and no source, it simply loads the byte code directly. Because of this, the compile step is bypassed if possible, to speed program startup. If you change the source code, Python will automatically regenerate the byte code the next time your program is run. Moreover, you can ship a program as just byte code files, and avoid sending source.

Notice that compilation happens when a file is being *imported*. Because of this, you will not usually see a *.pyc* byte code file for the top-level file of your program, unless it is also imported elsewhere—only imported files leave behind a *.pyc* on your machine. The byte code of top-level files is used internally and discarded; byte-code of imported files is saved in files to speed future imports.

Top-level files are often designed to be executed directly and not imported at all. Later, we'll see that it is possible to design a file that serves both as the top-level code of a program, and a module of tools to be imported. Such files may be both executed and imported, and thus generate a *.pyc*. To learn how, watch for the discussion of the special _ _name_ _ attribute and " _ _main_ _ " in Chapter 18.

3. Run It

The final step of an import operation executes the byte code of the module. All statements in the file execute in turn, from top to bottom, and any assignments made to names during this step generate attributes of the resulting module object. This execution step generates all the tools that the module's code defines. For instance, def statements in a file are run at import time to create functions, and assign attributes within the module to those functions. The functions are called later in the program by importers.

Because this last import step actually runs the file's code, if any top-level code in a module file does real work, you'll see its results at import time. For example, top-level print statements in a module show output when the file is imported. Function def statements simply define objects for later use.

As you can see, import operations involve quite a bit of work—they search for files, possibly run a compiler, and run Python code. A given module is only imported once per process by default. Future imports skip all three import steps, and reuse the already-loaded module in memory.[*]

As you can also see, the import operation is at the heart of program architecture in Python. Larger programs are divided into multiple files, which are linked together at runtime by imports. Imports in turn use module search paths to locate your files, and modules define attributes for external use.

Of course, the whole point of imports and modules is to provide a structure to your program, which divides its logic into self-contained software components. Code in one module is isolated from code in another; in fact, no file can ever see the names defined in another, unless explicit import statements are run. To see what this all means in terms of actual code, let's move on to Chapter 16.

---

[*] Technically, Python keeps already-loaded modules in the built-in sys.modules dictionary, and checks that at the start of an import operation to know if the module is already loaded. If you want to see which modules are loaded, import sys, and print sys.modules.keys( ). More on this internal table in Chapter 18.

Module Coding Basics

Now that we've looked at the larger ideas behind modules, let's turn to a simple example of modules in action. Python modules are easy to *create*; they're just files of Python program code, created with your text editor. You don't need to write special syntax to tell Python you're making a module; almost any text file will do. Because Python handles all the details of finding and loading modules, modules are also easy to *use*; clients simply import a module, or specific names a module defines, and use the objects they reference.

Module Creation

To define a module, use your text editor to type Python code into a text file. Names assigned at the top level of the module become its attributes (names associated with the module object), and are exported for clients to use. For instance, if we type the def below into a file called *module1.py* and import it, we create a module object with one attribute—the name printer, which happens to be a reference to a function object:

```
def printer(x):          # Module attribute
    print x
```

A word on module filenames: you can call modules just about anything you like, but module filenames should end in a *.py* suffix if you plan to import them. The *.py* is technically optional for top-level files that will be run, but not imported; but adding it in all cases makes the file's type more obvious.

Since module names become variables inside a Python program without the *.py*, they should also follow the normal variable name rules we learned in Chapter 8. For instance, you can create a module file named *if.py*, but cannot import it, because if is a reserved word—when you try to run import if, you'll get a syntax error. In fact, both the names of module files and directories used in package imports must conform to the rules for variable names presented in Chapter 8. This becomes a larger concern for package directories; their names cannot contain platform-specific syntax such as spaces.

When modules are imported, Python maps the internal module name to an external filename, by adding directory paths in the module search path to the front, and a *.py* or other extension at the end. For instance, a module name M ultimately maps to some external file <directory>\M.<extension> that contains our module's code.

Module Usage

Clients can use the module file we just wrote by running import or from statements. Both find, compile, and run a module file's code if it hasn't yet been loaded. The chief difference is that import fetches the module as a whole, so you must qualify to fetch its names; instead, from fetches (or copies) specific names out of the module.

Let's see what this means in terms of code. All of the following examples wind up calling the printer function defined in the external module file *module1.py*, but in different ways.

The import Statement

In the first example, the name module1 serves two different purposes. It identifies an external file to be loaded and becomes a variable in the script, which references the module object after the file is loaded:

```
>>> import module1                    # Get module as a whole.
>>> module1.printer('Hello world!')   # Qualify to get names.
Hello world!
```

Because import gives a name that refers to the whole module object, we must go through the module name to fetch its attributes (e.g., module1.printer).

The from statement

By contrast, because from also copies names from one file over to another scope, we instead use the copied names directly without going through the module (e.g., printer):

```
>>> from module1 import printer       # Copy out one variable.
>>> printer('Hello world!')           # No need to qualify name.
Hello world!
```

The from * statement

Finally, the next example uses a special form of `from`: when we use a `*`, we get copies of *all* the names assigned at the top level of the referenced module. Here again, we use the copied name, and don't go through the module name:

```
>>> from module1 import *          # Copy out all variables.
>>> printer('Hello world!')
Hello world!
```

Technically, both `import` and `from` statements invoke the same import operation; `from` simply adds an extra copy-out step.

And that's it; modules really are simple to use. But to give you a better understanding of what really happens when you define and use modules, let's move on to look at some of their properties in more detail.

Imports Happen Only Once

One of the most common questions beginners seem to ask when using modules is: why won't my imports keep working? The first import works fine, but later imports during an interactive session (or program run) seem to have no effect. They're not supposed to, and here's why.

Modules are loaded and run on the first `import` or `from`. However, the import operation only happens on the first import, on purpose—since this is an expensive operation, Python does it just once per process by default. Later import operations simply fetch an already loaded module object.

As one consequence, because top-level code in a module file is usually executed only once, you can use it to initialize variables. Consider the file *simple.py*, for example:

```
print 'hello'
spam = 1                          # Initialize variable.
```

In this example, the `print` and `=` statements run the first time the module is imported, and variable spam is initialized at import time:

```
% python
>>> import simple                 # First import: loads and runs file's code
hello
>>> simple.spam                   # Assignment makes an attribute.
1
```

However, second and later imports don't rerun the module's code, but just fetch the already created module object in Python's internal modules table—variable spam is not reinitialized:

```
>>> simple.spam = 2               # Change attribute in module.
>>> import simple                 # Just fetches already-loaded module.
>>> simple.spam                   # Code wasn't rerun: attribute unchanged.
2
```

Of course, sometimes you really want a module's code to be rerun; we'll see how to do it with the reload built-in function later in this chapter.

import and from Are Assignments

Just like def, import and from are executable statements, not compile-time declarations. They may be nested in if tests, appear in function defs, and so on, and are not resolved or run until Python reaches them while your program executes. Imported modules and names are never available until import statements run. Also like def, import and from are implicit assignments:

- import assigns an entire module object to a single name.
- from assigns one or more names to objects of the same name in another module.

All the things we've already said about assignment apply to module access, too. For instance, names copied with a from become references to shared objects; like function arguments, reassigning a fetched name has no effect on the module it was copied from, but changing a fetched *mutable object* can change it in the module it was imported from. File *small.py* illustrates:

```
x = 1
y = [1, 2]

% python
>>> from small import x, y      # Copy two names out.
>>> x = 42                      # Changes local x only
>>> y[0] = 42                   # Changes shared mutable in-place
```

Here, we change a shared mutable object we got with the from assignment: name y in the importer and importee reference the same list object, so changing it from one place changes it in the other:

```
>>> import small               # Get module name (from doesn't).
>>> small.x                    # Small's x is not my x.
1
>>> small.y                    # But we share a changed mutable.
[42, 2]
```

In fact, for a graphical picture of what from assignments do, flip back to Figure 13-2 (function argument passing). Mentally replace "caller" and "function" with "imported" and "importer" to see what from assignments do with references. It's the exact same effect, except that here we're dealing with names in modules, not functions. Assignment works the same everywhere in Python.

Cross-File Name Changes

Note in the prior example how the assignment to x in the interactive session changes name x in that scope only, not the x in the file—there is no link from a name copied with `from` back to the file it came from. To really change a global name in another file, you must use `import`:

```
% python
>>> from small import x, y      # Copy two names out.
>>> x = 42                       # Changes my x only

>>> import small                 # Get module name.
>>> small.x = 42                 # Changes x in other module
```

Because changing variables in other modules like this is commonly confused (and often a bad design choice), we'll revisit this technique again later in this chapter. The change to y[0] in the prior session changes an object, not a name.

import and from Equivalence

Incidentally, notice that we also have to execute an `import` statement in the prior example after the `from`, in order to gain access to the small module name at all; `from` only copies names from one module to another, and does not assign the module name itself. At least conceptually, a `from` statement like this one:

```
from module import name1, name2      # Copy these two names out (only).
```

is equivalent to this sequence:

```
import module                        # Fetch the module object.
name1 = module.name1                 # Copy names out by assignment.
name2 = module.name2
del module                           # Get rid of the module name.
```

Like all assignments, the `from` statement creates new variables in the importer, which initially refer to objects of the same name in the imported file. We only get the names copied out, though, not the module itself.

Module Namespaces

Modules are probably best understood as simply packages of names—places to define names you want to make visible to the rest of a system. In Python, modules are a *namespace*—a place where names are created. Names that live in a module are called its *attributes*. Technically, modules usually correspond to files, and Python creates a module object to contain all the names assigned in the file; but in simple terms, modules are just namespaces.

Files Generate Namespaces

So how do files morph into namespaces? The short story is that every name that is assigned a value at the top level of a module file (i.e., not nested in a function or class body) becomes an attribute of that module.

For instance, given an assignment statement such as X=1 at the top level of a module file *M.py*, the name X becomes an attribute of M, which we can refer to from outside the module as M.X. The name X also becomes a global variable to other code inside *M.py*, but we need to explain the notion of module loading and scopes a bit more formally to understand why:

Module statements run on the first import.   The first time a module is imported anywhere in a system, Python creates an empty module object and executes the statements in the module file one after another, from the top of the file to the bottom.

Top-level assignments create module attributes.   During an import, statements at the top-level of the file that assign names (e.g., =, def) create attributes of the module object; assigned names are stored in the module's namespace.

Module namespace: attribute __dict__, or dir(M).   Module namespaces created by imports are dictionaries; they may be accessed through the built-in __dict__ attribute associated with module objects and may be inspected with the dir function. The dir function is roughly equivalent to the sorted keys list of an object's __dict__ attribute, but includes inherited names for classes, may not be complete, and is prone to change from release to release.

Modules are a single scope (local is global).   As we saw in Chapter 13, names at the top level of a module follow the same reference/assignment rules as names in a function, but the local and global scopes are the same (or, more accurately, it's the LEGB rule, but without the L and E lookup layers). But in modules, the module *scope* becomes an attribute dictionary of a module *object*, after the module has been loaded. Unlike functions (where the local namespace exists only while the function runs), a module file's scope becomes a module object's attribute namespace and lives on after the import.

Here's a demonstration of these ideas. Suppose we create the following module file with a text editor and call it *module2.py*:

```
print 'starting to load...'

import sys
name = 42

def func(): pass

class klass: pass

print 'done loading.'
```

The first time this module is imported (or run as a program), Python executes its statements from top to bottom. Some statements create names in the module's namespace as a side effect, but others may do actual work while the import is going on. For instance, the two `print` statements in this file execute at import time:

```
>>> import module2
starting to load...
done loading.
```

But once the module is loaded, its scope becomes an attribute namespace in the module object we get back from `import`—we access attributes in this namespace by qualifying them with the name of the enclosing module:

```
>>> module2.sys
<module 'sys'>
>>> module2.name
42
>>> module2.func, module2.klass
(<function func at 765f20>, <class klass at 76df60>)
```

Here, `sys`, `name`, `func`, and `klass` were all assigned while the module's statements were being run, so they're attributes after the import. We'll talk about classes in Part VI, but notice the `sys` attribute; `import` statements really *assign* module objects to names and any type of assignment to a name at the top level of a file generates a module attribute. Internally, module namespaces are stored as dictionary objects. In fact, we can access the namespace dictionary through the module's `__dict__` attribute; it's just a normal dictionary object, with the usual methods:

```
>>> module2.__dict__.keys( )
['__file__', 'name', '__name__', 'sys', '__doc__', '__builtins__', 'klass',
'func']
```

The names we assigned in the module file become dictionary keys internally. Some of the names in the module's namespace are things Python adds for us; for instance, `__file__` gives the name of the file the module was loaded from, and `__name__` gives its name as known to importers (without the *.py* extension and directory path).

Attribute Name Qualification

Now that you're becoming more familiar with modules, we should clarify the notion of name *qualification*. In Python, you can access attributes in any object that has attributes, using the qualification syntax `object.attribute`.

Qualification is really an expression that returns the value assigned to an attribute name associated with an object. For example, the expression `module2.sys` in the previous example fetches the value assigned to `sys` in `module2`. Similarly, if we have a built-in list object `L`, `L.append` returns the method associated with the list.

So what does attribute qualification do to the scope rules we studied in Chapter 13? Nothing, really: it's an independent concept. When you use qualification to access names, you give Python an explicit object to fetch from. The LEGB rule applies only to bare, unqualified names. Here are the rules:

Simple variables
   X means search for name X in the current scopes (LEGB rule).

Qualification
   X.Y means find X in the current scopes, then search for attribute Y in the object X (not in scopes).

Qualification paths
   X.Y.Z means look up name Y in object X, then look up Z in object X.Y.

Generality
   Qualification works on all objects with attributes: modules, classes, C types, etc.

In Part VI, we'll see that qualification means a bit more for classes (it's also the place where something called inheritance happens), but in general, the rules here apply to all names in Python.

Imports Versus Scopes

It is never possible to access names defined in another module file without first importing that file. That is, you never automatically get to see names in another file, regardless of the structure of imports or function calls in your program.

For example, consider the following two simple modules. The first, *moda.py*, defines a variable X global to code in its file only, along with a function that changes the global X in this file:

```
X = 88              # My X: global to this file only

def f():
    global X        # Change my X.
    X = 99          # Cannot see names in other modules
```

The second module, *modb.py*, defines its own global variable X, and imports and calls the function in the first module:

```
X = 11              # My X: global to this file only

import moda         # Gain access to names in moda.
moda.f()            # Sets moda.X, not my X
print X, moda.X
```

When run, moda.f changes the X in moda, not the X in modb. The global scope for moda.f is always the file enclosing it, regardless of which module it is ultimately called from:

```
% python modb.py
11 99
```

In other words, import operations never give upward visibility to code in imported files—it cannot see names in the importing file. More formally:

- Functions can never see names in other functions, unless they are physically enclosing.
- Module code can never see names in other modules unless they are explicitly imported.

Such behavior is part of the *lexical scoping* notion—in Python, the scopes surrounding a piece of code are completely determined from the code's physical position in your file. Scopes are never influenced by function calls, or module imports.*

Namespace Nesting

In some sense, although imports do not nest namespaces upward, they do nest downward. Using attribute qualification paths, it's possible to descend into arbitrarily nested modules, and access their attributes. For example, consider the next three files. *mod3.py* defines a single global name and attribute by assignment:

```
X = 3
```

mod2.py imports the first and uses qualification to access the imported module's attribute:

```
X = 2
import mod3

print X,           # My global X
print mod3.X       # mod3's X
```

And *mod1.py* imports the second, and fetches attributes in both the first and second files:

```
X = 1
import mod2

print X,           # My global X
print mod2.X,      # mod2's X
print mod2.mod3.X  # Nested mod3's X
```

Really, when mod1 imports mod2 here, it sets up a two-level namespace nesting. By using a path of names mod2.mod3.X, it descends into mod3, which is nested in the imported mod2. The net effect is that mod1 can see the Xs in all three files, and hence has access to all three global scopes:

```
% python mod1.py
2 3
1 2 3
```

---

* Some languages act differently and provide for dynamic scoping, where scopes really may depend on runtime calls. This tends to make code trickier, though, because the meaning of a variable can differ over time.

Conversely, mod3 cannot see names in mod2, and mod2 cannot see names in mod1. This example may be easier to grasp if you don't think in terms of namespaces and scopes; instead, focus on the objects involved. Within mod1, mod2 is just a name that refers to an object with attributes, some of which may refer to other objects with attributes (import is an assignment). For paths like mod2.mod3.X, Python simply evaluates left to right, fetching attributes from objects along the way.

Note that mod1 can say import mod2 and then mod2.mod3.X, but cannot say import mod2.mod3—this syntax invokes something called package (directory) imports, described in the next chapter. Package imports also create module namespace nesting, but their import statements are taken to reflect directory trees, not simple import chains.

Reloading Modules

A module's code is run only once per process by default. To force a module's code to be reloaded and rerun, you need to ask Python explicitly to do so, by calling the reload built-in function. In this section, we'll explore how to use reloads to make your systems more dynamic. In a nutshell:

- Imports (both import and from statements) load and run a module's code only the first time the module is imported in a process.

- Later imports use the already loaded module object without reloading or rerunning the file's code.

- The reload function forces an already loaded module's code to be reloaded and rerun. Assignments in the file's new code change the existing module object in-place.

Why all the fuss about reloading modules? The reload function allows parts of programs to be changed without stopping the whole program. With reload, the effects of changes in components can be observed immediately. Reloading doesn't help in every situation, but where it does, it makes for a much shorter development cycle. For instance, imagine a database program that must connect to a server on startup; since program changes can be tested immediately after reloads, you need to connect only once while debugging.

Because Python is interpreted (more or less), it already gets rid of the compile/link steps you need to go through to get a C program to run: modules are loaded dynamically, when imported by a running program. Reloading adds to this, by allowing you to also change parts of running programs without stopping. We should note that reload currently only works on modules written in Python; C extension modules can be dynamically loaded at runtime too, but they can't be reloaded.

Reload Basics

Unlike `import` and `from`:

- `reload` is a built-in function in Python, not a statement.
- `reload` is passed an existing module object, not a name.

Because `reload` expects an object, a module must have been previously imported successfully before you can reload it. In fact, if the import was unsuccessful due to a syntax or other error, you may need to repeat an import before you can reload. Furthermore, the syntax of import statements and `reload` calls differs: reloads require parenthesis, but imports do not. Reloading looks like this:

```
import module                # Initial import
...use module.attributes...
...                          # Now, go change the module file.
...
reload(module)              # Get updated exports.
...use module.attributes...
```

You typically import a module, then change its source code in a text editor and reload. When you call `reload`, Python rereads the module file's source code and reruns its top-level statements. But perhaps the most important thing to know about `reload` is that it changes a module object in-place; it does not delete and recreate the module object. Because of that, every reference to a module object anywhere in your program is automatically affected by a reload. The details:

`reload` runs a module file's new code in the module's current namespace. Rerunning a module file's code overwrites its existing namespace, rather than deleting and recreating it.

Top-level assignments in the file replace names with new values. For instance, rerunning a `def` statement replaces the prior version of the function in the module's namespace, by reassigning the function name.

Reloads impact all clients that use `import` to fetch modules. Because clients that use `import` qualify to fetch attributes, they'll find new values in the module object after a reload.

Reloads impact future `from` clients only. Clients that used `from` to fetch attributes in the past won't be affected by a `reload`; they'll still have references to the old objects fetched before the reload.

Reload Example

Here's a more concrete example of `reload` in action. In the following example, we change and reload a module file without stopping the interactive Python session. Reloads are used in many other scenarios, too (see the sidebar "Why You Will Care:

Module Reloads"), but we'll keep things simple for illustration here. First, let's write a module file named *changer.py* with the text editor of our choice:

```
message = "First version"

def printer():
    print message
```

This module creates and exports two names—one bound to a string, and another to a function. Now, start the Python interpreter, import the module, and call the function it exports; the function prints the value of the global variable message:

```
% python
>>> import changer
>>> changer.printer()
First version
>>>
```

Next, keep the interpreter active and edit the module file in another window:

```
...modify changer.py without stopping Python...
% vi changer.py
```

Here, change the global message variable, as well as the printer function body:

```
message = "After editing"

def printer():
    print 'reloaded:', message
```

Finally, come back to the Python window and reload the module to fetch the new code we just changed. Notice that importing the module again has no effect; we get the original message even though the file's been changed. We have to call reload in order to get the new version:

```
...back to the Python interpreter/program...

>>> import changer
>>> changer.printer()          # No effect: uses loaded module
First version

>>> reload(changer)            # Forces new code to load/run
<module 'changer'>
>>> changer.printer()          # Runs the new version now
reloaded: After editing
```

Notice that reload actually returns the module object for us; its result is usually ignored, but since expression results are printed at the interactive prompt, Python shows a default <module name> representation.

CHAPTER 17

Module Packages

So far, when we've imported a module, we've been loading files. This represents typi-cal module usage, and is what you will probably use for most imports you'll code early on in your Python career. The module import story is a bit more rich than we have thus far implied.

Imports can name a directory path, in addition to a module name. When they do, they are known as *package imports*—a directory of Python code is said to be a pack-age. This is a somewhat advanced feature, but turns out to be handy for organizing the files in a large system, and tends to simplify module search path settings. As we'll see, package imports are also sometimes required in order to resolve ambiguities when multiple programs are installed on a single machine.

Package Import Basics

Here's how package imports work. In the place where we have been naming a simple file in `import` statements, we can instead list a path of names separated by periods:

```
import dir1.dir2.mod
```

The same goes for `from` statements:

```
from dir1.dir2.mod import x
```

The "dotted" path in these statements is assumed to correspond to a path through the directory hierarchy on your machine, leading to the file *mod.py* (or other file type). That is, there is directory `dir1`, which has a subdirectory `dir2`, which contains a module file *mod.py* (or other suffix).

Furthermore, these imports imply that `dir1` resides within some container directory `dir0`, which is accessible on the Python module search path. In other words, the two import statements imply a directory structure that looks something like this (shown with DOS backslash separators):

```
dir0\dir1\dir2\mod.py            # Or mod.pyc,mod.so,...
```

The container directory dir0 still needs to be added to your module search path (unless it's the home directory of the top-level file), exactly as if dir1 were a module file. From there down the import statements in your script give the directory path leading to the module explicitly.

Packages and Search Path Settings

If you use this feature, keep in mind that the directory paths in your import statements can only be variables separated by periods. You cannot use any platform-specific path syntax in your import statements; things like C:\dir1, My Documents. dir2, and ../dir1, do not work syntactically. Instead, use platform-specific syntax in your module search path settings to name the container directory.

For instance, in the prior example, dir0—the directory name you add to your module search path—can be an arbitrarily long and platform-specific directory path leading up to dir1. Instead of using an invalid statement like this:

```
import C:\mycode\dir1\dir2\mod      # Error: illegal syntax
```

add C:\mycode to your PYTHONPATH variable or .pth files, unless it is the program's home directory, and say this:

```
import dir1.dir2.mod
```

In effect, entries on the module search path provide platform-specific directory path prefixes, which lead to the leftmost names in import statements. Import statements provide directory path tails in a platform neutral fashion.[*]

Package _ _init_ _.py Files

If you choose to use package imports, there is one more constraint you must follow. Each directory named within the path of a package import statement must also contain a file named _ _init_ _.py, or else your package imports will fail. In the example we've been using, both dir1 and dir2 must contain a file called _ _init_ _.py; the container directory dir0 does not require such a file, because it's not listed in the import statement itself. More formally, for a directory structure such as:

```
dir0\dir1\dir2\mod.py
```

and an import statement of the form:

```
import dir1.dir2.mod
```

---

[*] The dot path syntax was chosen partly for platform neutrality, but also because paths in import statements become real nested object paths. This syntax also means that you get odd error messages if you forget to omit the .py in your import statements: import mod.py is assumed to be a directory path import—it loads mod.py, then tries to load a mod\py.py, and ultimately issues a potentially confusing error message.

the following rules apply:

- dir1 and dir2 both must contain an _ _*init*_ _.*py* file.
- dir0, the container, does not require an _ _*init*_ _.*py*; it will simply be ignored if present.
- dir0 must be listed on the module search path (home directory, PYTHONPATH, etc.), not dir0\dir1.

The net effect is that this example's directory structure should be as follows, with indentation designating directory nesting:

```
dir0\                    # Container on module search path
    dir1\
        __init__.py
        dir2\
            __init__.py
            mod.py
```

These _ _*init*_ _.*py* files contain Python code, just like normal module files. They are partly present as a declaration to Python, and can be completely empty. As a *declaration*, these files serve to prevent directories with a common name from unintentionally hiding true modules that occur later on the module search path. Otherwise, Python may pick a directory that has nothing to do with your code, just because it appears in an earlier directory on the search path.

More generally, this file serves as a hook for package initialization-time actions, serves to generate a module namespace for a directory, and implements the behavior of from* (i.e., from ... import *) statements when used with directory imports:

Package initialization
> The first time Python imports through a directory, it automatically runs all the code in the directory's _ _*init*_ _.*py* file. Because of that, these files are a natural place to put code to initialize the state required by files in the package. For instance, a package might use its initialization file to create required data files, open connections to databases, and so on. Typically, _ _*init*_ _.*py* files are not meant to be useful if executed directly; they are run automatically during imports, the first time Python goes through a directory.

Module namespace initialization
> In the package import model, the directory paths in your script become real nested object paths after the import. For instance, in the example above, the expression dir1.dir2 works, and returns a module object whose namespace contains all the names assigned by dir2's _ _*init*_ _.*py* file. Such files provide a namespace for modules that have no other file.

From statement behavior*
> As an advanced feature, you can use _ _all_ _ lists in _ _*init*_ _.*py* files to define what is exported when a directory is imported with the from* statement form. (We'll meet _ _all_ _ in Chapter 18.) In an _ _*init*_ _.*py* file, the _ _all_ _ list is

taken to be the list of submodule names that should be imported when from* is used on the package (directory) name. If __all__ is not set, the from* does not automatically load submodules nested in the directory, but instead loads just names defined by assignments in the directory's __init__.py file, including any submodules explicitly imported by code in this file. For instance, a statement from submodule import X in a directory's __init__.py makes name X available in that directory's namespace.

You can also simply leave these files empty, if their roles are beyond your needs. They must really exist, though, for your directory imports to work at all.

Package Import Example

Let's actually code the example we've been talking about to show how initialization files and paths come into play. The following three files are coded in a directory dir1 and its subdirectory dir2:

```
#File: dir1\__init__.py
print 'dir1 init'
x = 1

#File: dir1\dir2\__init__.py
print 'dir2 init'
y = 2

#File: dir1\dir2\mod.py
print 'in mod.py'
z = 3
```

Here, dir1 will either be a subdirectory of the one we're working in (i.e., the home directory), or a subdirectory of a directory that is listed on the module search path (technically, on sys.path). Either way, dir1's container does not need an __init__.py file.

As for simple module files, import statements run each directory's initialization file as Python descends the path, the first time a directory is traversed; we've added print statements to trace their execution. Also like module files, already-imported directories may be passed to reload to force re-execution of that single item—reload accepts a dotted path name to reload nested directories and files:

```
% python
>>> import dir1.dir2.mod     # First imports run init files.
dir1 init
dir2 init
in mod.py
>>>
>>> import dir1.dir2.mod     # Later imports do not.
>>>
>>> reload(dir1)
dir1 init
```

```
<module 'dir1' from 'dir1\__init__.pyc'>
>>>
>>> reload(dir1.dir2)
dir2 init
<module 'dir1.dir2' from 'dir1\dir2\__init__.pyc'>
```

Once imported, the path in your import statement becomes a *nested object path* in your script; mod is an object nested in object dir2, nested in object dir1:

```
>>> dir1
<module 'dir1' from 'dir1\__init__.pyc'>
>>> dir1.dir2
<module 'dir1.dir2' from 'dir1\dir2\__init__.pyc'>
>>> dir1.dir2.mod
<module 'dir1.dir2.mod' from 'dir1\dir2\mod.pyc'>
```

In fact, each directory name in the path becomes a variable, assigned to a module object whose namespace is initialized by all the assignments in that directory's __init__.py file. dir1.x refers to the variable x assigned in *dir1__init__.py*, much as mod.z refers to z assigned in *mod.py*:

```
>>> dir1.x
1
>>> dir1.dir2.y
2
>>> dir1.dir2.mod.z
3
```

from Versus import with Packages

import statements can be somewhat inconvenient to use with packages, because you must retype paths frequently in your program. In the prior section's example, you must retype and rerun the full path from dir1 each time you want to reach z. In fact, we get errors here if we try to access dir2 or mod directly at this point.

```
>>> dir2.mod
NameError: name 'dir2' is not defined
>>> mod.z
NameError: name 'mod' is not defined
```

Because of that, it's often more convenient to use the from statement with packages, to avoid retyping paths at each access. Perhaps more importantly, if you ever restructure your directory tree, the from statement requires just one path update in your code, whereas the import may require many. The import as extension, discussed in the next chapter, can also help here, by providing a shorter synonym for the full path:

```
% python
>>> from dir1.dir2 import mod        # Code the path here only.
dir1 init
dir2 init
in mod.py
>>> mod.z                            # Don't repeat path.
```

```
3
>>> from dir1.dir2.mod import z
>>> z
3
>>> import dir1.dir2.mod as mod        # Use shorter name.
>>> mod.z
3
```

Why Use Package Imports?

If you're new to Python, make sure that you've mastered simple modules before step-ping up to packages, as they are a somewhat advanced feature of Python. They do serve useful roles, especially in larger programs: they make imports more informa-tive, serve as an organizational tool, simplify your module search path, and can resolve ambiguities.

First of all, because package imports give some directory information in program files, they both make it easier to locate your files, and serve as an organizational tool. Without package paths, you must resort to consulting the module search to find files more often. Moreover, if you organize your files into subdirectories for functional areas, package imports make it more obvious what role a module plays, and so make your code more readable. For example, a normal import of a file in a directory some-where on the module search path:

```
import utilities
```

bears much less information than an import that includes path information:

```
import database.client.utilities
```

Package imports can also greatly simplify your PYTHONPATH or .pth file search path set-tings. In fact, if you use package imports for all your cross-directory imports, and you make those package imports relative to a common root directory where all your Python code is stored, you really only need a single entry on your search path: the common root.

A Tale of Three Systems

The only time package imports are actually required, though, is in order to resolve ambiguities that may arise when multiple programs are installed on a single machine. This is something of an install issue, but can also become a concern in general prac-tice. Let's turn to a hypothetical scenario to illustrate.

Suppose that a programmer develops a Python program that contains a file called *utilities.py* for common utility code, and a top-level file named *main.py* that users launch to start the program. All over this program, its files say import utilities to load and use the common code. When this program is shipped, it arrives as a single *tar* or *zip* file containing all the program's files; when it is installed, it unpacks all its files into a single directory named system1 on the target machine:

```
system1\
    utilities.py        # Common utility functions, classes
    main.py             # Launch this to start the program.
    other.py            # Import utilities to load my tools
```

Now, suppose that a second programmer does the same thing: he or she develops a different program with files *utilities.py* and *main.py*, and uses import utilities to load the common code file again. When this second system is fetched and installed, its files unpack into a new directory called system2 somewhere on the receiving machine, such that its files do not overwrite same-named files from the first system. Eventually, both systems become so popular that they wind up commonly installed in the same computer:

```
system2\
    utilities.py        # Common utilities
    main.py             # Launch this to run.
    other.py            # Imports utilities
```

So far, there's no problem: both systems can coexist or run on the same machine. In fact, we don't even need to configure the module search path to use these programs— because Python always searches the home directory first (that is, the directory containing the top-level file), imports in either system's files will automatically see all the files in that system's directory. For instance, if you click on *system1\main.py*, all imports will search system1 first. Similarly, if you launch *system2\main.py*, then system2 is searched first instead. Remember, module search path settings are only needed to import across directory boundaries.

But now, suppose that after you've installed these two programs on your machine, you decide that you'd like to use code in the *utilities.py* files of either of the two in a system of your own. It's common utility code, after all, and Python code by nature wants to be reused. You want to be able to say the following from code that you're writing in a third directory:

```
import utilities
utilities.func('spam')
```

to load one of the two files. And now the problem starts to materialize. To make this work at all, you'll have to set the module search path to include the directories containing the *utilities.py* files. But which directory do you put first in the path—system1 or system2?

The problem is the *linear* nature of the search path; it is always scanned left to right. No matter how long you may ponder this dilemma, you will always get *utilities.py* from the directory listed *first* (leftmost) on the search path. As is, you'll never be able to import it from the other directory at all. You could try changing sys.path within your script before each import operation, but that's both extra work, and highly error-prone. By default, you're stuck.

And this is the issue that packages actually fix. Rather than installing programs as a flat list of files in standalone directories, package and install them as *subdirectories*, under a common root. For instance, you might organize all the code in this example as an install hierarchy that looks like this:

```
root\
    system1\
        __init__.py
        utilities.py
        main.py
        other.py
    system2\
        __init__.py
        utilities.py
        main.py
        other.py
    system3\                    # Here or elsewhere
        __init__.py             # Your new code here
        myfile.py
```

Why You Will Care: Module Packages

Now that packages are a standard part of Python, it's common to see larger third-party extensions shipped as a set of package directories, rather than a flat list of modules. The win32all Windows extensions package for Python, for instance, was one of the first to jump on the package bandwagon. Many of its utility modules reside in packages imported with paths; for instance, to load client-side COM tools:

```
from win32com.client import constants, Dispatch
```

this line fetches names from the client module of the win32com package (an install subdirectory). Package imports are also pervasive in code run under the Jython Java-based implementation of Python, because Java libraries are organized into a hierarchy as well. We'll see more of COM and Jython later in Part VIII. In recent Python releases, the email and XML tools are also organized into packaged subdirectories in the standard library.

Now, add just the common root directory to your search path. If your code's imports are relative to this common root, you can import *either* system's utility file with package imports—the enclosing directory name makes the path (and hence the module reference) unique. In fact, you can import *both* utility files in the same module, as long as you use the import statement and repeat the full path each time you reference the utility modules:

```
import system1.utilities
import system2.utilities
system1.utilities.function('spam')
system2.utilities.function('eggs')
```

Notice that __init__.py_ files were added to the system1 and system2 directories to make this work, but not to the root: only directories listed within import statements require these files.

Technically, your system3 directory doesn't have to be under root—just the packages of code from which you will import. However, because you never know when your own modules might be useful in other programs, you might as well place them under the common root to avoid similar name-collision problems in the future.

Also, notice that both of the two original systems' imports will keep working as is and unchanged: because their *home* directory is searched first, the addition of the common root on the search path is irrelevant to code in system1 and system2. They can keep saying just import utilities and expect to find their own file. Moreover, if you're careful to unpack all your Python systems under the common root like this, path configuration becomes simple: you'll only need to add the common root, once.

## CHAPTER 18

Advanced Module Topics

Part V concludes with a collection of more advanced module-related topics, along with the standard set of gotchas and exercises. Just like functions, modules are more effective when their interfaces are defined well, so this chapter also takes a brief look at module design concepts. Some of the topics here, such as the _ _name_ _ trick, are very widely used, despite the word "advanced" in this chapter's title.

Data Hiding in Modules

As we've seen, Python modules export all names assigned at the top level of their file. There is no notion of declaring which names should and shouldn't be visible outside the module. In fact, there's no way to prevent a client from changing names inside a module if they want to.

In Python, data hiding in modules is a convention, not a syntactical constraint. If you want to break a module by trashing its names, you can, but we have yet to meet a programmer who would want to. Some purists object to this liberal attitude towards data hiding and claim that it means Python can't implement encapsulation. However, encapsulation in Python is more about packaging than about restricting.

Minimizing from* damage: _X and _ _all_ _

As a special case, prefixing names with a single underscore (e.g., _X) prevents them from being copied out when a client imports with a from* statement. This really is intended only to minimize namespace pollution; since from* copies out all names, you may get more than you bargained for (including names that overwrite names in the importer). But underscores aren't "private" declarations: you can still see and change such names with other import forms such as the import statement.

A module can achieve a hiding effect similar to the _X naming convention, by assigning a list of variable name strings to the variable _ _all_ _ at the top level of the module. For example:

```
    __all__ = ["Error", "encode", "decode"]    # Export these only.
```

When this feature is used, the from* statement will only copy out those names listed in the __all__ list. In effect, this is the converse of the _X convention: __all__ contains names to be copied, but _X identifies names to not be copied. Python looks for an __all__ list in the module first; if one is not defined, from* copies all names without a single leading underscore.

The __all__ list also only has meaning to the from* statement form, and is not a privacy declaration. Module writers can use either trick, to implement modules that are well-behaved when used with from*. See the discussion of __all__ lists in package __init__.py files in Chapter 17; there, they declare submodules to be loaded for a from*.

Enabling Future Language Features

Changes to the language that may potentially break existing code in the future are introduced gradually. Initially, they appear as optional extensions, which are disabled by default. To turn on such extensions, use a special import statement of this form:

```
from __future__ import featurename
```

This statement should generally appear at the top of a module file (possibly after a docstring), because it enables special compilation of code on a per-module basis. It's also possible to submit this statement at the interactive prompt to experiment with upcoming language changes; the feature will then be available for the rest of the interactive session.

For example, we had to use this in Chapter 14 to demonstrate generator functions, which require a keyword that is not yet enabled by default (they use a featurename of generators). We also used this statement to activate true division for numbers in Chapter 4.

Mixed Usage Modes: __name__ and __main__

Here's a special module-related trick that lets you both import a file as a module, and run it as a standalone program. Each module has a built-in attribute called __name__, which Python sets automatically as follows:

- If the file is being run as a top-level program file, __name__ is set to the string "__main__" when it starts.
- If the file is being imported, __name__ is instead set to the module's name as known by its clients.

The upshot is that a module can test its own __name__ to determine whether it's being run or imported. For example, suppose we create the following module file, named *runme.py*, to export a single function called tester:

```
def tester():
    print "It's Christmas in Heaven..."

if __name__ == '__main__':      # Only when run
    tester()                    # Not when imported
```

This module defines a function for clients to import and use as usual:

```
% python
>>> import runme
>>> runme.tester()
It's Christmas in Heaven...
```

But the module also includes code at the bottom that is set up to call the function when this file is run as a program:

```
% python runme.py
It's Christmas in Heaven...
```

Perhaps the most common place you'll see the __name__ test applied is for *self-test* code: you can package code that tests a module's exports in the module itself, by wrapping it in a __name__ test at the bottom. This way, you can use the file in clients by importing it, and test its logic by running it from the system shell or other launching schemes. Chapter 26 will discuss other commonly used options for testing Python code.

Another common role for the __name__ trick, is for writing files whose functionality can be used as *both* a command-line utility, and a tool library. For instance, suppose you write a file finder script in Python; you can get more mileage out of your code, if you package your code in functions, and add a __name__ test in the file to automatically call those functions when the file is run standalone. That way, the script's code becomes reusable in other programs.

Changing the Module Search Path

In Chapter 15, we mentioned that the module search path is a list of directories initialized from environment variable PYTHONPATH, and possibly *.pth* path files. What we haven't shown you until now is how a Python program can actually change the search path, by changing a built-in list called sys.path (the path attribute in the built-in sys module). sys.path is initialized on startup, but thereafter, you can delete, append, and reset its components however you like:

```
>>> import sys
>>> sys.path
['', 'D:\\PP2ECD-Partial\\Examples', 'C:\\Python22', ...more deleted...]
```

```
>>> sys.path = [r'd:\temp']                    # Change module search path
>>> sys.path.append('c:\\lp2e\\examples')      # for this process only.
>>> sys.path
['d:\\temp', 'c:\\lp2e\\examples']

>>> import string
Traceback (most recent call last):
  File "<stdin>", line 1, in ?
ImportError: No module named string
```

You can use this to dynamically configure a search path inside a Python program. Be careful: if you delete a critical directory from the path, you may lose access to critical utilities. In the last command in the example, we no longer have access to the string module, since we deleted the Python source library's directory from the path. Also remember that such settings only endure for the Python session or program that made them; they are not retained after Python exits.

The import as Extension

Both the import and from statements have been extended to allow a module to be given a different name in your script:

```
import longmodulename as name
```

is equivalent to:

```
import longmodulename
name = longmodulename
del longmodulename          # Don't keep original name.
```

After the import, you can (and in fact must) use the name after the as to refer to the module. This works in a from statement too:

```
from module import longname as name
```

to assign the name from the file to a different name in your script. This extension is commonly used to provide short synonyms for longer names, and to avoid name clashes when you are already using a name in your script that would otherwise be overwritten by a normal import statement. This also comes in handy for providing a short, simple name for an entire directory path, when using the package import feature described in Chapter 17.

Module Design Concepts

Like functions, modules present design tradeoffs: deciding which functions go in which module, module communication mechanisms, and so on. Here are a few general ideas that will become clearer when you start writing bigger Python systems:

You're always in a module in Python.   There's no way to write code that doesn't live in some module. In fact, code typed at the interactive prompt really goes in a

---

built-in module called __main__; the only unique things about the interactive prompt is that code runs and is discarded immediately, and that expression results are printed.

Minimize module coupling: global variables. Like functions, modules work best if they're written to be closed boxes. As a rule of thumb, they should be as independent of global names in other modules as possible.

Maximize module cohesion: unified purpose. You can minimize a module's couplings by maximizing its cohesion; if all the components of a module share its general purpose, you're less likely to depend on external names.

Modules should rarely change other modules' variables. It's perfectly okay to use globals defined in another module (that's how clients import services), but changing globals in another module is often a symptom of a design problem. There are exceptions of course, but you should try to communicate results through devices such as function return values, not cross-module changes. Otherwise your globals' values become dependent on the order of arbitrarily remote assignments.

As a summary, Figure 18-1 sketches the environment in which modules operate. Modules contain variables, functions, classes, and other modules (if imported). Functions have local variables of their own. You'll meet classes—another object that lives within modules—in Chapter 19.

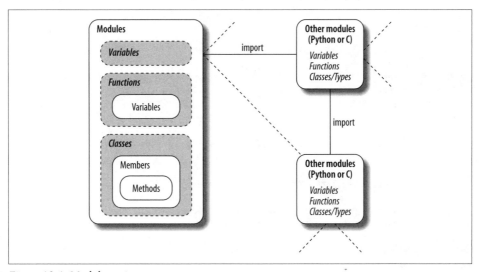

Figure 18-1. Module environment

Modules Are Objects: Metaprograms

Because modules expose most of their interesting properties as built-in attributes, it's easy to write programs that manage other programs. We usually call such manager programs *metaprograms*, because they work on top of other systems. This is also referred to as *introspection*, because programs can see and process object internals. Introspection is an advanced feature, but can be useful for building programming tools.

For instance, to get to an attribute called name in a module called M, we can either use qualification, or index the module's attribute dictionary exposed in the built-in __dict__ attribute. Further, Python also exports the list of all loaded modules as the sys.modules dictionary (that is, the modules attribute of the sys module), and provides a built-in called getattr that lets us fetch attributes from their string names (it's like saying object.attr, but attr is a runtime string). Because of that, all the following expressions reach the same attribute and object:

```
M.name                    # Qualify object.
M.__dict__['name']        # Index namespace dictionary manually.
sys.modules['M'].name     # Index loaded-modules table manually.
getattr(M, 'name')        # Call built-in fetch function.
```

By exposing module internals like this, Python helps you build programs about programs.* For example, here is a module named *mydir.py* that puts these ideas to work, to implement a customized version of the built-in dir function. It defines and exports a function called listing, which takes a module object as an argument and prints a formatted listing of the module's namespace:

```
# A module that lists the namespaces of other modules

verbose = 1

def listing(module):
    if verbose:
        print "-"*30
        print "name:", module.__name__, "file:", module.__file__
        print "-"*30

    count = 0
    for attr in module.__dict__.keys():     # Scan namespace.
        print "%02d) %s" % (count, attr),
        if attr[0:2] == "__":
            print "<built-in name>"          # Skip __file__, etc.
        else:
            print getattr(module, attr)      # Same as .__dict__[attr]
        count = count+1

    if verbose:
        print "-"*30
```

---

* Notice that because a function can access its enclosing module by going through the sys.modules table like this, it's possible to emulate the effect of the global statement you met in Chapter 13. For instance, the effect of global X; X=0 can be simulated by saying, inside a function: import sys; glob=sys.modules[__name__]; glob.X=0 (albeit with much more typing). Remember, each module gets a __name__ attribute for free; it's visible as a global name inside functions within a module. This trick provides another way to change both local and global variables of the same name, inside a function.

```
        print module.__name__, "has %d names" % count
        print "-"*30

if __name__ == "__main__":
    import mydir
    listing(mydir)        # Self-test code: list myself
```

We've also provided self-test logic at the bottom of this module, which narcissistically imports and lists itself. Here's the sort of output produced:

```
C:\python> python mydir.py
-------------------------------
name: mydir file: mydir.py
-------------------------------
00) __file__ <built-in name>
01) __name__ <built-in name>
02) listing <function listing at 885450>
03) __doc__ <built-in name>
04) __builtins__ <built-in name>
05) verbose 1
-------------------------------
mydir has 6 names
-------------------------------
```

We'll meet getattr and its relatives again. The point to notice here is that mydir is a program that lets you browse other programs. Because Python exposes its internals, you can process objects generically.[*]

Module Gotchas

Here is the usual collection of boundary cases, which make life interesting for beginners. Some are so obscure it was hard to come up with examples, but most illustrate something important about Python.

Importing Modules by Name String

The module name in an import or from statement is a hardcoded variable name. Sometimes, though, your program will get the name of a module to be imported as a string at runtime (e.g., if a user selects a module name from within a GUI). Unfortunately, you can't use import statements directly to load a module given its name as a string—Python expects a variable here, not a string. For instance:

```
>>> import "string"
    File "<stdin>", line 1
```

---

[*] Tools such as mydir.listing can be preloaded into the interactive namespace, by importing them in the file referenced by the PYTHONSTARTUP environment variable. Since code in the startup file runs in the interactive namespace (module __main__), imports of common tools in the startup file can save you some typing. See Appendix A for more details.

```
    import "string"
              ^
  SyntaxError: invalid syntax
```

It also won't work to put the string in a variable name:

```
x = "string"
import x
```

Here, Python will try to import a file *x.py*, not the string module.

To get around this, you need to use special tools to load modules dynamically from a string that exists at runtime. The most general approach is to construct an import statement as a string of Python code and pass it to the exec statement to run:

```
>>> modname = "string"
>>> exec "import " + modname       # Run a string of code.
>>> string                         # Imported in this namespace
<module 'string'>
```

The exec statement (and its cousin for expressions, the eval function) compiles a string of code, and passes it to the Python interpreter to be executed. In Python, the byte code compiler is available at runtime, so you can write programs that construct and run other programs like this. By default, exec runs the code in the current scope, but you can get more specific by passing in optional namespace dictionaries.

The only real drawback to exec is that it must compile the import statement each time it runs; if it runs many times, your code may run quicker if it uses the built-in __import__ function to load from a name string instead. The effect is similar, but __import__ returns the module object, so assign it to a name here to keep it:

```
>>> modname = "string"
>>> string = __import__(modname)
>>> string
<module 'string'>
```

from Copies Names but Doesn't Link

The from statement is really an assignment to names in the importer's scope—a name-copy operation, not a name aliasing. The implications of this are the same as for all assignments in Python, but subtle, especially given that the code that shares objects lives in different files. For instance, suppose we define the following module (*nested1.py*):

```
X = 99
def printer(): print X
```

If we import its two names using from in another module (*nested2.py*), we get copies of those names, not links to them. Changing a name in the importer resets only the binding of the local version of that name, not the name in *nested1.py*:

```
from nested1 import X, printer    # Copy names out.
X = 88                            # Changes my "X" only!
printer()                         # nested1's X is still 99
```

```
% python nested2.py
99
```

If you use `import` to get the whole module and assign to a qualified name, you change the name in *nested1.py*. Qualification directs Python to a name in the module object, rather than a name in the importer (*nested3.py*):

```
import nested1                    # Get module as a whole.
nested1.X = 88                    # Okay: change nested1's X
nested1.printer()

% python nested3.py
88
```

Statement Order Matters in Top-Level Code

When a module is first imported (or reloaded), Python executes its statements one by one, from the top of file to the bottom. This has a few subtle implications regarding forward references that are worth underscoring here:

- Code at the top level of a module file (not nested in a function) runs as soon as Python reaches it during an import; because of that, it can't reference names assigned lower in the file.

- Code inside a function body doesn't run until the function is called; because names in a function aren't resolved until the function actually runs, they can usually reference names anywhere in the file.

Generally, forward references are only a concern in top-level module code that executes immediately; functions can reference names arbitrarily. Here's an example that illustrates forward reference:

```
func1()                # Error: "func1" not yet assigned

def func1():
    print func2()      # Okay:  "func2" looked up later

func1()                # Error: "func2" not yet assigned

def func2():
    return "Hello"

func1()                # Okay:  "func1" and "func2" assigned
```

When this file is imported (or run as a standalone program), Python executes its statements from top to bottom. The first call to func1 fails because the func1 def hasn't run yet. The call to func2 inside func1 works as long as func2's def has been reached by the time func1 is called (it hasn't when the second top-level func1 call is run). The last call to func1 at the bottom of the file works, because func1 and func2 have both been assigned.

Mixing `defs` with top-level code is not only hard to read, it's dependent on statement ordering. As a rule of thumb, if you need to mix immediate code with `defs`, put your defs at the top of the file and top-level code at the bottom. That way, your functions are defined and assigned by the time code that uses them runs.

Recursive "from" Imports May Not Work

Because imports execute a file's statements from top to bottom, you sometimes need to be careful when using modules that import each other (something called *recursive imports*). Since the statements in a module have not all been run when it imports another module, some of its names may not yet exist. If you use `import` to fetch a module as a whole, this may or may not matter; the module's names won't be accessed until you later use qualification to fetch their values. But if you use `from` to fetch specific names, you only have access to names already assigned.

For instance, take the following modules `recur1` and `recur2`. `recur1` assigns a name X, and then imports `recur2`, before assigning name Y. At this point, `recur2` can fetch `recur1` as a whole with an `import` (it already exists in Python's internal modules table), but it can see only name X if it uses `from`; the name Y below the `import` in `recur1` doesn't yet exist, so you get an error:

```
#File: recur1.py
X = 1
import recur2              # Run recur2 now if it doesn't exist.
Y = 2
```

```
#File: recur2.py
from recur1 import X       # Okay: "X" already assigned
from recur1 import Y       # Error: "Y" not yet assigned
```

```
>>> import recur1
Traceback (innermost last):
  File "<stdin>", line 1, in ?
  File "recur1.py", line 2, in ?
    import recur2
  File "recur2.py", line 2, in ?
    from recur1 import Y   # Error: "Y" not yet assigned
ImportError: cannot import name Y
```

Python avoids rerunning `recur1`'s statements when they are imported recursively from `recur2` (or else the imports would send the script into an infinite loop), but `recur1`'s namespace is incomplete when imported by `recur2`.

Don't use `from` in recursive imports…really! Python won't get stuck in a cycle, but your programs will once again be dependent on the order of statements in modules. There are two ways out of this gotcha:

- You can usually eliminate import cycles like this by careful design; maximizing cohesion and minimizing coupling are good first steps.

- If you can't break the cycles completely, postpone module name access by using `import` and qualification (instead of `from`), or running your `from`s inside functions (instead of at the top level of the module) or near the bottom of your file to defer their execution.

reload May Not Impact from Imports

The `from` statement is the source of all sorts of gotchas in Python. Here's another: because `from` copies (assigns) names when run, there's no link back to the module where the names came from. Names imported with `from` simply become references to objects, which happen to have been referenced by the same names in the importee when the `from` ran.

Because of this behavior, reloading the importee has no effect on clients that use `from`; the client's names still reference the original objects fetched with `from`, even though names in the original module have been reset:

```
from module import X       # X may not reflect any module reloads!
...
reload(module)             # Changes module, but not my names
X                          # Still references old object
```

Don't do it that way. To make reloads more effective, use `import` and name qualification, instead of `from`. Because qualifications always go back to the module, they will find the new bindings of module names after reloading:

```
import module              # Get module, not names.
...
reload(module)             # Changes module in-place.
module.X                   # Get current X: reflects module reloads
```

reload and from and Interactive Testing

Chapter 3 warned readers that it's usually better to not launch programs with imports and reloads, because of the complexities involved. Things get even worse with `from`. Python beginners often encounter this gotcha: after opening a module file in a text edit window, they launch an interactive session to load and test their module with `from`:

```
from module import function
function(1, 2, 3)
```

After finding a bug, they jump back to the edit window, make a change, and try to reload this way:

```
reload(module)
```

Except this doesn't work—the from statement assigned the name function, not module. To refer to the module in a reload, you have to first load it with an import statement, at least once:

```
import module
reload(module)
function(1, 2, 3)
```

Except this doesn't quite work either—reload updates the module object, but names like function copied out of the module in the past still refer to old objects (in this case, the original version of the function). To really get the new function, either call it module.function after the reload, or rerun the from:

```
import module
reload(module)
from module import function
function(1, 2, 3)
```

And now, the new version of the function finally runs. But there are problems inherent in using reload with from; not only do you have to remember to reload after imports, you also have to remember to rerun your from statements after reloads; this is complex enough to even trip up an expert once in a while.

You should not expect reload and from to play together nicely. Better yet, don't combine them at all—use reload with import, or launch programs other ways, as suggested in Chapter 3 (e.g., use the Edit/Runscript option in IDLE, file icon clicks, or system command lines).

reload Isn't Applied Transitively

When you reload a module, Python only reloads that particular module's file; it doesn't automatically reload modules that the file being reloaded happens to import. For example, if you reload some module A, and A imports modules B and C, the reload only applies to A, not B and C. The statements inside A that import B and C are rerun during the reload, but they'll just fetch the already loaded B and C module objects (assuming they've been imported before). In actual code, here's file *A.py*:

```
import B          # Not reloaded when A is
import C          # Just an import of an already loaded module

% python
>>> . . .
>>> reload(A)
```

Don't depend on transitive module reloads. Use multiple reload calls to update sub-components independently. If desired, you can design your systems to reload their subcomponents automatically by adding reload calls in parent modules like A.

Better still, you could write a general tool to do transitive reloads automatically, by scanning module _ _dict_ _s (see the section "Modules Are Objects: Metaprograms" earlier in this chapter), and checking each item's type( ) (see Chapter 7) to find nested modules to reload recursively. Such a utility function could call itself, recursively, to navigate arbitrarily shaped import dependency chains.

Module *reloadall.py*, listed below, has a reload_all function that automatically reloads a module, every module that the module imports, and so on, all the way to the bottom of the import chains. It uses a dictionary to keep track of modules already reloaded, recursion to walk the import chains, and the standard library's types module (introduced at the end of Chapter 7), which simply predefines type( ) result for built-in types.

To use this utility, import its reload_all function, and pass it the name of an already-loaded module, much like the built-in reload function; when the file runs stand-alone, its self-test code tests itself—it has to import itself, because its own name is not defined in the file without an import. We encourage you to study and experiment with this example on your own:

```python
import types

def status(module):
    print 'reloading', module.__name__

def transitive_reload(module, visited):
    if not visited.has_key(module):          # Trap cycles, dups.
        status(module)                        # Reload this module
        reload(module)                        # and visit children.
        visited[module] = None
        for attrobj in module.__dict__.values():   # For all attrs
            if type(attrobj) == types.ModuleType:   # Recur if module
                transitive_reload(attrobj, visited)

def reload_all(*args):
    visited = {}
    for arg in args:
        if type(arg) == types.ModuleType:
            transitive_reload(arg, visited)

if __name__ == '__main__':
    import reloadall             # Test code: reload myself
    reload_all(reloadall)        # Should reload this, types
```

Part V Exercises

1. *Basics, import.* Write a program that counts lines and characters in a file (similar in spirit to "wc" on Unix). With your text editor, code a Python module called *mymod.py*, which exports three top-level names:

   - A countLines(name) function that reads an input file and counts the number of lines in it (hint: file.readlines( ) does most of the work for you, and len does the rest)

   - A countChars(name) function that reads an input file and counts the number of characters in it (hint: file.read( ) returns a single string)

   - A test(name) function that calls both counting functions with a given input filename. Such a filename generally might be passed-in, hardcoded, input with raw_input, or pulled from a command line via the sys.argv list; for now, assume it's a passed-in function argument.

   All three mymod functions should expect a filename string to be passed in. If you type more than two or three lines per function, you're working much too hard—use the hints listed above!

   Next, test your module interactively, using import and name qualification to fetch your exports. Does your PYTHONPATH need to include the directory where you created mymod.py? Try running your module on itself: e.g., test("mymod.py"). Note that test opens the file twice; if you're feeling ambitious, you may be able to improve this by passing an open file object into the two count functions (hint: file.seek(0) is a file rewind).

2. *from/from*.* Test your mymod module from Exercise 1 interactively, by using from to load the exports directly, first by name, then using the from* variant to fetch everything.

3. *__main__.* Add a line in your mymod module that calls the test function automatically only when the module is run as a script, not when it is imported. The line you add will probably test the value of __name__ for the string "__main__", as shown in this chapter. Try running your module from the system command line; then, import the module and test its functions interactively. Does it still work in both modes?

4. *Nested imports.* Write a second module, myclient.py, which imports mymod and tests its functions; run myclient from the system command line. If myclient uses from to fetch from mymod, will mymod's functions be accessible from the top level of myclient? What if it imports with import instead? Try coding both variations in myclient and test interactively, by importing myclient and inspecting its __dict__.

5. *Package imports.* Import your file from a package. Create a subdirectory called mypkg nested in a directory on your module import search path, move the mymod.py module file you created in Exercise 1 or 3 into the new directory, and try to import it with a package import of the form: import mypkg.mymod.

You'll need to add an _ _init_ _.py file in the directory your module was moved to in order to make this go, but it should work on all major Python platforms (that's part of the reason Python uses "." as a path separator). The package directory you create can be simply a subdirectory of the one you're working in; if it is, it will be found via the home directory component of the search path, and you won't have to configure your path. Add some code to your _ _init_ _.py, and see if it runs on each import.

6. *Reload.* Experiment with module reloads: perform the tests in Chapter 16's changer.py example, changing the called function's message and/or behavior repeatedly, without stopping the Python interpreter. Depending on your system, you might be able to edit changer in another window, or suspend the Python interpreter and edit in the same window (on Unix, a Ctrl-Z key combination usually suspends the current process, and a fg command later resumes it).

7. *Circular imports.*[*] In the section on recursive import gotchas, importing recur1 raised an error. But if you restart Python and import recur2 interactively, the error doesn't occur: test and see this for yourself. Why do you think it works to import recur2, but not recur1? (Hint: Python stores new modules in the built-in sys.modules table (a dictionary) before running their code; later imports fetch the module from this table first, whether the module is "complete" yet or not.) Now try running recur1 as a top-level script file: % python recur1.py. Do you get the same error that occurs when recur1 is imported interactively? Why? (Hint: when modules are run as programs they aren't imported, so this case has the same effect as importing recur2 interactively; recur2 is the first module imported.) What happens when you run recur2 as a script?

---

[*] Note that circular imports are extremely rare in practice. In fact, this author has never coded or come across a circular import in a decade of Python coding. On the other hand, if you can understand why it's a potential problem, you know a lot about Python's import semantics.

Classes and OOP

In Part VI, we study the basics of *object-oriented programming* (OOP), as well as the code you write to use OOP in Python—the class statement. As you'll see, OOP is an option in Python, but a good one: no other construct in the language supports code reuse to the degree that the class statement does. Especially in larger programs, OOP's notion of programming by *customizing* is a powerful paradigm to apply, and can cut development time substantially when used well.

## CHAPTER 19

OOP: The Big Picture

So far in this book, we've been using the term "object" generically. Really, the code written up to this point has been *object-based*—we've passed objects around, used them in expressions, called their methods, and so on. To qualify as being truly *object-oriented* (OO), though, objects generally need to also participate in something called an inheritance hierarchy.

This chapter begins the exploration of the Python *class*—a device used to implement new kinds of objects in Python. Classes are Python's main *object-oriented programming* (OOP) tool, so we'll also look at OOP basics along the way in this part of the book. In Python, classes are created with a new statement: the class. As we'll see, the objects defined with classes can look a lot like the built-in types we saw earlier in the book. They will also support inheritance—a mechanism of code customization and reuse, above and beyond anything we've seen so far.

One note up front: Python OOP is entirely optional, and you don't need to use classes just to get started. In fact, you can get plenty of work done with simpler constructs such as functions, or even simple top-level script code. But classes turn out to be one of the most useful tools Python provides, and we will show you why here. They're also employed in popular Python tools like the Tkinter GUI API, so most Python programmers will usually find at least a working knowledge of class basics helpful.

Why Use Classes?

Remember when we told you that programs do things with stuff? In simple terms, classes are just a way to define new sorts of stuff, which reflect real objects in your program's domain. For instance, suppose we've decided to implement that hypothetical pizza-making robot we used as an example in Chapter 12. If we implement it using classes, we can model more of its real-world structure and relationships:

Inheritance

Pizza-making robots are a kind of robot, and so possess the usual robot-y properties. In OOP terms, we say they inherit properties from the general category of all robots. These common properties need to be implemented only once for the general case and reused by all types of robots we may build in the future.

Composition

Pizza-making robots are really collections of components that work together as a team. For instance, for our robot to be successful, it might need arms to roll dough, motors to maneuver to the oven, and so on. In OOP parlance, our robot is an example of composition; it contains other objects it activates to do its bidding. Each component might be coded as a class, which defines its own behavior and relationships.

General OOP ideas like inheritance and composition apply to any application that can be decomposed into a set of objects. For example, in typical GUI systems, interfaces are written as collections of widgets—buttons, labels, and so on—which are all drawn when their container is drawn (*composition*). Moreover, we may be able to write our own custom widgets—buttons with unique fonts, labels with new color schemes, and the like—which are specialized versions of more general interface devices (*inheritance*).

From a more concrete programming perspective, classes are a Python program unit, just like functions and modules. They are another compartment for packaging logic and data. In fact, classes also define a new namespace much like modules. But compared to other program units we've already seen, classes have three critical distinctions that make them more useful when it comes to building new objects:

Multiple instances

Classes are roughly factories for generating one or more objects. Every time we call a class, we generate a new object, with a distinct namespace. Each object generated from a class has access to the class's attributes and gets a namespace of its own for data that varies per object.

Customization via inheritance

Classes also support the OOP notion of inheritance; they are extended by redefining their attributes outside the class itself. More generally, classes can build up namespace hierarchies, which define names to be used by objects created from classes in the hierarchy.

Operator overloading

By providing special protocol methods, classes can define objects that respond to the sorts of operations we saw work on built-in types. For instance, objects made with classes can be sliced, concatenated, indexed, and so on. Python provides hooks classes can use to intercept and implement any built-in type operation.

OOP from 30,000 Feet

Before we show what this all means in terms of code, we'd like to say a few words about the general ideas behind OOP here. If you've never done anything object-oriented in your life before now, some of the words we'll be using in this chapter may seem a bit perplexing on the first pass. Moreover, the motivation for using such words may be elusive, until you've had a chance to study the ways that programmers apply them in larger systems. OOP is as much an experience as a technology.

Attribute Inheritance Search

The good news is that OOP is much simpler to understand and use in Python than in other languages such as C++ or Java. As a dynamically-typed scripting language, Python removes much of the syntactic clutter and complexity that clouds OOP in other tools. In fact, most of the OOP story in Python boils down to this expression:

    object.attribute

We've been using this all along in the book so far, to access module attributes, call methods of objects, and so on. When we say this to an object that is derived from a class statement, the expression kicks off a *search* in Python—it searches a tree of linked objects, for the first appearance of the *attribute* that it can find. In fact, when classes are involved, the Python expression above translates to the following in natural language:

> Find the first occurrence of *attribute* by looking in *object*, and all classes above it, from bottom to top and left to right.

In other words, attribute fetches are simply tree searches. We call this search procedure *inheritance*, because objects lower in a tree inherit attributes attached to objects higher in a tree, just because the attribute search proceeds from bottom to top in the tree. In a sense, the automatic search performed by inheritance means that objects linked into a tree are the union of all the attributes defined in all their tree parents, all the way up the tree.

In Python, this is all very literal: we really do build up trees of linked objects with code, and Python really does climb this tree at runtime searching for attributes, every time we say *object.attribute*. To make this more concrete, Figure 19-1 sketches an example of one of these trees.

In this figure, there is a tree of five objects labeled with variables, all of which have attached attributes, ready to be searched. More specifically, this tree links together three *class objects* (the ovals: C1, C2, C3), and two *instance objects* (the rectangles: I1, I2), into an inheritance search tree. In the Python object model, classes, and the instances you generate from them, are two distinct object types:

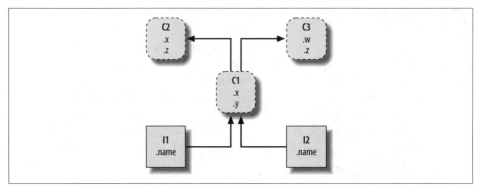

Figure 19-1. A class tree

Classes

  Serve as instance factories. Their attributes provide behavior—data and functions—that is inherited by all the instances generated from them (e.g., a function to compute employee salary from pay and hours).

Instances

  Represent the concrete items in a program's domain. Their attributes record data that varies per specific object (e.g., an employee's social security number).

In terms of search trees, an instance inherits attributes from its class, and a class inherits attributes from all classes above it in the tree.

In Figure 19-1, we can further categorize the ovals by their relative position in the tree. We usually call classes higher in the tree (like C2 and C3) *superclasses*; classes lower in the tree (like C1) are known as *subclasses*.* These terms refer both to relative tree positions and roles. By virtue of inheritance search, superclasses provide behavior shared by all their subclasses. Because the search proceeds bottom-up, subclasses may override behavior defined in their superclasses by redefining superclass names lower in the tree.

Since these last few words are really the crux of the matter of software customization in OOP, let's expand on this concept. Suppose we've built up the tree in Figure 19-1, and then say this:

```
I2.w
```

Right away, we're doing inheritance here. Because this is one of those object. attribute expressions, it triggers a search of the tree in Figure 19-1. Python will search for attribute w, by looking in I2 and above. Specifically, it will search the linked objects in this order:

```
I2, C1, C2, C3
```

---

* In other literature, you may also occasionally see the terms *base class* and *derived class* to describe superclasses and subclasses, respectively.

and stop at the first attached w it finds (or raise an error if it can't be found at all). For this expression, w won't be found until it searches C3 as a last step, because it only appears in that object. In other words, I2.w resolves to C3.w, by virtue of the automatic search. In OOP terminology, I2 "inherits" attribute w from C3. Other attribute references will wind up following different paths in the tree; for example:

- I1.x and I2.x both find x in C1 and stop, because C1 is lower than C2.
- I1.y and I2.y both find y in C1, because that's the only place y appears.
- I1.z and I2.z both find z in C2, because C2 is more to the left than C3.
- I2.name finds name in I2, without climbing the tree at all.

Ultimately, the two instances inherit four attributes from their classes: w, x, y, and z. Trace these searches through the tree in Figure 19-1 to get a feel for how inheritance does its search in Python. The first in the list above is perhaps the most important to notice—because C1 redefines attribute x lower in the tree, it effectively *replaces* the version above in C2. As you'll see in a moment, such redefinitions are at the heart of software customization in OOP.

All of the class and instance objects we put in these trees are just packages of names known as *namespaces*—places where we can attach attributes. If that sounds like modules, it should; the only major difference here is that objects in class trees also have automatically-searched links to other namespace objects.

Coding Class Trees

Although we are speaking in the abstract here, there is tangible code behind all these ideas. We construct such trees and their objects with class statements and class calls, which we'll meet in more detail. But in short:

- Each class statement generates a new class object.
- Each time a class is called, it generates a new instance object.
- Instances are automatically linked to the class they are created from.
- Classes are linked to their superclasses, by listing them in parenthesis in a class header line; the left-to-right order there gives the order in the tree.

To build the tree in Figure 19-1, for example, we would run Python code of this form (we've omitted the guts of the class statements here):

```
class C2: ...          # Make class objects (ovals).
class C3: ...
class C1(C2, C3): ...   # Links to superclasses

I1 = C1( )             # Make instance objects (rectangles).
I2 = C1( )             # Linked to their class
```

Here, we build the three class objects by running three class statements, and make the two instance objects by calling a class twice as though it were a function. The instances remember the class they were made from, and class C1 remembers its listed superclasses.

Technically, this example is using something called *multiple inheritance,* which simply means that a class has more than one superclass above it in the class tree. In Python, the left-to-right order of superclasses listed in parenthesis in a class statement (like C1's here) gives the order in which superclasses are searched, if there is more than one.

Because of the way inheritance searches, the object you attach an attribute to turns out to be crucial—it determines the name's scope. Attributes attached to instances only pertain to a single instance, but attributes attached to classes are shared by all their subclasses and instances. Later, we'll study the code that hangs attributes on these objects in depth. As we'll find:

- Attributes are usually attached to classes by assignments made within class statements.
- Attributes are usually attached to instances by assignments to a special argument passed to functions inside classes, called self.

For example, classes provide behavior for their instances with functions, created by coding def statements inside class statements. Because such nested defs assign names within the class, they wind up attaching attributes to the class object that will be inherited by all instances and subclasses:

```
class C1(C2, C3):              # Make and link class C1.
    def setname(self, who):   # Assign name: C1.setname
        self.name = who       # Self is either I1 or I2.

I1 = C1()                     # Make two instances.
I2 = C1()
I1.setname('bob')            # Sets I1.name to 'bob'
I2.setname('mel')            # Sets I2.name to 'mel'
print I1.name                 # Prints 'bob'
```

There's nothing syntactically unique about def in this context. Operationally, when a def appears inside a class like this, it is usually known as a *method,* and automatically receives a special first argument—called self by convention—which provides a handle back to the instance to be processed.[*]

Because classes are factories for multiple instances, their methods usually go through this automatically passed-in self argument, whenever they need to fetch or set attributes of the particular instance being processed by a method call. In the code above, self is used to store a name on one of two instances.

---

[*] If you've ever used C++ or Java, Python's self is the same as the this pointer, but self is always explicit in Python to make attribute access more obvious.

Like simple variables, attributes of classes and instances are not declared ahead of time, but spring into existence the first time they are assigned a value. When methods assign to self attributes, they create or change an attribute in an instance at the bottom of the class tree (i.e., the rectangles), because self automatically refers to the instance being processed.

In fact, because all the objects in class trees are just namespace objects, we can fetch or set any of their attributes by going through the appropriate names. Saying C1.setname is as valid as saying I1.setname, as long as names C1 and I1 are in your code's scopes.

If a class wants to guarantee that an attribute like name is always set in its instances, it more typically would fill out the attribute at construction time like this:

```
class C1(C2, C3):
    def __init__(self, who):    # Set name when constructed.
        self.name = who         # Self is either I1 or I2

I1 = C1('bob')                  # Sets I1.name to 'bob'
I2 = C1('mel')                  # Sets I2.name to 'mel'
```

If coded and inherited, a method named __init__ is called automatically by Python each time an instance is generated from a class. The new instance is passed in to the self argument of __init__ as usual, and any values listed in parenthesis in the class call go to arguments two and beyond. The effect here is to initialize instances when made, without requiring extra method calls.

The __init__ method is known as a *constructor*, because of when it is run. It's the most commonly used representative of a larger class of methods called *operator overloading* methods. Such methods are inherited in class trees as usual, and have double underscores at the start and end of their names to make them distinct. They're run by Python automatically when objects appear in expressions, and are mostly an alternative to using simple method calls. They're also optional: if omitted, the operation is not supported.

For example, to implement set intersection, a class might either provide a method named intersect, or overload the & expression operator to dispatch to the required logic by coding a method named __and__. Because the operator scheme makes instances look and feel more like built-in types, it allows some classes to provide a consistent and natural interface, and be compatible with code that expects a built-in type.

OOP Is About Code Reuse

And that, along with a few syntax details, is most of the OOP story in Python. There's a bit more to OOP in Python than inheritance; for example, operator overloading is much more general than described so far—classes may also provide the implementation of indexing, attribute fetches, printing, and more. By and large, though, OOP is about looking up attributes in trees.

So why would we be interested in building and searching trees of objects? Although it takes some experience to see how, when used well, classes support code *reuse* in ways that other Python program components cannot. With classes, we code by *customizing* existing software, instead of either changing existing code in-place, or starting from scratch for each new project.

At a fundamental level, classes are really just packages of functions and other names, much like a module. However, the automatic attribute inheritance search that we get from classes, supports customization of software above and beyond modules and functions. Moreover, classes provide a natural structure for code that localizes logic and names, and so aids in debugging.

For instance, because methods are simply functions with a special first argument, we could mimic some of their behavior by manually passing objects to be processed to simple functions. The participation of methods in class *inheritance*, though, allows us to naturally customize existing software by coding subclasses with new method definitions, rather than changing existing code in-place. There is really no such concept with modules and functions.

Here's an example: suppose you're assigned the task of implementing an employee database application. As a Python OOP programmer, you might begin by coding a general superclass that defines default behavior common to all the kinds of employees in your organization:

```
class Employee:                     # General superclass
    def computeSalary(self): ...    # Common or default behavior
    def giveRaise(self): ...
    def promote(self): ...
    def retire(self): ...
```

Once you've coded this general behavior, you can specialize it for each specific kind of employee that differs from the norm. You code subclasses that customize just the bits of behavior that differ per employee type; the rest of employee behavior will be inherited from the more general class. For example, if engineers have a unique salary computation rule (maybe it's not hours times rate), replace just that one method in a subclass:

```
class Engineer(Employee):           # Specialized subclass
    def computeSalary(self): ...    # Something custom here
```

Because the computeSalary version here is lower in the class tree, it will replace (override) the general version in Employee. Create instances of the kind of employee class that a real employee belongs to, to get the correct behavior. Notice that we can make instances of any class in a tree, not just the ones at the bottom—the class you make an instance from determines the level at which attribute search will begin:

```
bob = Employee()                    # Default behavior
```

```
    mel = Engineer()                      # Custom salary calculator
```

Ultimately, these two instance objects might wind up embedded in a larger container object (e.g., a list, or an instance of another class) that represents a department or company, using the *composition* idea mentioned at the start of this chapter. When we later ask for salaries, they will be computed according to the class the object was made from, due to inheritance search—yet another instance of the *polymorphism* idea for functions introduced in Chapter 12:*

```
    company = [bob, mel]                   # A composite object
    for emp in company:
        print emp.computeSalary()         # Run this object's version
```

Polymorphism means that the meaning of an operation depends on the object being operated on. Here, method computeSalary is located by inheritance in each object before it is called. In other applications, polymorphism might also be used to hide (i.e., *encapsulate*) interface differences. For example, a program that processes data streams might be coded to expect objects with input and output methods, without caring what those methods actually do:

```
    def processor(reader, converter, writer):
        while 1:
            data = reader.read()
            if not data: break
            data = converter(data)
            writer.write(data)
```

By passing in instances of subclasses that specialize the required read and write method interfaces for various data sources, the processor function can be reused for any data source we need to use, both now and in the future:

```
    class Reader:
        def read(self): ...               # Default behavior and tools
        def other(self): ...
    class FileReader(Reader):
        def read(self): ...               # Read from a local file
    class SocketReader(Reader):
        def read(self): ...               # Read from a network socket
    ...
    processor(FileReader(...),   Converter,  FileWriter(...))
    processor(SocketReader(...), Converter,  TapeWriter(...))
    processor(FtpReader(...),    Converter,  XmlWriter(...))
```

Moreover, the internal implementation of those read and write methods can be changed without impacting code such as this that uses them. In fact, the processor function might itself be a class, to allow the conversion logic of converter to be filled in by inheritance, and embed readers and writers by composition (we'll see how later in this part of the book).

---

* Note that the company list in this example could be stored on a file with Python object pickling, introduced later in this book, to yield a persistent employee database.

Once you get used to programming by *software customization* this way, you'll find that when it's time to write a new program, much of your work may already be done—your task largely becomes mixing together existing superclasses that already implement the behavior required by your program. For example, both the Employee and reader and writer classes in these examples may have already been written by someone else, for use in a completely different program. If so, you'll get all their code "for free."

In fact, in many application domains, you can fetch or purchase collections of super-classes, known as *frameworks*, which implement common programming tasks as classes, ready to be mixed into your applications. These frameworks might provide database interfaces, testing protocols, GUI toolkits, and so on. With frameworks, you often simply code a subclass that fills in an expected method or two; the frame-work classes higher in the tree do most of the work for you. Programming in such an OOP world is just a matter of combining and specializing already-debugged code by writing subclasses of your own.

Of course, it takes awhile to learn how to leverage classes to achieve such OOP uto-pia. In practice, object-oriented work also entails substantial design to fully realize the code reuse benefits of classes. To this end, programmers have begun cataloging common OOP structures, known as *design patterns*, to help with design issues. The actual code you write to do OOP in Python is so simple that it will not, by itself, pose an additional obstacle to your OOP quests. To see why, you'll have to move on to Chapter 20.

Class Coding Basics

Now that we've talked about OOP in the abstract, let's move on to the details of how this translates to actual code. In this chapter and in Chapter 21, we fill in the syntax details behind the class model in Python.

If you've never been exposed to OOP in the past, classes can be somewhat complicated if taken in a single dose. To make class coding easier to absorb, we'll begin our detailed look at OOP by taking a first look at classes in action in this chapter. We'll expand on the details introduced here in later chapters of this part of the book; but in their basic form, Python classes are easy to understand.

Classes have three primary distinctions. At a base level, they are mostly just *namespaces*, much like the modules studied in Part V. But unlike modules, classes also have support for generating multiple objects, namespace inheritance, and operator overloading. Let's begin our class statement tour by exploring each of these three distinctions in turn.

Classes Generate Multiple Instance Objects

To understand how the multiple objects idea works, you have to first understand that there are two kinds of objects in Python's OOP model—*class* objects and *instance* objects. Class objects provide default behavior and serve as factories for instance objects. Instance objects are the real objects your programs process; each is a namespace in its own right, but inherits (i.e., has automatic access to) names in the class it was created from. Class objects come from statements, and instances from calls; each time you call a class, you get a new instance of that class.

This object generation concept is very different from any of the other program constructs we've seen so far in this book. In effect, classes are factories for making many instances. By contrast, there is only one copy of each module imported (in fact, this is one reason that we have to call reload, to update the single module object).

Next, we'll summarize the bare essentials of Python OOP. Classes are in some ways similar to both def and modules, but they may be quite different than what you're used to in other languages.

Class Objects Provide Default Behavior

*The **class** statement creates a class object and assigns it a name.* Just like the function def statement, the Python class statement is an *executable statement*. When reached and run, it generates a new class object and assigns it to the name in the class header. Also like def, class statements typically run when the file they are coded in is first imported.

*Assignments inside **class** statements make class attributes.* Just like module files, *assignments* within a class statement generate *attributes* in a class object. After running a class statement, class attributes are accessed by name qualification: object.name.

Class attributes provide object state and behavior. Attributes of a class object record state information and behavior, to be shared by all instances created from the class; function def statements nested inside a class generate *methods*, which process instances.

Instance Objects Are Concrete Items

Calling a class object like a function makes a new instance object. Each time a class is called, it creates and returns a new instance object. Instances represent concrete items in your program's domain.

Each instance object inherits class attributes and gets its own namespace. Instance objects created from classes are new namespaces; they start out empty, but inherit attributes that live in the class object they were generated from.

*Assignments to attributes of **self** in methods make per-instance attributes.* Inside class method functions, the first argument (called self by convention) references the instance object being processed; assignments to attributes of self create or change data in the instance, not the class.

A First Example

Let's turn to a real example to show how these ideas work in practice. To begin, let's define a class named FirstClass, by running a Python class statement interactively:

```
>>> class FirstClass:              # Define a class object.
...     def setdata(self, value):  # Define class methods.
...         self.data = value      # self is the instance.
...     def display(self):
...         print self.data        # self.data: per instance
```

We're working interactively here, but typically, such a statement would be run when the module file it is coded in is imported. Like functions, your class won't even exist until Python reaches and runs this statement.

Like all compound statements, class starts with a header line that lists the class name, followed by a body of one or more nested and (usually) indented statements. Here, the nested statements are defs; they define functions that implement the behavior the class means to export. As we've learned, def is really an assignment; here, it assigns to the names setdata and display in the class statement's scope, and so generates attributes attached to the class: FirstClass.setdata, and FirstClass.display.

Functions inside a class are usually called *methods*; they're normal defs, but the first argument automatically receives an implied instance object when called—the subject of a call. We need a couple of instances to see how:

```
>>> x = FirstClass()          # Make two instances.
>>> y = FirstClass()          # Each is a new namespace.
```

By *calling* the class this way (notice the parenthesis), it generates instance objects, which are just namespaces that have access to their class's attributes. Properly speaking, at this point we have three objects—two instances and a class. Really, we have three linked namespaces, as sketched in Figure 20-1. In OOP terms, we say that x "is a" FirstClass, as is y.

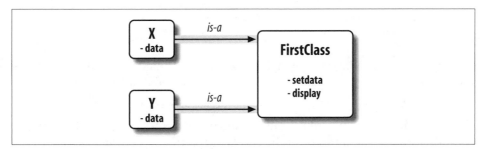

Figure 20-1. Classes and instances are linked namespace objects

The two instances start empty, but have links back to the class they were generated from. If we qualify an instance with the name of an attribute that lives in the class object, Python fetches the name from the class by inheritance search (unless it also lives in the instance):

```
>>> x.setdata("King Arthur")   # Call methods: self is x
>>> y.setdata(3.14159)         # Runs: FirstClass.setdata(y, 3.14159)
```

Neither x nor y has a setdata of its own; instead, Python follows the link from instance to class if an attribute doesn't exist in an instance. And that's about all there is to *inheritance* in Python: it happens at attribute qualification time, and just involves looking up names in linked objects (e.g., by following the is-a links in Figure 20-1).

In the setdata function inside FirstClass, the value passed in is assigned to self. data. Within a method, self—the name given to the leftmost argument by convention—automatically refers to the instance being processed (x or y), so the assignments store values in the instances' namespaces, not the class (that's how the data names in Figure 20-1 are created).

Since classes generate multiple instances, methods must go through the self argument to get to the instance to be processed. When we call the class's display method to print self.data, we see that it's different in each instance; on the other hand, display is the same in x and y, since it comes (is inherited) from the class:

```
>>> x.display()                    # self.data differs in each.
King Arthur
>>> y.display()
3.14159
```

Notice that we stored different object types in the data member (a string and a floating-point). Like everything else in Python, there are no declarations for instance attributes (sometimes called members); they spring into existence the first time they are assigned a value, just like simple variables. In fact, we can change instance attributes either in the class itself by assigning to self in methods, or outside the class by assigning to an explicit instance object:

```
>>> x.data = "New value"           # Can get/set attributes
>>> x.display()                    # outside the class too.
New value
```

Although less common, we could even generate a brand new atribute on the instance, by assigning to its name outside the class's method functions:

```
>>> x.anothername = "spam"         # Can get/set attributes
```

This would attach a new attribute called anothername to the instance object x, which may or may not be used by any of the class's methods. Classes usually create all the instance's attributes by assignment to the self argument, but they don't have to; programs can fetch, change, or create attributes on any object that they have a reference to.

Classes Are Customized by Inheritance

Besides serving as object generators, classes also allow us to make changes by introducing new components (called subclasses), instead of changing existing components in place. Instance objects generated from a class inherit the class's attributes. Python also allows classes to inherit from other classes, and this opens the door to coding *hierarchies* of classes, that specialize behavior by overriding attributes lower in the hierarchy. Here, too, there is no parallel in modules: their attributes live in a single, flat namespace.

In Python, instances inherit from classes, and classes inherit from superclasses. Here are the key ideas behind the machinery of attribute inheritance:

Superclasses are listed in parentheses in a **class** *header.* To inherit attributes from another class, just list the class in parentheses in a class statement's header. The class that inherits is called a *subclass*, and the class that is inherited from is its *superclass*.

Classes inherit attributes from their superclasses. Just like instances, a class gets all the attribute names defined in its superclasses; they're found by Python automatically when accessed, if they don't exist in the subclass.

Instances inherit attributes from all accessible classes. Instances get names from the class they are generated from, as well as all of that class's superclasses. When looking for a name, Python checks the instance, then its class, then all superclasses above.

Each **object.attribute** *reference invokes a new, independent search.* Python performs an independent search of the class tree, for each attribute fetch expression. This includes both references to instances and classes made outside class statements (e.g., X.attr), as well as references to attributes of the self instance argument in class method functions. Each self.attr in a method invokes a new search for attr in self and above.

Logic changes are made by subclassing, not by changing superclasses. By redefining superclass names in subclasses lower in a hierarchy (tree), subclasses replace, and thus, customize inherited behavior.

A Second Example

The next example builds on the one before. Let's define a new class, SecondClass, which inherits all of FirstClass's names and provides one of its own:

```
>>> class SecondClass(FirstClass):          # Inherits setdata
...     def display(self):                   # Changes display
...         print 'Current value = "%s"' % self.data
```

SecondClass defines the display method to print with a different format. But because SecondClass defines an attribute of the same name, it effectively overrides and *replaces* the display attribute in FirstClass.

Recall that inheritance works by searching *up* from instances, to subclasses, to superclasses, and stops at the first appearance of an attribute name it finds. Since it finds the display name in SecondClass before the one in FirstClass, we say that SecondClass overrides FirstClass's display. Sometimes we call this act of replacing attributes by redefining them lower in the tree *overloading*.

The net effect here is that SecondClass specializes FirstClass, by changing the behavior of the display method. On the other hand, SecondClass (and instances created from it) still inherits the setdata method in FirstClass verbatim. Figure 20-2 sketches the namespaces involved; let's make an instance to demonstrate:

```
>>> z = SecondClass()
>>> z.setdata(42)              # setdata found in FirstClass
>>> z.display()                # finds overridden method in SecondClass.
Current value = "42"
```

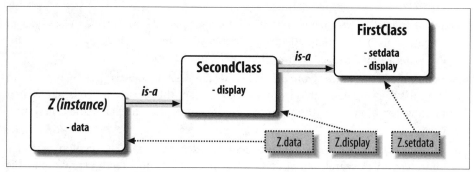

Figure 20-2. Specialization by overriding inherited names

As before, we make a SecondClass instance object by calling it. The setdata call still runs the version in FirstClass, but this time the display attribute comes from SecondClass and prints a custom message.

Here's a very important thing to notice about OOP: the specialization introduced in SecondClass is completely *external* to FirstClass; it doesn't affect existing or future FirstClass objects—like x from the prior example:

```
>>> x.display()        # x is still a FirstClass instance (old message).
New value
```

Rather than changing FirstClass, we customized it. Naturally, this is an artificial example; but as a rule, because inheritance allows us to make changes like this in external components (i.e., in subclasses), classes often support extension and reuse better than functions or modules can.

Classes and Modules

Before we move on, remember that there's nothing magic about a class name. It's just a variable assigned to an object when the class statement runs, and the object can be referenced with any normal expression. For instance, if our FirstClass was coded in a module file instead of being typed interactively, we could import and use its name normally in a class header line:

```
from modulename import FirstClass      # Copy name into my scope.
class SecondClass(FirstClass):         # Use class name directly.
    def display(self): ...
```

Or, equivalently:

```
import modulename                           # Access the whole module.
class SecondClass(modulename.FirstClass):   # Qualify to reference
    def display(self): ...
```

Like everything else, class names always live within a module, and so follow all the rules we studied in Part V. For example, more than one class can be coded in a single module file—like other names in a module, they are run and defined during imports, and become distinct module attributes. More generally, each module may arbitrarily mix any number of variables, functions, and classes, and all names in a module behave the same way. File *food.py* demonstrates:

```
var = 1          # food.var
def func():      # food.func
    ...
class spam:      # food.spam
    ...
class ham:       # food.ham
    ...
class eggs:      # food.eggs
    ...
```

This holds true even if the module and class happen to have the same name. For example, given the following file, *person.py*:

```
class person:
    ...
```

We need to go through the module to fetch the class as usual:

```
import person            # Import module
x = person.person()      # class within module.
```

Although this path may look redundant, it's required: person.person refers to the person class inside the person module. Saying just person gets the module, not the class, unless the from statement is used:

```
from person import person    # Get class from module.
x = person()                 # Use class name.
```

Like other variables, we can never see a class in a file without first importing and somehow fetching from its enclosing file. If this seems confusing, don't use the same name for a module and a class within it.

Also keep in mind that although classes and modules are both namespaces for attaching attributes, they correspond to very different source code structures: a module reflects an entire file, but a class is a statement within a file. We'll say more about such distinctions later in this part of the book.

Classes Can Intercept Python Operators

Let's take a look at the third major distinction of classes: operator overloading. In simple terms, operator overloading lets objects coded with classes intercept and respond to operations that work on built-in types: addition, slicing, printing, qualification, and so on. It's mostly just an automatic dispatch mechanism: expressions route control to implementations in classes. Here, too, there is nothing similar in modules: modules can implement function calls, but not the behavior of expressions.

Although we could implement all class behavior as method functions, operator overloading lets objects be more tightly integrated with Python's object model. Moreover, because operator overloading makes our own objects act like built-ins, it tends to foster object interfaces that are more consistent and easier to learn. Here are the main ideas behind overloading operators:

Methods with names such as _ _X_ _ are special hooks. Python operator overloading is implemented by providing specially named methods to intercept operations.

Such methods are called automatically when Python evaluates operators. For instance, if an object inherits an _ _add_ _ method, it is called when the object appears in a + expression.

Classes may override most built-in type operations. There are dozens of special operator method names, for intercepting and implementing nearly every operation available for built-in types.

Operators allow classes to integrate with Python's object model. By overloading type operations, user-defined objects implemented with classes act just like built-ins, and so provide consistency.

A Third Example

On to another example. This time, we define a subclass of SecondClass, which implements three specially-named attributes that Python will call automatically: _ _init_ _ is called when a new instance object is being constructed (self is the new ThirdClass object), and _ _add_ _ and _ _mul_ _ are called when a ThirdClass instance appears in + and * expressions, respectively:

```
>>> class ThirdClass(SecondClass):              # is-a SecondClass
...     def __init__(self, value):              # On "ThirdClass(value)"
...         self.data = value
...     def __add__(self, other):               # On "self + other"
...         return ThirdClass(self.data + other)
...     def __mul__(self, other):
...         self.data = self.data * other        # On "self * other"

>>> a = ThirdClass("abc")         # New __init__ called
>>> a.display()                   # Inherited method
Current value = "abc"
```

```
>>> b = a + 'xyz'              # New __add__: makes a new instance
>>> b.display()
Current value = "abcxyz"

>>> a * 3                      # New __mul__: changes instance in-place
>>> a.display()
Current value = "abcabcabc"
```

ThirdClass is a SecondClass, so its instances inherit display from SecondClass. But
ThirdClass generation calls pass an argument now (e.g., "abc"); it's passed to the
value argument in the __init__ constructor and assigned to self.data there. Further, ThirdClass objects can show up in + and * expressions; Python passes the
instance object on the left to the self argument and the value on the right to other,
as illustrated in Figure 20-3.

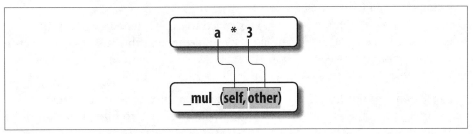

Figure 20-3. Operators map to special methods

Specially-named methods such as __init__ and __add__ are inherited by subclasses
and instances, just like any other name assigned in a class. If the methods are not
coded in a class, Python looks for such names in all superclasses as usual. Operator
overloading method names are also not built-in or reserved words: they are just
attributes that Python looks for when objects appear in various contexts. They are
usually called by Python automatically, but may occasionally be called by your code
as well.

Notice that the __add__ method makes and returns a *new* instance object of its class
(by calling ThirdClass with the result value), but __mul__ *changes* the current
instance object in place (by reassigning a self attribute). This is different than the
behavior of built-in types such as numbers and strings, which always make a new
object for the * operator. Because operator overloading is really just an expression-
to-method dispatch mechanism, you can interpret operators any way you like in your
own class objects.*

---

* But you probably shouldn't. Common practice dictates that overloaded operators should work the same way
  built-in operator implementations do. In this case, that means our __mul__ method should return a *new*
  object as its result, rather than changing the instance (self) in place; for in-place changes, a mul method call
  may be better style than a * overload here (e.g., a.mul(3) instead of a * 3).

Why Operator Overloading?

As a class designer, you can choose to use operator overloading or not. Your choice simply depends on how much you want your object to look and feel like a built-in type. If you omit an overloading operator method and do not inherit it from a superclass, the corresponding operation is not supported for your instances, and will simply throw an exception (or use a standard default) if attempted.

Frankly, many operator overloading methods tend to be used only when implementing objects that are mathematical in nature; a vector or matrix class may overload addition, for example, but an employee class likely would not. For simpler classes, you might not use overloading at all, and rely instead on explicit method calls to implement your object's behavior.

On the other hand, you might also use operator overloading if you need to pass a user-defined object to a function that was coded to expect the operators available on a built-in type like a list or a dictionary. By implementing the same operator set in your class, your objects will support the same expected object interface, and so will be compatible with the function.

Typically, one overloading method seems to show up in almost every realistic class: the __init__ constructor method. Because it allows classes to fill out the attributes in their newly-created instances immediately, the constructor is useful for almost every kind of class you might code. In fact, even though instance attributes are not declared in Python, you can usually find out which attributes an instance will have by inspecting its class's __init__ method code. We'll see additional inheritance and operator overloading techniques in action in Chapter 21.

Class Coding Details

Did all of Chapter 20 make sense? If not, don't worry; now that we've had a quick tour, we're going to dig a bit deeper and study the concepts we've introduced in further detail. This chapter takes a second pass, to formalize and expand on some of the class coding ideas introduced in Chapter 20.

The Class Statement

Although the Python class statement seems similar to other OOP languages on the surface, on closer inspection it is quite different than what some programmers are used to. For example, as in C++, the class statement is Python's main OOP tool. Unlike C++, Python's class is not a declaration. Like def, class is an object builder, and an implicit assignment—when run, it generates a class object, and stores a reference to it in the name used in the header. Also like def, class is true executable code—your class doesn't exist until Python reaches and runs the class statement (typically, while importing the module it is coded in, but not until).

General Form

class is a compound statement with a body of indented statements usually under it. In the header, superclasses are listed in parentheses after the class name, separated by commas. Listing more than one superclass leads to multiple inheritance (which we'll say more about in the next chapter). Here is the statement's general form:

```
class <name>(superclass,...):    # Assign to name.
    data = value                 # Shared class data
    def method(self,...):        # Methods
        self.member = value      # Per-instance data
```

Within the class statement, any assignment generates a class attribute, and specially-named methods overload operators; for instance, a function called __init__ is called at instance object construction time, if defined.

Example

Classes are mostly just namespaces—a tool for defining names (i.e., attributes) that export data and logic to clients. So how do you get from the class statement to a namespace?

Here's how. Just as with modules files, the statements nested in a class statement body create its attributes. When Python executes a class statement (not a call to a class), it runs all the statements in its body, from top to bottom. Assignments that happen during this process create names in the class's local scope, which become attributes in the associated class object. Because of this, classes resemble both modules and functions:

- Like functions, class statements are a local scope where names created by nested assignments live.
- Like modules, names assigned in a class statement become attributes in a class object.

The main distinction for classes is that their namespaces are also the basis of inheritance in Python; attributes are fetched from other classes if not found in a class or instance object.

Because class is a compound statement, any sort of statement can be nested inside its body—print, =, if, def, and so on. All the statements inside the class statement run when the class statement itself runs (not when the class is later called to make an instance). Any name assigned inside the class statement makes a class attribute. Nested defs make class methods, but other assignments make attributes, too. For example:

```
>>> class SharedData:
...     spam = 42                    # Generates a class attribute.
...
>>> x = SharedData()                 # Make two instances.
>>> y = SharedData()
>>> x.spam, y.spam                   # They inherit and share spam.
(42, 42)
```

Here, because the name spam is assigned at the top-level of a class statement, it is attached to the class, and so will be shared by all instances. Change it by going through the class name; refer to it through either instances or the class.*

```
>>> SharedData.spam = 99
>>> x.spam, y.spam, SharedData.spam
(99, 99, 99)
```

---

* If you've used C++, you may recognize this as similar to the notion of C++'s "static" class data—members that are stored in the class, independent of instances. In Python, it's nothing special: all class attributes are just names assigned in the class statement, whether they happen to reference functions (C++'s "methods") or something else (C++'s "members").

Such class attributes can be used to manage information that spans all the instances—a counter of the number of instances generated, for example (we'll expand on this idea in Chapter 23). Now, watch what happens if we assign name spam through an instance instead of the class:

```
>>> x.spam = 88
>>> x.spam, y.spam, SharedData.spam
(88, 99, 99)
```

Assignments to instance attributes create or change that name in the instance, rather than the shared class. More generally, inheritance search occurs only on attribute *reference*, not assignment: assigning to an object's attribute always changes that object, and no other.[*] For example, y.spam is looked up in the class by inheritance, but the assignment to x.spam attaches a name to x itself.

Here's a more comprehensive example of this behavior, that stores the same name in two places. Suppose we run the following class:

```
class MixedNames:                       # Define class.
    data = 'spam'                       # Assign class attr.
    def __init__(self, value):         # Assign method name.
        self.data = value              # Assign instance attr.
    def display(self):
        print self.data, MixedNames.data   # Instance attr, class attr
```

This class contains two defs, which bind class attributes to method functions. It also contains an = assignment statement; since this class-level assignment assigns the name data inside the class, it lives in the class's local scope and becomes an attribute of the class object. Like all class attributes, this data is inherited and shared by all instances of the class that don't have a data of their own.

When we make instances of this class, the name data is also attached to instances, by the assignment to self.data in the constructor method:

```
>>> x = MixedNames(1)      # Make two instance objects.
>>> y = MixedNames(2)      # Each has its own data.
>>> x.display(); y.display()   # self.data differs, Subclass.data same.
1 spam
2 spam
```

The net result is that data lives in two places: in instance objects (created by the self.data assignment in __init__), and in the class they inherit names from (created by the data assignment in the class). The class's display method prints both versions, by first qualifying the self instance, and then the class.

By using these techniques to store attributes on different objects, you determine their scope of visibility. When attached to classes, names are shared; in instances, names

---

[*] Unless the attribute assignment operation has been redefined by a class with the __setattr__ operator overloading method to do something unique.

record per-instance data, not shared behavior or data. Although inheritance looks up names for us, we can always get to an attribute anywhere in a tree, by accessing the desired object directly.

In the example, x.data and self.data will choose an instance name, which normally hides the same name in the class. But MixedNames.data grabs the class name explicitly. We'll see various roles for such coding patterns later; the next section describes one of the most common.

Methods

Since you already know about functions, you also know about methods in classes. Methods are just function objects created by def statements nested in a class statement's body. From an abstract perspective, methods provide behavior for instance objects to inherit. From a programming perspective, methods work in exactly the same way as simple functions, with one crucial exception: their first argument always receives the instance object that is the implied subject of a method call.

In other words, Python automatically maps instance method calls to class method functions as follows. Method calls made through an instance:

```
instance.method(args...)
```

are automatically translated to class method function calls of this form:

```
class.method(instance, args...)
```

where the class is determined by locating the method name using Python's inheritance search procedure. In fact, both call forms are valid in Python.

Beside the normal inheritance of method attribute names, the special first argument is the only real magic behind method calls. In a class method, the first argument is usually called self by convention (technically, only its position is significant, not its name). This argument provides methods with a hook back to the instance—because classes generate many instance objects, they need to use this argument to manage data that varies per instance.

C++ programmers may recognize Python's self argument as similar to C++'s "this" pointer. In Python, though, self is always explicit in your code. Methods must always go through self to fetch or change attributes of the instance being processed by the current method call. This explicit nature of self is by design—the presence of this name makes it obvious that you are using attribute names in your script, not a name in the local or global scope.

Example

Let's turn to an example; suppose we define the following class:

```
class NextClass:                     # Define class.
    def printer(self, text):         # Define method.
```

```
        self.message = text            # Change instance.
        print self.message             # Access instance.
```

The name printer references a function object; because it's assigned in the class statement's scope, it becomes a class object attribute and is inherited by every instance made from the class. Normally, because methods like printer are designed to process instances, we call them through instances:

```
>>> x = NextClass( )               # Make instance

>>> x.printer('instance call')     # Call its method
instance call

>>> x.message                      # Instance changed
'instance call'
```

When called by qualifying an instance like this, printer is first located by inheritance, and then its self argument is automatically assigned the instance object (x); the text argument gets the string passed at the call ('instance call'). When called this way, we pass one fewer argument than it seems we need—Python automatically passes the first argument to self for us. Inside printer, the name self is used to access or set per-instance data, because it refers back to the instance currently being processed.

Methods may be called in one of two ways—through an instance, or through the *class* itself. For example, we can also call printer by going through the class name, provided we pass an instance to the self argument explicitly:

```
>>> NextClass.printer(x, 'class call')    # Direct class call
class call

>>> x.message                             # Instance changed again
'class call'
```

Calls routed through the instance and class have the exact same effect, as long as we pass the same instance object ourselves in the class form. By default, in fact, you get an error message if you try to call a method without any instance:

```
>>> NextClass.printer('bad call')
TypeError: unbound method printer( ) must be called with NextClass instance...
```

Calling Superclass Constructors

Methods are normally called through instances. Calls to methods through the class, though, show up in a variety of special roles. One common scenario involves the constructor method. The __init__ method, like all attributes, is looked up by inheritance. This means that at construction time, Python locates and calls just one `__init__`; if subclass constructors need to guarantee that superclass construction-time logic runs too, they generally must call it explicitly through the class:

```
class Super:
    def __init__(self, x):
        ...default code...

class Sub(Super):
    def __init__(self, x, y):
        Super.__init__(self, x)        # Run superclass init.
        ...custom code...              # Do my init actions.

I = Sub(1, 2)
```

This is one of the few contexts in which your code calls an overload method directly. Naturally, you should only call the superclass constructor this way if you really *want* it to run—without the call, the subclass replaces it completely.*

Other Method Call Possibilities

This pattern of calling through a class is the general basis of extending (instead of completely replacing) inherited method behavior. In Chapter 23, we'll also meet a new option in Python 2.2, *static* and *class* methods, which allows you to code methods that do not expect an instance object in their first argument. Such methods can act like simple instance-less functions, with names that are local to the class they are coded in. This is an advanced and optional extension, though; normally, you must always pass an instance to a method, whether it is called through the instance or the class.

Inheritance

The whole point of a namespace tool like the class statement is to support name inheritance. This section expands on some of the mechanisms and roles of attribute inheritance.

In Python, inheritance happens when an object is qualified, and involves searching an attribute definition tree (one or more namespaces). Every time you use an expression of the form object.attr where object is an instance or class object, Python searches the namespace tree at and above object, for the first attr it can find. This includes references to self attributes in your methods. Because lower definitions in the tree override higher ones, inheritance forms the basis of specialization.

---

* On a somewhat related note, you can also code multiple `__init__` methods within the same single class, but only the last definition will be used; see Chapter 22 for more details.

Attribute Tree Construction

Figure 21-1 summarizes the way namespace trees are constructed and populated with names. Generally:

- Instance attributes are generated by assignments to self attributes in methods.
- Class attributes are created by statements (assignments) in class statements.
- Superclass links are made by listing classes in parentheses in a class statement header.

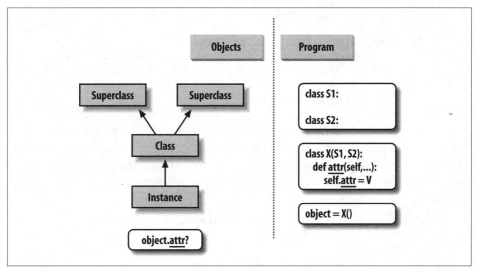

Figure 21-1. Namespaces tree construction and inheritance

The net result is a tree of attribute namespaces, which grows from an instance, to the class it was generated from, to all the superclasses listed in the class headers. Python searches upward in this tree from instances to superclasses, each time you use qualification to fetch an attribute name from an instance object.*

Specializing Inherited Methods

The tree-searching model of inheritance just described turns out to be a great way to specialize systems. Because inheritance finds names in subclasses before it checks superclasses, subclasses can replace default behavior by redefining the superclass's attributes. In fact, you can build entire systems as hierarchies of classes, which are

---

* This description isn't 100% complete, because instance and class attributes can also be created by assigning to objects outside class statements. But that's much less common and sometimes more error prone (changes aren't isolated to class statements). In Python all attributes are always accessible by default; we talk more about name privacy in Chapter 23.

extended by adding new external subclasses rather than changing existing logic in place.

The idea of redefining inherited names leads to a variety of specialization techniques. For instance, subclasses may *replace* inherited attributes completely, *provide* attributes that a superclass expects to find, and *extend* superclass methods by calling back to the superclass from an overridden method. We've already seen replacement in action; here's an example that shows how extension works:

```
>>> class Super:
...     def method(self):
...         print 'in Super.method'
...
>>> class Sub(Super):
...     def method(self):                    # Override method.
...         print 'starting Sub.method'      # Add actions here.
...         Super.method(self)               # Run default action.
...         print 'ending Sub.method'
...
```

Direct superclass method calls are the crux of the matter here. The Sub class replaces Super's method function with its own specialized version. But within the replacement, Sub calls back to the version exported by Super to carry out the default behavior. In other words, Sub.method just extends Super.method behavior, rather than replacing it completely:

```
>>> x = Super()          # Make a Super instance.
>>> x.method()           # Runs Super.method
in Super.method

>>> x = Sub()            # Make a Sub instance.
>>> x.method()           # Runs Sub.method, which calls Super.method
starting Sub.method
in Super.method
ending Sub.method
```

This extension coding pattern is also commonly used with constructors; see the "Methods" section for an example.

Class Interface Techniques

Extension is only one way to interface with a superclass; the following file, *specialize.py,* defines multiple classes that illustrate a variety of common techniques:

Super
: Defines a method function and a delegate that expects an action in a subclass

Inheritor
: Doesn't provide any new names, so it gets everything defined in Super

Replacer
: Overrides Super's method with a version of its own

Extender

Customizes Super's method by overriding and calling back to run the default

Provider

Implements the action method expected by Super's delegate method

Study each of these subclasses to get a feel for the various ways they customize their common superclass:

```
class Super:
    def method(self):
        print 'in Super.method'        # Default behavior
    def delegate(self):
        self.action()                  # Expected to be defined

class Inheritor(Super):                # Inherit method verbatim.
    pass

class Replacer(Super):                 # Replace method completely.
    def method(self):
        print 'in Replacer.method'

class Extender(Super):                 # Extend method behavior.
    def method(self):
        print 'starting Extender.method'
        Super.method(self)
        print 'ending Extender.method'

class Provider(Super):                 # Fill in a required method.
    def action(self):
        print 'in Provider.action'

if __name__ == '__main__':
    for klass in (Inheritor, Replacer, Extender):
        print '\n' + klass.__name__ + '...'
        klass().method()

    print '\nProvider...'
    x = Provider()
    x.delegate()
```

A few things are worth pointing out here. The self-test code at the end of this example creates instances of three different classes in a for loop. Because classes are objects, you can put them in a tuple and create instances generically (more on this idea later). Classes also have the special __name__ attribute like modules; it's just preset to a string containing the name in the class header.

```
% python specialize.py

Inheritor...
in Super.method

Replacer...
in Replacer.method
```

```
Extender...
starting Extender.method
in Super.method
ending Extender.method

Provider...
in Provider.action
```

Abstract Superclasses

Notice how the `Provider` class in the prior example works. When we call the delegate method through a `Provider` instance, *two* independent inheritance searches occur:

1. On the initial `x.delegate` call, Python finds the delegate method in `Super`, by searching at the `Provider` instance and above. The instance `x` is passed into the method's `self` argument as usual.

2. Inside the `Super.delegate` method, `self.action` invokes a new, independent inheritance search at `self` and above. Because `self` references a `Provider` instance, the `action` method is located in the `Provider` subclass.

This "filling in the blanks" sort of coding structure is typical of OOP frameworks. At least in terms of the `delegate` method, the superclass in this example is what is sometimes called an *abstract superclass*—a class that expects parts of its behavior to be provided by subclasses. If an expected method is not defined in a subclass, Python raises an undefined name exception after inheritance search fails. Class coders sometimes make such subclass requirements more obvious with `assert` statements, or raising the built-in `NotImplementedError` exception:

```
class Super:
    def method(self):
        print 'in Super.method'
    def delegate(self):
        self.action()
    def action(self):
        assert 0, 'action must be defined!'
```

We'll meet `assert` in Chapter 24; in short, if its expression evaluates to false, it raises an exception with an error message. Here, the expression is always false (0), so as to trigger an error message if a method is not redefined and inheritance locates the version here. Alternatively, some classes simply raise a `NotImplemented` exception directly in such method stubs; we'll study the `raise` statement in Chapter 24.

For a somewhat more realistic example of this section's concepts in action, see the "Zoo Animal Hierarchy" exercise at the end of Part VI and its solution in Appendix B. Such taxonomies are a traditional way to introduce OOP, but are a bit removed from most developers' job descriptions.

Operator Overloading

We introduced operator overloading in the prior chapter; let's fill in more details here and look at a few commonly used overloading methods. Here's a review of the key ideas behind overloading:

- Operator overloading lets classes intercept normal Python operations.
- Classes can overload all Python expression operators.
- Classes can also overload operations: printing, calls, qualification, etc.
- Overloading makes class instances act more like built-in types.
- Overloading is implemented by providing specially named class methods.

Here's a simple example of overloading at work. When we provide specially named methods in a class, Python automatically calls them when instances of the class appear in the associated operation. For instance, the Number class in file *number.py* below provides a method to intercept instance construction (__init__), as well as one for catching subtraction expressions (__sub__). Special methods are the hook that lets you tie into built-in operations:

```
class Number:
    def __init__(self, start):          # On Number(start)
        self.data = start
    def __sub__(self, other):           # On instance - other
        return Number(self.data - other) # result is a new instance

>>> from number import Number           # Fetch class from module.
>>> X = Number(5)                       # Number.__init__(X, 5)
>>> Y = X - 2                           # Number.__sub__(X, 2)
>>> Y.data                             # Y is new Number instance.
3
```

Common Operator Overloading Methods

Just about everything you can do to built-in objects such as integers and lists has a corresponding specially named method for overloading in classes. Table 21-1 lists a few of the most common; there are many more. In fact, many overload methods come in multiple versions (e.g., __add__, __radd__, and __iadd__ for addition). See other Python books or the Python Language Reference Manual for an exhaustive list of special method names available.

Table 21-1. Common operator overloading methods

Method	Overloads	Called for
__init__	Constructor	Object creation: Class()
__del__	Destructor	Object reclamation
__add__	Operator '+'	X + Y, X += Y

Table 21-1. Common operator overloading methods (continued)

Method	Overloads	Called for
__or__	Operator ' | ' (bitwise or)	X | Y, X |= Y
__repr__, __str__	Printing, conversions	print X, `X`, str(X)
__call__	Function calls	X( )
__getattr__	Qualification	X.undefined
__setattr__	Attribute assignment	X.any = value
__getitem__	Indexing	X[key], for loops, in tests
__setitem__	Index assignment	X[key] = value
__len__	Length	len(X), truth tests
__cmp__	Comparison	X == Y, X < Y
__lt__	Specific comparison	X < Y (or else __cmp__)
__eq__	Specific comparison	X == Y (or else __cmp__)
__radd__	Right-side operator '+'	Noninstance + X
__iadd__	In-place (augmented) addition	X += Y (or else __add__)
__iter__	Iteration contexts	for loops, in tests, others

All overload methods have names that start and end with two underscores, to keep them distinct from other names you define in your classes. The mapping from special method name to expression or operations is simply predefined by the Python language (and documented in the standard language manual). For example, name __add__ always maps to + expressions by Python language definition, regardless of what an __add__ method's code actually does.

All operator overloading methods are optional—if you don't code one, that operation is simply unsupported by your class (and may raise an exception if attempted). Most overloading methods are only used in advanced programs that require objects to behave like built-ins; the __init__ constructor tends to appear in most classes, however. We've already met the __init__ initialization-time constructor method, and a few others in Table 21-1. Let's explore some of the additional methods in the table by example.

__getitem__ Intercepts Index References

The __getitem__ method intercepts instance indexing operations. When an instance X appears in an indexing expression like X[i], Python calls a __getitem__ method inherited by the instance (if any), passing X to the first argument and the index in brackets to the second argument. For instance, the following class returns the square of an index value:

```
>>> class indexer:
...     def __getitem__(self, index):
...         return index ** 2
```

```
...
>>> X = indexer( )
>>> X[2]                        # X[i] calls __getitem__(X, i).
4
>>> for i in range(5):
...     print X[i],
...
0 1 4 9 16
```

__getitem__ and __iter__ Implement Iteration

Here's a trick that isn't always obvious to beginners, but turns out to be incredibly useful: the for statement works by repeatedly indexing a sequence from zero to higher indexes, until an out-of-bounds exception is detected. Because of that, __getitem__ also turns out to be one way to overload iteration in Python—if defined, for loops call the class's __getitem__ each time through, with successively higher offsets. It's a case of "buy one, get one free": any built-in or user-defined object that responds to indexing also responds to iteration:

```
>>> class stepper:
...     def __getitem__(self, i):
...         return self.data[i]
...
>>> X = stepper( )              # X is a stepper object.
>>> X.data = "Spam"
>>>
>>> X[1]                        # Indexing calls __getitem__.
'p'
>>> for item in X:             # for loops call __getitem__.
...     print item,            # for indexes items 0..N.
...
S p a m
```

In fact, it's really a case of "buy one, get a bunch for free": any class that supports for loops automatically supports all iteration contexts in Python, many of which we've seen in earlier chapters. For example, the in membership test, list comprehensions, the map built-in, list and tuple assignments, and type constructors, will also call __getitem__ automatically if defined:

```
>>> 'p' in X                    # All call __getitem__ too.
1

>>> [c for c in X]              # List comprehension
['S', 'p', 'a', 'm']

>>> map(None, X)                # map calls
['S', 'p', 'a', 'm']

>>> (a,b,c,d) = X               # Sequence assignments
>>> a, c, d
('S', 'a', 'm')
```

```
>>> list(X), tuple(X), ''.join(X)
(['S', 'p', 'a', 'm'], ('S', 'p', 'a', 'm'), 'Spam')

>>> X
<__main__.stepper instance at 0x00A8D5D0>
```

In practice, this technique can be used to create objects that provide a sequence interface, and add logic to built-in sequence type operations; we'll revisit this idea when extending built-in types in Chapter 23.

User-defined iterators

Today, all iteration contexts in Python will first try to find a __iter__ method, which is expected to return an object that supports the new iteration protocol. If provided, Python repeatedly calls this object's next method to produce items, until the StopIteration exception is raised. If no such method is found, Python falls back on the __getitem__ scheme and repeatedly indexes by offsets as before, until an IndexError exception.

In the new scheme, classes implement user-defined iterators by simply implementing the iterator protocol introduced in Chapter 14 for functions. For example, the following file, *iters.py*, defines a user-defined iterator class that generates squares:

```
class Squares:
    def __init__(self, start, stop):
        self.value = start - 1
        self.stop  = stop
    def __iter__(self):                    # Get iterator object
        return self
    def next(self):                        # on each for iteration.
        if self.value == self.stop:
            raise StopIteration
        self.value += 1
        return self.value ** 2
```

```
% python
>>> from iters import Squares
>>> for i in Squares(1,5):
...     print i,
...
1 4 9 16 25
```

Here, the iterator object is simply the instance, self, because the next method is part of this class. The end of the iteration is signaled with a Python raise statement (more on raising exceptions in the next part of this book).

An equivalent coding with __getitem__ might be less natural, because the for would then iterate through offsets zero and higher; offsets passed in would be only indirectly related to the range of values produced (0..N would need to map to start..stop). Because __iter__ objects retain explicitly-managed state between next calls, they can be more general than __getitem__.

On the other hand, __iter__-based iterators can sometimes be more complex and less convenient than __getitem__. They are really designed for iteration, not random indexing. In fact, they don't overload the indexing expression at all:

```
>>> X = Squares(1,5)
>>> X[1]
AttributeError: Squares instance has no attribute '__getitem__'
```

The __iter__ scheme implements the other iteration contexts we saw in action for __getitem__ (membership tests, type constructors, sequence assignment, and so on). However, unlike __getitem__, __iter__ is designed for a single traversal, not many. For example, the Squares class is a one-shot iteration; once iterated, it's empty. You need to make a new iterator object for each new iteration:

```
>>> X = Squares(1,5)
>>> [n for n in X]              # Exhausts items
[1, 4, 9, 16, 25]
>>> [n for n in X]              # Now it's empty.
[]
>>> [n for n in Squares(1,5)]
[1, 4, 9, 16, 25]
>>> list(Squares(1,3))
[1, 4, 9]
```

For more details on iterators, see Chapter 14. Notice that this example would probably be simpler if coded with *generator functions*—a topic introduced in Chapter 14 and related to iterators:

```
>>> from __future__ import generators   # Need in 2.2
>>>
>>> def gsquares(start, stop):
...     for i in range(start, stop+1):
...         yield i ** 2
...
>>> for i in gsquares(1, 5):
...     print i,
...
1 4 9 16 25
```

Unlike the class, the function automatically saves its state between iterations. Classes may be better at modeling more complex iterations, though, especially when they can benefit from inheritance hierarchies. Of course, for this artificial example, you might as well skip both techniques, and simply use a for loop, map, or list comprehension, to build the list all at once; the best and fastest way to accomplish a task in Python is often also the simplest:

```
>>> [x ** 2 for x in range(1, 6)]
[1, 4, 9, 16, 25]
```

_ _getattr_ _ and _ _setattr_ _ Catch Attribute References

The _ _getattr_ _ method intercepts attribute qualifications. More specifically, it's called with the attribute name as a string, whenever you try to qualify an instance on an *undefined* (nonexistent) attribute name. It is not called if Python can find the attribute using its inheritance tree-search procedure. Because of its behavior, _ _getattr_ _ is useful as a hook for responding to attribute requests in a generic fashion. For example:

```
>>> class empty:
...     def __getattr__(self, attrname):
...         if attrname == "age":
...             return 40
...         else:
...             raise AttributeError, attrname
...
>>> X = empty()
>>> X.age
40
>>> X.name
...error text omitted...
AttributeError: name
```

Here, the empty class and its instance X have no real attributes of their own, so the access to X.age gets routed to the _ _getattr_ _ method; self is assigned the instance (X), and attrname is assigned the undefined attribute name string ("age"). The class makes age look like a real attribute by returning a real value as the result of the X.age qualification expression (40). In effect, age becomes a *dynamically computed attribute*.

For other attributes the class doesn't know how to handle, it raises the built-in AttributeError exception, to tell Python that this is a bona fide undefined name; asking for X.name triggers the error. You'll see _ _getattr_ _ again when we show delegation and properties at work in the next two chapters, and we will say more about exceptions in Part VII.

A related overloading method, _ _setattr_ _, intercepts *all* attribute assignments. If this method is defined, self.attr=value becomes self._ _setattr_ _('attr',value). This is a bit more tricky to use, because assigning to any self attributes within _ _setattr_ _ calls _ _setattr_ _ again, causing an infinite recursion loop (and eventually, a stack overflow exception!). If you want to use this method, be sure that it assigns any instance attributes by indexing the attribute dictionary, discussed in the next section. Use self._ _dict_ _['name']=x, not self.name=x:

```
>>> class accesscontrol:
...     def __setattr__(self, attr, value):
...         if attr == 'age':
...             self.__dict__[attr] = value
...         else:
```

```
...                    raise AttributeError, attr + ' not allowed'
...
>>> X = accesscontrol()
>>> X.age = 40                    # Calls __setattr__
>>> X.age
40
>>> X.name = 'mel'
...text omitted...
AttributeError: name not allowed
```

These two attribute access overloading methods tend to play highly specialized roles, some of which we'll meet later in this book; in general, they allow you to control or specialize access to attributes in your objects.

__repr__ and __str__ Return String Representations

The next example exercises the __init__ constructor and the __add__ overload methods we've already seen, but also defines a __repr__ that returns a string representation for instances. String formatting is used to convert the managed self.data object to a string. If defined, __repr__, or its sibling __str__, is called automatically when class instances are printed or converted to strings; they allow you to define a better print string for your objects than the default instance display.

```
>>> class adder:
...     def __init__(self, value=0):
...         self.data = value                # Initialize data.
...     def __add__(self, other):
...         self.data += other               # Add other in-place.

>>> class addrepr(adder):                    # Inherit __init__, __add__.
...     def __repr__(self):                  # Add string representation.
...         return 'addrepr(%s)' % self.data # Convert to string as code.

>>> x = addrepr(2)          # Runs __init__
>>> x + 1                   # Runs __add__
>>> x                       # Runs __repr__
addrepr(3)
>>> print x                 # Runs __repr__
addrepr(3)
>>> str(x), repr(x)         # Runs __repr__
('addrepr(3)', 'addrepr(3)')
```

So why two display methods? Roughly, __str__ is tried first for user-friendly displays, such as the print statement and the str built-in function. The __repr__ method should in principle return a string that could be used as executable code to recreate the object, and is used for interactive prompt echoes and the repr function. Python falls back on __repr__ if no __str__ is present, but not vice-versa:

```
>>> class addstr(adder):
...     def __str__(self):                   # __str__ but no __repr__
...         return '[Value: %s]' % self.data # Convert to nice string.
```

```
>>> x = addstr(3)
>>> x + 1
>>> x                                    # Default repr
<__main__.addstr instance at 0x00B35EF0>
>>> print x                              # Runs __str__
[Value: 4]
>>> str(x), repr(x)
('[Value: 4]', '<__main__.addstr instance at 0x00B35EF0>')
```

Because of this, __repr__ may be best if you want a single display for all contexts. By defining both methods, though, you can support different displays in different contexts:

```
>>> class addboth(adder):
...     def __str__(self):
...         return '[Value: %s]' % self.data    # User-friendly string
...     def __repr__(self):
...         return 'addboth(%s)' % self.data     # As-code string

>>> x = addboth(4)
>>> x + 1
>>> x                              # Runs __repr__
addboth(5)
>>> print x                        # Runs __str__
[Value: 5]
>>> str(x), repr(x)
('[Value: 5]', 'addboth(5)')
```

__radd__ Handles Right-Side Addition

Technically, the __add__ method in the prior example does not support the use of instance objects on the right side of the + operator. To implement such expressions, and hence support *commutative* style operators, code the __radd__ method as well. Python calls __radd__ only when the object on the right of the + is your class instance, but the object on the left is not an instance of your class. The __add__ method for the object on the left is called instead in all other cases:

```
>>> class Commuter:
...     def __init__(self, val):
...         self.val = val
...     def __add__(self, other):
...         print 'add', self.val, other
...     def __radd__(self, other):
...         print 'radd', self.val, other
...
>>> x = Commuter(88)
>>> y = Commuter(99)
>>> x + 1                    # __add__:  instance + noninstance
add 88 1
>>> 1 + y                    # __radd__: noninstance + instance
radd 99 1
>>> x + y                    # __add__:  instance + instance
add 88 <__main__.Commuter instance at 0x0086C3D8>
```

Notice how the order is reversed in `__radd__`: self is really on the right of the +, and other is on the left. Every binary operator has a similar right-side overloading method (e.g., `__mul__` and `__rmul__`). Typically, a right-side method like `__radd__` usually just converts if needed and reruns a + to trigger `__add__`, where the main logic is coded. Also note that x and y are instances of the same class here; when instances of different classes appear mixed in an expression, Python prefers the class of the one on the left.

Right-side methods are an advanced topic, and tend to be fairly rarely used; you only code them when you need operators to be commutative, and then only if you need to support operators at all. For instance, a Vector class may use these tools, but an Employee or Button class probably would not.

__call__ Intercepts Calls

The `__call__` method is called when your instance is called. No, this isn't a circular definition—if defined, Python runs a `__call__` method for function call expressions applied to your instances. This allows class instances to emulate the look and feel of things like functions:

```
>>> class Prod:
...     def __init__(self, value):
...         self.value = value
...     def __call__(self, other):
...         return self.value * other
...
>>> x = Prod(2)
>>> x(3)
6
>>> x(4)
8
```

In this example, the `__call__` may seem a bit gratuitous—a simple method provides similar utility:

```
>>> class Prod:
...     def __init__(self, value):
...         self.value = value
...     def comp(self, other):
...         return self.value * other
...
>>> x = Prod(3)
>>> x.comp(3)
9
>>> x.comp(4)
12
```

However, `__call__` can become more useful when interfacing with APIs that expect functions. For example, the Tkinter GUI toolkit we'll meet later in this book allows you to register functions as event handlers (a.k.a., callbacks); when events occur,

Tkinter calls the registered object. If you want an event handler to retain state between events, you can either register a class's bound method, or an instance that conforms to the expected interface with __call__. In our code, both x.comp from the second example and x from the first can pass as function-like objects this way. More on bound methods in the next chapter.

__del__ Is a Destructor

The __init__ constructor is called whenever an instance is generated. Its counterpart, destructor method __del__, is run automatically when an instance's space is being reclaimed (i.e., at "garbage collection" time):

```
>>> class Life:
...     def __init__(self, name='unknown'):
...         print 'Hello', name
...         self.name = name
...     def __del__(self):
...         print 'Goodbye', self.name
...
>>> brian = Life('Brian')
Hello Brian
>>> brian = 'loretta'
Goodbye Brian
```

Here, when brian is assigned a string, we lose the last reference to the Life instance, and so, trigger its destructor method. This works, and may be useful to implement some cleanup activities such as terminating server connections. However, destructors are not as commonly used in Python as in some OOP languages, for a number of reasons.

For one thing, because Python automatically reclaims all space held by an instance when the instance is reclaimed, destructors are not necessary for space management.* For another, because you cannot always easily predict when an instance will be reclaimed, it's often better to code termination activities in an explicitly-called method (or try/finally statement, described in the next part of the book); in some cases, there may be lingering references to your objects in system tables, which prevent destructors from running.

That's as many overloading examples as we have space for here. Most work similarly to ones we've already seen, and all are just hooks for intercepting built-in type operations; some overload methods have unique argument lists or return values. You'll see a few others in action later in the book, but for a complete coverage, we'll defer to other documentation sources.

---

* In the current C implementation of Python, you also don't need to close files objects held by the instance in destructors, because they are automatically closed when reclaimed. However, as mentioned in Chapter 7, it's better to explicitly call file close methods, because auto-close-on-reclaim is a feature of the implementation, not the language itself (and can vary under Jython).

Namespaces: The Whole Story

Now that we've seen class and instance objects, the Python namespace story is complete; for reference, let's quickly summarize all the rules used to resolve names. The first things you need to remember are that qualified and unqualified names are treated differently, and that some scopes serve to initialize object namespaces:

- Unqualified names (e.g., X) deal with scopes.
- Qualified attribute names (e.g., object.X) use object namespaces.
- Some scopes initialize object namespaces (modules and classes).

Unqualified Names: Global Unless Assigned

Unqualified names follow the LEGB lexical scoping rules outlined for functions in Chapter 13:

Assignment: X = value
> Makes names local: creates or changes name X in the current local scope, unless declared global

Reference: X
> Looks for name X in the current local scope, then any and all enclosing functions, then the current global scope, then the built-in scope

Qualified Names: Object Namespaces

Qualified names refer to attributes of specific objects and obey the rules for modules and classes. For class and class instance objects, the reference rules are augmented to include the inheritance search procedure:

Assignment: object.X = value
> Creates or alters the attribute name X in the namespace of the object being qualified, and no other. Inheritance tree climbing only happens on attribute reference, not on attribute assignment.

Reference: object.X
> For class-based objects, searches for the attribute name X in the object, then in all accessible classes above it, using the inheritance search procedure. For non-class objects such as modules, fetches X from object directly.

Assignments Classify Names

With distinct search procedures for qualified and unqualified names, and multiple lookup layers for both, it can sometimes be confusing to know where a name will wind up going. In Python, the place where you assign a name is crucial—it fully determines which scope or which object a name will reside in. File *manynames.py* illustrates and summarizes how this translates to code:

```
X = 11                  # Module (global) name/attribute

class c:
    X = 22              # Class attribute
    def m(self):
        X = 33          # Local variable in method
        self.X = 44     # Instance attribute

def f():
    X = 55              # Local variable in function

def g():
    print X             # Access module X (11)
```

Because this file assigns the same name, X, in five different locations, there are actually five completely different Xs in this program. From top to bottom, the assignments to X names generate a module attribute, a class attribute, a local variable in a method, an instance attribute, and a local in a function.

You should take enough time to study this example carefully, because it collects ideas we've been exploring throughout the last few parts of this book. When it makes sense to you, you will have achieved Python namespace nirvana. Of course, an alternative route to nirvana is to simply run this and see what happens. Here's the remainder of this file, which makes an instance, and prints all the Xs that it can fetch:

```
obj = c()
obj.m()

print obj.X         # 44: instance
print c.X           # 22: class     (a.k.a. obj.X if no X in instance)
print X             # 11: module    (a.k.a. manynames.X outside file)

#print c.m.X        # FAILS: only visible in method
#print f.X          # FAILS: only visible in function
```

Notice that we can go through the class to fetch its attribute (c.X), but can never fetch local variables in functions or methods from outside their def statements. Locals are only visible to other code within the def, and in fact only live in memory while a call to the function or method is executing.

Namespace Dictionaries

In Chapter 16, we learned that module namespaces are actually implemented as dictionaries and exposed with the built-in __dict__ attribute. The same holds for class and instance objects: attribute qualification is really a dictionary indexing operation internally, and attribute inheritance is just a matter of searching linked dictionaries. In fact, instance and class objects are mostly just dictionaries with links inside

Python. Python exposes these dictionaries, as well as the links between them, for use in advanced roles (e.g., for coding tools).

To help you understand how attributes work internally, let's work through an interactive session that traces the way namespace dictionaries grow when classes are involved. First, let's define a superclass and a subclass with methods that will store data in their instances:

```
>>> class super:
...     def hello(self):
...         self.data1 = 'spam'
...
>>> class sub(super):
...     def hola(self):
...         self.data2 = 'eggs'
...
```

When we make an instance of the subclass, the instance starts out with an empty namespace dictionary, but has links back to the class for the inheritance search to follow. In fact, the inheritance tree is explicitly available in special attributes, which you can inspect: instances have a __class__ attribute that links to their class, and classes have a __bases__ attribute that is a tuple containing links to higher superclasses:

```
>>> X = sub( )
>>> X.__dict__
{ }

>>> X.__class__
<class __main__.sub at 0x00A48448>

>>> sub.__bases__
(<class __main__.super at 0x00A3E1C8>,)

>>> super.__bases__
( )
```

As classes assign to self attributes, they populate the instance object—that is, attributes wind up in the instance's attribute namespace dictionary, not in the classes. Instance object namespaces record data that can vary from instance to instance, and self is a hook into that namespace:

```
>>> Y = sub( )

>>> X.hello( )
>>> X.__dict__
{'data1': 'spam'}

>>> X.hola( )
>>> X.__dict__
{'data1': 'spam', 'data2': 'eggs'}

>>> sub.__dict__
{'__module__': '__main__', '__doc__': None, 'hola': <function hola at
 0x00A47048>}
```

```
>>> super.__dict__
{'__module__': '__main__', 'hello': <function hello at 0x00A3C5A8>,
 '__doc__': None}

>>> sub.__dict__.keys(), super.__dict__.keys()
(['__module__', '__doc__', 'hola'], ['__module__', 'hello', '__doc__'])

>>> Y.__dict__
{}
```

Notice the extra underscore names in the class dictionaries; these are set by Python automatically. Most are not used in typical programs, but some are utilized by tools (e.g., __doc__ holds the docstrings discussed in Chapter 11).

Also observe that Y, a second instance made at the start of this series, still has an empty namespace dictionary at the end, even though X's has been populated by assignments in methods. Each instance is an independent namespace dictionary, which starts out empty, and can record completely different attributes than other instances of the same class.

Now, because attributes are actually dictionary keys inside Python, there are really two ways to fetch and assign their values—by qualification, or key indexing:

```
>>> X.data1, X.__dict__['data1']
('spam', 'spam')

>>> X.data3 = 'toast'
>>> X.__dict__
{'data1': 'spam', 'data3': 'toast', 'data2': 'eggs'}

>>> X.__dict__['data3'] = 'ham'
>>> X.data3
'ham'
```

This equivalence only applies to attributes attached to the instance, though. Because attribute qualification also performs *inheritance*, it can access attributes that namespace dictionary indexing cannot. The inherited attribute X.hello, for instance, cannot be had by X.__dict__['hello'].

And finally, here is the built-in dir function we met in Chapters 3 and 11 at work on class and instance objects. This function works on anything with attributes: dir(object) is similar to an object.__dict__.keys() call. Notice though, that dir sorts its list, and includes some system attributes; as of Python 2.2, dir also collects *inherited* attributes automatically.*

```
>>> X.__dict__
{'data1': 'spam', 'data3': 'ham', 'data2': 'eggs'}
```

---

* The content of attribute dictionaries and dir call results is prone to change over time. For example, because Python now allows built-in types to be subclassed like classes, the contents of dir results for built-in types expanded to include operator overloading methods. In general, attribute names with leading and trailing double underscores are interpreter-specific. More on type subclasses in Chapter 23.

```
>>> X.__dict__.keys()
['data1', 'data3', 'data2']

>>>> dir(X)
['__doc__', '__module__', 'data1', 'data2', 'data3', 'hello', 'hola']
>>> dir(sub)
['__doc__', '__module__', 'hello', 'hola']
>>> dir(super)
['__doc__', '__module__', 'hello']
```

Experiment with these special attributes on your own to get a better feel for how namespaces actually do their attribute business. Even if you will never use these in the kinds of programs you write, it helps demystify the notion of namespaces in general when you see that they are just normal dictionaries.

Namespace Links

The prior section introduced the special __class__ and __bases__ instance and class attributes without really telling why you might care about them. In short, they allow you to inspect inheritance hierarchies within your own code. For example, they can be used to display a class tree, as in the following example, file *classtree.py*:

```
def classtree(cls, indent):
    print '.'*indent, cls.__name__       # Print class name here.
    for supercls in cls.__bases__:       # Recur to all superclasses
        classtree(supercls, indent+3)    # May visit super > once

def instancetree(inst):
    print 'Tree of', inst                # Show instance.
    classtree(inst.__class__, 3)         # Climb to its class.

def selftest():
    class A: pass
    class B(A): pass
    class C(A): pass
    class D(B,C): pass
    class E: pass
    class F(D,E): pass
    instancetree(B())
    instancetree(F())

if __name__ == '__main__': selftest()
```

The classtree function in this script is *recursive*—it prints a class's name using __name__, and then climbs up to superclasses by calling itself. This allows the function to traverse arbitrarily shaped class trees; the recursion climbs to the top, and stops at root superclasses that have empty __bases__. Most of this file is self-test code; when run standalone, it builds an empty class tree, makes two instance from it, and prints their class tree structures:

```
% python classtree.py
Tree of <__main__.B instance at 0x00ACB438>
```

```
... B
...... A
Tree of <__main__.F instance at 0x00AC4DA8>
... F
...... D
......... B
............ A
......... C
............ A
...... E
```

Here, indentation marked by periods is used to denote class tree height. We can import these functions anywhere we want a quick class tree display:

```
>>> class Emp: pass
>>> class Person(Emp): pass
>>> bob = Person( )
>>> import classtree
>>> classtree.instancetree(bob)
Tree of <__main__.Person instance at 0x00AD34E8>
... Person
...... Emp
```

Of course, we could improve on this output format, and perhaps even sketch it in a GUI display. Whether or not you will ever code or use such tools, this example demonstrates one of the many ways that we can make use of special attributes that expose interpreter internals. We'll meet another when we code a general purpose attribute listing class, in the multiple inheritance section of Chapter 22.

Designing with Classes

So far, we've concentrated on the OOP tool in Python—the class. But OOP is also about design issues—how to use classes to model useful objects. This section will touch on a few OOP core ideas, and look at some additional examples that are more realistic than the examples shown so far. Many of the design terms mentioned here require more explanation than we can provide; if this section sparks your curiosity, we suggest exploring a text on OOP design or design patterns as a next step.

Python and OOP

Python's implementation of OOP can be summarized by three ideas:

Inheritance
> Is based on attribute lookup in Python (in X.name expressions).

Polymorphism
> In X.method, the meaning of method depends on the type (class) of X.

Encapsulation
> Methods and operators implement behavior; data hiding is a convention by default.

By now, you should have a good feel for what inheritance is all about in Python. We've talked about Python's polymorphism a few times already; it flows from Python's lack of type declarations. Because attributes are always resolved at runtime, objects that implement the same interfaces are interchangeable. Clients don't need to know what sort of object is implementing a method they call.

Encapsulation means packaging in Python—hiding implementation details behind an object's interface; it does not mean enforced privacy, as you'll see in Chapter 23. Encapsulation allows the implementation of an object's interface to be changed, without impacting the users of that object.

Overloading by Call Signatures (or Not)

Some OOP languages also define polymorphism to mean overloading functions based on the type signatures of their arguments. Since there is no type declaration in Python, the concept doesn't really apply; polymorphism in Python is based on object *interfaces*, not types. For example, you can try to overload methods by their argument lists:

```
class C:
    def meth(self, x):
        ...
    def meth(self, x, y, z):
        ...
```

This code will run, but because the def simply assigns an object to a name in the class's scope, the last definition of a method function is the only one retained (it's just as if you say X=1, and then X=2; X will be 2).

Type-based selections can always be coded using the type testing ideas we met in Chapter 7, or the argument list tools in Chapter 13:

```
class C:
    def meth(self, *args):
        if len(args) == 1:
            ...
        elif type(arg[0]) == int:
            ...
```

You normally shouldn't do this, though—as described in Chapter 12, write your code to expect an object interface, not a specific datatype. That way, it becomes useful for a broader category of types and applications, now and in the future:

```
class C:
    def meth(self, x):
        x.operation()       # Assume x does the right thing.
```

It's also generally considered better to use distinct method names for distinct operations, rather than relying on call signatures (no matter what language you code in).

Classes as Records

Chapter 6 showed you how to use dictionaries to record properties of entities in your program. Let's explore this in more detail. Here is the example for dictionary-based records used earlier:

```
>>> rec = {}
>>> rec['name'] = 'mel'
>>> rec['age']  = 40
>>> rec['job']  = 'trainer/writer'
>>>
>>> print rec['name']
mel
```

This code emulates things like "records" and "structs" in other languages. It turns out that there are multiple ways to do the same with classes. Perhaps the simplest is this:

```
>>> class rec: pass
...
>>> rec.name = 'mel'
>>> rec.age  = 40
>>> rec.job  = 'trainer/writer'
>>>
>>> print rec.age
40
```

This code has substantially less syntax than the dictionary equivalent. It uses an empty class statement to generate an empty namespace object (notice the pass statement—we need a statement syntactically even though there is no logic to code in this case). Once we make the empty class, we fill it out by assigning to class attributes over time.

This works, but we'll need a new class statement for each distinct record we will need. Perhaps more typically, we can instead generate *instances* of an empty class to represent each distinct entity:

```
>>> class rec: pass
...
>>> pers1 = rec( )
>>> pers1.name = 'mel'
>>> pers1.job  = 'trainer'
>>> pers1.age    = 40
>>>
>>> pers2 = rec( )
>>> pers2.name = 'dave'
>>> pers2.job  = 'developer'
>>>
>>> pers1.name, pers2.name
('mel', 'dave')
```

Here, we make two records from the same class; instances start out life empty, just like classes. We fill in the record by assigning to attributes. This time, though, there are two separate objects, and hence two separate name attributes. In fact, instances of the same class don't even have to have the same set of attribute names; in this example, one has a unique age name. Instances really are distinct namespaces—each has a distinct attribute dictionary. Although they are normally filled out consistently by class methods, they are more flexible than you might expect.

Finally, you might instead code a more full-blown class to implement your record:

```
>>> class Person:
...     def __init__(self, name, job):
...         self.name = name
...         self.job  = job
...     def info(self):
```

```
...             return (self.name, self.job)
...
>>> mark = Person('ml', 'trainer')
>>> dave = Person('da', 'developer')
>>>
>>> mark.job, dave.info()
('trainer', ('da', 'developer'))
```

This scheme also makes multiple instances, but the class is not empty this time: we've added logic (methods) to initialize instances at construction time, and collect attributes into a tuple. The constructor imposes some consistency on instances here, by always setting name and job attributes.

Eventually, we might add additional logic to compute salaries, parse names, and so on. Ultimately, we might link the class into a larger hierarchy to inherit an existing set of methods by the automatic attribute search of classes, and may even store instances of the class in a file with Python object pickling to make them persistent (more on pickling and persistence in a sidebar, and again later in the book). In the end, although things like dictionaries are flexible, classes allow us to add behavior to objects in ways that built-in types and simple functions do not directly support.

OOP and Inheritance: "is-a" Relationships

We've talked about the mechanics of inheritance in depth already, but we'd like to show you an example of how it can be used to model real-world relationships. From a programmer's point of view, inheritance is kicked off by attribute qualifications, and triggers a search for a name in an instance, its class, and then its superclasses. From a designer's point of view, inheritance is a way to specify set membership: a class defines a set of properties that may be inherited and customized by more specific sets (i.e., subclasses).

To illustrate, let's put that pizza-making robot we talked about at the start of this part of the book to work. Suppose we've decided to explore alternative career paths and open a pizza restaurant. One of the first things we'll need to do is hire employees to serve customers, make the pizza, and so on. Being engineers at heart, we've also decided to build a robot to make the pizzas; but being politically and cybernetically correct, we've also decided to make our robot a full-fledged employee, with a salary.

Our pizza shop team can be defined by the following classes in the example file *employees.py*. It defines four classes and some self-test code. The most general class, Employee, provides common behavior such as bumping up salaries (giveRaise) and printing (__repr__). There are two kinds of employees, and so two subclasses of Employee—Chef and Server. Both override the inherited work method to print more specific messages. Finally, our pizza robot is modeled by an even more specific class:

PizzaRobot is a kind of Chef, which is a kind of Employee. In OOP terms, we call these relationships "is-a" links: a robot is a chef, which is a(n) employee.

```python
class Employee:
    def __init__(self, name, salary=0):
        self.name   = name
        self.salary = salary
    def giveRaise(self, percent):
        self.salary = self.salary + (self.salary * percent)
    def work(self):
        print self.name, "does stuff"
    def __repr__(self):
        return "<Employee: name=%s, salary=%s>" % (self.name, self.salary)

class Chef(Employee):
    def __init__(self, name):
        Employee.__init__(self, name, 50000)
    def work(self):
        print self.name, "makes food"

class Server(Employee):
    def __init__(self, name):
        Employee.__init__(self, name, 40000)
    def work(self):
        print self.name, "interfaces with customer"

class PizzaRobot(Chef):
    def __init__(self, name):
        Chef.__init__(self, name)
    def work(self):
        print self.name, "makes pizza"

if __name__ == "__main__":
    bob = PizzaRobot('bob')       # Make a robot named bob.
    print bob                     # Runs inherited __repr__
    bob.work()                    # Run type-specific action.
    bob.giveRaise(0.20)           # Give bob a 20% raise.
    print bob; print

    for klass in Employee, Chef, Server, PizzaRobot:
        obj = klass(klass.__name__)
        obj.work()
```

When we run this module's self-test code, we create a pizza-making robot named bob, which inherits names from three classes: PizzaRobot, Chef, and Employee. For instance, printing bob runs the Employee.__repr__ method, and giving bob a raise invokes Employee.giveRaise, because that's where inheritance finds it.

```
C:\python\examples> python employees.py
<Employee: name=bob, salary=50000>
bob makes pizza
<Employee: name=bob, salary=60000.0>
```

```
Employee does stuff
Chef makes food
Server interfaces with customer
PizzaRobot makes pizza
```

In a class hierarchy like this, you can usually make instances of any of the classes, not just the ones at the bottom. For instance, the for loop in this module's self-test code creates instances of all four classes; each responds differently when asked to work, because the work method is different in each. Really, these classes just simulate real world objects; work prints a message for the time being, but could be expanded to really work later.

OOP and Composition: "has-a" Relationships

We introduced the notion of composition in Chapter 19. From a programmer's point of view, composition involves embedding other objects in a container object and activating them to implement container methods. To a designer, composition is another way to represent relationships in a problem domain. But rather than set membership, composition has to do with components—parts of a whole. Composition also reflects the relationships between parts; it's usually called a "has-a" relationship. Some OO design texts refer to composition as aggregation (or distinguish between the two terms by using aggregation for a weaker dependency between container and contained); in this text, "composition" simply refers to a collection of embedded objects.

Now that we've implemented our employees, let's put them in the pizza shop and let them get busy. Our pizza shop is a composite object; it has an oven, and employees like servers and chefs. When a customer enters and places an order, the components of the shop spring into action—the server takes an order, the chef makes the pizza, and so on. The following example, file *pizzashop.py*, simulates all the objects and relationships in this scenario:

```python
from employees import PizzaRobot, Server

class Customer:
    def __init__(self, name):
        self.name = name
    def order(self, server):
        print self.name, "orders from", server
    def pay(self, server):
        print self.name, "pays for item to", server

class Oven:
    def bake(self):
        print "oven bakes"
```

```
class PizzaShop:
    def __init__(self):
        self.server = Server('Pat')          # Embed other objects.
        self.chef  = PizzaRobot('Bob')       # A robot named bob
        self.oven  = Oven( )

    def order(self, name):
        customer = Customer(name)            # Activate other objects.
        customer.order(self.server)          # Customer orders from server.
        self.chef.work( )
        self.oven.bake( )
        customer.pay(self.server)

if __name__ == "__main__":
    scene = PizzaShop( )                     # Make the composite.
    scene.order('Homer')                     # Simulate Homer's order.
    print '...'
    scene.order('Shaggy')                    # Simulate Shaggy's order.
```

The PizzaShop class is a container and controller; its constructor makes and embeds
instances of the employee classes we wrote in the last section, as well as an Oven class
defined here. When this module's self-test code calls the PizzaShop order method,
the embedded objects are asked to carry out their actions in turn. Notice that we
make a new Customer object for each order, and pass on the embedded Server object
to Customer methods; customers come and go, but the server is part of the pizza shop
composite. Also notice that employees are still involved in an inheritance relationship; composition and inheritance are complementary tools:

```
C:\python\examples> python pizzashop.py
Homer orders from <Employee: name=Pat, salary=40000>
Bob makes pizza
oven bakes
Homer pays for item to <Employee: name=Pat, salary=40000>
...
Shaggy orders from <Employee: name=Pat, salary=40000>
Bob makes pizza
oven bakes
Shaggy pays for item to <Employee: name=Pat, salary=40000>
```

When we run this module, our pizza shop handles two orders—one from Homer,
and then one from Shaggy. Again, this is mostly just a toy simulation, but the objects
and interactions are representative of composites at work. As a rule of thumb, classes
can represent just about any objects and relationships you can express in a sentence;
just replace *nouns* with classes and *verbs* with methods, and you have a first cut at a
design.

Stream Processors Revisited

For a more realistic composition example, recall the generic data stream processor function partially coded in the introduction to OOP in Chapter 19:

```
def processor(reader, converter, writer):
    while 1:
        data = reader.read( )
        if not data: break
        data = converter(data)
        writer.write(data)
```

Rather than using a simple function here, we might code this as a class that uses composition to do its work, to provide more structure, and support inheritance. File *streams.py* demonstrates one way to code this:

```
class Processor:
    def __init__(self, reader, writer):
        self.reader = reader
        self.writer = writer
    def process(self):
        while 1:
            data = self.reader.readline( )
            if not data: break
            data = self.converter(data)
            self.writer.write(data)
    def converter(self, data):
        assert 0, 'converter must be defined'
```

Coded this way, reader and writer objects are embedded within the class instance (*composition*), and we supply the converter logic in a subclass rather than passing in a converter function (*inheritance*). File *converters.py* shows how:

```
from streams import Processor

class Uppercase(Processor):
    def converter(self, data):
        return data.upper( )

if __name__ == '__main__':
    import sys
    Uppercase(open('spam.txt'), sys.stdout).process( )
```

Here, the Uppercase class inherits the stream processing loop logic (and anything else that may be coded in its superclasses). It needs to define only the thing that is unique about it—the data conversion logic. When this file is run, it makes and runs an instance, which reads from file *spam.txt* and writes the uppercase equivalent of that file to the stdout stream:

```
C:\lp2e> type spam.txt
spam
Spam
SPAM!
```

```
C:\lp2e> python converters.py
SPAM
SPAM
SPAM!
```

To process different sorts of streams, pass in different sorts of objects to the class construction call. Here, we use an output file instead of a stream:

```
C:\lp2e> python
>>> import converters
>>> prog = converters.Uppercase(open('spam.txt'), open('spamup.txt', 'w'))
>>> prog.process()

C:\lp2e> type spamup.txt
SPAM
SPAM
SPAM!
```

But as suggested earlier, we could also pass in arbitrary objects wrapped up in classes that define the required input and output method interfaces. Here's a simple example that passes in a writer class that wraps up the text inside HTML tags:

```
C:\lp2e> python
>>> from converters import Uppercase
>>>
>>> class HTMLize:
...     def write(self, line):
...         print '<PRE>%s</PRE>' % line[:-1]
...
>>> Uppercase(open('spam.txt'), HTMLize()).process()
<PRE>SPAM</PRE>
<PRE>SPAM</PRE>
<PRE>SPAM!</PRE>
```

If you trace through this example's control flow, you'll see that we get both upper-case conversion (by *inheritance*) and HTML formatting (by *composition*), even though the core processing logic in the original Processor superclass knows nothing about either step. The processing code only cares that writers have a write method, and that a method named convert is defined; it doesn't care what those calls do. Such polymorphism and encapsulation of logic is behind much of the power of classes.

As is, the Processor superclass only gives a file-scanning loop. In more real work, we might extend it to support additional programming tools for its subclasses, and in the process turn it into a full-blown *framework*. By coding such tools once in a super-class, they can be reused in all your programs. Even in this simple example, because so much is packaged and inherited with classes, all we had to code here was the HTML formatting step; the rest is free.[*]

---

[*] For another example of composition at work, see this part's "Dead Parrot Sketch" exercise and solution; it's similar to the Pizza shop example.

OOP and Delegation

Object-oriented programmers often talk about something called delegation, which usually implies controller objects that embed other objects, to which they pass off operation requests. The controllers can take care of administrative activities such as keeping track of accesses and so on. In Python, delegation is often implemented with the __getattr__ method hook; because it intercepts accesses to nonexistent attributes, a wrapper class can use __getattr__ to route arbitrary accesses to a wrapped object. Consider file *trace.py*, for instance:

```
class wrapper:
    def __init__(self, object):
```

```
        self.wrapped = object                          # Save object.
    def __getattr__(self, attrname):
        print 'Trace:', attrname                        # Trace fetch.
        return getattr(self.wrapped, attrname)          # Delegate fetch.
```

Recall that __getattr__ gets the attribute name as a string. This code makes use of the getattr built-in function to fetch an attribute from the wrapped object by name string—getattr(X,N) is like X.N, except that N is an expression that evaluates to a string at runtime, not a variable. In fact, getattr(X,N) is similar to X.__dict__[N], but the former also performs inheritance search like X.N (see the prior namespace dictionaries section).

You can use the approach of this module's wrapper class to manage access to any object with attributes—lists, dictionaries, and even classes and instances. Here, the class simply prints a trace message on each attribute access, and delegates the attribute request to the embedded wrapped object:

```
>>> from trace import wrapper
>>> x = wrapper([1,2,3])          # Wrap a list.
>>> x.append(4)                    # Delegate to list method.
Trace: append
>>> x.wrapped                      # Print my member.
[1, 2, 3, 4]

>>> x = wrapper({"a": 1, "b": 2})  # Wrap a dictionary.
>>> x.keys()                       # Delegate to dictionary method.
Trace: keys
['a', 'b']
```

We'll revive the notions of wrapped object and delegated operations as one way to extend built-in types in Chapter 23.

Multiple Inheritance

In the class statement, more than one superclass can be listed in parentheses in the header line. When you do this, you use something called *multiple inheritance*—the class and its instances inherit names from all listed superclasses.

When searching for an attribute, Python searches superclasses in the class header from left to right until a match is found. Technically, the search proceeds depth-first all the way to the top, and then left to right, since any of the superclasses may have superclasses of its own.

In general, multiple inheritance is good for modeling objects that belong to more than one set. For instance, a person may be an engineer, a writer, a musician, and so on, and inherit properties from all such sets.

Perhaps the most common way multiple inheritance is used is to "mix in" general-purpose methods from superclasses. Such superclasses are usually called *mixin classes*—they provide methods you add to application classes by inheritance. For instance, Python's default way to print a class instance object isn't incredibly useful:

```
>>> class Spam:
...     def __init__(self):              # No __repr__
...         self.data1 = "food"
...
>>> X = Spam( )
>>> print X                              # Default: class, address
<__main__.Spam instance at 0x00864818>
```

As seen in the previous section on operator overloading, you can provide a __repr__ method to implement a custom string representation of your own. But rather than code a __repr__ in each and every class you wish to print, why not code it once in a general-purpose tool class, and inherit it in all your classes?

That's what mixins are for. The following code, file *mytools.py*, defines a mixin class called Lister that overloads the __repr__ method for each class that includes Lister in its header line. It simply scans the instance's attribute dictionary (remember, it's exported in __dict__) to build up a string showing the names and values of all instance attributes. Since classes are objects, Lister's formatting logic can be used for instances of any subclass; it's a generic tool.

Lister uses two special tricks to extract the instance's classname and address. Instances have a built-in __class__ attribute that references the class the instance was created from, and classes have a __name__ that is the name in the header, so self.__class__.__name__ fetches the name of an instance's class. You get the instance's memory address by calling the built-in id function, which returns any object's address (by definition, a unique object identifier):

```
############################################
# Lister can be mixed-in to any class to
# provide a formatted print of instances
# via inheritance of __repr__ coded here;
# self is the instance of the lowest class;
############################################

class Lister:
    def __repr__(self):
        return ("<Instance of %s, address %s:\n%s>" %
                       (self.__class__.__name__,      # My class's name
                        id(self),                     # My address
                        self.attrnames()) )           # name=value list
    def attrnames(self):
        result = ''
        for attr in self.__dict__.keys():             # Instance namespace dict
            if attr[:2] == '__':
                result = result + "\tname %s=<built-in>\n" % attr
```

```
        else:
            result = result + "\tname %s=%s\n" % (attr, self.__dict__ [attr])
    return result
```

When derived from this class, instances display their attributes automatically when
printed, which gives a bit more information than a simple address:

```
>>> from mytools import Lister
>>> class Spam(Lister):
...     def __init__(self):
...         self.data1 = 'food'
...
>>> x = Spam( )
>>> x
<Instance of Spam, address 8821568:
    name data1=food
>
```

Now, the Lister class is useful for any class you write—even classes that already
have a superclass. This is where multiple inheritance comes in handy: by adding
(mixing in) Lister to the list of superclasses in a class header, you get its __repr__
for free, while still inheriting from the existing superclass. File *testmixin.py* demonstrates:

```
from mytools import Lister          # Get tool class

class Super:
    def __init__(self):             # superclass __init__
        self.data1 = "spam"

class Sub(Super, Lister):           # Mix-in a __repr__
    def __init__(self):             # Lister has access to self
        Super.__init__(self)
        self.data2 = "eggs"         # More instance attrs
        self.data3 = 42

if __name__ == "__main__":
    X = Sub( )
    print X                         # Mixed-in repr
```

Here, Sub inherits names from both Super and Lister; it's a composite of its own
names and names in both its superclasses. When you make a Sub instance and print
it, you automatically get the custom representation mixed in from Lister:

```
C:\lp2e> python testmixin.py
<Instance of Sub, address 7833392:
    name data3=42
    name data2=eggs
    name data1=spam
>
```

Lister works in any class it's mixed into, because self refers to an instance of the subclass that pulls Lister in, whatever that may be. If you later decide to extend Lister's __repr__ to also print all the class attributes that an instance inherits, you're safe; because it's an inherited method, changing Lister.__repr__ automatically updates the display of each subclass that imports the class and mixes it in.[*]

In some sense, mixin classes are the class equivalent of modules—packages of methods useful in a variety of clients. Here is Lister working again in single-inheritance mode, on a different class's instances; OOP is about code reuse:

```
>>> from mytools import Lister
>>> class x(Lister):
...     pass
...
>>> t = x()
>>> t.a = 1; t.b = 2; t.c = 3
>>> t
<Instance of x, address 7797696:
    name b=2
    name a=1
    name c=3
>
```

Mix-in classes are a powerful technique. In practice, multiple inheritance is an advanced tool and can become complicated if used carelessly or excessively. Like almost everything else in programming, it can be a useful device when applied well. We'll revisit this topic as a *gotcha* at the end of this part of the book. In Chapter 23, we'll also meet an option (new style classes) that modifies the search order for one special multiple inheritance case.

Classes Are Objects: Generic Object Factories

Because classes are objects, it's easy to pass them around a program, store them in data structures, and so on. You can also pass classes to functions that generate arbitrary kinds of objects; such functions are sometimes called *factories* in OOP design circles. They are a major undertaking in a strongly typed language such as C++, but almost trivial in Python: the apply function and syntax we met in Chapter 14 can call

---

[*] If you're curious how, flip back to Chapter 21's section on namespace dictionaries for hints. We saw there that classes have a built-in attribute called __bases__, which is a tuple of the class's superclass objects. A general-purpose class hierarchy lister or browser can traverse from an instance's __class__ to its class, and then from the class's __bases__ to all superclasses recursively, much like the classtree.py example shown earlier. In Python 2.2 and later it may be even simpler: the built-in dir function now includes inherited attribute names automatically. If you don't care about displaying tree structure, you might just scan the dir list instead of the dictionary keys list, and use getattr to fetch attributes by name string instead of dictionary key indexing. We'll rehash this idea in an exercise and its solution.

---

any class with any number of constructor arguments in one step, to generate any sort of instance:[*]

```
def factory(aClass, *args):              # varargs tuple
    return apply(aClass, args)           # Call aClass.

class Spam:
    def doit(self, message):
        print message

class Person:
    def __init__(self, name, job):
        self.name = name
        self.job  = job

object1 = factory(Spam)                  # Make a Spam.
object2 = factory(Person, "Guido", "guru")   # Make a Person.
```

In this code, we define an object generator function, called factory. It expects to be passed a class object (any class will do), along with one or more arguments for the class's constructor. The function uses apply to call the function and return an instance.

The rest of the example simply defines two classes and generates instances of both by passing them to the factory function. And that's the only factory function you ever need write in Python; it works for any class and any constructor arguments. One possible improvement worth noting: to support keyword arguments in constructor calls, the factory can collect them with a **args argument and pass them as a third argument to apply:

```
def factory(aClass, *args, **kwargs):    # +kwargs dict
    return apply(aClass, args, kwargs)   # Call aClass.
```

By now, you should know that everything is an "object" in Python; even things like classes, which are just compiler input in languages like C++. However, as mentioned at the start of Part VI, only objects derived from classes are OOP objects in Python.

Why Factories?

So what good is the factory function (besides giving us an excuse to illustrate class objects in this book)? Unfortunately, it's difficult to show you applications of this design pattern, without listing much more code than we have space for here. In general, though, such a factory might allow code to be insulated from the details of dyamically-configured object construction.

---

[*] Actually, apply can call any callable object; that includes functions, classes, and methods. The factory function here can run any callable, not just a class (despite the argument name).

For instance, recall the processor example presented in the abstract in Chapter 19, and then again as a has-a composition example in this chapter. It accepted reader and writer objects for processing arbitrary data streams. The original version of this example manually passed in instances of specialized classes like FileWriter and SocketReader to customize the data streams being processed; later, we passed in hardcoded file, stream, and formatter objects. In a more dynamic scenario, streams might be configured by external devices such as configuration files or GUIs.

In such a dynamic world, we might not be able to hardcode the creation of stream interface objects in our script, but might instead create them at runtime according to the contents of a configuration file. For instance, the file might simply give the string name of a stream class to be imported from a module, plus an optional constructor call argument. Factory-style functions or code may come in handy here, because we can fetch and pass in classes that are not hardcoded in our program ahead of time. Indeed, those classes might not even have existed at all when we wrote our code:

```
classname = ...parse from config file...
classarg  = ...parse from config file...

import streamtypes                        # Customizable code
aclass = getattr(streamtypes, classname)  # Fetch from module
reader = factory(aclass, classarg)        # or aclass(classarg).
processor(reader, ...)
```

Here, the getattr built-in is used to fetch a module attribute given a string name again (it's like saying obj.attr, but attr is a string). Because this code snippet assumes a single constructor argument, it doesn't strictly need either factory or apply (we could make an instance with just aclass(classarg)); they may prove more useful in the presence of unknown argument lists. The general factory coding pattern, though, can improve code flexibility. For more details on such things, please consult books that cover OOP design and design patterns.

Methods Are Objects: Bound or Unbound

Methods are a kind of object, much like functions. Class methods can be accessed from either an instance or a class; because of this, they actually come in two flavors in Python:

Unbound class method objects: no self
: Accessing a class's function attribute by qualifying a class returns an unbound method object. To call it, you must provide an instance object explicitly as its first argument.

Bound instance method objects: self + *function pairs*
: Accessing a class's function attribute by qualifying an instance returns a bound method object. Python automatically packages the instance with the function in the bound method object, so we don't need to pass an instance to call the method.

Both kinds of methods are full-fledged objects; they can be passed around, stored in lists, and so on. Both also require an instance in their first argument when run (i.e., a value for `self`). This is why we've had to pass in an instance explicitly when calling superclass methods from subclass methods in the previous chapter; technically, such calls produce unbound method objects.

When calling a bound method object, Python provides an instance for you automatically—the instance used to create the bound method object. This means that bound method objects are usually interchangeable with simple function objects, and makes them especially useful for interfaces written originally for functions (see the sidebar on callbacks for a realistic example).

To illustrate, suppose we define the following class:

```
class Spam:
    def doit(self, message):
        print message
```

Now, in normal operation, we make an instance, and call its method in a single step to print the passed argument:

```
object1 = Spam( )
object1.doit('hello world')
```

Really, though, a *bound* method object is generated along the way—just before the method call's parenthesis. In fact, we can fetch a bound method without actually calling it. An `object.name` qualification is an object expression. In the following, it returns a bound method object that packages the instance (`object1`) with the method function (`Spam.doit`). We can assign the bound method to another name, and call it as though it were a simple function:

```
object1 = Spam( )
x = object1.doit        # Bound method object: instance+function
x('hello world')        # Same effect as object1.doit('...')
```

On the other hand, if we qualify the class to get to `doit`, we get back an *unbound* method object, which is simply a reference to the function object. To call this type of method, pass in an instance in the leftmost argument:

```
object1 = Spam( )
t = Spam.doit           # Unbound method object
t(object1, 'howdy')     # Pass in instance.
```

By extension, the same rules apply within a class's method if we reference `self` attributes that refer to functions in the class. A `self.method` is a bound method object, because `self` is an instance object:

```
class  Eggs:
    def m1(self, n):
        print n
    def m2(self):
```

```
        x = self.m1        # Another bound method object
        x(42)              # Looks like a simple function

  Eggs().m2()              # Prints 42
```

Most of the time, you call methods immediately after fetching them with qualification, so you don't always notice the method objects generated along the way. But if you start writing code that calls objects generically, you need to be careful to treat unbound methods specially—they normally require an explicit instance object to be passed in.[*]

Documentation Strings Revisited

Chapter 11 covered docstrings in detail in our look at documentation sources and tools. Docstrings are string literals that show up at the top of various structures, and are saved by Python automatically in object __doc__ attributes. This works for module files, function defs, and classes and methods. Now that we know more about classes and methods, file *docstr.py* provides a quick but comprehensive example that summarizes the places where docstrings can show up in your code; all can be triple-quoted blocks:

```
"I am: docstr.__doc__"

class spam:
    "I am: spam.__doc__ or docstr.spam.__doc__"

    def method(self, arg):
        "I am: spam.method.__doc__ or self.method.__doc__"
        pass

def func(args):
    "I am: docstr.func.__doc__"
    pass
```

The main advantage of documentation strings is that they stick around at runtime; if it's been coded as a documentation string, you can qualify an object to fetch its documentation.

```
>>> import docstr
>>> docstr.__doc__
'I am: docstr.__doc__'

>>> docstr.spam.__doc__
'I am: spam.__doc__ or docstr.spam.__doc__'
```

---

[*] See the upcoming discussion of the *static* and *class* methods extension in Python 2.2, for an optional exception to this rule. Like bound methods, both of these can masquerade as basic functions too, because they do not expect an instance when called.

```
>>> docstr.spam.method.__doc__
'I am: spam.method.__doc__ or self.method.__doc__'

>>> docstr.func.__doc__
'I am: docstr.func.__doc__'
```

The discussion of the PyDoc tool that knows how to format all these strings in reports appears in Chapter 11. Documentation strings are available at runtime, but they are also less flexible syntactically than # comments (which can appear anywhere in a program). Both forms are useful tools, and any program documentation is good (as long as it's accurate).

Why You Will Care: Bound Methods and Callbacks

Because bound methods automatically pair an instance with a class method function, you can use them in any place that a simple function is expected. One of the most common places you'll see this idea put to work is in code that registers methods as event callback handlers in the Tkinter GUI interface. Here's the simple case:

```
def handler():
    ...use globals for state...
...
widget = Button(text='spam', command=handler)
```

To register a handler for button click events, we usually pass a callable object that takes no arguments to the command keyword argument. Function names (and lambdas) work here; so do class methods, as long they are bound methods:

```
class MyWidget:
    def handler(self):
        ...use self.attr for state...
    def makewidgets(self):
        b = Button(text='spam', command=self.handler)
```

Here, the event handler is self.handler—a bound method object that remembers both self and MyGui.handler. Because self will refer to the original instance when handler is later invoked on events, the method will have access to instance attributes that can retain state between events. With simple functions, state normally must be retained in global variables instead. See also the discussion of __call__ operator overloading in Chapter 21 for another way to make classes compatible with function-based APIs.

Classes Versus Modules

Finally, let's wrap up this chapter by comparing the topics of this book's last two parts—modules and classes. Since they're both about namespaces, the distinction can sometimes be confusing. In short:

Modules

- Are data/logic packages
- Are created by writing Python files or C extensions
- Are used by being imported

Classes

- Implement new objects
- Are created by class statements
- Are used by being called
- Always live within a module

Classes also support extra features modules don't, such as operator overloading, multiple instance generation, and inheritance. Although both are namespaces, we hope you can tell by now that they are very different things.

## CHAPTER 23

Advanced Class Topics

Part VI concludes our look at OOP in Python by presenting a few more advanced class-related topics, along with the gotchas and exercises for this part of the book. We encourage you to do the exercises, to help cement the ideas we've studied. We also suggest working on or studying larger OOP Python projects as a supplement to this book. Like much in computing, the benefits of OOP tend to become more apparent with practice.

Extending Built-in Types

Besides implementing new kinds of objects, classes are sometimes used to extend the functionality of Python's built-in types in order to support more exotic data structures. For instance, to add queue insert and delete methods to lists, you can code classes that wrap (embed) a list object, and export insert and delete methods that process the list specially, like the delegation technique studied in Chapter 22. As of Python 2.2, you can also use inheritance to specialize built-in types. The next two sections show both techniques in action.

Extending Types by Embedding

Remember those set functions we wrote in Part IV? Here's what they look like brought back to life as a Python class. The following example, file *setwrapper.py*, implements a new set object type, by moving some of the set functions to methods, and adding some basic operator overloading. For the most part, this class just wraps a Python list with extra set operations. Because it's a class, it also supports multiple instances and customization by inheritance in subclasses.

```
class Set:
    def __init__(self, value = []):    # Constructor
        self.data = []                 # Manages a list
        self.concat(value)
```

```
    def intersect(self, other):        # other is any sequence.
        res = [ ]                       # self is the subject.
        for x in self.data:
            if x in other:              # Pick common items.
                res.append(x)
        return Set(res)                 # Return a new Set.

    def union(self, other):             # other is any sequence.
        res = self.data[:]              # Copy of my list
        for x in other:                 # Add items in other.
            if not x in res:
                res.append(x)
        return Set(res)

    def concat(self, value):            # value: list, Set...
        for x in value:                 # Removes duplicates
            if not x in self.data:
                self.data.append(x)

    def __len__(self):        return len(self.data)          # len(self)
    def __getitem__(self, key): return self.data[key]        # self[i]
    def __and__(self, other): return self.intersect(other)   # self & other
    def __or__(self, other):  return self.union(other)       # self | other
    def __repr__(self):       return 'Set:' + `self.data`    # Print
```

By overloading indexing, the set class can often masquerade as a real list. Since you will interact with and extend this class in an exercise at the end of this chapter, we won't say much more about this code until Appendix B.

Extending Types by Subclassing

Beginning with Python 2.2, all the built-in types can now be subclassed directly. Type conversion functions such as list, str, dict, and tuple, have become built-in type names—although transparent to your script, a type conversion call (e.g., list('spam')) is now really an invocation of a type's object constructor.

This change allows us to customize or extend the behavior of built-in types with user-defined class statements: simply subclass the new type names to customize them. Instances of your type subclasses can be used anywhere that the original built-in type can appear. For example, suppose you have trouble getting used to the fact that Python list offsets begin at 0 instead of 1. Not to worry—you can always code your own subclass that customizes this core behavior of lists. File *typesubclass.py* shows how:

```
# Subclass built-in list type/class.
# Map 1..N to 0..N-1; call back to built-in version.

class MyList(list):
    def __getitem__(self, offset):
        print '(indexing %s at %s)' % (self, offset)
        return list.__getitem__(self, offset - 1)
```

```
if __name__ == '__main__':
    print list('abc')
    x = MyList('abc')               # __init__ inherited from list
    print x                         # __repr__ inherited from list

    print x[1]                      # MyList.__getitem__
    print x[3]                      # Customizes list superclass method

    x.append('spam'); print x       # Attributes from list superclass
    x.reverse();      print x
```

In this file, the MyList subclass extends the built-in list's __getitem__ indexing method only, in order to map indexes 1 to N back to the required 0 to N-1. All it really does is decrement the index submitted, and call back to the superclass's version of indexing, but it's enough to do the trick:

```
% python typesubclass.py
['a', 'b', 'c']
['a', 'b', 'c']
(indexing ['a', 'b', 'c'] at 1)
a
(indexing ['a', 'b', 'c'] at 3)
c
['a', 'b', 'c', 'spam']
['spam', 'c', 'b', 'a']
```

This output also includes tracing text the class prints on indexing. Whether or not changing indexing this way is a good idea in general is another issue—users of your MyList class may very well be confused by such a core departure from Python sequence behavior. The fact that you can customize built-in types this way can be a powerful tool in general, though.

For instance, this coding pattern gives rise to an alternative way to code sets—as a subclass of the built-in list type, rather than a standalone class that manages an embedded list object. The following class, coded in file *setsubclass.py*, customizes lists, to add just methods and operators related to set processing; because all other behavior is inherited from the built-in list superclass, this makes for a shorter and simpler alternative:

```
class Set(list):
    def __init__(self, value = []):     # Constructor
        list.__init__([])               # Customizes list
        self.concat(value)              # Copies mutable defaults

    def intersect(self, other):         # other is any sequence.
        res = []                        # self is the subject.
        for x in self:
            if x in other:              # Pick common items.
                res.append(x)
        return Set(res)                 # Return a new Set.
```

```
    def union(self, other):          # other is any sequence.
        res = Set(self)              # Copy me and my list.
        res.concat(other)
        return res

    def concat(self, value):         # value: list, Set...
        for x in value:              # Removes duplicates
            if not x in self:
                self.append(x)

    def __and__(self, other): return self.intersect(other)
    def __or__(self, other):  return self.union(other)
    def __repr__(self):       return 'Set:' + list.__repr__(self)

if __name__ == '__main__':
    x = Set([1,3,5,7])
    y = Set([2,1,4,5,6])
    print x, y, len(x)
    print x.intersect(y), y.union(x)
    print x & y, x | y
    x.reverse(); print x
```

Here is the output of this script's self-test code at the end of the file. Because subclassing core types is an advanced feature, we will omit further details here, but invite you to trace through these results in the code, to study its behavior:

```
% python setsubclass.py
Set:[1, 3, 5, 7] Set:[2, 1, 4, 5, 6] 4
Set:[1, 5] Set:[2, 1, 4, 5, 6, 3, 7]
Set:[1, 5] Set:[1, 3, 5, 7, 2, 4, 6]
Set:[7, 5, 3, 1]
```

There are more efficient ways to implement sets with dictionaries in Python, that replace the linear scans in the set implementations we've shown, with dictionary index operations (hashing), and so run much quicker. (For more details, see *Programming Python, Second Edition* [O'Reilly]). If you're interested in sets, also see the new set module that was added in Python 2.3 release; this module provides a set object and set operations as built-in tools. Sets are fun to experiment with, but are no longer strictly required as of Python 2.3.

For another type subclass example, see the implementation of the new bool type in Python 2.3: as mentioned earlier, bool is a subclass of int, with two instances True and False that behave like integers 1 and 0, but inherit custom string representation methods that display their names.

Pseudo-Private Class Attributes

In Part IV, we learned that every name assigned at the top level of a file is exported by a module. By default, the same holds for classes—data hiding is a convention, and clients may fetch or change any class or instance attribute they like. In fact, attributes are all "public" and "virtual" in C++ terms; they're all accessible everywhere and all looked up dynamically at runtime.[*]

That's still true today. However, Python also includes the notion of name "mangling" (i.e., expansion), to localize some names in classes. This is sometimes misleadingly called private attributes—really, it's just a way to *localize* a name to the class that created it, and does not prevent access by code outside the class. That is, this feature is mostly intended to avoid namespace collisions in instances, not to restrict access to names in general.

Pseudo-private names are an advanced feature, entirely optional, and probably won't be very useful until you start writing large class hierarchies in multi-programmer projects. But because you may see this feature in other people's code, you need to be somewhat aware of it even if you don't use it in your own.

Name Mangling Overview

Here's how name mangling works. Names inside a class statement that start with two underscores (and don't end with two underscores) are automatically expanded to include the name of the enclosing class. For instance, a name like _ _X within a class named Spam is changed to _Spam_ _X automatically: a single underscore, the enclosing class's name, and the rest of the original name. Because the modified name is prefixed with the name of the enclosing class, it's somewhat unique; it won't clash with similar names created by other classes in a hierarchy.

Name mangling happens only in class statements and only for names you write with two leading underscores. Within a class, though, it happens to every name preceded with double underscores wherever they appear. This includes both method names and instance attributes. For example, an instance attribute reference self._ _X is transformed to self._Spam_ _X. Since more than one class may add attributes to an instance, this mangling helps avoid clashes; but we need to move on to an example to see how.

Why Use Pseudo-Private Attributes?

The problem that the pseudo-private attribute feature is meant to alleviate has to do with the way instance attributes are stored. In Python, all instance attributes wind up in the single instance object at the bottom of the class tree. This is very different from the C++ model, where each class gets its own space for data members it defines.

---

[*] This tends to scare C++ people unnecessarily. In Python, it's even possible to change or completely delete a class method at runtime. On the other hand, nobody ever does, in practical programs. As a scripting language, Python is more about enabling, than restricting.

Within a class method in Python, whenever a method assigns to a self attribute (e.g., self.attr=value), it changes or creates an attribute in the instance (inheritance search only happens on reference, not assignment). Because this is true even if multiple classes in a hierarchy assign to the same attribute, collisions are possible.

For example, suppose that when a programmer codes a class, she assumes that she owns the attribute name X in the instance. In this class's methods, the name is set and later fetched:

```
class C1:
    def meth1(self): self.X = 88        # Assume X is mine.
    def meth2(self): print self.X
```

Suppose further that another programmer, working in isolation, makes the same assumption in a class that he codes:

```
class C2:
    def metha(self): self.X = 99        # Me too
    def methb(self): print self.X
```

Both of these classes work by themselves. The problem arises if these two classes are ever mixed together in the same class tree:

```
class C3(C1, C2): ...
I = C3()                                # Only 1 X in I!
```

Now, the value that each class will get back when it says self.X depends on which class assigned it last. Because all assignments to self.X refer to the same single instance, there is only one X attribute—I.X, no matter how many classes use that attribute name. To guarantee that an attribute belongs to the class that uses it, prefix the name with double underscores everywhere it is used in the class, as in this file, *private.py*:

```
class C1:
    def meth1(self): self.__X = 88      # Now X is mine.
    def meth2(self): print self.__X     # Becomes _C1__X in I

class C2:
    def metha(self): self.__X = 99      # Me too
    def methb(self): print self.__X     # Becomes _C2__X in I

class C3(C1, C2): pass
I = C3()                                # Two X names in I

I.meth1(); I.metha()
print I.__dict__
I.meth2(); I.methb()
```

When thus prefixed, the X attributes are expanded to include the name of the class, before being added to the instance. If you run a dir call on I or inspect its namespace dictionary after the attributes have been assigned, you see the expanded names: _C1__X and _C2__X, but not X. Because the expansion makes the names unique within the instance, the class coders can assume they truly own any names that they prefix with two underscores:

```
% python private.py
{'_C2__X': 99, '_C1__X': 88}
88
99
```

This trick can avoid potential name collisions in the instance, but note that it is not true privacy at all. If you know the name of the enclosing class, you can still access these attributes anywhere you have a reference to the instance, by using the fully expanded name (e.g., I._C1__X=77). On the other hand, this feature makes it less likely that you will *accidentally* step on a class's names.

We should note that this feature tends to become more useful for larger, multi-programmer projects, and then only for selected names. That is, don't clutter your code unnecessarily; only use this feature for names that truly need to be controlled by a single class. For simpler programs, it's probably overkill.

"New Style" Classes in Python 2.2

In Release 2.2, Python introduced a new flavor of classes, known as "new style" classes; the classes covered so far in this part of the book are known as "classic classes" when comparing them to the new kind.

New style classes are only slightly different than classic classes, and the ways in which they differ are completely irrelevent to the vast majority of Python users. Moreover, the classic class model, which has been with Python for over a decade, still works exactly as we have described previously.

New style classes are almost completely backward-compatible with classic classes, in both syntax and behavior; they mostly just add a few advanced new features. However, because they modify one special case of inheritance, they had to be introduced as a distinct tool, so as to avoid impacting any existing code that depends on the prior behavior.

New style classes are coded with all the normal class syntax we have studied. The chief coding difference is that you subclass from a built-in type (e.g., list) to produce a new style class. A new built-in name, object, is provided to serve as a super-class for new style classes if no other built-in type is appropriate to use:

```
class newstyle(object):
    ...normal code...
```

More generally, any object *derived* from object or other built-in type is automatically treated as a new style class. By derived, we mean that this includes subclasses of object, subclasses of subclasses of object, and so on—as long as a built-in is somewhere in the superclass tree. Classes not derived from built-ins are considered classic.

Diamond Inheritance Change

Perhaps the most visible change in new style classes is their slightly different treatment of inheritance for the so-called *diamond* pattern of multiple inheritance trees—where more than one superclass leads to the same higher superclass further above. The diamond pattern is an advanced design concept, which we have not even discussed for normal classes.

In short, with classic classes inheritance search is strictly depth first, and then left to right—Python climbs all the way to the top before it begins to back up and look to the right in the tree. In new style classes, the search is more breadth-first in such cases—Python chooses a closer superclass to the right before ascending all the way to the common superclass at the top. Because of this change, lower superclasses can overload attributes of higher superclasses, regardless of the sort of multiple inheritance trees they are mixed into.

Diamond inheritance example

To illustrate, consider this simplistic incarnation of the diamond inheritance pattern for classic classes:

```
>>> class A:      attr = 1          # Classic
>>> class B(A):   pass
>>> class C(A):   attr = 2
>>> class D(B,C): pass              # Tries A before C
>>> x = D()
>>> x.attr
1
```

The attribute here was found in superclass A, because inheritance climbs as high as it can before backing up and moving right—it searches D, B, A, then C (and stops when attr is found in A above B). With the new style classes derived from a built-in like object, though, inheritance looks in C first (to the right) before A (above B)—it searches D, B, C, then A (and in this case stops in C):

```
>>> class A(object): attr = 1      # New style
>>> class B(A):      pass
>>> class C(A):      attr = 2
>>> class D(B,C):    pass          # Tries C before A
>>> x = D()
>>> x.attr
2
```

This change in inheritance is based upon the assumption that if you mix in C lower in the tree, you probably intend to grab its attributes in preference to A's. It also assumes that C probably meant to override A's attribute *always*—it does when used standalone, but not when mixed into a diamond with classic classes. You might not know that C may be mixed-in like this at the time you code it.

Explicit conflict resolution

Of course, the problem with assumptions is that they assume things. If this search order deviation seems too subtle to remember, or if you want more control over the search process, you can always force the selection of an attribute from anywhere in the tree by assigning or otherwise naming the one you want at the place where classes are mixed together:

```
>>> class A:      attr = 1          # Classic
>>> class B(A):   pass
>>> class C(A):   attr = 2
>>> class D(B,C): attr = C.attr     # Choose C, to the right.
>>> x = D()
>>> x.attr                          # Works like new style
2
```

Here, a tree of classic classes is emulating the search order of new style classes; the assignment to the attribute in D picks the version in C, thereby subverting the normal inheritance search path (D.attr will be lowest in the tree). New style classes can similarly emulate classic classes, by choosing the attribute above at the place where the classes are mixed together:

```
>>> class A(object): attr = 1       # New style
>>> class B(A):      pass
>>> class C(A):      attr = 2
>>> class D(B,C):    attr = B.attr  # Choose A.attr, above.
>>> x = D()
>>> x.attr                          # Works like classic
1
```

If you are willing to always resolve conflicts like this, you can largely ignore the search order difference, and not rely on assumptions about what you meant when you coded your classes. Naturally, the attributes we pick this way can also be method functions—methods are normal, assignable objects:

```
>>> class A:
...     def meth(s): print 'A.meth'
>>> class C(A):
...     def meth(s): print 'C.meth'
>>> class B(A):
...     pass

>>> class D(B,C): pass              # Use default search order.
>>> x = D()                         # Will vary per class type
>>> x.meth()                        # Defaults to classic order
A.meth

>>> class D(B,C): meth = C.meth     # Pick C's method: new style.
>>> x = D()
>>> x.meth()
C.meth
```

```
>>> class D(B,C): meth = B.meth      # Pick B's method: classic.
>>> x = D( )
>>> x.meth( )
A.meth
```

Here, we select methods by assignments to same names lower in the tree. We might also simply call the desired class explicity; in practice, this pattern might be more common, especially for things like constructors:

```
class D(B,C):
    def meth(self):                # Redefine lower.
        ...
        C.meth(self)              # Pick C's method by calling.
```

Such selections by assignment or call at mix-in points can effectively insulate your code from this difference in class flavors. By explicitly resolving the conflict this way, your code won't vary per Python version in the future (apart from perhaps needing to derive classes from a built-in for the new style).[*]

By default, the diamond pattern is searched differently in classic and new style classes, and this is a non-backward compatible change. However, keep in mind that this change only affects diamond pattern cases; new style class inheritance works unchanged for all other inheritance tree structures. Further, it's not impossible that this entire issue may be of more theoretical than practical importance—since it wasn't significant enough to change until 2.2, it seems unlikely to impact much Python code.

Other New Style Class Extensions

Beyond this change in the diamond inheritance pattern (which is itself too obscure to matter to most readers of this book), new style classes open up a handful of even more advanced possibilities. Here's a brief look at each.

Static and class methods

It is possible to define methods within a class that can be called without an instance: *static* methods work roughly like simple instance-less functions inside a class, and *class* methods are passed a class instead of an instance. Special built-in functions must be called within the class to enable these method modes: staticmethod and classmethod. Because this is also a solution to a longstanding gotcha in Python, we'll

---

[*] Even without the classic/new divergence, this technique may sometimes come in handy in *multiple inheritance* scenarios in general. If you want part of a superclass on the left, and part of a superclass on the right, you might need to tell Python which same-named attributes to choose by such explicit assignments in subclasses. We'll revisit this notion in a gotcha at the end of this chapter. Also note that diamond inheritance can be more problematic in some cases than we've implied (e.g., what if B and C both have required constructors that call to A's?), but this is beyond this book's scope.

present these calls later in this chapter in the "Class Gotchas" section. Note that the new static and class methods also work for classic classes in Python release 2.2.

Instance slots

By assigning a list of string attribute names to a special _ _slots_ _ class attribute, it is possible for new style classes to limit the set of legal attributes that instances of the class will have. This special attribute is typically set by assigning to variable _ _slots_ _ at the top level of a class statement. Only those names in the _ _slots_ _ list can be assigned as instance attributes. However, like all names in Python, instance attribute names must still be assigned before they can be referenced, even if listed in _ _slots_ _. Here's an example to illustrate:

```
>>> class limiter(object):
...     __slots__ = ['age', 'name', 'job']

>>> x = limiter()
>>> x.age                        # Must assign before use
AttributeError: age

>>> x.age = 40
>>> x.age
40
>>> x.ape = 1000                 # Illegal: not in slots
AttributeError: 'limiter' object has no attribute 'ape'
```

This feature is envisioned as a way to catch "typo" errors (assignment to illegal attribute names not in _ _slots_ _ is detected) and as a possible optimization mechanism in the future. Slots are something of a break with Python's dynamic nature, which dictates that any name may be created by assignment. They also have additional constraints and implications that are far too complex for us to discuss here (e.g., some instances with slots may not have an attribute dictionary _ _dict_ _); see Python 2.2 release documents for details.

Class properties

A mechanism known as properties provides another way for new style classes to define automatically called methods for access or assignment to instance attributes. This feature is an alternative for many current uses of the _ _getattr_ _ and _ _setattr_ _ overloading methods studied in Chapter 21. Properties have a similar effect to these two methods, but incur an extra method call only for access to names that require dynamic computation. Properties (and slots) are based on a new notion of attribute descriptors, which is too advanced for us to cover here.

In short, properties are a type of object assigned to class attribute names. They are generated by calling a property built-in with three methods (handlers for get, set, and delete operations), as well as a docstring; if any argument is passed as None or omitted, it is not supported. Properties are typically assigned at the top level of a class statement (e.g., name=property(...)). When thus assigned, accesses to the class attribute itself (e.g., obj.name) are automatically routed to one of the accessor methods passed into the property. For example, the __getattr__ method allows classes to intercept undefined attribute references:

```
>>> class classic:
...     def __getattr__(self, name):
...         if name == 'age':
...             return 40
...         else:
...             raise AttributeError
...
>>> x = classic()
>>> x.age                          # Runs __getattr__
40
>>> x.name                         # Runs __getattr__
AttributeError
```

Here is the same example, coded with properties instead:

```
>>> class newprops(object):
...     def getage(self):
...         return 40
...     age = property(getage, None, None, None)      # get,set,del,docs
...
>>> x = newprops()
>>> x.age                          # Runs getage
40
>>> x.name                         # Normal fetch
AttributeError: newprops instance has no attribute 'name'
```

For some coding tasks, properties can be both less complex and quicker to run than the traditional techniques. For example, when we add attribute *assignment* support, properties become more attractive—there's less code to type, and you might not incur an extra method call for assignments to attributes you don't wish to compute dynamically:

```
>>> class newprops(object):
...     def getage(self):
...         return 40
...     def setage(self, value):
...         print 'set age:', value
...         self._age = value
...     age = property(getage, setage, None, None)
...
>>> x = newprops()
>>> x.age                # Runs getage
40
>>> x.age = 42           # Runs setage
set age: 42
>>> x._age               # Normal fetch; no getage call
42
>>> x.job = 'trainer'    # Normal assign; no setage call
```

```
>>> x.job                    # Normal fetch; no getage call
'trainer'
```

The equivalent classic class might trigger extra method calls, and may need to route attribute assignments through the attribute dictionary to avoid loops:

```
>>> class classic:
...     def __getattr__(self, name):           # On undefined reference
...         if name == 'age':
...             return 40
...         else:
...             raise AttributeError
...     def __setattr__(self, name, value):    # On all assignments
...         print 'set:', name, value
...         if name == 'age':
...             self.__dict__['_age'] = value
...         else:
...             self.__dict__[name] = value
...
>>> x = classic()
>>> x.age                    # Runs __getattr__
40
>>> x.age = 41               # Runs __setattr__
set: age 41
>>> x._age                   # Defined: no __getattr__ call
41
>>> x.job = 'trainer'        # Runs __setattr__ again
>>> x.job                    # Defined: no __getattr__ call
```

Properties seem like a win for this simple example. However, some applications of __getattr__ and __setattr__ may still require more dynamic or generic interfaces than properties directly provide. For example, in many cases, the set of attributes to be supported cannot be determined when the class is coded, and may not even exist in any tangible form at all (e.g., when delegating arbitrary method references to a wrapped/embedded object generically). In such cases, a generic __getattr__ or __setattr__ attribute handler with a passed-in attribute name may be an advantage. Because such generic handlers can also handle simpler cases, properties are largely an optional extension.

New __getattribute__ overload method

The __getattribute__ method, available for new style classes only, allows a class to intercept all attribute references, not just undefined references like __getattr__. It is also substantially trickier to use than both __getattr__ or __setattr__ (it is prone to loops). We'll defer to Python's standard documentation for more details.

Besides all these feature additions, new style classes integrate with the notion of subclassable types that we met earlier in this chapter; subclassable types and new style classes were both introduced in conjunction with a merging of the type/class dichotomy in 2.2 and beyond.

Because new style class features are all advanced topics, we are going to skip further details in this introductory text. Please see Python 2.2 release documentation and the language reference for more information.

It is not impossible that new style classes might be adopted as the single class model in future Python releases. If they are, you might simply need to make sure your top-level superclasses are derived from object or other built-in type name (if even that will be required at all); everything else we've studied in this part of the book should continue to work as described.

Class Gotchas

Most class issues can usually be boiled down to namespace issues (which makes sense, given that classes are just namespaces with a few extra tricks). Some of the topics in this section are more like case studies of advanced class usage than problems, and one or two of these have been eased by recent Python releases.

Changing Class Attributes Can Have Side Effects

Theoretically speaking, classes (and class instances) are all *mutable* objects. Just as with built-in lists and dictionaries, they can be changed in place, by assigning to their attributes. And like lists and dictionaries, this also means that changing a class or instance object may impact multiple references to it.

That's usually what we want (and is how objects change their state in general), but this becomes especially critical to know when changing class attributes. Because all instances generated from a class share the class's namespace, any changes at the class level are reflected in all instances, unless they have their own versions of changed class attributes.

Since classes, modules, and instances are all just objects with attribute namespaces, you can normally change their attributes at runtime by assignments. Consider the following class; inside the class body, the assignment to name a generates an attribute X.a, which lives in the class object at runtime and will be inherited by all of X's instances:

```
>>> class X:
...     a = 1        # Class attribute
...
>>> I = X()
>>> I.a              # Inherited by instance
1
>>> X.a
1
```

So far so good—this is the normal case. But notice what happens when we change the class attribute dynamically outside the class statement: it also changes the attribute in every object that inherits from the class. Moreover, new instances created from the class during this session or program get the dynamically set value, regardless of what the class's source code says:

```
>>> X.a = 2          # May change more than X
>>> I.a              # I changes too.
2
>>> J = X()          # J inherits from X's runtime values
>>> J.a              # (but assigning to J.a changes a in J, not X or I).
2
```

Is this a useful feature or a dangerous trap? You be the judge, but you can actually get work done by changing class attributes, without ever making a single instance. This technique can simulate "records" or "structs" in other languages. As a refresher on this technique, consider the following unusual but legal Python program:

```
class X: pass                       # Make a few attribute namespaces.
class Y: pass

X.a = 1                             # Use class attributes as variables.
X.b = 2                             # No instances anywhere to be found
X.c = 3
Y.a = X.a + X.b + X.c

for X.i in range(Y.a): print X.i    # Prints 0..5
```

Here, classes X and Y work like "file-less" modules—namespaces for storing variables we don't want to clash. This is a perfectly legal Python programming trick, but is less appropriate when applied to classes written by others; you can't always be sure that class attributes you change aren't critical to the class's internal behavior. If you're out to simulate a C "struct," you may be better off changing instances than classes, since only one object is affected:

```
class Record: pass
X = Record()
X.name = 'bob'
X.job  = 'Pizza maker'
```

Multiple Inheritance: Order Matters

This may be obvious, but is worth underscoring: if you use multiple inheritance, the order in which superclasses are listed in a class statement header can be critical. Python always searches your superclasses left to right, according to the order in the class header line.

For instance, in the multiple inheritance example we saw in Chapter 22, suppose that the Super implemented a __repr__ method too; would we then want to inherit Lister's or Super's? We would get it from whichever class is listed first in Sub's class header, since inheritance searches left to right. Presumably, we would list Lister first, since its whole purpose is its custom __repr__:

```
class Lister:
    def __repr__(self): ...

class Super:
    def __repr__(self): ...

class Sub(Lister, Super):  # Get Lister's __repr__ by listing it first.
```

But now suppose Super and Lister have their own versions of other same-named attributes, too. If we want one name from Super and another from Lister, no order in the class header will help—we will have to override inheritance by manually assigning to the attribute name in the Sub class:

```
class Lister:
    def __repr__(self): ...
    def other(self): ...

class Super:
    def __repr__(self): ...
    def other(self): ...

class Sub(Lister, Super):  # Get Lister's __repr__ by listing it first
    other = Super.other    # but explicitly pick Super's version of other.
    def __init__(self):
        ...


x = Sub()                  # Inheritance searches Sub before Super/Lister.
```

Here, the assignment to other within the Sub class creates Sub.other—a reference back to the Super.other object. Because it is lower in the tree, Sub.other effectively hides Lister.other, the attribute that inheritance would normally find. Similarly, if we listed Super first in the class header to pick up its other, we would then need to select Lister's method:

```
class Sub(Super, Lister):      # Get Super's other by order.
    __repr__ = Lister.__repr__ # Explicitly pick Lister.__repr__.
```

Multiple inheritance is an advanced tool. Even if you understood the last paragraph, it's still a good idea to use it sparingly and carefully. Otherwise, the meaning of a name may depend on the order in which classes are mixed in an arbitrarily far removed subclass. For another example of the technique shown here in action, see the discussion of explicit conflict resolution in the section "'New Style' Classses in Python 2.2" earlier in this chapter.

As a rule of thumb, multiple inheritance works best when your mix-in classes are as self-contained as possible—since they may be used in a variey of contexts, they should not make assumptions about the names related to other classes in a tree. Moreover, the pseudo-private attributes feature we studied earlier can help by localizing names that the a class relies on owning, and limiting the names that your mix-in classes add to the mix. In the example, if `Lister` only means to export its custom `__repr__`, it could name its other method `__other` to avoid clashing with other classes.

Class Function Attributes Are Special: Static Methods

This gotcha has been fixed by a new optional feature in Python 2.2, *static* and *class* methods, but we retain it here for readers with older Python releases, and because it gives us as good a reason as any for presenting the new static and class methods advanced feature.

In Python releases prior to 2.2, class method functions can never be called without an instance. (In Python 2.2 and later, this is also the default behavior, but it can be modified if necessary.) In the prior chapter, we talked about *unbound* methods: when we fetch a method function by qualifying a class (instead of an instance), we get an unbound method object. Even though they are defined with a def statement, unbound method objects are not simple functions; they cannot be called without an instance.

For example, suppose we want to use class attributes to count how many instances are generated from a class (file *spam.py*, shown below). Remember, class attributes are shared by all instances, so we can store the counter in the class object itself:

```
class Spam:
    numInstances = 0
    def __init__(self):
        Spam.numInstances = Spam.numInstances + 1
    def printNumInstances():
        print "Number of instances created: ", Spam.numInstances
```

But this won't work: the `printNumInstances` method still expects an instance to be passed in when called, because the function is associated with a class (even though there are no arguments in the def header):

```
>>> from spam import *
>>> a = Spam()
>>> b = Spam()
>>> c = Spam()
>>> Spam.printNumInstances()
Traceback (innermost last):
  File "<stdin>", line 1, in ?
TypeError: unbound method must be called with class instance 1st argument
```

Solution (prior to 2.2, and in 2.2 normally)

Don't expect this: unbound instance methods aren't exactly the same as simple functions. This is mostly a knowledge issue, but if you want to call functions that access class members without an instance, probably the best advice is to just make them simple functions, not class methods. This way, an instance isn't expected in the call:

```
def printNumInstances():
    print "Number of instances created: ", Spam.numInstances
```

```
class Spam:
    numInstances = 0
    def __init__(self):
        Spam.numInstances = Spam.numInstances + 1

>>> import spam
>>> a = spam.Spam()
>>> b = spam.Spam()
>>> c = spam.Spam()
>>> spam.printNumInstances()
Number of instances created:  3
>>> spam.Spam.numInstances
3
```

We can also make this work by calling through an instance, as usual, although this can be inconvenient if making an instance changes the class data:

```
class Spam:
    numInstances = 0
    def __init__(self):
        Spam.numInstances = Spam.numInstances + 1
    def printNumInstances(self):
        print "Number of instances created: ", Spam.numInstances

>>> from spam import Spam
>>> a, b, c = Spam(), Spam(), Spam()
>>> a.printNumInstances()
Number of instances created:  3
>>> b.printNumInstances()
Number of instances created:  3
>>> Spam().printNumInstances()
Number of instances created:  4
```

Some language theorists claim that this means Python doesn't have class methods, only instance methods. We suspect they really mean Python classes don't work the same as in some other language. Python really has bound and unbound method objects, with well-defined semantics; qualifying a class gets you an unbound method, which is a special kind of function. Python does have class attributes, but functions in classes expect an instance argument.

Moreover, since Python already provides *modules* as a namespace partitioning tool, there's usually no need to package functions in classes unless they implement object behavior. Simple functions within modules usually do most of what instance-less class methods could. For example, in the first code sample in this section, printNumInstances is already associated with the class, because it lives in the same module. The only lost functionality is that the function name has a broader scope—the entire module, rather than the class.

Static and class methods in Python 2.2

As of Python 2.2, you can code classes with both static and class methods, neither of which require an instance to be present when they are invoked. To designate such methods, classes call the built-in functions staticmethod and classmethod, as hinted in the earlier discussion of new style classes. For example:

```
class Multi:
    def imeth(self, x):        # Normal instance method
        print self, x
    def smeth(x):              # Static: no instance passed
        print x
    def cmeth(cls, x):         # Class: gets class, not instance
        print cls, x
    smeth = staticmethod(smeth)  # Make smeth a static method.
    cmeth = classmethod(cmeth)   # Make cmeth a class method.
```

Notice how the last two assignments in this code simply *reassign* the method names smeth and cmeth. Attributes are created and changed by any assignment in a class statement, so these final assignments overwrite the assignments made earlier by the defs.

Technically, Python 2.2 supports three kinds of class-related methods: instance, static, and class. *Instance methods* are the normal (and default) case that we've seen in this book. With instance methods, you always must call the method with an instance object. When you call through an instance, Python passes the instance to the first (leftmost) argument automatically; when called through the class, you pass along the instance manually:

```
>>> obj = Multi()          # Make an instance
>>> obj.imeth(1)           # Normal call, through instance
<__main__.Multi instance...> 1
>>> Multi.imeth(obj, 2)    # Normal call, through class
<__main__.Multi instance...> 2
```

By contrast, *static methods* are called without an instance argument; their names are local to the scope of the class they are defined in, and may be looked up by inheritance; mostly, they work like simple functions that happen to be coded inside a class:

```
>>> Multi.smeth(3)         # Static call, through class
3
>>> obj.smeth(4)           # Static call, through instance
4
```

Class methods are similar, but Python automatically passes the class (not an instance) in to the method's first (leftmost) argument:

```
>>> Multi.cmeth(5)         # Class call, through class
__main__.Multi 5
>>> obj.cmeth(6)           # Class call, through instance
__main__.Multi 6
```

Static and class methods are new and advanced features of the language. They have highly specialized roles that we don't have space to document here. Static methods are commonly used in conjunction with class attributes to manage information that spans all instances generated from the class.

For example, to keep track of the number of instances generated from a class (as in the earlier example), you may use static methods to manage a counter attached as a class attribute. Since such a count has nothing to do with any particular instance, it is inconvenient to have to access methods that process it through an instance (especially since making an instance to access the counter may change the counter). Moreover, static methods' proximity to the class provides a more natural solution than coding class-oriented functions outside the class. Here is the static method equivalent of this section's original example:

```
class Spam:
    numInstances = 0
    def __init__(self):
        Spam.numInstances += 1
    def printNumInstances():
        print "Number of instances:", Spam.numInstances
    printNumInstances = staticmethod(printNumInstances)
```

```
>>> a = Spam()
>>> b = Spam()
>>> c = Spam()
>>> Spam.printNumInstances()
Number of instances: 3
>>> a.printNumInstances()
Number of instances: 3
```

Compared to simply moving printNumInstances outside the class as prescribed earlier, this version requires an extra staticmethod call, but localizes the function name in the class scope, and moves the function code closer to where it is used (inside the class statement). You should judge for yourself whether this is a net improvement or not.

Methods, Classes, and Nested Scopes

This gotcha went away in Python 2.2, with the introduction of nested function scopes, but we retain it here for historical perspective, for readers working with older Python releases, and because it demonstrates what happens to the new nested function scope rules when a class is a layer of the nesting.

Classes introduce a local scope just as functions do, so the same sorts of scope behavior can happen in a class statement body. Moreover, methods are further nested functions, so the same issues apply. Confusion seems to be especially common when classes are nested.

In the following example, file *nester.py*, the generate function returns an instance of the nested Spam class. Within its code, the class name Spam is assigned in the generate function's local scope. But within the class's method function, the class name Spam is not visible in Python prior to 2.2 where method has access only to its own local scope, the module surrounding generate, and built-in names:

```
def generate():
    class Spam:
        count = 1
        def method(self):          # Name Spam not visible:
            print Spam.count       # not local(def),global(module), built-in
    return Spam()

generate().method()
```

```
C:\python\examples> python nester.py
Traceback (innermost last):
  File "nester.py", line 8, in ?
    generate().method()
  File "nester.py", line 5, in method
    print Spam.count               # Not local(def),global(module), built-in
NameError: Spam
```

As a solution, either upgrade to Python 2.2, or don't nest code this way. This example works in Python 2.2 and later, because the local scopes of all enclosing function defs are automatically visible to nested defs, including nested *method* defs, as in this example.

Note that even in 2.2, method defs cannot see the local scope of the enclosing *class*, only the local scope of enclosing defs. That's why methods must go through the self instance or the class name, to reference methods and other attributes defined in the enclosing class statement. For example, code in the method must use self.count or Spam.count, not just count.

Prior to release 2.2, there are a variety of ways to get the example above to work. One of the simplest is to move the name Spam out to the enclosing module's scope with global declarations; since method sees global names in the enclosing module, references work:

```
def generate():
    global Spam                    # Force Spam to module scope.
    class Spam:
        count = 1
        def method(self):
            print Spam.count       # Works: in global (enclosing module)
    return Spam()

generate().method()                # Prints 1
```

Perhaps better, we can also restructure the code such that class Spam is defined at the top level of the module by virtue of its nesting level, rather than global declarations. Both the nested method function and the top level generate find Spam in their global scopes:

```
def generate():
    return Spam()
```

```
    class Spam:                     # Define at module top-level.
        count = 1
        def method(self):
            print Spam.count        # Works: in global (enclosing module)

    generate().method()
```

In fact, this is what we prescribe for all Python releases—your code tends to be simpler in general if you avoid nesting of classes and functions.

If you want to get complicated and tricky, you can also get rid of the Spam reference in method altogether, by using the special __class__ attribute, which returns an instance's class object:

```
    def generate():
        class Spam:
            count = 1
            def method(self):
                print self.__class__.count      # Works: qualify to get class
        return Spam()

    generate().method()
```

Overwrapping-itis

Sometimes, the abstraction potential of OOP can be abused to the point of making code difficult to understand. If your classes are layered too deeply, it can make code obscure; you may have to search through many classes to discover what an operation does. For example, one of your authors once worked in a C++ shop with thousands of classes (some generated by machine), and up to 15 levels of inheritance; deciphering a method call in such a complex system was often a monumental task. Multiple classes had to be consulted for even the most basic of operations.

The most general rule of thumb applies here too: don't make things complicated unless they truly must be. Wrapping your code in multiple layers of classes to the point of incomprehensibility is always a bad idea. Abstraction is the basis of polymorphism and encapsulation, and can be a very effective tool when used well. But you'll simplify debugging and aid maintainability, if you make your class interfaces intuitive, avoid making code overly abstract, and keep your class hierarchies short and flat unless there is a good reason to do otherwise.

Part VI Exercises

These exercises ask you to write a few classes and experiment with some existing code. Of course, the problem with existing code is that it must be existing. To work with the set class in exercise 5, either pull down the class source code off the Internet (see the Preface) or type it up by hand (it's fairly small). These programs are starting to get more sophisticated, so be sure to check the solutions at the end of the book for pointers.

Why You Will Care: OOP by the Masters

When I (Mark) teach Python classes, invariably, about halfway through the class, people who have used OOP in the past are following along intensely; people who have not are beginning to glaze over (or nod off completely). The point behind the technology just isn't apparent.

In a book like this, we have the luxury of adding overview material like the new "Big Picture" overview in Chapter 19, and you should probably review that section if you're starting to feel like OOP is just some computer science mumbo-jumbo.

In real classes, however, to help get the newcomers on board (and awake), I have been known to stop and ask the experts in the audience why they use OOP at all. The answers they've given might help shed some light on the purpose of OOP, if you are new to the subject.

Here, then, with only a few embellishments, are the most common reasons to use OOP, as cited by my students over the years:

Code reuse

> This one's easy (and is the main reason for using OOP). By supporting inheritance, classes allow you to program by customization, instead of starting each project from scratch.

Encapsulation

> By wrapping up implementation details behind object interfaces, users of a class are insulated from code changes.

Structure

> Classes provide a new local scope, which minimizes name clashes. They also provide a natural place to write and look for implementation code, and manage object state.

Maintenance

> Thanks both to the structure and code reuse support of classes, there is usually only one copy of code to be changed.

Consistency

> Classes and inheritance allow you to implement common interfaces, and hence a common look-and-feel in your code; this eases debugging, comprehension, and maintenance.

Polymorphism

> This is more a property of OOP than a reason; but by supporting generality of code, polymorphism makes that code more flexible and widely applicable, and hence more reusable.

And of course, the number-one reason students gave for using OOP: it looks good on a resume.

Finally, keep in mind what we said at the beginning of Part VI: you won't fully appreciate OOP until you've used it for a while. Pick a project, study larger examples, work through the exercises—whatever it takes to get your feet wet with OO code; it's worth the effort.

1. *Inheritance.* Write a class called `Adder` that exports a method `add(self, x, y)` that prints a "Not Implemented" message. Then define two subclasses of `Adder` that implement the add method:

   `ListAdder`
   > With an `add` method that returns the concatenation of its two list arguments

   `DictAdder`
   > With an `add` method that returns a new dictionary with the items in both its two dictionary arguments (any definition of addition will do)

   Experiment by making instances of all three of your classes interactively and calling their add methods.

   Now, extend your `Adder` superclass to save an object in the instance with a constructor (e.g., assign `self.data` a list or a dictionary) and overload the + operator with an `__add__` to automatically dispatch to your add methods (e.g., X+Y triggers X.add(X.data,Y)). Where is the best place to put the constructors and operator overload methods (i.e., in which classes)? What sorts of objects can you add to your class instances?

   In practice, you might find it easier to code your add methods to accept just one real argument (e.g., `add(self,y)`), and add that one argument to the instance's current data (e.g., `self.data+y`). Does this make more sense than passing two arguments to `add`? Would you say this makes your classes more "object-oriented"?

2. *Operator overloading.* Write a class called `Mylist` that shadows ("wraps") a Python list: it should overload most list operators and operations including +, indexing, iteration, slicing, and list methods such as `append` and `sort`. See the Python reference manual for a list of all possible methods to support. Also, provide a constructor for your class that takes an existing list (or a `Mylist` instance) and copies its components into an instance member. Experiment with your class interactively. Things to explore:

   a. Why is copying the initial value important here?

   b. Can you use an empty slice (e.g., `start[:]`) to copy the initial value if it's a `Mylist` instance?

   c. Is there a general way to route list method calls to the wrapped list?

   d. Can you add a `Mylist` and a regular list? How about a list and a `Mylist` instance?

   e. What type of object should operations like + and slicing return; how about indexing?

   f. If you are working with a more recent Python release (Version 2.2 or later), you may implement this sort of wrapper class either by embedding a real list in a standalone class, or by extending the built-in list type with a subclass. Which is easier and why?

3. *Subclassing*. Make a subclass of `Mylist` from Exercise 2 called `MylistSub`, which extends `Mylist` to print a message to `stdout` before each overloaded operation is called and counts the number of calls. `MylistSub` should inherit basic method behavior from `Mylist`. Adding a sequence to a `MylistSub` should print a message, increment the counter for + calls, and perform the superclass's method. Also, introduce a new method that displays the operation counters to `stdout` and experiment with your class interactively. Do your counters count calls per instance, or per class (for all instances of the class)? How would you program both of these? (Hint: it depends on which object the count members are assigned to: class members are shared by instances, `self` members are per-instance data.)

4. *Metaclass methods*. Write a class called `Meta` with methods that intercept every attribute qualification (both fetches and assignments) and prints a message with their arguments to `stdout`. Create a `Meta` instance and experiment with qualifying it interactively. What happens when you try to use the instance in expressions? Try adding, indexing, and slicing the instance of your class.

5. *Set objects*. Experiment with the set class described in the section "Extending Types by Embedding." Run commands to do the following sorts of operations:

    a. Create two sets of integers, and compute their intersection and union by using & and | operator expressions.

    b. Create a set from a string, and experiment with indexing your set; which methods in the class are called?

    c. Try iterating through the items in your string set using a `for` loop; which methods run this time?

    d. Try computing the intersection and union of your string set and a simple Python string; does it work?

    e. Now, extend your set by subclassing to handle arbitrarily many operands using a `*args` argument form (Hint: see the function versions of these algorithms in Chapter 13). Compute intersections and unions of multiple operands with your set subclass. How can you intersect three or more sets, given that & has only two sides?

    f. How would you go about emulating other list operations in the set class? (Hints: `__add__` can catch concatenation, and `__getattr__` can pass most list method calls off to the wrapped list.)

6. *Class tree links*. In the section "Namespaces: The Whole Story" in Chapter 21, and in the section "Multiple Inheritance" in Chapter 22, we mentioned that classes have a `__bases__` attribute that returns a tuple of the class's superclass objects (the ones in parentheses in the class header). Use `__bases__` to extend the `Lister` mixin class (see Chapter 22), so that it prints the names of the immediate superclasses of the instance's class. When you're done, the first line of the string representation should look like this (your address may vary):

```
<Instance of Sub(Super, Lister), address 7841200:
```

How would you go about listing inherited class attributes too? (Hint: classes have a __dict__.) Try extending your Lister class to display all accessible super-classes and their attributes as well; see Chapter 21's *classtree.py* example for hints on climbing class trees, and the Lister footnote about using dir and getattr in Python 2.2 for hints on climbing trees.

7. *Composition*. Simulate a fast-food ordering scenario by defining four classes:

Lunch
> A container and controller class

Customer
> The actor that buys food

Employee
> The actor that a customer orders from

Food
> What the customer buys

To get you started, here are the classes and methods you'll be defining:

```
class Lunch:
    def __init__(self)        # Make/embed Customer and Employee.
    def order(self, foodName) # Start a Customer order simulation.
    def result(self)          # Ask the Customer what kind of Food it has.

class Customer:
    def __init__(self)                        # Initialize my food to None.
    def placeOrder(self, foodName, employee)  # Place order with an Employee.
    def printFood(self)                       # Print the name of my food.

class Employee:
    def takeOrder(self, foodName)    # Return a Food, with requested name.

class Food:
    def __init__(self, name)       # Store food name.
```

The order simulation works as follows:

a. The Lunch class's constructor should make and embed an instance of Customer and Employee, and export a method called order. When called, this order method should ask the Customer to place an order, by calling its placeOrder method. The Customer's placeOrder method should in turn ask the Employee object for a new Food object, by calling the Employee's takeOrder method.

b. Food objects should store a food name string (e.g., "burritos"), passed down from Lunch.order to Customer.placeOrder, to Employee.takeOrder, and finally to Food's constructor. The top-level Lunch class should also export a method called result, which asks the customer to print the name of the food it received from the Employee via the order (this can be used to test your simulation).

Note that Lunch needs to either pass the Employee to the Customer, or pass itself to the Customer, in order to allow the Customer to call Employee methods.

Experiment with your classes interactively by importing the Lunch class, calling its order method to run an interaction, and then calling its result method to verify that the Customer got what he or she ordered. If you prefer, you can also simply code test cases as self-test code in the file where your classes are defined, using the module __name__ trick in Chapter 18. In this simulation, the Customer is the active agent; how would your classes change if Employee were the object that initiated customer/ employee interaction instead?

8. *Zoo Animal Hierarchy*: Consider the class tree shown in Figure 23-1. Code a set of six class statements to model this taxonomy with Python inheritance. Then, add a speak method to each of your classes that prints a unique message, and a reply method in your top-level Animal superclass that simply calls self.speak to invoke the category-specific message printer in a subclass below (this will kick off an independent inheritance search from self). Finally, remove the speak method from your Hacker class, so that it picks up the default above it. When you're finished, your classes should work this way:

```
% python
>>> from zoo import Cat, Hacker
>>> spot = Cat( )
>>> spot.reply( )              # Animal.reply; calls Cat.speak
meow
>>> data = Hacker( )           # Animal.reply; calls Primate.speak
>>> data.reply( )
Hello world!
```

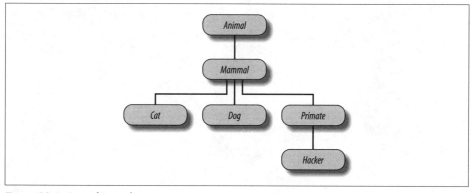

Figure 23-1. A zoo hierarchy

9. *The Dead Parrot Sketch*: Consider the object embedding structure captured in Figure 23-2. Code a set of Python classes to implement this structure with composition. Code your Scene object to define an action method, and embed instances of Customer, Clerk, and Parrot classes—all three of which should define a line method that prints a unique message. The embedded objects may

either inherit from a common superclass that defines line and simply provide message text, or define line themselves. In the end, your classes should operate like this:

```
% python
>>> import parrot
>>> parrot.Scene().action()          # Activate nested objects.
customer: "that's one ex-bird!"
clerk: "no it isn't..."
parrot: None
```

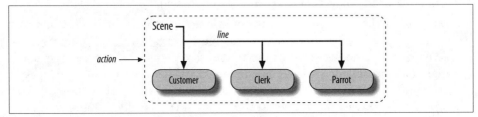

Figure 23-2. A scene composite

Exceptions and Tools

In Part VII, we study exceptions, which are software events generated by Python on errors, or by your program on demand. Exceptions can be caught and ignored, or allowed to pass and terminate a program with a standard error message. Because of this, Part VII is also a part of the debugging story in Python. As we'll see, although standard error messages are often enough to analyse a problem, exception handling is a lightweight tool that offers more control.

Part VII also begins the transition from core language topics to peripheral tool topics. Strictly speaking, exceptions are the last core language topic we'll meet in the book; after Part VII, we deal with tools in the standard library and public domain, beyond the language itself. We conclude Part VII with an overview of tools that are useful when developing larger applications in Python.

## CHAPTER 24

Exception Basics

Part VII deals with *exceptions*, which are events that can modify the flow of control through a program. In Python, exceptions are triggered automatically on errors, and can be both triggered and intercepted by your code. They are processed by three statements we'll study in this part, the first of which has two variations:

try/except
: Catch and recover from exceptions raised by Python, or by you.

try/finally
: Perform cleanup actions whether exceptions occur or not.

raise
: Trigger an exception manually in your code.

assert
: Conditionally trigger an exception in your code.

With a few exceptions (pun intended), we'll find that exception handling is simple in Python, because it's integrated into the language itself as another high-level tool.

Why Use Exceptions?

In a nutshell, exceptions let us jump out of arbitrarily large chunks of a program. Consider the pizza-making robot we talked about earlier in the book. Suppose we took the idea seriously and actually built such a machine. To make a pizza, our culinary automaton would need to execute a plan, which we implement as a Python program. It would take an order, prepare the dough, add toppings, bake the pie, and so on.

Now, suppose that something goes very wrong during the "bake the pie" step. Perhaps the oven is broken. Or perhaps our robot miscalculates its reach and spontaneously bursts into flames. Clearly, we want to be able to jump to code that handles such states quickly. Since we have no hope of finishing the pizza task in such unusual cases, we might as well abandon the entire plan.

That's exactly what exceptions let you do; you can jump to an exception handler in a single step, abandoning all suspended function calls. They're a sort of structured "super-goto."* An exception handler (try statement) leaves a marker and executes some code. Somewhere further ahead in the program, an exception is raised that makes Python jump back to the marker immediately, without resuming any active functions that were called since the marker was left. Code in the exception handler can respond to the raised exception as appropriate (calling the fire department, for instance). Moreover, because Python jumps to the handler statement immediately, there is usually no need to check status codes after every call to a function that could possibly fail.

Exception Roles

In Python programs, exceptions are typically used for a variety of purposes. Here are some of their most common roles:

Error handling

Python raises exceptions whenever it detects errors in programs at runtime. You can either catch and respond to the errors in your code, or ignore the exception. If the error is ignored, Python's default exception-handling behavior kicks in—it stops the program and prints an error message. If you don't want this default behavior, code a try statement to catch and recover from the exception—Python jumps to your try handler when the error is detected, and your program resumes execution after the try.

Event notification

Exceptions can also signal a valid condition, without having to pass result flags around a program or test them explicitly. For instance, a search routine might raise an exception on failure, rather than returning an integer result code (and hoping that the code will never be a valid result).

Special-case handling

Sometimes a condition may happen so rarely that it's hard to justify convoluting your code to handle it. You can often eliminate special-case code by handling unusual cases in exception handlers instead.

Termination actions

As we'll see, the try/finally statement allows us to guarantee that required closing-time operations will be performed, regardless of the presence or absence of exceptions in our program.

---

* If you've used C, you may be interested to know that Python exceptions are roughly similar to C's setjmp/longjmp standard function pair. The try statement acts much like a setjmp, and raise works like a longjmp. But in Python, exceptions are based on objects and are a standard part of the execution model.

Unusual control-flows

And finally, because exceptions are a sort of high-level "goto," you can use them as the basis for implementing exotic control flows. For instance, although back-tracking is not part of the language itself, it can be implemented in Python with exceptions and a bit of support logic to unwind assignments.*

We'll see such typical uses in action later in this part of the book. First, let's get started with a look at Python's exception-processing tools.

Exception Handling: The Short Story

Compared to some other core language topics we've met, exceptions are a fairly light-weight tool in Python. Because they are so simple, let's jump right into an initial example. Suppose you've coded the following function:

```
>>> def fetcher(obj, index):
...     return obj[index]
```

There's not much to this function—it simply indexes an object on a passed-in index. In normal operation, it returns the result of legal indexes:

```
>>> x = 'spam'
>>> fetcher(x, 3)         # Like x[3]
'm'
```

However, if you ask this function to index off the end of your string, you will trigger an exception when your function tries to run obj[index]. Python detects out-of-bounds sequence indexing, and reports it by *raising* (triggering) the built-in IndexError exception:

```
>>> fetcher(x, 4)
Traceback (most recent call last):
  File "<stdin>", line 1, in ?
  File "<stdin>", line 2, in fetcher
IndexError: string index out of range
```

Technically, because this exception is not caught by your code, it reaches the top level of the program and invokes the *default exception handler*—which simply prints the standard error message. By this point in the book, you've probably seen your share of standard error messages. They include the exception that was raised, along with a *stack trace*—a list of the lines and functions active when the exception occurred. When coding interactively, the file is just "stdin" (standard input stream) or "pyshell" (in IDLE), so file line numbers are not very meaningful here.

---

* True backtracking is an advanced topic that is not part of the Python language (even with addition of generator functions in 2.2), so we won't say more about it here. Roughly, backtracking undoes all computation before it jumps; Python exceptions do not (e.g., variables assigned between the time a try statement is entered and an exception is raised are not reset to their prior values). See a book on artificial intelligence or the Prolog or icon programming languages if you're curious.

In a more realistic program launched outside the interactive prompt, the default handler at the top also *terminates* the program immediately. That course of action makes sense for simple scripts; errors often should be fatal, and the best you can do is inspect the standard error message. Sometimes this isn't what you want, though. Server programs, for instance, typically need to remain active even after internal errors. If you don't want the default exception behavior, wrap the call in a try statement to catch the exception yourself:

```
>>> try:
...     fetcher(x, 4)
... except IndexError:
...     print 'got exception'
...
got exception
>>>
```

Now, Python jumps to your *handler* (the block under the except clause that names the exception raised) automatically when the exception is triggered while the try block runs. When working interactively like this, after the except clause runs we wind up back at the Python prompt. In a more realistic program, try statements not only *catch* exceptions, but also *recover* from them:

```
>>> def catcher():
...     try:
...         fetcher(x, 4)
...     except IndexError:
...         print 'got exception'
...     print 'continuing'
...
>>> catcher()
got exception
continuing
>>>
```

This time, after the exception is caught and handled, the program resumes execution after the entire try statement that caught it—which is why we get the "continuing" message here. You won't see the standard error message, and your program will continue on its way normally.

Exceptions can be raised both by Python and you, and can be caught or not. To trigger an exception manually, simply run a raise (or assert) statement; user-defined exceptions are caught the same way as built-ins:

```
>>> bad = 'bad'
>>> try:
...     raise bad
... except bad:
...     print 'got bad'
...
got bad
```

If not caught, user-defined exceptions reach the top-level default exception handler, and terminate your program with a standard error message. In this case, the standard message includes the text of the string used to identify the exception:

```
>>> raise bad
Traceback (most recent call last):
  File "<pyshell#18>", line 1, in ?
    raise bad
bad
```

In other cases, the error message may include text provided by *classes* used to identify exceptions. As we'll see in the next chapter, class-based exceptions allow scripts to build exception categories (and other things):

```
>>> class Bad: pass
...
>>> def doomed(): raise Bad()
...
>>> try:
...     doomed()
... except Bad:
...     print 'got Bad'
...
got Bad
>>>
```

Finally, try statements can also say finally: the try/finally combination specifies termination actions that always execute "on the way out"—whether an exception happens in the try block or not:

```
>>> try:
...     fetcher(x, 3)
... finally:
...     print 'after fetch'
...
'm'
after fetch
```

Here, when the try block finishes without an exception, the finally block runs, and then the program resumes after the entire try. In this case, this statement seems a bit silly—we might as well have simply typed the print right after a call to the function, and skipped try altogether:

```
fetcher(x, 3)
print 'after fetch'
```

There is a problem with coding this way, though: if the function call raises an exception, we will never reach the print. The try/finally lets us do better—when an exception does occur in the try block, finally blocks are executed while the program is being unwound:

```
>>> def after():
...     try:
...         fetcher(x, 4)
```

```
...      finally:
...          print 'after fetch'
...      print 'after try?'
...
>>> after()
after fetch
Traceback (most recent call last):
  File "<stdin>", line 1, in ?
  File "<stdin>", line 3, in after
  File "<stdin>", line 2, in fetcher
IndexError: string index out of range
```

Here, we didn't get the "after try?" message, because control does not resume after the try/finally when an exception occurs. Instead, Python jumps back to run the finally action, but then keeps *propagating* the exception to a prior handler (in this case, to the default handler at the top). If you change the call inside this function so as not to trigger an exception, the finally code still runs, but the program continues after the try:

```
>>> def after():
...      try:
...          fetcher(x, 3)
...      finally:
...          print 'after fetch'
...      print 'after try?'
...
>>> after()
after fetch
after try?
>>>
```

In practice, try/except combinations are useful for catching and recovering from exceptions, and try/finally comes in handy to guarantee that termination actions will fire regardless of the exceptions that may occur in the try block's code. For instance, you might use try/except to catch errors raised by code that you import from a third-party library, and try/finally to ensure that calls to close files or terminate server connections are always run. We'll see some such practical examples later in this part of the book.

That is a majority of the exception story; it really is a simple tool. In the rest of this part, we'll fill in some of the details of the statements involved, show you the other sorts of clauses that can appear under a try, and discuss string and class-based exception objects.

Python exceptions are a high-level control flow device. They may be raised either by Python or by your own programs; in both cases, they may be ignored (to trigger the default error message), or may be caught by try statements (to be processed by your code). Python's raise and assert statements trigger exceptions on demand. The try statement comes in two formats—one that handles exceptions and one that executes finalization code whether exceptions occur or not. Let's take a deeper look at these statements' general forms.

The try/except/else Statement

The try is another compound statement; its most complete form is sketched below. It starts with a try header line followed by a block of (usually) indented statements, then one or more except clauses that identify exceptions to be caught, and an optional else clause at the end. The words try, except, and else are associated by indenting them the same—they line up vertically. For reference, here's the general format:

```
try:
    <statements>          # Run this action first.
except <name1>:
    <statements>          # Run if name1 is raised during try block.
except <name2>, <data>:
    <statements>          # Run if name2 is raised, and get extra data.
except (name3, name4):
    <statements>          # Run if any of these exceptions occur.
except:
    <statements>          # Run for all (other) exceptions raised.
else:
    <statements>          # Run if no exception was raised by try block.
```

In this statement, the block under the try header represents that *main action* of the statement—the code you're trying to run. The except clauses define *handlers* for exceptions raised during the try block, and the else clause (if coded) provides a handler to be run if *no* exception occurs. The <data> entry here has to do with a feature of raise statements we will discuss later in this chapter.

Here's how try statements work. When a try statement is started, Python marks the current program context, so it can come back if an exception occurs. The statements nested under the try header are run first. What happens next depends on whether exceptions are raised while the try block's statements are running:

- If an exception occurs while the try block's statements are running, Python jumps back to the try and runs the statements under the first except clause that matches the raised exception. Control continues past the entire try statement after the except block runs (unless the except block raises another exception).

- If an exception happens in the try block and *no* except clause matches, the exception is propagated up to a try that was entered earlier in the program, or to the top level of the process (which makes Python kill the program and print a default error message).

- If no exception occurs while the statements under the try header run, Python runs the statements under the else line (if present), and control then resumes past the entire try statement.

In other words, except clauses catch exceptions that may happen while the try block is running, and the else clause is run only if no exceptions happen while the try block runs.

The except clauses are focused exception handlers—they catch exceptions that occur only within the statements in the associated try block. However, since the try block's statements can call functions coded elsewhere in a program, the source of an exception may be outside the try statement itself. More on this when we explore try nesting in Chapter 26.

Try Statement Clauses

When you write try statements, a variety of clauses can appear after the try statement block; Table 24-1 summarizes all the possible forms, and you must use at least one. We've already met some of these—except clauses catch exceptions, finally runs on the way out, and so on. Syntactically, there may be any number of except clauses, but there should be only one else. Moreover, the finally clause must appear alone (without else or except); it's really a different statement.

Table 24-1. try statement clause forms

Clause form	Interpretation
except:	Catch all (other) exception types.
except name:	Catch a specific exception only.
except name, value:	Catch exception and its extra data.
except (name1, name2):	Catch any of the listed exceptions.
except (name1, name2), value	Catch any, and get the extra data.
else:	Run block if no exceptions raised.
finally:	Always perform block.

We'll explore the entries with the extra value part when we meet the raise statement. The first and fourth entries in Table 24-1 are new here:

- except clauses that list no exception name catch *all* exceptions not previously listed in the try statement (except:).

- except clauses that list a set of exceptions in parenthesis catch *any* of the listed exceptions (except (e1,e2,e3)).

Since Python looks for a match within a given try by inspecting except clauses from top to bottom, the parenthesized version is like listing each exception in its own except clause, but the statement body needs to be coded only once. Here's an example of multiple except clauses at work, which demonstrates just how specific your handlers can be:

```
try:
    action( )
except NameError:
    ...
except IndexError:
    ...
```

```
        except KeyError:
            ...
        except (AttributeError, TypeError, SyntaxError):
            ...
        else:
            ...
```

In this example, when an exception is raised while the call to the action function is running, Python returns to the try and searches for the first except that names the exception raised. It inspects except clauses from top to bottom and left to right, and runs the statements under the first one that matches. If none match, the exception is propagated past this try.

Note that the else runs only when *no* exception occurred in action, not for other exceptions raised. If you really want a general *catch-all* clause, an *empty* except does the trick:

```
        try:
            action()
        except NameError:
            ...                    # Handle NameError.
        except IndexError:
            ...                    # Handle IndexError.
        except:
            ...                    # Handle all other exceptions.
        else:
            ...                    # Handle the no-exception case.
```

The empty except clause is a sort of wildcard feature—because it catches everything, it allows your handlers to be as general or specific as you like. In some scenarios, this form may be more convenient than listing all possible exceptions in a try. For example, the following catches everything without listing anything:

```
        try:
            action()
        except:
            ...            # Catch all possible exceptions.
```

Empty excepts also raise some design issues. Although convenient, they may also catch unexpected system exceptions unrelated to your code, and may inadvertently intercept exceptions meant for another handler. For example, even system exit calls in Python trigger exceptions, and you usually want these to pass. We'll revisit this as a gotcha at the end of Part VII. For now, we'll just say: use with care.

The try/else Clause

At first glance, the purpose of the else clause is not always obvious. Without it, though, there is no way to tell, without setting and checking Boolean flags, whether we wound up past a try statement because no exception happened, or because an exception occurred and was handled:

```
try:
    ...run code...
except IndexError:
    ...handle exception...
# Did we get here because the try failed or not?
```

Much like else clauses in loops, the else provides syntax here that makes this case obvious and unambiguous:

```
try:
    ...run code...
except IndexError:
    ...handle exception...
else:
    ...no exception occurred...
```

You can *almost* emulate an else clause by moving its code to the end of the try block:

```
try:
    ...run code...
    ...no exception occurred...
except IndexError:
    ...handle exception...
```

This can lead to incorrect exception classifications, though. If the "no exception occurred" action triggers IndexError, it will register as a failure of the try block, and hence erroneously trigger the exception handler below the try (subtle, but true!). By using an explicit else clause instead, you make the logic more obvious, and guarantee that except handlers only run for real failures in the code you're wrapping in try, not for failures in the else case's action.

Example: Default Behavior

Since control flow through a program is easier to capture in Python than in English, let's run some examples that further illustrate exception basics. Exceptions not caught by try statements reach the top level of a Python process and run Python's default exception-handling logic. Python terminates the running program and prints a standard error message. For example, running the following module, *bad.py*, generates a divide-by-zero exception:

```
def gobad(x, y):
    return x / y

def gosouth(x):
    print gobad(x, 0)

gosouth(1)
```

Since the program ignores the exception it triggers, Python kills the program and prints a message—this time, with useful file and line number information:[*]

```
% python bad.py
Traceback (most recent call last):
  File "bad.py", line 7, in ?
    gosouth(1)
  File "bad.py", line 5, in gosouth
    print gobad(x, 0)
  File "bad.py", line 2, in gobad
    return x / y
ZeroDivisionError: integer division or modulo by zero
```

When an uncaught exception occurs, Python ends the program, and prints a stack trace and the name and any extra data of the exception that was raised. The stack trace lists all lines active when the exception occurred, from oldest to newest. For example, you can see that the bad divide happens at the last entry in the trace—line 2 of file *bad.py*, a return statement.

Because Python detects and reports all errors at runtime by raising exceptions, exceptions are intimately bound up with the idea of error handling in general. For instance, if you've worked through the examples, you've undoubtedly seen an exception or two along the way—even typos usually generate a SyntaxError or other exception when a file is imported or executed (that's when the compiler is run). By default, you get a useful error display like the one above, which helps track down the problem.

Often this standard error message is all you need to resolve a problem in your code. For more heavy duty debugging jobs, you can catch exceptions with try statements, or use debugging tools we'll introduce in Chapter 26.

Example: Catching Built-in Exceptions

Python's default exception handling is often exactly what you want—especially for code in top-level script files, an error generally should terminate your program immediately. For many programs, there is no need to be more specific about errors in your code.

Sometimes, though, you'll want to catch errors and recover from them instead. If you don't want your program terminated when an exception is raised by Python, simply catch it by wrapping program logic in a try. For example, the following code catches

---

[*] We should point out that the text of error messages and stack traces tends to vary slightly over time. Don't be alarmed if your error messages don't exactly match ours.

and recovers from the TypeError Python raises immediately when we try to concatenate a list and a string (the + operator wants the same sequence type on both sides):

```
def kaboom(x, y):
    print x + y                    # Trigger TypeError.

try:
    kaboom([0,1,2], "spam")
except TypeError:                  # Catch and recover here.
    print 'Hello world!'
print 'resuming here'             # Continue here if exception or not.
```

When the exception occurs in function kaboom, control jumps to the try statement's except clause, which prints a message. Since an exception is "dead" after it's been caught like this, the program continues past the whole try, rather than being terminated by Python. In effect, your code processes and clears the error.

Notice that once you've caught the error, control resumes at the place where you caught it, after the try; there is no direct way to go back to the place where the exception occurred (function kaboom). In a sense, this makes exceptions more like simple jumps than function calls—there is no way to return to the code that triggered the error.

The try/finally Statement

The other flavor of the try statement is a specialization and has to do with finalization actions. If a finally clause is used in a try, its block of statements are always run by Python "on the way out," whether an exception occurred while the try block was running or not. Its general form:

```
try:
    <statements>       # Run this action first.
finally:
    <statements>       # Always run this code on the way out.
```

Here's how this variant works. Python begins by running the statement block associated with the try header line first. The remaining behavior of this statement depends on whether an exception occurs during the try block or not:

- If no exception occurs while the try block is running, Python jumps back to run the finally block, and then continues execution past the entire try statement.

- If an exception *does* occur during the try block's run, Python comes back and runs the finally block, but then propagates the exception to a higher try or the top-level default handler; the program does not resume execution past the try statement.

The try/finally form is useful when you want to be completely sure that an action happens after some code runs, regardless of the exception behavior of the program.

Note that the `finally` clause cannot be used in the same `try` statement as except and else, so it is best thought of as a distinct statement form.

Example: Coding Termination Actions with try/finally

We saw simple `try/finally` examples earlier. Here's a more realistic example that illustrates a typical role for this statement:

```
MyError = "my error"

def stuff(file):
    raise MyError

file = open('data', 'r')      # Open an existing file.
try:
    stuff(file)               # Raises exception
finally:
    file.close()              # Always close file.
...                           # Continue here if no exception.
```

In this code, we've wrapped a call to a file-processing function in a `try` with a `finally` clause, to make sure that the file is always closed, whether the function triggers an exception or not.

This particular example's function isn't all that useful (it just raises an exception), but wrapping calls in `try/finally` statements is a good way to ensure that your closing-time (i.e., termination) activities always run. Python always runs the code in your `finally` blocks, regardless of whether an exception happens in the try block or not.[*] For example, if the function here did not raise an exception, the program would still execute the `finally` block to close your file, and then continue past the entire try statement.

The raise Statement

To trigger exceptions explicitly, you code `raise` statements. Their general form is simple—the word `raise`, optionally followed by both the name of the exception to be raised and an extra data item to pass with the exception:

```
raise <name>              # Manually trigger an exception.
raise <name>, <data>      # Pass extra data to catcher too.
raise                     # Reraise the most recent exception.
```

The second form allows you to pass an extra data item along with the exception, to provide details for the handler. In the `raise`, the data is listed after the exception

---

[*] Unless Python crashes completely, of course. Python does a good job of avoiding crashes, by checking all possible errors as a program runs. When a program does crash hard, it is often due to a bug in linked-in C extension code, outside of Python's scope.

name; back in the try statement, the data is obtained by including a variable to receive it. For instance, in except name,X:, X will be assigned the extra data item listed at the raise. The third raise form simply reraises the current exception; it's handy if you want to propagate an exception you've caught to another handler.

So what's an exception name? It might be the name of a built-in exception from the built-in scope (e.g., IndexError), or the name of an arbitrary string object you've assigned in your program. It can also reference a user-defined class or class instance—a possibility that further generalizes raise statement formats. We'll postpone the details of this generalization until after we have a chance to study class exceptions in the next chapter.

Regardless of how you name exceptions, they are always identified by normal objects, and at most one is active at any given time. Once caught by an except clause anywhere in the program, an exception dies (won't propagate to another try), unless reraised by another raise statement or error.

Example: Raising and Catching User-Defined Exceptions

Python programs can trigger both built-in and user-defined exceptions, using the raise statement. In their simplest form, user-defined exceptions are string objects, like the one that variable MyBad is assigned to in the following:

```
MyBad = "oops"

def stuff():
    raise MyBad            # Trigger exception manually.

try:
    stuff()                # Raises exception
except MyBad:
    print 'got it'         # Handle exception here.
    ...                    # Resume execution here.
```

This time, the raise occurs inside a function, but it makes no real difference—control jumps back to the except block immediately. Notice that user-defined exceptions are caught with try statements just like built-in exceptions.

Example: Passing Extra Data with raise

As suggested earlier, raise statements can pass an extra data item along with the exception for use in a handler. In general, the extra data allows you to send context information about the exception to a handler. If you're writing a data file parser, for example, you might raise a syntax error exception on errors, and also pass along an object that gives line and file information to the handler (we'll meet an example of such later in this part).

Strictly speaking, every exception has the extra data: much like function return values, it defaults to the special None object if nothing was passed explicitly. The following code, *raisedata.py*, illustrates this concept at work:

```
myException = 'Error'                    # String object

def raiser1():
    raise myException, "hello"           # Raise, pass data.

def raiser2():
    raise myException                    # Raise, None implied.

def tryer(func):
    try:
        func()
    except myException, extraInfo:       # Run func; catch exception+data.
        print 'got this:', extraInfo
```

```
% python
>>> from raisedata import *
>>> tryer(raiser1)                       # Explicitly passed extra data
got this: hello
>>> tryer(raiser2)                       # Extra data is None by default.
got this: None
```

Here, the tryer function always requests the extra data object; it comes back as an explicit string from raiser1, but defaults to None in raiser2's raise statement. Later, we'll see that the same hook can be used to access instances raised in conjunction with class-based exceptions.

Example: Propagating Exceptions with raise

A raise statement without an exception name or extra data value simply reraises the current exception. It's typically used if you need to catch and handle an exception, but don't want the exception to die in your code:

```
>>> try:
...     raise IndexError, 'spam'
... except IndexError:
...     print 'propagating'
...     raise
...
propagating
Traceback (most recent call last):
  File "<stdin>", line 2, in ?
IndexError: spam
```

By running a raise this way, the exception will be reraised and thus propagated to a higher handler, or to the default handler at the top, which stops the program with a standard error message.

The assert Statement

As a somewhat special case, Python includes the assert statement. It is mostly syntactic shorthand for a common raise usage pattern, and can be thought of as a *conditional raise* statement. A statement of the form:

```
assert <test>, <data>        # The <data> part is optional.
```

works like the following code:

```
if __debug__:
    if not <test>:
        raise AssertionError, <data>
```

In other words, if the test evaluates to false, Python raises an exception, with the data item as the exception's extra data (if provided). Like all exceptions, the assertion error exception raised will kill your program if not caught with a try.

As an added feature, assert statements may also be removed from the compiled program's byte code if the -O Python command-line flag is used, thereby optimizing the program. AssertionError is a built-in exception, and the __debug__ flag is a built-in name that is automatically set to 1 (true) unless the -O flag is used.

Example: Trapping Constraints (but Not Errors)

Assertions are typically used to verify program conditions during development. When displayed, their error message text automatically includes source code line information, and the value you listed in the assert statement. Consider *asserter.py*:

```
def f(x):
    assert x < 0, 'x must be negative'
    return x ** 2

% python
>>> import asserter
>>> asserter.f(1)
Traceback (most recent call last):
  File "<stdin>", line 1, in ?
  File "asserter.py", line 2, in f
    assert x < 0, 'x must be negative'
AssertionError: x must be negative
```

It's important to keep in mind that assert is mostly intended for trapping user-defined constraints, not for catching genuine programming errors. Because Python traps programming errors itself, there is usually no need to code asserts to catch things like out-of-bounds indexes, type mismatches, and zero divides:

```
def reciprocal(x):
    assert x != 0    # a useless assert!
    return 1 / x     # python checks for zero automatically
```

Such asserts are generally superfluous. Because Python raises exceptions on errors automatically, you might as well let Python do the job for you.[*] For another example of assert common usage, see the abstract superclass example of Chapter 21; there, we used assert to make calls to undefined methods fail with a message.

---

[*] In most cases, at least. As suggested in Part IV, if a function has to perform long-running or unrecoverable actions before it reaches the place where an exception will be triggered, you still might want to test for errors. Even in this case, though, be careful not to make your tests overly specific or restrictive, or you will limit your code's utility.

CHAPTER 25

Exception Objects

So far, we've been deliberately vague about what an exception actually *is*. Python generalizes the notion of exceptions—they may be identified by either string or class objects. Both have merits, but classes tend to provide a better solution when it comes to maintaining exception hierarchies.

String-Based Exceptions

In all the examples we've seen up to this point, user-defined exceptions have been strings. This is the simpler way to code an exception—any string value can be used to identify an exception:

```
>>> myexc = "My exception string"
>>> try:
...     raise myexc
... except myexc:
...     print 'caught'
...
caught
```

Technically, the exception is identified by the string *object*, not the string value—you must use the same variable (i.e., reference) to raise and catch the exception (we'll expand on this idea in a gotcha at the conclusion of Part VII). Here, the exception name myexc is just a normal variable—it can be imported from a module, and so on. The text of the string is almost irrelevant, except that it shows up in standard error messages:

```
>>> raise myexc
Traceback (most recent call last):
  File "<stdin>", line 1, in ?
My exception string
```

The text of the string exception here is printed as the exception message. If your string exceptions may print like this, you'll want to use more meaningful text than most of the examples shown in this book.

Class-Based Exceptions

Strings are a simple way to define your exceptions. Exceptions may also be identified with classes. Like some other topics we've met in this book, class exceptions are an advanced topic you can choose to use or not in Python 2.2. However, classes have some added value that merits a quick look; in particular, they allow us to identify exception *categories* that are more flexible to use and maintain than simple strings. Moreover, classes are likely to become the prescribed way to identify your exceptions in the future.

The chief difference between string and class exceptions has to do with the way that exceptions raised are matched against except clauses in try statements:

- String exceptions are matched by simple *object identity*: the raised exception is matched to except clauses by Python's is test (not ==).
- Class exceptions are matched by *superclass relationships*: the raised exception matches an except clause, if that except clause names the exception's class or any superclass of it.

That is, when a try statement's except clause lists a superclass, it catches instances of that superclass, as well as instances of all its subclasses lower in the class tree. The net effect is that class exceptions support the construction of exception hierarchies: superclasses become *category* names, and subclasses become specific kinds of exceptions within a category. By naming a general exception superclass, an except clause can catch an entire category of exceptions—any more specific subclass will match.

Class Exception Example

Let's look at an example to see how class exceptions work in code. In the following file, *classexc.py*, we define a superclass General and two subclasses of it called Specific1 and Specific2. We're illustrating the notion of exception categories here: General is a category name, and its two subclasses are specific types of exceptions within the category. Handlers that catch General will also catch any subclasses of it, including Specific1 and Specific2.

```
class General:          pass
class Specific1(General): pass
class Specific2(General): pass

def raiser0():
    X = General()       # Raise superclass instance.
    raise X

def raiser1():
    X = Specific1()     # Raise subclass instance.
    raise X
```

```
def raiser2():
    X = Specific2()        # Raise different subclass instance.
    raise X

for func in (raiser0, raiser1, raiser2):
    try:
        func()
    except General:        # Match General or any subclass of it.
        import sys
        print 'caught:', sys.exc_type
```

```
C:\python> python classexc.py
caught: __main__.General
caught: __main__.Specific1
caught: __main__.Specific2
```

Notice that we call classes to make *instances* in the raise statements here; as we'll see when we formalize raise statement forms later in this section, an instance is always present when raising class-based exceptions. This code also includes functions that raise instances of all three classes as exceptions, and a top-level try that calls the functions and catches General exceptions. The same try catches General and the two specific exceptions, because the two specific exceptions are subclasses of General.

Why Class Exceptions?

Since there are only three possible exceptions in the prior section's example, it doesn't really do justice to the utility of class exceptions. In fact, we can achieve the same effects by coding a list of string exception names in parenthesis within the except clause. File *stringexc.py* shows how:

```
General   = 'general'
Specific1 = 'specific1'
Specific2 = 'specific2'

def raiser0(): raise General
def raiser1(): raise Specific1
def raiser2(): raise Specific2

for func in (raiser0, raiser1, raiser2):
    try:
        func()
    except (General, Specific1, Specific2):     # Catch any of these.
        import sys
        print 'caught:', sys.exc_type
```

```
C:\python> python stringexc.py
caught: general
caught: specific1
caught: specific2
```

But for large or high exception hierarchies, it may be easier to catch categories using classes than to list every member of a category in a single except clause. Moreover, exception hierarchies can be extended by adding new subclasses, without breaking existing code.

Suppose you code a numeric programming library in Python, to be used by a large number of people. While you are writing your library, you identify two things that can go wrong with numbers in your code—division by zero, and numeric overflow. You document these as the two exceptions that your library may raise, and define them as simple strings in your code:

```
divzero = 'Division by zero error in library'
oflow   = 'Numeric overflow error in library'
...
raise divzero
```

Now, when people use your library, they will typically wrap calls to your functions or classes in try statements that catch your two exceptions (if they do not catch your exceptions, exceptions from the library kill their code):

```
import mathlib
...
try:
    mathlib.func(...)
except (mathlib.divzero, mathlib.oflow):
    ...report and recover...
```

This works fine and people use your library. Six months down the road, you revise your library; along the way, you identify a new thing that can go wrong—underflow—and add that as a new string exception:

```
divzero = 'Division by zero error in library'
oflow   = 'Numeric overflow error in library'
uflow   = 'Numeric underflow error in library'
```

Unfortunately, when you rerelease your code, you've just created a maintenance problem for your users. Assuming they list your exceptions explicitly, they have to now go back and change every place they call your library, to include the newly added exception name:

```
try:
    mathlib.func(...)
except (mathlib.divzero, mathlib.oflow, mathlib.uflow):
    ...report and recover...
```

Now, maybe this isn't the end of the world. If your library is used only in-house, you can make the changes yourself. You might also ship a Python script that tries to fix such code automatically (it would be a few dozen lines, and would guess right at least some of the time). If many people have to change their code each time you alter your exceptions set, though, this is not exactly the most polite of upgrade policies.

Your users might try to avoid this pitfall by coding empty except clauses:

```
try:
    mathlib.func(...)
```

```
except:                          # Catch everything here.
    ...report and recover...
```

The problem with this workaround is that it may catch more than they bargained for—even things like memory errors and system exits trigger exceptions, and you want such things to pass, not be caught and erroneously classified as a library error. As a rule of thumb, it's usually better to be specific than general in exception handlers (an idea we'll revisit in the gotchas).

So what to do, then? Class exceptions fix this dilemma completely. Rather than defining your library's exceptions as a simple set of strings, arrange them into a class tree, with a common superclass to encompass the entire category:

```
class NumErr: pass
class Divzero(NumErr): pass
class Oflow(NumErr): pass
...
raise DivZero()
```

This way, users of your library simply need to list the common superclass (i.e., category), to catch all of your library's exceptions—both now and in the future:

```
import mathlib
...
try:
    mathlib.func(...)
except mathlib.NumErr:
    ...report and recover...
```

When you go back and hack your code again, new exceptions are added as new subclasses of the common superclass:

```
class Uflow(NumErr): pass
```

The end result is that user code that catches your library's exceptions will keep working, *unchanged*. In fact, you are then free to add, delete, and change your exceptions arbitrarily in the future—as long as clients name the superclass, they are insulated from changes in your exceptions set. In other words, class exceptions provide a better answer to maintenance issues than strings do. Class-based exceptions can also support state retention and inheritance in ways that strings cannot—a concept we'll explore by example later in this section.

Built-in Exception Classes

We didn't really pull the prior section's examples out of thin air. Although user-defined exceptions may be identified by string or class objects, all built-in exceptions that Python itself may raise are predefined class objects, instead of strings. Moreover, they are organized into a shallow hierarchy with general superclass categories and specific subclass types, much like the exceptions class tree in the prior section.

All the familiar exceptions you've seen (e.g., SyntaxError) are really just predefined classes, available both as built-in names (in module __builtin__), and as attributes of the standard library module exceptions. In addition, Python organizes the built-in exceptions into a hierarchy, to support a variety of catching modes. For example:

Exception
> Top-level root superclass of exceptions

StandardError
> The superclass of all built-in error exceptions

ArithmeticError
> The superclass of all numeric errors

OverflowError
> A subclass that identifies a specific numeric error

And so on—you can read further about this structure in either the library manual, or the help text of the exceptions module (see Chapter 11 for help on help):

```
>>> import exceptions
>>> help(exceptions)
...lots of text omitted...
```

The built-in class tree allows you to choose how specific or general your handlers will be. For example, the built-in exception ArithmeticError is a superclass to more specific exceptions such as OverflowError and ZeroDivisionError. By listing ArithmeticError in a try, you will catch any kind of numeric error raised; by listing just OverflowError, you will intercept just that specific type of error, and no others.

Similarly, because StandardError is the superclass of all built-in error exceptions, you can generally use it to select between built-in errors and user-defined exceptions in a try:

```
try:
    action( )
except StandardError:
    ...handle Python errors...
except:
    ...handle user exceptions...
else:
    ...handle no exception case...
```

You can also almost simulate an empty except clause (that catches everything) by catching root class Exception, but not quite—string exceptions, as well as stand-alone user-defined exceptions, are not subclasses of the Exception root class today.* Whether or not you will use categories in the built-in class tree, it serves as a good

---

* Note that current Python documentation says that "It is recommended that user-defined class-based exceptions be derived from the Exception class, although this is currently not enforced." That is, Exception subclasses are preferred to standalone exception classes, but not required. The defensive programmer might infer that it may be a good idea to adopt this policy anyhow.

example; by using similar techniques for class exceptions in your own code, you can provide exception sets that are flexible, and easily modified.

Other than this, built-in exceptions are largely indistinguishable from strings. In fact, you normally don't need to care that they are classes, unless you assume built-in exception are strings and try to concatenate without converting (e.g., KeyError+"spam" fails, but str(KeyError)+"spam" works).

Specifying Exception Text

When we met string-based exceptions at the start of this section, we saw that the text of the string shows up in the standard error message when the exception is not caught. For an uncaught class exception, by default you get the class's name, and a not very pretty display of the instance object that was raised:

```
>>> class MyBad: pass

>>> raise MyBad()
Traceback (most recent call last):
  File "<pyshell#30>", line 1, in ?
    raise MyBad
MyBad: <__main__.MyBad instance at 0x00B58980>
```

To do better, define the __repr__ or __str__ string representation overload methods in your class, to return the string you want to display for your exception if it reaches the default handler at the top:

```
>>> class MyBad:
...     def __repr__(self):
...         return "Sorry--my mistake!"
...
>>> raise MyBad()
Traceback (most recent call last):
  File "<pyshell#43>", line 1, in ?
    raise MyBad()
MyBad: Sorry--my mistake!
```

The __repr__ overload method is called for printing, and string conversion requests made to your class's instances. See the "Operator Overloading" section in Chapter 21.

Sending Extra Data in Instances

Besides supporting flexible hierarchies, class exceptions also provide storage for extra *state* information as instance attributes. When a class-based exception is raised, Python automatically passes the class instance object along with the exception, as the extra data item. As for string exceptions, you can access the raised instance by listing an extra variable back in the try statement. This provides a natural hook for supplying data and behavior to the handler.

Example: extra data with classes and strings

Let's demonstrate the notion of extra data by an example, and compare string and class-based approaches along the way. A program that parses datafiles might signal a formatting error by raising an exception instance that is filled out with extra details about the error:

```
>>> class FormatError:
...     def __init__(self, line, file):
...         self.line = line
...         self.file = file
...
>>> def parser():
...     # when error found
...     raise FormatError(42, file='spam.txt')
...
>>> try:
...     parser()
... except FormatError, X:
...     print 'Error at', X.file, X.line
...
Error at spam.txt 42
```

In the except clause here, variable X is assigned a reference to the instance that was generated where the exception was raised. In practice, though, this isn't noticeably more convenient than passing compound objects (e.g., tuples, lists, or dictionaries) as extra data with string exceptions, and may not by itself be compelling enough to warrant class-based exceptions:

```
>>> formatError = 'formatError'

>>> def parser():
...     # when error found
...     raise formatError, {'line':42, 'file':'spam.txt'}
...
>>> try:
...     parser()
... except formatError, X:
...     print 'Error at', X['file'], X['line']
...
Error at spam.txt 42
```

This time, variable X in the except clause is assigned the dictionary of extra details listed at the raise statement. The net effect is similar, without having to code a class along the way. The class approach might be more convenient, if the exception should also have behavior—the exception class can also define *methods* to be called in the handler:

```
class FormatError:
    def __init__(self, line, file):
        self.line = line
        self.file = file
    def logerror(self):
```

```
        log = open('formaterror.txt', 'a')
        print >> log, 'Error at', self.file, self.line

def parser():
    raise FormatError(40, 'spam.txt')

try:
    parser()
except FormatError, exc:
    exc.logerror()
```

In such a class, methods (like `logerror`) may also be *inherited* from superclasses, and instance attributes (like `line` and `file`) provide a place to save *state* for use in later method calls. Here, we can mimic much of this effect by passing simple *functions* in the string-based approach:

```
formatError = "formatError"

def logerror(line, file):
    log = open('formaterror.txt', 'a')
    print >> log, 'Error at', file, line

def parser():
    raise formatError, (41, 'spam.txt', logerror)

try:
    parser()
except formatError, data:
    data[2](data[0], data[1])        # Or simply: logerror()
```

Naturally, such functions would not participate in inheritance like class methods do, and would not be able to retain state in instance attributes (lambdas and global variables are usually the best we can do for stateful functions). We could, of course, pass a class instance in the extra data of string-based exceptions to achieve the same effect. But if we go this far to mimic class-based exceptions, we might as well adopt them—we'd be coding a class anyhow.

In general, the choice between string- and class-based exceptions is much like the choice to use classes at all; not every program requires the power of OOP. String-based exceptions are a simpler tool for simpler tasks. Class-based exceptions become most useful for defining *categories*, and in advanced applications that can benefit from *state* retention and attribute *inheritance*. As usual in Python, the choice to use OOP or not is mostly yours to make (although this might change in a future release of Python).

General raise Statement Forms

With the addition of class-based exceptions, the raise statement can take the following five forms: the first two raise string exceptions, the next two raise class exceptions, and the last reraises the current exception (useful if you need to propagate an arbitrary exception).

```
raise string          # Matches except with same string object
raise string, data    # Pass optional extra data (default=None).

raise instance        # Same as: raise instance.__class__ instance.
raise class, instance # Matches except with this class or its superclass

raise                 # Reraise the current exception.
```

For class-based exceptions, Python always requires an instance of the class. Raising an instance really raises the instance's class; the instance is passed along with the class as the extra data item (it's a good place to store information for the handler). For backward compatibility with Python versions in which built-in exceptions were strings, you can also use these forms of the raise statement:

```
raise class            # Same as: raise class()
raise class, arg       # Same as: raise class(arg)
raise class, (arg, arg,...)  # Same as: raise class(arg, arg,...)
```

These are all the same as saying raise class(arg...), and therefore the same as the raise instance form above. Specifically, if you list a class instead of an instance, and the extra data item is not an instance of the class listed, Python automatically calls the class with the extra data items as constructor arguments to create and raise an instance for you.

For example, you may raise an instance of the built-in KeyError exception by saying simply raise KeyError, even though KeyError is now a class; Python calls KeyError to make an instance along the way. In fact, you can raise KeyError, and any other class-based exception, in a variety of ways:

```
raise KeyError()             # Normal: raise an instance
raise KeyError, KeyError()   # Class, instance: uses instance
raise KeyError               # Class: instance will be generated
raise KeyError, "bad spam"   # Class, arg: instance is generated
```

For all of these raise forms, a try statement of the form:

```
try:
    ...
except KeyError, X:
    ...
```

assigns X to the KeyError instance raised.

If that sounds confusing, just remember that exceptions may be identified by string or class instance objects. For strings, you may pass extra data with the exception or not. For classes, if there is no instance object in the raise statement, Python makes an instance for you.

## CHAPTER 26

Designing with Exceptions

This chapter rounds out Part VII, with a collection of exception design topics and examples, followed by this part's gotchas and exercises. Because this chapter also closes out the core language material of this book, it also includes a brief overview of development tools, by way of migration to the rest of this book.

Nesting Exception Handlers

Our examples so far have used only a single try to catch exceptions, but what happens if one try is physically nested inside another? For that matter, what does it mean if a try calls a function that runs another try? Technically, try statements can *nest* in terms of both syntax, and the runtime control flow through your code.

Both these cases can be understood if you realize that Python *stacks* try statements at runtime. When an exception is raised, Python returns to the most recently entered try statement with a matching except clause. Since each try statement leaves a marker, Python can jump back to earlier trys by inspecting the markers stacked. This nesting of active handlers is what we mean by "higher" handlers—try statements entered earlier in the program's execution flow.

For example, Figure 26-1 illustrates what occurs when try/except statements nest at runtime. Because the amount of code that can go into a try clause block can be substantial (e.g., function calls), it will typically invoke other code that may be watching for the same exception. When the exception is eventually raised, Python jumps back to the most recently entered try statement that names that exception, runs that statement's except clauses, and then resumes after that try.

Once the exception is caught, its life is over—control does not jump back to all matching trys that names the exception, just *one*. In Figure 26-1, for instance, the raise in function func2 sends control back to the handler in func1, and then the program continues within func1.

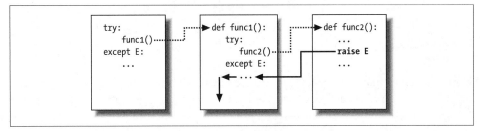

Figure 26-1. nested try/except

By contrast, when try/finally statements are used, control runs the finally block on exceptions, but then continues propagating the exception to other trys, or to the top-level default handler (standard error message printer). As Figure 26-2 illustrates, the finally clauses do not kill the exception—they just specify code to be run on the way out, during the exception propagation process. If there are many try/finally clauses active when an exception occurs, they will *all* be run (unless a try/except catches the exception somewhere along the way).

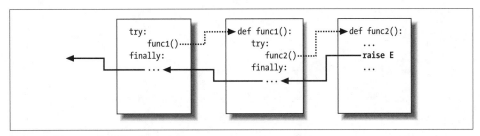

Figure 26-2. nested try/finally

Example: Control-Flow Nesting

Let's turn to an example to make this nesting concept more concrete. The following module, file *nestexc.py*, defines two functions; action2 is coded to trigger an exception (you can't add numbers and sequences), and action1 wraps a call to action2 in a try handler, to catch the exception:

```
def action2():
    print 1 + []          # Generate TypeError.

def action1():
    try:
        action2()
    except TypeError:      # Most recent matching try
        print 'inner try'

try:
    action1()
```

```
    except TypeError:          # Here, only if action1 reraises.
        print 'outer try'

% python nestexc.py
inner try
```

Notice, though, that the top-level module code at the bottom of the file wraps a call to action1 in a try handler too. When action2 triggers the TypeError exception, there will be two active try statements—the one in action1, and the one at the top level of the module. Python picks and runs just the most recent with a matching except, which in this case is the try inside action1.

In general, the place where an exception winds up jumping to depends on the control flow through a program at runtime. In other words, to know where you will go, you need to know *where you've been*—exceptions are more a function of control flow than statement syntax.

Example: Syntactic Nesting

It's also possible to nest try statements syntactically:

```
try:
    try:
        action2()
    except TypeError:          # Most recent matching try
        print 'inner try'
except TypeError:              # Here, only if nested handler reraises.
    print 'outer try'
```

But really, this just sets up the same handler nesting structure as, and behaves identical to, the prior example. In fact, syntactic nesting works just like the cases we sketched in Figures 26-1 and 26-2. The only difference is that the nested handlers are physically embedded in a try block, not coded in a called function elsewhere. For example, nested finally handlers all fire on an exception, whether they are nested syntactically, or by the runtime flow through physically separated parts of your code:

```
>>> try:
...     try:
...         raise IndexError
...     finally:
...         print 'spam'
... finally:
...     print 'SPAM'
...
spam
SPAM
Traceback (most recent call last):
  File "<stdin>", line 3, in ?
IndexError
```

See Figure 26-2 for a graphic illustration of this code's operation; it's the same effect, but function logic has been inlined as nested statements here. For a more useful example of syntactic nesting at work, consider the following file, *except-finally.py*:

```
def raise1():  raise IndexError
def noraise(): return
def raise2():  raise SyntaxError

for func in (raise1, noraise, raise2):
    print '\n', func
    try:
        try:
            func()
        except IndexError:
            print 'caught IndexError'
    finally:
        print 'finally run'
```

This code catches an exception if it is raised, and performs a finally termination time action regardless of whether any exception occurred or not. This takes a few moments to digest, but the effect is much like combining an except and finally clause in a single try statement, even though such a combination would be syntactically illegal (they are mutually exclusive):

```
% python except-finally.py

<function raise1 at 0x00867DF8>
caught IndexError
finally run

<function noraise at 0x00868EB8>
finally run

<function raise2 at 0x00875B80>
finally run
Traceback (most recent call last):
  File "except-finally.py", line 9, in ?
    func()
  File "except-finally.py", line 3, in raise2
    def raise2(): raise SyntaxError
SyntaxError
```

Exception Idioms

We've seen the mechanics behind exceptions. Now, let's take a look at some of the other ways they are typically used.

Exceptions Aren't Always Errors

In Python, all errors are exceptions, but not all exceptions are errors. For instance, we saw in Chapter 7 that file object read methods return empty strings at the end of a file. The built-in `raw_input` function that we first met in Chapter 3, and deployed in an interactive loop in Chapter 10, reads a line of text from the standard input stream (`sys.stdin`). Unlike file methods, `raw_input` raises the built-in `EOFError` at end of file, instead of returning an empty string (an empty string from `raw_input` means an empty line).

Despite its name, the `EOFError` exception is just a signal in this context, not an error. Because of this behavior, unless end-of-file should terminate a script, `raw_input` often appears wrapped in a `try` handler and nested in a loop, as in the following code.

```
while 1:
    try:
        line = raw_input()       # Read line from stdin.
    except EOFError:
        break                    # Exit loop at end of file
    else:
        ...process next line here...
```

Other built-in exceptions are similarly signals, not errors. Python also has a set of built-in exceptions that represent *warnings*, rather than errors. Some of these are used to signal use of deprecated (phased out) language features. See the standard library manual's description of built-in exceptions and the `warnings` module for more on warnings.

Functions Signal Conditions with raise

User-defined exceptions can also signal nonerror conditions. For instance, a search routine can be coded to raise an exception when a match is found, instead of returning a status flag that must be interpreted by the caller. In the following, the try/except/else exception handler does the work of an if/else return value tester:

```
Found = "Item found"

def searcher():
    if ...success...:
        raise Found
    else:
        return

try:
    searcher()
except Found:                # Exception if item was found
    ...success...
else:                        # else returned: not found
    ...failure...
```

More generally, such a coding structure may also be useful for any function that cannot return a sentinel value to designate success or failure. For instance, if all objects are potentially valid return values, it's impossible for any return value to signal unusual conditions. Exceptions provide a way to signal results without a return value:

```
failure = "not found"

def searcher():
    if ...success...:
        return ...founditem...
    else:
        raise failure

try:
    item = searcher()
except failure:
    ...report...
else:
    ...use item here...
```

Because Python is dynamically typed and polymorphic to the core, exceptions, rather than sentinel return values, are the generally preferred way to signal conditions.

Debugging with Outer try Statements

You can also make use of exception handlers to replace Python's default top-level exception-handling behavior. By wrapping an entire program (or a call to it) in an outer try in your top-level code, you can catch any exception that may occur while your program runs, thereby subverting the default program termination.

In the following, the empty except clause catches any uncaught exception raised while the program runs. To get hold of the actual exception that occurred, fetch the exc_type and exc_value attributes from the built-in sys module; they're automatically set to the current exception's name and extra data:*

```
try:
    ...run program...
except:                    # All uncaught exceptions come here.
    import sys
    print 'uncaught!', sys.exc_type, sys.exc_value
```

This structure is commonly used during development, to keep your program active even after errors occur—you can run additional tests without having to restart. It's also used when testing code, as described in the next section.

---

* The built-in traceback module allows the current exception to be processed in a generic fashion, and a sys.exc_info() function returns a tuple containing the current exception's type, data, and traceback. sys.exc_type and sys.exc_value still work, but manage a single, global exception; exc_info() keeps track of each thread's exception information and so is thread-specific. This distinction matters only when using multiple threads in Python programs (a subject beyond this footnote's scope). See the Python library manual for more details.

Running in-Process Tests

You might combine some of these coding patterns in a test-driver application, which tests other code within the same process:

```
import sys
log = open('testlog', 'a')
from testapi import moreTests, runNextTest, testName

def testdriver():
    while moreTests():
        try:
            runNextTest()
        except:
            print >> log, 'FAILED', testName(), sys.exc_type
        else:
            print >> log, 'PASSED', testName()

testdriver()
```

The testdriver function here cycles through a series of test calls (module testapi is left abstract in this example). Because an uncaught exception in a test case would normally kill this test driver, we need to wrap test case calls in a try if we want to continue the testing process after a test fails. As usual, the empty except catches any uncaught exception generated by a test case, and uses sys.exc_type to log the exception to a file; the else clause is run when no exception occurs—the test success case.

Such boilerplate code is typical of systems that test functions, modules, and classes, by running them in the same process as the test driver. In practice, testing can be much more sophisticated than this. For instance, to test *external programs*, we would instead check status codes or outputs generated by program launching tools such as os.system and os.popen, covered in the standard library manual; such tools do not generally raise exceptions for errors in the external program (in fact, the test cases may run in parallel with the test driver). At the end of this chapter, we'll also meet more complete testing frameworks provided by Python, such as doctest and PyUnit, which provide tools for comparing expected outputs with actual results.

Exception Design Tips

By and large, exceptions are easy to use in Python. The real art behind them is deciding how specific or general your except clauses should be, and how much code to wrap up in try statements. Let's address the second of these first.

Why You Will Care: Error Checks

One way to see why exceptions are useful is to compare coding styles in Python and languages without exceptions. For instance, if you want to write robust programs in the C language, you generally have to test return values or status codes after every operation that could possibly go astray:

```
doStuff( )
{                                        # C program:
    if (doFirstThing( ) == ERROR)        # Detect errors everywhere
        return ERROR;                    # even if not handled here.
    if (doNextThing( ) == ERROR)
        return ERROR;
    ...
    return doLastThing( );
}

main( )
{
    if (doStuff( ) == ERROR)
        badEnding( );
    else
        goodEnding( );
}
```

In fact, realistic C programs often have as much code devoted to error detection as to doing actual work. But, in Python, you don't have to be so methodical; instead, you can wrap arbitrarily vast pieces of a program in exception handlers and write the parts that do the actual work to assume all is well:

```
def doStuff( ):         # Python code
    doFirstThing( )     # We don't care about exceptions here,
    doNextThing( )      # so we don't need to detect them here.
    ...
    doLastThing( )

if __name__ == '__main__':
    try:
        doStuff( )      # This is where we care about results,
    except:             # so it's the only place we must check.
        badEnding( )
    else:
        goodEnding( )
```

Because control jumps immediately to a handler when an exception occurs, there's no need to instrument all your code to guard for errors. Moreover, because Python detects errors automatically, your code usually doesn't need to check for errors in the first place. The upshot is that exceptions let you largely ignore the unusual cases and avoid much error-checking code.

What Should Be Wrapped

In principle, you could wrap every statement in your script in its own try, but that would just be silly (the try statements would then need to be wrapped in try statements!). This is really a design issue that goes beyond the language itself, and becomes more apparent with use. But here are a few rules of thumb:

- Operations that commonly fail are generally wrapped in try statements. For example, things that interface with system state, such as file opens, socket calls, and the like, are prime candidates for try.

- However, there are exceptions to the prior rule—in simple scripts, you may *want* failures of such operations to kill your program, instead of being caught and ignored. This is especially true if the failure is a show-stopper. Failure in Python means a useful error message (not a hard crash), and this is often the best outcome you could hope for.

- Implement termination actions in try/finally statements, in order to guarantee their execution. This statement form allows you to run code whether exceptions happen or not.

- It is sometimes more convenient to wrap the *call* to a large function in a single try statement, rather than littering the function itself with many try statements. That way, all exceptions in the function percolate up to the try around the call, and you reduce the amount of code within the function.

Catching Too Much

On to the issue of handler generality. Because Python lets you pick and choose which exceptions to catch, you sometimes have to be careful to not be too inclusive. For example, you've seen that an empty except clause catches *every* exception that might be raised while the code in the try block runs.

That's easy to code and sometimes desirable, but you may also wind up intercepting an error that's expected by a try handler higher up in the exception nesting structure. For example, an exception handler such as the following catches and stops every exception that reaches it—whether or not another handler is waiting for it:

```
def func():
    try:
        ...              # IndexError is raised in here.
    except:
        ...              # But everything comes here and dies!

try:
    func()
except IndexError:       # Needed here
    ...
```

Perhaps worse, such code might also catch system exceptions. Even things like memory errors, programming mistakes, iteration stops, and system exits raise exceptions in Python. Such exceptions should not usually be intercepted.

For example, scripts normally exit when control falls off the end of the top-level file. However, Python also provides a built-in sys.exit call to allow early terminations. This actually works by raising a built-in SystemExit exception to end the program, so that try/finally handlers run on the way out, and special types of programs can intercept the event.[*] Because of this, a try with an empty except might unknowingly prevent a crucial exit, as in file *exiter.py*:

```
import sys

def bye():
    sys.exit(40)              # Crucial error: abort now!

try:
    bye()
except:
    print 'got it'           # Oops--we ignored the exit
print 'continuing...'
```

```
% python exiter.py
got it
continuing...
```

You simply might not expect all the kinds of exceptions that could occur during an operation. In fact, an empty except will also catch genuine programming errors, which should also be allowed to pass most of the time:

```
mydictionary = {...}
...
try:
    x = myditctionary['spam']    # Oops: misspelled
except:
    x = None                     # Assume we got KeyError.
...continue here...
```

The coder here assumes the only sort of error that can happen when indexing a dictionary is a key error. But because the name myditctionary is misspelled (it should say mydictionary), Python raises a NameError instead for the undefined name reference, which will be silently caught and ignored by the handler. The event will incorrectly fill in a default for the dictionary access, masking the program error. If this

---

[*] A related call, os._exit also ends a program, but is an immediate termination—it skips cleanup actions and cannot be intercepted with try/except or try/finally. It is usually only used in spawned child processes—a topic beyond this book's scope. See the library manual or *Programming Python*, Second Edition (O'Reilly) for details.

happens in code that is far removed from the place where the fetched values are used, it might make for a very interesting debugging task.

As a rule of thumb, be specific in your handlers—empty except clauses are handy, but potentially error-prone. In the last example, for instance, you should usually say except KeyError: to make your intentions explicit, and avoid intercepting unrelated events. In simpler scripts, the potential for problems might not be significant enough to outweigh the convenience of a catch-all. But in general, general handlers are generally trouble.

Catching Too Little

Conversely, handlers also shouldn't be too specific. When listing specific exceptions in a try, you catch only what you actually list. This isn't necessarily a bad thing either, but if a system evolves to raise other exceptions in the future, you may need to go back and add them to exception lists elsewhere in the code.

For instance, the following handler is written to treat myerror1 and myerror2 as normal cases, and treat everything else as an error. If a myerror3 is added in the future, it is processed as an error unless you update the exception list:

```
try:
    ...
except (myerror1, myerror2):     # What if I add a myerror3?
    ...                          # Nonerrors
else:
    ...                          # Assumed to be an error
```

Careful use of class-based exceptions can make this trap go away completely. As we learned in the prior chapter, if you catch a general superclass, you can add and raise more specific subclasses in the future without having to extend except clause lists manually:

```
try:
    ...
except SuccessCategoryName:      # What if I add a myerror3?
    ...                          # Nonerrors
else:
    ...                          # Assumed to be an error
```

Whether you use classes here or not, a little design goes a long way. The moral of the story is that you have to be careful not to be too general or too specific in exception handlers, and have to pick the granularity of your try statement wrapping wisely. Especially in larger systems, exception policies should be a part of the overall design.

Exception Gotchas

There isn't much to trip over with exceptions, but here are two general pointers on use, one of which summarizes concepts we've already met.

String Exceptions Match by Identity, Not Value

When an exception is raised (by you or by Python itself), Python searches for the most recently entered try statement with a matching except clause, where matching means the same string object, the same class, or a superclass of the raised class. It's important to notice that matching is performed by identity, not equality. For instance, suppose we define two string objects we want to raise as exceptions:

```
>>> ex1 = 'Error: Spam Exception'
>>> ex2 = 'Error: Spam Exception'
>>>
>>> ex1 == ex2, ex1 is ex2
(1, 0)
```

Applying the == test returns true (1) because they have equal values, but is returns false (0) since they are two distinct string objects in memory. Now, an except clause that names the same string object will always match:

```
>>> try:
...     raise ex1
... except ex1:
...     print 'got it'
...
got it
```

But one that lists an equal value, but not an identical object, will fail (assuming the string values are long enough to defeat Python's string object caching mechanism, which is described in Chapters 4 and 7:

```
>>> try:
...     raise ex1
... except ex2:
...     print 'Got it'
...
Traceback (innermost last):
  File "<stdin>", line 2, in ?
    raise ex1
Error: Spam Exception
```

Here, the exception isn't caught, so Python climbs to the top level of the process and prints a stack trace and the exception's text automatically. For strings, be sure to use the same object in the raise and the try. For class exceptions, the behavior is similar, but Python generalizes the notion of exception matching to include superclass relationships.

Catching the Wrong Thing

Perhaps the most common gotchas related to exceptions involve the design guidelines of the prior section. Remember, try to avoid empty except clauses (or you may catch things like system exits), and overly-specific except clauses (use superclass categories instead, to avoid maintenance issues in the future).

Core Language Summary

Congratulations! This concludes your look at the core Python programming language. If you've gotten this far, you may consider yourself an Official Python Programmer (and should feel free to add Python to your resume the next time you dig it out). You've already seen just about everything there is to see in the language itself—all in much more depth than many practicing Python programmers. In Part II through Part VII of the book, you studied built-in types, statements, and exceptions, as well as tools used to build-up larger program units—functions, modules, and classes and explored design issues, OOP, program architecture, and more.

The Python Toolset

From this point forward, your future Python career will largely consist of becoming proficient with the *toolset* available for application-level Python programmming. You'll find this to be an ongoing task. The standard library, for example, contains some 200 modules and the public domain offers more tools still. Because new tools appear constantly, it's possible to spend a decade or more becoming proficient in all these tools. We speak from personal experience here.

In general, Python provides a hierarchy of tool sets:

Built-ins
> Built-in types like strings, lists, and dictionaries make it easy to write simple programs fast.

Python extensions
> For more demanding tasks, you can extend Python, by writing your own functions, modules, and classes.

C extensions
> Although not covered in this book, Python can also be extended with modules written in C or C++.

Because Python layers its tool sets, you can decide how deeply your programs need to delve into this hierarchy for any given task—use built-ins for simple scripts, add Python-coded extensions for larger systems, and code C extensions for advanced work. You've covered the first two of these categories above in this book already, and that's plenty to do substantial programming in Python.

The next part of this book takes you on a tour of standard modules and common tasks in Python. Table 26-1 summarizes some of the sources of built-in or existing functionality available to Python programmers, and topics you'll explore in the remainder of this book. Up until now, most of our examples have been very small and self-contained. We wrote them that way on purpose to help you master the basics. But now that you know all about the core language, it's time to start learning how to use Python's built-in interfaces to do real work. You'll find that with a simple language like Python, common tasks are often much easier than you might expect.

Table 26-1. Python's toolbox categories

Category	Examples
Object types	Lists, dictionaries, files, strings
Functions	`len`, `range`, `apply`, `open`
Exceptions	`IndexError`, `KeyError`
Modules	`string`, `os`, `Tkinter`, `pickle`, `re`
Attributes	`__dict__`, `-name-`, `__class__`
Peripheral tools	NumPy, SWIG, Jython, PythonWin, etc.

Development Tools for Larger Projects

Finally, once you've mastered the basics, you'll find that your Python programs become substantially larger than the examples you've experimented with so far. For developing larger systems, a set of development tools is available in both Python and the public domain. You've seen some of these in action, and we've talked about others. To help you on your way, here is a summary of some of the most commonly used tools in this domain, many of which you've already seen:

PyDoc and docstrings

We introduced the PyDoc help function and HTML interfaces in Chapter 11. PyDoc provides a documentation system for your modules and objects, and integrates with the docstings feature of Python. PyDoc is a standard part of the Python system. See the library manual for more details. Be sure to also refer back to the documentation source hints listed in Chapter 11, for Python information resources in general.

PyChecker

Because Python is such a dynamic language, some programming errors are not reported until your program runs (e.g., syntax errors are caught when a file is run or imported). This isn't a big downside—like most languages, it just means that you have to test your Python code before shipping it. Furthermore, Python's dynamic nature, automatic error messages, and exception model, makes it easier and quicker to find and fix errors than in some languages (unlike C, Python does not crash on errors).

However, the PyChecker system provides support for catching a large set of common errors ahead of time, before your script runs. It serves similar roles to the "lint" program in C development. Some Python groups run their code through PyChecker prior to testing or delivery, to catch any lurking potential problems. In fact, the Python standard library is regularly run through

PyChecker before release. PyChecker is a third party package; find it at either *http://www.python.org*, or the Vaults of Parnassus web site.

PyUnit (a.k.a. unittest)

In Part V, we demonstrated how to add self-test code to Python files, by using the __name__ =='__main__' trick at the bottom of the file. For more advanced testing purposes, Python comes with two testing support tools. The first, PyUnit (called unittest in the library manual), provides an object-oriented class framework, for specifying and customizing test cases and expected results. It mimics the JUnit framework for Java. This is a large class-based system; see the Python library manual for details.

Doctest

The doctest standard library module provides a second and simpler approach to regression testing. It is based upon the docstrings feature of Python. Roughly, under doctest, you cut and paste a log of an interactive testing session into the docstrings of your source files. Doctest then extracts your docstrings, parses out test cases and results, and reruns the tests to verify the expected results. Doctest's operation can be tailored in a variety of ways; see the library manual for more on its operation.

IDEs

We discussed IDEs for Python in Chapter 3. IDEs, such as IDLE, provide a graphical environment for editing, running, debugging, and browsing your Python programs. Some advance IDEs such as Komodo support additional development tasks, such as source control integration, interactive GUI builders, project files, and more. See Chapter 3, the text editors page at *http://www.python.org*, and the Vaults of Parnassus web site for more on available IDEs and GUI builders for Python.

Profilers

Because Python is so high-level and dynamic, intuitions about performance gleaned from experience with other languages is usually wrong. To truly isolate performance bottlenecks in your code, you need to either add timing logic with clock tools in the time module, or run your code under the profile module.

profile is a standard library module that implements a source code profiler for Python; it runs a string of code you provide (e.g., a script file import, or a call to a function), and then, by default, prints a report to the standard output stream that gives performance statistics—number of calls to each function, time spent in each function, and more. The profile module can be customized in various ways; for example, it can save run statistics to a file, to be later analyzed with the pstats module.

Debuggers

The Python standard library also includes a command line source code debugger module, called pdb. This module works much like a command line C language debugger (e.g., dbx, gdb). You import the module, start running code by calling a pdb function (e.g., `pdb.run("main( )")`), and then type debugging commands from an interactive prompt. Because IDEs such as IDLE include point-and-click debugging interfaces, pdb seems to be used infrequently today; see Chapter 3 for tips on using IDLE's debugging GUI interfaces.*

Shipping options

In Chapter 2, we introduced common tools for packaging Python programs. Py2Exe, Installer, and freeze, can package byte-code and the Python Virtual Machine into "frozen binary" stand alone executables, which don't require that Python be installed in the target machine, and fully hide your system's code. In addition, you learned in Chapter 2 and Part V that Python programs may be shipped in their source (*.py*) or byte-code (*.pyc*) forms, and import hooks support special packaging techniques such as zip files and byte-code encryption. A system known as *distutils* also provides packaging options for Python modules and packages, and C-coded extensions; see the Python manuals for more details.

Optimization options

For optimizing your programs, the Psyco system described in Chapter 2 (and still experimental), provides a just-in-time compiler for Python byte-code to binary machine code. You may also occasionally see *.pyo* optimized byte-code files, generated and run with the -0 Python command line flag discussed in Chapter 15; because this provides a very modest performance boost, it is not commonly used. As a last resort, you can also move parts of your program to a compiled language such as C to boost performance; see the book *Programming Python* and the Python standard manuals for more on C extensions. In general, Python's speed also improves over time, so be sure to upgrade to the most recent release when possible (Version 2.3 has been clocked at 15–20% faster them 2.2).

Other hints for larger projects

Finally, we've met a variety of language features that tend to become more useful once you start coding larger projects. Among these are: module packages (Chapter 17); class-based exceptions (Chapter 25); class pseudo-private attributes (Chapter 23); documentation strings (Chapter 11); module path configuration files (Chapter 15); hiding names from `from*` with `__all__` lists and `_X` style names (Chapter 18); adding self-test code with the `-name-=='__main__'` trick (Chapter 18); using common design rules for functions and modules (Chapters 5 and 6); and so on.

---

* To be honest, IDLE's debugger is not used very often either. Most practicing Python programmers end up debugging their code by inserting strategic `print` statements, and running again. Because turnaround from change to execution is so quick in Python, adding prints is usually faster than either typing pdb debugger commands, or starting a GUI debugging session. Another valid debugging technique is to do nothing at all—because Python prints useful error messages instead of crashing on program errors, you usually get enough information to analyze and repair errors.

For additional large-scale Python development tools available in the public domain, be sure to also browse the pages at the Vaults of Parnassus web site.

Part VII Exercises

Since we're at the end of the core language coverage, we'll work on a few short exception exercises to give you a chance to practice the basics. Exceptions really are a simple tool, so if you get these, you've got exceptions mastered.

1. *try/except*. Write a function called oops that explicitly raises an IndexError exception when called. Then write another function that calls oops inside a try/except statement to catch the error. What happens if you change oops to raise KeyError instead of IndexError? Where do the names KeyError and IndexError come from? (Hint: recall that all unqualified names come from one of four scopes, by the LEGB rule.)

2. *Exception objects and lists*. Change the oops function you just wrote to raise an exception you define yourself, called MyError, and pass an extra data item along with the exception. You may identify your exception with either a string or a class. Then, extend the try statement in the catcher function to catch this exception and its data in addition to IndexError, and print the extra data item. Finally, if you used a string for your exception, go back and change it to a class instance; what now comes back as the extra data to the handler?

3. *Error handling*. Write a function called safe(func,*args) that runs any function using apply, catches any exception raised while the function runs, and prints the exception using the exc_type and exc_value attributes in the sys module. Then, use your safe function to run the oops function you wrote in exercises 1 and/or 2. Put safe in a module file called *tools.py*, and pass it the oops function interactively. What sort of error messages do you get? Finally, expand safe to also print a Python stack trace when an error occurs by calling the built-in print_exc( ) function in the standard traceback module (see the Python library reference manual for details).

## PART VIII

The Outer Layers

So far, we have covered the core of the Python language. With this knowledge, you should be able to read almost all Python code, with few language-related surprises. However, as anyone who's ever worked with existing programs knows, understanding the syntax of a language doesn't guarantee a clear and easy understanding of a program, even if it is well-written. Indeed, knowing which tools are being used—be they simple functions, coherent packages, or even complex frameworks—is the important step between a theoretical understanding of a language and a practical, effective mastery of a system.

How can you make this transition? No amount of reading woodworking magazines will turn a novice into a master woodworker. For that to happen, you have to have talent, of course, but you also have to spend years examining furniture, taking furniture apart, building new pieces, and learning from your mistakes and others' successes. The same is true in programming. The role of textbooks is to give a bird's eye view of the kinds of problems and appropriate solutions, to show some of the basic tricks of the trade, and to motivate the frustrated beginner by showing some of the nicer pieces of work others have built. Part VIII presents a different view of the Python landscape in each chapter and gives plentiful pointers to other sources of information.

## CHAPTER 27

Common Tasks in Python

At this point in the book, you have been exposed to a fairly complete survey of the more formal aspects of the language (the syntax, the data types, etc.). In this chapter, we'll "step out of the classroom" by looking at a set of basic computing tasks and examining how Python programmers typically solve them, hopefully helping you ground the theoretical knowledge with concrete results.

Python programmers don't like to reinvent wheels when they already have access to nice, round wheels in their garage. Thus, the most important content in this chapter is the description of selected tools that make up the Python standard library—built-in functions, library modules, and their most useful functions and classes. While you most likely won't use all of these in any one program, no useful program avoids all of these. Just as Python provides a list object type because sequence manipulations occur in all programming contexts, the library provides a set of modules that will come in handy over and over again. Before designing and writing any piece of generally useful code, check to see if a similar module already exists. If it's part of the standard Python library, you can be assured that it's been heavily tested; even better, others are committed to fixing any remaining bugs—for free.

The goal of this chapter is to expose you to a lot of different tools, so that you know that they exist, rather than to teach you everything you need to know in order to use them. There are very good sources of complementary knowledge once you've finished this book. If you want to explore more of the standard library, the definitive reference is the Python Library Reference, currently over 600 pages long. It is the ideal companion to this book; it provides the completeness we don't have the room for, and, being available online, is the most up-to-date description of the standard Python toolset. Three other O'Reilly books provide excellent additional information: the *Python Pocket Reference*, written by Mark Lutz, which covers the most important modules in the standard library, along with the syntax and built-in functions in compact form; Fredrik Lundh's *Python Standard Library*, which takes on the formidable task of both providing additional documentation for each module in the standard library as well as providing an example program showing how to use each module; and finally, Alex Martelli's *Python in a Nutshell* provides a thorough yeteminently readable and concise description of the language and standard library. As we'll see in the section "Exploring on Your Own," Python comes with tools that make self-learning easy as well.

Just as we can't cover every standard module, the set of tasks covered in this chapter is necessarily limited. If you want more, check out the *Python Cookbook* (O'Reilly), edited by David Ascher and Alex Martelli. This Cookbook covers many of the same problem domains we touch on here but in much greater depth and with much more discussion. That book, leveraging the collective knowledge of the Python community, provides a much broader and richer survey of Pythonic approaches to common tasks.

This chapter limits itself to tools available as part of standard Python distributions. The next two chapters expand the scope to third party modules and libraries, since many such modules can be just as valuable to the Python programmer.

This chapter starts by covering common tasks which apply to fundamental programming concepts—types, data structures, strings, moving on to conceptually higher-level topics like files and directories, Internet-related operations and process launching before finishing with some nonprogramming tasks such as testing, debugging, and profiling.

Exploring on Your Own

Before digging into specific tasks, we should say a brief word about self-exploration. We have not been exhaustive in coverage of object attributes or module contents in order to focus on the most important aspects of the objects under discussion. If you're curious about what we've left out, you can look it up in the Library Reference, or you can poke around in the Python interactive interpreter, as shown in this section.

The dir built-in function returns a list of all of the attributes of an object, and, along with the type built-in, provides a great way to learn about the objects you're manipulating. For example:

```
>>> dir([ ])                            # What are the attributes of lists?
['__add__', '__class__', '__contains__', '__delattr__', '__delitem__',
'__delslice__', '__doc__', '__eq__', '__ge__', '__getattribute__', '__getitem__',
'__getslice__', '__gt__', '__hash__', '__iadd__', '__imul__', '__init__',
'__le__', '__len__', '__lt__', '__mul__', '__ne__', '__new__', '__reduce__',
'__repr__', '__rmul__', '__setattr__', '__setitem__', '__setslice__', '__str__',
'append', 'count', 'extend', 'index', 'insert', 'pop', 'remove', 'reverse', 'sort']
```

What this tells you is that the empty list object has a few methods: append, count, extend, index, insert, pop, remove, reverse, sort, and a lot of "special methods" that start with an underscore (_) or two (__). These are used under the hood by Python when performing operations like +. Since these special methods are not needed very often, we'll write a simple utility function that will not display them:

```
>>> def mydir(obj):
...     orig_dir = dir(obj)
...     return [item for item in orig_dir if not item.startswith('_')]
...
>>>
```

Using this new function on the same empty list yields:

```
>>> mydir([ ])                          # What are the attributes of lists?
['append', 'count', 'extend', 'index', 'insert', 'pop', 'remove', 'reverse', 'sort']
```

You can then explore any Python object:

```
>>> mydir(( ))                          # What are the attributes of tuples?
[ ]                                     # Note: no "normal" attributes
>>> import sys                          # What are the attributes of files?
>>> mydir(sys.stdin)                    # What are the attributes of files?
['close', 'closed', 'fileno', 'flush', 'isatty', 'mode', 'name', 'read', 'readinto',
'readline', 'readlines', 'seek', 'softspace', 'tell', 'truncate', 'write',
'writelines', 'xreadlines']
 >>> mydir(sys)                         # Modules are objects too.
['argv', 'builtin_module_names', 'byteorder', 'copyright', 'displayhook',
'dllhandle', 'exc_info', 'exc_type', 'excepthook', 'exec_prefix', 'executable',
'exit', 'getdefaultencoding', 'getrecursionlimit', 'getrefcount', 'hexversion',
'last_traceback', 'last_type', 'last_value', 'maxint', 'maxunicode', 'modules',
'path', 'platform', 'prefix', 'ps1', 'ps2', 'setcheckinterval', 'setprofile',
'setrecursionlimit', 'settrace', 'stderr', 'stdin', 'stdout', 'version',
'version_info', 'warnoptions', 'winver']
>>> type(sys.version)                   # What kind of thing is 'version'?
<type 'string'>
>>> print repr(sys.version)             # What is the value of this string?
'2.3a1 (#38, Dec 31 2002, 17:53:59) [MSC v.1200 32 bit (Intel)]'
```

Recent versions of Python also contain a built-in that is very helpul to beginners, named (appropriately enough) help:

```
>>> help(sys)
Help on built-in module sys:
NAME
    sys

FILE
     (built-in)

DESCRIPTION
    This module provides access to some objects used or maintained by the
    interpreter and to functions that interact strongly with the
    interpreter.

    Dynamic objects:

    argv—command line arguments; argv[0] is the script pathname if known
    path—module search path; path[0] is the script directory, else ''
    modules—dictionary of loaded modules
```

```
    displayhook—called to show results in an interactive session
    excepthook—called to handle any uncaught exception other than
    SystemExit

    To customize printing in an interactive session or to install a
    custom top-level exception handler, assign other functions to replace
    these.
    ...
```

There is quite a lot to the online help system. We recommend that you start it first in its "modal" state, just by typing **help( )**. From then on, any string you type will yield its documentation. Type **quit** to leave the help mode.

```
>>> help( )
Welcome to Python 2.2! This is the online help utility
...
help> socket
Help on module socket:

NAME
    socket

FILE
    c:\python22\lib\socket.py

DESCRIPTION
    This module provides socket operations and some related functions.
    On Unix, it supports IP (Internet Protocol) and Unix domain sockets.
    On other systems, it only supports IP. Functions specific for a
    socket are available as methods of the socket object.

    Functions:

    socket( ) -- create a new socket object
    fromfd( ) -- create a socket object from an open file descriptor [*]
    gethostname( ) -- return the current hostname
    gethostbyname( ) -- map a hostname to its IP number
    gethostbyaddr( ) -- map an IP number or hostname to DNS info
    getservbyname( ) -- map a service name and a protocol name to a port
    ...
help> keywords

Here is a list of the Python keywords.  Enter any keyword to get more help.

and             elif            global          or
assert          else            if              pass
break           except          import          print
class           exec            in              raise
continue        finally         is              return
def             for             lambda          try
del             from            not             while
help> topics

Here is a list of available topics.  Enter any topic name to get more help.
```

```
ASSERTION            DEBUGGING           LITERALS         SEQUENCEMETHODS1
ASSIGNMENT           DELETION            LOOPING          SEQUENCEMETHODS2
ATTRIBUTEMETHODS     DICTIONARIES        MAPPINGMETHODS   SEQUENCES
ATTRIBUTES           DICTIONARYLITERALS  MAPPINGS         SHIFTING
AUGMENTEDASSIGNMENT  ELLIPSIS            METHODS          SLICINGS
BACKQUOTES           EXCEPTIONS          MODULES          SPECIALATTRIBUTES
BASICMETHODS         EXECUTION           NAMESPACES       SPECIALIDENTIFIERS
BINARY               EXPRESSIONS         NONE             SPECIALMETHODS
BITWISE              FILES               NUMBERMETHODS    STRINGMETHODS
BOOLEAN              FLOAT               NUMBERS          STRINGS
CALLABLEMETHODS      FORMATTING          OBJECTS          SUBSCRIPTS
CALLS                FRAMEOBJECTS        OPERATORS        TRACEBACKS
CLASSES              FRAMES              PACKAGES         TRUTHVALUE
CODEOBJECTS          FUNCTIONS           POWER            TUPLELITERALS
COERCIONS            IDENTIFIERS         PRECEDENCE       TUPLES
COMPARISON           IMPORTING           PRINTING         TYPEOBJECTS
COMPLEX              INTEGER             PRIVATENAMES     TYPES
CONDITIONAL          LISTLITERALS        RETURNING        UNARY
CONVERSIONS          LISTS               SCOPING          UNICODE
help> TYPES
   3.2 The standard type hierarchy

   Below is a list of the types that are built into Python. Extension
   modules written in C can define additional types. Future versions of
   Python may add types to the type hierarchy (e.g., rational numbers,
   efficiently stored arrays of integers, etc.).
   ...

help> quit
>>>
```

Conversions, Numbers, and Comparisons

While we've covered data types, one of the common issues when dealing with any type system is how one converts from one type to another. These conversions happen in a myriad of contexts—reading numbers from a text file, computing integer averages, interfacing with functions that expect different types than the rest of an application, etc.

We've seen in previous chapters that we can create a string from a nonstring object by simply passing the nonstring object to the str string constructor. Similarly, unicode converts any object to its Unicode string form and returns it.*

---

* As we're not going to be subclassing from built-in types in this chapter, it makes no difference to us whether these conversion calls are functions (which they were until recent versions of Python) or class creators (which they are in Python 2.2 or later)—either way, they take objects as input and return new objects of the appropriate type (assuming the specific conversion is allowed). In this section we'll refer to them as functions as a matter of convenience.

In addition to the string creation functions, we've seen list and tuple, which take sequences and return list and tuple versions of them, respectively. int, complex, float, and long take any number and convert it to their respective types. int, long, and float have additional features that can be confusing. First, int and long truncate their numeric arguments, if necessary, to perform the operation, thereby losing information and performing a conversion that may not be what you want (the round built-in rounds numbers the standard way and returns a float). Second, int, long, and float can also convert strings to their respective types, provided the strings are valid integer (or long, or float) literals. Literals are the text strings that are converted to numbers early in the Python compilation process. So, the string 1244 in your Python program file (which is necessarily a string) is a valid integer literal, but def foo( ): isn't.

```
>>> int(1.0), int(1.4), int(1.9), round(1.9), int(round(1.9))
(1, 1, 1, 2.0, 2)
>>> int("1")
1
>>> int("1.2")                          # This doesn't work.
Traceback (most recent call last):
  File "<stdin>", line 1, in ?
ValueError: invalid literal for int( ): 1.2
```

What's a little odd is that the rule about conversion (if it's a valid integer literal) is more important than the feature about truncating numeric arguments, thus:

```
>>> int("1.0")                          # Neither does this
Traceback (most recent call last):      # since 1.0 is also not a valid
  File "<stdin>", line 1, in ?          # integer literal.
ValueError: invalid literal for int( ): 1.0
```

Given the behavior of int, it may make sense in some cases to use a custom variant that does only conversion, refusing to truncate:

```
>>> def safeint(candidate):
...     converted = float(candidate)
...     rounded = round(converted)
...     if converted == rounded:
...             return int(converted)
...     else:
...             raise ValueError, "%s would lose precision when cast"%candidate
...
>>> safeint(3.0)
3
>>> safeint("3.0")
3
>>> safeint(3.1)
Traceback (most recent call last):
  File "<stdin>", line 1, in ?
  File "<stdin>", line 8, in safeint
ValueError: 3.1 would lose precision when cast
```

Converting numbers to strings can be done in a variety of ways. In addition to using str or unicode, one can use hex or oct, which take integers (whether int or long) as arguments and return string representations of them in hexadecimal or octal format, respectively.

```
>>> hex(1000), oct(1000)
('0x3e8', '01750')
```

The abs built-in returns the absolute value of scalars (integers, longs, floats) and the magnitude of complex numbers (the square root of the sum of the squared real and imaginary parts):

```
>>> abs(-1), abs(-1.2), abs(-3+4j)
(1, 1.2, 5.0)                              # 5 is sqrt(3*3 + 4*4).
```

The ord and chr functions return the ASCII value of single characters and vice versa:

```
>>> map(ord, "test")     # Remember that strings are sequences
[116, 101, 115, 116]     # of characters, so map can be used.
>>> chr(64)
'@'
>>> ord('@')
64
# map returns a list of single characters, so it
# needs to be "joined" into a str.
>>> map(chr, (83, 112, 97, 109, 33))
['S', 'p', 'a', 'm', '! ']
# Can also be spelled using list comprehensions
>>> [chr(x) for x in (83, 112, 97, 109, 33)]
['S', 'p', 'a', 'm', '! ']
>>> ''.join([chr(x) for x in (83, 112, 97, 109, 33)])
'Spam!'
```

The cmp built-in returns a negative integer, 0, or a positive integer, depending on whether its first argument is less than, equal to, or greater than its second one. It's worth emphasizing that cmp works with more than just numbers; it compares characters using their ASCII values, and sequences are compared by comparing their elements. Comparisons can raise exceptions, so the comparison function is not guaranteed to work on all objects, but all reasonable comparisons will work.* The comparison process used by cmp is the same as that used by the sort method of lists. It's also used by the built-ins min and max, which return the smallest and largest elements of the objects they are called with, dealing reasonably with sequences:

```
>>> min("pif", "paf", "pof")      # When called with multiple arguments,
'paf'                             # return appropriate one.
>>> min("ZELDA!"), max("ZELDA!")  # when called with a sequence,
'!', 'Z'                          # return the min/max element of it.
```

---

* For a variety of mostly historical reasons, even some unreasonable comparisons (1 > "2") will yield a value.

Table 27-1 summarizes the built-in functions dealing with type conversions. Many of these can also be called with no argument to return a false value; for example, str( ) returns the empty string.

Table 27-1. Type conversion built-in functions

Function name	Behavior

str(string)
unicode(string)
	Returns the string representation of any object:
	<pre>>>> str(dir( ))
	"['__builtins__', '__doc__', '__name__']"
	>>> unicode('tomato')
	u' tomato'</pre>

list(seq)	Returns the list version of a sequence:
	<pre>>>> list("tomato")
	['t', 'o', 'm', 'a', 't', 'o']
	>>> list((1,2,3))
	[1, 2, 3]</pre>

tuple(seq)	Returns the tuple version of a sequence:
	<pre>>>> tuple("tomato")
	('t', 'o', 'm', 'a', 't', 'o')
	>>> tuple([0])
	(0,)</pre>

dict( )
dict(mapping)
dict(seq)
dict(**kwargs)
	Creates a dictionary from its argument, which can be a mapping, a sequence, keyword arguments or nothing (yielding the empty dictionary):
	<pre>>>> dict( )
	{ }
	>>> dict([('a', 2), ('b', 5)])
	{'a': 2, 'b': 5}
	>>> dict(a=2, b=5) # In Python 2.3 or later
	{'a': 2, 'b': 5}</pre>

int(x)	Converts a string or number to a plain integer; truncates floating-point values. The string needs to be a valid string literal (i.e., no decimal point).
	<pre>>>> int("3")
	3</pre>

long(x)	Converts a string or number to a long integer; truncates floating-point values:
	<pre>>>> long("3")
	3L</pre>

float(x)	Converts a string or a number to floating point:
	<pre>>>> float("3")
	3.0</pre>

complex(real,imag)	Creates a complex number with the value real + imag*j:
	<pre>>>> complex(3,5)
	(3+5j)</pre>

hex(i)	Converts an integer number (of any size) to a hexadecimal string:
	<pre>>>> hex(10000)
	'0x2710'</pre>

Table 27-1. Type conversion built-in functions (continued)

Function name	Behavior

oct(i)	Converts an integer number (of any size) to an octal string:
	
	``
	>>> oct(10000)
	'023420'
	``

ord(char)	Returns the numeric value of a string of one character (using the current default encoding, often ASCII):
	
	``
	>>> ord('A')
	65
	``

chr(i)	Returns a string of one character whose numeric code in the current encoding (often ASCII) is the integer i:
	
	``
	>>> chr(65)
	'A'
	``

min(i [, i]*)	Returns the smallest item of a nonempty sequence:
	
	``
	>>> min([5,1,2,3,4])
	1
	>>> min(5,1,2,3,4)
	1
	``

max(i [, i]*)	Returns the largest item of a nonempty sequence:
	
	``
	>>> max([5,1,2,3,4])
	5
	>>> max(5,1,2,3,4)
	5
	``

file(name [, mode [,buffering])	Opens a file.
	
	``
	>>> data = file('contents.txt', 'r').read( )
	``

Manipulating Strings

The vast majority of programs perform string operations. We've covered most of the properties and variants of string objects in Chapter 5, but there are two areas that we haven't touched on thus far, the string module, and regular expressions. As we'll see the first is simple and mostly a historical note, while the second is complex and powerful.

The string Module

The string module is somewhat of a historical anomaly. If Python were being designed today, the string module would not exist—it is mostly a remnant of a less civilized age before everything was a first-class object. Nowadays, string objects have methods like split and join, which replace the functions that are still defined in the string module. The string module does define a convenient function, maketrans, used to automatically do string "mapping" operations with the translate method of string objects. maketrans/translate is useful when you want to translate several characters in a string at once. For example, if you want to replace all occurrences of the space character with an underscore, change underscores to minus signs, and change minus signs to plus signs. Doing so with repeated `.replace()` operations is in fact quite tricky, but doing it with maketrans is trivial:

```
>>> import string
>>> conversion = string.maketrans(" _-", " _-+")
>>> input_string = "This is a two_part - one_part"
>>> input_string.translate(conversion)
'This_is_a_two-part_+_one-part'
```

In addition, the string module defines a few useful constants, which haven't been implemented as string attributes yet. These are shown in Table 27-2.

Table 27-2. String module constants

Constant name	Value
digits	'0123456789'
octdigits	'01234567'
hexdigits	'0123456789abcdefABCDEF'
lowercase	'abcdefghijklmnopqrstuvwxyz'
uppercase	'ABCDEFGHIJKLMNOPQRSTUVWXYZ'
Letters	lowercase + uppercase
whitespace	'\t\n\r\v' (all whitespace characters)

The constants in Table 27-2 are useful to test whether specific characters fit a criterion—for example, x in string.whitespace returns true only if x is one of the whitespace characters. Note that the values given above aren't always the values you'll find—for example, the definition of 'uppercase' depends on the locale: if you're running a French operating system, string.lowercase will include ç and ê.

Complicated String Matches with Regular Expressions

If strings and their methods aren't enough (and they do get clumsy in many perfectly normal use cases), Python provides a specialized string-processing tool in the form of a regular expression engine.

Regular expressions are strings that let you define complicated pattern matching and replacement rules for strings. The syntax for regular expressions emphasizes compact notation over mnemonic value. For example, the single character . means "match any single character." The character + means "one or more of what just preceded me." Table 27-3 lists some of the most commonly used regular expression symbols and their meanings in English. Describing the full set of regular expression tokens and their meaning would take quite a few pages—instead, we'll cover a simple use case and walk through how to solve the problem using regular expressions.

Table 27-3. Common elements of regular expression syntax

Special character	Meaning
.	Matches any character except newline by default
^	Matches the start of the string
$	Matches the end of the string
*	"Any number of occurrences of what just preceded me"
+	"One or more occurrences of what just preceded me"
|	"Either the thing before me or the thing after me"
\w	Matches any alphanumeric character
\d	Matches any decimal digit
tomato	Matches the string tomato

A real regular expression problem

Suppose you need to write a program to replace the strings "green pepper" and "red pepper" with "bell pepper" if and only if they occur together in a paragraph before the word "salad" and not if they are followed (with no space) by the string "corn." Although the specific requirements are silly, the general kind (conditional replacement of subparts of text based on specific contextual constraints) is surprisingly common in computing. We will explain each step of the program that solves this task.

Assume that the file you need to process is called *pepper.txt*. Here's an example of such a file:

```
This is a paragraph that mentions bell peppers multiple times. For
one, here is a red pepper and dried tomato salad recipe. I don't like
to use green peppers in my salads as much because they have a harsher
flavor.

This second paragraph mentions red peppers and green peppers but not
the "s" word (s-a-l-a-d), so no bells should show up.

This third paragraph mentions red peppercorns and green peppercorns,
which aren't vegetables but spices (by the way, bell peppers really
aren't peppers, they're chilies, but would you rather have a good cook
or a good botanist prepare your salad?).
```

The first task is to open the file and read in the text:

```
file = open('pepper.txt')
text = file.read()
```

We read the entire text at once and avoid splitting it into lines, since we will assume that paragraphs are defined by two consecutive newline characters. This is easy to do using the split function of the string module:

```
paragraphs = text.split('\n\n')
```

At this point we've split the text into a list of paragraph strings, and all there is left to do is perform the actual replacement operation. Here's where regular expressions come in:

```
import re
matchstr = re.compile(
    r"""\b(red|green)        # 'red' or 'green' starting new words
       (\s+                  # followed by whitespace
       pepper                # The word 'pepper',
       (?!corn)              # if not followed immediately by 'corn'
       (?=.*salad))""",      # and if followed at some point by 'salad',
       re.IGNORECASE |       # allow pepper, Pepper, PEPPER, etc.
       re.DOTALL |           # Allow dots to match newlines as well.
       re.VERBOSE)           # This allows the comments and the newlines above.
for paragraph in paragraphs:
    fixed_paragraph = matchstr.sub(r'bell\2', paragraph)
    print fixed_paragraph+'\n'
```

The first line is simple but key: all of Python's regular expression smarts are in the `re` module.

The bold statement is the hardest one; it creates a regular expression pattern, which is like a program (that's the raw string), and compiles it. Such a pattern specifies two things: which parts of the strings we're interested in and how they should be grouped. Let's go over these in turn. The `re.compile( )` call takes a string (although the syntax of that string is quite particular) and returns an object called a compiled regular expression object, which corresponds to that string.

Defining which parts of the string we're interested in is done by specifying a pattern of characters that defines a match. This is done by concatenating smaller patterns, each of which specifies a simple matching criterion (e.g., "match the string 'pepper'," "match one or more whitespace characters," "don't match 'corn'," etc.). We're looking for the words "red" or "green" followed by the word "pepper" that is itself followed by the word "salad," as long as "pepper" isn't followed immediately by "corn." Let's take each line of the `re.compile( ... )` expression in turn.

The first thing to notice about the string in the `re.compile( )` is that it's a "raw" string (the quotation marks are preceded by an r). Prepending such an r to a string (single- or triple-quoted) turns off the interpretation of the backslash characters within the string.* We could have used a regular string instead and used \\b instead of \b and \\s instead of \s. In this case, it makes little difference; for complicated regular expressions, raw strings allow for much clearer syntax than escaped backslashes.

The first line in the pattern is \b(red|green). \b stands for "the empty string, but only at the beginning or end of a word"; using it here prevents matches that have red

---

* Raw strings can't end with an odd number of backslash characters. That's unlikely to be a problem when using raw strings for regular expressions, however, since regular expressions can't end with backslashes.

or green as the final part of a word (as in "tired pepper"). The (red|green) pattern specifies an alternation: either 'red' or 'green'. Ignore the left parenthesis that follows for now. \s is a special symbol that means "any whitespace character," and + means "one or more occurrence of whatever comes before me," so, put together, \s+ means "one or more whitespace characters." Then, pepper just means the string 'pepper'. (?!corn) prevents matches of "patterns that have 'corn' at this point," so we prevent the match on 'peppercorn'. Finally, (?=.*salad) says that for the pattern to match, it must be followed by any number of arbitrary characters (that's what .* means), followed by the word salad. The ?= specifies that while the pattern should determine whether the match occurs, it shouldn't be "used up" by the match process; it's a subtle point that we won't cover in detail here. At this point we've defined the pattern corresponding to the substring.

Now, note that there are two parentheses—the one before \s+ and the last one. What these two do is define a "group," which starts after the red or green and go to the end of the pattern. We'll use that group in the next operation, the actual replacement. The three flags are joined by the | symbol (the bitwise "or" operation) to form the second argument to re.compile. These specify kinds of pattern matches. The first, re.IGNORECASE, says that the text comparisons should ignore whether the text and the match have similar or different cases. The second, re.DOTALL, specifies that the . character should match any character, including the newline character (that's not the default behavior). The third, re.VERBOSE, allows us to insert extra newlines and # comments in the regular expression, making it easier to read and understand. We could have written the statement more compactly as:

```
matchstr = re.compile(r"\b(red|green)(\s+pepper(?!corn)(?=.*salad))", re.I | re.S)
```

The actual replacement operation is done with the line:

```
fixed_paragraph = matchstr.sub(r'bell\2', paragraph)
```

We're calling the sub method of the matchstr object. That object is a compiled regular expression object, meaning that some of the processing of the expression has already been done (in this case, outside the loop), thus speeding up the total program execution. We use a raw string again to write the first argument to the method. The \2 is a reference to group 2 in the regular expression—the second group of parentheses in the regular expression—in our case, everything starting with whitespace followed by 'pepper' and up to and including the word 'salad'. Therefore, this line means, "Replace the occurrences of the matched substring with the string that is 'bell' followed by whatever starts with whitespace followed by 'pepper' and goes up to the end of the matched string, throughout the paragraph string."

So, does it work? The *pepper.txt* file had three paragraphs: the first satisfied the requirements of the match twice, the second didn't because it didn't mention the word 'salad', and the third didn't because the 'red' and 'green' words are before peppercorn, not pepper. As it was supposed to, our program (saved in a file called *pepper.py*) modifies only the first paragraph:

```
/home/David/book$ python pepper.py
This is a paragraph that mentions bell peppers multiple times. For
one, here is a bell pepper and dried tomato salad recipe. I don't like
to use bell peppers in my salads as much because they have a harsher
flavor.

This second paragraph mentions red peppers and green peppers but not
the "s" word (s-a-l-a-d), so no bells should show up.

This third paragraph mentions red peppercorns and green peppercorns,
which aren't vegetables but spices (by the way, bell peppers really
aren't peppers, they're chilies, but would you rather have a good cook
or a good botanist prepare your salad?).
```

This example, while artificial, shows how regular expressions can compactly express complicated matching rules. If this kind of problem occurs often in your line of work, mastering regular expressions can be a worthwhile investment of time and effort.

A more thorough coverage of regular expressions is beyond the scope of this book. Jeffrey Friedl provides excellent coverage of regular expressions in his book *Mastering Regular Expressions* (O'Reilly). This book is a must-have for anyone doing serious text processing. For the casual user, the descriptions in the Library Reference or *Python in a Nutshell* do the job most of the time. Be sure to use the re module, not the regex, or regsub modules, which are deprecated (they probably won't be around in a later version of Python):

```
>>> import regex
__main__:1: DeprecationWarning: the regex module is deprecated; please use the re
module
```

Data Structure Manipulations

One of Python's greatest features is that it provides the list, tuple, and dictionary built-in types. They are so flexible and easy to use that once you've grown used to them, you'll find yourself reaching for them automatically. While we covered all of the operations on each data structure as we introduced them, now's a good time to go over tasks that can apply to all data structures, such as how to make copies, sort objects, randomize sequences, etc. Many functions and algorithms (theoretical procedures describing how to implement a complex task in terms of simpler basic tasks) are designed to work regardless of the type of data being manipulated. It is therefore useful to know how to do generic things for all data types.

Making Copies

Making copies of objects is a reasonable task in many programming contexts. Often, the only kind of copy that's needed is just another reference to an object, as in:

```
x = 'tomato'
y = x                    # y is now 'tomato'.
x = x + ' and cucumber' # x is now 'tomato and cucumber', but y is unchanged.
```

Due to Python's reference management scheme, the statement a = b doesn't make a copy of the object referenced by b; instead, it makes a new reference to that same object. When the object being copied is an immutable object (e.g., a string), there is no real difference. When dealing with mutable objects like lists and dictionaries, however, sometimes a real, new copy of the object, not just a shared reference, is needed. How to do this depends on the type of the object in question. The simplest way of making a copy is to use the list( ) or tuple( ) constructors:

```
newList = list(myList)
newTuple = tuple(myTuple)
```

As opposed to the simplest, the most common way to make copies of sequences like lists and tuples is somewhat odd. If myList is a list, then to make a copy of it, you can use:

```
newList = myList[:]
```

which you can read as "slice from beginning to end," since the default index for the start of a slice is the beginning of the sequence (0), and the default index for the end of a slice is the end of sequence (see Chapter 3). Since tuples support the same slicing operation as lists, this same technique can also be applied to tuples, except that if x is a tuple, then x[:] is the same object as x, since tuples are immutable. Dictionaries, on the other hand, don't support slicing. To make a copy of a dictionary myDict, you can either use:

```
newDict = myDict.copy( )
```

or the dict( ) constructor:

```
newDict = dict(myDict)
```

For a different kind of copying, if you have a dictionary oneDict, and want to update it with the contents of a different dictionary otherDict, simply type oneDict. update(otherDict). This is the equivalent of:

```
for key in otherDict.keys( ):
    oneDict[key] = otherDict[key]
```

If oneDict shared some keys with otherDict before the update( ) operation, the old values associated with the keys in oneDict are obliterated by the update. This may be what you want to do (it usually is). If it isn't, the right thing to do might be to raise an exception. To do this, make a copy of one dictionary, then look over each entry in the second. If we find shared keys, we raise an exception, if not, we just add the key-value mapping to the new dictionary.

```
def mergeWithoutOverlap(oneDict, otherDict):
    newDict = oneDict.copy()
    for key in otherDict:
        if key in oneDict:
            raise ValueError, "the two dictionaries share keys!"
        newDict[key] = otherDict[key]
    return newDict
```

or, alternatively, combine the values of the two dictionaries, with a tuple, for example. Using the same logic as in mergeWithoutOverlap, but combining the values instead of throwing an exception:

```
def mergeWithOverlap(oneDict, otherDict):
    newDict = oneDict.copy()
    for key in otherDict:
        if key in oneDict:
            newDict[key] = oneDict[key], otherDict[key]
        else:
            newDict[key] = otherDict[key]
    return newDict
```

To illustrate the differences between the preceding three algorithms, consider the following two dictionaries:

```
phoneBook1 = {'michael': '555-1212', 'mark': '554-1121', 'emily': '556-0091'}
phoneBook2 = {'latoya': '555-1255', 'emily': '667-1234'}
```

If phoneBook1 is possibly out of date, and phoneBook2 is more up to date but less complete, the right usage is probably phoneBook1.update(phoneBook2). If the two phoneBooks are supposed to have nonoverlapping sets of keys, using newBook = mergeWithoutOverlap(phoneBook1, phoneBook2) lets you know if that assumption is wrong. Finally, if one is a set of home phone numbers and the other a set of office phone numbers, chances are newBook = mergeWithOverlap(phoneBook1, phoneBook2) is what you want, as long as the subsequent code that uses newBook can deal with the fact that newBook['emily'] is the tuple ('556-0091', '667-1234').

The copy module

The [:] and .copy() tricks will get you copies in 90% of the cases. If you are writing functions that, in true Python spirit, can deal with arguments of any type, it's sometimes necessary to make copies of x, regardless of what x is. In comes the copy module. It provides two functions, copy and deepcopy. The first is just like the [:] sequence slice operation or the copy method of dictionaries. The second is more subtle and has to do with deeply nested structures (hence the term deepcopy). Take the example of copying a list (listOne) by slicing it from beginning to end using the [:] construct. This technique makes a new list that contains references to the same objects contained in the original list. If the contents of that original list are immutable objects, such as numbers or strings, the copy is as good as a "true" copy. However, suppose that the first element in listOne is itself a dictionary (or any other mutable object). The first element of the copy of listOne is a new reference to the same dictionary. So if you then modify that dictionary, the modification is evident in both listOne and the copy of listOne. An example makes it much clearer:

```
>>> import copy
>>> listOne = [{"name": "Willie", "city": "Providence, RI"}, 1, "tomato", 3.0]
>>> listTwo = listOne[:]                # Or listTwo=copy.copy(listOne)
>>> listThree = copy.deepcopy(listOne)
>>> listOne.append("kid")
>>> listOne[0]["city"] = "San Francisco, CA"
>>> print listOne, listTwo, listThree
[{'name': 'Willie', 'city': 'San Francisco, CA'}, 1, 'tomato', 3.0, 'kid']
[{'name': 'Willie', 'city': 'San Francisco, CA'}, 1, 'tomato', 3.0]
[{'name': 'Willie', 'city': 'Providence, RI'}, 1, 'tomato', 3.0]
```

As you can see, modifying listOne directly modified only listOne. Modifying the first entry of the list referenced by listOne led to changes in listTwo, but not in listThree; that's the difference between a shallow copy ([:]) and a deep copy. The copy module functions know how to copy all the built-in types that are reasonably copyable,* including classes and instances.

Sorting

Lists have a sort method that does an in-place sort. Sometimes you want to iterate over the sorted contents of a list, without disturbing the contents of this list. Or you may want to list the sorted contents of a tuple. Because tuples are immutable, an operation such as sort, which modifies it in place, is not allowed. The only solution is to make a list copy of the elements, sort the list copy, and work with the sorted copy, as in:

```
listCopy = list(myTuple)
listCopy.sort()
for item in listCopy:
    print item                      # Or whatever needs doing
```

This solution is also the way to deal with data structures that have no inherent order, such as dictionaries. One of the reasons that dictionaries are so fast is that the implementation reserves the right to change the order of the keys in the dictionary. It's really not a problem, however, given that you can iterate over the keys of a dictionary using an intermediate copy of the keys of the dictionary:

```
keys = myDict.keys()                # Returns an unsorted list of
                                    # the keys in the dict.
```

---

* Some objects don't qualify as "reasonably copyable," such as modules, file objects, and sockets. Remember that file objects are different from files on disk as they are opened at a particular point, and are possibly not even fully written to disk yet. For copying files on disk, the shutil module is introduced later in this chapter.

```
    keys.sort()
    for key in keys:                          # Print key/value pairs
        print key, myDict[key]                # sorted by key.
```

The sort method on lists uses the standard Python comparison scheme. Sometimes, however, that scheme isn't what's needed, and you need to sort according to some other procedure. For example, when sorting a list of words, case (lower versus UPPER) may not be significant. The standard comparison of text strings, however, says that all uppercase letters come before all lowercase letters, so 'Baby' is less than 'apple', but 'baby' is greater than 'apple'. In order to do a case-independent sort, you need to define a comparison function that takes two arguments, and returns −1, 0, or 1 depending on whether the first argument is smaller than, equal to, or greater than the second argument. So, for case-independent sorting, you can use:

```
>>> def caseIndependentSort(something, other):
...     something, other = something.lower(), other.lower()
...     return cmp(something, other)
...
>>> testList = ['this', 'is', 'A', 'sorted', 'List']
>>> testList.sort()
>>> print testList
['A', 'List', 'is', 'sorted', 'this']
>>> testList.sort(caseIndependentSort)
>>> print testList
['A', 'is', 'List', 'sorted', 'this']
```

We're using the built-in function cmp, which does the hard part of figuring out that 'a' comes before 'b', 'b' before 'c', etc. Our sort function simply converts both items to lowercase and compares the lowercase versions. Also note that the conversion to lowercase is local to the comparison function, so the elements in the list aren't modified by the sort.

Randomizing

What about randomizing a sequence, such as a list of lines? The easiest way to randomize a sequence is to call the shuffle function in the random module, which randomizes a sequence in-place:[*]

```
    random.shuffle(myList)
```

If you need to shuffle a nonlist object, it's usually easiest to convert that object to a list and shuffle the list version of the same data, rather than come up with a new strategy for each data type. This might seem a wasteful strategy, given that it involves building intermediate lists that might be quite large. In general, however, what seems large to you probably won't seem so to the computer, thanks to the reference system. Also,

---

[*] Another useful function in the random module is the choice function, which returns a random element in the sequence passed in as argument.

consider the time saved by not having to come up with a different strategy for each data type! Python is designed to save programmer time; if that means running a slightly slower or bigger program, so be it. If you're handling enormous amounts of data, it may be worthwhile to optimize. But never optimize until the need for optimization is clear; that would be a waste of your time.

Making New Data Structures

This chapter emphasizes the silliness involved in reinventing wheels. This point is especially important when it comes to data structures. For example, Python lists and dictionaries might not be the lists and dictionaries or mappings you're used to, but you should avoid designing your own data structure if these structures will suffice. The algorithms they use have been tested under wide ranges of conditions, and they're fast and stable. Sometimes, however, the interface to these algorithms isn't convenient for a particular task.

For example, computer science textbooks often describe algorithms in terms of other data structures such as queues and stacks. To use these algorithms, it may make sense to come up with a data structure that has the same methods as these data structures (such as pop and push for stacks or enqueue/dequeue for queues). However, it also makes sense to reuse the built-in list type in the implementation of a stack. In other words, you need something that acts like a stack but is based on a list. A simple solution is to use a class wrapper around a list. For a minimal stack implementation, you can do this:

```
class Stack:
    def __init__(self, data):
        self._data = list(data)
        self.push = self._data.append
        self.pop = self._data.pop
```

The following is simple to write, to understand, to read, and to use:

```
>>> thingsToDo = Stack(['write to mom', 'invite friend over', 'wash the kid'])
>>> thingsToDo.push('do the dishes')
>>> print thingsToDo.pop()
do the dishes
>>> print thingsToDo.pop()
wash the kid
```

Two standard Python naming conventions are used in the Stack class above. The first is that class names start with an uppercase letter, to distinguish them from functions. The other is that the _data attribute starts with an underscore. This is a half-way point between public attributes (which don't start with an underscore), private attributes (which start with two underscores; see Chapter 7), and Python-reserved identifiers (which both start and end with two underscores). What it means is that _data is an attribute of the class that shouldn't be needed by clients of the class. The class designer expects such pseudo-private attributes to be used only by the class methods and by the methods of any eventual subclass.

Making New Lists and Dictionaries

The Stack class presented earlier does its minimal job just fine. It assumes a fairly minimal definition of what a stack is, specifically, something that supports just two operations, a push and a pop. Some of the features of lists would be nice to use, such as the ability to iterate over all the elements using the for...in... construct. While you could continue in the style of the previous class and delegate to the "inner" list object, at some point it makes more sense to simply reuse the implementation of list objects directly, through subclassing. In this case, you should derive a class from the list base class. The dict base class can also be used to create dictionary-like classes.

```
# Subclass the list class.
class Stack(list):
    push = list.append
```

This Stack is a subclass of the list class. The list class implements the pop methods among others. You don't need to define your own __init__ method because list defines a perfectly good default. The push method is defined just by saying that it's the same as list's append method. Now we can do list-like things as well as stack-like things:

```
>>> thingsToDo = Stack(['write to mom', 'invite friend over', 'wash the kid'])
>>> print thingsToDo             # Inherited from list base class
['write to mom', 'invite friend over', 'wash the kid']
>>> thingsToDo.pop()
'wash the kid'
>>> thingsToDo.push('change the oil')
>>> for chore in thingsToDo:      # We can also iterate over the contents.
...     print chore
...
write to mom
invite friend over
change the oil
```

Manipulating Files and Directories

So far so good—we know how to create objects, we can convert between different data types, and we can perform various kinds of operations on them. In practice, however, as soon as one leaves the computer science classroom one is faced with tasks that involve manipulating data that lives outside of the program and performing processes that are external to Python. That's when it becomes very handy to know how to talk to the operating system, explore the filesystem, read and modify files.

The os and os.path Modules

The os module provides a generic interface to the operating system's most basic set of tools. Different operating systems have different behaviors. This is true at the programming interface as well. This makes it hard to write so-called "portable" programs, which run well regardless of the operating system. Having generic interfaces independent of the operating system helps, as does using an interpreted language like Python. The specific set of calls it defines depend on which platform you use. (For example, the permission-related calls are available only on platforms that support them, such as Unix and Windows.) Nevertheless, it's recommended that you always use the os module, instead of the platform-specific versions of the module (called by such names as posix, nt, and mac). Table 27-4 lists some of the most often used functions in the os module. When referring to files in the context of the os module, one is referring to filenames, not file objects.

Table 27-4. Most frequently used functions from the os module

Function name	Behavior

getcwd( )	Returns a string referring to the current working directory (cwd):
	```>>> print os.getcwd( )```
	```h:\David\book```

listdir(path)	Returns a list of all of the files in the specified directory:
	```>>> os.listdir(os.getcwd( ))```
	```['preface.doc', 'part1.doc', 'part2.doc']```

chown(path, uid, gid)	Changes the owner ID and group ID of specified file
chmod(path, mode)	Changes the permissions of specified file with numeric mode mode (e.g., 0644 means read/write for owner, read for everyone else)
rename(src, dest)	Renames file named src with name dest
remove(path) or unlink(path)	Deletes specified file (see rmdir( ) to remove directories)
rmdir(path)	Deletes specified directory
removedirs(path)	Works like rmdir( ) except that if the leaf directory is successfully removed, directories corresponding to rightmost path segments will be pruned away.
mkdir(path[, mode])	Creates a directory named path with numeric mode mode (see os.chmod): ```>>> os.mkdir('newdir')```

makedirs(path[, mode])	Like mkdir( ), but makes all intermediate-level directories needed to contain the leaf directory:
	```>>> os.makedirs('newdir/newsubdir/```
	```newsubsubdir')```

system(command)	Executes the shell command in a subshell; the return value is the return code of the command
symlink(src, dest)	Creates soft link from file src to file dest
link(src, dest)	Creates hard link from file src to file dest

Table 27-4. Most frequently used functions from the os module (continued)

Function name	Behavior

stat(path)	Returns data about the file, such as size, last modified time, and ownership:
	
	```>>> os.stat('TODO.txt')```
	# It returns something like a tuple.
	```(33206, 0L, 3, 1, 0, 0, 1753L, 1042186004, 1042186004, 1042175785)```
	```>>> os.stat('TODO.txt').st_size```
	# Just look at the size.
	1753L
	```>>> time.asctime(time.localtime```
	``` (os.stat('TODO.txt').st_mtime))```
	'Fri Jan 10 00:06:44 2003'

walk(top, topdown=True, onerror=None) (Python 2.3 and later)	For each directory in the directory tree rotted at top (including top itself, but excluding '.' and '..'), yield a 3-tuple: dirpath, dirnames, filenames

With just these modules, you can find out a lot about the current state of the filesystem, as well as modify it:

```
>>> print os.getcwd()        # Where am I?
C:\Python22
>>> print os.listdir('.')     # What's here?
['DLLs', 'Doc', 'include', 'Lib', 'libs', 'License.txt', ...]
>>> os.chdir('Lib')           # Let's go explore the library.
>>> print os.listdir('.')     # What's here?
['aifc.py', 'anydbm.py', 'anydbm.pyc', 'asynchat.py',
 'asyncore.py', 'atexit.py', 'atexit.pyc', 'atexit.pyo',
 'audiodev.py', 'base64.py', ...]
>>> os.remove('atexit.pyc')  # We can remove .pyc files safely.
>>>
```

There are many other functions in the os module; in fact, just about any function that's part of the POSIX standard and widely available on most Unix and Unix-like platforms is supported by Python on Unix. The interfaces to these routines follow the POSIX conventions. You can retrieve and set UIDs, PIDs, and process groups; control nice levels; create pipes; manipulate file descriptors; fork processes; wait for child processes; send signals to processes; use the execv variants; etc (if you don't know what half of the words in this paragraph mean, don't worry, you probably don't need to).

The os module also defines some important attributes that aren't functions:

- The os.name attribute defines the current version of the platform-specific operating-system interface. Registered values for os.name are 'posix', 'nt', 'dos', and 'mac'. It's different from sys.platform, primarily in that it's less specific—for example, Solaris and Linux will have the same value ('posix') for os.name, but different values of sys.platform.

- os.error defines an exception class used when calls in the os module raise errors. It's the same thing as OSError, one of the built-in exception classes. When this exception is raised, the value of the exception object contains two variables. The first is the number corresponding to the error (known as errno), and the second is a string message explaining it (known as strerror):

```
>>> os.rmdir('nonexistent_directory')       # How it usually shows up
Traceback (innermost last):
  File "<stdin>", line 1, in ?
os.error: (2, 'No such file or directory')
>>> try:                                     # We can catch the error and take
...     os.rmdir('nonexistent directory')    # it apart.
... except os.error, value:
...     print value[0], value[1]
...
2 No such file or directory
```

- The os.environ dictionary contains key/value pairs corresponding to the environment variables of the shell from which Python was started. Because this environment is inherited by the commands that are invoked using the os.system call, modifying the os.environ dictionary modifies the environment:

```
>>> print os.environ['SHELL']
/bin/sh
>>> os.environ['STARTDIR'] = 'MyStartDir'
>>> os.system('echo $STARTDIR')             # 'echo %STARTDIR%' on DOS/Win
MyStartDir                                   # Printed by the shell
0                                            # Return code from echo
```

The os module also includes a set of strings that define portable ways to refer to directory-related parts of filename syntax, as shown in Table 27-5.

Table 27-5. String attributes of the os module

Attribute name	Meaning and values
curdir	A string that denotes the current directory: ' . ' on Unix, DOS, and Windows; ' : ' on the Mac
pardir	A string that denotes the parent directory: ' .. ' on Unix, DOS, and Windows; ' :: ' on the Mac
sep	The character that separates pathname components: ' / ' on Unix, ' \ ' on DOS and Windows, ' : ' on the Mac
altsep	An alternate character to sep when available; set to None on all systems except DOS and Windows, where it's ' / '
pathsep	The character that separates path components: ' : ' on Unix, ' ; ' on DOS and Windows

These strings are used by the functions in the os.path module, which manipulate file paths in portable ways (see Table 27-6). Note that the os.path module is an attribute of the os module, not a sub-module of an os package; it's imported automatically when the os module is loaded, and (unlike packages) you don't need to import it explicitly. The outputs of the examples in Table 27-6 correspond to code run on a Windows or DOS machine. On another platform, the appropriate path separators would be used instead. A useful relevant bit of knowledge is that the forward slash (/) can be used safely in Windows to indicate directory traversal, even though the native separator is the backwards slash (\)—Python and Windows both do the right thing with it.

Table 27-6. Most frequently used functions from the os.path module

Function name	Behavior

`split(path)` is equivalent to the tuple: `(dirname(path), basename(path))`	Splits the given path into a pair consisting of a head and a tail; the head is the path up to the directory, and the tail is the filename:
	
	`>>> os.path.split("h:/David/book/part2.doc"`
	`('h:/David/book', 'part2.doc')`

`splitdrive(p)`	Splits a pathname into drive and path specifiers:
	
	`>>> os.path.splitdrive(r"C:\foo\bar.txt")`
	`('C:', '\\foo\\bar.txt')`

`splitext(p)`	Splits the extension from a pathname:
	
	`>>> os.path.splitext(r"C:\foo\bar.txt")`
	`('C:\\foo\\bar', '.txt')`

`splitunc(p)`	Splits a pathname into UNC mount point and relative path specifiers:
	
	`>>> os.path.splitunc(r"\\machine\mount\directory`
	`                         \file.txt")`
	`('\\\\machine\\mount', '\\directory\\file.txt')`

`join(path, ...)`	Joins path components intelligently:
	
	`>>> print os.path.join(os.getcwd(),`
	`... os.pardir, 'backup', 'part2.doc')`
	`h:\David\book\..\backup\part2.doc`

`exists(path)`	Returns true if path corresponds to an existing path

`expanduser(path)`	Expands the argument with an initial argument of ~ followed optionally by a username:
	
	`>>> print os.path.expanduser('~/mydir')`
	`h:\David\mydir`

`expandvars(path)`	Expands the path argument with the variables specified in the environment:
	
	`>>> print os.path.expandvars('$TMP')`
	`C:\TEMP`

`isfile(path)`
`isdir(path)`
`islink(path)`
`ismount(path)`
`isabs(path)`
	Returns true if the specified path is a file, directory, link, mount point, or an absolute path, respectively

`getatime(filename)`
`getmtime(filename)`
`getsize(filename)`
	Gets the last access time, last modification time, and size of a file, respectively

`normpath(path)`	Normalizes the given path, collapsing redundant separators and uplevel references:
	
	`>>> print os.path.normpath("/foo/bar\\../tmp")`
	`\foo\tmp`

Table 27-6. Most frequently used functions from the os.path module (continued)

Function name	Behavior

normcase(s)	Normalizes case of pathname; makes all characters lowercase and all slashes into backslashes:
	
	`>>> print os.path.normcase(r'c:/foo\BAR.txt')`
	`c:\foo\bar.txt`

samefile(p, q)	Returns true if both arguments refer to the same file

walk(p, visit, arg)	Calls the function visit with arguments (arg, dirname, names) for each directory in the directory tree rooted at p (including p itself, if it's a directory); the argument dirname specifies the visited directory; the argument names lists the files in the directory:
	
	`>>> def test_walk(arg, dirname, names):`
	`...     print arg, dirname, names`
	`...`
	`>>> os.path.walk('..', test_walk, 'show')`
	`show ..\logs ['errors.log', 'access.log']`
	`show ..\cgi-bin ['test.cgi']`
	`...`

Copying Files and Directories: The shutil Module

The keen-eyed reader might have noticed that the os module, while it provides lots of file-related functions, doesn't include a copy function. In DOS, copying a file is basically the same thing as opening one file in read/binary mode, reading all its data, opening a second file in write/binary mode, and writing the data to the second file. On Unix and Windows, making that kind of copy fails to copy the *stat bits* (permissions, modification times, etc.) associated with the file. On the Mac, that operation won't copy the resource fork, which contains data such as icons and dialog boxes. In other words, copying files is just more complicated than one could reasonably believe. Nevertheless, often you can get away with a fairly simple function that works on Windows, DOS, Unix, and Mac, as long as you're manipulating just data files with no resource forks. That function, called copyfile, lives in the shutil module. This module includes a few generally useful functions, shown in Table 27-7.

Table 27-7. Functions of the shutil module

Function name	Behavior
copyfile(src, dest)	Makes a copy of the file src and calls it dest (straight binary copy).
copymode(src, dest)	Copies mode information (permissions) from src to dest.
copystat(src, dest)	Copies all stat information (mode, utime) from src to dest.
copy(src, dest)	Copies data and mode information from src to dest (doesn't include the resource fork on Macs).

Table 27-7. Functions of the shutil module (continued)

Function name	Behavior
copy2(src, dest)	Copies data and stat information from `src` to `dest` (doesn't include the resource fork on Macs).
copytree(src, dest, symlinks=0)	Copies a directory recursively using `copy2`. The `symlinks` flag specifies whether symbolic links in the source tree must result in symbolic links in the destination tree, or whether the files being linked to must be copied. The destination directory must not already exist.
rmtree(path, ignore_errors=0, onerror=None)	Recursively deletes the directory indicated by path. If `ignore_error` is set to `0` (the default behavior), errors are ignored. Otherwise, if `onerror` is set, it's called to handle the error; if not, an exception is raised on error.

Filenames and Directories

While the previous section lists common functions for working with files, many tasks require more than a single function call.

Let's take a typical example: you have lots of files, all of which have a space in their name, and you'd like to replace the spaces with underscores. All you need is the os. curdir attribute (which returns an operating-system specific string that corresponds to the current directory), the os.listdir function (which returns the list of filenames in a specified directory), and the os.rename function:

```
import os
if len(sys.argv) == 1:                    # If no filenames are specified,
    filenames = os.listdir(os.curdir)     # use current dir;
else:                                     # otherwise, use files specified
    filenames = sys.argv[1:]              # on the command line.
for filename in filenames:
    if ' ' in filename:
        newfilename = filename.replace(' ', '_')
        print "Renaming", filename, "to", newfilename, "..."
        os.rename(filename, newfilename)
```

This program works fine, but it reveals a certain Unix-centrism. That is, if you call it with wildcards, such as:

```
python despacify.py *.txt
```

you find that on Unix machines, it renames all the files with names with spaces in them and that end with .txt. In a DOS-style shell, however, this won't work because the shell normally used in DOS and Windows doesn't convert from *.txt to the list of filenames; it expects the program to do it. This is called globbing, because the * is said to match a glob of characters. Luckily, Python helps us make the code portable.

Matching Sets of Files

The glob module exports a single function, also called glob, which takes a filename pattern and returns a list of all the filenames that match that pattern (in the current working directory):

```
import sys, glob
print sys.argv[1:]
sys.argv = [item for arg in sys.argv for item in glob.glob(arg)]
print sys.argv[1:]
```

Running this on Unix and DOS shows that on Unix, the Python glob didn't do anything because the globbing was done by the Unix shell before Python was invoked, and in DOS, Python's globbing came up with the same answer:

```
/usr/python/book$ python showglob.py *.py
['countlines.py', 'mygrep.py', 'retest.py', 'showglob.py', 'testglob.py']
['countlines.py', 'mygrep.py', 'retest.py', 'showglob.py', 'testglob.py']

C:\python\book> python showglob.py *.py
['*.py']
['countlines.py', 'mygrep.py', 'retest.py', 'showglob.py', 'testglob.py']
```

It's worth looking at the bold line in *showglob.py* and understanding exactly what happens there, especially if you're new to the list comprehension concept (discussed in Chapter 14).

Using Temporary Files

If you've ever written a shell script and needed to use intermediary files for storing the results of some intermediate stages of processing, you probably suffered from directory litter. You started out with 20 files called *log_001.txt*, *log_002.txt*, etc., and all you wanted was one summary file called *log_sum.txt*. In addition, you had a whole bunch of *log_001.tmp*, *log_001.tm2*, etc. files that, while they were labeled temporary, stuck around. To put order back into your directories, use temporary files in specific directories and clean them up afterwards.

To help in this temporary file management problem, Python provides a nice little module called tempfile that publishes two functions: mktemp() and TemporaryFile(). The former returns the name of a file not currently in use in a directory on your computer reserved for temporary files (such as /tmp on Unix or C:\TEMP on Windows). The latter returns a new file object directly. For example:

```
# Read input file
inputFile = open('input.txt', 'r')

import tempfile
# Create temporary file
tempFile = tempfile.TemporaryFile()                # We don't even need to
first_process(input = inputFile, output = tempFile) # know the filename...
```

```
# Create final output file
outputFile = open('output.txt', 'w')
second_process(input = tempFile, output = outputFile)
```

Using tempfile.TemporaryFile( ) works well in cases where the intermediate steps manipulate file objects. One of its nice features is that when the file object is deleted, it automatically deletes the file it created on disk, thus cleaning up after itself. One important use of temporary files, however, is in conjunction with the os.system call, which means using a shell, hence using filenames, not file objects. For example, let's look at a program that creates form letters and mails them to a list of email addresses (on Unix only):

```
formletter = """Dear %s,\nI'm writing to you to suggest that ...."""     # etc.
myDatabase = [('Michael Jackson', 'michael@neverland.odd'),
              ('Bill Gates', 'bill@microsoft.com'),
              ('Bob', 'bob@subgenius.org')]
for name, email in myDatabase:
    specificLetter = formletter % name
    tempfilename = tempfile.mktemp( )
    tempfile = open(tempfilename, 'w')
    tempfile.write(specificLetter)
    tempfile.close( )
    os.system('/usr/bin/mail %(email)s -s "Urgent!" < %(tempfilename)s' % vars( ))
    os.remove(tempfilename)
```

The first line in the for loop returns a customized version of the form letter based on the name it's given. That text is then written to a temporary file that's emailed to the appropriate email address using the os.system call. Finally, to clean up, the temporary file is removed.

The vars( ) function is a built-in function that returns a dictionary corresponding to the variables defined in the current local namespace. The keys of the dictionary are the variable names, and the values of the dictionary are the variable values. vars( ) comes in quite handy for exploring namespaces. It can also be called with an object as an argument (such as a module, a class, or an instance), and it will return the namespace of that object. Two other built-ins, locals( ) and globals( ), return the local and global namespaces, respectively. In all three cases, modifying the returned dictionaries doesn't guarantee any effect on the namespace in question, so view these as read-only and you won't be surprised. You can see that the vars( ) call creates a dictionary that is used by the string interpolation mechanism; it's thus important that the names inside the %(...)s bits in the string match the variable names in the program.

Modifying Input and Outputs

The argv attribute of the sys module holds one set of inputs to the current program—the command-line arguments, more precisely a list of the words input on the command line, excluding the reference to Python itself if it exists. In other words, if you type at the shell:

```
csh> python run.py a x=3 foo
```

then when *run.py* starts, the value of the sys.argv attribute is ['run.py', 'a', 'x=3', 'foo']. The sys.argv attribute is mutable (after all, it's just a list). Common usage involves iterating over the arguments of the Python program, that is, sys.argv[1:]; slicing from index 1 till the end gives all of the arguments to the program itself, but doesn't include the name of the program (module) stored in sys.argv[0]. There are two modules that help you process command line options. The first, an older module called getopt, is replaced in Python 2.3 by a similar but more powerful module called optparse. Check the library reference for further details on how to use them.

Experienced programmers will know that there are other inputs to a program, especially the standard input stream, with siblings for output and error messages. Python lets the programmer access and modify these through three file attributes in the sys module: sys.stdin, sys.stdout, and sys.stderr. Standard input is generally associated by the operating system with the user's keyboard; standard output and standard error are usually associated with the console. The print statement in Python outputs to standard output (sys.stdout), while error messages such as exceptions are output on the standard error stream (sys.stderr). Python lets you modify these on the fly: you can redirect the output of a Python program to a file simply by assigning to sys.stdout:

```
sys.stdout = open('log.out', 'w')
```

After this line, any output will be written to the file log.out instead of showing up on the console. Note that if you don't save it first, the reference to the "original" standard out stream is lost. It's generally a good idea to save a reference before reallocating any of the standard streams, as in:

```
old_stdout = sys.stdout
sys.stdout = open('log.out', 'w')
```

Using Standard I/O to Process Files

Why have a standard input stream? After all, it's not that hard to type open('input.txt') in the program. The major argument for reading and writing with standard streams is that you can chain programs so that the standard output from one becomes the standard input of the next, with no file used in the transfer. This facility, known as *piping*, is at the heart of the Unix philosophy. Using standard I/O this way means that you can write a program to do a specific task once, and then use it to process files or the intermediate results of other programs at any time in the future.

As an example, a simple program that counts the number of lines in a file could be written as:

```
import sys
data = sys.stdin.readlines()
print "Counted", len(data), "lines."
```

On Unix, you could test it by doing something like:

```
% cat countlines.py | python countlines.py
Counted 3 lines.
```

On Windows or DOS, you'd do:

```
C:\> type countlines.py | python countlines.py
Counted 3 lines.
```

You can get each line in a file simply by iterating over a file object. This comes in very handy when implementing simple filter operations. Here are a few examples of such filter operations.

Finding all lines that start with a

```
# Show comment lines (lines that start with a #, like this one).
import sys
for line in sys.stdin:
    if line[0] == '#':
        print line,
```

Note that a final comma is added after the print statement to indicate that the print operation should not add a newline, which would result in double-spaced output since the line string already includes a newline character as its last character.

The last two programs can easily be combined using pipes to combine their power. To count the number of comment lines in *commentfinder.py*:

```
C:> type commentfinder.py | python commentfinder.py | python countlines.py
Counted 1 lines.
```

Some other filtering tasks that take from standard input and write to standard output follow.

Extracting the fourth column of a file (where columns are defined by whitespace)

```
import sys
for line in sys.stdin:
    words = line.split()
    if len(words) >= 4:
        print words[3]
```

We look at the length of the words list to find if there are indeed at least four words. The last two lines could also be replaced by the try/except statement, which is quite common in Python:

```
try:
    print words[3]
```

```
        except IndexError:                        # There aren't enough words.
            pass
```

Extracting the fourth column of a file, where columns are separated by colons, and making it lowercase

```
import sys, string
for line in sys.stdin:
    words = line.split(':')
    if len(words) >= 4:
        print words[3].lower()
```

If iterating over all of the lines isn't what you want, just use the readlines() or read() methods of file objects.

Printing the first 10 lines, the last 10 lines, and every other line

```
import sys
lines = sys.stdin.readlines()
sys.stdout.writelines(lines[:10])          # First 10 lines
sys.stdout.writelines(lines[-10:])         # Last 10 lines
for lineIndex in range(0, len(lines), 2):  # Get 0, 2, 4, ...
    sys.stdout.write(lines[lineIndex])     # Get the indexed line.
```

Counting the number of times the word "Python" occurs in a file

```
text = open(fname).read()
print text.count('Python')
```

Changing a list of columns into a list of rows

In this more complicated example, the task is to transpose a file; imagine you have a file that looks like:

```
Name:   Willie  Mark   Guido  Mary  Rachel  Ahmed
Level:    5       4      3      1      6      4
Tag#:   1234    4451   5515   5124   1881   5132
```

And you really want it to look like the following instead:

```
Name: Level: Tag#:
Willie 5      1234
Mark   4      4451
...
```

You could use code like the following:

```
import sys
lines = sys.stdin.readlines()
wordlists = [line.split() for line in lines]
for row in zip(*wordlists):
    print '\t'.join(row)
```

Of course, you should really use much more defensive programming techniques to deal with the possibility that not all lines have the same number of words in them, that there may be missing data, etc. Those techniques are task-specific and are left as an exercise to the reader.

Choosing chunk sizes

All the preceding examples assume you can read the entire file at once. In some cases, however, that's not possible, for example, when processing really huge files on computers with little memory, or when dealing with files that are constantly being appended to (such as log files). In such cases, you can use a while/readline combination, where some of the file is read a bit at a time, until the end of file is reached. In dealing with files that aren't line-oriented, you must read the file a character at a time:

```
# Read character by character.
while 1:
    next = sys.stdin.read(1)        # Read a one-character string
    if not next:                    # or an empty string at EOF.
        break
    # Process character 'next'.
```

Notice that the read( ) method on file objects returns an empty string at end of file, which breaks out of the while loop. Most often, however, the files you'll deal with consist of line-based data and are processed a line at a time:

```
# Read line by line.
while 1:
    next = sys.stdin.readline( )    # Read a one-line string
    if not next:                    # or an empty string at EOF.
        break
    # Process line 'next'.
```

Doing Something to a Set of Files Specified on the Command Line

Being able to read stdin is a great feature; it's the foundation of the Unix toolset. However, one input is not always enough: many tasks need to be performed on sets of files. This is usually done by having the Python program parse the list of arguments sent to the script as command-line options. For example, if you type:

```
% python myScript.py input1.txt input2.txt input3.txt output.txt
```

you might think that *myScript.py* wants to do something with the first three input files and write a new file, called *output.txt*. Let's see what the beginning of such a program could look like:

```
import sys
inputfilenames, outputfilename = sys.argv[1:-1], sys.argv[-1]
for inputfilename in inputfilenames:
    inputfile = open(inputfilename, "r")
    do_something_with_input(inputfile)
inputfile.close( )
```

```
    outputfile = open(outputfilename, "w")
    write_results(outputfile)
    outputfile.close()
```

The second line extracts parts of the argv attribute of the sys module. Recall that it's a list of the words on the command line that called the current program. It starts with the name of the script. So, in the example above, the value of sys.argv is:

```
['myScript.py', 'input1.txt', 'input2.txt', 'input3.txt', 'output.txt'].
```

The script assumes that the command line consists of one or more input files and one output file. So the slicing of the input file names starts at 1 (to skip the name of the script, which isn't an input to the script in most cases), and stops before the last word on the command line, which is the name of the output file. The rest of the script should be pretty easy to understand (but won't work until you provide the do_something_with_input() and write_results() functions).

Note that the preceding script doesn't actually read in the data from the files, but passes the file object down to a function to do the real work. A generic version of do_something_with_input() is:

```
def do_something_with_input(inputfile):
    for line in inputfile:
        process(line)
```

Processing Each Line of One or More Files

The combination of this idiom with the preceding one regarding opening each file in the sys.argv[1:] list is so common that there is a module, fileinput, to do just this task:

```
import fileinput
for line in fileinput.input():
    process(line)
```

The fileinput.input() call parses the arguments on the command line, and if there are no arguments to the script, uses sys.stdin instead. It also provides several useful functions that let you know which file and line number you're currently manipulating, as we can see in the following script:

```
import fileinput, sys
# Take the first argument out of sys.argv and assign it to searchterm.
searchterm, sys.argv[1:] = sys.argv[1], sys.argv[2:]
for line in fileinput.input():
    num_matches = line.count(searchterm)
    if num_matches:                        # A nonzero count means there was a match.
        print "found '%s' %d times in %s on line %d." % (searchterm, num_matches,
                fileinput.filename(), fileinput.filelineno())
```

Running *mygrep.py* on a few Python files produces:

```
% python mygrep.py in *.py
found 'in' 2 times in countlines.py on line 2.
```

```
found 'in' 2 times in countlines.py on line 3.
found 'in' 2 times in mygrep.py on line 1.
found 'in' 4 times in mygrep.py on line 4.
found 'in' 2 times in mygrep.py on line 5.
found 'in' 2 times in mygrep.py on line 7.
found 'in' 3 times in mygrep.py on line 8.
found 'in' 3 times in mygrep.py on line 12.
```

Dealing with Binary Data: The struct Module

A file is considered a binary file if it's not a text file or a file written in a format based on text, such as HTML and XML. Image and sound files are prototypical examples of binary files. A frequent question about file manipulation is "How do I process binary files in Python?" The answer to that question usually involves the struct module. It has a simple interface, since it exports just three functions: pack, unpack, and calcsize.

Let's start with the task of decoding a binary file. Imagine a binary file *bindat.dat* that contains data in a specific format: first there's a float corresponding to a version number, then a long integer corresponding to the size of the data, and then the number of unsigned bytes corresponding to the actual data. The key to using the struct module is to define a *format* string, which corresponds to the format of the data you wish to read, and find out which subset of the file corresponds to that data. For example:

```
import struct
data = open('bindat.dat').read()
start, stop = 0, struct.calcsize('fl')
version_number, num_bytes = struct.unpack('fl', data[start:stop])
start, stop = stop, start + struct.calcsize('B'*num_bytes)
bytes = struct.unpack('B'*num_bytes, data[start:stop])
```

'f' is a format string for a single floating-point number (a C float, to be precise), 'l' is for a long integer, and 'B' is a format string for an unsigned char. The available unpack format strings are listed in Table 27-8. Consult the library reference manual for usage details.

Table 27-8. Common format codes used by the struct module

Format	C type	Python
x	pad byte	No value
c	char	String of length 1
b	signed char	Integer
B	unsigned char	Integer
h	short	Integer
H	unsigned short	Integer
i	int	Integer

Table 27-8. Common format codes used by the struct module (continued)

Format	C type	Python
I	unsigned int	Integer
l	long	Integer
L	unsigned long	Integer
f	float	Float
d	double	Float
s	char[ ]	String
p	char[ ]	String
P	void *	Integer

At this point, bytes is a tuple of num_bytes Python integers. If we know that the data is in fact storing characters, we could use chars = map(chr, bytes). To be more efficient, we could change the last unpack to use 'c' instead of 'B', which would do the conversion and return a tuple of num_bytes single-character strings. More efficiently still, we could use a format string that specifies a string of characters of a specified length, such as:

```
chars = struct.unpack(str(num_bytes)+'s', data[start:stop])
```

The packing operation (struct.pack) is the exact converse; instead of taking a format string and a data string, and returning a tuple of unpacked values, it takes a format string and a variable number of arguments and packs those arguments using that format string into a new packed string.

Note that the struct module can process data that's encoded with either kind of byte-ordering,* thus allowing you to write platform-independent binary file manipulation code. For large files, also consider using the array module.

Internet-Related Modules

Python is used in a wide variety of Internet-related tasks, from making web servers to crawling the Web to "screen-scraping" web sites for data. This section briefly describes the most often used modules used for such tasks that ship with Python's core. For more detailed examples of their use, we recommend Lundh's *Standard Python Library* and Martelli and Ascher's *Python Cookbook* (O'Reilly). There are many third-party add-ons worth knowing about before embarking on a significant web- or Internet-related project.

---

* The order with which computers list multibyte words depends on the chip used (so much for standards). Intel and DEC systems use little-endian ordering, while Motorola and Sun-based systems use big-endian ordering. Network transmissions also use big-endian ordering, so the struct module comes in handy when doing network I/O on PCs.

The Common Gateway Interface: The cgi Module

Python programs often process forms from web pages. To make this task easy, the standard Python distribution includes a module called cgi. Chapter 28 includes an example of a Python script that uses the CGI, so we won't cover it any further here.

Manipulating URLs: The urllib and urlparse Modules

Universal resource locators are strings such as *http://www.python.org* that are now ubiquitous. Three modules—urllib, urllib2, and urlparse—provide tools for processing URLs.

The urllib module defines a few functions for writing programs that must be active users of the Web (robots, agents, etc.). These are listed in Table 27-9.

Table 27-9. Functions of the urllib module

Function name	Behavior

urlopen(url [, data])	Opens (for reading) a network object denoted by a URL; it can also open local files:
	<pre>>>> page = urlopen('http://www.python.org')
	>>> page.readline()
	'<HTML>\012'
	>>> page.readline()
	'<!-- THIS PAGE IS AUTOMATICALLY GENERATED.DO NOT EDIT.
	-->\012'</pre>

urlretrieve(url [, filename][, hook])	Copies a network object denoted by a URL to a local file (uses a cache):
	<pre>>>> urllib.urlretrieve('http://www.python.org/',
	'wwwpython.html')</pre>

urlcleanup()	Cleans up the cache used by urlretrieve.

quote(string[, safe])	Replaces special characters in string using the %xx escape. The optional safe parameter specifies additional characters that shouldn't be quoted; its default value is:
	<pre>>>> quote('this & that @ home')
	'this%20%26%20that%20%40%20home'</pre>

quote_plus(string[, safe])	Like quote( ), but also replaces spaces by plus signs.

unquote(string)	Replaces %xx escapes by their single-character equivalent:
	<pre>>>> unquote('this%20%26%20that%20%40%20home')
	'this & that @ home'</pre>

urlencode(dict)	Converts a dictionary to a URL-encoded string, suitable to pass to urlopen( ) as the optional data argument:
	<pre>>>> locals()
	{'urllib': <module 'urllib'>, '__doc__': None, 'x':
	3, '__name__': '__main__', '__builtins__': <module
	'__builtin__'>}
	>>> urllib.urlencode(locals())
	'urllib=%3cmodule+%27urllib%27%3e&__doc__=None&x=3&
	__name__=__main__&__builtins__=%3cmodule+%27
	__builtin__%27%3e'</pre>

The module `urllib2` focuses on the tasks of opening URLs that the simpler `urllib` doesn't know how to deal with, and provides an extensible framework for new kinds of URLs and protocols. It is what you should use if you want to deal with passwords, digest authentication, proxies, HTTPS URLs, and other fancy URLs.

The module `urlparse` defines a few functions that simplify taking URLs apart and putting new URLs together. These are listed in Table 27-10.

Table 27-10. Functions of the urlparse module

Function name	Behavior

`urlparse(urlstring[,`
`default_scheme[,allow fragments]])`
	Parses a URL into six components, returning a six tuple (addressing scheme, network location, path, parameters, query, fragment identifier):
	
	`>>> urlparse('http://www.python.org/`
	`FAQ.html')`
	`('http', 'www.python.org', '/FAQ.html', '',`
	`'', '')`

`urlunparse(tuple)`	Constructs a URL string from a tuple as returned by `urlparse()`

`urljoin(base, url[,allow fragments])`	Constructs a full (absolute) URL by combining a base URL (`base`) with a relative URL (`url`):
	
	`>>> urljoin('http://www.python.org',`
	`'doc/lib')`
	`'http://www.python.org/doc/lib'`

Specific Internet Protocols

The most commonly used protocols built on top of TCP/IP are supported with modules named after them. The `telnetlib` module lets you act like a Telnet client. The `httplib` module lets you talk to web servers with the HTTP protocol. The `ftplib` module is for transferring files using the FTP protocol. The `gopherlib` module is for browsing Gopher servers (now fairly rare). In the domains of mail and news, you can use the `poplib` and `imaplib` modules for reading mail files on POP3 and IMAP servers, respectively and the `smtplib` module for sending mail, and the `nntplib` module for reading and posting Usenet news from NNTP servers.

There are also modules that can build Internet servers, specifically a generic socket-based IP server (`SocketServer`), a simple web server (`SimpleHTTPServer`), a CGI-compliant HTTP server (`CGIHTTPSserver`), and a module for building asynchronous socket handling services (`asyncore`).

Support for web services currently consists of a core library to process XML-RPC client-side calls (`xmlrpclib`), as well as a simple XML-RPC server implementation (`SimpleXMLRPCServer`). Support for SOAP is likely to be added when the SOAP standard becomes more stable.

Processing Internet Data

Once you use an Internet protocol to obtain files from the Internet (or before you serve them to the Internet), you often must process these files. They come in many different formats. Table 27-11 lists each module in the standard library that processes a specific kind of Internet-related file format (there are others for sound and image format processing; see the library reference manual).

Table 27-11. Modules dedicated to Internet file processing

Module name	File format
sgmllib	A simple parser for SGML files.
htmllib	A parser for HTML documents.
formatter	Generic output formatter and device interface.
rfc822	Parse RFC-822 mail headers (i.e., "Subject: hi there!").
mimetools	Tools for parsing MIME-style message bodies (a.k.a. file attachments).
multifile	Support for reading files that contain distinct parts.
binhex	Encode and decode files in binhex4 format.
uu	Encode and decode files in uuencode format.
binascii	Convert between binary and various ASCII-encoded representations.
xdrlib	Encode and decode XDR data.
mailcap	Mailcap file handling.
mimetypes	Mapping of filename extensions to MIME types.
base64	Encode and decode MIME base64 encoding.
quopri	Encode and decode MIME quoted-printable encoding.
mailbox	Read various mailbox formats.
mimify	Convert mail messages to and from MIME format.
mail	A package for parsing, handling, and generating email messages.

XML Processing

Python comes with a rich set of XML-processing tools. These include parsers, DOM interfaces, SAX interfaces, and more, as shown in Table 27-12.

Table 27-12. Some of the XML modules in the core distribution

Module name	Description
xml.parsers.expat	An interface to the Expat nonvalidating XML parser
xml.dom	Document Object Model (DOM) API for Python
xml.dom.minidom	Lightweight DOM implementation
xml.dom.pulldom	Support for building partial DOM trees from SAX events
xml.sax	Package containing SAX2 base classes and convenience functions

Table 27-12. Some of the XML modules in the core distribution (continued)

Module name	Description
xml.sax.handlers	Base classes for SAX event handlers.
xml.sax.saxutils	Convenience functions and classes for use with SAX.
xml.sax.xmlreader	Interface that SAX-compliant XML parsers must implement.
xmllib	A parser for XML documents.

See the standard library reference for details, or the *Python Cookbook* (O'Reilly) for example tasks easily solved using the standard XML libraries. The XML facilities are developed by the XML Special Interest Group, which publishes versions of the XML package in-between Python releases. See *http://www.python.org/topics/xml* for details and the latest version of the code. For expanded coverage, consider *Python and XML*, by Christopher A. Jones and Fred L. Drake, Jr. (O'Reilly).

Executing Programs

The last set of built-in functions in this section have to do with creating, manipulating, and calling Python code. See Table 27-13.

Table 27-13. Ways to execute Python code

Name	Behavior
import	Executes the code in a module as part of the importing and binds it to a name in the scope in which it is executed. You can choose what name is chosen by using the import *modulename* as *name* form.
exec code [in globaldict [, localdict]]	Executes the specified code (string, file, or compiled code object) in the optionally specified global and local namespaces. This is sometimes useful when reading programs from user-entered code as in an interactive shell or "macro" window.
compile(string, filename, kind)	Compiles the string into a code object. This function is only useful as an optimization.
execfile(filename[, globaldict[, localdict]])	Executes the program in the specified filename, using the optionally specified global and local namespaces. This function is sometimes useful in systems which use Python as an extension language for the users of the system.
eval(code[, globaldict[, localdict]])	Evaluates the specified expression (string or compiled code object) in the optionally specified global and local namespaces, and returns the expression's result. Calculator-type programs that ask the users for an expression to compute often use eval.

It's a simple matter to write programs that run other programs. Shortly, we'll talk about ways to call any program from within a Python program. There are several mechanisms that let you execute arbitrary Python code. The most important is one statement we've used throughout the book, import, which executes code existing in files on the Python path. There are several other ways to execute Python code in-process. The first is the exec statement:

```
exec code [ in globaldict [, localdict]]
```

exec takes between one and three arguments. The first argument must contain Python code—either in a string, as in the following example; in an open file object; or in a compiled code object. For example:

```
>>> code = "x = 'Something'"
>>> x = "Nothing"                    # Sets the value of x
>>> exec code                        # Modifies the value of x!
>>> print x
'Something'
```

exec can take optional arguments. If a single dictionary argument is provided (after the then-mandatory in word), it's used as both the local and global namespaces for the execution of the specified code. If two dictionary arguments are provided, they are used as the global and local namespaces, respectively. If both arguments are omitted, as in the previous example, the current global and local namespaces are used.

When exec is called, Python needs to parse the code that is being executed. This can be a computationally expensive process, especially if a large piece of code needs to be executed thousands of times. If this is the case, it's worth compiling the code first (once), and executing it as many times as needed. The compile function takes a string containing the Python code and returns a compiled code object, which can then be processed efficiently by the exec statement.

compile takes three arguments. The first is the code string. The second is the file-name corresponding to the Python source file (or '<string>' if it wasn't read from a file); it's used in the traceback in case an exception is generated when executing the code. The third argument is one of 'single', 'exec', or 'eval', depending on whether the code is a single statement whose result would be printed (just as in the interactive interpreter), a set of statements, or an expression (creating a compiled code object for use by the eval function).

A related function is the execfile built-in function. Its first argument must be the filename of a Python script instead of a file object or string (remember that file objects are the things the open built-in returns when it's passed a filename). Thus, if you want your Python script to start by running its arguments as Python scripts, you can do something like:

```
import sys
for argument in sys.argv[1:]:      # We'll skip ourselves, or it'll go forever!
    execfile(argument)             # Do whatever.
```

Two warnings are warranted with respect to execfile. First, it is logical but sometimes surprising that execfile executes by default in its local scope—thus, calling execfile from inside a function will often have much more localized effects than users expect. Second, execfile is almost never the right answer—if you're writing the code being executed, you should really put it in a module and import it. The behavior you'll get will be much more predictable, safe, and maintainable—it's just too easy for execfile( ) code to wreak havoc with the module calling execfile.

Two more functions can execute Python code. The first is the eval function, which takes a code string (and the by now expected optional pair of dictionaries) or a compiled code object and returns the evaluation of that expression. For example:

```
>>> word = 'xo'
>>> z = eval("word*10")
>>> print z
'xoxoxoxoxoxoxoxoxoxo'
```

The eval function can't work with statements, as shown in the following example, because expressions and statements are different syntactically:

```
>>> z = eval("x = 3")
Traceback (innermost last):
File "<stdin>", line 1, in ?
File "<string>", line 1
x = 3
    ^
SyntaxError: invalid syntax
```

The last function that executes code is apply. It's called with a callable object, an optional tuple of the positional arguments, and an optional dictionary of the keywords arguments. A callable object is any function (standard functions, methods, etc.), any class object (they create an instance when called), or any instance of a class that defines a __call__ method. apply is slowly being deprecated because it is no longer necessary or the most efficient way of doing what it does—you can always replace it by simple calls, optionally using the * and ** argument markers. As we've seen in the chapter on OOP, one can call a method defined in a base class using:

```
class Derived(Base):
    def __init__(self, arg, *args, **kw):
        self.__init__(self, *args, **kw)
```

This code used to be written using apply as in:

```
class Derived(Base):
    def __init__(self, arg, *args, **kw):
        apply(self.__init__, (self,) + args, kw)
```

As you can see, the new variant is much cleaner, which is why apply is quickly becoming obsolete.

If you're not sure if an object is callable (e.g., if it's an argument to a function), test it using the callable built-in, which returns true if the object it's called with is callable.[*]

```
>>> callable(sys.exit), type(sys.exit)
(1, <type 'builtin_function_or_method'>)
>>> callable(sys.version), type(sys.version)
(0, <type 'string'>)
```

There are other built-in functions we haven't covered; if you're curious, check a reference source such as the library reference manual (Section 2.3).

Debugging, Testing, Timing, Profiling

To wrap up our overview of common Python tasks, we'll cover some tasks that are common for Python programmers even though they're not programming tasks per se—debugging, testing, timing, and optimizing Python programs.

Debugging with pdb

The first task is, not surprisingly, debugging. Python's standard distribution includes a debugger called pdb. Using pdb is fairly straightforward. You import the pdb module and call its run method with the Python code the debugger should execute. For example, if you're debugging the program in *spam.py*, do this:

```
>>> import spam                          # Import the module we want to debug.
>>> import pdb                           # Import pdb.
>>> pdb.run('instance = spam.Spam()')   # Start pdb with a statement to run.
> <string>(0)?()
(Pdb) break spam.Spam.__init__          # We can set break points.
(Pdb) next
>    <string>(1)?()
(Pdb) n                                 # 'n' is short for 'next'.
> spam.py(3)__init__()
-> def __init__(self):
(Pdb) n
> spam.py(4)__init__()
-> Spam.numInstances = Spam.numInstances + 1
(Pdb) list                              # Show the source code listing.
  1     class Spam:
  2         numInstances = 0
  3 B     def __init__(self):           # Note the B for Breakpoint.
  4 ->        Spam.numInstances = Spam.numInstances + 1  # Where we are
  5         def printNumInstances(self):
  6             print "Number of instances created: ", Spam.numInstances
  7
```

---

[*] You can find many things about callable objects, such as how many arguments they expect and what the names and default values of their arguments are by checking the Language Reference for details, especially Section 3. 2, which describes all attributes for each type. Even easier is using the inspect module, which is designed for that.

```
[EOF]
(Pdb) where                              # Show the calling stack.
<string>(1)?()
> spam.py(4)__init__()
-> Spam.numInstances = Spam.numInstances + 1
(Pdb) Spam.numInstances = 10             # Note that we can modify variables
(Pdb) print Spam.numInstances            # while the program is being debugged.
10
(Pdb) continue                           # This continues until the next break-
--Return--                               # point, but there is none, so we're
-> <string>(1)?()->None                  # done.
(Pdb) c                                  # This ends up quitting Pdb.
<spam.Spam instance at 80ee60>           # This is the returned instance.
>>> instance.numInstances                # Note that the change to numInstance
11                                       # was before the increment op.
```

As the session above shows, with pdb you can list the current code being debugged (with an arrow pointing to the line about to be executed), examine variables, modify variables, and set breakpoints. Chapter 9 in the Library Reference covers the debugger in detail. Alternative debuggers abound, from the one in IDLE, to the more full-featured debuggers you'll find in commercial IDEs for Python.

Testing with unittest

Testing software is, in the general case, a very hard problem. For software that takes user input or more generally interacts with the outside world, doing comprehensive testing of any medium-sized program quickly becomes hard to do completely. Luckily, one can get many benefits from doing nonexhaustive testing. The easiest kind of testing to do is called *unit testing*, and it is supported in Python by the module unittest. In unit testing, one writes very small scripts that test one fact about the program being tested at a time. The trick is to write lots of these simple tests, learn how to write useful unit tests as opposed to silly tests, and to run these tests in between every change to the program. If you have a test suite with good coverage, you'll gain confidence that each change you make is not going to break another part of the system.

unittest is documented as part of the standard library, as well as on the PyUnit web site (*http://pyunit.sourceforge.net*).

Timing

Even when a program is working, it can sometimes be too slow. If you know what the bottleneck in your program is, and you know of alternative ways to code the same algorithm, then you might time the various alternative methods to find out which is fastest. The time module, which is part of the standard distribution, provides many time-manipulation routines. We'll use just one, which returns the time since a fixed epoch with the highest precision available on your machine. As we'll use just relative times to compare algorithms, the precision isn't all that important. Here's two different ways to create a list of 10,000 zeros:

```
def lots_of_appends():
    zeros = [ ]
    for i in range(10000):
        zeros.append(0)

def one_multiply():
    zeros = [0] * 10000
```

How can we time these two solutions? Here's a simple way:

```
import time, makezeros
def do_timing(num_times, *funcs):
    totals = {}
    for func in funcs:
        totals[func] = 0.0
        starttime = time.clock()          # Record starting time.
        for x in range(num_times):
            for func in funcs:
                apply(func)
        stoptime = time.clock ()          # Record ending time.
        elapsed = stoptime-starttime      # Difference yields time elapsed
        totals[func] = totals[func] + elapsed
    for func in funcs:
        print "Running %s %d times took %.3f seconds" % (func.__name__, num_times
totals[func])

do_timing(100, (makezeros.lots_of_appends, makezeros.one_multiply))
```

And running this program yields:

```
csh> python timings.py
Running lots_of_appends 100 times took 7.891 seconds
Running one_multiply 100 times took 0.120 seconds
```

As you might have suspected, a single list multiplication is much faster than lots of appends. Note that in timings, it's always a good idea to compare lots of runs of functions instead of just one. Otherwise, the timings are likely to be heavily influenced by things that have nothing to do with the algorithm, such as network traffic on the computer or GUI events. Python 2.3 introduces a new module called timeit that provides a very simple way to do precise code timing correctly.

What if you've written a complex program, and it's running slower than you'd like, but you're not sure where the problem spot is? In that case, what you need to do is profile the program: determine which parts of the program are the time-sinks and see if they can be optimized, or if the program structure can be modified to even out the bottlenecks. The Python distribution includes just the right tools for that, the profile module, documented in the Library Reference, and another module, hotshot, which is unfortunately not well documented as of this writing. Assuming that you want to profile a given function in the current namespace, do this:

```
>>> from timings import *
>>> from makezeros import *
>>> profile.run('do_timing(100, (lots_of_appends, one_multiply))')
Running lots_of_appends 100 times took 8.773 seconds
Running one_multiply 100 times took 0.090 seconds
    203 function calls in 8.823 CPU seconds
Ordered by: standard name
ncalls  tottime  percall  cumtime  percall filename:lineno(function)
   100    8.574    0.086    8.574    0.086 makezeros.py:1(lots_of_appends)
   100    0.101    0.001    0.101    0.001 makezeros.py:6(one_multiply)
     1    0.001    0.001    8.823    8.823 profile:0(do_timing(100,
(lots_of_appends, one_multiply)))
     0    0.000             0.000          profile:0(profiler)
     1    0.000    0.000    8.821    8.821 python:0(194.C.2)
     1    0.147    0.147    8.821    8.821 timings.py:2(do_timing)
```

As you can see, this gives a fairly complicated listing, which includes such things as per-call time spent in each function and the number of calls made to each function. In complex programs, the profiler can help find surprising inefficiencies. Optimizing Python programs is beyond the scope of this book; if you're interested, however, check the Python newsgroup: periodically, a user asks for help speeding up a program and a spontaneous contest starts up, with interesting advice from expert users.

Exercises

This chapter is full of programs we encourage you to type in and play with. However, here are a few more challenging exercises:

1. *Avoiding regular expressions.* Write a program that obeys the same requirements as *pepper.py* but doesn't use regular expressions to do the job. This is somewhat difficult, but a useful exercise in building program logic.

2. *Wrapping a text file with a class.* Write a class that takes a filename and reads the data in the corresponding file as text. Make it so that this class has three attributes: paragraph, line, word, each of which take an integer argument, so that if mywrapper is an instance of this class, printing mywrapper.paragraph(0) prints the first paragraph of the file, mywrapper.line(-2) prints the next-to-last line in the file, and mywrapper.word(3) prints the fourth word in the file.

3. *Describing a directory.* Write a function that takes a directory name and describes the contents of the directory, recursively (in other words, for each file, print the name and size, and proceed down any eventual directories).

4. *Modifying the prompt.* Modify your interpreter so that the prompt is, instead of the >>> string, a string describing the current directory and the count of the number of lines entered in the current Python session. Two hints: the prompt variables (e.g., sys.ps1) doesn't have to be a string but can be any object; printing an

instance can have side effects, and is done by calling the instance's __repr__ method.

5. *Writing a shell.* Using the Cmd class in the cmd module and the functions described in this chapter for manipulating files and directories, write a little shell that accepts the standard Unix commands (or DOS commands): ls (dir) for listing the current directory, cd for changing directory, mv (or ren) for moving/renaming a file, and cp (copy) for copying a file.

6. *Redirecting stdout.* Modify the *mygrep.py* script to output to the last file specified on the command line instead of to the console.

## CHAPTER 28

Frameworks

All the examples in this book so far have been quite small and they may seem toys compared to real-world applications. This chapter shows some of the frameworks that are available to Python programmers who wish to build such applications in some specific domains. A *framework* can be thought of as a domain-specific set of classes and expected patterns of interactions between these classes. We mention just three here: the COM framework for interacting with Microsoft's Component Object Model, the Tkinter graphical user interface (GUI), and the Swing Java GUI toolkit.

We will illustrate the power of frameworks using a hypothetical scenario, that of a small company's web site, and the need to collect, maintain, and respond to customer input about the product through a web form. We will describe three programs in this scenario. The first program is a web-based data entry form that asks the user to enter some information in their web browser, and then saves that information on disk. The second program uses the same data and automatically uses Microsoft Word to print out a customized form letter based on that information. The final example is a simple browser for the saved data built with the Tkinter module, which uses the Tk GUI, a powerful, portable toolkit for managing windows, buttons, menus, etc. Hopefully, these examples will make you realize how these kinds of toolkits, when combined with the rapid development power of Python, can truly let you build real applications fast. Each program builds on the previous one, so we strongly recommend that you read through each program, even if you don't wish to get them up and running on your computer.

The last section of this chapter covers Jython, the Java port of Python. The chapter closes with a medium-sized Jython program that allows users to manipulate mathematical functions graphically using the Swing toolkit.

An Automated Complaint System

The scenario for this example is that of a startup company, Joe's Toothpaste, Inc., which sells the latest in 100% organic, cruelty-free, tofu-based toothpaste. Since there is only one employee, and that employee is quite busy shopping for the best tofu he can find, the tube doesn't say "For customer complaints or comments, call 1-800-TOFTOOT," but instead, says, "If you have a complaint or wish to make a comment, visit our web site at www.toftoot.com." The web site has all the usual glossy pictures and an area where the customer can enter a complaint or comment. This page looks like Figure 28-1.

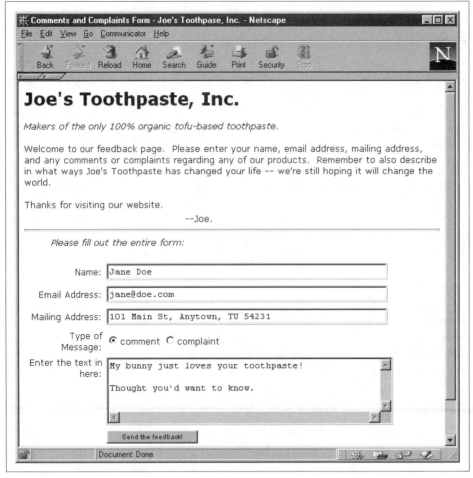

Figure 28-1. What the customer finds at http://www.toftoot.com/comment.html

Excerpt from the HTML File

The key parts of the HTML code that generated this page are:

```html
<form method="post" action="http://toftoot.com/cgi-bin/feedback.py">
<ul><i>Please fill out the entire form:</i></ul>
<center><table width="100%" >
<tr>
    <td align="right" width="20%">Name:</td>
    <td>
        <input type="text" name="name" size="50" value="">
    </td>
</tr>
<tr>
    <td align="right">Email Address:</td>
    <td>
        <input type="text" name="email" size="50" value="">
    </td>
</tr>
<tr>
    <td align="right">Mailing Address:</td>
    <td>
        <input type="text" name="address" size="50" value="">
    </td>
</tr>
<tr>
    <td align="right">Type of Message:</td>
    <td>
        <input type="radio" name="type" checked
                value="comment">comment </input>
        <input type="radio" name="type"
                value="complaint">complaint</input>
    </td>
</tr>
<tr>
    <td align="right" valign="top">
        Enter the text in here:</td>
    <td><textarea name="text" rows="5" cols="50" value="">
        </textarea></td></tr>
<tr>
    <td></td>
    <td>
    <input type="submit" name="send" value="Send the feedback!">
    </td>
</tr>
</table></center>
</form>
```

We assume that you know enough about CGI and HTML to follow this discussion. The HTML code generates the web page shown in Figure 28-1:

- The form line specifies what CGI program should be invoked when the form is submitted; specifically, the URL points to a script called *feedback.py*.

- The input tags indicate the names of the fields in the form (name, address, email, and text, as well as type). The values of these fields are whatever the user enters, except for the type, which takes either the value 'comment' or 'complaint', depending on which radio button the user selected.

- The input type="submit" tag is for the submission button, which actually calls the CGI script.

We now get to the interesting part as far as Python is concerned: the processing of the request. Here is the entire *feedback.py* program:

```
1    #!c:/python23/python.exe
2    import cgi, cgitb, os, sys, string, time
3    cgitb.enable( )

4    def gush(data):
5        print """Content-type: text/html\n
6    <h3>Thanks, %(name)s!</h3>
7    Our customer's comments are always appreciated.
8    They drive our business directions, as well as
9    help us with our karma.
10   <p>Thanks again for the feedback!<p>
11   And feel free to enter more comments if you wish.""" % vars(data)
12       print "<p>"+10*" "+"--Joe."
13
14   def whimper(data):
15       print """Content-type: text/html\n
16   <h3>Sorry, %(name)s!</h3>
17   We're very sorry to read that you had a complaint"
18   regarding our product__We'll read your comments"
19   carefully and will be in touch with you."
20   <p>Nevertheless, thanks for the feedback.<p>""" % vars(data)
21       print "<p>"+10*" "+"--Joe."

22   def bail( ):
23       print """<h3>Error filling out form</h3>
24   Please fill in all the fields in the form.<p>
25   <a href="http://localhost/comment.html">
26   Go back to the form</a>"""
27       sys.exit( )

28   class FormData:
29       """ A repository for information gleaned from a CGI form """
30       def __init__(self, form):
31           self.time = time.asctime( )
```

```
32          for fieldname in self.fieldnames:
33              if fieldname not in form or form[fieldname].value == "":
34                  bail()
35              else:
36                  setattr(self, fieldname, form[fieldname].value)

37  class FeedbackData(FormData):
38      """ A FormData generated by the comment.html form. """
39      fieldnames = ('name', 'address', 'email', 'type', 'text')
40      def __repr__(self):
41          return "%(type)s from %(name)s on %(time)s" % vars(self)

42  DIRECTORY = r'C:\complaintdir'

43  if __name__ == '__main__':
44      sys.stderr = sys.stdout
45      form = cgi.FieldStorage()
46      data = FeedbackData(form)
47      if data.type == 'comment':
48          gush(data)
49      else:
50          whimper(data)

51      # Save the data to file.
52      import tempfile, pickle
53      tempfile.tempdir = DIRECTORY
54      pickle.dump(data, open(tempfile.mktemp(), 'w'))
```

The output of this script clearly depends on the input, but the output with the form filled out with the parameters shown in Figure 28-1 is displayed in Figure 28-2.

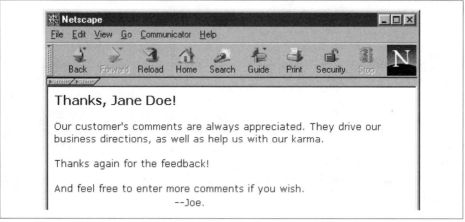

Figure 28-2. What the user sees after pressing the Send the feedback button

How does the *feedback.py* script work? There are a few aspects of the script common to all CGI programs, and those are highlighted in bold. To start, the first line of the program needs to refer to the Python executable. This is a requirement of the web server we're using here, and it might not apply in your case; even if it does, the specific location of your Python program is likely to be different from this. The second line includes imports of cgi and cgitb. The cgi module deals with the hard parts of CGI, such as parsing the environment variables and handling escaped characters. The cgitb module stands for "CGI Traceback," and it makes debugging CGI applications much easier. It needs to be enabled (line 3) to turn exceptions in the script into prettily-printed tracebacks. The documentation for the cgi module describes a very straightforward and easy way to use it. For this example, however, mostly because we're going to build on it, the script is somewhat more complicated than strictly necessary.

Let's just go through the code in the if __name__ == '__main__' block one statement at a time.[*] The first statement (line 44) redirects the sys.stderr stream to whatever standard output is. This is done for debugging because the output of the stdout stream in a CGI program goes back to the web browser, and the stderr stream goes to the server's error log, which can be harder to read than simply looking at the web page. This way, if a runtime exception occurs, we can see it on the web page, as opposed to having to guess what it was.

The second line (line 45) is crucial and does all of the hard CGI work: it returns a dictionary-like object (called a FieldStorage object) whose keys are the names of the variables filled out in the form, while the value of each field in the form can be obtained by asking for the value attribute of the entries in the FieldStorage object. Sounds complicated, but all it means is that for our form, the form object has keys 'name', 'type', 'email', 'address', and 'text', and that to find out what the user entered in the Name field of the web form, we need to look at form['name'].value.

The third line in the if block (line 46) creates an instance of our user-defined class FeedbackData, passing the form object as an argument. If you now look at the definition of the FeedbackData class, you'll see that it's a very simple subclass of FormData, which is also a user-defined class. All we've defined in the FeedbackData subclass is a class attribute fieldnames and a __repr__ function (used by the print statement, among others). Clearly, the __init__ method of the FormData class must do something with the FieldStorage argument. Indeed, it looks at each of the field names defined in the fieldnames class attribute of the instance (that's what self.fieldnames refers to), and for each field name, checks whether the FieldStorage object has a corresponding nonempty key. If it does, it sets an attribute with the same name as the field in the instance, giving it as value the text entered by the user. If it doesn't, it calls the bail function.

---

[*] You'll remember that this if statement is true only when the program is run as a script, not when it's imported. CGI programs qualify as scripts, so the code in the if block runs when this program is called by the web server. We use it later as an imported script.

Now, let's walk through the usual case, when the user dutifully enters all of the required data. In those cases, FieldStorage has all of the keys ('name', 'type', etc.), which the FeedbackData class needs. The FormData class' _ _init_ _ method in turn sets attributes for each field name in the instance. So, when the data = FeedbackData(form) call returns, data is guaranteed to be an instance of FeedbackData, which is a subclass of FormData, and data has the attributes name, type, email, etc., with the corresponding values the user entered. In addition, the instance will also have an attribute (time) corresponding to the time at which the instance was created.

A similar effect could have been obtained with code like:

```
form = cgi.FieldStorage( )
form_ok = 1
if 'name' not in form or form["name"].value == "":
    form_ok = 0
else:
    data_name = form["name"].value
if 'email' not in form or form["email"].value == "":
    form_ok = 0
else:
    data_email = form["email"].value
...
```

but it should be clear that this kind of programming can get very tedious, repetitive, and error-prone. With our scheme, when Joe changes the set of field names in the web page, all we need to change is the fieldnames attribute of the FeedbackData class. Also, we can use the same FormData class in any other CGI script, and thus reuse code.

What if the user didn't enter all of the required fields? Either the FieldStorage dictionary will be missing a key, or its value will be the empty string. The FormData._ _init_ _ method then calls the bail function, which displays a polite error message and exits the script. Control never returns back to the main function, so there is no need to test the validity of the data variable; if we got something back from FeedbackData( ), it's a valid instance.

With the data instance, we check to see if the feedback type was a comment, in which case we thank the user for their input. If the feedback type was a complaint, we apologize profusely and promise to get back in touch with them.

We now have a basic CGI infrastructure in place. To save the data to file is remarkably easy:

- First, we define the DIRECTORY variable outside the if test because we'll use it from another script that will import this one, so we wish it to be defined even if this script is not run as a program.
- At line 52, we import the tempfile and pickle modules. The tempfile module comes up with filenames currently not in use; that way we don't need to worry

about "collisions" in any filename generation scheme. The pickle module will allow us to serialize (i.e., save) any Python object.

- Line 53: The next line sets the tempdir attribute of the tempfile module to the value of the DIRECTORY variable, which is where we want our data to be saved. This is an example of customizing an existing module by directly modifying its namespace, just as we modified the stderr attribute of the sys module earlier.

- Line 54: The last line does the actual saving; it opens in write mode the file with a name generated by the tempfile module and dumps the instance data into it, using the pickle module. The pickle module is one of the gems that makes using a high-level language like Python so productive—*pickling* means taking arbitrary Python objects and converting them into streams of bytes in a format that Python knows how to "unpickle." Since they're streams of bytes, they can be written to disk, as we're doing here, or sent over a network, or otherwise stored or transmitted for later unpickling. There was no need to come with a file format specific to this application. As you can see on line 54, all it takes to save a Python object is to pass it to pickle.dump( ), take the result and stuff it in a file. Now the specified file contains a pickled instance, which we'll unpickle in the next section.

Interfacing with COM: Cheap Public Relations

At this point, we have a program that is run whenever users fill in the feedback form and that writes out instances of the feedback data to files on the server. We'll use this data to do two things. First, a program that's run periodically (say, at 2 a.m., every night)* will look through the saved data, find out which saved pickled files correspond to complaints, and print out a customized letter to the complainer. The second use we'll make of that data is a GUI browser to look through the stored feedback entries. All this sounds sophisticated, but you'll be surprised at how simple it is using the right tools. Joe's web site is on a Windows machine, but other platforms work in similar ways.

Before we talk about how to write this program, a word about the technology it uses, namely Microsoft's Component Object Model (COM). COM is, among other things, a standard for interaction between programs, which allows COM-compliant programs to talk to, access the data in, and execute commands in other COM-compliant programs. Roughly speaking, the program doing the calling is called a COM client, and the program doing the executing is called a COM server. All major Microsoft products are COM-aware and can act as servers. Microsoft Word is one of

---

* Setting up this kind of automatic regularly scheduled program is easily done on most platforms, using, for example, cron on Unix or the AT scheduler in Windows NT/2000/XP.

these, and the one we'll use here, since Microsoft Word is just fine for writing letters, which is what we're doing. Luckily for us, Python can be made COM-aware as well, on Windows. Mark Hammond and Greg Stein have made available a set of extensions to Python for Windows called win32com, which allow Python programs to do almost everything you can do with COM from any other language. You can write COM clients, servers, ActiveX scripting hosts, debuggers, and more, all in Python. We only need to do the first of these tasks, which is also the simplest. The basic tasks that our form letter generator program needs to do are:

1. Open all of the pickled files in the appropriate directory and unpickle them to turn them back into Python objects.

2. For each unpickled instance, test if the feedback is a complaint. If it is, find out the name and address of the person who filled out the form and go on to Step 3. If not, skip it.

3. Open a Word document containing a template of the letter we want to send, and fill in the appropriate pieces with the customized information.

4. Print the document and close it.

This task is almost as simple to express in Python with win32com. Here's a program called *formletter.py*:

```python
from win32com.client import gencache, constants
WORD = 'Word.Application'
False, True = 0, -1

class Word:
    def __init__(self):
        self.app = gencache.EnsureDispatch(WORD)
    def open(self, doc):
        self.app.Documents.Open(FileName=doc)
    def replace(self, source, target):
        self.app.Selection.HomeKey(Unit=constants.wdLine)
        find = self.app.Selection.Find
        find.Text = "%"+source+"%"
        find.Execute()
        self.app.Selection.TypeText(Text=target)
    def printdoc(self):
        self.app.Application.PrintOut()
    def close(self):
        self.app.ActiveDocument.Close(SaveChanges=False)

def print_formletter(data):
    word.open(r"h:\David\Book\tofutemplate.doc")
    word.replace("name", data.name)
    word.replace("address", data.address)
    word.replace("firstname", data.name.split()[0])
    word.printdoc()
    word.close()
```

```
if __name__ == '__main__':
    import os, pickle
    from feedback import DIRECTORY, FormData, FeedbackData
    word = Word()
    for filename in os.listdir(DIRECTORY):
        data = pickle.load(open(os.path.join(DIRECTORY, filename)))
        if data.type == 'complaint':
            print "Printing letter for %(name)s." % vars(data)
            print_formletter(data)
        else:
            print "Got comment from %(name)s, skipping printing." % vars(data)
```

The first few lines of the main program show the power of a well-designed framework. The first line is a standard import statement, except that it's worth noting that win32com is a package, not a module. It is, in fact, a collection of subpackages, modules, and functions. We need two things from the win32com package: the EnsureDispatch function in the gencache module, a function that allows us to dispatch functions to other objects (COM servers), and the constants submodule of the same module, which holds the constants defined by the COM objects we want to talk to.

The second line simply defines a variable that contains the name of the COM server we're interested in. It's called Word.Application, as you can find out from using a COM browser or reading Word's API (see the sidebar "Finding Out About COM Interfaces"). Using gencache.EnsureDispatch ensures that late binding is used for the Word library, and also ensures that all Word related constants are loaded.

Let's focus now on the if __name__ == '__main__' block, which is the next statement after the class and function definitions.

The first task is to read the data. We import the os and pickle modules because we're going to need functions they define, and then three references from the feedback module we just wrote: the DIRECTORY where the data is stored (this way if we change it in *feedback.py*, this module reflects the change the next time it's run), and the FormData and FeedbackData classes. The next line creates an instance of the Word class; this opens a connection with the Word COM server, starting the server if necessary.

The for loop is a simple iteration over the files in the directory with all the saved files. It's important that this directory contain only the pickled instances, since we're not doing any error checking. (We should make the code more robust, but we've ignored stability for simplicity.)

The first line in the for loop does the unpickling. It uses the load function from the pickle module, which takes a single argument, the file which is being unpickled. It returns as many references as were stored in the file—in our case, just one. The data that was stored was just the instance of the FeedbackData class. The definition of the class itself isn't stored in the pickled file, just the instance values and a reference to the class. This design reduces the total size of pickled objects, and more importantly, it allows you to unpickle instances of previous versions of a class and automatically upgrade them to the newer class definitions.

The `if` statement inside the loop is straightforward.

The `print_formletter` function simply calls the various methods of the `word` instance of the `Word` class with the data extracted from the data instance. Note that we use the `split` method to extract the first name of the user, just to make the letter more friendly, but this risks strange behavior for nonstandard names.

In the `Word` class, the `__init__` method appears simple yet hides a lot of work. It creates a connection with the COM server and stores a reference to that COM server in an instance variable app. Now, there are two ways in which the subsequent code might use this server: dynamic dispatch and nondynamic dispatch. In dynamic dispatch, Python doesn't know at the time the program is running what the interface to the COM server (in this case Microsoft Word) is. That's not a problem because COM allows Python to query the server and determine the number and kinds of arguments each function expects.

To explain the `Word` class methods, let's start with a possible template document, shown in Figure 28-3. so that we can see what needs to be done to it to customize it.

As you can see, it's a pretty average document, with the exception of some text in between % signs. We've used this notation just to make it easy for a program to find the parts that need customization, but any other technique could work as well. To use this template, we need to open the document, customize it, print it, and close it. Opening it is done by the open method of the Word class. The printing and closing are done similarly. To customize, we replace the %name%, %firstname%, and %address% text with the appropriate strings. That's what the `replace` method of the `Word` class does (we won't cover how we figured out what the exact sequence of calls should be; see the sidebar "Finding Out About COM Interfaces" for details).

Putting all of this at work, the program, when run, outputs text like:

```
C:\Programs> python formletter.py
Printing letter for John Doe.
Got comment from Your Mom, skipping printing.
Printing letter for Susan B. Anthony.
```

and prints two customized letters, ready to be sent in the mail. Note that the Word program doesn't show up on the desktop; by default, COM servers are invisible, so Word just acts behind the scenes. If Word is currently active on the desktop, each step is visible to the user.

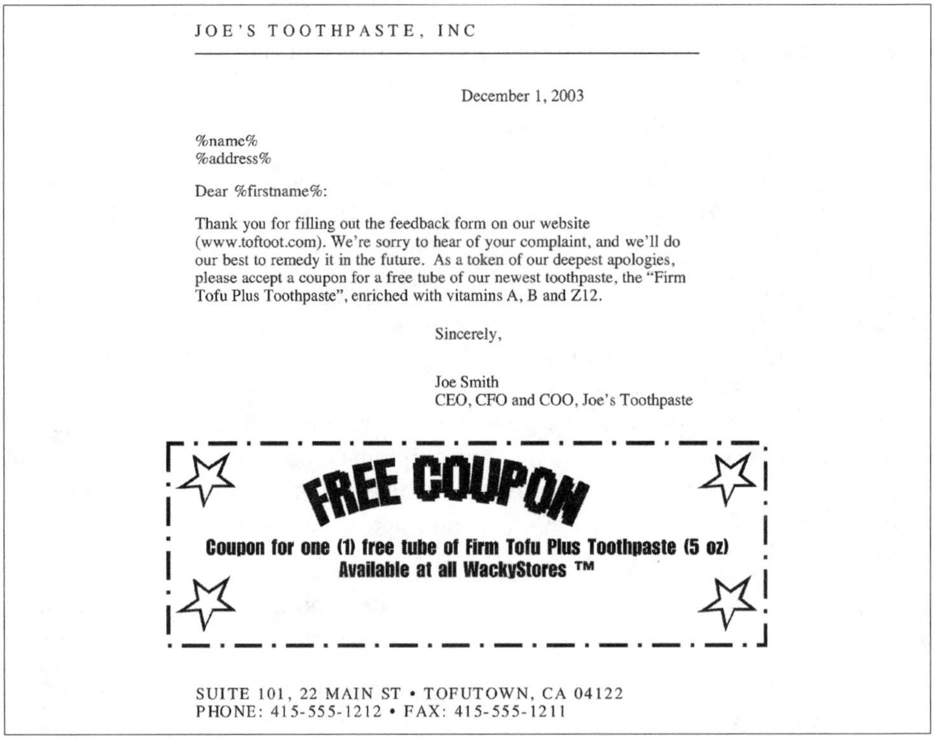

JOE'S TOOTHPASTE, INC

December 1, 2003

%name%
%address%

Dear %firstname%:

Thank you for filling out the feedback form on our website (www.toftoot.com). We're sorry to hear of your complaint, and we'll do our best to remedy it in the future. As a token of our deepest apologies, please accept a coupon for a free tube of our newest toothpaste, the "Firm Tofu Plus Toothpaste", enriched with vitamins A, B and Z12.

Sincerely,

Joe Smith
CEO, CFO and COO, Joe's Toothpaste

FREE COUPON

Coupon for one (1) free tube of Firm Tofu Plus Toothpaste (5 oz)
Available at all WackyStores ™

SUITE 101, 22 MAIN ST • TOFUTOWN, CA 04122
PHONE: 415-555-1212 • FAX: 415-555-1211

Figure 28-3. Joe's template letter to complainers

A Tkinter-Based GUI Editor for Managing Form Data

Let's recap: we wrote a CGI program (*feedback.py*) that takes the input from a web form and stores the information on disk on our server. We then wrote a program (*formletter.py*) that takes some of those files and generates apologies to those deserving them. The next task is to construct a program to allow a human to look at the comments and complaints, using the Tkinter toolkit to build a GUI browser for these files.

The Tkinter toolkit is a Python-specific interface to a non-Python GUI library called Tk. Tk is the GUI toolkit most commonly chosen by Python programmers because it provides professional-looking GUIs within a fairly easy-to-use system and because the Python/Tk interface comes with most Python distributions. The interfaces it generates don't look exactly like Windows, the Mac, or any Unix toolkit, but they look very close to each of them, and the same Python program works on all those platforms, an impossible task with any platform-specific toolkit. Two other portable toolkits worth considering are wxPython (*http://www.wxPython.org*) and PyQt.

Tk, therefore, is what we'll use in this example. It's a toolkit developed by John Ousterhout, originally as a companion to Tcl, another scripting language. Since then, Tk has been adopted by many other scripting languages including Python and Perl.

The goals of this program are simple: to display in a window a description of each feedback instance, allowing the user to select one to examine in greater detail (e.g., seeing the contents of the text widget). Furthermore, Joe wants to be able to discard items once they have been dealt with. A screenshot of the finished program in action is shown in Figure 28-4.

The Main Program

We'll work through one possible way of coding the program to manage form data. Our entire program, called *feedbackeditor.py*, is:

```
from FormEditor import FormEditor
from feedback import FeedbackData, FormData
```

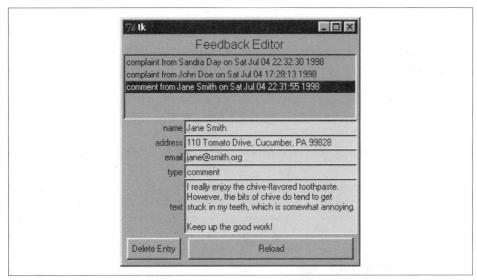

Figure 28-4. A sample screen dump of the feedbackeditor.py program

```
from Tkinter import mainloop
FormEditor("Feedback Editor", FeedbackData, feedback.DIRECTORY)
mainloop()
```

The point of breaking these five lines out into a separate file is that we've broken out all that is specific to our form. As we'll see, the FormEditor program is completely independent of the specific CGI form. A further point made explicit by this microprogram is that it shows how to interact with Tkinter; you create widgets and windows, and then call the mainloop function, which sets the GUI running. Every change in the program that follows happens as a result of GUI actions. As for *formletter.py*, this program imports the class objects from the feedback module, for the same reason (unpickling). Then, an instance of the FormEditor class is created, passing to its initialization function the name of the editor, the class of the objects being unpickled, and the location of the pickled instances.

The Form Editor

The code for *FormEditor.py* is just a class definition, which we'll show all at once and then describe in parts, one method at a time:

```
from Tkinter import *
import os, pickle

class FormEditor:

    def __init__(self, name, dataclass, storagedir):
        self.storagedir = storagedir      # Stash away some references.
```

```
        self.dataclass = dataclass
        self.row = 0
        self.current = None

        self.root = root = Tk()          # Create window and size it.
        root.minsize(300,200)

        root.rowconfigure(0, weight=1)   # Define how columns and rows scale
        root.columnconfigure(0, weight=1) # when the window is resized.
        root.columnconfigure(1, weight=2)

        # Create the title Label.
        Label(root, text=name, font='bold').grid(columnspan=2)
        self.row = self.row + 1
        # Create the main listbox and configure it.
        self.listbox = Listbox(root, selectmode=SINGLE)
        self.listbox.grid(columnspan=2, sticky=E+W+N+S)
        self.listbox.bind('<ButtonRelease-1>', self.select)
        self.row = self.row + 1

        # Call self.add_variable once per variable in the class's fieldnames var.
        for fieldname in dataclass.fieldnames:
            setattr(self, fieldname, self.add_variable(root, fieldname))

        # Create a couple of buttons, with assigned commands.
        self.add_button(self.root, self.row, 0, 'Delete Entry', self. delentry)
        self.add_button(self.root, self.row, 1, 'Reload', self.load_data)

        self.load_data()

    def add_variable(self, root, varname):
        Label(root, text=varname).grid(row=self.row, column=0, sticky=E)
        value = Label(root, text='', background='gray90',
                        relief=SUNKEN, anchor=W, justify=LEFT)
        value.grid(row=self.row, column=1, sticky=E+W)
        self.row = self.row + 1
        return value

    def add_button(self, root, row, column, text, command):
        button = Button(root, text=text, command=command)
        button.grid(row=row, column=column, sticky=E+W, padx=5, pady=5)

    def load_data(self):
        self.listbox.delete(0,END)
        self.items = []
        for filename in os.listdir(self.storagedir):
            item = pickle.load(open(os.path.join(self.storagedir, filename)))
            item._filename = filename
            self.items.append(item)
            self.listbox.insert('end', repr(item))
        self.listbox.select_set(0)
        self.select(None)
```

```
def select(self, event):
    selection = self.listbox.curselection( )
    self.selection = self.items[int(selection[0])]
    for fieldname in self.dataclass.fieldnames:
        label = getattr(self, fieldname)              # GUI field
        labelstr = getattr(self.selection, fieldname)  # instance attribute
        labelstr = labelstr.replace('\r', '')
        label.config(text=labelstr)

def delentry(self):
    os.remove(os.path.join(self.storagedir,self.selection._filename))
    self.load_data( )
```

You'll notice that the first line uses the from … import * construct we warned you about earlier. In Tkinter programs, it's usually fairly safe, because Tkinter only exports variables that are fairly obviously GUI-related (Label, Widget, etc.), and they all start with uppercase letters.

Understanding the __init__ method is best done by comparing the structure of the code to the structure of the window screen dump shown in Figure 28-4. As you move down the __init__ method lines, you should be able to match many statements with their graphical consequences.

The first few lines simply stash away a few things in instance variables and assign default values to variables. The next set of lines access a Toplevel widget (basically, a window; the Tk( ) call returns the currently defined top-level widget), set its minimum size and a few properties. The row and column configuration options allow the widgets inside the window to scale if the user changes the size of the window and determines the relative width of the two columns of internal widgets.

The next call creates a Label widget, which is defined in the Tkinter module, and which, as you can see in the screen dump, is just a text label. It spans both columns of widgets, meaning that it extends from the leftmost edge of the window to the rightmost edge. Specifying the locations of graphical elements is responsible for the majority of GUI calls, due to the wide array of possible arrangements.

The Listbox widget is created next; it's a list of text lines, which can be selected by the user using arrow keys and the mouse button. This specific listbox allows only one line to be selected at a time (selectmode=SINGLE) and fills all the space available to it (the sticky option).

The for loop block, by iterating over the fieldnames attribute of the dataclass variable (the fieldnames class of the FeedbackData class), finds out which variables are in the instance data, and for each, calls the add_variable method of the FormEditor class and takes the returned value and stuffs it in an instance variable. This is equivalent in our case to:

```
    ...
self.name = self.add_variable(root, 'name')
self.email = self.add_variable(root, 'email')
```

```
    self.address = self.add_variable(root, 'address')
    self.type = self.add_variable(root, 'type')
    self.text = self.add_variable(root, 'text')
```

The version in the code sample, however, is better, because the list of field names is already available to the program and retyping anything is usually an indicator of bad design. Furthermore, there is nothing about FormData that is specific to our forms. It can be used to browse any instance of a class that defines a variable fieldnames. Making the program generic like this makes it more likely to be reused in other contexts for other tasks.

Finishing off with the __init__ method, we see that two buttons finish the graphical layout of the window, each associated with a command that's executed when it's clicked. One is the delentry method, which deletes the current entry, and the other is a reloading function that rereads the data in the storage directory.

Finally, the data is loaded by a call to the load_data method. We'll describe it as soon as we're done with the calls that set up widgets, namely add_variable and add_button.

add_variable creates two Label widgets on the same row. The first displays the name of the field, and the second will contain the value of the corresponding field in the entry selected in the listbox:

```
def add_variable(self, root, varname):
    Label(root, text=varname).grid(row=self.row, column=0, sticky=E)
    value = Label(root, text='', background='gray90',
                  relief=SUNKEN, anchor=W, justify=LEFT)
    value.grid(row=self.row, column=1, sticky=E+W)
    self.row = self.row + 1
    return value
```

add_button is simpler, as it needs to create only one widget:

```
def add_button(self, root, row, column, text, command):
    button = Button(root, text=text, command=command)
    button.grid(row=row, column=column, sticky=E+W, padx=5, pady=5)
```

The load_data function is called when the Refresh button is selected. Before loading the data from the pickled file, it first cleans up any contents in the listbox (the graphical list of items) corresponding to possibly out-of-date data and resets the items attribute (which is a Python list that will contain references to the actual data instances). The loop that fills in the listbox and items attribute is quite similar to that used for *formletter.py*:

```
def load_data(self):
    self.listbox.delete(0,END)
    self.items = [ ]
    for filename in os.listdir(self.storagedir):
        item = pickle.load(open(os.path.join(self.storagedir, filename)))
        item._filename = filename
```

```
        self.items.append(item)
        self.listbox.insert('end', repr(item))
    self.listbox.select_set(0)
    self.select(None)
```

Note that:

- The name of the file in which an instance is stored is attached as an attribute to that instance.
- The instance is added to the items instance attribute.
- The string representation of the item is added to the listbox.
- The first item in the listbox is selected.

We now get to the select method. It's called in one of two circumstances. The first, as we just showed, is the last thing to happen when the data is loaded. The second is a consequence of the binding operation in the __init__ method, which we reprint here:

```
self.listbox.bind('<ButtonRelease-1>', self.select)
```

This call binds the occurrence of a specific event ('<ButtonRelease-1>') in a specific widget (self.listbox) to a call to self.select. In other words, whenever you let go of the left mouse button on an item in the listbox, the select method of your editor is called. It's called with an argument of type Event, which can let us know such things as when the button click occurred, but since we don't need to know anything about the event except that it occurred, we'll ignore it. What must happen on selection? First, the instance corresponding to the item being selected in the GUI element must be identified, and then the fields corresponding to the values of that instance must be updated. This is performed by iterating over each field name (looking back to the fieldnames class variable again), finding the value of the field in the selected instance, and configuring the appropriate label widget to display the right text:[*]

```
def select(self, event):
    selection = self.listbox.curselection( )
    self.selection = self.items[int(selection[0])]
    for fieldname in self.dataclass.fieldnames:
        label = getattr(self, fieldname)               # GUI field
        labelstr = getattr(self.selection, fieldname)  # instance attribute
        labelstr = string.replace(labelstr,'\r', '')
        label.config(text=labelstr)
```

The reload functionality is exactly that of the load_data method, which is why that's what was passed as the command to be called when the Reload button is clicked. The deletion of an entry, however, is a tad more difficult. The first thing we do when loading an instance from disk is to give it an attribute that corresponds to the filename

---

[*] The replace operation is needed because Tk treats the \r\n sequence that occurs on Windows machines as two carriage returns instead of one.

---

whence it came. We use this information to delete the file before asking for a reload; the listbox is automatically updated:

```
def delentry(self):
    os.remove(os.path.join(self.storagedir,self.selection._filename))
    self.load_data()
```

This program is probably the hardest to understand of any in this book, simply because it uses the complex and powerful Tkinter library extensively. There is documentation for Tkinter, as well as for Tk itself.

- The most complete documentation is Fredrik Lundh's documentation, available on the Web at *http://www.pythonware.com/library/tkinter/introduction/index.htm.*

- Several books cover Tkinter. John Grayson wrote a book devoted to Tkinter programming, *Python and Tkinter Programming* (Manning Publications). O'Reilly's *Programming Python* also has extensive coverage of Tkinter, including a 260-page section devoted to basic widgets and complete example programs. Finally, *Python in a Nutshell* (O'Reilly) has concise documentation covering most of Tkinter.

- The New Mexico Institute of Mining and Technology created its own 84-page Tkinter manual. It is available in PDF and PostScript form from *http://www.nmt. edu/tcc/help/lang/python/docs.html.* Look under "Locally written documentation."

- Also, see the Python web site section on Tkinter at *http://www.python.org/topics/ tkinter/.*

Design Considerations

Think of the CGI script *feedback.py* and the GUI program *FormEditor.py* as two different ways of manipulating a common dataset (the pickled instances on disk). When should you use a web-based interface, and when should you use a GUI? The choice should be based on a couple of factors:

- How easy is it to implement the needed functionality in a given framework?

- What software can you require the user to install in order to access or modify the data?

The web frontend is well suited to cases where the complexity of the data manipulation requirements is low and where it's more important that users be able to work the program than that the program be full-featured. Building a real program on top of a GUI toolkit, on the other hand, allows maximum flexibility, at the cost of having to teach the user how to use it and/or installing specific programs. One reason for Python's success among experienced programmers is that Python allows them to design programs on such reasoned bases, as opposed to forcing them to use one type of programming framework just because it's what the language designer had in mind.

Jython: The Felicitous Union of Python and Java

Jython is a version of Python written entirely in Java. Jython is very exciting for both the Python community and the Java community. Python users are happy that their current Python knowledge can be applied in Java-based projects; Java programmers are happy that they can use the Python scripting language as a way to control their Java systems, test libraries, and learn about Java libraries by working in a powerful interactive environment.

Jython is available from *http://www.jython.org*, with license and distribution terms similar to those of CPython (which is what the reference implementation of Python is called when contrasted with Jython).

The Jython installation includes several parts:

- *jython*, which is the equivalent of the python program used throughout the book.
- *jythonc*, which takes a Jython program and compiles it to Java class files. The resulting Java class files can be used as any Java class file can, for example, as applets, as servlets, or as beans.
- A set of modules that provide the Jython user with the vast majority of the modules in the standard Python library.
- A few programs demonstrating various aspects of Jython programming.

Using Jython is very similar to using Python:

```
~/book> jython
Jython 2.1 on java1.3.1_03 (JIT: null)
Type "copyright", "credits" or "license" for more information.
>>> 2 + 3
5
```

In fact, Jython works almost identically to CPython. For an up-to-date listing of the differences between the two, see *http://www.jython.org/docs/differences.html*. The most important differences are:

- Jython is currently slower than CPython. How much slower depends on the test code used and on the Java Virtual Machine Jython is using.
- Some of the built-ins or library modules aren't available for Jython. For example, the os.system( ) call is not implemented yet, as doing so is difficult given Java's interaction with the underlying operating system. Also, some of the largest extension modules, such as the Tkinter GUI framework, aren't available, because the underlying tools (the Tk/Tcl toolkit, in the case of Tkinter) aren't available in Java.

Jython Gives Python Programmers Access to Java Libraries

The most important difference between Jython and CPython, however, is that Jython offers the Python programmer seamless access to Java libraries. Consider the following program, *jythondemo.py*, the output of which is shown in Figure 28-5.

```
from pawt import swing
import java

def exit(e): java.lang.System.exit(0)

frame = swing.JFrame('Swing Example', visible=1)
button = swing.JButton('This is a Swinging example!', actionPerformed=exit)
frame.contentPane.add(button)
frame.pack()
```

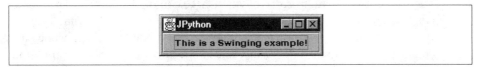

Figure 28-5. The output of jythondemo.py

This simple program demonstrates how easy it is to write a Python program that uses the Swing Java GUI framework.* The first line imports the swing Java package (the pawt module figures out the exact location of Swing in your particular Java installation, which can be in java.awt.swing, in com.sun.java.swing, or maybe in javax. swing—it also includes some utility code such as the GridBag class, which we use in the *grapher.py* program below). The second line imports the java package that we need for the java.lang.System.exit() call. The fourth line creates a JFrame, setting its bean property visible to true. The fifth line creates a JButton with a label and specifies what function should be called when the button is clicked. Finally, the last two lines put the JButton in the JFrame and make them both visible.

Experienced Java programmers might be a bit surprised at some of the code in *jythondemo.py*, as it has some differences from the equivalent Java program. In order to make using Java libraries as easy as possible for Python users, Jython performs a lot of work behind the scenes. For example, when Jython imports a Java package, it actively tracks down the appropriate package, and then, using the Java Reflection API, finds the contents of packages, and the signatures of classes and methods. Jython also performs on-the-fly conversion between Python types and Java types. In *jythondemo.py*, for example, the text of the button ('This is a Swinging example!')

---

* Documentation for Swing and the Java Foundation Classes is available online at *http://java.sun.com/ products/jfc/index.html*. Alternatively, Robert Eckstein, Marc Loy, and Dave Wood have written a thorough review of the Swing toolkit for Java: *Java Swing* (O'Reilly).

is a Python string. Before the constructor for JButton is called, Jython finds which variant of the constructor can be used (e.g., by rejecting the version that accepts an Icon as a first argument), and automatically converts the Python string object to a Java string object. More sophisticated mechanisms allow the convenient `actionPerformed=exit` keyword argument to the JButton constructor. This idiom isn't possible in Java, since Java can't manipulate functions (or methods) as first-class objects. Jython makes it unnecessary to create an `ActionListener` class with a single `actionPerformed` method, although you can use the more verbose form if you wish.

Jython as a Java Scripting Language

Jython is gaining in popularity because it allows programmers to explore the myriad Java libraries that are becoming available in an interactive, rapid turnaround environment. It also is proving useful to embed Python as a scripting language in Java frameworks, for customization, testing, and other programming tasks by end users (as opposed to systems developers). For an example of a Python interpreter embedded in a Java program, see the program in the demo/embed directory of the Jython distribution.

A Real Jython/Swing Application: grapher.py

The *grapher.py* program (output shown in Figure 28-6) allows users to graphically explore the behavior of mathematical functions. It's also based on the Swing GUI toolkit. There are two text-entry widgets in which Python code should be entered. The first is an arbitrary Python program that's invoked before the function is drawn; it imports the needed modules and defines any functions that might be needed in computing the value of the function. The second text area (labeled `Expression:`) should be a Python expression (as in `sin(x)`), not a statement. It's called for each data point, with the value of the variable x set to the horizontal coordinate.

The user can control whether to draw a line graph or a filled graph, the number of points to plot, and what color to plot the graph in. Finally, the user can save configurations to disk and reload them later (using the `pickle` module). Here is the *grapher.py* program:

```
from pawt import swing, awt, colors, GridBag
RIGHT = swing.JLabel.RIGHT
APPROVE_OPTION = swing.JFileChooser.APPROVE_OPTION
import java.io
import pickle, os

default_setup = """from math import *
def squarewave(x,order):
    total = 0.0
    for i in range(1, order*2+1, 2):
```

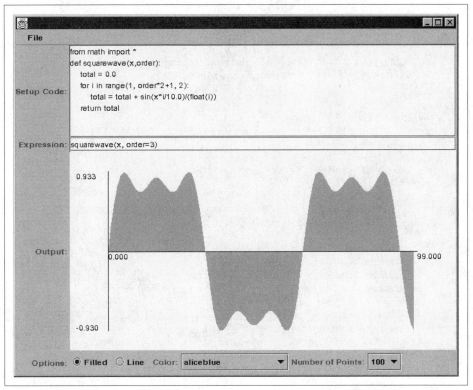

Figure 28-6. Output of grapher.py

```
        total = total + sin(x*i/10.0)/(float(i))
    return total
"""

default_expression = "squarewave(x, order=3)"

class Chart(awt.Canvas):
    color = colors.darkturquoise
    style = 'Filled'

    def getPreferredSize(self):
        return awt.Dimension(600,300)

    def paint(self, graphics):
        clip = self.bounds
        graphics.color = colors.white
        graphics.fillRect(0, 0, clip.width, clip.height)

        width = int(clip.width * .8)
        height = int(clip.height * .8)
        x_offset = int(clip.width * .1)
        y_offset = clip.height - int(clip.height * .1)

        N = len(self.data); xs = [0]*N; ys = [0]*N
```

```
            xmin, xmax = 0, N-1
            ymax = max(self.data)
            ymin = min(self.data)

            zero_y = y_offset - int(-ymin/(ymax-ymin)*height)
            zero_x = x_offset + int(-xmin/(xmax-xmin)*width)

            for i in range(N):
                xs[i] = int(float(i)*width/N) + x_offset
                ys[i] = y_offset - int((self.data[i]-ymin)/(ymax-ymin)*height)
            graphics.color = self.color
            if self.style == "Line":
                graphics.drawPolyline(xs, ys, len(xs))
            else:
                xs.insert(0, xs[0]); ys.insert(0, zero_y)
                xs.append(xs[-1]); ys.append(zero_y)
                graphics.fillPolygon(xs, ys, len(xs))

            # Draw axes.
            graphics.color = colors.black
            graphics.drawLine(x_offset,zero_y, x_offset+width, zero_y)
            graphics.drawLine(zero_x, y_offset, zero_x, y_offset-height)

            # Draw labels.
            leading = graphics.font.size
            graphics.drawString("%.3f" % xmin, x_offset, zero_y+leading)
            graphics.drawString("%.3f" % xmax, x_offset+width, zero_y+leading)
            graphics.drawString("%.3f" % ymin, zero_x-50, y_offset)
            graphics.drawString("%.3f" % ymax, zero_x-50, y_offset-height+leading)

class GUI:
    def __init__(self):
        self.numelements = 100
        self.frame = swing.JFrame(windowClosing=self.do_quit)

        # Build menu bar.
        menubar = swing.JMenuBar( )
        file = swing.JMenu("File")
        file.add(swing.JMenuItem("Load", actionPerformed = self.do_load))
        file.add(swing.JMenuItem("Save", actionPerformed = self.do_save))
        file.add(swing.JMenuItem("Quit", actionPerformed = self.do_quit))
        menubar.add(file)
        self.frame.JMenuBar = menubar

        # Create widgets.
        self.chart = Chart(visible=1)
        self.execentry = swing.JTextArea(default_setup, 8, 60)
        self.evalentry = swing.JTextField(default_expression,
                                          actionPerformed = self.update)

        # Create options panel.
        optionsPanel = swing.JPanel(awt.FlowLayout(
            alignment=awt.FlowLayout.LEFT))
```

```python
        # Whether the plot is a line graph or a filled graph
        self.filled = swing.JRadioButton("Filled",
                                actionPerformed=self.set_filled)
        optionsPanel.add(self.filled)
        self.line = swing.JRadioButton("Line",
                                    actionPerformed=self.set_line)
        optionsPanel.add(self.line)
        styleGroup = swing.ButtonGroup()
        styleGroup.add(self.filled)
        styleGroup.add(self.line)

        # Color selection
        optionsPanel.add(swing.JLabel("Color:", RIGHT))
        colorlist = filter(lambda x: x[0] != '_', dir(colors))
        self.colorname = swing.JComboBox(colorlist)
        self.colorname.itemStateChanged = self.set_color
        optionsPanel.add(self.colorname)

        # Number of points
        optionsPanel.add(swing.JLabel("Number of Points:", RIGHT))
        self.sizes = [50, 100, 200, 500]
        self.numpoints = swing.JComboBox(self.sizes)
        self.numpoints.selectedIndex = self.sizes.index(self.numelements)
        self.numpoints.itemStateChanged = self.set_numpoints
        optionsPanel.add(self.numpoints)

        # Do the rest of the layout in a GridBag.
        self.do_layout(optionsPanel)

    def do_layout(self, optionsPanel):
        bag = GridBag(self.frame.contentPane, fill='BOTH',
                    weightx=1.0, weighty=1.0)
        bag.add(swing.JLabel("Setup Code: ", RIGHT))
        bag.addRow(swing.JScrollPane(self.execentry), weighty=10.0)
        bag.add(swing.JLabel("Expression: ", RIGHT))
        bag.addRow(self.evalentry, weighty=2.0)
        bag.add(swing.JLabel("Output: ", RIGHT))
        bag.addRow(self.chart, weighty=20.0)
        bag.add(swing.JLabel("Options: ", RIGHT))
        bag.addRow(optionsPanel, weighty=2.0)
        self.update(None)
        self.frame.visible = 1
        self.frame.size = self.frame.getPreferredSize()

        self.chooser = swing.JFileChooser()
        self.chooser.currentDirectory = java.io.File(os.getcwd())

    def do_save(self, event=None):
        self.chooser.rescanCurrentDirectory()
        returnVal = self.chooser.showSaveDialog(self.frame)
        if returnVal == APPROVE_OPTION:
            object = (self.execentry.text,  self.evalentry.text,
```

```
                            self.chart.style,
                            self.chart.color.RGB,
                            self.colorname.selectedIndex,
                            self.numelements)
            file = open(os.path.join(self.chooser.currentDirectory.path,
                        self.chooser.selectedFile.name), 'w')
            pickle.dump(object, file)
            file.close()

    def do_load(self, event=None):
        self.chooser.rescanCurrentDirectory()
        returnVal = self.chooser.showOpenDialog(self.frame)
        if returnVal == APPROVE_OPTION:
            file = open(os.path.join(self.chooser.currentDirectory.path,
                        self.chooser.selectedFile.name))
            (setup, each, style, color,
             colorname, self.numelements) = pickle.load(file)
            file.close()
            self.chart.color = java.awt.Color(color)
            self.colorname.selectedIndex = colorname
            self.chart.style = style
            self.execentry.text = setup
            self.numpoints.selectedIndex = self.sizes.index(self.numelements)
            self.evalentry.text = each
            self.update(None)

    def do_quit(self, event=None):
        import sys
        sys.exit(0)

    def set_color(self, event):
        self.chart.color = getattr(colors, event.item)
        self.chart.repaint()

    def set_numpoints(self, event):
        self.numelements = event.item
        self.update(None)

    def set_filled(self, event):
        self.chart.style = 'Filled'
        self.chart.repaint()

    def set_line(self, event):
        self.chart.style = 'Line'
        self.chart.repaint()

    def update(self, event):
        context = {}
        exec self.execentry.text in context
        each = compile(self.evalentry.text, '<input>', 'eval')
        numbers = [0]*self.numelements
```

```
        for x in xrange(self.numelements):
            context['x'] = float(x)
            numbers[x] = eval(each, context)
        self.chart.data = numbers
        if self.chart.style == 'Line':
            self.line.setSelected(1)
        else:
            self.filled.setSelected(1)
        self.chart.repaint( )

GUI( )
```

The logic of this program is fairly straightforward, and the class and method names make it easy to follow the flow of control. Most of this program could have been written in fairly analogous (but quite a bit longer) Java code. The parts in bold, however, show the power of having Python available: at the top of the module, default values for the Setup and Expression text widgets are defined. The former imports the functions in the math module and defines a function called squarewave. The latter specifies a call to this function, with a specific order parameter (as that parameter grows, the resulting graph looks more and more like a square wave, hence the name of the function). If you have Java, Swing, and Jython installed, play around with other possibilities for both the Setup and Expression text widgets.

The key asset of using Jython instead of Java in this example is in the update method: it simply calls the standard Python exec statement with the Setup code as an argument, and then calls eval with the compiled version of the Expression code for each coordinate. The user is free to use any Python code in these text widgets!

Jython is still very much a work in progress; the Jython developers are constantly refining the interface between Python and Java, optimizing it, and keeping up with Python upgrades. Jython, by being the second implementation of Python, is also forcing Guido van Rossum to decide what aspects of Python are core to the language and what aspects are features of his implementation.

Exercises

Most of the topics this chapter are not really good topics for exercises without first covering the frameworks they cover. A couple of things can be done with the knowledge you already have, however:

1. *Faking the Web*. You may not have a web server running, which makes using *formletter.py* and *FormEditor.py* difficult, since they use data generated by the CGI script. As an exercise, write a program that creates files with the same properties as those created by the CGI script.

2. *Cleaning up*. There's a serious problem with the *formletter.py* program: namely, if, it's run nightly, any complaint is going to cause a letter to be printed. That will happen every night, since there is no mechanism for indicating that a letter

has been generated and that no more letters need be generated regarding that specific complaint. Fix this problem.

3. *Adding parametric plotting to grapher.py*. Modify *grapher.py* to allow the user to specify expressions that return both *x* and *y* values, instead of the current just *y* solution. For example, the user should be able to write in the Expression widget: `sin(x/3. 1),cos(x/6.15)` (note the comma: this is a tuple!) and get a picture like that shown in Figure 28-7.

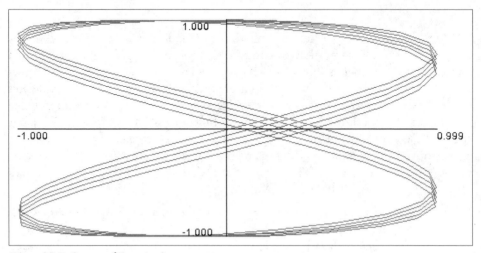

Figure 28-7. Output of Exercise 3

## CHAPTER 29

Python Resources

Programming languages, like natural languages, grow tight-knit communities—speakers of the same language have a natural affinity for each other. Programming languages, being the result of individual choice rather than accident of birth, lead to stronger feelings of kinship than might seem reasonable for what some see as a purely technological topic. Open source languages, which are never chosen because of a marketing campaign, but instead after a process of deliberation and comparison, seem to elicit even more enthusiasm (some would even say fanaticism) from their users. This chapter is about the community that defines itself as being "The Python Community," from the inner sanctum of people who dream about Python daily to the occasional Python user.

Because writing shareable Python code is so easy, much of this community shares their enthusiasm and their work, quite often in the form of yet more free software. The resulting snowball effect (or, to use a more trendy term, the "network effect") makes writing even large programs a snap compared to many other language choices. This chapter will point out some of the most valuable third-party offerings, from small modules to interfaces to operating system libraries to module repositories.

Layers of Community

In this section, we will discuss the various layers of the community, from the core of very serious programmers who implement the official Python interpreter, out through the Python Software Foundation, special interest groups and user groups, and out to the broad spectrum of participants, which is known as "python-list." You'll probably find that you belong in one or more of these neighborhoods, and may want to visit some of the neighborhoods you don't yet know. Regardless of where you choose to settle, welcome to our community!

The Core

Unlike many language communities, the Python world has a very clear center. This center has grown over the years, with Guido van Rossum as the permanent core, surrounded physically by a trusty cohort called "Pythonlabs," and surrounded virtually by the "python-dev group." Pythonlabs consists of a few key Python developers(Tim Peters, Barry Warsaw, Jeremy Hylton, and Fred Drake) who were recruited by Guido to work with him on Python and Python-related projects, first at BeOpen.com, and then at Zope Corporation. Along with Guido, they have generally been the ones making the most radical changes to the Python internals, although there have been some notable exceptions from other contributors.

Python is too big for so few people to manage and grow as fast as its users would like (especially as Python is only a part-time job, even for Guido). A supporting cast, generally referred to as the python-dev crowd after the mailing list that anchors the discussions, is available to help in design discussions, implementing, testing, and, most of all, arguing (all in good faith, though).

To most Python users, however, the work of Pythonlabs and Python-dev is gratefully acknowledged but somewhat mysterious. Many more people live in one of the outer layers of Pythondom, either virtual or physical (or, hopefully, both). We'll get back to the technically "deep" layers later—it's far more reasonable to learn about a community from the tourism bureau than from the city planning committee, however.

Local User Groups

While most Python-related communications occur on the Internet, it's nice to ground the names with faces and accents, and to get a feel for the real-world personalities behind the online personas. There are two great ways to do that, each with their own benefits: user groups and conferences.

You may have a local Python or Zope user group in your neighborhood. There is a list at *http://www.python.org/UserGroups.html*, but check with your local computer society, Linux users group or other such organization for possibly more up-to-date information. If there isn't one yet, chances are quite good that there is pent-up demand for it, and they're easy to organize. It's a great occasion to learn more about Python, find out who else is using Python locally (which can be helpful at resume-passing time), and meet people with whom you share at least one interest. Both of the authors visit local user groups on a regular basis.

Conferences and Workshops

Whether or not you partake in an occasional beer with local Pythoneers, we encourage you to go to Python conferences. There are several regular conferences, all worth attending.

The oldest conference, the International Python Conference (IPC), is now part of the O'Reilly Open Source Convention (OSCON) (see *http://conferences.oreillynet.com* for information). IPC has grown over the years from a very small informal gathering to a large, very well attended meeting where Python experts, enthusiasts and novices from around the world come to mingle. For many, it is the only occasion to talk to their Python acquaintances in real life, and it's well worth it.

A new conference, PyCon, has recently been started. Meant to complement the track at OSCON, it is a low-cost, hacker's conference, emphasizing technical discussions and foregoing the more commercial aspects of trade shows such as an exhibit hall and fancy lunches. When not writing this chapter, I (David) am helping to plan the second PyCon event, which promises to have very high-quality presentations.

Both of the two conferences mentioned are based in the U.S. An alternative for some is to head to Europe for some of the Python conferences there: EuroPython (*http://www.europython.org*), and the Python UK Conference (*http://www.python-uk.org*). More conferences may have sprung up to accommodate the crowds. See *http://www.python.org/workshops/* for updates.

Where to Get Help

As easy as Python is to learn, no book or website can give all the answers. If you have a Python-related question, there are a few avenues for free and paid support. Information about all of the mailing lists mentioned below, including how to subscribe, is available at *http://www.python.org/psa/MailingLists.html*.

Python-help

Should you have a Python question that you can't get an answer for through the usual means, you can send an email to *Python-help@python.org*. Your email will be sent to a set of volunteers around the world who will do their best to answer you. Be as detailed as possible in your questions, copy and paste your code and the errors you get into your email (as opposed to often confusing paraphrases), and be patient as you await an answer. You'll find python-help can be quite a useful resource.

Python-tutor

While python-help provides one-on-one help, python-tutor is a mailing list for people who are looking for help in the early stages of learning about Python or even learning about programming by using Python. It's a friendly list where no question is deemed too basic and still is fairly low-volume. See *http://www.python.org/psa/MailingLists.html#tutor* for details.

Python-list

Python-list is the commons of Python development. It's available either as a mailing list or as the Usenet newsgroup *comp.lang.python*. Over the years it's grown to be a *very* popular destination, with thousands of messages a month. Conversations tend to be about Python, although some interesting excursions through the oddest topics do occur. It's a good place to hang out on the net with like minded folk. Python-list defines the public face of the Python community to a large extent.

Special Interest Groups

All of the resources mentioned thus far have been generalist resources. Two kinds of more focused discussion groups also need to be mentioned. The first and most essential one is the discussion around the implementation of the language itself, on a list called python-dev. Additionally, some specialized topics naturally lead to long-term discussions, which can get quite technical but still remain within a well-defined domain. Typical examples of this kind of special interest group are the discussions aimed at defining specialized libraries that should be added to Python, such as those for scientific processing, database interfaces, XML or Unicode support. People interested in working on such areas typically form a special interest group(s) mailing list to coordinate their activities, get access to an area of *http://www.python.org* to publicize their results, and, when they have reached internal agreement, lobby the greater Python community (and Guido in particular) for inclusion of a particular functionality (as the Numeric SIG did for some syntactic changes) or just to report an agreement (as the Database SIG did to announce the definition of the DB-API standard). These days, many satellite discussions occur in other mailing lists that aren't "official" SIGs, although those tend to not feed back to the language core quite as much. Information about SIGs is always available at *http://www.python.org/sigs*.

python-dev

Apart from those few "physical" conversations that happen in the Reston, VA area (where Pythonlabs team members are located), daily discussion about the development of Python itself happens on a mailing list called python-dev. The number of people participating in this list is considerably larger (dozens of active contributors, probably thousands of regular readers), and provides a very good forum for people who already know most of what there is to know about Python today, and want to participate in shaping tomorrow's Python. If you're curious, you can subscribe to the mailing list (*http://mail.python.org/mailman/listinfo/python-dev*), read it through a mail/web interface (e.g., *http://aspn.activestate.com/ASPN/Mail/Browse/Threaded/python-dev/*) or through a mail/news interfaces (see e.g. *http://www.gmane.org*). However, most readers of this book will find the discussions on python-dev to be much too detailed and technical. To get a feel for what's keeping the core Python developers busy while staying awake, you're better off reading the edited summaries that get posted to python-dev and python-list on a periodic basis and that are archived at *http://www.python.org/dev/summary/* (you can also ask to receive them by email). It's important to keep in mind that Python-dev is a *working group*. If you are a Python novice, you're welcome to read, but you probably shouldn't post except in very rare circumstances. You should definitely *not* ask for help on python-dev—as we've seen, there are many other, more appropriate places to go for help. Similarly, requests for new syntax or new features are in large part inappropriate on python-dev.

News Sources

If you're too busy to follow python-list on a regular basis, there are several options to make sure that you learn of all new developments in the Python world.

Major announcements typically get sent both to python-list and to python-announce, which is a moderated list. That's the primary forum to announce new Python packages or modules, new conferences, and other major announcements of broad interest to the community.

Several people report on Python developments, such as Fredrik Lundh, a longstanding web log of Python news at *http://www.pythonware.com/daily/*.

A rotating volunteer also monitors python-list and summarizes it on a weekly basis. Sponsored by *Doctor Dobb's Journal*, archives and information on how to subscribe are available at *http://www.ddj.com/topics/pythonurl/*.

The Process

The topic of how Python is developed is a fascinating one, as Python is one of the better run open source projects, but it is mostly off-topic for this book. If you're interested in learning more (whether you think you can contribute to Python yourself or not), read some of the information at *http://www.python.org/dev*—you'll find everything from descriptions of the Python developer culture to specific technical details on how to contribute.

As a user of Python, however, you can play a role in the (unlikely) event that you find a bug in Python. If you do, you should isolate the code that's causing you headaches or not behaving according to specification to the bare minimum, and post it as a bug on Python's bug tracker. As of this writing, Python is using the bug tracker run by Sourceforge, although there is talk to move to something else. The bug manager is located at *http://sourceforge.net/bugs/?group_id=5470*, and instructions on how to submit a bug report are at *http://www.python.org/doc/current/ext/reporting-bugs.html*.

Services and Products

There are hundreds of thousands or perhaps millions of people using Python, and thousands of companies relying on it. Several commercial vendors, both corporations and individual consultants provide support of various kinds to help people and companies work with Python, from training to development tools to on-call support. Not altogether surprisingly, the first author's main job is to teach Python to individuals and companies worldwide and the second author's company provides developer tools and enterprise-level support for Python. Many other vendors exist—consult your usual channels to find the provider most suited to your needs.

The Legal Framework: The Python Software Foundation

Python is, at its core, a programming language. As a technology, Python needs an owner—a person or entity who can define it to the world, protect it from attack, and nurture its growth. While Guido van Rossum is the recognized father of Python, Guido doesn't want to be the sole person responsible for Python. The "what if Guido gets hit by a bus?" discussions have been dealt with by, over the years, defining a legal entity called the Python Software Foundation (PSF) to act as Python's legal owner. Thus, all of the Python intellectual property is being assigned to the PSF. The PSF has received provisional non-profit status from the US IRS, thus making donations to the organization tax-deductible. The PSF is composed of individual members (invited by the existing membership because of their contribution to Python) and is funded by corporate sponsorships. Information about the PSF is available at *http://www.python.org/psf/*. Both of the authors are members of the PSF and the second author is a director of the PSF. Essentially, what this means is that the PSF is an organization we believe is important to the long-term health of Python.

Software

This book's task was to present the Python language, including brief overviews of some of the most important modules and libraries that come with Python. There are countless other such supporting software packages available, most of them for free, on the Internet. In this section, we give you pointers as to what this landscape of software looks like, what maps are available to help you find what you're looking for, and finally some notable software packages that can make choosing Python such a high-value choice.

One of Python's weaknesses has been the lack of a single, authoritative repository for such third-party software. While there are volunteers working hard to solve that problem, the best we can do at time of writing is to point you to the several alternative methods that can be used to find out what's available and where.

Search the Web

It used to be hard to find things on the Internet. Some of us remember days before the Web, when word of mouth and secret handshakes seemed to be required to find particular pieces of software. These days, search engines like Google do 95% of the hard work. Regardless of the topic, searches on Google are very likely to get you what you want.

Search the Mailing List Archives

Software that's available on the Web has typically been announced in public, or at the very least discussed in public. You can search the various mailing lists mentioned above with specialized search engines, such as Google's Groups interface (although that doesn't cover all of the Python mailing lists, only those mirrored as newsgroups), *http://search.python.org*, or the mailing list archives at *http://www.ASPN.ActiveState.com*.

Look in the Vaults of Parnassus

"The Vaults of Parnassus" is a fairly old (in Internet years) and well-established directory of Python software. It uses a library-style directory of Python software and Python-related tools. The vaults are at: *http://py.vaults.ca/*. Note that the vaults archive only metadata finding something on the vaults is no guarantee that the pages it refers you to are still around, or that the information on the vaults are necessarily up to date.

Check the Python Package Index (PyPI)

A new project which, unlike some of its predecessors, seems likely to succeed is called PyPI (Python Package Index). Hosted at *http://www.python.org/pypi*, the current prototype lets people register their python package either manually, or, preferably, using the package description software distutils, which is part of the standard library. As of this writing there are only a few dozen packages listed, but by the time you read this the catalog is likely to be much larger.

Look in the Python Cookbook

The Python Cookbook is a joint project combining the efforts of ActiveState, O'Reilly and Associates, and the Python community. ActiveState hosts a web site (*aspn.ActiveState.com/Python/Cookbook*), which lets anyone post their favorite recipe of Python code, and solicit feedback from readers of the site. O'Reilly published a book from selected, edited, and expanded recipes called the *Python Cookbook*, coedited by Alex Martelli and David Ascher. The book contains hundreds of well-motivated recipes explained in detail, and has become a favorite even of long-time Python programmers. The online site contains hundreds more recipes, and is constantly being updated. Both are excellent resources for that smallest kind of software package, the snippets and idioms that define the fluent speaker of a language.

Popular Third-Party Software

In this section, we list some of the most popular third-party add-ons to Python. Some are small yet deeply useful modules, others are full fledged applications with massive internal complexity. Each is what we consider a good tool.

URLs change, so don't be dissapointed if the URLs we mention are no longer valid by the time you type them in. Instead, go to Google and type python *name of the package*—you're more than likely to find it.

Interfaces to Windows and the MacOS

While each operating system provides a wide variety of interfaces, Unix and related operating systems like Linux tend to provide that interface through command-line tools and special-purpose files, both of which tend to vary too much across versions to allow for useful programmatic interfaces. Windows and Macintosh use a more API-oriented approach, and as a result make the operating system more naturally accessible from a programming language like Python. There are Python interfaces to pretty much every corner of Windows and the Macintosh APIs.

Windows

Core Python comes with some interfaces to basic Windows interfaces like the os module for basic operating system functions and the _regedit low-level API to the Windows Registry. Serious Windows programming, however, requires access to many more Windows libraries. Most of these are exposed by the win32all package by Mark Hammond. win32all is available either as an add-on to the Python distribution from *http://www.python.org*, or bundled as part of ActivePython from ActiveState (*http://www.ActiveState.com/Python*). win32all also includes a Window-only IDE for Python, Pythonwin.

Not all Windows APIs are exposed by win32all. Should you wish to use one of these, you can use Thomas Heller's ctypes module, which provides a foreign function interface from Python to dynamically loaded shared libraries. ctypes is described below.

Macintosh

The Macintosh port of Python, maintained by Jack Jansen, and available at *http://www.cwi.nl/~jack/macpython.html*, comes in two kinds as of this writing. There is a new version that runs from the Mac OS X command line, as well as a version which runs on Mac OS 9 or OS X, although there are plans to merge the two. The documentation for the Macintosh library, the *Macintosh Library Modules*, is part of the standard library reference. Recent versions of Mac OS X come with Python preinstalled.

Special-Purpose Libraries

There are some domains of computing that lend themselves to well-defined libraries. These typically involve specialized data types (e.g., arrays of numbers, dates) or special-purpose algorithms (e.g., three-dimensional graphics engines). In this section we survey some of the most popular such libraries.

Scientific computing libraries

Python has a significant following in the scientific and engineering fields. Its fairly mathematically reasonable syntax and ease of extensibility make it a good match for scientists who need to combine easy to use syntax with the ability to attach high-power computational engines.

The granddaddy of scientific libraries in Python is called Numeric Python, NumPy, or Numeric for short. Numeric consists of a set of Python and C extension modules that provide very powerful and high performance array operations. With Numeric, one can do "en masse" operations on very large multidimensional arrays of numbers much faster than one can do in pure Python. Numeric is the current standard solution for doing such operations in Python, although many are looking to its proposed replacement, numarray.

Here's an example of typical NumPy code, *numpytest.py*, and one representation of the data in generates:

```
from Numeric import *
coords = arange(-6, 6, .02)              # Create a range of coordinates.
xs = sin(coords)                         # Take the sine of all of the x's.
ys = cos(coords)*exp(-coords*coords/18.0) # Take a complex function of the y's.
zx = xs * ys[:,NewAxis]                   # Multiply the x row with the y column.
```

If you remember your math, you might figure out that xs is an array of the sines of the numbers between –6 and 6, and ys is an array of the cosines of those same numbers scaled by an exponential function centered at 0. zs is simply the outer product of those two arrays of numbers. If you're curious as to what that might look like, you could convert the array zs into an image and obtain the image shown in Figure 29-1.

NumPy lets you manipulate very large arrays of numbers very efficiently. The preceding code runs orders of magnitude faster than comparable code using large lists of numbers and uses a fraction of the memory. Many Python users never have to deal with these kinds of issues, but many scientists and engineers require such capabilities daily.

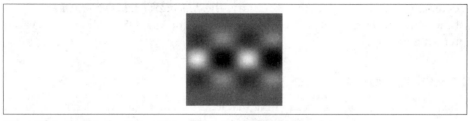

Figure 29-1. Graphical representation of the array zs in numpytest.py

Numarray (*http://stsdas.stsci.edu/numarray/*) is a reimplementation of the basic functionality of Numeric, while aiming to fix some of the problems with the original having to do with type conversions, extensibility, memory efficiency and other factors. It's too early to tell, but our sources indicate that numarray is well positioned to take over Numeric's market share in a nice, progressive, and orchestrated transition.

For those interested in doing more with numbers, the SciPy project is worth looking at. SciPy supplements the core array-crunching modules with a variety of high-level scientific and engineering modules, such as solvers, optimizers, statistical routines, and a very interesting inlining tool that compiles expressions using C++ in a semi-transparent way, called weave. SciPy also includes the most Pythonic scientific graphing software, called Chaco. Information about SciPy can be found at its web site, *http://www.scipy.org*.

Finally, there are other scientific libraries for Python not listed above—some for dealing with Fortran libraries, some for doing specialized processing in the fields of chemistry, genetics, etc. Use the resources mentioned to look for software in your particular field.

Relational database interfaces

Relational databases are a very common mode of storing and manipulating data, although as we've seen in this book, there are other, simpler ways of storing at least small amounts of data (such as using `pickle`, or the related `marshal` and `shelve` modules—see their documentation for details). All popular scripting languages have interfaces to common database engines, and Python is no exception. There is even a standard interface that allows Python programmers to talk to a variety of databases in a database-independent way, called the DB-API. Details on the DB-API, including references to current modules, are available at *http://www.python.org/topics/database/* . You will find that there are interfaces to Oracle, Postgres, MySQL, SAP DB, Informix, and many others.

There are other, less standard databases that are worth knowing about in case you don't have a particular reason to use a SQL server. The two most commonly used ones are Gadfly and MetaKit. Gadfly (*http://gadfly.sourceforge.net/gadfly.html*), is a SQL server written entirely in Python (with some C extensions), which provides a very simple SQL solution for people who have relatively small databases (Gadfly stores its data in memory), and don't require multiuser capabilities, but still want transactional support. MetaKit (*http://www.equi4.com/metakit/python.html*) is a C++ database engine with very good Python bindings. MetaKit has a more record-oriented view of the world, and is remarkably fast at a remarkable set of operations. A third and more recent entry half-way between Gadfly and full-fledged SQL databases is PySQLite, an interface to the popular embedded SQL engine SQLite.

A final player worth mentioning here is the set of tools from eGenix.com. These include mxODBC (an interface to the ODBC database layer), mxDateTime (a high-power date/time library), and other add-ons. These are all available at *http://www.egenix.com*).

Graphics libraries

There are several types of packages that can help produce graphical output of various kinds, from image processing tools to game frameworks to visualization toolkits.

Python Imaging Library (PIL). The Python Imaging Library is an extensive framework written by Fredrik Lundh for creating, manipulating, converting, and saving bit-mapped images in a variety of formats such as GIF, JPEG, and PNG. It has interfaces to Tk and Pythonwin, so that one can use either Tk widgets or Pythonwin code to display PIL-generated images. Alternatively, the images can be saved to disk in a variety of formats. The home for PIL is at *http://www. pythonware.com*.

PyGame and PyOpenGL. Two of the most popular selections for graphics work are PyGame for two-dimensional and gaming software, and PyOpenGL for 3-D graphics, especially in the area of scientific visualization. Pygame (*http://pygame.org*) is a set of Python modules written on top of the free, cross-platform SDL library. It has been used for a variety of game and nongame software, and provides excellent interfaces to the screen, the mouse, the keyboard and sound output. People have written some remarkable games with PyGame, as well as used it for nongaming applications that have heavy emphasis on game-like animations, controls etc. A simple example of PyGame programming is the following snippet, which plays the first five seconds of the first track of the first CD player it finds, and then ejects it.

```
import pygame
pygame.cdrom.init( )
cd_object = pygame.cdrom.CD(pygame.cdrom.get_count( )-1)
cd_object.init( )
if cd_object.get_track_audio(i):
    audio_track_found = 1
    cd_object.play(i)
    pygame.time.delay(5000)
cd_object.eject( )
cd_object.quit( )
```

PyOpenGL is a fairly different tool—it is a wrapper around OpenGL, the standard for cross-platform high-performance 2-D and 3-D graphics. PyOpenGL, available from *http://pyopengl.sourceforge.net*, provides Python-level interfaces to a very large number of OpenGL APIs as well as related libraries such as GLU, GLUT, and more. PyOpenGL, especially when combined with Numeric Python arrays and used with a graphics card that provides hardware acceleration of OpenGL, can produce stunningly fast graphics. Anyone looking to do scientific or engineering visualization should explore this option.

Interfaces to GUI Toolkits

Working with a GUI toolkit is a requirement for many people who write end-user-software. The decision of which GUI toolkit to use is typically quite a complex one, involving such factors as portability, performance, look and feel, licensing and cost, threading models, etc. Suffice it to say that Python has interfaces to all of the popular GUI toolkits on the major platforms.

There are several popular cross-platform toolkits with Python interfaces:

- Tk has an interface that ships with standard Python called Tkinter. While Tk's widget set isn't as rich as others, there are ways to extend it using megawidget tools such as Pmw (*http://pmw.sf.net*).

- wxPython, the interface to the wxWindows GUI toolkit, has become very popular of late (see *http://www.wxPython.org* for details).

- PyQt on top of Qt (see *http://www.riverbankcomputing.co.uk/pyqt/* for details; note the somewhat restrictive licensing terms and purchasing options).

Another cross-platform solution is:

- FXPy (*http://fxpy.sourceforge.net/*), the bindings to the FOX GUI library

For the most native Windows look and feel, you can use either low-level Win32 calls through the win32ui and win32gui modules, or the higher-level Microsoft Foundation Classes (MFC). Both interfaces are available with win32all, either standalone or bundled with ActivePython.

Jython users can use the native Java toolkits (AWT and Swing).

Unix/Linux users can also use:

- Python-GTK (*http://www.daa.com.au/~james/pygtk/*), bindings to GTK + and GNOME.

- PyKDE, bindings for the KDE desktop environment (*http://www.riverbankcomputing.co.uk/pykde/index.php*).

Several other toolkit interfaces are available, but have been omitted here because they are not as popular or battle-tested.

Interfaces to C/C++/Fortran

Many of the libraries mentioned are wrappers around third-party libraries written in a compiled language like C, C++ or Fortran. There are several options available to those wishing to expose such libraries to Python.

SWIG and f2py

The oldest, but still very useful package is SWIG (Simple Wrapper Interface Generator), available from *http://www.swig.org*. SWIG, unlike all of the other packages mentioned in this section, works with other languages in addition to Python. SWIG takes (a sometimes tweaked version of) C or C++ header files and automatically produces the interfacing code that exposes the C/C++ APIs to Python. It is especially well-suited to large code bases with clean APIs, such as OpenGL, the Windows API, and other well-defined codebases. SWIG makes writing such interfaces quite simple even for nonexperts, and takes care of many of the tedious details such as reference counting, error checking and the like.

People interested in wrapping Fortran 77/90/95 should investigate f2py, available from *http://cens.ioc.ee/projects/f2py2e/*.

CXX and Boost::Python

Sometimes one wants to write extensions in C or C++. C extension writers tend to use the API that comes with Python (documented in Extending and Embedding the Python Interpreter, which is part of the standard documentation set, available at *http://www.python.org/doc/current/ext/ext.html*). C++ extension writers tend to use one of two popular tools, CXX and Boost::Python. CXX was designed to write extensions in C++ instead of C. Standard CXX code looks like a hybrid of C++ and Python—one manipulates Python-style data structures using C++ syntax. CXX takes care of reference counting and of mapping C++ exceptions to Python and vice-versa. Boost::Python is a more recent library, part of the well-respected Boost C++ library, and probably more actively maintained than CXX as of this writing. Boost::Python is a framework for interfacing Python and C++, designed to let you to quickly and seamlessly expose C++ classes functions and objects to Python, and vice-versa, using no special tools. Because it aims to wrap C++ interfaces unintrusively, you should not have to change the C++ code at all in order to wrap it. To compare the two, CXX is probably the right choice when trying to write an extension from scratch whose only purpose is to be a Python extension, while Boost::Python is more appropriate for wrapping C++ code and making a Python interface to that interface. Your mileage may vary, and you are encouraged to study both before embarking on a significant project.

Pyrex, Weave, and Psyco

SWIG and Boost::Python are designed mostly to wrap existing codes. CXX, while it can be used to interface to C++ libraries, is more of a straight port of the C extension mechanism to C++. Given that many C extensions are written strictly to optimize away some bottlenecks, an alternative approach is to use C or C++ to write special-purpose code strictly for performance reasons. Three other systems target this case: Pyrex, Weave and Psyco.

Pyrex is a language specially designed to write extensions for Python. Pyrex can be summarized as Python with C data types. It's best illustrated with a simple example:

```
def primes(int kmax):
    cdef int n, k, i
    cdef int p[1000]
    result = [ ]
    if kmax > 1000:
        kmax = 1000
    k = 0
    n = 2
    while k < kmax:
        i = 0
        while i < k and n % p[i] <> 0:
            i = i + 1
        if i == k:
            p[k] = n
            k = k + 1
            result.append(n)
        n = n + 1
    return result
```

When Pyrex runs this code, it notices the cdef statements that tell it that n, k and i are C integers, and that p is an array of 1,000 C integers. The rest of the function is straight Python code, but thanks to those declarations, Pyrex can compile the code to C, making the key loop run *much* faster than if this same program had run in Python.

Weave takes a different approach to solve the same fundamental problem—how to insert C/C++ code inside of otherwise perfectly fine, logical Python code. Unlike Pyrex, Weave uses no new syntax, but instead requires you to insert C or C++ code in a Python string, and to call out to a specialized module to do compilation and loading behind the scenes. So the straightforward but slow binary search routine written in Python as:

```
def binary_search(seq, t):
    min = 0; max = len(seq) - 1
    while 1:
        if max < min:
            return -1
        m = (min + max) / 2
        if seq[m] < t:
            min = m + 1
```

```
        elif seq[m] > t:
            max = m  - 1
        else:
            return m
```

can be written in Weave as:

```
def c_int_binary_search(seq,t):
    # Do a little type checking in Python.
    assert(type(t) == type(1))
    assert(type(seq) == type([ ]))

    # Now the C code
    code = """
            # Line 29 "binary_search.py"
            int val, m, min = 0;
            int max = seq.length( ) - 1;
            PyObject *return_val;
            for(;;) {
                if (max < min) {
                    return_val =  Py::new_reference_to(Py::Int(-1));
                    break;
                }
                m =  (min + max) /2;
                val = py_to_int(PyList_GetItem(seq.ptr( ),m),"val");
                if (val  < t)
                    min = m  + 1;
                else if (val >  t)
                    max = m - 1;
                else {
                    return_val = Py::new_reference_to(Py::Int(m));
                    break;
                }
            }
            """
    return inline(code,['seq','t'])
```

Weave is part of SciPy, available from *http://www.scipy.org/site_content/weave*.

Psyco is the most ambitious of any of the projects mentioned here, and, as a result the least practically useful at this stage. Psyco is a specializing compiler for Python. The details are much beyond the level of this book, and Psyco isn't of much use today, but it offers great promise for the future, including the possibility of making Python code run faster than C code, which is considered the benchmark for interpreted languages. The curious can read up on the current Psyco project at *http://psyco.sourceforge.net/*, as well as a related project, pypy, which aims to write a new implementation of Python in Python, and to build Psyco-style technology to compile it (see *http://codespeak.net/pypy/*).

ctypes

The latest entry in this set of tools is ctypes. ctypes uses a completely different approach to interfacing—unlike SWIG, Boost::Python or the standard C extension module system, ctypes is designed to call directly from Python into shared libraries. Using platform-specific tricks (ctypes currently runs only on Windows, Linux and OS/X, although more platforms may be added), ctypes lets you load arbitrary shared libraries and call arbitrary functions, as long as you know the signature of these functions:

```
>>> from ctypes import cdll, c_double
>>> printf = cdll.msvcrt.printf
>>> printf("An int %d, a double %f\n", 1234, c_double(3.14))
An int 1234, a double 3.140000
```

There is a lot more to ctypes that makes this approach realistic for a wide variety of applications. See *http://starship.python.net/crew/theller/ctypes.html* for details.

Little Gems

In this section, we'll list some modules that, while not necessarily deeply complex or major efforts, provide nice solutions to common problems.

The platform module (part of the standard library in Python 2.3 but available for earlier python version at *http://www.egenix.com/files/python/platform.py*) is a module that lets you find out many more subtle variations of what your current platform, compared to sys.platform. Instead of just saying win32, it lets you know that you're running on e.g. "Windows-2000-5.0.2195-SP3". Sometimes this sort of information is crucial, and it's hard to identify without code like that in *platform.py*.

turtle.py, which is part of the standard distribution but unknown to many, provides a simple LOGO-like system for interactive drawing and beginning programmers. Built on Tkinter, it provides a nice first step for teaching programming.

Trent Mick's go (at *http://starship.python.net/crew/tmick/*) is a simple command line tool that makes it trivial to build bookmarks of often-used directories. Instead of having to remember long path names, you can teach go which directories you use often and then use two-word commands to go there (go home, go python23, etc.).

Packaging Tools

Python developers who wish to share their Python code with other Python developers should learn how to use the distutils package, which lets people build distributions of their programs that are easy for other developers to install. distutils is documented as part of the standard Python library (*http://www.python.org/doc/current/dist/dist.html*).

Python developers who are building standalone applications for use by non-Python developers have a variety of approaches available to them. To make it easy for end users, it is generally a good idea to ship a single file that installs everything the users need—this may include all or a part of the Python distribution. While you can do it the hard way, by shipping the hundreds of files that make up this distribution, it is much easier to use a tool that packages the program and the part of the standard distribution that the program needs.

The Python distribution includes such a program, called freeze, which, while it should work, has far fewer features than the alternatives.

Installer

The most popular packaging tool is probably Gordon McMillan's *Installer* tool. Installer inspects your source code to find out all of the modules that it imports, as well as the modules that they import and so on, until it has built a list of all of the files it thinks your program needs. Those files, including the shared libraries that contain the Python interpreter and extension modules you use, are then packaged in an executable, which you can ship to your users. When the executable is run, it unpacks its contents in a temporary directory and runs the code from there. Installer works on Windows and Linux.

py2exe

Windows users have an alternative to Installer that has a more standard approach—it leverages the existing distutils mechanisms for defining the contents of a package, extends it with a few special purpose options, but generally performs the same task as Installer. py2exe has specialized support for packaging Windows NT Services.

Web Application Frameworks

Anyone who has used the Internet recently knows that it's very possible to develop full-featured applications that happen to use web browsers as their GUI. In the last few years, a plethora of web application development frameworks for Python have been developed. They span a huge gamut, from simple hacks to elaborate systems. Many allow embedding of Python code in HTML, others generate HTML from Python code. Many provide support for persistence, cookie management, URL rewriting, and more. A comparative review of all of these is far beyond the scope of this book. We'll simply mention some of the more commonly used frameworks.

Zope

Zope is the grand-daddy of Python web application frameworks. While Zope is open source, it is very much the product of a company called Zope Corp., in collaboration with a vast user community. Zope is a very powerful tool for building content management systems, including such advanced features as replication, transactional support, sophisticated security models and workflow. Zope often stumps people who expect it to be a simple system. While efforts are under way to redesign part of Zope to make learning Zope easier, those who find Zope most useful are typically those with very large or complex websites to build. Information about the Zope software is available at *http://www.zope.org*, and information about Zope Corp. is at *http://www.zope.com*.

Twisted

If Zope is the web application server for sites with sophisticated workflow, Twisted is more of a swiss army knife for networked application development. Not strictly focused on the web and the HTTP/HTML standards that anchor the web, Twisted is a framework for building networked applications. Using Twisted, it is relatively easy to build high-performance clients and servers for any protocol, from instant messaging to IRC to HTTP to NNTP. The Twisted framework, like all frameworks, requires a certain learning curve. Those who do learn it do tend to be passionate about it, and it seems to perform admirably. Twisted's home is *http://www.twistedmatrix.com*.

Quixote

Quixote is a dynamic web application framework built by Python programmers for Python programmers. Unlike many of the alternatives such as Zope, Quixote deliberately does not try to cater to web designers. To use Quixote means to program in Python, even for HTML generation. To those of us who are more comfortable with Python modules and classes than with HTTP redirects, however, that's a great benefit. Quixote has wonderfully clear documentation (at least if you are comfortable with Python) at *http://www.mems-exchange.org/software/quixote/*.

Webware, Spyce, and More

The three systems, Zope, Twisted, and Quixote, while probably among the most popular, do not cover the extent of Python/web frameworks. If embarking on a new project, you owe it to yourself to compare the various frameworks and figure out which one is best for you. Programming on the Web is a complex task with lots of variables—it's very possible that in your particular case, you'd want to use something more like a PHP-style system such as Spyce (*http://spyce.sourceforge.net*), or more of a component-oriented system like WebWare for Python (*http://webware. sourceforge.net/*).

Tools for Python Developers

Given the large number of Python developers and the large number of Python programs that need editing and debugging, there is a wide variety of editing and development tools available for Python programmers. They range from customization files for free general-purpose editors like Emacs and Vim to specialized integrated development environments. They can be free, such as Idle (which comes with Python) and Pythonwin (part of win32all and ActivePython), or commercial products like Archaeopteryx's Wing IDE and ActiveState's Komodo and Visual Python .NET. Be sure to research what's available at the time you need it, as this is an area where new tools and new revisions of existing tools show up fairly often.

Appendixes

Part IX includes two appendixes. Appendix A presents a list of Python installation and configuration hints. Appendix B provides answers to all the exercises that appear at the end of each part of the book. Some exercise solutions provide information that is not included in the rest of the book, so you should also consider these as supplemental reading.

Installation and Configuration

This appendix provides additional installation and configuration details, as a resource for people new to such topics.

Installing the Python Interpreter

Because you need the Python interpreter to run Python scripts, your first step to using Python is usually installing Python. Unless a Python is already available on your machine, you'll need to fetch, install, and possibly configure a Python on your computer. You only need to do this once per machine, and perhaps not at all, if you will be running a frozen binary.

Where to Get Python

First off, before doing anything, make sure you don't already have a recent Python on your machine. For instance, if you are working on Linux, or some Unix systems, Python is probably already installed. Type **python** at a shell prompt and see what happens; alternatively, try searching the usual places (*/usr/bin*, */usr/local/bin*, etc.). On Windows, check if there is a Python entry in the programs menu you find in your Start button, at the bottom left of the screen. Make sure the Python you find is version 2.2 or later; you'll need that to run some of the examples in this edition.

If there is no Python to be found, you will need to install one yourself. You can always fetch the latest and greatest standard Python release from *http://www.python. org*, Python's official web site; look for the Downloads link on that page, and grab a release for the platform you will be working on. There, you'll find prebuilt Python executables (unpack and run); self-installer executables for Windows (click to install); RPMs for Linux (unpack with rpm); the full source-code distribution (compile on your machine to generate an interpreter); and more. For some platforms such as PalmOS and PocketPC, Python's web site links to an offsite page where these versions are maintained.

You can also find Python on CD-ROMs supplied with Linux distributions, included with some products and computer systems, sold by commercial outlets such as *Dr. Dobb's Journal*, and enclosed with other Python books. These tend to lag behind the current release somewhat, but usually not seriously so.

In addition, a company called ActiveState also distributes Python, as part of its *ActivePython* package. This package combines standard CPython with extensions for Windows development, an IDE called PythonWin (described in Chapter 3), and other commonly used extensions. See ActiveState's web site, *www.activestate.com*, for more details on the ActivePython package.

Finally, if you are interested in alternative Python implementations, try *www.jython.org* for Jython, and AciveState's web site for Python.NET; installation of these systems is beyond the scope of this book.

Installation Steps

Once you have your Python, it must be installed. Installation steps are very platform-specific, but here are a few pointers for major Python platforms:

Windows

On Windows, Python comes as a self-installer executable program file—simply double-click on its file icon, and answer Yes or Next to every prompt, to perform a default install. The default install includes Python's documentation set, and support for Tkinter GUIs, shelve databases, the IDLE development GUI, and other things we'll describe later. After the install, Python shows up in the programs menu of your Start button.

Figure A-1 shows where Python appears in the Start button on a Windows XP machine after installation. Python's menu has five entries that give quick access to common tasks: starting the IDLE user interface; reading module documentation; starting an interactive session; reading Python's standard manuals in a web broswer; and uninstalling. Most of these actions involve concepts we explore in detail elsdewhere in this text.

When installed on Windows, Python also automatically registers itself to be the program that opens Python files when their icons are clicked—a program launch technique described in Chapter 3. It is also possible to build Python from its source-code on Windows, but this is not common.

Linux

On Linux, Python is available as one or more RPM files, which you unpack in the usual way. Consult your RPM man page for more details. Depending on which RPMs you download, there may be one for Python itself, and another that adds support for Tkinter GUIs and the IDLE environment. Since Linux is a Unix-like system, the next paragraph applies as well.

Unix

On Unix systems, Python is usually compiled from its full C source-code distribution. This usually only requires unpacking the file, and running simple config and make commands; Python configures its own build procedure automatically, according to the system it is being compiled on. However, be sure to see the package's *README* file for more details on this process. Because Python is Open Source, its source code may be used and distributed free of charge.

On other platforms, these details can differ widely; installing the "Pippy" port of Python for the PalmOS, for example, requires a hot synch operation with your PDA, and Python for the Sharp Zaurus Linux-based PDA comes as one or more *.ipk* files, which you simply run to install. Because additional install procedures for both executable and source forms are well documented, though, we'll skip further details here.

Configuration Steps

After you've installed Python, you can also configure system settings that impact the way Python runs your code. When you are just getting started with the language, you can probably skip this section completely; there is usually no need to make any system settings at all for basic programs.

Generally speaking, though, parts of the Python interpreter's behaviour can be configured both with *environment variable* settings, and *command-line options*. In this section, we take a brief look at Python environment variables. Python command-line options—words listed when you launch a Python program from a system prompt—are used more rarely, and have very specialized roles; see other documentation sources for Python's command-line option details.

Python environment variables

Environment variables—known to some as shell variables, or DOS variables—live outside Python, and thus can be used to customize the interpreter's behavior each time it is run on a given computer. Python recognizes a handful of environment variable settings, but only a few are used often enough to warrant explanation here. Table A-1 summarizes the main Python-related environment variable settings.

Table A-1. Important environment variables

Variable	Role
PATH (or path)	System shell search path (for finding "python")
PYTHONPATH	Python module search path (for imports)
PYTHONSTARTUP	Path to Python interactive startup file
TCL_LIBRARY, TK_LIBRARY	GUI extension variables (Tkinter)

These variables are straightforward to use, but here are a few pointers:

- The PATH setting lists a set of directories that the operating system searches for executable programs. It should normally include the directory where your Python interpreter lives (the python program on Unix, or the *python.exe* file on Windows). You don't need to set this variable at all, if you are willing to either work in the directory where Python resides, or type the full path to Python in command-lines. On Windows, for instance, the PATH is irrelevant if you run cd C:\Python22 before running any code (to change to the directory where Python lives), or always type **C:\Python22\python** instead of just python (to give a full path). Also note thet PATH settings are mostly for launching programs from command lines; they are usually irrelevent for running with icon clicks and IDEs.

- The PYTHONPATH setting serves a role similar to PATH: the Python interpreter consults the PYTHONPATH variable to locate module files when you import them in a program. (We talked about the module search path in Chapter 15.) If used, this variable is set to a platform-dependent list of directory names, separated by colons on Unix, and semicolons on Windows. This list normally includes just your own source-code directories. You don't need to set this variable either, unless you will be performing cross-directory imports—because Python always searches the home directory of the program's top-level file automatically, this setting is only required if a module needs to import another module that lives in a different directory. As mentioned in Chapter 15, *.pth* files are a recent alternative to PYTHONPATH.

- If PYTHONSTARTUP is set to the pathname of a file of Python code, Python executes the file's code automatically whenever you start the interactive interpreter, as though you had typed it at the interactive command line. This is a rarely used, but handy way to make sure you always load utilities whenever working interactively; it saves an import.

- If you wish to use the Tkinter GUI toolkit, you might have to set the two GUI variables in Table A-1 to the name of the source library directories of the Tcl and Tk systems (much like PYTHONPATH). However, these settings are not required on Windows systems (where Tkinter support is installed alongside Python), and are usually not required elsewhere if Tcl and Tk reside in standard directories.

Note that because these environment settings (as well as *.pth* files) are external to Python itself, the *time* at which you set these is usually irrelevant. They may be set before or after Python is installed—just as long as they are set the way you require before Python is actually *run*.

How to Set Configuration Options

The way to set these variables, and what to set them to, depends on the type of computer you will work on. And again, remember that you don't necessarily have to set these at all right away; especially when working under IDLE (described in Chapter 3), configuration is not required up-front.

But suppose, for illustration, that you have generally useful module files in directories called *utilities* and *package1* somewhere on your machine, and you want to be able to import these modules from files located in any other directory. To load a file called *spam.py* from the *utilities* directory, you want to be able to say:

```
import spam
```

from another file located anywhere on your computer. To make this work, you'll have to configure your module search path one way or another to imclude the directory contaiing spam.py. Here are a few tips on this process.

UNIX/Linux shell variables

On Unix systems the way to set envoronment variables depends on the shell you use. Under the csh shell, you might add a line like the following in your *.cshrc* or *.login* file, to set the Python module search path:

```
setenv PYTHONPATH /usr/home/pycode/utilities:/usr/lib/pycode/package1
```

This tells Python to look for imported modules in two user-defined directories. But if you're using the ksh shell, the setting might instead appear in your *.kshrc* file, and look like this:

```
export PYTHONPATH="/usr/home/pycode/utilities:/usr/lib/pycode/package1"
```

Other shells may use different, but analogous syntax.

DOS variables (Windows)

If you are using MS-DOS or some older flavors of MS-Windows, you may need to add an environment variable configuration command to your *C:\autoexec.bat* file, and reboot your machine for the changes to take effect. The configuration command on such machines would have a syntax unique to DOS:

```
set PYTHONPATH=c:\pycode\utilities;d:\pycode\package1
```

You can type such a command in a DOS console window too, but the setting will then be active only for that one console window. Changing your *.bat* file makes the change permanent, and global to all programs.

Other Windows options

On more recent versions of Windows, you may instead set PYTHONPATH and others by navigating to the system *environment variable GUI*, without having to edit files or reboot. On XP, select Control Panel, choose the System icon, pick the Advanced tab, and click the Environment Variables button to edit or add new variables (PYTHONPATH is usually a user variable). You do not need to reboot your machine, but be sure to restart Python if open, so that it picks up your changes (it configures its path at start-up time only).

If you are an experienced Windows user, you may also be able to configure the module search path by using the Windows Registry Editor. Type **regedit** in the Run... option of your Start button to see if the typical registry tool is on your machine, and navigate to Python's entries. This is a delicate and error-prone procedure—unless you're familiar with the registry, we suggest other options.

Path files

Finally, if you choose to extend the module search path with a *.pth* file instead of the PYTHONPATH variable, you might instead code a text file that looks like the following on Windows (file *C:\Python22\mypath.pth*). Its contents will differ per platform, and its container directory may differ per both platform and Python release. Python locates this file automatically when it starts up:

```
c:\pycode\utilities
d:\pycode\package1
```

Directory names in path files may be absolute, or relative to the directory containing the path file; multiple *.pth* files can be used (all their directories are added); and *.pth* files may appear in various automatically-checked directories that are platform and version-specific. For example, Release 2.2 typically looks for path files in *C:\Python22* and *C:\Python22\Lib\site-packages* on Windows, and in */usr/local/lib/python2.2/site-packages* and */usr/local/lib/site-python* on Unix and Linux.

Because these settings are often optional, though, and because this isn't a book on operating system shells, we're going to defer to other sources for more details. Consult your system shell's manpages or other documentation for details. And if you have trouble figuring out what your settings must be, ask your system administrator or other local expert for help.

Solutions to Exercises

Part I, Getting Started

1. *Interaction*. Assuming Python is configured properly, interaction should look something like the following. You can run this any way you like: in IDLE, from a shell prompt, and so on:

```
% python
...copyright information lines...
>>> "Hello World!"
'Hello World!'
>>>                     # Ctrl-D or Ctrl-Z to exit, or window close
```

2. *Programs*. Your code (i.e., module) file *module1.py* and shell interactions should look like:

```
print 'Hello module world!'
```

```
% python module1.py
Hello module world!
```

Again, feel free to run this other ways—by clicking its icon, by IDLE's Edit/Run-Script menu option, and so on.

3. *Modules*. The following interaction listing illustrates running a module file by importing it.

```
% python
>>> import module1
Hello module world!
>>>
```

Remember that you need to reload the module to run again without stopping and restarting the interpreter. The questions about moving the file to a different directory and importing it again is a trick question: if Python generates a *module1.pyc* file in the original directory, it uses that when you import the module, even if the source code file (*.py*) has been moved to a directory not on Python's search path. The *.pyc* file is written automatically if Python has access to the source file's directory and contains the compiled byte-code version of a module. See Part V for more on modules.

4. *Scripts.* Assuming your platform supports the #! trick, your solution will look like the following (although your #! line may need to list another path on your machine):

```
#!/usr/local/bin/python          (or #!/usr/bin/env python)
print 'Hello module world!'

% chmod +x module1.py

% module1.py
Hello module world!
```

5. *Errors.* The interaction below demonstrates the sort of error messages you get when you complete this exercise. Really, you're triggering Python exceptions; the default exception handling behavior terminates the running Python program and prints an error message and stack trace on the screen. The stack trace shows where you were in a program when the exception occurred. In Part VII, you will learn that you can catch exceptions using try statements and process them arbitrarily; you'll also see that Python includes a full-blown source code debugger for special error detection requirements. For now, notice that Python gives meaningful messages when programming errors occur (instead of crashing silently):

```
% python
>>> 1 / 0
Traceback (innermost last):
  File "<stdin>", line 1, in ?
ZeroDivisionError: integer division or modulo
>>>
>>> x
Traceback (innermost last):
  File "<stdin>", line 1, in ?
NameError: x
```

6. *Breaks.* When you type this code:

```
L = [1, 2]
L.append(L)
```

you create a cyclic data structure in Python. In Python releases before Version 1.5.1, the Python printer wasn't smart enough to detect cycles in objects, and it would print an unending stream of [1, 2, [1, 2, [1, 2, [1, 2,—and so on, until you hit the break key combination on your machine (which, technically, raises a keyboard-interrupt exception that prints a default message). Beginning with Python Version 1.5.1, the printer is clever enough to detect cycles and prints [[...]] instead.

The reason for the cycle is subtle and requires information you will gain in Part II. But in short, assignment in Python always generates references to objects (which you can think of as implicitly followed pointers). When you run the first assignment above, the name L becomes a named reference to a two-item list

---

object. Python lists are really arrays of object references, with an append method that changes the array in place by tacking on another object reference. Here, the append call adds a reference to the front of L at the end of L, which leads to the cycle illustrated in Figure B-1. Believe it or not, cyclic data structures can sometimes be useful (but not when printed!).

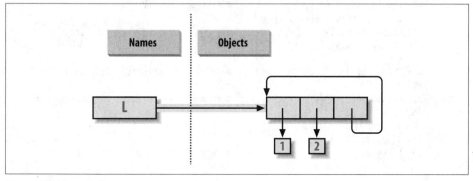

Figure B-1. A cyclic list

Part II, Types and Operations

1. *The basics.* Here are the sort of results you should get, along with a few comments about their meaning. Note that ; is used in a few of these to squeeze more than one statement on a single line; the ; is a statement separator.

```
Numbers

>>> 2 ** 16              # 2 raised to the power 16
65536
>>> 2 / 5, 2 / 5.0       # Integer / truncates, float / doesn't
(0, 0.40000000000000002)

Strings

>>> "spam" + "eggs"      # Concatenation
'spameggs'
>>> S = "ham"
>>> "eggs " + S
'eggs ham'
>>> S * 5                # Repetition
'hamhamhamhamham'
>>> S[:0]                # An empty slice at the front--[0:0]
''
>>> "green %s and %s" % ("eggs", S)  # Formatting
'green eggs and ham'

Tuples
```

```
>>> ('x',)[0]                        # Indexing a single-item tuple
'x'
>>> ('x', 'y')[1]                    # Indexing a 2-item tuple
'y'
```

Lists

```
>>> L = [1,2,3] + [4,5,6]            # List operations
>>> L, L[:], L[:0], L[-2], L[-2:]
([1, 2, 3, 4, 5, 6], [1, 2, 3, 4, 5, 6], [], 5, [5, 6])
>>> ([1,2,3]+[4,5,6])[2:4]
[3, 4]
>>> [L[2], L[3]]                     # Fetch from offsets; store in a list
[3, 4]
>>> L.reverse( ); L                  # Method: reverse list in-place
[6, 5, 4, 3, 2, 1]
>>> L.sort( ); L                     # Method: sort list in-place
[1, 2, 3, 4, 5, 6]
>>> L.index(4)                       # Method: offset of first 4 (search)
3
```

Dictionaries

```
>>> {'a':1, 'b':2}['b']             # Index a dictionary by key.
2
>>> D = {'x':1, 'y':2, 'z':3}
>>> D['w'] = 0                       # Create a new entry.
>>> D['x'] + D['w']
1
>>> D[(1,2,3)] = 4                   # A tuple used as a key (immutable)
>>> D
{'w': 0, 'z': 3, 'y': 2, (1, 2, 3): 4, 'x': 1}
>>> D.keys( ), D.values( ), D.has_key((1,2,3))          # Methods
(['w', 'z', 'y', (1, 2, 3), 'x'], [0, 3, 2, 4, 1], 1)
```

Empties

```
>>> [[]], ["",[],(),{},None]         # Lots of nothings: empty objects
([[]], ['', [], (), {}, None])
```

2. *Indexing and slicing.* Indexing out-of-bounds (e.g., L[4]) raises an error; Python always checks to make sure that all offsets are within the bounds of a sequence.

On the other hand, slicing out of bounds (e.g., L[-1000:100]) works, because Python scales out-of-bounds slices so that they always fit (they're set to zero and the sequence length, if required).

Extracting a sequence in reverse—with the lower bound greater than the higher bound (e.g., L[3:1])—doesn't really work. You get back an empty slice ([ ]), because Python scales the slice limits to make sure that the lower bound is always less than or equal to the upper bound (e.g., L[3:1] is scaled to L[3:3], the empty insertion point at offset 3). Python slices are always extracted from left to right, even if you use negative indexes (they are first converted to positive indexes by adding the length). Note that Python 2.3 three-limit slices modify this behavior somewhat: L[3:1:-1] does extract from right to left.

```
>>> L = [1, 2, 3, 4]
>>> L[4]
Traceback (innermost last):
  File "<stdin>", line 1, in ?
IndexError: list index out of range
>>> L[-1000:100]
[1, 2, 3, 4]
>>> L[3:1]
[]
>>> L
[1, 2, 3, 4]
>>> L[3:1] = ['?']
>>> L
[1, 2, 3, '?', 4]
```

3. *Indexing, slicing, and del.* Your interaction with the interpreter should look something like the following code. Note that assigning an empty list to an offset stores an empty list object there, but assigning an empty list to a slice deletes the slice. Slice assignment expects another sequence, or you'll get a type error; it inserts items *inside* the sequence assigned, not the sequence itself:

```
>>> L = [1,2,3,4]
>>> L[2] = [ ]
>>> L
[1, 2, [ ], 4]
>>> L[2:3] = [ ]
>>> L
[1, 2, 4]
>>> del L[0]
>>> L
[2, 4]
>>> del L[1:]
>>> L
[2]
>>> L[1:2] = 1
Traceback (innermost last):
  File "<stdin>", line 1, in ?
TypeError: illegal argument type for built-in operation
```

4. *Tuple assignment.* The values of X and Y are swapped. When tuples appear on the left and right of an assignment symbol (=), Python assigns objects on the right to targets on the left, according to their positions. This is probably easiest to understand by noting that targets on the left aren't a real tuple, even though they look like one; they are simply a set of independent assignment targets. The items on the right are a tuple, which get unpacked during the assignment (the tuple provides the temporary assignment needed to achieve the swap effect).

```
>>> X = 'spam'
>>> Y = 'eggs'
>>> X, Y = Y, X
>>> X
```

```
'eggs'
>>> Y
'spam'
```

5. *Dictionary keys*. Any immutable object can be used as a dictionary key—integers, tuples, strings, and so on. This really is a dictionary, even though some of its keys look like integer offsets. Mixed type keys work fine too.

```
>>> D = {}
>>> D[1] = 'a'
>>> D[2] = 'b'
>>> D[(1, 2, 3)] = 'c'
>>> D
{1: 'a', 2: 'b', (1, 2, 3): 'c'}
```

6. *Dictionary indexing*. Indexing a nonexistent key (D['d']) raises an error; assigning to a nonexistent key (D['d']='spam') creates a new dictionary entry. On the other hand, out-of-bounds indexing for lists raises an error too, but so do out-of-bounds assignments. Variable names work like dictionary keys; they must have already been assigned when referenced, but are created when first assigned. In fact, variable names can be processed as dictionary keys if you wish (they're made visible in module namespace or stack-frame dictionaries).

```
>>> D = {'a':1, 'b':2, 'c':3}
>>> D['a']
1
>>> D['d']
Traceback (innermost last):
  File "<stdin>", line 1, in ?
KeyError: d
>>> D['d'] = 4
>>> D
{'b': 2, 'd': 4, 'a': 1, 'c': 3}
>>>
>>> L = [0,1]
>>> L[2]
Traceback (innermost last):
  File "<stdin>", line 1, in ?
IndexError: list index out of range
>>> L[2] = 3
Traceback (innermost last):
  File "<stdin>", line 1, in ?
IndexError: list assignment index out of range
```

7. *Generic operations*. Question answers:

- The + operator doesn't work on different/mixed types (e.g., string + list, list + tuple).

- + doesn't work for dictionaries, because they aren't sequences.

- The append method works only for lists, not strings, and keys works only on dictionaries. append assumes its target is mutable, since it's an in-place extension; strings are immutable.

- Slicing and concatenation always return a new object of the same type as the objects processed:

```
>>> "x" + 1
Traceback (innermost last):
  File "<stdin>", line 1, in ?
TypeError: illegal argument type for built-in operation
>>>
>>> {} + {}
Traceback (innermost last):
  File "<stdin>", line 1, in ?
TypeError: bad operand type(s) for +
>>>
>>> [ ].append(9)
>>> "".append('s')
Traceback (innermost last):
  File "<stdin>", line 1, in ?
AttributeError: attribute-less object
>>>
>>> {}.keys( )
[ ]
>>> [ ].keys( )
Traceback (innermost last):
  File "<stdin>", line 1, in ?
AttributeError: keys
>>>
>>> [ ][:]
[ ]
>>> ""[:]
''
```

8. *String indexing*. Since strings are collections of one-character strings, every time you index a string, you get back a string, which can be indexed again. S[0][0][0][0][0] just keeps indexing the first character over and over. This generally doesn't work for lists (lists can hold arbitrary objects), unless the list contains strings.

```
>>> S = "spam"
>>> S[0][0][0][0][0]
's'
>>> L = ['s', 'p']
>>> L[0][0][0]
's'
```

9. *Immutable types*. Either of the solutions below work. Index assignment doesn't, because strings are immutable.

```
>>> S = "spam"
>>> S = S[0] + 'l' + S[2:]
>>> S
'slam'
>>> S = S[0] + 'l' + S[2] + S[3]
>>> S
'slam'
```

10. *Nesting*. Here is a sample:

```
>>> me = {'name':('mark', 'e', 'lutz'), 'age':'?', 'job':'engineer'}
>>> me['job']
'engineer'
>>> me['name'][2]
'lutz'
```

11. *Files*. Here's one way to create and read back a text file in Python (ls is a Unix command; use dir on Windows):

```
#File: maker.py
file = open('myfile.txt', 'w')
file.write('Hello file world!\n')      # Or: open().write()
file.close()                           # close not always needed

#File: reader.py
file = open('myfile.txt', 'r')
print file.read()                      # Or print open().read()

% python maker.py
% python reader.py
Hello file world!

% ls -l myfile.txt
-rwxrwxrwa   1 0        0              19 Apr 13 16:33 myfile.txt
```

12. *The dir function revisited*: Here's what you get for lists; dictionaries do the same (but with different method names). Note that the dir result expanded in Python 2.2—you'll see a large set of additional underscore names that implement expression operators, and support the subclassing in Part VI. The __methods__ attribute disappeared in 2.2 as well, because it wasn't consistently implemented—use dir to to fetch attribute lists today instead:

```
>>> [].__methods__
['append', 'count', 'index', 'insert', 'remove', 'reverse', 'sort',...]
>>> dir([])
['append', 'count', 'index', 'insert', 'remove', 'reverse', 'sort',...]
```

Part III, Statements and Syntax

1. *Coding basic loops*. As you work through this exercise, you'll wind up with code that looks like the following:

```
>>> S = 'spam'
>>> for c in S:
...     print ord(c)
...
115
112
97
109
```

```
>>> x = 0
>>> for c in S: x = x + ord(c)          # Or: x += ord(c)
...
>>> x
433

>>> x = []
>>> for c in S: x.append(ord(c))
...
>>> x
[115, 112, 97, 109]

>>> map(ord, S)
[115, 112, 97, 109]
```

2. *Backslash characters*. The example prints the bell character (\a) 50 times; assuming your machine can handle it, and when run outside of IDLE, you may get a series of beeps (or one long tone, if your machine is fast enough). Hey—we warned you.

3. *Sorting dictionaries*. Here's one way to work through this exercise (see Chapter 6 if this doesn't make sense). Remember, you really do have to split the keys and sort calls up like this, because sort returns None. In Python 2.2, you can iterate through dictionary keys directly without calling keys (e.g., for key in D:), but the keys list will not be sorted like it is by this code:

```
>>> D = {'a':1, 'b':2, 'c':3, 'd':4, 'e':5, 'f':6, 'g':7}
>>> D
{'f': 6, 'c': 3, 'a': 1, 'g': 7, 'e': 5, 'd': 4, 'b': 2}
>>>
>>> keys = D.keys( )
>>> keys.sort( )
>>> for key in keys:
...        print key, '=>', D[key]
...
a => 1
b => 2
c => 3
d => 4
e => 5
f => 6
g => 7
```

4. *Program logic alternatives*. Here's sample code for the solutions. Your results may vary a bit; this exercise is mostly designed to get you playing with code alternatives, so anything reasonable gets full credit:

```
L = [1, 2, 4, 8, 16, 32, 64]
X = 5

i = 0
while i < len(L):
    if 2 ** X == L[i]:
        print 'at index', i
```

```
            break
        i = i+1
else:
    print X, 'not found'


L = [1, 2, 4, 8, 16, 32, 64]
X = 5

for p in L:
    if (2 ** X) == p:
        print (2 ** X), 'was found at', L.index(p)
        break
else:
    print X, 'not found'


L = [1, 2, 4, 8, 16, 32, 64]
X = 5

if (2 ** X) in L:
    print (2 ** X), 'was found at', L.index(2 ** X)
else:
    print X, 'not found'


X = 5
L = []
for i in range(7): L.append(2 ** i)
print L

if (2 ** X) in L:
    print (2 ** X), 'was found at', L.index(2 ** X)
else:
    print X, 'not found'


X = 5
L = map(lambda x: 2**x, range(7))
print L

if (2 ** X) in L:
    print (2 ** X), 'was found at', L.index(2 ** X)
else:
    print X, 'not found'
```

Part IV, Functions

1. *The basics.* There's not much to this one, but notice that using print (and hence your function) is technically a *polymorphic* operation, which does the right thing for each type of object:

```
% python
>>> def func(x): print x
```

```
...
>>> func("spam")
spam
>>> func(42)
42
>>> func([1, 2, 3])
[1, 2, 3]
>>> func({'food': 'spam'})
{'food': 'spam'}
```

2. *Arguments.* Here's a sample solution. Remember that you have to use print to see results in the test calls, because a file isn't the same as code typed interactively; Python doesn't normally echo the results of expression statements in files.

```
def adder(x, y):
    return x + y

print adder(2, 3)
print adder('spam', 'eggs')
print adder(['a', 'b'], ['c', 'd'])

% python mod.py
5
spameggs
['a', 'b', 'c', 'd']
```

3. *varargs.* Two alternative adder functions are shown in the following file, *adders. py.* The hard part here is figuring out how to initialize an accumulator to an empty value of whatever type is passed in. The first solution, uses manual type testing to look for an integer and an empty slice of the first argument (assumed to be a sequence) otherwise. The second solution, uses the first argument to initialize and scan items 2 and beyond, much like one of the min function variants shown in Chapter 13.

The second solution is better. Both of these assume all arguments are the same type and neither works on dictionaries; as we saw in Part II, + doesn't work on mixed types or dictionaries. We could add a type test and special code to add dictionaries too, but that's extra credit.

```
def adder1(*args):
    print 'adder1',
    if type(args[0]) == type(0):    # Integer?
        sum = 0                     # Init to zero.
    else:                           # else sequence:
        sum = args[0][:0]           # Use empty slice of arg1.
    for arg in args:
        sum = sum + arg
    return sum

def adder2(*args):
    print 'adder2',
    sum = args[0]                   # Init to arg1.
    for next in args[1:]:
```

```
        sum = sum + next          # Add items 2..N.
    return sum

for func in (adder1, adder2):
    print func(2, 3, 4)
    print func('spam', 'eggs', 'toast')
    print func(['a', 'b'], ['c', 'd'], ['e', 'f'])

% python adders.py
adder1 9
adder1 spameggstoast
adder1 ['a', 'b', 'c', 'd', 'e', 'f']
adder2 9
adder2 spameggstoast
adder2 ['a', 'b', 'c', 'd', 'e', 'f']
```

4. *Keywords.* Here is our solution to the first part of this exercise (file *mod.py*). To iterate over keyword arguments, use a **args form in the function header and use a loop like: for x in args.keys( ): use args[x].

```
def adder(good=1, bad=2, ugly=3):
    return good + bad + ugly

print adder( )
print adder(5)
print adder(5, 6)
print adder(5, 6, 7)
print adder(ugly=7, good=6, bad=5)

% python mod.py
6
10
14
18
18
```

5 and 6. Here are our solutions to exercises 5 and 6 (file *dicts.py*). These are just coding exercises, though, because Python 1.5 added dictionary methods, to do things like copying and adding (merging) dictionaries: D.copy( ), and D1. update(D2). (See Python's library manual or the *Python Pocket Reference* for more details). X[:] doesn't work for dictionaries, since they're not sequences (see Chapter 6 for details). Also remember that if we assign (e = d) rather than copy, we generate a reference to a *shared* dictionary object; changing d changes e, too.

```
def copyDict(old):
    new = { }
    for key in old.keys( ):
        new[key] = old[key]
    return new

def addDict(d1, d2):
    new = { }
    for key in d1.keys( ):
```

```
        new[key] = d1[key]
    for key in d2.keys():
        new[key] = d2[key]
    return new

% python
>>> from dicts import *
>>> d = {1:1, 2:2}
>>> e = copyDict(d)
>>> d[2] = '?'
>>> d
{1: 1, 2: '?'}
>>> e
{1: 1, 2: 2}

>>> x = {1:1}
>>> y = {2:2}
>>> z = addDict(x, y)
>>> z
{1: 1, 2: 2}
```

7. *More argument matching examples.* Here is the sort of interaction you should get, along with comments that explain the matching that goes on:

```
def f1(a, b): print a, b            # Normal args

def f2(a, *b): print a, b           # Positional varargs

def f3(a, **b): print a, b          # Keyword varargs

def f4(a, *b, **c): print a, b, c   # Mixed modes

def f5(a, b=2, c=3): print a, b, c  # Defaults

def f6(a, b=2, *c): print a, b, c   # Defaults and positional varargs


% python
>>> f1(1, 2)                    # Matched by position (order matters)
1 2
>>> f1(b=2, a=1)               # Matched by name (order doesn't matter)
1 2

>>> f2(1, 2, 3)               # Extra positionals collected in a tuple
1 (2, 3)

>>> f3(1, x=2, y=3)          # Extra keywords collected in a dictionary
1 {'x': 2, 'y': 3}

>>> f4(1, 2, 3, x=2, y=3)    # Extra of both kinds
1 (2, 3) {'x': 2, 'y': 3}

>>> f5(1)                     # Both defaults kick in.
1 2 3
>>> f5(1, 4)                  # Only one default used
1 4 3
```

```
>>> f6(1)                          # One argument: matches "a"
1 2 ()
>>> f6(1, 3, 4)                    # Extra positional collected
1 3 (4,)
```

8. *Primes revisited.* Below is the primes example wrapped up in a function and
   module (file *primes.py*) so it can be run multiple times. We added an if test to
   trap negatives, 0, and 1. We also changed / to // to make this immune from the
   Python 3.0 / "true" division changes we studied in Chapter 4, and support floating-point numbers. The // operator works in both the current and future division scheme, but the future / operator fails (uncomment the from and change //
   to / to see the differences in 2.2 and 3.0).

```
#from __future__ import division

def prime(y):
    if y <= 1:                          # For some y > 1
        print y, 'not prime'
    else:
        x = y // 2                      # Future / fails
        while x > 1:
            if y % x == 0:              # No remainder?
                print y, 'has factor', x
                break                   # Skip else.
            x -= 1
        else:
            print y, 'is prime'

prime(13); prime(13.0)
prime(15); prime(15.0)
prime(3);  prime(2)
prime(1);  prime(-3)
```

   Here is the module in action; the // operator allows it to works for floating-point
   numbers too, even though it perhaps should not:

```
% python primes.py
13 is prime
13.0 is prime
15 has factor 5
15.0 has factor 5.0
3 is prime
2 is prime
1 not prime
-3 not prime
```

   This function still isn't very reusable yet—it could return values instead of printing—but it's enough to run experiments. It's also still not a strict mathematical
   prime (floating-points work), and is still inefficient. Improvements are left as
   exercises for more mathematically-minded readers. Hint: a for loop over
   range(y, 1, -1) may be a bit quicker than the while (in fact, it's roughly twice as
   fast in 2.2), but the algorithm is the real bottleneck here. To time alternatives,

use the built-in `time` module, and coding patterns like those used in this general function-call timer (see the library manual for details):

```
def timer(reps, func, *args):
    import time
    start = time.clock()
    for i in xrange(reps):
        apply(func, args)
    return time.clock() - start
```

9. *List comprehensions.* Here is the sort of code you should write; we may have a preference, but we're not telling:

```
>>> values = [2, 4, 9, 16, 25]
>>> import math

>>> res = []
>>> for x in values: res.append(math.sqrt(x))
...
>>> res
[1.4142135623730951, 2.0, 3.0, 4.0, 5.0]

>>> map(math.sqrt, values)
[1.4142135623730951, 2.0, 3.0, 4.0, 5.0]

>>> [math.sqrt(x) for x in values]
[1.4142135623730951, 2.0, 3.0, 4.0, 5.0]
```

Part V, Modules

1. *Basics, import.* This one is simpler than you may think. When you're done, your file and interaction should look close to the following code (file *mymod.py*); remember that Python can read a whole file into a string or lines list, and the `len` built-in returns the length of strings and lists:

```
def countLines(name):
    file = open(name, 'r')
    return len(file.readlines())

def countChars(name):
    return len(open(name, 'r').read())

def test(name):                                # Or pass file object
    return countLines(name), countChars(name)  # Or return a dictionary

% python
>>> import mymod
>>> mymod.test('mymod.py')
(10, 291)
```

On Unix, you can verify your output with a `wc` command; on Windows, right-click on your file to views its properties. But note that your script may report fewer characters than Windows does—for portability, Python converts Windows

\r\n line-end markers to \n, thereby dropping one byte (character) per line. To match byte counts with Windows exactly, you have to open in binary mode (rb) or add back the number of lines.

Incidentally, to do the "ambitious" part (passing in a file object, so you only open the file once), you'll probably need to use the seek method of the built-in file object. We didn't cover it in the text, but it works just like C's fseek call (and calls it behind the scenes): seek resets the current position in the file to an offset passed in. After a seek, future input/output operations are relative to the new position. To rewind to the start of a file without closing and reopening, call file.seek(0); the file read methods all pick up at the current position in the file, so you need to rewind to reread. Here's what this tweak would look like:

```
def countLines(file):
    file.seek(0)                         # Rewind to start of file.
    return len(file.readlines())

def countChars(file):
    file.seek(0)                         # Ditto (rewind if needed)
    return len(file.read())

def test(name):
    file = open(name, 'r')                          # Pass file object.
    return countLines(file), countChars(file)       # Open file only once.

>>> import mymod2
>>> mymod2.test("mymod2.py")
(11, 392)
```

2. *from/from**. Here's the from* part. Replace * with countChars to do the rest.

```
% python
>>> from mymod import *
>>> countChars("mymod.py")
291
```

3. __main__. If you code it properly, it works in either mode (program run or module import):

```
def countLines(name):
    file = open(name, 'r')
    return len(file.readlines())

def countChars(name):
    return len(open(name, 'r').read())

def test(name):                                    # Or pass file object
    return countLines(name), countChars(name)      # Or return a dictionary

if __name__ == '__main__':
    print test('mymod.py')

% python mymod.py
(13, 346)
```

4. *Nested imports*. Here is our solution (file *myclient.py*):

```
from mymod import countLines, countChars
print countLines('mymod.py'), countChars('mymod.py')
```

```
% python myclient.py
13 346
```

As for the rest of this one: mymod's functions are accessible (that is, importable) from the top level of myclient, since from simply assigns to names in the importer (it works almost as though mymod's defs appeared in myclient). For example, another file can say this:

```
import myclient
myclient.countLines(...)
```

```
from myclient import countChars
countChars(...)
```

If myclient used import instead of from, you'd need to use a path to get to the functions in mymod through myclient:

```
import myclient
myclient.mymod.countLines(...)
```

```
from myclient import mymod
mymod.countChars(...)
```

In general, you can define *collector* modules that import all the names from other modules, so they're available in a single convenience module. Using the following code, you wind up with three different copies of name somename: mod1. somename, collector.somename, and __main__.somename; all three share the same integer object initially, and only the name somename exists at the interactive prompt as is:

```
#File: mod1.py
somename = 42
```

```
#File: collector.py
from mod1 import *      # Collect lots of names here.
from mod2 import *      # from assigns to my names.
from mod3 import *
```

```
>>> from collector import somename
```

5. *Package imports*. For this, we put the *mymod.py* solution file listed for exercise 3 into a directory package. The following is what we did to set up the directory and its required *__init__.py* file in a Windows console interface; you'll need to interpolate for other platforms (e.g., use mv and vi instead of move and edit). This works in any directory (we just happened to run our commands in Python's install directory), and you can do some of this from a file explorer GUI, too.

When we were done, we had a *mypkg* subdirectory, which contained files *__init__.py* and *mymod.py*. You need an *__init__.py* in the *mypkg* directory, but not in its parent; *mypkg* is located in the home directory component of the module search path.

Notice how a print statement coded in the directory's initialization file only fires the first time it is imported, not the second:

```
C:\python22> mkdir mypkg
C:\Python22> move mymod.py mypkg\mymod.py
C:\Python22> edit mypkg\__init__.py
...coded a print statement...

C:\Python22> python
>> import mypkg.mymod
initializing mypkg
>>> mypkg.mymod.countLines('mypkg\mymod.py')
13
>>> from mypkg.mymod import countChars
>>> countChars('mypkg\mymod.py')
346
```

6. *Reload*. This exercise just asks you to experiment with changing the *changer.py* example in the book, so there's nothing to show here.

7. *Circular imports*. The short story is that importing recur2 first works, because the recursive import then happens at the import in recur1, not at a from in recur2.

The long story goes like this: importing recur2 first works, because the recursive import from recur1 to recur2 fetches recur2 as a whole, instead of getting specific names. recur2 is incomplete when imported from recur1, but because it uses import instead of from, you're safe: Python finds and returns the already created recur2 module object and continues to run the rest of recur1 without a glitch. When the recur2 import resumes, the second from finds name Y in recur1 (it's been run completely), so no error is reported. Running a file as a script is not the same as importing it as a module; these cases are the same as running the first import or from in the script interactively. For instance, running recur1 as a script is the same as importing recur2 interactively, since recur2 is the first module imported in recur1.

Part VI, Classes and OOP

1. *Inheritance*. Here's the solution code for this exercise (file *adder.py*), along with some interactive tests. The __add__ overload has to appear only once, in the superclass, since it invokes type-specific add methods in subclasses.

```
class Adder:
    def add(self, x, y):
        print 'not implemented!'
    def __init__(self, start=[ ]):
        self.data = start
    def __add__(self, other):                # Or in subclasses?
        return self.add(self.data, other)    # Or return type?
```

```
class ListAdder(Adder):
    def add(self, x, y):
        return x + y

class DictAdder(Adder):
    def add(self, x, y):
        new = { }
        for k in x.keys( ): new[k] = x[k]
        for k in y.keys( ): new[k] = y[k]
        return new
```

```
% python
>>> from adder import *
>>> x = Adder( )
>>> x.add(1, 2)
not implemented!
>>> x = ListAdder( )
>>> x.add([1], [2])
[1, 2]
>>> x = DictAdder( )
>>> x.add({1:1}, {2:2})
{1: 1, 2: 2}

>>> x = Adder([1])
>>> x + [2]
not implemented!
>>>
>>> x = ListAdder([1])
>>> x + [2]
[1, 2]
>>> [2] + x
Traceback (innermost last):
  File "<stdin>", line 1, in ?
TypeError: __add__ nor __radd__ defined for these operands
```

Notice in the last test that you get an error for expressions where a class instance appears on the right of a +; if you want to fix this, use __radd__ methods as described in the section "Operator Overloading" in Chapter 21.

If you are saving a value in the instance anyhow, you might as well rewrite the add method to take just one argument, in the spirit of other examples in Part VI:

```
class Adder:
    def __init__(self, start=[ ]):
        self.data = start
    def __add__(self, other):        # Pass a single argument.
        return self.add(other)       # The left side is in self.
    def add(self, y):
        print 'not implemented!'

class ListAdder(Adder):
    def add(self, y):
        return self.data + y
```

```
class DictAdder(Adder):
    def add(self, y):
        pass  # Change me to use self.data instead of x.

x = ListAdder([1,2,3])
y = x + [4,5,6]
print y                  # Prints [1, 2, 3, 4, 5, 6]
```

Because values are attached to objects rather than passed around, this version is arguably more object-oriented. And once you've gotten to this point, you'll probably see that you could get rid of add altogether, and simply define type-specific __add__ methods in the two subclasses.

2. *Operator overloading.* The solution code (file *mylist.py*) uses a few operator overload methods we didn't say much about, but they should be straightforward to understand. Copying the initial value in the constructor is important, because it may be mutable; you don't want to change or have a reference to an object that's possibly shared somewhere outside the class. The __getattr__ method routes calls to the wrapped list. For hints on an easier way to code this as of Python 2.2, see the section "Extending Types by Subclassing" in Chapter 23.

```
class MyList:
    def __init__(self, start):
        #self.wrapped = start[:]        # Copy start: no side effects
        self.wrapped = []               # Make sure it's a list here.
        for x in start: self.wrapped.append(x)
    def __add__(self, other):
        return MyList(self.wrapped + other)
    def __mul__(self, time):
        return MyList(self.wrapped * time)
    def __getitem__(self, offset):
        return self.wrapped[offset]
    def __len__(self):
        return len(self.wrapped)
    def __getslice__(self, low, high):
        return MyList(self.wrapped[low:high])
    def append(self, node):
        self.wrapped.append(node)
    def __getattr__(self, name):        # Other members: sort/reverse/etc
        return getattr(self.wrapped, name)
    def __repr__(self):
        return `self.wrapped`

if __name__ == '__main__':
    x = MyList('spam')
    print x
    print x[2]
    print x[1:]
    print x + ['eggs']
    print x * 3
    x.append('a')
    x.sort()
    for c in x: print c,
```

```
% python mylist.py
['s', 'p', 'a', 'm']
a
['p', 'a', 'm']
['s', 'p', 'a', 'm', 'eggs']
['s', 'p', 'a', 'm', 's', 'p', 'a', 'm', 's', 'p', 'a', 'm']
a a m p s
```

Note that it's important to copy the start value by appending instead of slicing here, because the result may other wise not be a true list, and so would not respond to expected list methods such as append (e.g., slicing a string returns another string, not a list). You would be able to copy a MyList start value by slicing, because its class overloads the slicing operation and provides the expected list interface. You need to avoid sliced-based copying for things such as strings, however.

3. *Subclassing*. Our solution (*mysub.py*) appears below. Your solution should be similar.

```
from mylist import MyList

class MyListSub(MyList):
    calls = 0                                    # Shared by instances

    def __init__(self, start):
        self.adds = 0                            # Varies in each instance
        MyList.__init__(self, start)

    def __add__(self, other):
        MyListSub.calls = MyListSub.calls + 1    # Class-wide counter
        self.adds = self.adds + 1                # Per instance counts
        return MyList.__add__(self, other)

    def stats(self):
        return self.calls, self.adds             # All adds, my adds

if __name__ == '__main__':
    x = MyListSub('spam')
    y = MyListSub('foo')
    print x[2]
    print x[1:]
    print x + ['eggs']
    print x + ['toast']
    print y + ['bar']
    print x.stats()
```

```
% python mysub.py
a
['p', 'a', 'm']
['s', 'p', 'a', 'm', 'eggs']
['s', 'p', 'a', 'm', 'toast']
['f', 'o', 'o', 'bar']
(3, 2)
```

4. *Metaclass methods.* We worked through this exercise as follows. Notice that operators try to fetch attributes through __getattr__ too; you need to return a value to make them work.

```
>>> class Meta:
...     def __getattr__(self, name):
...         print 'get', name
...     def __setattr__(self, name, value):
...         print 'set', name, value
...
>>> x = Meta()
>>> x.append
get append
>>> x.spam = "pork"
set spam pork
>>>
>>> x + 2
get __coerce__
Traceback (innermost last):
  File "<stdin>", line 1, in ?
TypeError: call of non-function
>>>
>>> x[1]
get __getitem__
Traceback (innermost last):
  File "<stdin>", line 1, in ?
TypeError: call of non-function

>>> x[1:5]
get __len__
Traceback (innermost last):
  File "<stdin>", line 1, in ?
TypeError: call of non-function
```

5. *Set objects.* Here's the sort of interaction you should get. Comments explain which methods are called.

```
% python
>>> from setwrapper import Set
>>> x = Set([1,2,3,4])          # Runs __init__
>>> y = Set([3,4,5])

>>> x & y                       # __and__, intersect, then __repr__
Set:[3, 4]
>>> x | y                       # __or__, union, then __repr__
Set:[1, 2, 3, 4, 5]

>>> z = Set("hello")            # __init__ removes duplicates.
>>> z[0], z[-1]                 # __getitem__
('h', 'o')

>>> for c in z: print c,        # __getitem__
...
h e l o
>>> len(z), z                   # __len__, __repr__
(4, Set:['h', 'e', 'l', 'o'])
```

```
>>> z & "mello", z | "mello"
(Set:['e', 'l', 'o'], Set:['h', 'e', 'l', 'o', 'm'])
```

Our solution to the multiple-operand extension subclass looks like the class below (file *multiset.py*). It only needs to replace two methods in the original set. The class's documentation string explains how it works.

```
from setwrapper import Set

class MultiSet(Set):
    """
    inherits all Set names, but extends intersect
    and union to support multiple operands; note
    that "self" is still the first argument (stored
    in the *args argument now); also note that the
    inherited & and | operators call the new methods
    here with 2 arguments, but processing more than
    2 requires a method call, not an expression:
    """

    def intersect(self, *others):
        res = [ ]
        for x in self:                       # Scan first sequence
            for other in others:             # for all other args.
                if x not in other: break     # Item in each one?
            else:                            # No: break out of loop
                res.append(x)                # Yes: add item to end
        return Set(res)

    def union(*args):                        # self is args[0].
        res = [ ]
        for seq in args:                     # For all args
            for x in seq:                    # For all nodes
                if not x in res:
                    res.append(x)            # Add new items to result.
        return Set(res)
```

Your interaction with the extension will be something along the following lines. Note that you can intersect by using & or calling intersect, but must call intersect for three or more operands; & is a binary (two-sided) operator. Also note that we could have called MutiSet simply Set to make this change more transparent if we used setwrapper.Set to refer to the original within multiset:

```
>>> from multiset import *
>>> x = MultiSet([1,2,3,4])
>>> y = MultiSet([3,4,5])
>>> z = MultiSet([0,1,2])

>>> x & y, x | y                            # Two operands
(Set:[3, 4], Set:[1, 2, 3, 4, 5])

>>> x.intersect(y, z)                       # Three operands
Set:[ ]
>>> x.union(y, z)
Set:[1, 2, 3, 4, 5, 0]
```

```
>>> x.intersect([1,2,3], [2,3,4], [1,2,3])      # Four operands
Set:[2, 3]
>>> x.union(range(10))                          # non-MultiSets work too.
Set:[1, 2, 3, 4, 0, 5, 6, 7, 8, 9]
```

6. *Class tree links.* Below is the way we changed the Lister class, and a rerun of the test to show its format. To display inherited class attributes too, you'd need to do something like what the attrnames method currently does, but recursively, at each class reached by climbing __bases__ links. Because dir includes inherited attributes in Python 2.2, you might also simply loop through its result: say for x in dir(self) and use getattr(self,x). This won't directly help, if you wish to represent the class tree's structure in your display like the *classtree.py* example in Chapter 21.

```
class Lister:
    def __repr__(self):
        return ("<Instance of %s(%s), address %s:\n%s>" %
                        (self.__class__.__name__,   # My class's name
                         self.supers(),             # My class's supers
                         id(self),                  # My address
                         self.attrnames()) )        # name=value list
    def attrnames(self):
        ...unchanged...
    def supers(self):
        result = ""
        first = 1
        for super in self.__class__.__bases__:   # One level up from class
            if not first:
                result = result + ", "
            first = 0
            result = result + super.__name__       # name, not repr(super)
        return result


C:\python\examples> python testmixin.py
<Instance of Sub(Super, Lister), address 7841200:
        name data3=42
        name data2=eggs
        name data1=spam
>
```

7. *Composition.* Our solution is below (file *lunch.py*), with comments from the description mixed in with the code. This is one case where it's probably easier to express a problem in Python than it is in English.

```
class Lunch:
    def __init__(self):             # Make/embed Customer and Employee.
        self.cust = Customer()
        self.empl = Employee()
    def order(self, foodName):      # Start a Customer order simulation.
        self.cust.placeOrder(foodName, self.empl)
    def result(self):              # Ask the Customer about its Food.
        self.cust.printFood()
```

```
class Customer:
    def __init__(self):                              # Initialize my food to None.
        self.food = None
    def placeOrder(self, foodName, employee):  # Place order with Employee.
        self.food = employee.takeOrder(foodName)
    def printFood(self):                             # Print the name of my food.
        print self.food.name

class Employee:
    def takeOrder(self, foodName):        # Return a Food, with requested name.
        return Food(foodName)

class Food:
    def __init__(self, name):             # Store food name.
        self.name = name

if __name__ == '__main__':
    x = Lunch()                           # Self-test code
    x.order('burritos')                   # If run, not imported
    x.result()
    x.order('pizza')
    x.result()

% python lunch.py
burritos
pizza
```

8. *Zoo Animal Hierarchy*. Here is the way we coded the taxonomy on Python (file *zoo.py*); it's artificial, but the general coding pattern applies to many real structures—from GUIs to employee databases. Notice that the self.speak reference in Animal triggers an independent inheritance search, which finds speak in a subclass. Test this interactively per the exercise description. Try extending this hierarchy with new classes, and making instances of various classes in the tree.

```
class Animal:
    def reply(self):     self.speak()        # Back to subclass
    def speak(self):     print 'spam'        # Custom message

class Mammal(Animal):
    def speak(self):     print 'huh?'

class Cat(Mammal):
    def speak(self):     print 'meow'

class Dog(Mammal):
    def speak(self):     print 'bark'

class Primate(Mammal):
    def speak(self):     print 'Hello world!'

class Hacker(Primate): pass                  # Inherit from Primate.
```

9. *The Dead Parrot Sketch*. Here's how we implemented this one (file *parrot.py*). Notice how the line method in the Actor superclass works: by accessing self

attributes twice, it sends Python back to the instance twice, and hence invokes *two* inheritance searches—self.name and self.says( ) find information in the specific subclasses.

```
class Actor:
    def line(self): print self.name + ':', `self.says( )`

class Customer(Actor):
    name = 'customer'
    def says(self): return "that's one ex-bird!"

class Clerk(Actor):
    name = 'clerk'
    def says(self): return "no it isn't..."

class Parrot(Actor):
    name = 'parrot'
    def says(self): return None

class Scene:
    def __init__(self):
        self.clerk    = Clerk( )        # Embed some instances.
        self.customer = Customer( )     # Scene is a composite.
        self.subject  = Parrot( )

    def action(self):
        self.customer.line( )           # Delegate to embedded.
        self.clerk.line( )
        self.subject.line( )
```

Part VII, Exceptions and Tools

1. *try/except*. Our version of the oops function (file *oops.py*) follows. As for the non-coding questions, changing oops to raise KeyError instead of IndexError means that the exception won't be caught by the try handler (it "percolates" to the top level and triggers Python's default error message). The names KeyError and IndexError come from the outermost built-in names scope. Import __builtin__ and pass it as an argument to the dir function to see for yourself.

```
def oops( ):
    raise IndexError

def doomed( ):
    try:
        oops( )
    except IndexError:
        print 'caught an index error!'
    else:
        print 'no error caught...'

if __name__ == '__main__': doomed( )
```

```
% python oops.py
caught an index error!
```

2. *Exception objects and lists*. Here's the way we extended this module for an exception of our own (here a string, at first):

```
MyError = 'hello'

def oops():
    raise MyError, 'world'

def doomed():
    try:
        oops()
    except IndexError:
        print 'caught an index error!'
    except MyError, data:
        print 'caught error:', MyError, data
    else:
        print 'no error caught...'

if __name__ == '__main__':
    doomed()
```

```
% python oops.py
caught error: hello world
```

To identify the exception with a class, we just changed the first part of the file to this, and saved it as *oop_oops.py*:

```
class MyError: pass

def oops():
    raise MyError()

...rest unchanged...
```

Like all class exceptions, the instance comes back as the extra data; our error message now shows both the class, and its instance (<...>).

```
% python oop_oops.py
caught error: __main__.MyError <__main__.MyError instance at 0x00867550>
```

Remember, to make this look nicer, you can define a __repr__ or __str__ method in your class to return a custom print string. See Chapter 21 for details.

3. *Error handling*. Here's one way to solve this one (file *safe2.py*). We did our tests in a file, rather than interactively, but the results are about the same.

```
import sys, traceback

def safe(entry, *args):
    try:
        apply(entry, args)                    # catch everything else
    except:
        traceback.print_exc()
        print 'Got', sys.exc_type, sys.exc_value
```

```
import oops
safe(oops.oops)

% python safe2.py
Traceback (innermost last):
  File "safe2.py", line 5, in safe
    apply(entry, args)                          # catch everything else
  File "oops.py", line 4, in oops
    raise MyError, 'world'
hello: world
Got hello world
```

Part VIII, The Outer Layers

Chapter 27, Common Tasks in Python

1. *Avoiding regular expressions.* This program is long and tedious, but not especially complicated. See if you can understand how it works. Whether this is easier for you than regular expressions depends on many factors, such as your familiarity with regular expressions and your comfort with the functions in the string module. Use whichever type of programming works for you.

```python
file = open('pepper.txt')
text = file.read()
paragraphs = text.split('\n\n')

def find_indices_for(big, small):
    indices = [ ]
    cum = 0
    while 1:
        index = big.find(small)
        if index == -1:
            return indices
        indices.append(index+cum)
        big = big[index+len(small):]
        cum = cum + index + len(small)

def fix_paragraphs_with_word(paragraphs, word):
    lenword = len(word)
    for par_no in range(len(paragraphs)):
        p = paragraphs[par_no]
        wordpositions = find_indices_for(p, word)
        if wordpositions == [ ]: return
        for start in wordpositions:
            # Look for 'pepper' ahead.
            indexpepper = p.find('pepper')
            if indexpepper == -1: return -1
            if p[start:indexpepper].strip():
                # Something other than whitespace in between!
                continue
            where = indexpepper+len('pepper')
            if p[where:where+len('corn')] == 'corn':
```

```
                # It's immediately followed by 'corn'!
                continue
            if p.find('salad') < where:
                # It's not followed by 'salad'.
                continue
            # Finally! We get to do a change!
            p = p[:start] + 'bell' + p[start+lenword:]
            paragraphs[par_no] = p          # Change mutable argument!

    fix_paragraphs_with_word(paragraphs, 'red')
    fix_paragraphs_with_word(paragraphs, 'green')

    for paragraph in paragraphs:
        print paragraph+'\n'
```

We won't repeat the output here; it's the same as that of the regular expression solution.

2. *Wrapping a text file with a class.* This one is surprisingly easy, if you understand classes and the split function in the string module. The following is a version that has one little twist over and beyond what we asked for:

```
    class FileStrings:
        def __init__(self, filename=None, data=None):
            if data == None:
                self.data = open(filename).read( )
            else:
                self.data = data
            self.paragraphs = self.data.split('\n\n')
            self.lines = self.data.split('\n')
            self.words = self.data.split( )
        def __repr__(self):
            return self.data
        def paragraph(self, index):
            return FileStrings(data=self.paragraphs[index])
        def line(self, index):
            return FileStrings(data=self.lines[index])
        def word(self, index):
            return self.words[index]
```

This solution, when applied to the file *pepper.txt*, gives:

```
>>> from FileStrings import FileStrings
>>> bigtext = FileStrings('pepper.txt')
>>> print bigtext.paragraph(0)
This is a paragraph that mentions bell peppers multiple times.  For
one, here is a red Pepper and dried tomato salad recipe.  I don't like
to use green peppers in my salads as much because they have a harsher
flavor.
>>> print bigtext.line(0)
This is a paragraph that mentions bell peppers multiple times.  For
>>> print bigtext.line(-4)
aren't peppers, they're chilies, but would you rather have a good cook
>>> print bigtext.word(-4)
botanist
```

How does it work? The constructor simply reads all the file into a big string (the instance attribute data) and then splits it according to the various criteria, keeping the results of the splits in instance attributes that are lists of strings. When returning from one of the accessor methods, the data itself is wrapped in a FileStrings object. This isn't required by the assignment, but it's nice because it means you can chain the operations, so that to find out what the last word of the third line of the third paragraph is, you can just write:

```
>>> print bigtext.paragraph(2).line(2).word(-1)
'cook'
```

3. *Describing a directory.* There are several solutions to this exercise, naturally. One simple solution is:

```
import os, sys, stat

def describedir(start):
    def describedir_helper(arg, dirname, files):
        """ Helper function for describing directories """
        print "Directory %s has files:" % dirname
        for file in files:
            # Find the full path to the file (directory + filename).
            fullname = os.path.join(dirname, file)
            if os.path.isdir(fullname):
                # If it's a directory, say so; no need to find the size.
                print '  '+ file + ' (subdir)'
            else:
                # Find out the size and print the info.
                size = os.stat(fullname)[stat.ST_SIZE]
                print '  '+file+' size=' + `size`

    # Start the 'walk'.
    os.path.walk(start, describedir_helper, None)
```

which uses the walk function in the os.path module, and works just fine:

```
>>> import describedir
>>> describedir.describedir2('testdir')
Directory testdir has files:
  describedir.py size=939
  subdir1 (subdir)
  subdir2 (subdir)
Directory testdir\subdir1 has files:
  makezeros.py size=125
  subdir3 (subdir)
Directory testdir\subdir1\subdir3 has files:
Directory testdir\subdir2 has files:
```

Note that you could have found the size of the files by doing len(open(fullname, 'rb').read( )), but this works only when you have read access to all the files and is quite inefficient. The stat call in the os module gives out all kinds of useful information in a tuple, and the stat module defines some names that make it unnecessary to remember the order of the elements in that tuple. See the *Library Reference* for details.

4. *Modifying the prompt.* The key to this exercise is to remember that the ps1 and ps2 attributes of the sys module can be anything, including a class instance with a __repr__ or __str__ method. For example:

```
import sys, os
class MyPrompt:
    def __init__(self, subprompt='>>> '):
        self.lineno = 0
        self.subprompt = subprompt
    def __repr__(self):
        self.lineno = self.lineno + 1
        return os.getcwd( )+'|%d'%(self.lineno)+self.subprompt


sys.ps1 = MyPrompt( )
sys.ps2 = MyPrompt('... ')
```

This code works as shown (use the –i option of the Python interpreter to make sure your program starts right away):

```
h:\David\book> python -i modifyprompt.py
h:\David\book|1>>> x = 3
h:\David\book|2>>> y = 3
h:\David\book|3>>> def foo( ):
h:\David\book|3...     x = 3                    # The secondary prompt is supported.
h:\David\book|3...
h:\David\book|4>>> import os
h:\David\book|5>>> os.chdir('..')
h:\David|6>>>                                   # Note that the prompt changed!
```

5. *Writing a simple shell.* Mostly, the following script, which implements the Unix set of commands (well, some of them) should be self-explanatory. Note that we've only put a "help" message for the ls command, but there should be one for all the other commands as well:

```
import cmd, os, sys, shutil

class UnixShell(cmd.Cmd):
    def do_EOF(self, line):
        """ The do_EOF command is called when the user presses Ctrl-D (unix)
            or Ctrl-Z (PC). """
        sys.exit( )

    def help_ls(self):
        print "ls <directory>: list the contents of the specified directory"
        print "               (current directory used by default)"

    def do_ls(self, line):
        # 'ls' by itself means 'list current directory'
        if line == '': dirs = [os.curdir]
        else: dirs = line.split( )
        for dirname in dirs:
            print 'Listing of %s:' % dirname
            print '\n'.join(os.listdir(dirname)
```

```
    def do_cd(self, dirname):
        # 'cd' by itself means 'go home'.
        if dirname == '': dirname = os.environ['HOME']
        os.chdir(dirname)

    def do_mkdir(self, dirname):
        os.mkdir(dirname)

    def do_cp(self, line):
        words = line.split()
        sourcefiles,target = words[:-1], words[-1] # target could be a dir
        for sourcefile in sourcefiles:
            shutil.copy(sourcefile, target)

    def do_mv(self, line):
        source, target = line.split()
        os.rename(source, target)

    def do_rm(self, line):
        [os.remove(arg) for arg in line.split()]

class DirectoryPrompt:
    def __repr__(self):
        return os.getcwd()+'> '

cmd.PROMPT = DirectoryPrompt()
shell = UnixShell()
shell.cmdloop()
```

Note that we've reused the same trick as in exercise 5 of Chapter 8 to have a prompt that adjusts with the current directory, combined with the trick of modifying the attribute PROMPT in the cmd module itself. Of course those weren't part of the assignment, but it's hard to just limit oneself to a simple thing when a full-featured one will do. It works, too!

```
h:\David\book> python -i shell.py
h:\David\book> cd ../tmp
h:\David\tmp> ls
Listing of .:
api
ERREUR.DOC
ext
giant_~1.jpg
icons
index.html
lib
pythlp.hhc
pythlp.hhk
ref
tut
h:\David\tmp> cd ..
h:\David> cd tmp
h:\David\tmp> cp index.html backup.html
h:\David\tmp> rm backup.html
h:\David\tmp> ^Z
```

Of course, to be truly useful, this script needs a lot of error checking and many more features, all of which is left, as math textbooks say, as an exercise for the reader.

6. *Redirecting stdout.* This is simple: all you have to do is to replace the first line with:

```
import fileinput, sys                    # No change here
sys.stdout = open(sys.argv[-1], 'w')     # Open the output file.
del sys.argv[-1]                         # We've dealt with this argument.
...                                      # Continue as before.
```

Chapter 28, Frameworks

1. *Faking the Web.* What you need to do is to create instances of a class that has the fieldnames attribute and appropriate instance variables. One possible solution is:

```
class FormData:
    def __init__(self, dict):
        for k, v in dict.items():
            setattr(self, k, v)
class FeedbackData(FormData):
    """ A FormData generated by the comment.html form. """
    fieldnames = ('name', 'address', 'email', 'type', 'text')
    def __repr__(self):
        return "%(type)s from %(name)s on %(time)s" % vars(self)

fake_entries = [
    {'name': "John Doe",
     'address': '500 Main St., SF CA 94133',
     'email': 'john@sf.org',
     'type': 'comment',
     'text': 'Great toothpaste!'},
    {'name': "Suzy Doe",
     'address': '500 Main St., SF CA 94133',
     'email': 'suzy@sf.org',
     'type': 'complaint',
     'text': "It doesn't taste good when I kiss John!"},
    ]

DIRECTORY = r'C:\complaintdir'
if __name__ == '__main__':
    import tempfile, pickle, time
    tempfile.tempdir = DIRECTORY
    for fake_entry in fake_entries:
        data = FeedbackData(fake_entry)
        filename = tempfile.mktemp()
        data.time = time.asctime(time.localtime(time.time()))
        pickle.dump(data, open(filename, 'w'))
```

As you can see, the only thing you really had to change was the way the constructor for FormData works, since it has to do the setting of attributes from a dictionary as opposed to a FieldStorage object.

2. *Cleaning up.* There are many ways to deal with this problem. One easy one is to modify the *formletter.py* program to keep a list of the filenames that it has already processed (in a pickled file, of course!). This can be done by modifying the if __main__ == '__name__' test to read something like this (new lines are in bold):

```
if __name__ == '__main__':
    import os, pickle
    CACHEFILE = 'C:\cache.pik'
    from feedback import DIRECTORY#, FormData, FeedbackData
    if os.path.exists(CACHEFILE):
        processed_files = pickle.load(open(CACHEFILE))
    else:
        processed_files = [ ]
    for filename in os.listdir(DIRECTORY):
        if filename in processed_files: continue   # Skip this filename.
        processed_files.append(filename)
        data = pickle.load(open(os.path.join(DIRECTORY, filename)))
        if data.type == 'complaint':
            print "Printing letter for %(name)s." % vars(data)
            print_formletter(data)
        else:
            print "Got comment from %(name)s, skipping printing." % \
                    vars(data)
    pickle.dump(processed_file, open(CACHEFILE, 'w'))
```

As you can tell, you simply load a list of the previous filenames if it exists (and use an empty list otherwise) and compare the filenames with entries in the list to determine which to skip. If you don't skip one, it needs to be added to the list. Finally, at program exit, pickle the new list.

3. *Adding parametric plotting to grapher.py.* This exercise is quite simple, as all that's needed is to change the drawing code in the Chart class. Specifically, the code between xmin, xmax = 0, N-1 and graphics.fillPolygon(...) should be placed in an if test, so that the new code reads:

```
if not hasattr(self.data[0], '__len__'):   # It's probably a number (1D).
    xmin, xmax = 0, N-1
# Code from existing program, up to graphics.fillPolygon(xs, ys, len(xs))
elif len(self.data[0]) == 2:               # we'll only deal with 2-D
    xmin = reduce(min, map(lambda d: d[0], self.data))
    xmax = reduce(max, map(lambda d: d[0], self.data))

    ymin = reduce(min, map(lambda d: d[1], self.data))
    ymax = reduce(max, map(lambda d: d[1], self.data))

    zero_y = y_offset - int(-ymin/(ymax-ymin)*height)
    zero_x = x_offset + int(-xmin/(xmax-xmin)*width)
```

```
for i in range(N):
    xs[i] = x_offset + int((self.data[i][0]-xmin)/(xmax-xmin)*width)
    ys[i] = y_offset - int((self.data[i][1]-ymin)/(ymax-ymin)*height)
graphics.color = self.color
if self.style == "Line":
    graphics.drawPolyline(xs, ys, len(xs))
else:
    xs.append(xs[0]); ys.append(ys[0])
    graphics.fillPolygon(xs, ys, len(xs))
```

Index

Symbol

{ } (braces), 105
__add__ method, 327
+ (addition/concatenation) operator, 314
& (bitwise and) operator, 58
^ (bitwise exclusive or) operator, 58
| (bitwise or) operator, 58
: (colon), 149
== (comparison operator), 121
__dict__ attribute, 262, 263
/ (division) operator, 58
__getattr__ method, 332
__getitem__ method, 328
__init__ constructor, 315, 319, 324
__init__.py files, 271
>>> (input prompt), 26
* (multiplication) operator, 58, 314
... prompt, 166
' (quotation mark) for strings, 74
% (remainder/format) operator, 58
__repr__ method, 333
<< (shift left operator), 58
>> (shift right operator), 58

A

abs function, 445
abstract superclasses, 326
adding tests, 230
AI programming, 10
and operator, 58, 153
append method, 102, 107, 458
applications, internationalization of, 80
apply function, 224–227

architecture, 248–250
arguments, 191
    apply function, 224–227
    default values, 240
    matching, 210, 217
    mutable changes, 208
    passing, 207, 216, 217, 226
    shared references, 207
argv attribute (sys module), 85
arrays, 100
assert statement, 408
assignment statements, 134, 138, 140, 260
    forms, 135
    implicit, 135
    object references, 134
    variable name rules, 137
assignments, 68
    C, 161
    functions by, 191
    in-place object changes, 71
    lists, 101
    names, classifying, 337
    references, 125
attributes, 36
    architecture, 249
    classes, 376
    construction, 323
    inheritance searches, 299
    pseudo-private class, 366–369
    qualification, 263
augmented assignment statements, 139
automatic extensions, Windows, 30
automatic memory management, 13

We'd like to hear your suggestions for improving our indexes. Send email to *index@oreilly.com*.

B

backslashes, 77, 151
binary files, 472
bitwise operator, 58, 64
bitwise shift, numbers, 64
blank lines, 182
blocks
    delimiters, 150
    strings, 79
Boolean operators, 152
    lambdas, 222
    numbers, 64
bound instance methods, 358
break statement, 156
built-in apply functions, 225
built-in docstrings, 175
built-in exceptions
    catching, 403
    classes, 414
built-in functions, 480
    number tools, 67
built-in modules
    binary files, 472
    cgi module, 474
    debugging, 480
    Internet data processing, 476
    Internet protocols, 475
    profiling, 482
    string constants, 447
    string functions, 447
    time module, 481
    urllib, 474
    urlparse, 475
built-in object types, 55
built-in scope, 201
built-in string methods, 91
built-in tools, 57
built-in types, 53–55
    categories, 117
    extending, 363–366
    hierarchies, 123–125
    iterators, 236
    troubleshooting, 125–127
byte code, 6
    compiling, 19
    escape sequences, 76

C

C
    assignments, 161
    integration with, 13

C++ language, 9, 13
callback functions, 225
    bound methods, 361
call-by-reference argument passing, 209
calls
    apply function, 226
    built-in string methods, 91
    classes, 309
    embedding, 46–47
    functions, 193
    indirect, 237
    instances, 335
    list methods, 101
    methods, 322
    signatures, 344
    superclasses constructors, 321
case sensitivity, names, 137
case-independent sort, 456
catching
    built-in exceptions, 403
    exceptions, 428, 431
    user-defined exceptions, 406
categories
    exceptions, 411
    types, 117
CGI (Common Gateway Interface)
    modules, 111, 474
    scripts, 486, 503
characters
    encoding large sets, 80
    lists, 167
chr function, 445, 447
chunk sizes, selecting, 470
class statement, 317
classes
    _ _add_ _ method, 327
    _ _getattr_ _ method, 332
    _ _getitem_ _ method, 328
    _ _init_ _ constructor, 315, 319, 324
    _ _repr_ _ method, 333
    calling, 309
    designing with OOP, 343
    documentation strings, 360
    exceptions, 411–418
    generic object factories, 356
    inheritance, 310, 311, 356
    instances, 300
    interfaces, 324
    iteration, 329
    methods, 320, 372
    modules, 312, 362
    multiple instance objects, 307

J

Java/Jython, 504
  installation, 504
  Java libraries, 505
  Java scripting, 506
  Java, versus, 511
  swing application, grapher.py, 506
Jython, 21

K

keyword arguments, 210–217
  passing, 226
Komodo, 44
ksh shell, 539

L

lambdas, 219–224
  operators, 58
language tables, dictionaries, 107
languages
  comparisons to, 14
  enabling future features, 280
large character sets, encoding, 80
launching options, 47
LEGB rule, 199
len function, 82
lexical scoping, 265
LGB rule, 199
limitations, 6
  icon click, 35
lines, processing, 471
links, namespaces, 341
list comprehension expressions, 229–233
list function, 446
lists
  basic operations of, 99
  changing, in place, 101
  characters, 167
  common constants, 98
  creating, 458
  dictionaries, 109
  indexing and slicing, 100
  methods, 101
  objects, 121–123
  operations, 99–103
  sys.path, 253
  tuples, 115
literals, 54
  dictionaries, 105
  floating-point, 56

  lists, 98
  numbers, 55
  strings, 75–81
  tuples, 113
local scope, 198
local variables, 196
logical operators, 58
long, C, 444
long function, 446
long integers, 56, 65, 444
loops
  else, 146, 156, 161
  file scanners, 165
  for, 160–170
  formatting, 157–161
  nesting, 230
  ranges, 164
  string iteration, 82
  while, 155–157
Lundh, Fredrik, 523

M

management of automatic memory, 13
manuals (see documentation)
map function, 168, 227
mapping, 104
  functions, 227
matching
  arguments, 210, 217
  exceptions, 431
  files, 465
matrixes, 100
max function, 447
memory, automatic management of, 13
merging components, 23
metaprograms, 283, 285
methods
  calls, 322
  classes, 320
  dictionaries, 107
  lists, 101
  nested scope, 382
  operator overloading, 327
  strings, 90–95
Microsoft Common Object Model
    (see COM)
min function, 447
mixed operators, 58
mixed types, expression operators, 59
mixed usage modes, modules, 280
mixins, 354

O

P

About the Authors

Mark Lutz is an independent Python trainer, writer, and software developer. He is the author of the O'Reilly books *Programming Python* and *Python Pocket Reference*. Mark has been involved with Python since 1992, began teaching Python classes in 1997, and has instructed over 90 Python training sessions as of early 2003. In addition, he holds B.S. and M.S. degrees in computer science from the University of Wisconsin, and over the last two decades has worked on compilers, programming tools, scripting applications, and assorted client/server systems. Whenever Mark gets a break from spreading the Python word, he leads an ordinary, average life with his kids in Colorado. Mark can be reached by email at *lutz@rmi.net* or on the Web at *http://www.rmi.net/~lutz*.

Though a research scientist by training, **David Ascher** has spent the last few years in the software development business, focusing on providing professional tools for programmers using open source programming languages. After leading the development of the Komodo integrated development environment (for Python programmers, among others, and written mostly in Python), he is now responsible for the overall direction of the ActiveState division of Sophos, which produces language distributions, development tools, and services for Python, Perl, Tcl, PHP, and other languages. In addition, David has been a director of the Python Software Foundation since its inception and helps organize Python conferences and other events.

Colophon

Our look is the result of reader comments, our own experimentation, and feedback from distribution channels. Distinctive covers complement our distinctive approach to technical topics, breathing personality and life into potentially dry subjects.

The animal on the cover of *Learning Python*, Second Edition is a wood rat (*Neotoma*, family *Muridae*). The wood rat lives in a wide range of living conditions (mostly rocky, scrub, and desert areas) over much of North and Central America, generally at some distance from humans, though they occasionally damage some crops. They are good climbers, nesting in trees or bushes up to six meters off the ground; some species burrow underground or in rock crevices or inhabit other species' abandoned holes.

These grayish-beige, medium-sized rodents are the original pack rats: they carry anything and everything into their homes, whether or not it's needed, and are especially attracted to shiny objects such as tin cans, glass, and silverware.

Matt Hutchinson was the production editor for *Learning Python*, Second Edition. Argosy Publishing provided production services. Colleen Gorman, Emily Quill, and Mary Anne Mayo provided quality control.

Edie Freedman designed the cover of this book. The cover image is a 19th-century engraving from *Cuvier's Animals*. Emma Colby produced the cover layout with QuarkXPress 4.1 using Adobe's ITC Garamond font.

David Futato designed the interior layout. This book was converted by Julie Hawks to FrameMaker 5.5.6 with a format conversion tool created by Erik Ray, Jason McIntosh, Neil Walls, and Mike Sierra that uses Perl and XML technologies. The text font is Linotype Birka; the heading font is Adobe Myriad Condensed; and the code font is LucasFont's TheSans Mono Condensed. The illustrations that appear in the book were produced by Robert Romano and Jessamyn Read using Macromedia FreeHand 9 and Adobe Photoshop 6. The tip and warning icons were drawn by Christopher Bing. This colophon was written by Nancy Kotary.

Need in-depth answers fast?

Access over 2,000 of the newest and best technology books online

Safari Bookshelf is the premier electronic reference library for IT professionals and programmers—a must-have when you need to pinpoint exact answers in an instant.

Access over 2,000 of the top technical reference books by twelve leading publishers including O'Reilly, Addison-Wesley, Peachpit Press, Prentice Hall, and Microsoft Press. Safari provides the technical references and code samples you need to develop quality, timely solutions.

Try it today with a FREE TRIAL
Visit *www.oreilly.com/safari/max/*

For groups of five or more, set up a free, 30-day corporate trial
Contact: *corporate@oreilly.com*

Related Titles Available from O'Reilly

Scripting Languages

Exploring Expect

Jython Essentials

PHP 5 Essentials

PHP Cookbook

PHP Pocket Reference, *2nd Edition*

Programming PHP

Programming Python, *2nd Edition*

Python & XML

Python Cookbook

Python in a Nutshell

Python Pocket Reference, *2nd Edition*

Python Standard Library

Ruby in a Nutshell

Web Database Applications with PHP and MySQL, *2nd Edition*